Quantitative Analysis of Political Data

MERRILL POLITICAL SCIENCE SERIES

Under the editorship of

John C. Wahlke

Department of Political Science
The University of Iowa

Quantitative Analysis of Political Data

Samuel A. Kirkpatrick
University of Oklahoma

CHARLES E. MERRILL PUBLISHING COMPANY
A Bell & Howell Company
Columbus, Ohio

Published by
Charles E. Merrill Publishing Co.
A Bell & Howell Company
Columbus, Ohio 43216

ISBN: 0–675–08903–4

Library of Congress Catalog Card Number: 73–82657

1 2 3 4 5 6 7 8 — 81 80 79 78 77 76 75 74

Printed in the United States of America

TO:
Pamela Kirkpatrick
and
Oliver Benson

Preface

Scholarly research activity in political science has undergone a major transformation in modes of analysis. In some respects, this transformation was a gradual process evolving from social science activity in Europe and the behavioral movement in the United States. The trend reflects a growing commitment to the logic of scientific inquiry and to quantification. The application of these quantitative teohniques to political data developed in full during the past decade. All substantive areas within political science have discovered the utility of systematic analysis, and the various scholarly journals are replete with alternative uses of quantitative techniques. Undergraduate and graduate education in political science now recognizes the need for imparting methodological knowledge to students. Indeed, technical competence has not only become a necessity for research activity, but a certain level of sophistication is needed even if one is to grasp the substantive import evident in the discipline. These trends and needs have been primary motivating factors in writing and compiling this book.

The pedagogy of quantitative analysis is clearly in a developmental stage. More and more students are exposed to basic undergraduate laboratory courses on college campuses across the nation. These courses usually offer an appreciation for research design and analysis, as well as knowledge useful for substantive understanding in various areas of political science. The courses and thc books designed for them serve a vital function in our discipline. But where does the student go from there? Clearly, our level of sophistication in quantitative analysis extends considerably beyond an introductory course. By the time a political science major reaches upper division courses he discovers that an appreciation for empirical research is not sufficient. An even more difficult situation is faced by the graduate student. Whatever his substantive interests, he often finds it difficult and unrewarding to read scholarly materials which involve quantitative analysis. Yet, he is responsible for that substantive knowledge, and most important, he is expected to engage in research. When he finds a basic undergraduate laboratory course or a general scope and methods course contributing in only minor ways to his ability to apply research techniques, his options have not always been encouraging. More and more political science departments recognize this need by offering upper division and graduate level courses in research and analysis. This book is aimed primarily at that broad audience.

My own pedagogical understanding about how one can effectively teach and learn in this setting has shaped the coverage and organization of the book. While it is crucial for students to grasp the logic of inquiry and the various considerations involved in hypothesis formulation and data collection, there are many books on these subjects now being employed in political science courses. The gap which is most serious from a pedagogical viewpoint is in the area of data analysis. More and more undergraduates and graduate students are receiving training in basic statistics, but the types of topics covered or the extent of the coverage is often rendered inadequate when compared to the range and sophistication of the techniques now being applied.

In addition to inadequacies in the type and range of knowledge acquired, several other problems remain unattended. Although a few students become versed in the details of statistical and mathematical theory and its proofs, even fewer have the knowledge necessary for applying techniques. This book attempts to ease this problem by emphasizing techniques-in-use, rather than theoretical statistics or pure mathematics. By no means does this imply that mathematical theory or proofs are dysfunctional. Indeed, a little knowledge may be a dangerous thing. This approach recognizes a definite need in the area of data analysis — an understanding of when to use techniques, how to select them, and how to interpret the results. This should not imply that the book is atheoretical when it comes to technique understanding: I have tried to approach that understanding from an intuitive rather than a mathematical viewpoint.

Another major problem which the book addresses has to do with the meaning and utility of techniques. Far too often the techniques are taught in isolation — with little concept of application and the total research setting within which that application occurs. This is why the book has reading examples of technique applications following the text material. The text itself contains hypothetical as well as real examples. The hypothetical data serves an important function — it facilitates the description of various techniques, the options involved in applying them, and the alternative interpretations of possible findings. Yet the readings following the text and introductory notes serve a larger purpose: they facilitate an understanding of the entire research process, including previous research, theory, hypotheses, and data gathering. These readings were selected on the basis of several criteria: the use of techniques and the clarity of presentation; substantive applications in all areas of political science; attention to various levels of measurement; a mix of individual, group, and systemic data; and the overall importance of research questions to contemporary political science.

A final characteristic of the book is its breadth of coverage. There have been too few attempts in political science education to go beyond the more usual statistical application. Although this text clearly recognizes the importance of the more usual statistical techniques by containing a substantial chapter on statistics (which may be a review for some students), the remaining chapters attempt to extend these techniques through space and time. In addition to addressing such topics as bivariate and multivariate statistics, causal modeling, scalogram and factor analysis, unfolding analysis and multidimensional scaling, and the analysis of time series and panel data, the book begins with an overview of trends both within and without political science in order to place the analysis techniques in perspective. Two remaining features of organization should be useful to the reader who wishes to extend his methodological competence or his grasp of technique application: the text materials contain footnote references to methodological discussions and are followed by selected bibliographies of further research applications.

There have been many people who have contributed in various ways to the ideas found on the following pages. None of them bear the responsibility for accuracy or approach. Both Oliver Benson and Pamela Kirkpatrick have contributed in immeasurable and different ways. Surrounding oneself with an understanding wife and a competent scholar who grows with the discipline is comforting and reassuring. Several others have played an important role in developing my understanding at early stages, notably Lawrence K. Pettit, Fern K. Willits, and the teaching faculty associated with the Summer Program conducted by the Inter-University Consortium for Political Research at the University of Michigan. Over the years, both the University of Oklahoma and the University of Michigan have given me the opportunity to test the pedagogical soundness of the approach evident in this book. My graduate students have also assisted in this endeavor, especially Mary Ann Armour, Gary Cathey, Melvin Jones, William Lyons, Lelan McLemore, C. Kenneth Meyer, and Delbert Ringquist. I also appreciate the concrete and specific assistance offered by several colleagues who participated in reviewing the text and readings: Paul Allen Beck, Oliver Benson, Bruce Campbell, Lawerence Mayer, David Morgan, Stuart Rabinowitz, Rex Warland, Herbert Weisberg, Jonathan Wilkenfeld, and Fern Willits. A special note of appreciation is due John Wahlke for his assistance on the manuscript, and to Anne Hopkins and Jonathan Wilkenfeld for their original contributions to the readings. Finally, several secretaries have managed to endure this lengthy process and assist with typing and permissions: Eva Gunter, Vickie Craig, and Cherrie Flury.

Samuel A. Kirkpatrick

Contents

CHAPTER 1

Perspectives on Quantitative Trends in Political Science

The quantitative tradition in political science is neither new nor revolutionary. It is not delimited by disciplinary boundaries and it is not separable from trends in society or government. Its base is well established, yet the pervasiveness of quantitative modes of analysis is most evident in recent decades. In 1928 Stuart Rice wrote that "fashion and vogue are prevalent in scientific thought as well as in more ordinary human activities" and that quantitative methods had become fashionable among social scientists, but that in political science, specifically, it was a "comparatively new and rare means" for discovering truth.[1] If rich tradition, pervasiveness, the furtherance of knowledge, and a longitudinal evolution serve as the core of our criteria for assessing the quantitative method, we must surely conclude that it is no longer fad nor fancy. However, our present purpose is not to assess the merits of quantification but to trace the highlights of a rich and vastly complex evolution in a discipline. Perhaps the most discouraging, yet challenging aspect of the current state of political science is its increasingly complex methodology — in an attempt to grasp the meaning of social and political reality it has nearly become as complex as that reality. An understanding of the analysis techniques which are part of this methodology will bear the fruits of scientific judgement and contribute to our understanding of politics and political behavior.

Although the following discussion focuses on three broad themes — the evolution of quantification in political science, the development of specific techniques, and the utilization of these techniques in various political science fields — there is a variety of overarching factors which intersect and influence each of these topics.

The most general factors shaping the quantitative tradition in political science are the rise of natural science, the revolution in the methodology of knowledge,

---

1. *Quantitative Methods in Politics* (New York: Alfred A. Knopf, 1928), pp. 3–4.

and the growth of philosophies of science. The empirical trend in political science is a part of larger changes in social science emphasizing the empirical study of all aspects of human behavior. Daniel Lerner contends that "social *science* is a genuinely new way of looking at the world — replacing the successive methods of magic, religion, philosophy by the method of observation."[2] These changes do not merely include developments in technique, but rather, developments in broad gauge methodology — influenced by changes in science, mathematics, and philosophy. Although such trends are not unique to this century, the peak of the "revolution in methodology"[3] was in the early part of this century. It was an intellectual revolution characterized by new techniques for acquiring knowledge, new tools for enhancing the precision of logical inference, new standards for judging validity, and a rapidly developing discipline — the philosophy of science. These were trends signaling a departure from metaphysics and historicism and a movement toward empirical bases of knowledge. They led to an increased reliance on physical science and the philosophy of science in contemporary political research — not for the purpose of becoming an exact science, but rather, for improving modes of inquiry. This methodological departure has culminated in new bodies of empirically based frameworks, approaches, and theories, new means of measurement,[4] and new quantitative techniques of analysis.

Other factors shaping the quantitative mood in political science are part of general social science trends, both in the United States and Europe, which are, in turn, reflections of societal changes. Lerner contends that all communities and societies have developed means for self-observation in order to control and regulate societal activities.[5] Examples range from tribal genealogies to the modern census. In many respects, social science is a modern form of societal self observation and its contemporary political component is a consequence of transformations in social and political philosophy reflecting movements from rational speculation to empirical research. Although closely linked to the rise of scientific modes of analysis in social thought, the notion of self-observation entails a linkage with the reality of existing social and political phenomena. It was factors such as social mobility, urbanization and industrialization and their resultant human problems that encouraged social science to develop into an "empirical, quantitative, policy-related method of inquiry (not as a system of beliefs)."[6] Societies needed census data and statistical records, especially as their economies developed on a cash basis, both from a private point of view (e.g., family economics) and a public point of view (e.g., taxes). Subsequently, the critics of economic developments necessarily relied on new data to enhance their arguments. Robert Owen, for example, saw the need for detailed labor statistics in order to cope with the evils of capitalism. These factors, plus others closely aligned — the influence of the natural sciences, the rise of nation states, and the

---

2. Daniel Lerner, ed., Preface, *The Human Meaning of the Social Sciences* (New York: World, 1959), p. 6. Italics are mine.

3. Eugene J. Meehan, *The Theory and Method of Political Analysis* (Homewood, Ill.: Dorsey Press, 1965), pp. 9ff.

4. Although this chapter briefly discusses such developments, the primary focus of the book is data analysis.

5. "Social Science: Whence and Whither?" in *Human Meaning of the Sciences*, ed. Lerner, p. 13.

6. Ibid., p. 19.

need to understand social change — and the actors and ideas associated with them are discussed in greater detail below.

Several other themes can be considered here. (1) The evolutionary development of specific quantitative techniques, the nature of those techniques, their usage in other disciplines and the deficiencies in their development as well as the lags in their transference to political science have shaped the extent and nature of quantitative applications. (2) The changing mood and substantive interest in political science, characterized recently by the behavioral movement, has encouraged the development of new techniques. (3) The theoretical and methodological developments in other disciplines such as sociology and psychology, as well as more explicitly quantitative aspects of disciplines, such as biometrics, psychometrics, and econometrics, have had a profound impact on political data analysis. (4) Finally, factors internal to political science have contributed to its advancement, as well as its quantitative lag behind sister disciplines: the increasing availability of data; new trends in graduate education; improved, yet not pervasive, familiarity with new methods; a new mood of interdisciplinary cooperation; and the changing nature of mechanical, personnel, time, and financial resources affecting political research.

The Evolution of Quantitative Political Science

In many respects the roots of political quantification are similar to the roots of scientific sociology.[7] Although the roots began to grow most rapidly during the first half of the nineteenth century, there are important quantitative aspects to political philosophy before that time. Some of the more obvious examples can be found in the works of Aristotle and Hobbes, and they are closely tied to the development of mathematics. Even before Aristotle developed his "logical reasoning" — a series of logical syllogisms and the earliest components of mathematics and logic — there were evidences of mathematics applied for political purposes. For example, ropes with equidistant knots were used to measure the land of a king, and the Egyptian pyramids evidenced an application of geometry partially for political reasons.[8] Aristotle's mathematically related logic was used to link the causes of war between Athens and Persia. His propositions stated relations among predicates with various subjects. That is, "statements of fact, in classical terminology, were predicates asserted of particular objects. Specifying the *extent* to which these predicates applied, Aristotle showed, is equivalent to quantifying the universality of 'qualitative' judgement."[9] Other glimpses are evident in Greek thought. Equality and proportion were important notions; justice was given mathematical definitions by Pythagoras, Plato, and Aristotle; and the Greeks classified and ordered, as evidenced by Aristotle's study of constitutions.

Although the history of political ideas is replete with examples of empiricism, it was the work of Hobbes which brought mathematics back into the study of poli-

---

7. For an overview see John Madge, *The Origins of Scientific Sociology* (New York: Free Press of Glencoe, 1962).
8. Hayward R. Alker, Jr., *Mathematics and Politics* (New York: Macmillan, 1965), p. 2.
9. Ibid., p. 4.

tics.[10] Influenced by Euclid, Hobbes attempted to view social phenomena in a framework of exact formulation. His political theory, cast in a mechanistic and naturalistic framework, reflects his concern for social stability and his use of the mathematical method emphasized the role of empirical observation in determining cause and effect.

For the most part, however, the empirical aspects of normative philosophy were used for illustrative purposes. Data were used as examples to illustrate normatively derived truths about the social world. A systematic treatment of all relevant facts was missing, as was any idea of producing or collecting evidence beyond that which obviously existed.[11]

The beginning of the seventeenth century witnessed a rise of the quantification of social phenomena. What came to be called "political arithmetic" had its roots in demographic estimation, e.g., births, deaths, age, sex. Those involved at the earliest stages were natural scientists: the mortality research of the astronomer Halley, the economic research of the chemist Lavoisier and the population research of the mathematician Fourier.[12] However, the most important work in "political arithmetic" is credited to William Petty (1623–1687). He compared states from the viewpoint of the demographic bases of power, examined the relationship between social structure and government by studying political modernization in Ireland and sought to develop quantitative relationships such as those between wealth and population. In general, such emphases cannot be separated from Baconian philosophy, rationalistic capitalism, or the mercantilist concern for population size and political power.[13]

The development of statistics is dependent not only upon the work of Petty but also that of Hermann Conring (1606–1682) and his "university statistics." Conring was primarily interested in organizing facts in order to understand international relations; his concern for organizing knowledge led him to classify states on the basis of Aristotelian causes. Although both Petty and Conring sought an empirical basis for political ideas, the English root (Petty) developed into modern statistics and the German root (Conring) led to nineteenth-century German political science, laden with qualitative and taxonomic tendencies.[14]

The above are examples of close ties between politics and statistics, and in these respects, eighteenth-century statistics became a branch of political knowledge: an interest in statistics arose from an interest in the state.[15] As a consequence, the beginning of the nineteenth century saw the rise of political economy or the economy of the state, which was concerned with maximizing the profitability of the nation for

10. See William T. Bluhm, *Theories of the Political System* (Englewood Cliffs, N.J.: Prentice-Hall, 1965), pp. 260ff, and Harold T. Davis, *Political Statistics* (Evanston, Ill.: Principia Press of Illinois, 1954), p. 3.

11. Nathan Glazer, "The Rise of Social Research in Europe," in *Human Meaning of the Social Sciences*, ed. Lerner, p. 46.

12. Paul F. Lazarsfeld, "Notes on the History of Quantification in Sociology — Trends, Sources and Problems," in *Quantification: A History of the Meaning of Measurement in the Natural and Social Sciences*, ed. Harry Woolf (New York: Bobbs-Merrill, 1961), pp. 149ff.

13. Ibid., pp. 153ff.

14. Ibid., p. 155. Also see Hayward Alker's discussion in the context of causal analysis, "Statistics and Politics: The Need for Causal Data Analysis," in *Politics and the Social Sciences*, ed. Seymour M. Lipset (New York: Oxford University Press, 1969), pp. 245–48.

15. Lazarsfeld, in *Quantification*, ed. Woolf, p. 153.

the monarch's purposes, and it arose from the knowledge needs of the "monarchial mercantilist nation-state."[16] Regardless of its merits, it contained a heavy emphasis on the empirical. As Greer states, "if the people were his sheep, he (the monarch) did well to understand the conditions for their waxing fat and wooley."[17] Although much of the theoretical development of political economy is reflected in the works of Adam Smith, David Ricardo, and John Stuart Mill, it was not until the mid-nineteenth century that writers, such as W. S. Jevons (1871), called for a more scientific approach: "The deductive science of economy must be verified and rendered useful by the purely inductive science of statistics."[18] Political economy later split into separate disciplines of economics and political science reflecting an independent market economy, only to arise in new form in recent decades. In both its previous and present states, political economy has contributed heavily to statistical and mathematical schools of analysis.[19]

It was previously suggested that the nineteenth century was a landmark era for the quantitative mood. Glazer suggests that it entailed a new way of viewing society. Social factors were treated as unknowns. Truths had been doubted since the Renaissance, but men were now doubting facts which were previously of too little importance to be doubted. The mood contended that "it was necessary to collect all relevant facts, to consider the grounds on which one accepted these as facts, and, in the end, to test social knowledge by professionally investigating what had previously been casually observed."[20] There is no doubt that this mood had significant impact on political science, yet that impact occurred gradually and with a lag of nearly a century.

Although the word "statistics" appeared in use during the eighteenth century, as in the work of Sinclair (*Statistical Account of Scotland*, 1791–1799), it was not until the nineteenth century that various scientists became concerned about the methods and techniques of data collection and problems of validity.[21] This concern is best exemplified in the work of astronomer Adolphe Quetelet. His goal was to gather census data in order to develop laws reflecting all the facts relevant for a generalization and his data were not merely chosen to fit a thesis previously derived. Quetelet's more specific techniques also had profound influence: he used multivariate tabular analysis in the study of life cycles and longitudinal analysis in the study of crime rates; by making distinctions between observations over people and observations over time he contributed to a new field of sampling ideas; he was the intellectual father of stochastic processes; his measures of a state's "foresight" are not unlike contemporary measures of political development; and his attempts to quantify "penchants," e.g., for crime, were influential for later developments in attitude measurement.[22] Quetelet was also influential in the statistical society movement in

---

16. Seymour M. Lipset, "Politics and the Social Sciences: Introduction," in *Politics and the Social Sciences*, ed. Lipset, p. xviii.

17. Scott Greer, "Sociology and Political Science," in ibid., p. 51.

18. Quoted in Davis, *Political Statistics*, p. 4.

19. William C. Mitchell, "The Shape of Political Theory to Come: From Political Sociology to Political Economy," in *Politics and the Social Sciences*, ed. Lipset, pp. 101–37.

20. "The Rise of Social Research in Europe," in *Human Meaning of the Social Sciences*, ed. Lerner, p. 47.

21. Ibid., p. 48.

22. Lazarsfeld, in *Quantification*, ed. Woolf, pp. 172–79.

Great Britain (circa 1830) which was concerned with social reform and sought to use facts for that purpose. Led by men such as Malthus, refinements were made in census gathering, observation and interviewing techniques. In addition, the British factory inspection system collected data on characteristics of the working class, making the trend more advanced than on the Continent.

An exception on the Continent was the work of Laplace, a French mining engineer and social reformer. Laplace became famous for his empirical analyses of the economic and social life of workers and their families throughout Europe. He empirically analyzed the life style, history, economic and demographic aspects of families.[23] His goal was to change public policy, but in seeking it he cared not to sacrifice an objective treatment of social concerns. His methods continued to have lasting influence on case study and participant observer techniques. In England, his techniques were used by Beatrice Webb and Charles Booth in their factual treatments of London in the late nineteenth century. Webb and Booth made contributions in crude sampling procedures and in the use of indices. Their type of analysis spread quickly to the United States, to be used by early muckrakers like Lincoln Steffens and social reformers.

The above trends contributed to a school of thought emphasizing facts qua facts (logical positivism), and such thinking, its deficiencies aside, had an enduring impact. The positivist school contended that the natural and social sciences are similar in methodology and logic of inquiry, that the social order is mechanistic and that the scientist can reach objective knowledge in the study of social phenomena.[24] Coupled with the rise of social research in Europe, the forces of societal and the growth of the nation-state, social science and, in turn, political science profited from the new methodology of the nineteenth century.

The highlights of the quantitative tradition discussed to this point have not had an impact unique to political science; they represent important trends across social science disciplines. Compared to other social sciences, one finds political science turning to quantification rather late. The single most important element in the acceptance of quantification and the corresponding departure from traditional modes of analysis was behavioralism.[25] Although its roots are inseparable from the trends discussed previously, it acquired a uniqueness in political science.

Before 1900, the primary political science approach was historical and during the next two decades the nearest thing to quantification was a movement away from the historical analysis of institutions toward the description and evaluation of existing institutions. It was not until the following two decades that political scientists grasped the meaning of the previous century's revolution in methodology. World War I, the failures of Progressivism, and increasing pessimism about the inevitability of progress through gradual social change caused political scientists to look askance at traditional ways of accumulating and assessing knowledge. As a consequence of its need to understand irrationality and governmental power, the

23. Ibid., p. 182.

24. For an overview see Gideon Sjoberg and Roger Nett, *A Methodology for Social Research* (New York: Harper & Row, 1968), p. 7.

25. For general treatment see David Easton, "The Current Meaning of 'Behavioralism'," in *Contemporary Political Analysis*, ed. James C. Charlesworth (New York: Free Press, 1967), pp. 11–32, and Robert A. Dahl, "The Behavioral Approach in Political Science," *American Political Science Review* 55 (1961): 763–72.

discipline chose science as its guiding paradigm.[26] These decades witnessed the first major revolt against traditional political science, deductive reasoning, and historical approaches. The "revolt" began at the University of Chicago under the leadership of Charles Merriam and continued to develop through the efforts of his student, Harold Lasswell. In 1923 Merriam envisioned an increasing concern for observation and measurement, predicting future growth toward a science of politics.[27] The interdisciplinary social science and psychology and politics paradigm developed at the "Chicago School" had a lasting impact upon the discipline. Merriam constantly pushed for a new science of politics. It was he who organized conferences during the 1920s in an attempt to expose political scientists to scientific changes in related disciplines. Among others, he invited Thurstone and Allport, who "revolutionized political science by converting virtually every leader of the profession to the behavioral persuasion."[28] The results of these conferences suggest an eagerness to advance scientific methods, a realization of obstacles found in deficiencies of technique, and a firm belief in measurement and scientific generalization.

The "Chicago School" must not be viewed in isolation.[29] Earlier sociologists such as Spencer, Sumner, and Ward helped to make a science of politics plausible and their influence appears in the work of Bentley, Merriam, Rice, and Lasswell, as well as in the earlier works of Beard, Lowell, and Wilson. It was also during the early period that Graham Wallas (*Human Nature in Politics*, 1908) contributed a psychological thrust closely linked to concepts of quantification and natural science.

Although behavioralism came to be a broad mood encompassing substance, theory, and technique, its emphasis on quantification is of primary importance.[30] In an early description of the tenets of behavioralism Dwight Waldo used such words as models, research design, quantification, hypotheses, and replication.[31] A concern for observing, classifying, measuring, and analyzing became a primary component of scholarly research on political behavior. This quantitative aspect of behavioralism was highlighted by several landmark works. Aside from Merriam and Gosnell's classic in quantitative electoral behavioral (*Non-Voting*, 1924), Merriam's *New Aspects of Politics* argued forcefully for the use of quantitative methods as a means of problem verification. Stuart Rice's *Quantitative Methods in Politics* (1928) made skillful use of statistical techniques in the analysis of both survey and aggregate data. It was followed by his compilation of interdisciplinary research (*Methods in Social Science — A Case Book*, 1931) focusing on the philosophy of science, units and scales, spatial and temporal measurements, controlled and uncontrolled factors, and relationships between factors in existing works in social science.

26. These trends are discussed by Richard Jensen, "History and the Political Scientist," in *Politics and the Social Sciences*, ed. Lipset, pp. 1–29.

27. "Recent Advances in Political Methods," *American Political Science Review* 17 (1923): 286.

28. Jensen, in *Politics and the Social Sciences*, ed. Lipset, p. 5.

29. For detailed discussion see Bernard Crick, *The American Science of Politics: Its Origins and Conditions* (London: Routledge and Kegan Paul, 1959).

30. See Oliver Benson, "The Mathematical Approach to Political Science," in *Contemporary Political Analysis*, ed. Charlesworth, p. 108.

31. *Political Science in the United States of America: A Trend Report* (Paris: UNESCO, 1956), pp. 21–22.

While the above are landmarks in the quantitative tradition, the behavioral mood and the techniques associated with it did not receive wide acceptance until the post-World War II period. With a more widely accepted agreement on the substantive focus of political behavior, political scientists began to concentrate on technique development and the role of theory in research. The war and the flow of researchers to Washington enabled political scientists to confront theory with reality and to share the experiences of other social scientists.[32] As a consequence of this influx and the role of government in contemporary society, more interdisciplinary research was undertaken and the political scientist was forced to draw on the work of others, many of whom were familiar with quantification, statistical treatment, and mathematical approaches.[33] Aside from research stimulated by governmental agencies, such as the sample surveys of the Department of Agriculture and the Office of War Information, basic research and the funding for costly scientific research reflects a variety of institutional efforts: the financial capacities of private foundations such as the Rockefeller Foundation and Carnegie Corporation plus the resources of the National Science Foundation; the marketing research, attitude surveys, and content analysis contributions of business research units and even the basic research efforts of commercial units, as exemplified by Bell Telephone Laboratories and their development of multidimensional scaling; the evolution of important university institutes including the Institute for Social Research at the University of Michigan, the National Opinion Research Center at Chicago, and the Bureau of Applied Social Research at Columbia; plus a variety of research, funding, and data collection efforts by such intermediary agencies as the Social Science Research Council, the National Council of Social Science Data Archives, and the Inter-University Consortium for Political Research.[34]

The Development of Quantitative Techniques

While a predominant theme in the nineteenth-century trends in the evolution of quantified social science was empiricism and fact collection, this movement gained new meaning in the twentieth century by focusing on methods for analyzing such data. The primary modes of analysis adopted by political science were statistical — methods which assisted in the descriptive, inferential, and explanatory aspects of data analysis. There also was concern for new means of data collection and measurement as exemplified by developments in survey sampling and attitude scaling. Nevertheless, despite their concern for quantitative analysis, political scientists have played only a minor role in the development of techniques. Instead, they have borrowed heavily from sister disciplines and from others, such as mathematicians and statisticians outside the social sciences. The latter tended to develop such techniques either spontaneously or in response to demands from natural or social scientists. Karl Deutsch reminds political scientists of this inadequacy by contending that "what is new is usually only the application of this or that method to some problem

32. Dahl, "Behavioral Approach in Political Science."
33. Benson, "The Mathematical Approach to Political Science," in *Contemporary Political Analysis*, ed. Charlesworth, p. 109.
34. For an overview see Harry Alpert, "The Growth of Social Research in the United States," in *Human Meaning of the Social Sciences*, ed. Lerner, pp. 73–86.

in the field of political science followed by the increasing acceptance and application of this method or its results by other political scientists."[35]

Historians of science and statisticians themselves vary slightly in their account of the evolution of statistical techniques.[36] Yet a common set of important scholars inevitably arises: Laplace, Gauss, Quetelet, Galton, Pearson, Thorndike, Fisher, Yule, Gosset, and others. In turn, the innovations by these scholars emanated from such diverse sources as agriculture, biology, and gambling. For example, probability theory arose from the gaming table, the theory of errors was developed in astronomy, correlation in biology, time series in economics and meteorology, experimental design in agriculture, factor analysis in psychology, and significance tests in sociology.[37] Although we will focus on the highlights of statistical development, the tradition is rich in complexity.

Some of the earliest statistical developments are associated with the realization that patterns exist in a population of frequency distributions. This notion of a distribution of measurements eventually resulted in a set of descriptive statistics characterized by measures of central tendency (e.g., the mean) and dispersion (e.g., standard deviation). Early work is attributed to Galileo and eighteenth-century developments of the idea of continuous distributions. By the end of the nineteenth century Laplace and Gauss had discovered the normal distribution (bell-shaped curve), and subsequently research on skewed or asymmetrical frequency distributions took place.

Another important area of development was that of probability theory; its basic concepts now underlie a number of common statistical techniques such as tests of significance. Its early origins related to gambling and dice tossing, yet scientific developments were dependent upon Galileo (who evidenced some knowledge of probability theory) and particularly the eighteenth-century theoretical treatises of Bernoulli and Laplace. The application of probabilities to practical problems developed from the growing field of insurance where we find examples of more modern statistical analysis applied to demographic data. Even as early as 1785 Condorcet treated decision probabilities for various systems of voting. Today, more formal aspects of probability theory are evident in research on voting, attitudes, and decision making.

Although many fundamental statistical ideas were formulated before the twentieth century, it was during this century that extended theoretical treatment and, in turn, practical applications appeared. For example, the chi-square test of significance originated in the work of German geodesist Helmert around 1875, yet it was not fully developed until Pearson extended the treatment of chi-square distributions. Pearson (from ideas developed by Galton) also is credited with the primary contribution in the area of correlation.[38] As various scientists began to collect data

---

35. "Recent Trends in Research Methods in Political Science," in *A Design for Political Science: Scope, Objectives and Methods*, ed. James C. Charlesworth (Philadelphia: American Academy of Political and Social Science, 1966), p. 160. The author also has an informative discussion of new and extended sources of data.

36. The following discussion offers priority to the recent interpretation of M. G. Kendall, "The History of Statistical Method," in *International Encyclopedia of the Social Sciences*, vol. 15, ed. David L. Sills (New York: Crowell Collier and Macmillan, 1968), pp. 224–32.

37. Ibid., p. 224.

38. Ibid., p. 227.

on a large scale, there was a pressing need for techniques which would summarize more complex relationships between variables. Although Galton, Pearson, and others realized the usefulness of correlation in this context, it was not until between the World Wars that Fisher added rigor to the technique by deriving probability laws and techniques for estimation and testing.[39] This was followed by original contributions to more advanced forms of correlation and correlation-dependent techniques (e.g., factor analysis, canonical correlation) by Hotelling, Kendall, Spearman, and Thurstone.

It was also during this era that rapid and lasting developments occurred in measurement as well as analysis. Early examples of survey sampling procedures are evident in social science research on European workers. It was not until the 1930s that such techniques had a significant impact on American scholarship. These earlier studies were conducted with little knowledge of sampling reliability and therefore, inferences about the population from which samples were drawn was limited in its accuracy. It was Pearson, Gosset, and particularly Fisher who contributed to methods for dealing with sampling error and the distributional aspects of correlation coefficients, regression coefficients, and variance ratios.[40] Closely allied to sampling were problems of estimation and hypothesis testing. Before the work of Fisher, ideas about accurate sample inferences were unclear and it was usual for one to assume that a sample mean was an accurate estimate of a population mean. Concern for hypothesis testing also was fundamental to the evolution of inferential statistics; it was here that Neyman and Pearson contributed the standard procedures for comparing alternative hypotheses and testing for the existence of relationships. These techniques became particularly important to political science as survey sampling became the most important research method for the behavioral study of politics. After unfortunate experiences in the 1920s such as the Literary Digest poll, more scientific approaches were taken by Gallup as early as 1934 and two years later scholarly interest was sparked by the founding of the *Public Opinion Quarterly*. Political scientists began to use survey data in modest form by focusing on simple demographic characteristics[41] and later its usefulness was expanded to studies of political participation, voting, political elites, political ideology, political socialization, personality and politics, the legislative process, judicial behavior, and other subjects owing an intellectual heritage to the behavioral movement.[42]

Closely connected to refinements in survey research techniques were those of attitude measurement and scaling. The study of political behavior, drawing heavily from the fields of psychology and sociology,[43] encouraged the study of political

39. Harold Hotelling, "Correlation," in *Encyclopedia of Social Sciences*, vol. 10, ed. Sills, p. 538.

40. Kendall, "The History of Statistical Method," in *Encyclopedia of Social Sciences*, vol. 15, ed. Sills, p. 228.

41. Angus Campbell, "Recent Developments in Survey Studies of Political Behavior," in *Essays on the Behavioral Study of Politics*, ed. Austin Ranney (Urbana, Ill.: University of Illinois Press, 1962), pp. 31–46.

42. See Herbert McClosky, *Political Inquiry: The Nature and Uses of Survey Research* (New York: Macmillan, 1969), pp. 1–70.

43. See Calvin F. Schmid, "Scaling Techniques in Sociological Research," in *Scientific Social Surveys and Research*, Pauline V. Young, 4th ed. (Englewood Cliffs, N.J.: Prentice-Hall, 1966), pp. 348–87, and A. N. Oppenheim, *Questionnaire Design and Attitude Measurement* (New York: Basic Books, 1966), chap. 6.

attitudes in its many facets. An interest in scaling was derived from early works by Ernest Weber, a physiologist who measured pressure on the skin, and extensions of his concepts into psychological scales by Fechner during the 1850s. At the turn of the century psychologists were engaged in efforts to scale human abilities, such as intelligence, and in doing so they contributed to a growing body of measurement and test statistics originally developed in biometrics and traced to seventeenth-century studies in medicine (Kepler) and musical pitch (Galileo).[44] These developments led to the new subdiscipline of psychometrics from which Stevens' influential theory of measurement evolved. These efforts were followed by Thurstone's realization that scaling responses to questions could be methodologically apart from mere attempts at designing questions to measure attitudes. His equal-appearing interval concept was one of the first elaborate means for forming analysis scales. This development, and further research by Likert and Bogardus (1920–1930) stimulated interest in concepts of dimensionality. World War II and advancements by sociologists and psychologists working on troop morale, attitudes, and adjustment to the military added to a growing body of research on scaling. For example, it was during this era when Louis Guttman devised a measure of unidimensionality in sets of attitudes. A concern for multidimensionality and the variety of underlying factors in a large set of attitudes led to the development of factor analysis. Its origins were in a concern for factors underlying intelligence stimulated by Thurstone, but dependent upon previous ideas of Spearman.[45] As with other attitude scaling techniques factor analysis achieved new dimensions during the Army research studies. One of the first political applications reflected attempts to attain social utility while maintaining individual liberties and rights,[46] and it was followed by Thurstone's landmark study of the Supreme Court.[47] As is evident from our later discussion of factor analysis, it has subsequently been applied in such areas as voting, roll-call analysis, and international politics.

Our brief discussion has emphasized several important trends in the evolution of scientific techniques applied to politics. These techniques are largely based upon research by scholars in fields other than political science, and they reflect deeper changing methodological moods in the nineteenth century. For the most part, the era of specific and rapid accomplishments occurred during the first four decades of the twentieth century. By the end of that era the theory of statistical distributions and relationships was firmly established, as were the bases of sampling theory, experimental design, and problems of inference. Since that time, further advancements have been made in such areas as sampling and regression analysis, and new areas of development are evident in multivariate analysis, time series, decision function theory, and nonparametric statistics. Yet it does not follow that lags in data analysis are nonexistent: they are evident both within and between various

44. Edwin G. Boring, "The Beginning and Growth of Measurement in Psychology," in *Quantification*, ed. Woolf, pp. 108–28.

45. For more detailed treatment see Raymond Cattell, "Factor Analysis: An Introduction to Essentials," *Biometrics* 21 (1965): 191–212, and Harry H. Harman, *Modern Factor Analysis*, rev. ed. (Chicago: The University of Chicago Press, 1967), chap. 1.

46. Truman L. Kelley, "Talents and Tasks: Their Conjunction in a Democracy for Wholesome Living and National Defense," *Harvard Education Papers*, no. 1 (Cambridge: Harvard Graduate School of Education, 1940).

47. L. L. Thurstone and J. W. Degan, *A Factorial Study of the Supreme Court*, Research Report no. 64 (Chicago: University of Chicago Psychometric Laboratory, 1951).

disciplines. For example, the most developed aspect of statistics is its mathematical and theoretical base, yet there are lags in the development of easily used techniques and in the empirical study of the uses of techniques.[48] Evidence of the latter is the political scientist's scant knowledge of the interrelationships between statistical assumptions and political data.

As a consequence of quantitative advancements in fields outside political science, contemporary researchers in empirical politics utilize the fundamental language of mathematics; the inferential and explanatory power of mathematical, social, and psychological statistics; the matrix operations and stochastic models of econometrics; the experimental techniques, nonparametric statistics, and Markov chains of psychology and mathematical learning theory; the language of causal analysis from biometrics and sociology; and a host of other techniques unique to natural and social sciences. A primary purpose of this book is to encourage and facilitate greater transference of these techniques to the study of political phenomena.

Quantitative Applications in Contemporary Political Science

It is unnecessary to document in detail the pervasive use of quantitative techniques in contemporary political science. Even a brief and random perusal of political research reported in professional journals during the last decade attests to this extensiveness.[49] As recently as the early 1950s such writers on political statistics as Key and Davis[50] focused on what is now viewed as a rather limited list of substantive areas subjected to such analysis, e.g., forms of government, voting behavior, the composition of governing bodies, and issues of war and peace. Furthermore, the techniques used were largely those of descriptive and bivariate statistics. Today an extensive range of quantitative techniques is evident in every field of the discipline. It does not follow, however, that applications to substantive areas have been equally accepted nor that they are equally facilitated. In many respects the areas of study in political science differ significantly in the degree to which they have been subjected to quantitative analysis and to a large extent these parallel the receptivity and applicability of behavioral questions.[51] Although it is inherently difficult to arrange political topics treated quantitatively according to more traditionally accepted areas of the discipline,[52] we will do so briefly.

It is most difficult to analyze political theory in this substantive context. It reaches into all other substantive areas of the discipline and, as a body of knowledge, theory itself is multifaceted. Above all others, normative theory and the history of political ideas by their nature have been antagonistic to quantitative applications. Yet the philosophical propositions of classical theory are responsible for important hypothesis testing in political science. The most obvious development has occurred

---

48. John W. Tukey "Statistical and Quantitative Methodology," in *Trends in Social Science*, ed. Donald P. Ray (New York: Philosophical Library, 1961), pp. 88ff.

49. See the bibliography of substantive applications which appears throughout this book.

50. V. O. Key, Jr., *A Primer of Statistics for Political Scientists* (New York: Thomas Y. Crowell, 1954), and Davis, *Political Statistics*.

51. For a discussion of the latter see Waldo, *Political Science in the United States*, p. 23.

52. Benson, "The Mathematical Approach to Political Science," in *Contemporary Political Analysis*, ed. Charlesworth, p. 112.

in the vast literature on empirical modifications of democratic theory.[53] In conjunction with the behavioral movement, this literature established a basis for a growing interest in empirical theory. In its more formal forms, such as decision theory and game theory, it offers one of the more promising areas for *mathematical analysis.*[54]

Although examples of extensive quantitative advancements in public administration are rare, this area of inquiry has gradually responded to calls, by Simon and others, for more reliance on scientific methods.[55] Mathematical treatments have been constrained by a lack of communication with researchers in management science and organizational theory[56] as well as with those approaches developed in an industrial context, e.g., game theory and graph theory.[57] Nevertheless, new techniques are rapidly being applied to small group research, budgeting, cost-benefit analysis, decision making, and background studies of elite.[58]

The field of comparative politics is undergoing even more rapid changes in techniques of analysis.[59] The impact of the behavioral movement, the encouragement of interdisciplinary research on the emerging nations, and the increasing availability of data have led to extensive cross-national analyses using survey and aggregate research designs. Under the influence of Harold Lasswell, content analysis techniques are used in cross national contexts, and Karl Deutsch is credited with influencing a change from more qualitative analyses to those using ecological, census, and voting statistics. The availability of the latter has encouraged the use of regression, correlation, and factor analytic techniques, and recent attempts to gather survey data have opened comparative politics to the field of inferential statistics.

Another area of inquiry which has been even more receptive to scientific methods is international relations. Although most of its research continues to employ a traditional methodology, the field is dominated by an urgency to recognize the necessity for more theoretical and scientific research.[60] Furthermore, international relations specialists have been particularly alert to interdisciplinary approaches and even mathematical formulations.[61] Recent research has utilized time series and factor analysis to study systematic history; Guttman scaling, bloc and cluster analysis, simple correlation, multiple regression, and factor analysis to study voting

53. For an overview see Charles F. Cnudde and Deane E. Neubauer, eds., *Empirical Democratic Theory* (Chicago: Markham, 1969).

54. See Richard R. Fagen, "Some Contributions of Mathematical Reasoning to the Study of Politics," *American Political Science Review* 55 (1961): 889–900.

55. Dwight Waldo, "Public Administration," *Journal of Politics* 30 (1968): 455.

56. Benson, "The Mathematical Approach to Political Science," in *Contemporary Political Analysis*, ed. Charlesworth, p. 112.

57. Fagen, "Contributions of Mathematical Reasoning," p. 897.

58. See Robert T. Golembiewski, William A. Welsh, and William J. Crotty, *A Methodological Primer for Political Scientists* (Chicago: Rand McNally, 1969).

59. See Charles Andrain and David E. Apter, "Comparative Government: Developing New Nations," *Journal of Politics* 30 (1968): 372–416; Richard L. Merritt, *Systematic Approaches to Comparative Politics* (Chicago: Rand McNally, 1970); and C. L. Taylor, ed., *Aggregate Data Analysis: Political and Social Indicators in Cross-National Research* (Paris: Mouton & Co., 1968).

60. For a review see Harry H. Ransom, "International Relations," *Journal of Politics* 30 (1968): 345–71.

61. Benson, "The Mathematical Approach to Political Science," in *Contemporary Political Analysis*, ed. Charlesworth, p. 111.

in international organizations; and a host of other techniques, including simulation gaming, applied to aggregate, experimental, and survey data.[62]

Finally, there is no single field in political science which has relied more heavily on quantitative applications than American politics. The use of these methods reflects the predominant character of the behavioral movement, a large number of scholars engaged in research, institutional support, data availability, and the similar interests of other social scientists greatly influenced by empirical methodology. The study of voting behavior, public opinion, and political parties has been especially quantitative and based upon practically every form of data measurement and analysis technique. These include random sampling and panel interviewing, cross tabulation statistics, bivariate and multivariate correlation-regression, cumulative scaling, factor analysis, causal analysis, multidimensional scaling, simulation and mathematical modeling. In addition, roll calls have been subjected to a variety of correlational and scale analyses, and judicial decisions have been analyzed through cluster-bloc analysis, Guttman scaling, game theory, and multiple regression.[63]

Although our introductory discussion of quantitative techniques has been couched in general terms, there is evidence that methodological changes and their applications are practically as complex as the techniques themselves. For a variety of reasons both internal and external to political science, quantitative techniques have achieved considerable acceptance as a means to an end. That end is an improved understanding of political phenomena, and for many, an evaluation of political life and knowledge. These goals can only be reached through an improved working knowledge of *analysis* techniques, and it is to that task which we now turn.

62. See John E. Mueller, ed., *Approaches to Measurement in International Relations* (New York: Appleton-Century-Crofts, 1969), and J. David Singer, ed., *Quantitative International Politics: Insights and Evidence* (New York: Free Press, 1968).

63. For a review see William Keech and James Prothro, "American Government," *Journal of Politics* 30(1968): 417–42, and C. Herman Pritchett, "Public Law and Judicial Behavior," ibid., 480–509. These and other articles from the thirtieth anniversary issue of the *Journal of Politics* appear in Marian D. Irish, ed., *Political Science: Advance of the Discipline* (Englewood Cliffs, N.J.: Prentice-Hall, 1968).

CHAPTER 2

Statistics and Politics:
A Survey of Techniques

Our immediate focus is on only one of many stages in the scientific method as it is applied to the study of political phenomena: data analysis. Preceding it are the processes of problem formulation and data delineation and acquisition. These include conceptualization on a variety of levels, gathering of primary data through the use of various scientific instruments (e.g., mailed questionnaire, interview schedule), compilation of secondary data from published and unpublished sources, and derivation of specific variables and quantification of materials (e.g., coding, scaling). Ideally, these processes occur in the context of a comprehensive research design and scheme of analysis, characterized by a constant feedback of research information and ideas which result in incremental changes in the various stages of research. Although the elements of research design and execution have substantive, theoretical, and methodological aspects which are critical for the latter stage of data analysis, our attention assumes that the researcher is knowledgeable about the basics of these preceding processes.[1]

---

1. These preceding stages have been the subject of much discussion about the scientific method, the philosophy of social science, research design, and data collection. Particularly useful general references include the following: Abraham Kaplan, *The Conduct of Inquiry* (San Francisco: Chandler, 1964); Richard S. Rudner, *Philosophy of Social Science* (Englewood Cliffs, N.J.: Prentice-Hall, 1966); Scott Greer, *The Logic of Social Inquiry* (Chicago: Aldine, 1969); Alan C. Isaak, *Scope and Methods of Political Science* (Homewood, Ill.: The Dorsey Press, 1969); Fred M. Frohock, *The Nature of Political Inquiry* (Homewood, Ill.: The Dorsey Press, 1967); Eugene J. Meehan, *The Theory and Method of Political Analysis* (Homewood, Ill.: The Dorsey Press, 1965); Leon Festinger and Daniel Katz, eds., *Research Methods in the Behavioral Sciences* (New York: Holt, Rinehart and Winston, 1953); Claire Selltiz et al., *Research Methods in Social Relations*, rev. ed. (New York: Holt, Rinehart and Winston, 1959); Johan Galtung, *Theory and Methods of Social Research* (New York: Columbia University Press, 1967); Fred N. Kerlinger, *Foundations of Behavioral Research* (New York: Holt, Rinehart and Winston, 1964); Gideon Sjoberg and Roger Nett, *A Methodology for Social Research* (New York: Harper and Row, 1968); Robert T. Golembiewski, William A. Welsh, and William J. Crotty, *A Methodological Primer for Political Scientists* (Chicago: Rand McNally, 1969); Julian L. Simon, *Basic Research Methods in Social Science: The Art of Empirical Investigation* (New York: Random House, 1969); William Buchanan, *Understanding Political Variables* (New York: Charles Scribner's Sons, 1969); and Oliver Benson, *Political Science Laboratory* (Columbus, Ohio: Charles E. Merrill, 1969).

An empirical science depends upon concrete, experiential observations to provide the data for analysis. But, what is examined and how it is organized, analyzed, and evaluated is dependent upon the conceptual scheme of the observer. The scientist approaches his data with abstract concepts or theoretical propositions with which he wishes to deal. These need to be translated into elements that can be observed and assessed. Data theory deals with the correspondences between real world elements (individual, political system) and more abstract elements (numbers).[2] Measurement is a necessary part of this process: its goal is to match the formal, analytic features of model building (representations of reality) to the concrete, empirical, experiential observations by which we test relationships.[3] These data may refer to (1) recorded observations and (2) that which is analyzed. The latter definition has been advocated for behavioral research because "the same observations may frequently be interpreted as one of two or more different kinds of data."[4] From a universe of potential observations the scientist is selecting a "set of things" to record, yet for these recorded observations to be considered data (that which is analyzed) they must be classified (using a conceptual frame or taxonomic device) to be subsequently related, ordered, or structured.[5]

It is the scientist's decisions which determine the results of his analysis with each stage of the research process limiting the inferences to be drawn from analysis. The role of theory cannot be overemphasized, yet it is not the immediate object of our concern.[6] The structure of science is the interface of theory and data — the linkage (rules of correspondence) between observable phenomena and a network of constructs and systematic statements of relationships.[7] The researcher begins with a conceptual system of definable variables, a research design, and a set of hypotheses; the consequences of the research design then are compared with the hypotheses in the context of a theoretical framework.

Political data therefore are definable variables — characteristics or symbols of reality which have changing values. Conceptually, it is only one dimension of three dimensional space bounded by cases or units (e.g., a respondent), time, and characteristics of a case over time (a variable). Measurable political objects become points in space; a useful distinction for dimensional analysis discussed later. A variable is called independent when it is the influencing variable (conceptually and operationally) and the dependent variable is the outcome. Whereas a variable is a property in which members of a sample differ, a constant is an aspect of the sample which is common to everyone in that sample. For example, in a sample of the voting electorate, turnout (voting, not voting) is a constant.

---

2. For an extensive treatment of data theory see Clyde H. Coombs, *A Theory of Data* (New York: John Wiley, 1964), especially chap. 1.

3. S. S. Stevens, "Measurement, Statistics, and the Schemapiric View," *Science* 161 (1968): 849–56.

4. Coombs, *A Theory of Data*, p. 4. Scholars of sociolinguistics warn us that how someone talks may be more important than the subject of conversation. See Allen Grimshaw, "Sociolinguistics and the Sociologist," *American Sociologist* 4 (1969): 312–21.

5. Ibid.

6. Detailed treatment is available in Meehan, *Theory and Method of Political Analysis;* Frohock, *Nature of Political Inquiry;* Arthur L. Stinchcombe, *Constructing Social Theories* (New York: Harcourt, Brace & World, 1968); and Robert Dubin, *Theory Building* (New York: The Free Press, 1969).

7. For elaboration see Warren S. Torgerson, *Theory and Methods of Scaling* (New York: John Wiley, 1958), chap. 1.

Variables also may be characterized as continuous or discrete. The former have real number values which can be measured in fractions, such as a respondent's age, whereas discrete variables are classifications data in quantitative or qualitative form. There are also distinctions between extraneous and intervening variables. The former is an outside variable, unmeasured and not explicitly included in the scheme of analysis, which influences the dependent variable or the nature of the independent variable's impact on the dependent variable. In experimental analysis, the effects of such extraneous variables can be minimized through elimination, equalization, or randomization.[8] In most political science research the extraneous variables remain unidentified and uncontrolled. There are always many potentially influential factors which explain political behavior that are not part of our conceptual frame or are not measurable. An intervening variable is both conceptually and operationally defined. In some respects it is a mere refinement of the notion of independent variables. It is a factor which comes between an independent variable(s) and the dependent variable and tempers the impact of the former on the latter. In explanations of political behavior, psychological factors are frequently viewed as mediators between sociological independent variables and behavioral and attitudinal outcomes. The scheme is merely an adaptation of stimulus-organism-response theory in psychology.

Introduction to Statistical Analysis

Statistical techniques are the foundation for the analysis of quantifiable political data. Although various means of analysis and their uses are explored throughout this book, virtually all of them utilize statistics or statistically related concepts. Higher level mathematics is becoming increasingly important in the analysis of political data, but these developments are beyond our concern.[9] A student equipped with high school mathematics and introductory statistics will find the text and readings most useful, yet this does not exclude the student with only a smattering of statistics for whom this chapter is more than a review.

Among the goals of a science of politics are prediction and explanation of political phenomena (behavior, attitudes, events). Both imply the existence of an association between political or other variables, aspects of which are investigated by statistics. Prediction is not an association, but a projection that may be based on apparent association. The existence of a relationship does not necessarily imply causality. For prediction, two variables need only vary together; that is, they have only been observed to occur together. The imputing of explanatory value to this

---

8. Ralph H. Kolstoe, *Introduction to Statistics for the Behavioral Sciences* (Homewood, Ill.: The Dorsey Press, 1969), chap. 13; Kerlinger, *Foundations of Behavioral Research*, pp. 284–86; and Barry F. Anderson, *The Psychology Experiment* (Belmont, Calif.: Wadsworth, 1966).

9. The following are general and useful references: Hayward R. Alker, Jr., *Mathematics and Politics* (New York: Macmillan, 1965); Oliver Benson, "The Mathematical Approach to Political Science," in *Contemporary Political Analysis*, ed. James C. Charlesworth (New York: The Free Press, 1967), pp. 108–33; John M. Claunch, ed., *Mathematical Applications in Political Science* (Dallas: Arnold Foundation Monographs, Southern Methodist University, 1965); Joseph L. Bernd, ed., *Mathematical Applications in Political Science, II* (Dallas: Southern Methodist University Press, 1966); Joseph L. Bernd, ed., *Mathematical Applications in Political Science, III* (Charlottesville: The University Press of Virginia, 1967); John G. Kemeny and J. Laurie Snell, *Mathematical Models in the Social Sciences* (Waltham, Mass.: Blaisdell, 1962); and Paul F. Lazarsfeld and Neil W. Henry, eds., *Readings in Mathematical Social Science* (Chicago: Science Research Associates, 1966).

scheme may involve the notion of spuriousness. An oft-cited example is a correlation between a country's stork population and childbirth rates and the inherent predictive value of stork indices. On the other hand, a relationship is an actual association with predictive validity.[10] Explanation requires more than knowledge about covariation — it requires the infusion of substance.

Statistics is not a list of numbers: it is a method of analyzing data; a means for summarizing and extracting information, a tool for finding and evaluating patterns in data; a means of scholarly communication;[11] a way of making data speak and parsimoniously reducing masses of information; and it is a base upon which to build theory. Technically, a *statistic* is a computed measure of a characteristic or value of a sample. A population or universe is a group being generalized about. We speak of the characteristics or values of a population as *parameters*.[12]

More specifically, statistics performs descriptive, inductive, and analytical functions. It helps to describe data through the use of summarizing tools such as percentages or proportions, measures of central tendency (e.g., mean, median, mode) and dispersion (e.g., range and standard deviation). It aids in making inferences about the population by testing the statistical significance of an observed relationship to ascertain the probability of obtaining such a relationship by chance alone.[13] An analytical function is being performed with two or more variables when we examine the nature and degree to which they vary together, that is, the closeness of association between them. Statistics assists us in performing these functions by providing information about aspects of association: (1) the existence of a relationship (an association between characteristics); (2) the direction of a relationship (positive or negative); (3) the degree of the relationship (closeness of association); and (4) the nature of the relationship (either nonquantitative information or knowledge of changes in the interval measures of one variable associated with unit changes in another variable). An example of statistical usage indicates that tests of significance provide us with existence information; correlation coefficients tell us direction as well as closeness; and regression assists us in making judgements about the nature of the relationship.

A Functional-Scalar Approach to Political Statistics

Various kinds of statistics perform various functions and the types of statistical devices that are appropriate depend upon the nature of the problem we wish to address and the kinds of data the political scientist has collected. The phrase "kinds of data" implies different types of measurement or ways in which the data are

10. M. J. Hagood and D. O. Price, *Statistics for Sociologists* (New York: Henry Holt, 1952), pp. 343–55.

11. Unfortunately, statistics is sometimes a means of sanctification and obfuscation. See Darrell Huff, *How to Lie with Statistics* (New York: W. W. Norton, 1954), and William H. Kruskal, "Statistics, The Field," in *International Encyclopedia of the Social Sciences*, vol. 15, ed. David L. Sills (New York: Crowell Collier and Macmillan, 1968), pp. 209–10.

12. This technical term is frequently misused to apply to any social or political characteristic. To be sure, parametric jargonizing has become burdensome in the social sciences.

13. A readable discussion of induction and description appears in Hubert M. Blalock, *Social Statistics*, 2d ed. (New York: McGraw-Hill, 1972), chap. 1.

scaled. There are four widely accepted levels of measurement[14] which serve as statistical selection criteria. (1) *Nominal* scale: this is the lowest level of measurement and it is characterized by classification and categorization. For example, consider the following sets of categories: Democratic or Republican; East, West, North, or South; Catholic, Jew, or Protestant. (2) *Ordinal* scale: when data are scaled ordinally they maintain the lower level property of classification and add the property of order or rank which implies that some classes or categories are higher than others; for example, strong Democratic, moderate Democratic, weak Democratic; high, middle, low class. (An ordered metric scale[15] is a related level of measurement which occurs between an ordinal and interval scale. In this instance we know the rank of distances between classes, e.g., *c* is farther from *b* than *b* is from *a*.) (3) *Interval* scale: when data meet the interval criteria we not only have information about their classification and greater-lesser characteristics, we have an additional piece of information which implies real numbers: the distance between the classifications or ranks. These are real numbers which represent a particular unit of measurement, e.g., in years or votes. (4) *Ratio* scale: this highest level characteristic implies that interval scale data have a natural origin or zero-point, e.g., percentage of vote and income. This level of measurement permits the comparison of data based upon ratios of differences (e.g., $100 is to $50 as $1000 is to $500).[16]

The above "theory" of measurement, as a criterion for statistical selection, has not been consistently followed. Researchers dissatisfied with or unaware of the methods available for dealing with, e.g., ordinal data, have frequently ignored the requirement of interval scales for many of the tests and have incorporated ordinal data into primarily interval scale techniques. The frustration over the difficulty in applying higher level statistics and mathematics to data measured at lower levels is especially critical in social sciences where much data is measured with nominal and ordinal scales. Those who favor strict adherence to the measurement criteria emphasize the nature of reality as a determinant for measurement: the use of inappropriate statistics distorts the nature of social reality.[17] Moreover, statistical tests are based upon certain underlying assumptions concerning the nature of the measurement itself.[18] Other writers argue that any statistical tool can legitimately be applied to any level of data since the statistical test itself cannot be aware of the meaning of numbers. The basic problem is therefore one of interpretation.[19] Mathematics and statistics can be applied to many things, but to be useful the results must be interpretable. This has become a particularly vital issue with the availability of computer

---

14. The earliest complete formulation was by S. S. Stevens, "Mathematics, Measurement, and Psychophysics," in *Handbook of Experimental Psychology*, ed. S. S. Stevens (New York: John Wiley, 1951), pp. 1–49.

15. See Clyde H. Coombs, "Theory and Methods of Social Measurement," in *Research Methods in the Behavioral Sciences*, ed. Festinger and Katz, pp. 471–535. Finer distinctions are made in chapter 4 to follow.

16. Blalock, *Social Statistics*, p. 18 suggests that the interval-ratio distinction is often academic in the social sciences.

17. This argument is discussed in Sjoberg and Nett, *A Methodology for Social Research*, pp. 275–77.

18. For example, Sidney Siegel, *Nonparametric Statistics for the Behavioral Sciences* (New York: McGraw-Hill, 1956); Blalock, *Social Statistics;* and Theodore R. Anderson and Morris Zelditch, Jr., *A Basic Course in Statistics with Sociological Applications*, 2d ed. (New York: Holt, Rinehart and Winston, 1968).

19. William L. Hays, *Statistics for Psychologists* (New York: Holt, Rinehart and Winston, 1963), pp. 73–76.

routines; they will process any input irrespective of whether the results are meaningful or absurd. S. S. Stevens, in defense of his theory formulated twenty years previous, suggests that

> in the behavioral sciences, where the discernment for nonsense is perhaps less sharply
> honed than in the physical sciences, the vigil must remain especially alert against the in-
> trusion of a defective theory merely because it carries a mathematical visa. An absurdity
> in full formularized attire may be more seductive than an absurdity undressed.[20]

Although the entire issue is unsettled, the use of a variety of tests on similar data can
assist us in making judgments. Unfortunately, a grasp of the complexities of the
issue is only possible when the researcher understands data and data analysis. This
is only possible when the actual interpretive process is encountered. At that point,
the distinctions between semantic and scientific meaning become important.[21]
Many procedures can facilitate semantic meaning; however, the underlying assumptions become critical for generalization and scientific meaning. With these arguments
in mind, we cannot avoid measurement theory. Furthermore, measurement criteria
remain a useful means for cataloging the various statistical tools. The following
discussion therefore uses these criteria, accompanied by others, as a means for
structuring the presentation.

The above functions and scales imply several steps and criteria in the statistical
analysis of data. The data must be collected and measured; the researcher must
determine, conceptually and substantively, the scheme of analysis, the hypotheses
to be tested, and the kind of variables (independent-dependent) involved; and he
must select the proper kind of statistical analysis. This selection of statistical tests is
dealt with here as dependent upon (1) the level of measurement, (2) the function
which the researcher wishes to perform, and (3) the number of variables in his
scheme of analysis.

Nominal Measurement, Univariate Description

Using the above framework, we begin our survey with the smallest number of
variables, the lowest level of measurement, and the least sophisticated function.
In this category, there are three primary ways to describe data. (1) The most obvious
and least parsimonious type of presentation is the reporting of totals or N's. This
type of analysis characterized the earliest period of political data usage, e.g., number
of Republican and Democratic voters, partisan divisions on legislative roll calls.
(2) The *ratio* is less frequently used than other measures described here. Although
its purpose is to assist in the description of a relationship between two characteristics
of one variable it is less parsimonious because two or more numbers remain in the
description. For example, if our total N in a sample of 1964 voters is $N = 1111$ and
our variable is "vote direction," we may find that the Johnson voter $N = 750$ and
the Goldwater voter $N = 361$. In order to describe the relationship between Johnson
and Goldwater voters, the two characteristics (Johnson, Goldwater) of the variable

20. "Measurement, Statistics, and the Schemapiric View," pp. 161, 853.
21. Sjoberg and Nett, *A Methodology for Social Research*, p. 276, and Ernest W. Adams, Robert F.
Fagot, and Richard E. Robinson, "A Theory of Appropriate Statistics," *Psychometrika* 30 (1965):
99–127.

(vote) can be expressed as a ratio (750/361 or 750 : 361 further reduced to 208 : 100). (3) The *proportion* is used most often to express part-to-whole comparisons, e.g., 750 : 1111 or 0.67 or 67 percent.

Ordinal Measurement, Univariate Description

There are few descriptive alternatives to the analysis of data which involve only one variable at an ordinal level of measurement. The most frequently used is merely the presentation of rankings; for example, the listing of cities according to their level of income. However, the median and mode discussed below can be applied to ranked data.

Interval Measurement, Univariate Description

There are two categories of description subsumed under this classification: measures which indicate the central tendency of data and measures which indicate the dispersion about this central tendency. The heart of the descriptive function is summarization — finding a point to summarize masses of data — finding a *central tendency* in that data. There are three commonly used tools of analysis to perform this function and their calculation depends upon the form of the data.[22] The tools include the following. (1) The *mean:* the most frequently used and easiest understood device for describing the main thrust of data in this category. Although distorted by extreme values, it is based upon all observations; it is easy to calculate and easily subject to algebraic manipulation. (2) The *median:* whereas the mean is an arithmetic average, the median is a halfway or midpoint in the data array. Unlike the mean it is not a calculated value and it is not useful algebraically; however, its values are not affected by extreme observations and it is particularly useful for describing asymmetrical distributions. (3) The *mode* describes the most typical value in a data set, the value occurring most frequently. It is not affected by extreme values and it can yield information about data which is characterized by more than one point of clustering.

The laws of probability and areas under the normal curve[23] are subjects too detailed for this survey analysis; however, the above tools are related to fundamental notions of data distribution and the language of analysis (e.g., asymmetrical, clustering). Data distribution can be represented in two dimensions by graphic techniques. Typically, in the one variable case, the Y axis (ordinate) represents the number of observations (e.g., people) and the X axis (abscissa) represents a series of values (e.g., scores) so that the graph is a series of values plotted across observations or a series of frequency distributions. A common form of distribution is the normal, bell-shaped curve — one which is symmetrical (both halves are alike) and unimodal (one point of clustering), as shown in figure 2.1. In this distribution, or any symmetrical, unimodal distribution, the mean ($\bar{X}$), median (Md), and mode (Mo) are

---

22. A fourth tool is the less used and understood geometric mean, which is useful for treating variables which increase geometrically or for dealing with ratios. Others, including the harmonic mean and quadratic mean, are rarely used.

23. A brief and easy discussion appears in George H. Weinberg and John A. Schumaker, *Statistics, An Intuitive Approach* (Belmont, Calif.: Wadsworth, 1962). A more thorough treatment appears in Simon, *Basic Research Methods in Social Science*, pp. 362–420.

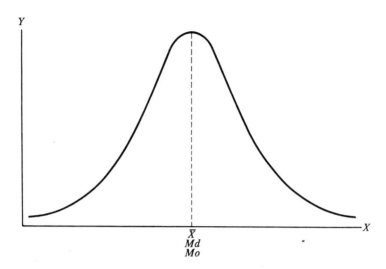

FIGURE 2.1 Normal Distribution

all equal to the same value. However, in distributions where the $\bar{X}$ is largest of the three, i.e., where extreme cases pull the $\bar{X}$ off center, the underlying data are skewed to the right, [24] as in figure 2.2. When $\bar{X}$ is smallest they cluster to the right and the distribution is skewed to the left. Furthermore, skewness can be measured and treated as a descriptive statistic.[25] More generally, it is a deviation from a purely symmetrical distribution. Kurtosis is also a distribution-related concept which can

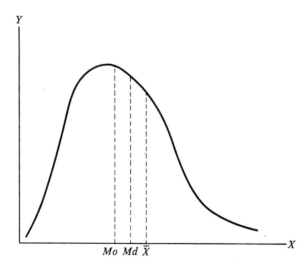

FIGURE 2.2 Skewed Distribution

---

24. This means that the tail of the distribution points to the right, i.e., the data cluster to the left. When $\bar{X}$ is smallest, they cluster to the right and the distribution is skewed to the left. In social research, skewed distributions are more often skewed to the right.

25. Dennis J. Palumbo, *Statistics in Political and Behavioral Science* (New York: Appleton-Century-Crofts, 1969), pp. 51–53.

be measured; it relates to a curve's peakedness (e.g., peaked or leptokurtic, flat or platykurtic).

When the underlying distribution is bi- or multimodal, there are two (or more) points of clustering and the mean and median become relatively useless for describing the data, as shown in figure 2.3.

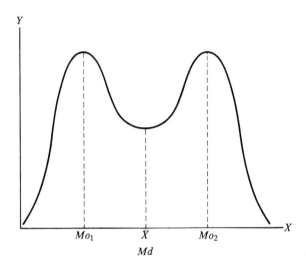

FIGURE 2.3 Bimodal Distribution

The calculation of descriptive statistics is facilitated by noting the extent to which data have been summarized or grouped into categories. These forms are in three classifications: *ungrouped, semigrouped,* and *grouped* data, and they each influence the calculation of the mean, median, and mode for interval data.

(1) Ungrouped data are merely raw numbers without any attempt at classification. For example, the researcher may develop a quantitative measure of past political participation with scores ranging from one through four. Arrayed from low to high the scores for five respondents might look like the following example.

$$
\begin{array}{c}
\underline{X} \\
1 \\
2 \\
3 \\
4 \\
\underline{4} \\
\Sigma X = 14
\end{array}
$$

The mean ($\bar{X}$) is calculated by summing the scores (ΣX) and dividing by the number of observations (N). Therefore,

$$\bar{X} = \frac{\Sigma X}{N} = \frac{14}{5} = 2.8$$

The median position is the midpoint in this distribution $(N + 1)/2$ and therefore, 6/2 or 3. The median is the value of X occupying the third rank position in the array. In this example the median is 3. The mode is the most frequently occurring value of X (4).

(2) Semi-grouped data is simply a concise way of expressing ungrouped information through the addition of a frequency value so the data array is of manageable length. Column (f) in table 2.1 indicates the number of times a particular value of

TABLE 2.1 Calculation of Mean and Median for Semi-Grouped Data

X	f	Xf	cf
1	1	1	1
2	1	2	2
3	1	3	3
4	2	8	5
	$N = 5$	$\Sigma Xf = 14$	

X occurs. To calculate the mean multiply the value of X by the frequencies and establish an Xf column. The sum of this column is the sum of the scores. Therefore,

$$\bar{X} = \frac{\Sigma Xf}{N} = 2.8.$$

A cumulative frequency column (cf) showing the accumulation of frequencies can then be established to locate the median such that the median position equals $(N + 1)/2$, locating the median in the third category $(X = 3)$. The mode is easily determined by scanning the frequency column to see which X occurs most frequently.

(3) Grouped data are not only characterized by a frequency, but the values of X are collapsed to enable ease of handling. Furthermore, the researcher will often encounter secondary data in grouped form only. If we have ungrouped data collapsed to facilitate manageability and description, we may lose data and accuracy. Using the same example where the mean (ungrouped and semi-grouped) participation scores was 2.8, the grouped mean is rounded at 2.7. The first and second values, and the third and fourth values have been arbitrarily grouped and the midpoint of the class interval (m) is now treated as X (table 2.2). The product of the f's and

TABLE 2.2 Calculation of Mean and Median for Grouped Data

X	f	m	mf	cf
1–2	2	1.5	3.0	2
3–4	3	3.5	10.5	5
	$\Sigma f = 5$		$\Sigma mf = 13.5$	

the m's yields a mf column which is analogous to our previous formula. The number of cases (N) equals Σf.

$$\bar{X} = \frac{\Sigma \, mf}{\Sigma f} = \frac{13.5}{5} = 2.7$$

The calculation of a mean for grouped data requires that all class intervals be closed. Also, the calculation of a median requires that its class be closed. As with semi-grouped data, a cumulative frequency (cf) column is determined, as presented in table 2.2. The median formula reads as follows:

$$Md = L_{md} + \left(\frac{\frac{N}{2} - cf_{md}}{f_{md}} \right) i_{md}$$

where the L_{md} is the lower theoretical limit of the median class; cf_{md} is the cumulative frequency to, but not through, the median class; f_{md} is the frequency of the median class; and i_{md} is the size of the median class interval. The median class is first determined by finding the median position ($N + 1$)/2 = 3, locating it on the cf column and observing the median class in the X column (3–4). The theoretical limits of this class range from 2.5 through 4.5; the value of cf up to the median class is 2, the frequency of the median class is 3, and the size of the interval is 2 (i.e., values can be either 3 or 4). Therefore, substituting these values in our formula we have

$$2.5 + \left(\frac{\frac{5}{2} - 2}{3} \right) 2 = 2.8$$

This method is particularly useful only for data arrays much larger than this brief example. Indeed, the fewer the categories defined, the greater the resultant error in the statistics calculated. This also may occur in calculating the mode in such form. It is accomplished by finding the modal class, i.e., that class with the greatest frequency (3–4) and reporting the midpoint of that modal class ($Mo = 3.5$).

A second set of measures useful for univariate description with interval data are *measures of dispersion*. They provide information about the spread of scores or X values. That is, they are measures of the degree of heterogeneity or homogeneity in the data. Two basic measures in this category are the *range* and the *standard deviation*. The former is usually stated in one of two ways: (1) the lowest value of X to the highest value of X (e.g., a range of 1 to 4), or (2) the highest value of X minus the lowest value of X (3). Although there are other measures of deviation (e.g., quartile deviation, average deviation[26]), the standard deviation is most universal and most useful for algebraic and statistical manipulation. It is frequently used as a comparison of data sets and can adequately compare data with similar mean values. In general, other things being equal, the higher its value, the greater the dispersion or scattering of the data around its mean value (see figure 2.4). A lower standard deviation indicates a more homogeneous data set, as shown in figure 2.5.

---

26. See George Simpson and Fritz Kafka, *Basic Statistics*, rev. ed. (New York: W. W. Norton, 1957), pp. 175–86.

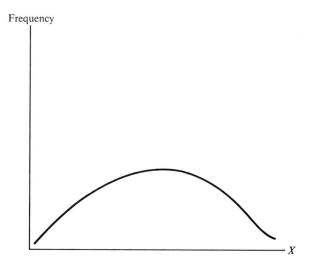

FIGURE 2.4   Relatively Heterogeneous Distribution

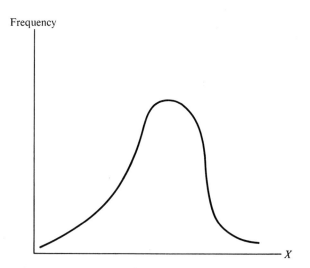

FIGURE 2.5   Relatively Homogeneous Distribution

Using categories and data similar to those discussed under measures of central tendency, the calculation becomes relatively straightforward:[27]

$$\hat{\sigma} = \sqrt{\frac{\Sigma\,x^2}{N-1}} \qquad \text{where } \Sigma\,x^2 = \Sigma\,X^2 - \frac{(\Sigma\,X)^2}{N}$$

Note that $\Sigma\,x^2$ is the sum of the squares of deviations about the mean, or $\Sigma\,x^2 = \Sigma\,(X - \bar{X})^2$. For example, with ungrouped data, the frequencies are arrayed, squared and summed (see table 2.3).

---

27. These procedures, as well as most others presented throughout this chapter, are designed to facilitate calculations manually or through the use of a desk calculator.

TABLE 2.3 Calculation of Standard Deviation for
Ungrouped Data

X	X^2
1	1
2	4
3	9
4	16
4	16

$\Sigma X = 14$ $\Sigma X^2 = 46$

$$\Sigma x^2 = 46 - \frac{14^2}{5} = 7$$

$$\hat{\sigma} = \sqrt{\frac{7}{4}} = 1.32$$

This $\hat{\sigma}$ value represents 1.32 standard deviation units from the mean (as it is described regarding areas under the normal curve). This is the equivalent of the differences between each score and the mean, squared, summed, divided by $N - 1$, and the square root taken. The procedures involved in obtaining individual deviations from a mean (x) are basic to many of the statistical tests we will review. Technically, the standard deviation which we are deriving here is for use with a universe of observations, i.e., an estimate of a population's standard deviation. By using N instead of $N - 1$ in the denominator we can derive s for describing a sample. With semi-grouped data (table 2.4), the example would appear as follows:

TABLE 2.4 Calculation of Standard Deviation for
Semi-Grouped Data

X	f	Xf	X^2	X^2f
1	1	1	1	1
2	1	2	4	4
3	1	3	9	9
4	2	8	16	32

$\Sigma Xf = 14$ $\Sigma X^2f = 46$

$$\Sigma x^2 = 46 - \frac{14^2}{5} = 7$$

$$s = \sqrt{\frac{7}{5}} = 1.18$$

If the data are grouped, calculation may be easier, yet information and accuracy are lost because we treat each X value as if it were at the class midpoint (see table 2.5). However, in instances of secondary analysis, this may be the form of the only available data. Inaccuracies become particularly evident where only a few groups are used. For example,

TABLE 2.5 Calculation of Standard Deviation for Grouped Data

X	f	d	d^2	d^2f	df
1–2	2	1.5	2.25	4.50	3.0
3–4	3	3.5	12.25	36.75	10.5

$$\Sigma\, d^2f = 41.25 \quad \Sigma\, df = 13.5$$

$$\Sigma\, x^2 = \Sigma\, d^2f - \frac{(\Sigma\, df)^2}{N} = 41.25 - \frac{13.5^2}{5} = 4.8$$

$$s = \sqrt{\frac{4.8}{5}} = .98$$

A related measure which serves the same purpose as a standard deviation is the variance. As the square of the standard deviation (s^2 for a sample, σ^2 for a population) it is most useful in a mathematical context, however, it does not facilitate visual representation of dispersion.

Univariate Induction

Inferential statistics involves the imputing of population values from a sample, i.e., statistics enable generalizations about parameters. In our example, we have drawn a hypothetical sample of five respondents from a particular universe and we want to know how the sample is like the population with regard to political participation rates. This question becomes very technical for the researcher engaged in sophisticated sampling;[28] however, the details are less important for our focus on the data analysis stage. Briefly, the researcher wants to know if the sample could reasonably have come from a population with a particular parameter. Therefore, a test of statistical significance of the difference between the sample and the population is calculated. If the calculated significance level is greater than .05, convention suggests that the researcher conclude that the sample is from the population. At .05 or less, however, he can conclude that the differences are too great and that the sample is not from the population.

For interval data, the choice of a test indicating significance level is dependent upon what we know about the standard deviation of the population. Whereas $\bar{X}$ and s are sample statistics, μ (mu) and σ (sigma) are the mean and standard deviation for the population. Sometimes the characteristics of the universe are known, as with aggregate voting data, but many times they are not, as with political attitudes. If σ is known, the statistical significance of the difference between $\bar{X}$ and μ can be tested by a one sample Z-test:

$$Z = \frac{\bar{X} - \mu}{\sigma/\sqrt{N}}$$

28. See Leslie Kish, *Survey Sampling* (New York: John Wiley, 1965).

If the parameters are unknown they may be estimated by a variety of techniques. The point or best estimate of $\hat{\mu}$ ($\hat{}$ = estimate) is $\bar{X}$; however, a more precise interval estimate can measure the certainty of μ falling within certain limits, e.g., 95 percent certain to fall within a particular range. The best estimate of $\hat{\sigma}$ is $\sqrt{\Sigma x^2}/(N - 1)$, with a t-test performed to test the inferential function.

$$t = \frac{\bar{X} - \mu}{\sigma/\sqrt{N}} \qquad \text{degrees of freedom } (df) = N - 1$$

If the data are measured at the nominal level, such as religious categories, a one sample chi-square (χ^2) can be performed to determine the extent to which the sample distribution differs from the population. Although the degrees of freedom vary (number of categories of the variable $- 1$),[29] the procedure is similar to that described below for two variable nominal data.

Bivariate Analysis of Nominal Data

Since predictive and explanatory power is based upon co-relationships, the two variable case is usually more important to the data analyst than the one variable case. In performing the three functions we are again seeking to (1) describe the relationship, (2) test to determine if it occurred by mere chance, and (3) measure the degree to which the variables relate to each other. To describe the relationship between nominally scaled variables, percentages or proportions can be calculated on the independent variable (whether it be by row or column). Such a procedure might yield the relationships in table 2.6 between level of education and vote direction, accompanied by a statement about the greater number of Republicans in higher educational categories.[30]

TABLE 2.6   Contingency Table for Educational Level
and Vote Direction by Party

EDUCATION	PARTY					
	Republican		Democrat		Total	
	%	N	%	N	%	N
Beyond college degree	80	(20)	20	(5)	100	(25)
College graduate	72	(18)	28	(7)	100	(25)
High school graduate	32	(8)	68	(17)	100	(25)
Less than high school graduate	40	(10)	60	(15)	100	(25)
Total		(56)		(44)		(100)

29. The mathematical meaning of degrees of freedom is tangential to our discussion. Its practical usage enables the researcher to utilize previously determined tables of critical values for significance levels. See Blalock, *Social Statistics*, p. 203, and Palumbo, *Statistics in Political and Behavioral Science*, pp. 155–56. Note also that expected frequencies are calculated differently in a one sample chi-square.

30. In order to ensure clarity and brevity of presentation, plus a variety of types of interrelationships, our examples are hypothetical, yet congruent with research findings. For details on table construction see Benson, *Political Science Laboratory*, pp. 22–37.

The basic statistical vehicle for making inferences about relationships that exist in a sample, and therefore in the population from which it was drawn, is the test of significance. The most frequently used test at the nominal level is chi-square (x^2) for contingency tables. It enables us to test the null hypothesis that there is no relationship between education and the vote. If the relationship is statistically significant, we reject the null hypothesis (H_0) and conclude that there is a relationship greater than no relationship between the two variables in the population. Chi-square is based on the differences between what we actually observe and what the laws of probability and chance say we should expect to observe. That is, it tests the differences between actual or observed frequencies on the one hand, and theoretical or expected frequencies on the other. The expected frequencies for each of the table cells can be calculated from the following verbalized formula:

$$fe = \frac{(\text{column total}) (\text{row total})}{\text{grand total}}$$

For example, for the first cell in table 2.6 (Republican with more than a college degree), the expected frequency is $56 \cdot 25$ divided by $100 = 14$. Similar calculations would be made for the other seven cells. After the observed (fo) and expected (fe) frequencies are listed, their difference is squared and divided by the expected frequencies (table 2.7). The formula for chi-square can therefore be represented as follows:

TABLE 2.7   Calculation of Contingency Chi-square

fo	fe	$fo\text{-}fe$	$(fo\text{-}fe)^2$	$(fo\text{-}fe)^2/fe$
20	14	6	36	2.57
18	14	4	16	1.14
8	14	6	36	2.57
10	14	4	16	1.14
5	11	6	36	3.27
7	11	4	16	1.46
17	11	6	36	3.27
15	11	4	16	1.46
$N = 100$				$x^2 = 16.88$

$$x^2 = \Sigma \frac{(fo - fe)^2}{fe} = 16.88$$

The pattern in table 2.7 is indicative of what is found when one of the variables (education) has equal numbers of observations in each category.

The degrees of freedom necessary for determining significance level are calculated as the number of table rows minus one times the number of table columns minus one: $df = (R - 1)(C - 1) = (4 - 1)(2 - 1) = 3$. The level of significance can now be determined by locating the x^2 value in a table designed for that purpose.[31] A signif-

---

31. Most statistics texts have a limited number of statistical tables, however, one of the most useful collections is by Herbert Arkin and Raymond R. Colton, *Tables for Statisticians* (New York: Barnes & Noble, 1963).

icance level of .001 for this χ^2 value suggests that the relationship is significant; that there is a relationship in the population. The probability of obtaining a relationship as close as the one in the sample if there is no relationship in the population is less than 1 in 1,000.

Before we investigate some of the norms for the use of chi-square and variations of the test, there are several distinctions which are basic to statistical analysis which have only been suggested in our previous discussion. Generally, statistical tools are of two types: *parametric* or *nonparametric*. The most basic distinction is that parametric tests make more assumptions about the population than nonparametric tests. The former assume normally distributed variables and equal variances (homoscedasticity). Unequal variances would occur when one variable has a high variance for some values of the other variable and a low variance for the other values. By avoiding such assumptions, nonparametric tests are less powerful or efficient, i.e., less likely to accept a true null hypothesis. In addition, the field of nonparametric statistics is relatively new and not as highly developed. At the time when Siegel wrote his landmark text[32] many of the tests were not suited for multiple relationships; however, recent developments, several of which are incorporated throughout this chapter, are encouraging to political scientists often faced with lower levels of measurement. since the requirements of normality and homoscedasticity are dependent upon a quantitative measurement, tests suited for interval variables are typically parametric (e.g., correlation-regression, analysis of variance), while those suited for nominal or ordinal data (e.g., chi-square, Spearman's rho for ties) are typically nonparametric. It also should be noted that the issue of underlying assumptions is rather complex since several parametric tests (e.g., t and F[33]) have been found to be functionally nonparametric or robust, i.e., depending on the circumstances, normal distributions and equal variances may be relatively unimportant.

Although chi-square is a nonparametric test, it assumes random sampling, independent observations, and a sample large enough to apply the chi-square distribution ($N \geq 50$). Because the value of χ^2 is dependent on sample size (directly proportional to N) and the number of rows and columns, several norms have developed for its usefulness. Most of these consider the minimum number of cases required. For example, cells should have expected frequencies of five or more; or no more than 20 percent of the cells should have frequencies less than five as long as these cells have at least one observation in them. If these criteria are not met, there are several alternatives for handling the data. The researcher may find that one set of cells are not meaningful for his analysis and therefore he can eliminate them (e.g., a "no answer" category) or he may find that the data can be analyzed by combining categories in order to meet the criteria (e.g., a multiplicity of religious groups collapsed into Catholic, Protestant, and Jewish). If either the original table or the collapsed/eliminated table is a 2 by 2 contingency table which fails to meet the criteria, a Fisher's Exact Probability Test can be performed as in table 2.8. The test is designed for sample sizes under fifty, yet when dealing with anything but very small N's, the factorial calculation becomes very involved. There-

32. *Nonparametric Statistics.*
33. C. Alan Boneau, "The Effects of Violations of Assumptions Underlying the *t* Test," *Psychological Bulletin* 57 (1960): 49–64.

TABLE 2.8 Computation of Fisher's Exact Test

Variable 2

a	b
c	d

Variable 1

$$p = \frac{(a+b)!(c+d)!(a+c)!(b+d)!}{N!a!b!c!d!}$$

fore, tables of critical values in the Fisher Test have been developed to assist in determining probability levels.[34]

In instances where a resultant 2 by 2 table meets cell criteria, it is generally accepted that a correction term is necessary to prevent an inflated χ^2 value. The Yates correction term or correction for continuity is therefore used where $df = 1$. Chi-square is corrected by subtracting .5 from the absolute value of the difference between each observed and expected frequency. The calculations in table 2.7 would be modified as follows: $(fo - fe) - .5$; $[(fo - fe) - .5]^2$ and $[(fo - fe) - .5]^2/fe$ summed to obtain the corrected χ^2 value.[35]

Our scheme for statistical analysis suggests that inferences about the existence of relationships in a population is a crucial element of data analysis. However, the usage of tests of significance has not endured without criticism. Few social scientists and even fewer political scientists are aware of the issues surrounding their use. Although the arguments have become too complex for detailed treatment here,[36] an awareness of controversies offers several warnings for scientific data analysis.

The controversy was initiated by Selvin in 1957,[37] when he contended that the assumptions of significance testing are not met by nonexperimental data and that we cannot derive proper inferences from them (e.g., survey data). Tests of significance were viewed as appropriate for experimental settings alone, where control and randomization of variables is possible. The basic thrust of his argument was that correlated biases must be controlled before such tests can be utilized. In other words, we need clear causal factors — ones which are not correlated with other disturbing influences. Unfortunately, Selvin implied that such causal concerns were the only legitimate ones in the scientific enterprise. Although he was critical of ex post facto research, such forms of analysis may be necessary. Most important, the

---

34. Siegel, *Nonparametric Statistics*, pp. 96–104, 256–70.

35. Although the correction for continuity is widely used, technical controversies exist over its application. See R. L. Plackett, "The Continuity Correction in 2 x 2 Tables," *Biometrika* 51 (1964): 427–38, and James E. Grizzle, "Continuity Correction in the χ^2 text for 2 x 2 Tables," *The American Statistician* 21 (1967): 28–32.

36. The appearance of a book on this subject, accompanied by many methodological articles (some of which are cited below) attests to the complexities of the issues. See Denton E. Morrison and Ramon E. Henkel, eds., *The Significance Test Controversy* (Chicago: Aldine, 1970). Also see Galtung, *Theory and Methods of Social Research*, pp. 358–89.

37. Hanan C. Selvin, "A Critique of Tests of Significance in Survey Research," *American Sociological Review* 22 (1957): 519–27.

basic problems are the fault of the researcher rather than the method. The inference of cause and broad explanatory power to significance tests is an error of interpretation. Important technical criticisms of Selvin's arguments contend that the correlated biases argument is fallacious, that probability sampling from known populations is an acceptable alternative to experimental randomizations, and that laboratory research, while important, is not the ideal since it is weak on representation and even incapable of inclusive control of all variables.[38] More recent refinements of the controversy remind us that tests of significance can only legitimately be used with probability samples from specified populations; that statistical and substantive significance are quite different; that causal inferences are unwarranted, especially in the light of differences between experimental randomization and random sampling; and that arbitary (and even conventional) decisions made on the basis of high significance levels are "more akin to religion than science."[39] Social scientists have been especially unimaginative with regard to variations on conventional statistical significance levels.[40] Although the equating of substance to significance is generally viewed as a sin, it has been argued that where relationships are not significant there are no relationships of substantive importance, and that such generalizations hold even for tests on universe data.[41] Although some disagree,[42] David Gold views significance testing as a necessary criterion for substantive importance and argues that meaningful interpretations can result despite sampling problems. However, most authors warn us that measures of the degree of association (analytical function) are most crucial for substantive significance.

The controversy continues and conclusive answers are not likely to be forthcoming in the immediate future. When they appear, the incorporation of changing moods about statistical significance will be a gradual process, constrained by the development of norms for political research. Although it has been suggested that we discontinue the "significance test" nomenclature, to be replaced by "auxiliary probability decision procedure,"[43] the remainder of this chapter adheres to conventional terminology for the sake of clarity and consistency with the substantive applications which appear in the readings. Nevertheless, there are strong arguments for the utilization of such statements as: "This finding signifies a basis for rejection of the null hypothesis at the .05 level."[44] The major thrust of these arguments is that statistical inference and scientific inference are not one and the same; yet our approach to the latter remains undefined and nebulous (replication? deductive theory?). Despite past sins and current warnings there is a mood which suggests that significance testing is only an index of reliability, that it is useful as a preliminary screening for hypotheses that must pass further tests, and that social scientists are

38. Robert McGinnis, "Randomization and Inference in Sociological Research," *American Sociological Review* 23 (1958): 408–14, and Leslie Kish, "Some Statistical Problems in Research Design," *American Sociological Review* 24 (1959): 328–38.

39. Denton E. Morrison and Ramon E. Henkel, "Significance Tests Reconsidered," *The American Sociologist* 4 (1969): 137.

40. See James K. Skipper, A. L. Guenther, and G. Nass, "The Sacredness of .05: A Note Concerning the Uses of Statistical Levels of Significance in Social Science," *The American Sociologist* 2 (1967): 16–18.

41. "Statistical Tests and Substantive Significance," *The American Sociologist* 4 (1969): 42–46.

42. For example, Morrison and Henkel, "Significance Tests Reconsidered," p. 136.

43. Ibid, p. 139.

44. Ibid.

"better off for using the significance test than for ignoring it."[45] It remains as a useful formal way of judging whether relationships are characterized by systematic or haphazard variations and its role in the initial stages of data analysis cannot be overlooked.

To this point, we have reviewed the descriptive functions treating the one variable case across the levels of measurement, the inferential function for the one variable case, and descriptive and inferential functions for the bivariate case. With two variables the analytical function can be performed in which we test the degree of association between the variables. The function involves making a statement about the degree to which the variables vary together, that is, the percent of shared variance between the variables — the degree and direction of their covariation. After describing the data and testing the statistical significance of the relationship to conclude that there is a relationship greater than no relationship, we then can attempt to make a statement about a certain amount of variation in one variable (e.g., vote) explained or caught by variation in another variable (e.g., education). Although direction and degree of association have limited meaning with nominal variables, the analytical function can be accomplished by calculating standardized values (e.g., from 0 to 1, or 1 percent to 100 percent). Several χ^2-based measures have been developed for this purpose: (1) *Phi coefficient*, where

$$\phi^2 = \frac{\chi^2}{N}$$

or using the distribution in table 2.6, $\phi^2 = .17$. (2) *Cramer's V^2*, where

$$V^2 = \frac{\chi^2}{N \cdot \text{minimum } (R - 1)(C - 1)}$$

and where the denominator equals N times whichever is smaller, the number of rows minus one or the number of columns minus one ($V^2 = .17$). The phi coefficient is most useful for 2 by 2 tables whereas Cramer's V^2 corrects for an inflated coefficient value that could result in larger tables. Another alternative is (3) *Pearson's contingency coefficient* (*C*) where, for the data in table 2.7,

$$C = \sqrt{\frac{\chi^2}{\chi^2 + N}} = \sqrt{\frac{16.9}{16.9 + 100}} = .12$$

A zero value for C indicates statistical independence, but when there is a relationship (as above), the contingency coefficient yields positive values between zero and one.

Although the usefulness of the analytical function is limited at this lowest level of measurement (nominal) the above tests enable statements about closeness of association. For example, an admittedly precise statement about a rather crude indicator would suggest that 17 percent of the fluctuation in vote direction is associated with fluctuation in levels of education. They also are useful for a series of

---

45. Robert F. Winch and Donald T. Campbell, "Proof? No. Evidence? Yes. The Significance of Tests of Significance," *The American Sociologist* 4 (1969): 140.

tables where sets of two variable relationships are to be compared, for example, the relative impact of education on the vote compared to the impact of sex on the vote. Although chi-square based measures of degree of association, as well as other nonparametric tests, are free from underlying assumptions regarding the shape of the population, they are constrained in usefulness by their chi-square base: they become functionally dependent on sample size, they should not be calculated unless chi-square can legitimately be calculated, and they depend on the number of rows and columns. Contingency coefficients are not comparable if based on tables of different size.[46] This variety of problems has led to the development of measures capable of performing the analytical function without dependence on chi-square.

One such measure designed specifically for nominal data in dichotomous contingency form is *Yule's Q*.[47] It is a measure of direction and degree of association (-1 to $+1$). Consider the previous data (table 2.6) in dichotomous form, as shown in table 2.9. Since Q is the difference between the cell cross products divided

TABLE 2.9 Dichotomous Contingency Table for
Education and Vote Direction

EDUCATION	PARTY					
	Republican		Democrat		Total	
	%	N	%	N	%	N
More than high school	76	38	24	12	100	50
High school or less	32	18	68	32	100	50
Total		56		44		100

by the sum of the cross products, it can be represented as:

$$Q = \frac{ad - bc}{ad + bc} = \frac{(38)(32) - (12)(18)}{(38)(32) + (12)(18)} = +.79$$

A comparable ϕ for this table equals the difference of cross products divided by the square root of the product of marginals:

$$\phi = \frac{(38)(32) - (12)(18)}{\sqrt{(50)(50)(56)(44)}} = +.40$$

In general, ϕ is more sensitive than Q and ϕ and Q do not correspond directly, e.g., Q can attain its upper and lower limits when any cell equals zero, and the ϕ upper limit decreases with greater discrepancy between column and row marginals.[48]

---

46. Siegel, *Nonparametric Statistics*, p. 201.

47. Although this test has not been widely used in political science, its usefulness is explored by Benson, *Political Science Laboratory*, pp. 151–52. Useful alternatives include epsilon (ϵ) and delta (δ) as described by Alker, *Mathematics and Politics*, pp. 55–65.

48. Further distinctions are explored by Blalock, *Social Statistics*, pp. 298–99.

Other newer measures are based on probability reasoning and the proportional reduction in errors (PRE) that result when certain cells in the table are known. Referring to the previous example with a sample of 100, we want to discover the relationship between education as an independent variable and vote direction as a dependent variable (table 2.6). Therefore, we want to place the respondents in our sample into categories of vote direction so that there are 56 Republicans and 44 Democrats. By assigning 56 respondents to the Republican column (i.e., so that 44 out of 100 do not belong there), over time, the expected error of doing this will be 56 (44/100) or 24.6. We also must assign 44 individuals to the Democratic column (and 56 out of 100 do not belong there), therefore, the expected error is 44 (56/100) or 24.6 again. Together the expected error is 24.6 + 24.6 = 49.2 errors in assigning the 100 respondents in the sample. This means that if you were given 100 cards with the partisan vote identified on the back of the card (without looking), you would make errors in properly assigning them to Republican and Democratic stacks about half of the time. If we have the information for the independent variable, we can discover to what extent it will reduce our errors in assigning respondents on the dependent variable, i.e., the proportional reduction in errors when the independent variable is taken into account. Using the card analogy again, if you know educational level will it help you to correctly assign voters to Republican and Democratic stacks? If there is a perfect relationship between education and the vote, you will assign them without making errors, that is, reducing the error to zero. A procedure similar to that used for vote direction can be used for education level. Twenty individuals must be placed in the "more than B.A." cell for Republicans, therefore, the expected long-run error is 20 (5/25) = 4.0. The calculations for remaining cells are as follows:

$$5 \, (20/25) = 4.0$$

$$18 \, (7/25) = 5.04$$

$$7 \, (18/25) = 5.04$$

$$8 \, (17/25) = 5.44$$

$$17 \, (8/25) = 5.44$$

$$10 \, (15/25) = 6.0$$

$$15 \, (10/25) = 6.0$$

The total error on the independent variable is the sum of these values (40.96). From these calculations, Goodman and Kruskal[49] define *tau beta* (τ_b) as a proportional reduction in error:

$$\tau_b = \frac{\text{errors without independent variable} - \text{errors with independent variable}}{\text{errors without independent variable}}$$

$$\text{or} \qquad \frac{49.20 - 40.96}{49.20} = \frac{8.2}{49.2} = .167$$

49. Leo. A. Goodman and William H. Kruskal, "Measures of Association for Cross Classifications," *Journal of the American Statistical Association* 49 (1954): 759–60. Also see Blalock, *Social Statistics*, pp. 232–34.

This indicates that we have eliminated 8.2 errors out of 49.2, i.e., the errors have been reduced by 16.7 percent. The higher this value, the more we have reduced the error in predicting the vote from education level, that is, they are more highly related. A comparable measure for testing the relationship in the other direction (predicting education levels from vote direction) is *tau alpha* (τ_a).

An alternative measure is *lambda b* (λ_b).[50] Whereas τ_b measures the absolute reduction in error, λ_b measures relative reduction of error so that its value varies between zero and one. Because the measure of relationship is asymmetrical and usually defined in terms of row comparisons, the subscript is used to identify the dependent variable, which is the column variable for λ_b and the row variable for λ_a. The following is the general formula:

$$\lambda_b = \frac{\Sigma \max f_{ij} - \max f \cdot j}{N - \max f \cdot j}$$

The expression $\Sigma \max f_{ij}$ means the sum of the maximum frequencies in each row, and $\max f \cdot i$ means the maximum column total. Applied to the data in table 2.6, we have the following:

$$\lambda_b = \frac{(20 + 18 + 17 + 15) - 56}{100 - 56} = \frac{14}{44} = .318$$

If the independent-dependent variables are reversed as in table 2.10 (which makes

TABLE 2.10   Computation of Lambda *b* for the Relationship Between Education and Vote Direction

PARTY	EDUCATION				
	B.A. +	College	High School	Grade School	Total
Republican	20	18	8	10	56
Democrat	5	7	17	15	44
Total	25	25	25	25	100

less sense substantively in our example), the *lambda a* (λ_a) value would equal

$$\lambda_a = \frac{(20 + 17) - 25}{100 - 25} = \frac{12}{75} = .160$$

Because λ_b has a range of 0 to 1, a .32 relationship between education and vote is only moderate. When the scheme of analysis is symmetrical, one may derive lambda (λ) from λ_b and λ_a by summing the numerator of λ_b and λ_a and dividing the sum by the sum of the denominators:

$$\lambda = \frac{14 + 12}{44 + 75} = \frac{26}{119} = .218$$

50. Ibid., pp. 740–47, and Palumbo, *Statistics in Political and Behavioral Science*, pp. 161–63.

indicating a relationship between two variables without regard for which is independent or dependent (like a correlation coefficient, but the range is 0 to 1. Lambda symmetric always lies between λ_a and λ_b, except when $\lambda_b = \lambda_a$).

Multivariate Analysis of Nominal Data

Although the above techniques have focused on the two variable case, often the political scientist will organize his research according to an underlying framework which suggests that there is a variety of factors which relate to a certain dependent variable. In performing the analytical function with a multiplicity of variables, we wish to measure the extent to which several independent variables together explain a dependent variable and the impact that each has on the final variable when others in the scheme have been controlled. One general approach which has been used without the advantages of parsimonious statistical measures is tabular control. For example, the impact of a third variable is treated by examining a relationship between two variables in one table and analyzing the changes that occur in that relationship when that table is decomposed for categories of the third variable. Such tabular controls for political data are thoroughly treated in other sources.[51]

Our immediate concern will focus on a nominal measure of partial and multiple determination. Limiting our example to a series of 2 by 2 tables for three variables, let us assume that we are interested in finding the impact of educational level and occupational prestige on vote direction in a particular election (or on party identification at one point in time). We have previously examined a hypothetical relationship between education and the vote reported in a fourfold scheme (table 2.9). Education and vote are related more than we would expect by chance ($\chi^2 = 16.2$ without Yates correction) and the ϕ^2 measure of association equals .16. Without working from a calculated χ^2 value, ϕ^2 can be restated as follows:

$$\phi^2 = \frac{(ad - bc)^2}{(a + b)(b + d)(a + c)(c + d)}$$

This value suggests that 16 percent of the variance in vote is associated with variation in education levels. What effect will a second independent variable such as occupational prestige have on the dependent variable? In answering such a question we must consider the independent effect of occupational prestige on vote, the way in which it now lessens the previous relationship between education and the vote, the interrelationship between the two independent variables, and the multiple effect that both have on the dependent variable. The relationship between occupation and the vote is depicted in table 2.11. A cursory examination indicates that occupation and education have similar effects on vote direction. You will note, for example, that the number of low educated voters who vote Democratic (64 percent) is similar to the percentage of low occupation voters who vote Democratic (62 percent). The ϕ^2 contingency coefficient for the relationship in table 2.11 (with second independent variable z and dependent variable y) is:

$$\phi^2_{yz} = \frac{(1111 - 161)^2}{(40)\,(44)\,(56)\,(60)} = .15$$

51. See Benson, *Political Science Laboratory*, chap. 9; Galtung, *Theory and Methods of Social Research*, chap. 5; and Alker, *Mathematics and Politics*, chap. 5.

TABLE 2.11   Contingency Relationship Between a
Second Independent Variable and the Dependent
Variable

OCCUPATIONAL PRESTIGE (z)	PARTY (y)					
	Republican		Democrat		Total	
	%	N	%	N	%	N
High	82	(33)	18	(7)	100	(40)
Low	38	(23)	62	(37)	100	(60)
Total	56		44		100	

Therefore, $\phi_{xy}^2 = .16$; $\phi_{yz}^2 = .15$; $\phi_{xy} = .40$ and $\phi_{yz} = .39$. From these estimates of coefficients of determination and coefficients of correlation, we might expect that the multiple correlation coefficient ($\phi_{y.xz}$) would equal the sum of the simple correlation coefficients ($\phi_{xy} + \phi_{yz} = .79$). However, this will not be the case if the two independent variables are interrelated, and hence their combined effect is less than the sum of their individual effects. The relationship between occupational prestige and educational level appears in table 2.12, and in fact, they are interrelated such

TABLE 2.12   Contingency Relationships Between Two
Independent Variables

OCCUPATIONAL PRESTIGE (z)	EDUCATION (x)		
	High	Low	Total
High	35	5	40
Low	15	45	60
Total	50	50	100

that, e.g., higher education is associated with higher occupational prestige and lower education with lower occupational prestige. The ϕ^2 value equals

$$\phi_{xz}^2 = \frac{(1575 - 75)^2}{(40)\,(50)\,(50)\,(60)} = .38$$

and $\phi_{xz} = .62$. We are now ready to measure the extent to which the introduction of z tempers the impact of x on y. A tabularly controlled scheme appears in table 2.13. The cells reflect the interrelationship between occupation and education in that there are few respondents with high occupation and low education or low occupational prestige and high education. However, the introduction of z has not changed the direction of association between x and y, i.e., the two control tables within table 2.13 do not show such marked differences in their distributions that we would conclude that x and y relate differently from one level of x to the next. When x's

TABLE 2.13   Tabular Controls with Three
Dichotomous Variables

EDUCA-TION (x)	OCCUPATIONAL PRESTIGE (z)								
	High				Low				
	Party (y)				Party (y)				
	Republican % N	Democrat % N	Total % N		Republican % N	Democrat % N	Total % N		
High	86 (30)	14 (5)	100 (35)		53 (8)	47 (7)	100 (15)		
Low	60 (3)	40 (2)	100 (5)		33 (15)	67 (30)	100 (45)		
Total	(33)	(7)	(40)		(23)	(37)	(60)		

impact on y differs for different levels of z we have the occurrence of interaction effects.[52] On the other hand, the percentage differences are now slightly greater with a control (but in the same direction) and we can expect that a measure of partial correlation (or a partial coefficient of determination) would indicate that z has some slight impact on the relationship between x and y. The partial correlation coefficient controlling for occupational prestige can be expressed as:

$$\phi_{xy.z} = \frac{\phi_{xy} - (\phi_{xz}\phi_{yz})}{\sqrt{(1 - \phi_{xz}^2)(1 - \phi_{yz}^2)}}$$

$$= \frac{.40 - (.62)(.39)}{\sqrt{(1 - .38)(1 - .15)}} = .22$$

The correlation between x and y ($\phi_{xy} = .40$) has been reduced to $\phi_{xy.z} = .22$ as a consequence of controlling for a variable (z) which is related to $y(\phi_{yz} = .32)$ and to $x(\phi_{xz} = .62)$. Whereas education alone explains 16 percent of the variation in vote direction, the introduction and control of occupational prestige reduces that effect to 5 percent.

We are now in a position to determine the multiple effect of x and z on y. A coefficient of multiple determination using the ϕ's and ϕ^2's is represented by the following:

$$\phi_{y.xz}^2 = \frac{\phi_{xy}^2 + \phi_{yz}^2 - 2\phi_{xy}\phi_{yz}\phi_{xz}}{1 - \phi_{xz}^2}$$

$$= \frac{.16 + .15 - 2(.40)(.39)(.62)}{1 - .38} = .20$$

---

52. Although partial correlation analysis does not measure interactive effects, they can be assessed by comparing $\phi_{xy.z}^2$ (.05) with ϕ_{xy}^2 for one level of Z (e.g., high prestige, .05) and ϕ_{xy}^2 for the other level of Z (e.g., low prestige, .03). If the $\phi_{xy.z}^2$ and ϕ_{xy}^2 values differ greatly, there is interaction. Another means for isolating interactive effects is by the covariance theorem developed by Lazarsfeld. See Alker, *Mathematics and Politics*, pp. 96–101.

Together, education level and occupational prestige explain 20 percent of the variation in vote direction.[53]

Bivariate Analysis of Ordinal Data

Although there are many instances in which political science measurements are less sophisticated than those in other sciences, there are many variables that have the property of order in addition to their property of classification. The most efficient means for analyzing these data is through a variety of ordinally based techniques. For example, education as a politically relevant independent variable may imply a ranking of education levels, not merely a categorization, yet it may be impossible for the researcher to adequately measure it on an interval level such as years of schooling. Furthermore, one might argue that it is not the years of schooling that are most important, but the completion of some specified level of work, i.e., education may be logically most meaningful as a set of ordered categories. There also are scaled measures such as authoritarianism, political conservatism, or political participation for which the researcher may be unable to assume a higher order of measurement, i.e., his data collection procedures could make it difficult to conclude that the distance between two rankings on the scale is the same as the distance between two other rankings on the same scale. Most of the ordinally based techniques are designed to perform the analytical function and measure the association between variables, but the analyst should keep the descriptive and inductive functions in mind. There is a variety of options available in performing the descriptive process, e.g., a comparison of median or modal rankings on two variables, a presentation of the array of ranked data for smaller samples, and the plotting of the rankings on a coordinate system. In performing the inductive function there are several statistical tests of significance which are separate from any measure of association. Some enable an automatic test of significance by looking up the critical values of a measure of association (e.g., Spearman's rho, r_s) while other measures of association have specially suited tests of significance for them (e.g., Z-tests).

Let us assume that we are interested in testing the relationship between authoritarianism and political conservatism, that such data have been collected on the basis of scale rankings, and that our theoretical framework suggests that conservatism is dependent upon an underlying psychological factor such as authoritarianism tested through the null hypothesis that there is no relationship between the two variables. When there are no ties on either of the variables, the most popular measure of rank order correlation is Spearman's rho (r_s). The technique involves taking the differences between ranks, squaring them and correcting the value so that it occurs between -1 and $+1$. Table 2.14 presents the computational scheme. When presenting such an array it is easiest to rank one of the variables in ascending order. A comparison of the rankings suggests that there are small differences between them and that as the ranks on the first variable increase, the ranks on the

53. Elaborations of related techniques appear in Herbert L. Costner and L. Wesley Wager, "The Multivariate Analysis of Dichotomized Variables," *American Journal of Sociology* 70 (1965): 455–66, and Leo A. Goodman, "On the Multivariate Analysis of Three Dichotomous Variables," *American Journal of Sociology* 71 (1965): 290–301.

TABLE 2.14   Computation of Spearman's Rho
without Ties

Respondent	Authori-tarianism (X) X Rank	Political Conservatism (Y) Y Rank	$d(X - Y)$	d^2
A	1	2	−1	1
B	2	3	−1	1
C	3	6	−3	9
D	4	1	+3	9
E	5	7	−2	4
F	6	4	+2	4
G	7	9	−2	4
H	8	5	+3	9
I	9	10	−1	1
J	10	8	+2	4
$N = 10$				$\Sigma d^2 = 46$

second generally increase. The value of Spearman's rho is computed for these data as follows:

$$r_s = 1 - \frac{6\Sigma d^2}{N(N^2 - 1)}$$

$$= 1 - \frac{(6)(46)}{10\,(100 - 1)} = +.72$$

Thus, there is a high and positive relationship between rank on authoritarianism and rank on political conservatism.[54] If the value is squared it suggests that 52 percent of the variation in political conservatism is associated with authoritarianism. In order to test our hypothesis of a relationship greater than no relationship, the significance level of r_s can be located on a table of critical values for r_s, or a Z-test can be calculated by the following formula.

$$Z = \frac{r_s}{1/\sqrt{N - 1}}$$

$$= \frac{.7213}{1/\sqrt{9}} = 2.16$$

With $Z_{.05} = 1.96$ and $Z_{.01} = 2.58$, the relationship between authoritarianism and political conservatism is statistically significant and likely to occur by chance in only 5 out of 100 times.

When there are ties on either or both variables, r_s will generally be inflated, especially for a large number of ties. Given a brief array of hypothetical data relating education rank and political participation rank, a Spearman's rho correction for ties can be computed (table 2.15). Note that there are only ties on the Y variable.

---

54. Spearman's rho and Pearson's r for interval data will be equal when the range and variance of X and Y are equal.

TABLE 2.15 Computation of Spearman's Rho
with Ties

| Respondents | Education Level (X) | Political Participation (Y) | | | |
	X Rank	Y Score	Y Rank	d	d^2
A	1	2	1.5	−.5	.25
B	2	2	1.5	+.5	.25
C	3	4	3.0	0	0
D	4	5	4.5	−.5	.25
E	5	5	4.5	+.5	.25
$N = 5$				$\Sigma d^2 = 1.0$	

Each time there are ties, the respective tied scores are assigned a rank based on the mean of their rank if there were no ties. That is, the 1.5 rankings on Y represent the mean of the rankings without ties $((1 + 2)/2)$. The rank differences are now computed on the basis of the "corrected" ranks, squared and summed. The corrected formula is

$$r_s = \frac{\Sigma x^2 + \Sigma y^2 - \Sigma d^2}{2\sqrt{\Sigma x^2 \, \Sigma y^2}}$$

where

$$\Sigma x^2 = \frac{N(N^2 - 1)}{12} - \Sigma Tx$$

and

$$\Sigma y^2 = \frac{N(N^2 - 1)}{12} - \Sigma Ty$$

where

$$T = \frac{t^3 - t}{12}$$

and t is the number of tied ranks on any given tied position. For example, the first tied position has two ties and the other tied position also has two ties, so that

$$\Sigma Ty = \frac{2^3 - 2}{12} + \frac{2^3 - 2}{12} = 1$$

Since there are no ties on X,

$$\Sigma x^2 = \frac{5 (5^2 - 1)}{12} - 0 = 10$$

and the correction for ties on $Y = 1$, therefore

$$\Sigma y^2 = \frac{5(5^2 - 1)}{12} - 1 = 9$$

and

$$r_s = \frac{10 + 9 - 1}{2\sqrt{(10)(9)}} = +.95$$

which is interpreted in the same manner as r_s without a correction for ties.

A sound alternative for Spearman's rank order correlation coefficient is Kendall's tau (τ) (to be distinguished from Goodman and Kruskal's tau for nominal data).[55] Looking at all pairs of ranks we want to determine if they are in the same order. It is useful to refer to the data in table 2.14 where one variable (authoritarianism) s in order. The formula for tau is

$$\tau_a = \frac{S}{\frac{1}{2} N(N - 1)}$$

where S is determined by reading down the unordered variable (political conservatism) and counting the number of ranks below each rank which are larger and subtracting the number of ranks below each rank which are smaller. For example, there are eight ranks on the dependent variable which are below and larger than rank number two, and one rank which is below and smaller, therefore $(8 - 1) = 7$. There are seven ranks below rank number three which are larger and one (rank 1) which is smaller, therefore $(7 - 1) = 6$. If this scheme is followed and the values are summed they equal:

$$(8 - 1) + (7 - 1) + (4 - 3) + (6 - 0) + (3 - 2) + (4 - 0) +$$

$$(1 - 2) + (2 - 0) + (0 - 1) = 25$$

and

$$\tau = \frac{25}{\frac{1}{2}(10)(9)} = +.55$$

Although the actual numerical values of τ and r_s differ for the same data they will both reject the null hypothesis of no relationship in the population at the same significance level.[56] As with r_s, a version of the Z-test establishes whether the re-

55. Maurice G. Kendall, *Rank Correlation Methods*, 3d ed. (London: Charles Griffin & Company Ltd., 1962), pp. 4–6. In addition to multivariate extensions of tau cited below, recent efforts have led to the development of a regression coefficient for this test. See Pranab Kumar Sen, "Estimates of the Regression Coefficient Based on Kendall's Tau," *Journal of the American Statistical Association* 63 (1968): 1379–89.

56. Siegel, *Nonparametric Statistics*, p. 219.

lationship between authoritarianism and political conservatism occurred by mere chance in the population. It is a most satisfactory test if there are no ties on the variables (or relatively few):

$$Z = \frac{S}{\sqrt{\frac{1}{18} N(N - 1)(2N + 5)}}$$

$$= \frac{25}{\sqrt{\frac{1}{18} (10)(9)(25)}} = 2.24 \qquad p < .05$$

The above coefficient (sometimes called tau_a) is applicable to ranked data without ties. If such data were in contingency table form, no two individuals would fall in the same row or column of the table. Such a table would be practically meaningless and furthermore, the untied conditions would be rare in social science examples with a small number of rankings. To correct this problem, Kendall's tau is adaptable to ties on either variable (τ_b) when there is an equal number of ranks on each variable. Using ties on the dependent variable (e.g., political participation) as we did with r_s in table 2.15, we follow the same procedure of assigning ranks based on the average of the ranks if there were no ties.[57] The S value is computed in the same manner as the example without ties. That is, there are three ranks on Y below and larger than the first rankings (1.5) and none below and smaller, therefore, $(3 - 0) = 3$.

$$S = (3 - 0) + (3 - 0) + (2 - 0) + (0 - 0) = 8$$

The denominator, however, is altered to become

$$\sqrt{\tfrac{1}{2}N(N - 1) - T_x} \cdot \sqrt{\tfrac{1}{2}N(N - 1) - T_y}$$

where

$$T_x = \tfrac{1}{2}\Sigma\, t(t - 1)$$

and

$$T_y = \tfrac{1}{2}\Sigma\, t(t - 1)$$

where t is the number of ties in each set of ties on either X or Y. Since there are no ties on X, $T_x = 0$, but there are ties on Y, so t must be determined. Scanning this short array we see that there are two ties at rank 1.5 and two ties at rank 4.5. Each of these sets must be accounted for in the formula and summed:

$$T_y = \tfrac{1}{2}[2(2 - 1) + 2(2 - 1)] = 2$$

---

57. Ibid., pp. 217–19.

Therefore,

$$\tau_b = \frac{8}{\sqrt{\frac{1}{2}(5)(4) - 0} \cdot \sqrt{\frac{1}{2}(5)(4) - 2}} = +.84$$

This indicates a high positive correlation between education and political participation, one which is suggested by a previous glance at the table which shows a close
relationship between rankings. A Z-test of significance is available for Kendall's
tau with ties but it is very involved and frequently it will show statistical significance
when the Z-test without ties is not significant. That is, in many instances, it is satisfactory to use the Z-test without ties for tied data because it is more conservative.[58]
When there is a large number of ties, the data can be grouped into contingency
table form (with an equal number of rows and columns) and a Kendall's tau can be
calculated in a manner similar to that above. If we are again comparing hypothetical
data on the relationship between authoritarianism and political conservatism, let
us assume that the data have been grouped into high, medium, and low categories
based upon cut-off points on the rankings, and they look like table 2.16. A cursory

TABLE 2.16 Contingency Data for Kendall's Tau$_b$

AUTHORITARIANISM (X)	POLITICAL CONSERVATISM (Y)			
	High	Medium	Low	Total
High	20	10	8	38
Medium	13	8	6	27
Low	4	6	25	35
Total	37	24	39	100

examination of the table (especially the high-high and low-low cells) suggests that
the two variables are at least moderately related in a positive direction and we see
that thirty-seven respondents are tied at high conservatism, twenty-four at medium,
and thirty-nine at low. In order to calculate S we use every cell below and not in
the same column or row of the cell we are calculating from. The cells below and to
the left are negative and those below and to the right are positive. Each cell value is
then multiplied by these values below it and summed to equal S. For example, the
cell values 8, 6, 6, and 25 are below and to the right of cell value 20; cell values 6 and
25 are below and to the right of value 10, but values 13 and 4 are below and to the
left (and therefore minus). S is calculated as follows:

$$20(8 + 6 + 6 + 25) + 10(6 + 25 - 13 - 4) + 8(-13 - 4 - 8 - 6)$$

$$+ 13(6 + 25) + 8(-4 + 25) + 6(-4 - 6) = 1303$$

---

58. Kendall, *Rank Correlation Methods*, pp. 55ff.

This S value represents the difference between concordant pairs (associated with the main diagonal of the table) and the discordant pairs (those associated with one of the off diagonals, i.e., inconsistent with the main diagonal). In an example (table 2.16), row totals are used to find the number of tied pairs for authoritarianism (X) and column totals are used to find ties on political conservatism (Y):

$$T_x = \tfrac{1}{2}[38(38 - 1) + 27(27 - 1) + 35(35 - 1)] = 1649$$

$$T_y = \tfrac{1}{2}[37(37 - 1) + 24(24 - 1) + 39(39 - 1)] = 3366$$

When these values are substituted in the τ_b formula we have:

$$\tau_b = \frac{1303}{\sqrt{\tfrac{1}{2} 100(100 - 1) - 1649} \cdot \sqrt{\tfrac{1}{2} 100(100 - 1) - 3366}} = +.57$$

We have specified τ_b as an appropriate measure of association between two ordinal variables with ties on either or both ranks. It also was noted that τ_b is most appropriate for contingency tables with an equal number of columns and rows — this is because τ_b can attain unity only under this condition (and when both variables are dichotomous, τ_b = phi). If we encounter data with an unequal number of rankings for each variable ($r \neq c$), Kendall's tau$_c$ employs a correction for the number of rows and columns. The formula for τ_c applicable to ordinal data with ties and an unequal number of rows and columns is:

$$\tau_c = \frac{S}{\tfrac{1}{2}N^2[(m - 1)/m]}$$

where m = min. (r,c), that is, whichever is smaller, the number of rows or the number of columns. This correction permits the coefficient to attain unity without requiring an equal number of rows and columns. The test of statistical significance for τ_c is the same Z-test applicable to τ_a.

Although the various tau's discussed above are flexible in their application to tied and non-tied cases, and square and rectangular tables, the tau coefficients lack an operational meaning comparable to many other measures of association. That is, the meaning of a τ_a value is judged only in relation to some other τ_a value, and τ_b's are only comparable with other τ_b's (and τ_c's with other τ_c's). Therefore, it is often desirable to employ a proportional reduction in error (PRE) statistic which has a meaning beyond its own class. Gamma (γ) is an ordinal measure of association which has this characteristic; furthermore, it allows for ties and it can attain unity without an equal number of rows and columns.[59] In the dichotomous case, gamma equals Yule's Q. Its values range from +1 to −1 and will approach +1 when values are concentrated in the extreme cells. High negative relationships appear when data are concentrated in low-high cells. A positive relationship moving toward +1 is evident from a cursory glance at the hypothetical grouped data on authori-

---

59. Goodman and Kruskal, "Association for Cross Classifications," pp. 784–54.

tarianism and conservatism (table 2.16). As with Goodman and Kruskal's tau and lambda for nominal data, it is based upon the idea of error reduction. That is, it is based upon selecting pairs of respondents at random, examining their order on authoritarianism and predicting their order on political conservatism. If the variables are highly related few errors will be made. The formula for gamma can be represented as

$$\gamma = \frac{S_+ - S_-}{S_+ + S_-}$$

where S_+ equals the proportion of pairs with similar ranks and S_- equals the proportion of pairs with different ranks. The calculation of S_+ and S_- is similar to that for S in the Kendall's τ_c formula. S_+ is each cell frequency times the cells below and to the right of it (i.e., cells representing lesser ranks), and S_- is each cell frequency times the cell values below and to the left of it (cells representing higher ranks). Such that, using the data on authoritarianism and conservatism, we derive the correct prediction minus the incorrect predictions as a proportion of all predictions:

$$S_+ = 20(8 + 6 + 6 + 25) + 10(6 + 25) + 13(6 + 25) + 8(25) = 1813$$

$$S_- = 10(13 + 4) + 8(13 + 4 + 8 + 6) + 8(4) + 6(4 + 6) = 510$$

$$\gamma = \frac{1813 - 510}{1813 + 510} = +.56$$

One final ordinal measure is Somers' d.[60] It is designed for ordered contingency tables like the above examples, but it has the advantage of being asymmetrical, like lambda$_a$ and lambda$_b$ for nominal data. This suggests a distinction between the independent and dependent variables (d_{xy} or d_{yx}). The numerator is the same as that for gamma and tau$_c$ ($S_+ - S_-$); that is, the excess of similar over dissimilar pairs. However, the denominator for d_{yx} is the number of pairs not tied on X regardless of Y and for d_{xy}, the number not tied on Y regardless of X, such that

$$d_{yx} = \frac{S_+ - S_-}{S_+ + S_- + Y_0}$$

and

$$d_{xy} = \frac{S_+ - S_-}{S_+ + S_- + X_0}$$

where

$$Y_0 = \text{those tied on } Y \text{ only}$$

$$X_0 = \text{those tied on } X \text{ only}$$

---

60. Robert H. Somers, "A New Asymmetric Measure of Association for Ordinal Variables," *American Sociological Review* 27 (1962): 799–811.

Using the grouped ordinal data (table 2.16) for authoritarianism as the independent variable (X) and conservatism as the dependent variable (Y), Y_0 (those tied on conservatism) $= 20(13 + 4) + (13 \cdot 4) + 10(8 + 6) + (8 \cdot 6) + 8(6 + 25) + (6 \cdot 25) = 978$; and X_0 (tied on authoritarianism) $= 20(10 + 8) + (10 \cdot 8) + 13(8 + 6) + (8 \cdot 6) + 4(6 + 25) + (6 \cdot 25) = 944.$[61] Therefore the relationship predicting Y from X (conservatism from authoritarianism) $=$

$$d_{yx} = \frac{1813 - 510}{1813 + 510 + 978} = \frac{1303}{3301} = +.39$$

and X from $Y =$

$$d_{xy} = \frac{1813 - 510}{1813 + 510 + 944} = \frac{1303}{3267} = +.40$$

Although these individual coefficients are interpreted as asymmetrical correlation coefficients, they are analogous to regression coefficients discussed later. Our hypothetical data suggest that similar levels of predictability will be achieved irrespective of the predictor variable chosen.

Since all of the above coefficients measure degree of relationship, it is important to keep distinctions between significance and association in mind following the inductive and analytical categories suggested previously. On the inductive level, a typical procedure for determining level of significance is to calculate χ^2 on some of the above tables, despite the ordinal level of measurement. However, several of the measures of association have related tests of significance as discussed above. The reader also is reminded that there is a body of nonparametric tests of significance for ordinal data designed to test whether two independent groups (e.g., Democrats, Republicans) have come from the same population. Such tests include the Kolmogorov-Smirnov Test, Mann-Whitney U Test, and the Wald-Wolfowitz Runs Test.[62]

Multivariate Analysis of Ordinal Data

Political scientists are often faced with the task of analyzing multivariate relationships between variables measured on an ordinal level. Most research designs treat a series of variables and the nature of social and political reality often suggests that data are less than interval. Despite the availability of multivariate tests for ordinal data,[63] the usual response is to either assume that data are interval, using multiple correlation-regression or to drop to a lower level of measurement, treating the data as nominal and employing partial coefficients based upon classifications or

---

61. As an alternative to calculating pairs tied only on Y (Y_0) it is possible to substitute the entire denominator which contains the Y_0 term with the number of pairs of observations that are not tied on X calculated by summing the products of marginal frequencies for X. For example, $(38)(27) + (38)(35) + (27)(35) = 3301$. Similarly, the denominator for d_{xy} can be the sum of the products of marginal frequencies for Y (3267).

62. Siegel, *Nonparametric Statistics*, pp. 116–45.

63. For general methods see Kendall, *Rank Correlation Methods*, pp. 117–22, and Siegel, *Nonparametric Statistics*, pp. 223–29.

dummy variable regression (discussed later). Several approaches to this problem
attempt to utilize as much ordinal information as possible, yet no more information
than is inherent in the data. One procedure for determining partial and multiple
effects with three or more ordered variables involves a manipulation of simple
tau's similar to the way in which we manipulate phi's in order to obtain partial
and multiple coefficients for nominal data. A hypothetical relationship between
authoritarianism and political conservatism has been examined previously (table
2.14). Let us assume that our data and hypotheses have led us to collect scale rankings on a third variable: political alienation. Previous theory and research might
suggest that such alienation factors as normlessness, meaninglessness, and lack of
political efficacy are positively associated with political conservatism and that they
also may be related to the independent variable, authoritarianism. The analysis
steps should indicate the simple relationships between three variables, including the
interrelationships between authoritarianism and alienation; the impact of authoritarianism on conservatism controlling for alienation; and the multiple effect of
both independent variables on the dependent variable.

The calculation of simple tau's satisfies the first step. The previous relationship
reported for authoritarianism and conservatism (tau$_a$) was $\tau_{xy} = +.55$. Since tau
is easiest to calculate when one of the variables in a pair of variables is placed in
ascending order, the reordered bivariate rankings appear in table 2.17. Following

TABLE 2.17   Bivariate Rankings of Three Ordered
Variables

Authoritarianism (X)	Political Alienation (Z)	Political Alienation (Z)	Political Conservatism (Y)
X Rank	Z Rank	Z Rank	Y Rank
1	4	1	4
2	6	2	5
3	5	3	9
4	8	4	2
5	10	5	6
6	1	6	3
7	3	7	10
8	2	8	1
9	7	9	8
10	9	10	7

the formula for tau:

$$\tau = \frac{S}{\frac{1}{2}N(N-1)}$$

where S is the sum of larger rankings below each rank minus the smaller rankings
below each, the S for $\tau_{xz} = (6-3) + (4-4) + (4-3) + (2-4) + (0-5)$
$+ (4-0) + (2-1) + (2-0) + (1-0) = 5$ and

$$\tau_{xz} = \frac{5}{\frac{1}{2}(10)(9)} = +.11$$

The S for τ_{zy} = $(6 - 3) + (5 - 3) + (1 - 6) + (5 - 1) + (3 - 2) + (3 - 1) + (0 - 3) + (2 - 0) + (0 - 1) = 5$ and $\tau_{zy} = +.11$. These simple tau's suggest low correlations between authoritarianism and alienation and conservatism and alienation. From these calculations we could examine our previous hypotheses and suggest, for example, that political alienation may cut across the entire political ideology spectrum and that authoritarianism does not imply a sense of alienation. These low correlations also suggest that when Z is controlled, the relationship between X and Y should be almost as strong as it was without the introduction of Z. Kendall's partial rank correlation coefficient $(\tau_{xy.z})$ measures this relationship.

$$\tau_{xy.z} = \frac{\tau_{xy} - \tau_{zy}\tau_{xz}}{\sqrt{(1 - \tau_{zy}^2)(1 - \tau_{xz}^2)}}$$

$$= \frac{.55 - (.11)(.11)}{\sqrt{[1 - (.11^2)][1 - (.11)^2]}} = +.55$$

When alienation is partialled out, the correlation between authoritarianism and conservatism remains the same. That is, the relationship between authoritarianism and conservatism is independent of effects of alienation.

The final step involves the derivation of a parsimonious figure which represents total multiple effects. Manipulating the tau's in a manner similar to the manipulation of phi's for a multiple coefficient of determination we get:

$$\tau_{y.xz}^2 = \frac{\tau_{xy}^2 + \tau_{yz}^2 - 2\,\tau_{xy}\tau_{xz}\tau_{yz}}{1 - \tau_{xz}^2}$$

$$= \frac{(.55)^2 + (.11)^2 - 2\,(.55)(.11)(.11)}{1 - (.11)^2} = .31$$

This coefficient indicates that 31 percent of the variance in political conservatism is caught by the independent variables authoritarianism and political alienation. The similarity of this value to τ_{xy}^2 (.30) suggests that alienation has added little to our explanatory power.[64]

If data can only be collected or presented in grouped rank form (i.e., with ties), a derivation of gamma can be applied to measure partial correlation.[65] When

---

64. A related measure which accomplishes the same purpose is Koppa, a multiple coefficient based upon multiple reduction in error prediction. See William H. Kruskal, "Ordinal Measures of Association," *Journal of the American Statistical Association* 52 (1958): 818–23. An application to political data appears in Roy T. Bowles and James T. Richardson, "Sources of Consistency of Political Opinion," *American Journal of Sociology* 74 (1969): 676–84. Our brief example of a multiple coefficient for Kendall's tau$_a$ is based on the logic of parametric tests and it should be used with caution. The development of multiple ordinal coefficients is a relatively new field marked by continuing research. Multiple coefficients have been derived for gamma, Somers' d and tau$_c$, but under some conditions their values (as well as those for tau$_a$) will be reduced by the addition of a meaningful control variable (nonzero partials). For a review of criteria and the extent to which they are met by the various multiple coefficients, see the development of gamma $-k$ in Raymond N. Morris, "Multiple Correlation and Ordinally Scaled Data," *Social Forces* 48 (1970): 299–311.

65. James A. Davis, "A Partial Coefficient for Goodman and Kruskal's Gamma," *Journal of the American Statistical Association* 62 (1967): 189–93. An extension of Kendall's tau also has been developed for the type of subgroup analysis employed by Davis. It is more effective for considering the ordinal nature of the control variable, yet it tends to yield discrepant findings in only unusual cases. See Robert H. Somers, "An Approach to the Multivariate Analysis of Ordinal Data," *American Sociological Review* 33 (1968): 971–77.

hypothetical data on authoritarianism and political conservatism were presented in tabular form with $N = 100$ (table 2.17), the gamma correlation coefficient yielded a $+.56$ relationship. We again wish to measure the affect of a third variable, political alienation, and the extent to which a control for this variable affects the relationship between the first independent variable and the dependent variable. The tabular controls are presented in table 2.18. A cursory examination of the fre-

TABLE 2.18 Contingency Relationships Between
Three Ordered Variables with a Tabular Control

AUTHORITAR-IANISM (X)	POLITICAL ALIENATION (Z)											
	High				Medium				Low			
	Political Conservatism (Y)											
	High	Medium	Low	Total	High	Medium	Low	Total	High	Medium	Low	Total
High	9	3	3	15	7	1	2	10	6	2	5	13
Medium	4	4	2	10	2	4	1	7	3	3	4	10
Low	1	1	10	12	2	3	5	10	3	3	7	13
Total	14	8	15	37	11	8	8	27	12	8	16	36

quencies and the percentages that could be calculated from them suggests that the impact of the third variable, alienation, on political conservatism, is rather stable across its values and that the important diagonal extremes are not drastically altered. This suggests that the ranked values of alienation have minimal impact on the relationship between authoritarianism and conservatism, yet we note less extreme diagonal values in the low alienation control table. The separate impact of high, medium, and low alienation on political conservatism can be measured by calculating gammas for each category. Furthermore, a disparity between the three gamma values indicates interaction. That is, the impact of one variable on another differs for differing levels of another variable.[66] These conditional gammas are calculated in the same manner as before: where S_+ is the sum of each cell multiplied by the sum of the cells below and to the right, and S_- is the sum of each cell multiplied by the sum of the cells below and to the left. Such that for high alienation:

$$S_+ = 9(4 + 2 + 1 + 10) + 3(2 + 10) + 4(1 + 10) + 4(10) = 276$$
$$S_- = 3(4 + 1) + 3(4 + 4 + 1 + 1) + 4(1) + 2(1 + 1) = 53$$

For medium alienation:

$$S_+ = 7(4 + 1 + 3 + 5) + 1(1 + 5) + 2(3 + 5) + 4(5) = 133$$
$$S_- = 1(2 + 2) + 2(2 + 4 + 2 + 3) + 4(2) + 1(2 + 3) = 39$$

66. When interactions are present, a partial gamma will give greater weight to classes of variable Z which have larger frequencies.

For low alienation:

$$S_+ = 6(3 + 4 + 3 + 7) + 2(4 + 7) + 3(3 + 7) + 3(7) = 175$$
$$S_- = 2(3 + 3) + 5(3 + 3 + 3 + 3) + 3(3) + 4(3 + 3) = 105$$

Therefore, following the $S_+ - S_-/S_+ + S_-$ formula for γ, the three coefficients for each level of the control variable equal $+.68$, $+.55$ and $+.25$. When each S_+ value and each S_- value for the three categories of alienation are added together to derive a total S_+ value, they can be treated as before and a partial coefficient is the result. For example,

$$\gamma_{xy.z} = \frac{\Sigma\, S_+ - \Sigma\, S_-}{\Sigma\, S_+ + \Sigma\, S_-}$$
$$= \frac{(276 + 133 + 175) - (53 + 39 + 105)}{(276 + 133 + 175) + (53 + 39 + 105)} = +.49$$

The impact of authoritarianism on conservatism controlling for alienation is $+.49$, representing only a minor change from the original zero order correlation coefficient between authoritarianism and conservatism $(+.56)$ and suggesting an effect between X and Y which is independent of control Z. If this partial correlation coefficient would have approached zero, we could have concluded that the previous relationship between X and Y vanished and that the previous relationship was dependent upon Z.

Other Combinations of Functions and Levels of Measurement

Before we discuss functions that can be performed in an analytical scheme where political data are measured on an interval scale, we will review an often neglected gap in statistical data analysis: combinations of variables at different levels of measurement. One of the most frequently occurring designs in social science research involves nominal and interval variables, yet statistical treatment of such designs has been neglected in political science. The most powerful tool which assists us in performing inductive as well as analytical functions at this level is the analysis of variance. At the same time, this parametric test is one of the most complex tools used in the social sciences, particularly with regard to assumptions and variations on different models. Most of the technical variations will be omitted for purposes of this survey; however, the researcher should acquaint himself with these factors if he is going to make extensive use of the tools. Particular attention should be paid to the development of analysis of variance as an experimental research tool.[67] Below we consider (1) one-way analysis of variance, (2) two-way analysis of variance, and (3) other procedures for various measurement levels.

---

67. For this development plus more technical considerations see Kerlinger, *Foundations of Behavioral Research*, pp. 187–256; Palumbo, *Statistics in Political and Behavioral Science*, pp. 223–49; George W. Snedecor and William G. Cochran, *Statistical Methods*, 6th ed. (Ames, Iowa: The Iowa State University Press, 1967), pp. 258–380; Blalock, *Social Statistics*, pp. 317–59; and Hays, *Statistics for Psychologists*, pp. 356–458.

(1) *One-way analysis of variance:* Inductively, analysis of variance provides for a test of significance between different sample means, thereby making inferences about population means. Analytically, an affiliated correlation coefficient tests the degree of association between variables. It is applicable for designs with a three or more category nominal independent variable[68] and an intervally measured dependent variable (one-way analysis of variance), as well as several nominal variables in combination with an interval variable (two-way analysis of variance). Many of the assumptions underlying the technique are common to parametric tests: normal population distributions, independent random samples, and equal population standard deviations.

In a hypothetical scheme meeting these restrictions, let us assume that we are testing the relationship between a rural-urban dimension measured as three categories,[69] and a liberal-conservative dimension measured on a scale which we are willing to assume is interval (1–15 points, where high scores are conservative). The data array necessary for calculation and description is shown in table 2.19.

TABLE 2.19   Data Array and Computation for
One-Way Analysis of Variance

| IDEOLOGY SCORES BY RESIDENCE | | | | | |
| Urban (X_u) | | Suburban (X_s) | | Rural (X_r) | |
X_u	$X_u{}^2$	X_s	$X_s{}^2$	X_r	$X_r{}^2$
0	0	0	0	3	9
1	1	3	9	4	16
2	4	4	16	5	25
4	16	6	36	7	49
4	16	8	64	9	81
6	36	11	121	10	100
7	49	12	144	12	144
		12	144	14	196
$\Sigma X_u = 24$	$\Sigma X_u{}^2 = 122$			15	225
		$\Sigma X_s = 56$	$\Sigma X_s{}^2 = 534$		
				$\Sigma X_r = 79$	$\Sigma X_r{}^2 = 845$
	$\bar{X} = 3.4$		$\bar{X} = 7.0$		$\bar{X} = 8.8$

In performing the descriptive function, the relative distribution of dependent variable scores can be shown in an array where the data are of manageable size. The array in table 2.19 suggests that higher conservatism scores are more frequent within the rural category of the independent variable. Means also can be calculated by summing the dependent variable scores in each category and dividing by the N of that category. We now have three more parsimonious figures to assist us in description: the rural subsample exhibits the highest mean conservatism score

---

68. For inferential purposes, a *t*-test for the difference between two means using a two-category variable will reject the null hypothesis at the same level of significance as the *F*-test for analysis of variance.

69. The independent variable categories are frequently called "treatments" in experimental research.

$(\bar{X} = 8.8)$ whereas the suburban, and particularly the urban group, have lower average scores ($\bar{X} = 7.0$ and 3.4).

To assess the significance of the differences among these means, that is, to test the null hypothesis of no relationship between place of residence and ideology, analysis of variance procedures can be utilized. In order to test the probability of such a relationship (described by the means) occurring by chance, several estimates of variance are calculated. One is an estimate of variance *within* each independent variable category, that is, a measure of the variation of individual observations about the mean of the category. The second is an estimate of variances *between or among* the categories of the independent variable, that is, a measure of the variation of each category mean from the grand mean for the total sample. The last is an estimate of *total* variation (defined as the sum of squared deviations from a mean) representing the sum of the within and among estimates. For ease of calculation, we will begin by obtaining the total sample sum of squares, and the among sum of squares, subtracting the among from the total to obtain the within estimate. The total is calculated by summing the squares of the dependent variable scores in each category of the independent variable and subtracting the total sum of the raw scores squared and divided by the total number of observations such that

$$\Sigma X^2 - \frac{(\Sigma X)^2}{N}$$

and utilizing the sums shown in the array, the values are

$$(122 + 534 + 845) - \frac{(24 + 56 + 79)^2}{(7 + 8 + 9)} = 447.63$$

The variation of each category mean from a grand mean $[(\Sigma X_g)^2/N_g]$ can be represented as

$$\frac{(\Sigma X_u)^2}{N_u} + \frac{(\Sigma X_s)^2}{N_s} + \frac{(\Sigma X_r)^2}{N_r} - \frac{(\Sigma X_g)^2}{N_g} \quad \text{or}$$

$$\frac{24^2}{7} + \frac{56^2}{8} + \frac{79^2}{9} - \frac{159^2}{24} = 114.36$$

The within sum of squares then is obtained by subtracting the among sum of squares from the total sum of squares ($447.63 - 114.36 = 333.27$). When the among sum of squares is divided by its respective degrees of freedom ($k - 1 =$ number of categories of independent variable $- 1$) the value represents the final estimate (sometimes called mean squares) of the variance of ideology accounted for by place of residence. The within sum of squares divided by its degrees of freedom ($N - k =$ total number of cases minus the number of categories of the independent variable) estimates the variance in the dependent variable not explained by the independent variable.

$$\text{Among Variance Estimate} = \frac{114.36}{3 - 1} = 57.18$$

$$\text{Within Variance Estimate} = \frac{333.27}{24 - 3} = 15.87$$

Although it appears that we have explained more variation than not, the rejection of the null hypothesis and the determination of significance level is dependent upon the magnitude of the difference between the two variance estimates. Therefore, a statistical test known as an *F*-test represents the ratio of among to within mean squares:

$$F = \frac{57.18}{15.87} = 3.60$$

Using a table of *F* values, the 3.60 value with 2 and 21 degrees of freedom is statistically significant at the .05 probability level, suggesting that there is something other than the forces of chance at work in the relationship between ideology and residence. For summary purposes the result of each analysis of variance step is entered in a one-way AOV table (table 2.20).

TABLE 2.20   One-Way Analysis of Variance Table

Source	Sum of Squares	Degrees of Freedom	Variance Estimate	*F* ratio	*p*
Total	447.63	N-1 = 23			
Among classes	114.36	k-1 = 2	57.18	3.60	<.05
Within classes	333.27	N-k = 21	15.87		

After the data have been described with an array and a comparison of means, and the probability level has been found to be significant, it is most useful to proceed with a measure of the magnitude of the relationship which is more accurate and parsimonious than a mere comparison of means. A commonly used measure of association for analysis of variance is the intraclass correlation coefficient. It is a measure of homogeneity in the categories of the independent variable vis-à-vis total variation in the dependent variable. As with other correlation coefficients, the researcher must be aware of the difficulties and fallacies of causal interpretation. This is especially true for analysis of variance used with social and political data where experimental control is difficult, i.e., where random assignment to categories of the independent variable has been impossible. Furthermore, the intraclass co-efficient (r_i) has theoretical limits of -1 and $+1$, yet the lower limit will frequently be less than unity. With high homogeneity in the categories of the independent variable, r_i will approach $+1$, and when the distribution of dependent variable scores is random, r_i will equal zero. The formula is:

$$r_i = \frac{\text{Among Variance Estimate} - \text{Within Variance Estimate}}{\text{Among Variance Estimate} + (\bar{N} - 1)(\text{Within Variance Estimate})}$$

where $\bar{N}$ is a simple mean of the number of cases in each category of the independent variable.[70] Using the estimates for the relationship between residence and ideology,

---

70. When these categories differ in size, more involved procedures are necessary for estimating $\bar{N}$. See E. A. Haggard, *Intraclass Correlation and the Analysis of Variance* (New York: Dryden Press, 1958), and our later example for two-way analysis of variance where subclass numbers differ greatly. The correction for $\bar{N}$ is not used in this one-way example because the subclasses are nearly equal.

the r_i value is

$$r_i = \frac{57.18 - 15.87}{57.18 + (8 - 1)(15.87)} = .245$$

We can conclude that there is a positive relationship between rural residence and conservatism, and that place of residence explains about 25 percent of the variability in liberalism-conservatism.[71]

Whereas the above measure has the drawback of lower limit variability, it does provide a correlation coefficient which measures degree of association. If direction has any particular meaning for nominal categories, the clues for direction must be taken from the array and means. This is also the case with an alternative measure (E). It is the square root of the ratio of explained sum of squares to total sum of squares. Therefore, it cannot equal a negative value. Nevertheless, this is an advantage for estimating a coefficient of determination (E^2).[72] For example:

$$E^2 = \frac{\text{Among Sum of Squares}}{\text{Total Sum of Squares}}$$

$$= \frac{114.36}{447.63} = .25 \qquad E = .5$$

Again, 25 percent of the variation in conservatism is caught by place of residence. Another similar measure is ω^2 (omega),

$$\omega^2 = \frac{\text{Among Sum of Squares} - (k - 1)\text{ Within Variance Estimate}}{\text{Total Sum of Squares} + \text{Within Variance Estimate}}$$

$$= \frac{114.36 - (3 - 1)(15.87)}{447.63 + 15.87} = .178$$

Any negative value of ω^2 is set equal to zero, and its upper limit is unity. In our example, it offers a more conservative estimate of the variance: about 18 percent of the variation in conservatism is attributable to residence location.

(2) *Two-way analysis of variance:* For explanatory purposes in the social sciences, we frequently find it useful to design the analysis of data in a multivariate setting. When a dependent variable is measured in real numbers, with two or more nominal independent variables, we can extend the assumptions and calculations of one-way analysis of variance to a two-way analysis of variance design. It is at this point that the procedures become complicated by model choices and adjustments for the varying size of subclasses. The extension of one-way analysis of variance is straightforward if all categories of the independent variables have an equal or proportionate number of observations. Because this rarely occurs in even the best controlled ex post facto analysis dealing with social science data, the example to follow will be

---

71. Since r_i is a correlation coefficient with a variable lower limit, such a percentage is difficult to interpret; nevertheless, the value of r_i is usually between zero and one.

72. This is sometimes called eta^2 (η^2). See Hays, *Statistics for Psychologists*, p. 547, and Blalock, *Social Statistics*, pp. 354–57.

more involved. In handling survey research (which meets analysis of variance assumptions) we not only find a large number of cases, but subclass categories are usually unequal. In order to examine the effect of each independent variable separately, there must be a correction for these disproportionate subclasses. One procedure for this correction uses proportional expected subclass numbers.[73] That is, expected subclass numbers are treated as if they were the original observed frequencies.

Let us assume that we desire to test the relationship between sex and residence as independent variables and voting turnout as a dependent variable. Sex is a two-category nominal scale, residence has three categories and voting turnout is a real number representing the number of times a respondent voted during five previous presidential and congressional elections. Hypothetical data for these relationships, accompanied by values necessary for calculation, are presented in table 2.21.

TABLE 2.21   Computation of Analysis of Variance
with Two Independent Variables

RESIDENCE	SEX		Total
	Male (m)	Female (f)	
	Voting Turnout Scores		
Rural (r)	$N = 242$ $\Sigma X = 486$ $\bar{X} = 2.01$ $N_e = 360.8$ $\Sigma X' = 724.5$	$N = 232$ $\Sigma X = 299$ $\bar{X} = 1.29$ $N_e = 113.2$ $\Sigma X' = 145.9$	$N = 474$ $\Sigma X = 785$ $\bar{X} = 1.66$ $\Sigma X' = 870.4$
Suburban (s)	$N = 630$ $\Sigma X = 1592$ $\bar{X} = 2.53$ $N_e = 555.7$ $\Sigma X' = 1404.2$	$N = 100$ $\Sigma X = 221$ $\bar{X} = 2.21$ $N_e = 174.3$ $\Sigma X' = 385.2$	$N = 730$ $\Sigma X = 1813$ $\bar{X} = 2.48$ $\Sigma X' = 1789.5$
Urban (u)	$N = 317$ $\Sigma X = 956$ $\bar{X} = 3.02$ $N_e = 272.5$ $\Sigma X' = 821.9$	$N = 41$ $\Sigma X = 127$ $\bar{X} = 3.10$ $N_e = 85.5$ $\Sigma X' = 264.8$	$N = 358$ $\Sigma X = 1083$ $\bar{X} = 3.03$ $\Sigma X' = 1086.7$
Total	$N = 1189$ $\Sigma X = 3034$ $\bar{X} = 2.55$ $\Sigma X' = 2950.6$	$N = 373$ $\Sigma X = 647$ $\bar{X} = 1.73$ $\Sigma X' = 795.9$	$N = 1562$ $\Sigma X = 3681$ $\bar{X} = 2.36$ $\Sigma X' = 3746.6$ $\Sigma X^2 = 114{,}812$

The mean turnout scores in each cell, as well as total means, can assist in the description of the data (as can the range and standard deviation). For example, the male-female mean differences decrease as we move from the rural category to the

73. For this and alternative procedures, such as the method of fitting constants and unweighted means, see Snedecor and Cochran, *Statistical Methods*, chap. 16.

urban category and the overall turnout mean for males is greater than for females (2.55 and 1.73). However, greater differences appear between the residence categories, i.e., as we move to the urban subclass mean turnout increases for both males and females. The researcher also may be interested in knowing whether the relationship between the two independent variables is statistically significant. Following the chi-square procedure described earlier, it can be concluded that there is a relationship between sex and residence in the population, with a disproportionate number of females living in rural areas. The expected frequencies themselves are utilized in the disproportionate subclass correction. Each cell's expected frequency is equal to the respective row total times the respective column total divided by the grand total. Therefore N_e for the rural-male cell is $(1189)(474)/1562 = 360.8$. These are the frequencies that would occur if variables were unrelated, i.e., the interrelationship has been removed. A revised sum of frequencies $(\Sigma X')$ then must be calculated as a product of the cell mean $(\bar{X})$ and the expected frequency value N_e. For example, in the rural-male cell $\Sigma X' = (2.01)(360.8) = 724.5$. These calculations have now provided us with the necessary values in each cell of table 2.21.

Although the calculations for two-way analysis of variance are more detailed than other statistical tests, computerized routines have eased this burden. More important, two-way analysis of variance has a variety of advantages over other tests. It not only provides several tests of significance, but unlike other procedures, it has associated routines for a coefficient of determination, plus the unique advantage of testing for interaction and controlling for interrelationship. These concepts of interrelationship and interaction are crucial to an understanding of multivariate analysis. Interrelationship is the linkage between independent variables, sometimes called multicollinearity. A desirable goal of multivariate analysis is the isolation of unique variance, and this is only possible when interrelationships are controlled. It assists us in determining the most meaningful independent variable. The concept of interaction, however, relates to the effect of one independent variable upon the dependent variable for different levels of another independent variable. In order for no interaction to be present in the hypothetical table, the mean differences between columns would be the same for each row and the mean differences between rows would be the same in each column. We see at a glance that these various differences are not equal in the table, yet they are not highly unequal. If mean differences are equal, we would conclude that the table displays the property of additivity. If we find that the relationship of sex to turnout varies with the different residence categories we would conclude that we have a statistical interaction.

At this point, procedures similar to those used in one-way analysis of variance can be followed, i.e., for total among and within sum of squares. We also will need a revised (based on $\Sigma X'$) sum of squares among all the cells and revised sums among the three residence categories and between the two sex categories, plus a test for interaction. The total sum of squares is obtained from the same formula used in one-way analysis of variance:

$$\Sigma X^2 - \frac{(\Sigma X)^2}{N}$$

$$= 114{,}812 - \frac{3681^2}{1562} = 16137.38$$

The among sum of squares for all groupings equals:

$$\frac{(\Sigma X_{mr})^2}{N_{mr}} + \frac{(\Sigma X_{fr})^2}{N_{fr}} + \frac{(\Sigma X_{ms})^2}{N_{ms}} + \frac{(\Sigma X_{fs})^2}{N_{fs}} + \frac{(\Sigma X_{mu})^2}{N_{mu}} + \frac{(\Sigma X_{fu})^2}{N_{fu}} - \frac{(\Sigma X_g)^2}{N_g}$$

$$= \frac{486^2}{242} + \frac{299^2}{232} + \frac{1592^2}{630} + \frac{221^2}{100} + \frac{956^2}{317} + \frac{127^2}{41} - \frac{3681^2}{1562} = 474.58$$

Again, the within total (unexplained variance) is the difference between total and among sum of squares ($16137.38 - 474.58 = 15662.80$). In order to isolate and remove interrelationships and in effect, control for each independent variable, we need a means for determining variability among the residence levels and between the sex levels using the revised frequency totals ($\Sigma X'$) for residence and sex categories. Among residence sum of squares equals:

$$\frac{(\Sigma X'_r)^2}{N_r} + \frac{(\Sigma X'_s)^2}{N_s} + \frac{(\Sigma X'_u)^2}{N_u} - \frac{(\Sigma X'_g)^2}{N_g}$$

$$= \frac{870.4^2}{474} + \frac{1789.5^2}{730} + \frac{1086.7^2}{358} - \frac{3746.6^2}{1562} = 297.15$$

Between sex sum of squares equals:

$$\frac{(\Sigma X'_m)^2}{N_m} + \frac{(\Sigma X'_f)^2}{N_f} - \frac{(\Sigma X'_g)^2}{N_g} = \frac{2950.6^2}{1189} + \frac{795.9^2}{373} - \frac{3746.6^2}{1562} = 34.29$$

We also need a total revised among sum of squares to assist in determining interaction.

Total revised among sum of squares equals:

$$\frac{(\Sigma X'_{mr})^2}{N_{e_{mr}}} + \frac{(\Sigma X'_{fr})^2}{N_{e_{fr}}} + \frac{(\Sigma X'_{ms})^2}{N_{e_{ms}}} + \frac{(\Sigma X'_{fs})^2}{N_{e_{fs}}} + \frac{(\Sigma X'_{mu})^2}{N_{e_{mu}}} + \frac{(\Sigma X'_{fu})^2}{N_{e_{fu}}} - \frac{(\Sigma X'_g)^2}{N_{e_g}}$$

$$= \frac{724.5^2}{360.8} + \frac{145.9^2}{113.2} + \frac{1404.2^2}{555.7} + \frac{385.2^2}{174.3} + \frac{821.9^2}{272.5} + \frac{264.8^2}{85.5} - \frac{3746.6^2}{1562} = 373.47$$

Now that we have preliminary revised sum of squares representing the unique contribution of residence (revised among residence) and sex (revised between sex), the difference between these contributions and the total contribution (total revised among) represents the interaction between the independent and dependent variable: Interaction Sum of Squares = Total Revised Among Sum of Squares − (Revised Among Residence + Revised Between Sex Sum of Squares) =

$$373.47 - (297.15 + 34.29) = 42.03$$

In order to collect these figures and proceed to obtain variance estimates and levels of significance, it is useful to present the data in an analysis of variance table such as table 2.22. In calculations similar to one-way analysis of variance the final variance estimate is determined by dividing each sum of squares by the respective degrees of freedom (where k = number of columns and l = number of rows).

TABLE 2.22 Two-Way Analysis of Variance Table

Source	Sum of Squares	Degrees of Freedom	Variance Estimate	F ratio	p
Total	16137.38	$N-1 = 1561$			
Among all classes	474.58	$kl-1 = 5$			
Among all revised	373.47	$kl-1 = 5$			
Among residence	297.15	$l-1 = 2$	129.26	12.85	<.01
Between sex	34.29	$k-1 = 1$	29.83	2.97	>.05
Interaction	42.03	$(k-1)(l-1) = 2$	18.28	1.82	>.05
Within classes	15662.80	$N-kl = 1556$	10.06		

You will note that the above explained variance estimates have been reduced slightly from their actual values after dividing degrees of freedom. This is accomplished by a frequently used reduction factor which is necessary as we move from real frequencies to revised frequencies, basically because we are assuming to have more N's than we really do. This factor can be used to either reduce each among variance estimate or to inflate the within variance estimate. The former option is reflected in the table. The formula for the reduction factor is:

$$\frac{N}{\Sigma \left(\frac{N_e^2}{N} \right)} = \frac{1562}{\frac{360.8^2}{242} + \frac{113.2^2}{232} + \frac{557.7^2}{630} + \frac{174.3^2}{100} + \frac{272.5^2}{317} + \frac{85.5^2}{41}} = .87$$

This value then is multiplied by the quotient of each among sum of squares (among residence and between sex) divided by their respective degrees of freedom to yield a corrected variance estimate. By an examination of the variance estimates in the table, we see that there is considerably more variation explained by residence alone than by sex or the interaction of sex and residence on the dependent variable. Significance levels then are derived by the F ratios which result from dividing the unexplained variance estimate (within) into the explained and interaction variance estimates, including main effects.[74]

$$\text{Among Residence } F = \frac{129.26}{10.06} = 12.85 \qquad \begin{array}{l} df = 2, 1556 \\ p < .01 \end{array}$$

$$\text{Between Sex } F = \frac{29.83}{10.06} = 2.97 \qquad \begin{array}{l} df = 1, 1556 \\ p > .05 \end{array}$$

$$\text{Interaction } F = \frac{18.28}{10.06} = 1.82 \qquad \begin{array}{l} df = 2, 1556 \\ p > .05 \end{array}$$

74. There are a variety of options for this procedure. If the interaction term is not significant, some statisticians suggest that additivity can be assumed and therefore the interaction sum of squares should be combined into the within sum of squares; also, the degrees of freedom for these two categories should be summed. This inflated unexplained variance then is used as the denominator to test the significance of explained variance. More technical questions arise when the interaction is significant. At this stage there is a choice of models for determining F Levels. One uses the within variance estimate as the denominator and the other uses the interaction variance estimate as the denominator. The first option is most appropriate for exhaustive numbers, that is, variables whose categories represent all possible categories. Many forms of sociopolitical data are measured in this fashion, e.g., sex and residence. On the other hand, if a variable represents only a sample of categories, e.g., several of many religious categories, the interaction term is used as the denominator to determine the F level. A brief discussion can be found in Blalock, *Social Statistics*, pp. 342–47, with more extended comments in Q. McNemar, *Psychological Statistics*, 2d ed. (New York: John Wiley, 1955), pp. 303–11.

We can therefore conclude that sex has no significant effect on voting turnout and that there is no significant interaction between residence and sex as they influence voting turnout. That is, sex and residence do not jointly relate to influence the dependent variable. Nevertheless, residence alone does have a significant relationship with voting turnout, reflecting greater differences between the means for each residence category. We can now move back to the descriptive level and present revised means $(\Sigma X')/N$ for the categories of the significant independent variable in table 2.23. These means indicate the direction of the relationship between residence and turnout. That is, urban residents vote more frequently than suburbanites, and they, in turn, have higher turnout rates than rural respondents.

TABLE 2.23 Table of Revised Means for Analysis of Variance

Residence	Mean Voting Turnout	
Rural	1.84	(870.4/474)
Suburban	2.45	(1789.5/730)
Urban	3.04	(1086.7/358)

One further step in two-way analysis of variance enables us to extend our generalizations to the analytical level, i.e., to a measure of the strength of the relationship or the degree of association between variables. For example, intraclass correlation coefficients can be computed to determine the degree of association between residence and turnout, sex and turnout, and the multiple effect of the independent variables on the dependent variable. Using the r_i formula given previously for one-way analysis of variance, the impact of residence on turnout can be isolated by substituting the among residence estimate for the among variance estimate in the one independent variable scheme. In addition, $\bar{N}$ should not equal a simple mean of the number of cases in each category of the independent variable being tested (residence). Since the size of the classes of residence differs, a correction for $\bar{N}$ is necessary, where

$$\bar{N} = \frac{1}{k-1}\left(\Sigma N - \frac{\Sigma N^2}{\Sigma N}\right)$$

therefore, in this example,

$$\bar{N} = \frac{1}{3-1}\left(1562 - \frac{474^2 + 730^2 + 358^2}{1562}\right) = 273.40$$

and,

$$r_{i_{residence}} = \frac{129.26 - 10.06}{129.26 + (273.40 - 1)(10.06)} = .042$$

This value represents the degree of association between residence and turnout without variation attributable to sex; that is, residence alone accounts for 4.3 percent of the variation in voter turnout. Although this figure is low, it is a logical step in many social science research projects once a significant relationship has been found. Because sex itself is not significantly related to turnout, its r_i value will be lower (.0034) and there is little reason to calculate it. If it would be necessary, its variance estimate would be substituted in the formula.

If the researcher so desires, it is also possible to estimate the multiple effects of the two independent variables on the dependent variable. By following the logic of the previous intraclass coefficients, we can divide the explained variance by the explained plus unexplained variance. The general formula for a multiple intraclass coefficient with subscripts denoting residence variance (r), sex variance (s), interaction variance (rs), and unexplained or within variance (w) is as follows:

$$r_i = \frac{\sigma_r^2 + \sigma_s^2 + \sigma_{rs}^2}{\sigma_r^2 + \sigma_s^2 + \sigma_{rs}^2 + \sigma_w^2}$$

Since the sizes of the variable classes in our example are so unequal, the variance associated with interaction should be weighted by the corrected "average" for six classes; the variance for residence should be weighted by the corrected average for three cells; and the variance for sex by the corrected average for two classes. Therefore,

$$\sigma_r^2 = \frac{\text{Residence Variance Estimate} - \text{Within Variance Estimate}}{\bar{N}}$$

and similarly,

$$\sigma_s^2 = \frac{VE_{\text{sex}} - VE_{\text{within}}}{\bar{N}}$$

and

$$\sigma_{sr}^2 = \frac{VE_{\text{interaction}} - VE_{\text{within}}}{\bar{N}}$$

where the average for the classes, $\bar{N}$, is calculated from the longer, corrected formula. Since we have previously obtained the corrected $\bar{N}$ for residence ($\bar{N} = 273.40$), we must now derive $\bar{N}$ for sex and interaction. The values substituted in the $\bar{N}$ formula are as follows:

$$\bar{N}_s = \frac{1}{2-1}\left(1562 - \frac{1189^2 + 373^2}{1562}\right) = 567.86$$

and,

$$N_{rs} = \frac{1}{6-1}\left(1562 - \frac{242^2 + 232^2 + 630^2 + 100^2 + 317^2 + 41^2}{1562}\right) = 278.57$$

We can now substitute these $\bar{N}$ values in the formulas for deriving a "weighted" variance for residence, sex, and interaction:

$$\sigma_r^2 = \frac{129.26 - 10.06}{273.40} = .4359$$

$$\sigma_s^2 = \frac{29.83 - 10.06}{567.86} = .0348$$

$$\sigma_{rs}^2 = \frac{18.28 - 10.06}{278.57} = .0295$$

By combining these variances with the unexplained or within variance, the multiple intraclass correlation coefficient equals:

$$r_i = \frac{.4359 + .0348 + .0295}{.4359 + .0348 + .0295 + 10.06} = .0473$$

Therefore, variation in sex and residence together accounts for 4.7 percent of the variation in voter turnout. The increase in explained variance over residence alone is, of course, small due to the minimal impact of sex differences on voter turnout.

Although we have taken a summary look at analysis of variance, the reader should be prepared for a more detailed understanding of this form of analysis. The technique has been used extensively in psychology and education, yet its use is almost nonexistent in political science literature — having been constrained by political scientists' lack of familiarity and understanding of the technique and its advantages at levels of measurement frequently encountered by the researcher.

(3) *Other procedures for various measurement levels:* A variety of tests of significance and measures of degree of association are available for different combinations of levels of measurement. With several exceptions, they do not provide the options and range of useful statistics as described above for analysis of variance. One exception is a computerized routine which includes combinations of multiple regression and analysis of variance called *multiple classification analysis.*[75] It requires only nominal independent variables, with an interval or dichotomous dependent variable. Another is a recently developed extension of one- and two-way analysis of variance to research designs where there are multiple nominal independent variables and multiple interval dependent variables. This *multivariate analysis of variance,* however, has not been widely used in the social sciences.[76] The last exception is the *analysis of covariance,* a combination of analysis of variance and correlational analysis techniques useful for various combinations of nominal and interval scales.[77] The use of *dummy variable regression,* discussed later, is also available for these

75. Frank Andrews, James Morgan, and John Sonquist, *Multiple Classification Analysis* (Ann Arbor: Institute for Social Research, University of Michigan, 1967).

76. See S. N. Roy and R. Gnanadesikan, "Some Contributions to ANOVA in One or More Dimensions: I & II," *Annals of Mathematical Statistics* 30 (1959): 304–40. The canonical correlation is also a technique designed for multiple dependent variables. See Maurice M. Tatsuoka, *Multivariate Analysis: Techniques for Educational and Psychological Research* (New York: John Wiley, 1971) pp. 183–93, and William W. Cooley and Paul R. Lohnes, *Multivariate Data Analysis* (New York: John Wiley, 1971), pp. 168–200.

77. Blalock, *Social Statistics,* chap. 20.

types of research designs. When nominal-interval combinations involve one two-category nominal variable, a *t-test* of significance can be performed; a difference of means test that will lead to the same decision about rejecting the null hypothesis as that reached by analysis of variance.[78] A parametric measure of association available at this level is the *point-biserial correlation coefficient* (r_{pb}) which is interpreted the same as Pearson's product-moment correlation discussed later. An extension of the point-biserial coefficient, known as *triserial r*, measures the strength of relationship between a three-category nominal variable and an interval dependent variable.[79] Finally, the *Kruskal-Wallis H* statistics has been designed specifically for testing statistical significance with one variable measured as an *ordinal* scale and one measured on a nominal scale.[80]

With some degree of selection, this chapter has reviewed a variety of statistical procedures which assist us in making judgements about political data on a variety of levels (descriptive, inductive, analytical) with several different kinds of measurement (nominal, ordinal, interval). The most inclusive, parsimonious, and sophisticated procedures, however, are those involving two or more interval variables.

Bivariate Analysis of Interval Data

In a two-variable research design, where data are measured at the interval or ratio level, we can take advantage of several parsimonious tests associated with correlation-regression analysis. Furthermore, the data can be analyzed on all functional levels. The data array, means, ranges, standard deviations for each variable, and a scatter diagram depicting the data distribution between variables are all useful for descriptive purposes. We are also able to reach a higher level of sophistication in our description with the assistance of regression analysis. By providing for a description of the nature or form of relationships, regression analysis enables a measure of prediction, an ultimate goal of all sciences. There is also a variety of tests of significance used to infer relationships in the population. Finally, correlation provides a measure of the direction and degree of relationship (r) and the percent of variance shared by variables.

Some researchers may only be interested in the degree of association between two variables (correlation) thereby avoiding regression analysis. If relationships are significant, however, it may be desirable to obtain regression coefficients in order to predict the level of one variable from the level of the other variable. Furthermore, most research designs at this level should encourage the preliminary use of regression, a concept viewed as being more theoretically relevant than the degree of association.[81] The calculations associated with regression are also important for basic descriptive analysis. Therefore, we will initially focus on this procedure.

As a parametric measure, the underlying assumptions of regression analysis are not unfamiliar: linear relationships, normality, and equal variances. If the actual distribution of the data is curvilinear, the application of linear regression will not

78. Hays, *Statistics for Psychologists*, chap. 10.
79. N. M. Downie and R. W. Heath, *Basic Statistical Methods*, 2d ed. (New York: Harper & Row, 1965), pp. 189–95.
80. Blalock, *Social Statistics*, pp. 349–53.
81. See chapter 3.

reflect the true distribution. However, there are related procedures for fitting a curve to such data.[82] If the data are skewed (non-normal), results will be distorted because the means used in calculations will be distorted. If the equal variances assumption is not met, there will be a nonuniform scatter of data points and a resulting spurious correlation. If none of the assumptions can be met, we can only describe the data at hand rather than making inferences about the parameters of the population.

For purposes of a hypothetical example we will again use voting turnout as a dependent variable (number of times the respondent voted in five past elections), but the independent variable is level of education attained in years. In order to measure variance, the data are arrayed with squared frequencies and values necessary for calculating sums of squares and cross products (see table 2.24).

TABLE 2.24   Computation of Simple
Correlation-Regression

Education (X)		Voting Turnout (Y)		
X	X^2	Y	Y^2	XY
3	9	1	1	3
5	25	1	1	5
6	36	4	16	24
8	64	3	9	24
10	100	4	16	40
12	144	2	4	24
12	144	3	9	36
15	225	3	9	45
15	225	4	16	60
16	256	5	25	80
$N = 10$ $\Sigma X = 102$	$\Sigma X^2 = 1228$	$\Sigma Y = 30$	$\Sigma Y^2 = 106$	$\Sigma XY = 341$

From the data array we can see that as education increases, turnout rates also increase, but that the turnout increase is not perfectly related to education. That is, there are exceptions in the progression from score one to five, yet the lowest values hold for low education and the highest values are related to the highest education levels. A scatterplot of the relationship assists in this description. This should be an integral part of the early stage of data analysis. The scatter diagram provides a graphic presentation showing the direction of the data cluster, the homogeneity of the cluster, and its shape (linear, curvilinear), as shown in figure 2.6. Extreme examples of linear scatterplots represent a strong positive correlation (A), a strong negative relationship (B), and no relationship (C).

Although our data array at least suggests a linear and positive relationship, for the data to approach example A, one variable would have to increase consistently with the other. The scatter diagram for education and voter turnout is linear and

82. For example, see Blalock, Social Statistics, pp. 408–13. Also note that with regard to the level of measurement assumption, Pearson's r exhibits robustness under certain ordinal data conditions; see Sanford Labovitz, "The Assignment of Numbers to Rank Order Categories," American Sociological Review 35 (1970): 515–24.

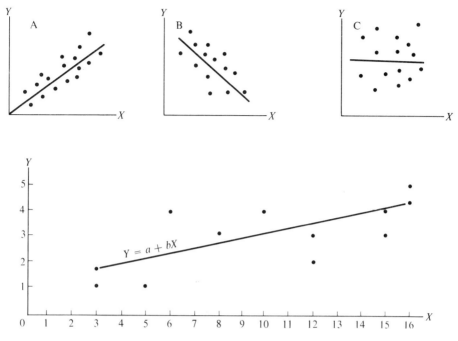

FIGURE 2.6 Scatter Diagram and Regression Lines for
Extreme Models and Hypothetical Data Distributions

positive (as one increases, the other increases), yet more dispersed. A further descriptive step is to actually plot a line which approximates the points. This regression line (or line of least squares or line of best fit) is drawn so that the distances from the points to the line are smaller than for any other single straight line that could be drawn. The slope of the line then represents the rate of change in turnout for each one unit change in level of education. The equation for this straight line is $Y = a + bX$, where a is the intercept of Y (where the line crosses Y) and b is the rate of change (slope) in Y relative to X. This latter value (b) is not only necessary for the plotting of a line which depicts slope but is the regression coefficient which provides information about the nature of the relationship. If the underlying assumptions are met, the a and b values are the best estimates of their respective values in the population (parameters). Theoretically, the scatterplot has two regression lines, one predicting Y from X and the other predicting X from Y. Both are rarely shown and the choice depends largely on the researcher's conceptual independent-dependent variable scheme and his hypothesis. For example, we have little reason to suspect that voting turnout influences educational attainment of the respondent. This also means that there are two possible regression coefficients: b_{yx} (predicting Y from X) or b_{xy} (predicting X from Y).[83] A highly homogeneous linear data distribution would produce regression lines which coincide, whereas a completely random scatter of points would yield lines at right angles to each other. The smaller the angle of scissoring, the more the lines coincide, and the greater the strength of the relationship between the variables (i.e., a high correlation coefficient).

---

83. The regression coefficient b_{xy} is calculated from the same formula as that for b_{yx}, except X and Y are interchanged.

Since we are predicting Y from X, the corresponding regression coefficient is

$$b_{yx} = \frac{\Sigma\, xy}{\Sigma\, x^2}$$

where

$$\Sigma\, x^2 = \Sigma\, X^2 - \frac{(\Sigma\, X)^2}{N}$$

and

$$\Sigma\, xy = \Sigma\, XY - \frac{(\Sigma\, X)(\Sigma\, Y)}{N}$$

therefore

$$\Sigma\, x^2 = 1228 - \frac{102^2}{10} = 187.6$$

and

$$\Sigma\, xy = 341 - \frac{(102)(30)}{10} = 35$$

and

$$b_{yx} = \frac{35}{187.6} = +.19$$

This regression coefficient measures the slope of the line of best fit through the data. Its value means that for every one unit increase in the independent variable there is a .19 unit increase in the dependent variable. The regression coefficient is only partially a function of strength of relationship (cluster) because it is also dependent on standard deviations. Therefore, there is little relationship between a regression coefficient and a correlation coefficient, except that when $b = 0$, $r = 0$ and the sign for both will be the same. Also note that $r^2 = b_{yx} \cdot b_{xy}$. Furthermore, it should be remembered that the regression coefficient is tied to the unit of measurement. It must be interpreted according to the units of the independent and dependent variables, e.g., for every one year increase in education there is a .19 increase in the number of times voting.

In order to plot the regression line shown on the scatter diagram (figure 2.6) we need a second value (a, the Y intercept) other than that which is a function of the regression coefficient (bX).

$$a_{yx} = \frac{\Sigma\, Y - b_{yx}\Sigma\, X}{N} = \frac{30 - (.19)(102)}{10} = 1.06$$

The a_{yx} and b_{yx} values then can be substituted in the line equation to equal $Y = 1.06 + .19X$. Since only two points are necessary to plot a straight line, two values of X can be chosen to plot its relationship to the Y axis. The lines should pass through all of the scatter points, therefore, extreme values of X are most useful. Using the lowest number of years of educational attainment and the highest value for education level, the corresponding Y values are as follows:

$$Y = 1.06 + (.19)(3) = 1.63$$

$$Y = 1.06 + (.19)(16) = 4.10$$

The coordinates of the first point are 3 and 1.63, and the coordinates of the second point are 16 and 4.10. That is, when $X = 3$, $Y = 1.63$ and when $X = 16$, $Y = 4.10$. For purposes of prediction, an X value can be used to predict a corresponding Y value. For example, the best estimate of the number of times a respondent with a tenth-grade education voted in past elections is $Y = 1.06 + (.19)(10) = 3$.

Although regression coefficients provide valuable information about the slope and direction ($\pm$) of the data, thereby facilitating predictions, the political scientist is frequently more interested in locating important variables. This is possible through the use of Pearson's product-moment correlation coefficient which measures the strength of relationship between the two variables (zero order). Whereas regression measures slope, correlation measures the goodness of fit of the line to the scatter diagram. As a goodness-of-fit measure, it reflects the spread about the linear regression line, i.e., how well the line fits the data points. It is usually wise to plot a scatter diagram so that we are certain that a linear coefficient is not being applied to curvilinear data. If a correlation coefficient is low, it may be that the data are highly related in a curvilinear fashion rather than unrelated at all. Furthermore, extreme values or a few homogeneous clusters of data points will distort the correlation coefficient. These can be inspected in a scatter diagram and we may conclude that certain values should be eliminated to prevent distortion. When values are adjusted, however, as with collapsing and omitting in chi-square frequency tables, we must carefully state our conclusions in specific terms according to the data being measured.

If the research purposes and goals demand it, the most inclusive procedure preliminary to measuring the degree of association includes describing the data array through means and other descriptive measures, plotting the scatter diagram, calculating the regression coefficient(s), determining the coordinants of the regression line and plotting that line. The subsequent derivation of the correlation coefficient utilizes previously derived values. However, if only the b_{yx} regression coefficient has been determined, the sum of the squares of deviations about the mean for the dependent variable must be calculated, where

$$\Sigma y^2 = \Sigma Y^2 - \frac{(\Sigma Y)^2}{N}$$

$$= 106 - \frac{30^2}{10} = 16.0$$

The product-moment correlation then represents the ratio of covariation in the independent and dependent variable to the square root of the product of X variation and Y variation.

$$r = \frac{\Sigma\ xy}{\sqrt{\Sigma\ x^2 \Sigma\ y^2}}$$

$$= \frac{35}{\sqrt{(187.6)(16.0)}} = +.64$$

This correlation coefficient, as others discussed previously, is standardized to vary between ± 1, and unlike the regression coefficient, it does not depend upon the unit of measurement. Highly positive, negative, and zero values correspond to scatter plot models, A, B, and C respectively (figure 2.6). If the relationship between the independent and dependent variable is unity, all of the data points fall on the line of best fit. If there is no relationship ($r = 0$), the data points are randomly distributed. From our example, we see that there is a high-moderate positive relationship between educational attainment and voting turnout. If other social science findings (usually below .7) become our criterion for assessing this relationship, it is quite strong. Furthermore, the sign of the coefficient tells us that as education increases, turnout increases. It should be remembered that this sign is tied to the data coding procedure. This must be closely examined especially for scaled data where it is essential to know, e.g., that high values represent conservatism rather than liberalism.

Although there is a variety of tests of significance[84] to be applied to r, a readily available determination can be made from a table of r values with corresponding probability levels. With $df = N - 2$ for a zero order correlation coefficient, an r of .64 is significant at the .01 level. This relationship could occur by chance in only 1 out of 100 times and we can conclude that a relationship exists in the population.

Two final coefficients derived from r can be used to make statements about variation in the variables. The coefficient of determination is $r^2 = .41$, representing the proportion of total variation in one variable explained by the other. We can conclude that 41 percent of the variation in voting turnout is associated with variation in educational attainment. The coefficient of nondetermination (or coefficient of alienation) is $1 - r^2 = .59$, indicating the percent of variance which remains unexplained.

Multivariate Analysis of Interval Data

The complexities of political and social phenomena have necessitated the increasing use of multivariate research design and analysis. The availability of aggregate data and our willingness to make interval assumptions about survey data have stimulated the use of multiple regression and correlation. These procedures are an extension of simple regression and correlation, yet they offer two distinct types of measures

---

84. Blalock, *Social Statistics*, chap. 18.

which are advantageous to the researcher. The first is a measure of multiple correlation indicating the variation in the dependent variable explained by all of the independent variables together. The second is a set of partial correlations which examine the relationship between two variables controlling for the others. In the bivariate case discussed previously, the regression and correlation coefficient excluded other possible independent variables; however, in multiple regression-correlation these other variables are brought into the analysis and controlled. This form of statistical control is not unlike that derived from two-way analysis of variance. You will recall also that similar measures were extended to the nominal and ordinal level earlier in this chapter. Its goal is to isolate the unique effects of variables and determine the validity of zero order relations. For example, there is a variety of information that controls can yield:[85] they may indicate that an original zero order relation (r_{xy}) is "real" or sustained by producing no change in the relationships; they may suggest that an initial weak relationship is more apparent than real; or they may clarify an original spurious correlation which disappears under control.

In order to keep our computations simple and comparable to the bivariate case, we will add a third variable to the research design discussed for simple correlation-regression. A variable which fits this context is political efficacy, a scale (which we treat as interval) measuring the degree to which respondents feel they can affect political outcomes (scale 1–5 toward higher efficacy). With the three-variable case it is conventional to denote the dependent variable as X_1 and the independent variables as X_2 and X_3, and so on. By arranging voting turnout (X_1) in ascending order, we can facilitate descriptive comparison with education (X_2) and political efficacy (X_3). Table 2.25 presents these frequency arrays, accompanied by the values whsch are extensions of bivariate analysis: squared frequencies, the sum of frequencies, cross products of variable frequencies, and values necessary for obtaining the sum of squares and the sum of cross products.[86]

An examination of the array suggests that all pairs of relationships between variables are positive, i.e., as one increases in value so does the other. The distribution of political efficacy scores in comparison to turnout scores also appears to be more related than education level to turnout. When variables have the same number of possible scores (e.g., 1→5), they can be compared descriptively by means and standard deviations. The mean turnout and efficacy values for our sample (and inferentially, the population) are similar (3.0 and 3.2). Unlike the bivariate case, the plotting of data points on a scatter diagram becomes difficult because we are dealing with three dimensions where a least squares plane intersecting the data points is analogous to the regression line. Nevertheless, the regression procedure is necessary for the derivation of regression coefficients describing the nature of the relationship for pairs of variables in consideration of the other variable. The regression equation also is used to predict levels of the dependent variable for specified levels of the independent variables.

Following the procedures outlined in the bivariate case, we can calculate sum of squares and sum of cross products necessary for regression and correlation:

85. See Benson, *Political Science Laboratory*, chap. 9, and Buchanan, *Understanding Political Variables*, pp. 126–30.
86. For ease of description, an $N = 10$ is used in the example; however, it is usually recommended that an N of 50 or greater is necessary for multiple regression-correlation.

TABLE 2.25 Computation of Multiple
Correlation-Regression

	Voting Turnout (X_1)		Education (X_2)		Political Efficacy (X_3)				
	X_1	X_1^2	X_2	X_2^2	X_3	X_3^2	X_1X_2	X_1X_3	X_2X_3
	1	1	3	9	1	1	3	1	3
	1	1	5	25	2	4	5	2	10
	2	4	12	144	1	1	24	2	12
	3	9	8	64	3	9	24	9	24
	3	9	12	144	4	16	36	12	48
$N = 10$	3	9	15	225	3	9	45	9	45
	4	16	6	36	4	16	24	16	24
	4	16	10	100	4	16	40	16	40
	4	16	15	225	5	25	60	20	75
	5	25	16	256	5	25	80	25	80

$\Sigma X_1 = 30$ $\Sigma X_1^2 = 106$ $\Sigma X_2 = 102$ $\Sigma X_2^2 = 1228$ $\Sigma X_3 = 32$ $\Sigma X_3^2 = 122$ $\Sigma X_1X_2 = 341$ $\Sigma X_1X_3 = 112$ $\Sigma X_2X_3 = 361$

$$\Sigma x_1^2 = \Sigma X_1^2 - \frac{(\Sigma X_1)^2}{N} = 106 - \frac{30^2}{10} = 16.0$$

$$\Sigma x_2^2 = \Sigma X_2^2 - \frac{(\Sigma X_2)^2}{N} = 1228 - \frac{(102)^2}{10} = 187.6$$

$$\Sigma x_3^2 = \Sigma X_3^2 - \frac{(\Sigma X_3)^2}{N} = 122 - \frac{32^2}{10} = 19.6$$

$$\Sigma x_1 x_2 = \Sigma X_1 X_2 - \frac{(\Sigma X_1)(\Sigma X_2)}{N} = 341 - \frac{(30)(102)}{10} = 35.0$$

$$\Sigma x_1 x_3 = \Sigma X_1 X_3 - \frac{(\Sigma X_1)(\Sigma X_3)}{N} = 112 - \frac{(30)(32)}{10} = 16.0$$

$$\Sigma x_2 x_3 = \Sigma X_2 X_3 - \frac{(\Sigma X_2)(\Sigma X_3)}{N} = 361 - \frac{(102)(32)}{10} = 34.6$$

The regression line (plane) equation is also an extension of regression in two dimensions, where the value of the dependent variable (X_1) is based upon a constant (a) plus a regression coefficient (b) times each independent variable (X_2, X_3):

$$X_1 = a + b_{12.3} X_2 + b_{13.2} X_3$$

The regression coefficients represent the nature of the relationship (slope) between education and turnout taking efficacy into account ($b_{12.3}$) and the relationship between efficacy and turnout controlling for education ($b_{13.2}$). These coefficients are therefore measures of the slopes when each independent variable in the regression is held constant (i.e., corrected for or removed arithmetically). Although it is possible to derive these coefficients from simple regression coefficients between pairs of variables,[87] the following procedure enables us to avoid simple relationships for the moment. In other words, we can solve for the values of $b_{12.3}$ and $b_{13.2}$ directly, yet the presence of two unknowns necessitates simultaneous equations. This pair of equations utilizing the information derived previously appears below:

$$b_{12.3} \Sigma x_2^2 + b_{13.2} \Sigma x_2 x_3 = \Sigma x_1 \Sigma x_2$$

$$b_{12.3} \Sigma x_2 x_3 + b_{13.2} \Sigma x_3^2 = \Sigma x_1 x_3$$

$$187.6 \, b_{12.3} + 34.6 \, b_{13.2} = 35.0$$

$$34.6 \, b_{12.3} + 19.6 \, b_{13.2} = 16.0$$

In order to solve for one b value we must cancel the other b value by dividing (or multiplying) the first value in the first equation into its other values and do the same for the second equation. That is, 187.6 is divided into each term of the first equation so that its $b_{12.3}$ value is canceled and 34.6 is divided into the second equa-

---

87. Palumbo, *Statistics in Political and Behavioral Science*, p. 212.

tion to eliminate its $b_{12.3}$ term. When the remaining equations are subtracted, we can solve $b_{13.2}$

$$.184\, b_{13.2} = .187$$

$$-\ .566\, b_{13.2} = .462$$

$$\overline{-.382\, b_{13.2} = -.275}$$

$$b_{13.2} = \frac{-.275}{-.382} = +.720$$

By substituting this $b_{13.2}$ value in either of the above original equations, we can derive $b_{12.3}$.

$$b_{12.3} + (.720)(.184) = .187$$

$$b_{12.3} = .187 - .132 = +.055$$

These respective regression coefficients represent the amount of change in the dependent variable associated with change in each independent variable, with the other independent variable taken into consideration. That is, for every one unit increase (since b is +) in political efficacy there is a corresponding .72 ($b_{13.2}$) unit increase in voting turnout controlling for the effect of education on turnout. Also, for every additional year of education there is a .06 increase in the number of times voting, controlling for efficacy.

If we wish to make full use of the predictive ability of the regression equation, the value of term a (the value of the dependent variable when all independent variables are zero) must be obtained through the following equation:

$$a_{1.23} = \bar{X}_1 - b_{12.3}\bar{X}_2 - b_{13.2}\bar{X}_3$$

By substituting the calculated regression coefficient and mean scores for turnout, education and efficacy, we have

$$a_{1.23} = 3.0 - (.055)(10.2) - (.720)(3.2) = .135$$

When these values are substituted in the original regression equation, we can predict a voting turnout score for any value of efficacy and education. For example, a respondent with a twelfth-grade education and an efficacy score of three will be most likely to have voted three times during the past five presidential and congressional elections:

$$x_1 = a_{1.23} + b_{12.3}X_2 + b_{13.2}X_3$$

$$= .135 + .055\,(12) + .720\,(3) = 3.0$$

Although the partial regression coefficients yield information about the slope of the regression line for each independent variable, plus predictive information, they do not enable comparison of variable strength because they are tied to the unit of measurement. That is, their meaning varies if the units of measurement are different (e.g., years, scale scores, income). In order to remedy this, the weight of each independent variable can be standardized by multiplying it by the ratio of standard deviations for the uncontrolled and dependent variables. In the context of our calculating procedures, it can be expressed as:

$$\beta_{12.3} = b_{12.3} \sqrt{\frac{\Sigma\, x_2^2}{\Sigma\, x_1^2}} = .055 \sqrt{\frac{187.6}{16.0}} = .19$$

$$\beta_{13.2} = b_{13.2} \sqrt{\frac{\Sigma\, x_3^2}{\Sigma\, x_1^2}} = .720 \sqrt{\frac{19.6}{16.0}} = .80$$

where β (beta) is frequently called a beta weight. These standardized regression coefficients suggests that political efficacy is a more important variable than education in relation to voting turnout. Furthermore, they will usually rank the importance of variables in the same order as partial correlation coefficients discussed below.

After the data are described and the changes in the dependent variable are associated with changes in independent variables, we can adapt the partialling concept to measures of strength of association in order to assess the amount of variation explained by each independent variable. Before this is attempted, however, it is usually helpful to examine all possible zero order correlations for purposes of analysis. Indeed, many researchers prefer to begin with a correlation analysis to determine level of significance before going to a regression analysis. We have previously determined the simple correlation between education and turnout as $+.64$ on a standardized scale of ± 1. We also might wish to determine the direction and degree of association between efficacy (X_3) and turnout (X_1), ignoring education (X_2) (i.e., permitting it to vary), and the relationship between the independent variables, efficacy and education, ignoring turnout. These zero order correlation coefficients are calculated the same as before:

$$r_{13} = \frac{\Sigma\, x_1 x_3}{\sqrt{\Sigma\, x_1^2 \Sigma\, x_3^2}}$$

$$= \frac{16.0}{\sqrt{(16.0)(19.6)}} = +.90 \qquad \begin{aligned} df &= N - 2, \\ p &< .01 \end{aligned}$$

and $\quad r_{23} = \dfrac{\Sigma\, x_2 x_3}{\sqrt{\Sigma\, x_2^2 \Sigma\, x_3^2}}$

$$= \frac{34.6}{\sqrt{(187.6)(19.6)}} = +.57 \qquad \begin{aligned} df &= N - 2, \\ p &> .05 \end{aligned}$$

The correlation coefficient between efficacy and turnout confirms our earlier guess based on the data array. In a simple relationship without controls or consideration of other independent variables, efficacy is more highly related to turnout than education is related to turnout ($+.90$ vs. $+.64$). Also note that the two independent variables are interrelated ($+.57$). Unless the independent variables are totally unrelated, a multivariate design usually necessitates the inclusion of all variables so that they can be accounted for and held off for control purposes. In order to determine the degree of association between each independent variable and the dependent variable, controlling for remaining independent variables, we utilize the partial correlation coefficient. By making an adjustment for the control variable, it can help to isolate unique effects of each independent variable, thereby clarifying interrelationships. This calculation of partial correlation coefficients, however, is facilitated if we know the total effect of the two independent variables on the dependent variable.[88] This value is known as a multiple correlation coefficient and it is usually presented as a squared value or coefficient of determination (R^2). It is similar to a simple correlation coefficient (or in its squared form, to a bivariate coefficient of determination) in that it measures the degree of association between variables, i.e., it measures the extent to which the least squares plane fits the data points in three-dimensional space. It can be derived from the zero order relations as follows:

$$R^2_{1.23} = \frac{r^2_{12} + r^2_{13} - 2r_{12}r_{13}r_{23}}{1 - r^2_{23}}$$

$$= \frac{.64^2 + .90^2 - 2(.64)(.90)(.57)}{1 - .57} = .83$$

This means that 83 percent of the variance in voting turnout is explained by education and political efficacy together. Its significance level can be determined by means of an F test similar to the analysis of variance test where the multiple coefficient of determination (explained) is analogous to between sum of squares and the multiple coefficient of nondetermination ($1 - .83 = 17$ percent unexplained) is analogous to within sum of squares.[89] Such an analysis of variance table can be expressed by formula as:

$$F = \frac{R^2_{1.23}}{(1 - R^2_{1.23})} \cdot \frac{(N - k - 1)}{k}$$

where N is the number of cases and k is the number of independent variables such that:

$$F = \frac{.834}{1 - .834} \cdot \frac{(10 - 2 - 1)}{2} = 17.57 \qquad p < .01$$

at k and $N - k - 1$ degrees of freedom. When a table of F is consulted, 17.57 with 2 and 7 degrees of freedom is significant at the .01 probability level. In only 1 out of 100 times would we account for this much variability according to the laws of chance.

With the multiple coefficient determined, the process of isolating independent effects for education and efficacy is straightforward. The two relevant partial cor-

---

88. All of the formulas can be extended to cases with more than two independent variables. See, for example, Blalock, *Social Statistics*, chap. 19.

89. It is also possible to locate the significance level of R^2 in a table designed for that purpose.

relation coefficients are $r_{13.2}$ and $r_{12.3}$: the relationship between variable 1 and 3, controlling for 2, and that between 1 and 2 controlling for 3. Because $R_{1.23}$ measures the impact of 2 and 3 together on 1, we can use a formula for the effect of 3 on 1 controlling for 2 by subtracting the amount explained by variable 2.

$$r_{13.2} = \sqrt{\frac{R_{1.23}^2 - r_{12}^2}{1 - r_{12}^2}}$$

$$= \sqrt{\frac{.834 - .64^2}{1 - .64^2}} = +.85$$

A similar procedure is used to measure the relationship between variable 1 and 2, controlling for variable 3.

$$r_{12.3} = \sqrt{\frac{R_{1.23}^2 - r_{13}^2}{1 - r_{13}^2}}$$

$$= \sqrt{\frac{.834 - .90^2}{1 - .90^2}} = +.36$$

The relationship between efficacy (X_3) and turnout (X_1), over and above the effect of education (X_2) on turnout, is equal to .85; the effect of education on turnout, controlling for efficacy, is .36. These values suggest the relative predictive utility of efficacy over education with regard to voting turnout. The relationship between efficacy and turnout controlling for education is the result of permitting education to explain all that it can of both variables. By squaring the partial correlation coefficients, we can conclude that 72 percent of the variation in turnout is explained by political efficacy and that this amount is left unexplained by education. Education alone explains only 13 percent of the variability in turnout. Similar types of analysis can be extended to multivariate designs with more than one control; however, calculations can become very tedious without shortcuts (e.g., the Dolittle method for solving simultaneous equations) or computer assistance. Furthermore, a large set of independent variables may frequently cloud the semantic meaning of the analysis due to interrelationships between the independent variables (mutlticollinearity). In performing multiple regression-correlation analysis, the researcher must rely more heavily on theory than we have here, i.e., the concept of control implies a conceptual distinction between control and zero order variables.[90] The partials described previously are of the first order (one control), but one with two control variables is a second order partial correlation coefficient, and so on. In designs with more than three variables it is also possible to calculate a multiple partial coefficient which explains the multiple effects of several independent variables on the dependent variable, controlling for several other independent variables (e.g., $r_{1(23).45}$).

---

90. For a discussion of partialling fallacies see Robert A. Gordon, "Issues in Multiple Regression," *American Journal of Sociology* 73 (1968): 592–616.

The significance of the partial correlations is determined by an F-test analogous to the analysis of variance, where the first degree of freedom is always one and the second is $N - k - 1$:

$$F_{13.2} = \frac{r_{13.2}^2}{1 - r_{13.2}^2} \cdot (N - k - 1)$$

$$= \frac{.848^2}{1 - .848^2} \cdot (10 - 2 - 1) = 17.91 \qquad \begin{array}{l} df = 1, 7 \\ p < .01 \end{array}$$

$$F_{12.3} = \frac{r_{12.3}^2}{1 - r_{12.3}^2} \cdot (N - k - 1)$$

$$= \frac{.355^2}{1 - .355^2} \cdot (10 - 2 - 1) = 1.01 \qquad \begin{array}{l} df = 1, 7 \\ p > .05 \end{array}$$

The level of a significance also may be found by using a table of r values with 1 and $N - k - 1$ degrees of freedom.

Although the simple zero order relationship between education and turnout was $+.64$ and statistically significant, we see that the inclusion of political efficacy as a variable explains more unique variations in turnout than that explained by education when efficacy is controlled. The partial regression coefficients and partial correlation coefficients confirm the salience of efficacy over education. Together the independent variables explain 83 percent of the variation in turnout. However, the inclusion of education in the design has not added a significant increment to our explanatory power. The effects of control are obviously not the same across research designs. For example, if education were unrelated to efficacy or turnout, the partial relationship between efficacy and turnout would equal its zero order relationship and the multiple relationship; or if efficacy and turnout were positively related, but education was negatively related to efficacy and positively related to turnout, the partial between efficacy and turnout controlling for education would be greater than the zero order correlation. More details about the nature of controlled relationships appear in the next chapter.

If we were dealing with more independent variables one of our goals might be a highly parsimonious explanation of turnout. That is, we might take as few variables as possible to maximize our predictions so long as they are congruent with the conceptual framework. This can be accomplished by step-wise multiple regression where only those partials which add a significant increment are kept in the prediction equation.

Further extensions of multiple regression-correlation are also possible through the use of *dummy variables* and *interaction terms*. As we noted in the discussion of analysis of variance, the political scientist may encounter independent variables which are only measured as categories (nominal). If one or possibly more of these are nominal variables a new set of artificial variables can be derived for use in the regression equation, taking advantage of the interval character of a dichotomy. For example, if one of our independent variables in a regression scheme represents three types of religious affiliation, it can be broken down into three dichotomized variables where the first may be scored as 0 or 1 (Protestant or not Protestant), the second as 0 or 1 (Catholic or not Catholic), and the third as 0 or 1 (Jew or not Jew). One of these must be dropped because it is automatically determined by the other two.[91] If we begin with a dependent variable (X_1), two interval independent variables (X_2, X_3), and a nominal independent variable (X_4), the latter could be reduced to X_4 and X_5, for Protestant and Catholic categories respectively, so that the partial denoting impact of religion with controls for X_2 and X_3 would equal $r_{1(45).23}$. Although the dichotomous nature of dummy variables issues warning to the researcher, it has been argued that they are sometimes better measures than real interval variables, e.g., when a real number variable is curvilinear the distortion caused by linear regression is more serious than that caused by the use of dummy variables.[92] More extensive use of dummy variable concepts has been incorporated into multiple classification analysis which is basically a regression procedure.

While multiple correlation is a very sophisticated means for statistical analysis, unlike analysis of variance, it does not automatically measure *interaction effects*. Interaction occurs when the impact of one independent variable on the dependent variable differs for various levels of the other independent variable. The data array in the example for turnout, education, and efficacy appears to indicate little interaction since the effect of the independent variables on turnout is about the same across their levels. That is, the independent variables affect the dependent variable similarly when they work together or separately. When interaction is obvious or when it is desirable to measure it, one or more new variables representing interaction can be added to the regression equation. For example, variable X_1 might be added to our equation to represent the interaction between X_2 and X_3 (X_2X_3).[93] Therefore, $r_{14.23}$ would measure the interactive effect of education and efficacy over and above the effect of education and efficacy alone.

Another regression-like procedure utilizing the notion of linear combinations is *discriminant analysis*. It is especially suited for analysis of dichotomous or more general nominal dependent variables which usually fail to meet the normality assumption of regression. Discriminant analysis serves to classify cases with respect to a nominal dependent variable based on a set of independent predictor variables. The analysis finds a linear combination of the independent variables which best discriminates between cases of the two or more classes comprising the dependent variable. In effect, it is finding a linear combination of predictor variables that shows large differences in group means.[94]

Summary

The above review of basic statistical procedures which have generally been accepted by social scientists is of necessity brief and noninclusive. Our goal has been to approach statistics from a "handbook" or applications point of view in order to

91. Daniel B. Suits, "Use of Dummy Variables in Regression Equations," *Journal of the American Statistical Association* 52 (1957): pp. 548–51.

92. For a discussion of curvilinear multiple regression-correlation techniques see Mordecai Ezekiel and Karl A. Fox, *Methods of Correlation and Regression Analysis*, 3d ed. (New York: John Wiley, 1959), pp. 204–79.

93. Hubert M. Blalock, "Theory Building and the Statistical Concept of Interaction," *American Sociological Review* 30 (1965): pp. 374–80.

94. See Tatsuoka, *Multivariate Analysis*, pp. 157–93, and Cooley and Lohnes, *Multivariate Data Analysis*, pp. 243–61. For an extension to political science, see Lawrence S. Mayer and Philip M. Burgess, *Contrasting Regression and Correlation Analysis with Discriminant Analysis for Investigating Nominal Measures of Behavior* (Columbus: Behavioral Science Laboratory, Ohio State University, 1970).

facilitate and encourage the use of techniques which assist in the analysis of political data. In doing so, we have avoided many theoretical and mathematical aspects of statistics, which at some point should become part of the researcher's genre of knowledge. Furthermore, the limitations and assumptions of such techniques should be recognized, and statistical techniques must be treated as only one, albeit important, class of analysis tools.

In keeping with the approach of this chapter, table 2.26 presents a summary outline of useful statistical tools based upon the three criteria for use discussed throughout the chapter. Alone, its primary use is as a review or summary table, but in conjunction with the text and readings to follow, it offers a broad perspective depicting the interrelationships between classes of techniques. It should not be viewed as an inclusive guide to the field of statistics; it is a summary of the tools discussed and mentioned in this chapter. Although it is easy to follow, several clarifications should be mentioned. The levels of measurement listed to the left refer to either the single variable case or to pairs (or groups) of similar levels in the bivariate and multivariate case; mixed variable systems include a variety of other combinations of levels of measurement outside similar pairs or groups. The descriptive tools column has not been divided with regard to the number of variables. That is, the entire range of descriptive tools is common to variable systems of differing size; exceptions are found in the text. Since our focus has been on the analysis stage rather than the data collection and measurement stage, mention of univariate inferential tools appears only in the text. Finally, regression coefficients appear under descriptive and analytical headings because of their close link with both concepts.

Research Examples and Introductory Notes

In the following section several complete research examples are presented illustrating the use of statistical techniques applied to political data. Since examples utilizing each technique overviewed in this chapter would indeed be cumbersome, the articles chosen for the readings attempt to include several basic classes of statistical analysis. The first article by Cole elaborates an analysis technique applied to a mixed variable system, i.e., a set of variables at different levels of measurement. The remaining research examples treat interval level political variables in the bivariate and multivariate case illustrating the use of simple, partial, and multiple correlation-regression applied to several kinds of political data: aggregate social, economic, and political factors, as well as political attitudes.

Although we have reviewed the basic computational and interpretation procedures for statistical analysis, each example to follow represents the entire research project — the overall design, concept, and theory building, hypothesis testing, and data analysis. The illustrations for each statistical technique employed earlier in this chapter were primarily devoid of these broader considerations. By presenting entire research articles, the various stages of the research process and the interrelationship between theory and data analysis techniques should become evident to the reader. Furthermore, by placing statistical techniques in a substantive context, you will be able to see how these techniques assist us in providing more scientific answers to important questions about politics. The fundamental purpose of these readings is to illustrate the way in which statistical techniques serve more fundamental substantive and theoretical goals in political science.

TABLE 2.26 Tabular Summary of Statistical Tool Selection

LEVELS OF MEASURE-MENT	FUNCTION				
	Descriptive	Inferential		Analytical	
		Size of Variable System			
	Differing Number of Variables	Bivariate	Multivariate	Bivariate	Multivariate
Nominal	Frequencies Ratios Proportions Percentages Mode (Mo) Contingency Table	Chi-Square (χ^2) Fisher's Exact Probability Test	Chi-Square (pooled)	Phi Coefficient (ϕ) Cramer's V Contingency Coefficient (C) Yule's Q Goodman & Kruskal's Tau, (τ_a,τ_b) Lambda ($\lambda,\lambda_a,\lambda_b$)	Partial & Multiple Phi (ϕ)
Ordinal	Rankings Median (Md) Mode (Mo) Scatter Diagram Contingency Table Frequency distribution (graphic)	Table of r_s Z-test	Z-test	Spearman's Rho (r_s) Kendall's Tau (τ_a,τ_b,τ_c) Gamma (γ) Somers' d	Partial and Multiple Tau (τ) Partial Gamma (γ) Multiple Gamma-k, Somers' d and Koppa
Interval	Mean ($\bar{X}$) Frequency distribution (graphic) Median (Md) Mode (Mo) Scatter Diagram Range Regression Line Standard Deviation (s) Regression Coefficients (b,β)	F-test Table of r	F-test	Preason Product-Moment Correlation Coefficient (r) Coefficient of Determination (r^2) Regression Coefficient (b,β)	Partial & Multiple Correlation Coefficients (r,R) Partial Regression Coefficients (b,β)
Mixed	Data Array Scatter Diagram Table of Means Standard Deviation Others — see above depending on combination	F-test t-test Kruskal-Wallis H Test Kolmogorov-Smirnov Test Mann-Whitney U Wald-Wolfowitz Runs Test	F-test	One-Way AOV Intraclass Correlation Coefficient (r_i) Eta Coefficient (E,η) Point-Biserial Correlation Coefficients	Two-Way AOV Intraclass Correlation Coefficient (r_i) Discriminant Analysis Multiple Classification Analysis (MCA) Analysis of Covariance Dummy Variable Regression

Selected Bibliography of Applications

Bivariate Analysis of Nominal Data

Baur, Jackson. "Opinion Change in a Public Controversy." *Public Opinion Quarterly* 26 (1962): 212–26. (Cramer's *V*)

Benjamin, Roger W., and Kautsky, John H. "Communism and Economic Development." *American Political Science Review* 62 (1968): 110–23. (contingency coefficient)

Downes, Bryan. "Municipal Social Rank and the Characteristics of Local Political Leaders." *Midwest Journal of Political Science* 12 (1968): 514–37. (contingency coefficient)

Fitzgibbon, Russell, and Johnson, Kenneth. "Measurement of Latin American Political Change." *American Political Science Review* 55 (1961): 515–26. (contingency coefficient)

Francis, Wayne L. "Influence and Interaction in a State Legislative Body." *American Political Science Review* 56 (1962): 953–60. (phi)

Nagel, Stuart. "Political Party Affiliation and Judge's Decisions." *American Political Science Review* 55 (1961): 843–50. (phi)

———. "Testing Relations Between Judicial Characteristics and Judicial Decision-Making." *Western Political Quarterly* 15 (1962): 425–37. (phi)

Parsons, Malcolm B. "Quasi-Partisan Conflict in a One-Party Legislative System: The Florida Senate." *American Political Science Review* 56 (1962): 605–14. (phi)

Tanenhaus, Joseph. "Supreme Court Attitudes Toward Federal Administrative Agencies." *Journal of Politics* 22 (1960): 503–24. (contingency coefficient)

Wiener, Phyllis R. "Doorbell-Ringing for a State Education Measure." *Western Political Quarterly* 15 (1962): 345–52. (lambda)

Bivariate Analysis of Ordinal Data

Barnes, Samuel. "Participation, Education and Political Competence: Evidence From a Sample of Italian Socialists." *American Political Science Review* 60 (1966): 348–53. (gamma)

Converse, Philip E., and Dupeux, Georges. "Politicization of the Electorate in France and the United States." *Public Opinion Quarterly* 26 (1962): 1–23. (tau *b*)

Dawson, Richard, and Robinson, James. "Inter-Party Competition, Economic Variables and Welfare Policies in the American States." *Journal of Politics* 25 (1963): 265–89. (rho)

Downes, Bryan. "Social and Political Characteristics of Riot Cities: A Comparative Study." *Social Science Quarterly* 49 (1968): 504–20. (gamma)

Eisinger, Peter K. "Protest Behavior and the Integration of Urban Political Systems." *Journal of Politics* 33 (1971): 980–1007. (gamma)

Hennessey, Timothy M. "Democratic Attitudinal Configurations Among Italian Youth." *Midwest Journal of Political Science* 13 (1969): 167–93. (tau *c* and partial tau)

Hofferbert, Richard I. "The Relationship Between Public Policy and Some Structural and Environmental Variables in the American States." *American Political Science Review* 60 (1966): 73–82. (rho)

Holsti, Ole R. "The Belief System and National Images: A Case Study." *Journal of Conflict Resolution* 6 (1962): 245–52. (rho)

Jaros, Dean; Hirsch, Herbert; and Fleron, Frederic J. "The Malevolent Leader: Political Socialization in an American Sub-Culture." *American Political Science Review* 62 (1968): 564–75. (tau *c*)

Jennings, M. Kent. "Parental Grievances and School Politics." *Public Opinion Quarterly* 32 (1968): 363–78. (gamma and rho)

Jennings, M. Kent, and Niemi, Richard G. "The Transmission of Political Values From Parent to Child." *American Political Science Review* 62 (1968): 169–84. (tau *b*)

Kessel, John H. "The Washington Congressional Delegation." *Midwest Journal of Political Science* 8 (1964): 1–21. (tau *c*)

Kornberg, Allan. "Caucus and Cohesion in Canadian Parliamentary Parties." *American Political Science Review* 60 (1966): 83–92. (gamma)

———. "Perception and Constituency Influence on Legislative Behavior." *Western Political Quarterly* 19 (1966): 285–92. (gamma)

Langton, Kenneth P. "Peer Groups and School and the Political Socialization Process." *American Political Science Review* 61 (1967): 751–58. (gamma)

Luttbeg, Norman, and Zeigler, Harmon. "Attitude Consensus and Conflict in an Interest Group." *American Political Science Review* 60 (1966): 655–66. (tau c)

McClosky, Herbert; Hoffman, Paul J.; and O'Hara, Rosemary. "Issue Conflict and Consensus Among Party Leaders and Followers." *American Political Science Review* 54 (1960): 406–27. (rho)

Moore, David W. "Legislative Effectiveness and Majority Party Size: A Test in the Indiana House." *Journal of Politics* 31 (1969): 1063–79. (Somers' *d*)

Moynihan, Daniel Patrick, and Wilson, James Q. "Patronage in New York State, 1955–59." *American Political Science Review* 58 (1964): 286 301. (tau)

Niemi, Richard G., and Jennings, M. Kent. "Intraparty Communication and the Selection of Delegates to a National Convention." *Western Political Quarterly* 22 (1969): 29–46. (gamma)

Olsen, Marvin E. "Alienation and Political Opinions." *Public Opinion Quarterly* 29 (1965): 200–212. (Somers' *d*)

Pettigrew, Thomas F., and Campbell, Ernest. "Faubus and Segregation: An Analysis of Arkansas Voting." *Public Opinion Quarterly* 24 (1960): 436–47. (tau and partial tau)

Putnam, Robert D. "Political Attitudes and the Local Community." *American Political Science Review* 60 (1966): 640–54. (tau c)

Scoble, Harry M. "Organized Labor In Electoral Politics." *Western Political Quarterly* 16 (1963): 666–85. (tau)

Soule, John W., and Clarke, James W. "Issue Conflict and Consensus: A Comparative Study of Democratic and Republican Delegates to the 1968 National Convention." *Journal of Politics* 33 (1971): 72–91. (gamma)

Bivariate Analysis of Interval Data

Alford, Robert R., and Lee, Eugene C. "Voting Turnout in American Cities." *American Political Science Review* 62 (1968): 796–814.

Dye, Thomas R. "Income Inequality and American State Politics." *American Political Science Review* 63 (1969): 157–62.

Eckhardt, William, and White, Ralph K. "A Test of the Mirror-Image Hypothesis: Kennedy and Khrushchev." *Journal of Conflict Resolution* 11 (1967): 325–32.

Flinn, Thomas A. "How Mr. Nixon Took Ohio." *Western Political Quarterly* 15 (1962): 274–79.

———. "Party Responsibility in the States: Some Causal Factors." *American Political Science Review* 58 (1964): 60–71.

Fried, Robert C. "Communism, Urban Budgets, and the Two Italies: A Case Study in Comparative Urban Government." *Journal of Politics* 33 (1971): 1008–51.

Hinckley, Barbara. "Seniority in the Committee Leadership Selection of Congress." *Midwest Journal of Political Science* 13 (1969): 613–30.

Hofferbert, Richard. "Ecological Development and Policy Change in the American States." *Midwest Journal of Political Science* 10 (1966): 464–84.

Mueller, John E. "The Politics of Fluoridation in Seven California Cities." *Western Political Quarterly* 19 (1966): 54–67.

Nagel, Stuart. "Sociometric Relations Among American Courts." *Southwestern Social Science Quarterly* 43 (1962): 136–42.

Nelson, Dalmas H., and Hoffman, Paul J. "Federal Employees and Voting in Federal Elections." *Western Political Quarterly* 22 (1969): 581–93.

Sharkansky, Ira. "Economic Development, Regionalism and State Political Systems." *Midwest Journal of Political Science* 12 (1968): 41–62.

Walton, John, and Sween, Joyce A. "Urbanization, Industrialization and Voting in Mexico: A Longitudinal Analysis of Official and Opposition Party Support." *Social Science Quarterly* 52 (1971): 721–45.

Wolfinger, Raymond E., and Field, John O. "Political Ethos and the Structure of City Government." *American Political Science Review* 60 (1966): 306–26.

Zikmund, Joseph. "Suburban Voting in Presidential Elections, 1948–64." *Midwest Journal of Political Science* 12 (1968): 239–59.

Multivariate Analysis of Interval Data

Clarke, James W. "Environment, Process and Policy: A Reconsideration." *American Political Science Review* 63 (1969): 1172–82.

Cnudde, Charles F., and McCrone, Donald J. "Party Competition and Welfare Policies in the American States." *American Political Science Review* 63 (1969): 858–66.

Conway, M. Margaret. "The White Backlash Re-Examined: Wallace and the 1964 Primaries." *Social Science Quarterly* 49 (1968): 710–19.

Cowart, Andrew T. "Anti-Poverty Expenditures in the American States." *Midwest Journal of Political Science* 13 (1969) 219–36.

Dye, Thomas, R. "Governmental Structure, Urban Environment and Education Policy." *Midwest Journal of Political Science* 11 (1967): 353–80.

———. "Malapportionment and Public Policy in the States." *Journal of Politics* 27 (1965): 586–601.

Erickson, Robert S. "The Electoral Impact of Congressional Roll Call Voting." *American Political Science Review* 65 (1971): 1018–32.

Gordon, Daniel N. "Immigrants and Municipal Voting Turnout: Implications for the Changing Ethnic Impact on Urban Politics." *American Sociological Review* 35 (1970): 665–81.

Jackson, John E. "Statistical Models of Senate Roll Call Voting." *American Political Science Review* 65 (1971): 451–70.

Hawkins, Brett W. "Life Style, Demographic Distance and Voter Support in City-County Consolidation." *Southwestern Social Science Quarterly* 48 (1967): 325–37.

Katz, Daniel, and Eldersveld, Samuel J. "The Impact of Local Party Activity Upon the Electorate." *Public Opinion Quarterly* 25 (1961): 1–24.

Kelley, Stanley; Ayres, Richard E.; and Bowen, William G. "Registration and Voting: Putting First Things First." *American Political Science Review* 61 (1967): 359–79.

Kramer, Gerald. "Short-Term Fluctuations in U.S. Voting Behavior, 1896–1964," *American Political Science Review* 65 (1971): 131–43.

Lee, Chae-Jin. "Socio-Economic Conditions and Party Politics in Japan: A Statistical Analysis of the 1969 General Election." *Journal of Politics* 33 (1971): 158–79.

Lineberry, Robert L., and Fowler, Edmund P. "Reformism and Public Policies in American Cities." *American Political Science Review* 61 (1967): 701–16.

Matthews, Donald R., and Prothro, James W. "Political Factors and Negro Voter Registration in the South." *American Political Science Review* 57 (1963): 355–68.

Murphey, Walter F., and Tanenhaus, Joseph. "Public Opinion and the Supreme Court: The Goldwater Campaign." *Public Opinion Quarterly* 32 (1968): 31–50.

Pulsipher, Allan G., and Weatherly, James. "Malapportionment, Party Competition, and the Functional Distribution of Governmental Expenditures." *American Political Science Review* 62 (1968): 1207–19.

Salisbury, Robert H., and Black, Gordon. "Class and Party in Partisan and Non-Partisan Elections." *American Political Science Review* 57 (1963): 584–92.

Sharkansky, Ira. "Government Expenditures and Public Services in the American States." *American Political Science Review* 61 (1967): 1066–78.

———. "Regional Patterns in the Expenditures of American States." *Western Political Quarterly* 20 (1967): 955–71.

Soares, Glaucio, and Hamblin, Robert L. "Socio-Economic Variables and Voting for the Radical Left: Chile, 1952." *American Political Science Review* 61 (1967): 1053–65.

Tanenhaus, Joseph et al. "The Supreme Court's Certiorari Jurisdiction." In *Judicial Decision-Making*, ed. Glendon Schubert, pp. 111–32. New York: The Free Press of Glencoe, 1963.

White, Elliott S. "Intelligence and Sense of Political Efficacy in Children." *Journal of Politics* 30 (1968): 710–31.

Bivariate and Multivariate Analysis at Different Levels of Measurement

Beck, Paul Allen, and Jennings, M. Kent. "Lowering the Voting Age: The Case of the Reluctant Electorate." *Public Opinion Quarterly* 33 (1969): 370–79. (Multiple Classification Analysis)

Bennett, Stephen E., and Klecka, William R. "Social Status and Political Participation: A Multivariate Analysis of Predictive Power." *Midwest Journal of Political Science* 14 (1970): 355–82. (Multiple Classification Analysis)

Burgess, Philip M., and Robinson, James A. "Alliances and the Theory of Collective Action: A Simulation of Coalition Processes." *Midwest Journal of Political Science* 13 (1969): 194–218. (Analysis of Variance)

Carter, Roy E., Jr., and Clarke, Peter. "Public Affairs Opinion Leadership Among Educational Television Viewers." *American Sociological Review* 27 (1962): 792–99. (Analysis of Variance)

Clausen, Aage R. "State Party Influence on Congressional Policy Decision." *Midwest Journal of Political Science* 16 (1972): 77–101. (dummy variable regression)

Cobb, Stephen A. "Defense Spending and Foreign Policy in the House of Representatives." *Journal of Conflict Resolution* 13 (1969): 358–69. (dummy variable regression)

Dogan, Mattei. "A Covariance Analysis of French Electoral Data." In *Quantitative Ecological Analysis in the Social Sciences*, ed. Mattei Dogan and Stein Rokkan, pp. 285–98. Cambridge: MIT Press, 1969. (Analysis of Variance)

Fisher, Franklin M. "The Mathematical Analysis of Supreme Court Decisions: The Use and Abuse of Quantitative Methods." *American Political Science Review* 52 (1958): 321–28. (discriminant analysis)

Kornberg, Allan, and Frasure, Robert C. "Policy Differences in British Parliamentary Parties." *American Political Science Review* 65 (1971): 694–703. (discriminant analysis)

Langton, Kenneth, and Jennings, M. Kent. "Political Socialization and the High School Civics Curriculum in the United States." *American Political Science Review* 62 (1968): 854–59. (Multiple Classification Analysis)

Luttbeg, Norman R. "Classifying the American States: An Empirical Attempt to Identify Internal Variations." *Midwest Journal of Political Science* 15 (1971): 703–21. (Analysis of Variance)

Muller, Edward N. "The Representation of Citizens by Political Authorities: Consequences of Regime Support." *American Political Science Review* 64 (1970): 1149–66. (Analysis of Variance)

Olsen, Marvin E. "Social and Political Participation of Blacks." *American Sociological Review* 35 (1970): 682–97. (Multiple Classification Analysis)

Paige, Jeffery M. "Political Orientation and Riot Participation." *American Sociological Review* 36 (1971): 810–20. (Analysis of Variance)

Segal, David R., and Knoke, David. "Class Inconsistency, Status Inconsistency, and Political Partisanship in America." *Journal of Politics* 33 (1971): 941–54. (Multiple Classification Analysis)

Sharkansky, Ira. "Regionalism, Economic Status and the Public Policies of American States." *Social Science Quarterly* 49 (1968): 9–26. (Analysis of Variance)

Stokes, Donald E. "Parties and the Nationalization of Electoral Forces." In *The American Party Systems*, ed. William N. Chambers and Walter Dean Burnham, pp. 182–202. New York: Oxford University Press, 1967. (Analysis of Variance)

———. "A Variance Components Model of Political Effects." In *Mathematical Applications in Political Science*, ed. John Claunch, pp. 61–85. Dallas: Southern Methodist University Press, 1965. (Analysis of Variance)

Stokes, Donald E., and Miller, Warren. "Party Government and the Saliency of Congress." *Public Opinion Quarterly* 26 (1962): 531–46. (Analysis of Variance)

Thomas, Norman C. "The Electorate and State Constitutional Revision." *Midwest Journal of Political Science* 12 (1968): 115–29. (Analysis of Variance)

———. "Voting Machines and Voter Participation in Four Michigan Constitutional Revision Referenda." *Western Political Quarterly* 21 (1968): 409–19. (Analysis of Variance)

Ulmer, S. Sidney. "Mathematical Models for Predicting Judicial Behavior." In *Mathematical Applications in Political Science III*, ed. Joseph L. Bernd, pp. 67–95. Charlottesville: University Press of Virginia, 1967. (discriminant analysis)

Zikmund, Joseph. "A Comparison of Political Attitude and Activity Patterns in Central Cities and Suburbs." *Public Opinion Quarterly* 31 (1967): 69–75. (Analysis of Variance)

RICHARD L. COLE

The Urban Policy Process:
A Note on Structural
and Regional Influences[1]

The following example employs one-way and two-way
analysis of variance to examine the relationships between region and
local governmental structure variables on policy outputs in U.S. cities
over 50,000. Region is measured as a four-category independent variable
(Northeast, South, Midwest, West) and form of local government is a
three-category nominal variable (mayor-council, council-manager,
commission), also measured in terms of levels of reformism (form of
government: mayor-council, council-manager or commission; mode of
election: partisan or nonpartisan; and districting: ward or at-large).
The dependent policy output measures include three interval variables
examined separately: proportion of local employees under civil service,
per capita urban renewal grants requested, and per capita planning
expenditures. In a one-way analysis of variance design the author creates
a two-category independent variable based upon reform (city manager and
commission) and unreformed (mayor-council) structures, compares mean
levels for the dependent variables by these categories and tests the
statistical significance of the difference between these means accompanied
by a measure of the degree of association (ω^2) for the statistically
significant relationship. A level of reform variable also is devised
based upon the number of reformed structures in each city (four categories)
and tested for its relationship to policy outputs through analysis of
variance. A two-way design then is utilized to test the impact of both
structure (reformism) and region on policy outputs.

Reprinted from Richard L. Cole, "The Urban Policy Process: A Note On Structural and Regional Influences," *Social Science Quarterly* 52 (1971): 646–55, by permission of the journal and the author.

1. The author wishes to express his appreciation to William Shaffer, Professor of Political Science, Purdue University, for his comments and technical advice upon an earlier draft of this paper. Any errors of omission or interpretation are, of course, mine alone.

Students of local politics have become increasingly interested in the relationships between various socioeconomic characteristics and forms of local government. Indeed, a large number of empirical studies exploring such relationships is now available[2] — many, perhaps most, indebted to the stimulating works of Banfield and Wilson[3] for their theoretical framework.

More recently students of urban political systems have been concerned with "policy outputs" and especially with the relationships between these outputs and various demographic and political variables.[4] Two of the most sophisticated of these analyses are the studies by Lineberry and Fowler and Wolfinger and Field.[5] Wolfinger and Field posit region to be one of the most important predictive variables of urban policy outputs; Lineberry and Fowler are interested in the influence of local governmental structure (among other "political factors") upon policy outcomes.[6]

The purpose of this study is to investigate more precisely the relationships between the independent variables of region and structure of local government and the dependent variable of policy outputs, employing the statistical tests of one-way and two-way analyses of variance. Since both "structure" and "region" are considered to be nominal data, these are the appropriate techniques that will allow us to determine which independent variables in fact are significantly related to which policy outputs and that will permit the calculation of the amount of inter-city variance "explained" by each independent variable.

2. For a sample of these studies see: John Kessel, "Governmental Structure and Political Environment: A Statistical Note About American Cities," *American Political Science Review*, 46 (Sept., 1962), pp. 615–620; Edgar Sherbenou, "Class, Participation, and the Council-Manager Plan," *Public Administration Review*, 21 (Summer, 1961), pp. 131–135; Leo Schnore and Robert Alford, "Forms of Government and Socio-economic Characteristics of Suburbs," *Administrative Science Quarterly*, 7 (June, 1963), p. 1017; and Robert Alford and Harry Scoble, "Political and Socio-economic Characteristics of Cities," *The Municipal Year Book, 1965* (Chicago: The International City Managers' Association, 1965), pp. 82–97. See also the collection of works presented by Charles M. Bonjean, Terry N. Clark, and Robert Lineberry, eds., *Community Politics: A Behavioral Approach* (New York: The Free Press, 1971), and especially the bibliographies prepared by Roland J. Pellegrin and Michael D. Grimes which are included in that volume.

3. I am referring, of course, to their notion of "ethos theory" best expressed in their works: Edward C. Banfield and James Q. Wilson, *City Politics* (Cambridge: Harvard University Press and M.I.T. Press, 1963); and James Q. Wilson and Edward C. Banfield, "Public-Regardingness as a Value Premise in Voting Behavior," *American Political Science Review*, 58 (Dec., 1964), pp. 876–87.

4. Actually the analysis of policy outputs on the state level appears much more advanced at present than does similar analysis at the local level. Nevertheless, several studies have dealt with local policy outputs. See, for example: Oliver P. Williams, Harold Herman, Charles S. Liebman, and Thomas R. Dye, *Suburban Differences and Metropolitan Politics: A Philadelphia Story* (Philadelphia: University of Pennsylvania Press, 1965); Thomas R. Dye, "City-Suburban Social Distance and Public Policy," *Social Forces*, 4 (1965), pp. 100–106; Raymond Wolfinger and John Osgood Field, "Political Ethos and the Structure of City Government," *American Political Science Review*, 60 (June, 1966), pp. 306–326; Bernard H. Booms, "City Governmental Form and Public Expenditure Levels," *National Tax Journal*, 19 (June, 1966), pp. 187–199; Robert L. Lineberry and Edmund P. Fowler, "Reformism and Public Policies in American Cities," *American Political Science Review*, 61 (Sept., 1967), pp. 701–716; and Lewis A. Froman, Jr., "An Analysis of Public Policies in Cities," *Journal of Politics*, 29 (Feb., 1967), pp. 94–108. See also Sherbenou, "Class, Participation, and the Council-Manager Plan."

5. Lineberry and Fowler, "Reformism and Public Policies in American Cities"; Wolfinger and Field, "Political Ethos and the Structure of City Government."

6. It is important to note that Lineberry and Fowler are primarily interested in the role of institutional features in mediating or "filtering" the relationships between socioeconomic characteristics and levels of public policy rather than with the direct effect of structure upon per capita expenditure data. Although their study is of obvious interest to students of the urban policy process, their findings and conclusions are not directly comparable to those presented in this paper.

Region is an obvious (if somewhat gross) measure. For the purposes of this research, cities were categorized as belonging to one of four regions: Northeast, South, Midwest, and West.[7] Form of local government refers to whether the city is administered by the mayor-council, council-manager, or commission system. In addition, structure of local government is more precisely calculated by ranking each city in terms of a "scale of reformism"[8] based upon the three measures of: form of local government (mayor-council, council-manager, or commission); mode of electing local officials (partisan or non-partisan); and manner of districting (ward or at-large).[9] Finally, measures of policy output are the same as those employed by the Wolfinger and Field survey. These include: proportion of municipal employees covered by civil service, per capita city planning expenditures, and urban renewal grants requested, per capita.[10] The relationships among these variables were examined for all U.S. cities over 50,000.[11]

Hypotheses

A fundamental assumption of governmental reformers and students of both state and local politics has been that governmental structures influence the policy outputs produced by the political system. Reformers assumed that the more "reformed" the city's political structure, the greater the probability that the policy outputs of that city would be more in the public or general interest than policy outputs of a city whose administrative structure is less reformed. Perhaps Banfield and Wilson (although they question these assumptions) have best interpreted this reformist philosophy:

> The reformers assumed that there existed an interest . . . that pertained to the city "as a whole" and that should always prevail over (private) interests. . . . The task of discovering

---

7. These categories are the same as those adopted by the International City Manager's Association for use in its 1966 *Municipal Yearbook*. Those states included in each region are as follows: (1) Northeast: Maine, Vermont, New Hampshire, Massachusetts, Rhode Island, Connecticut, New York, Pennsylvania, New Jersey; (2) South: Maryland, Delaware, Virginia, West Virginia, North Carolina, South Carolina, Georgia, Florida, Kentucky, Tennessee, Alabama, Mississippi, Arkansas, Louisiana, Oklahoma, Texas; (3) North Central: Michigan, Ohio, Indiana, Illinois, Wisconsin, Minnesota, Iowa, Missouri, Kansas, Nebraska, South Dakota, North Dakota; (4) West: Montana, Wyoming, Colorado, New Mexico, Arizona, Utah, Nevada, Idaho, Washington, Oregon, California.

8. Lineberry and Fowler ("Reformism and Public Policies in American Cities") were the first to construct and employ such a scale.

9. All data concerning form of local government (mayor-council, commission, or council-manager), mode of election (partisan or non-partisan), and manner of districting (ward or at-large) were taken from: *The Municipal Year Book, 1966* (Chicago: The International City Managers' Association, 1966). Consistent with the reformist thesis, commission cities were combined with council-manager cities for analysis.

10. Data concerning the proportion of municipal employees covered by civil service were taken from *The Municipal Year Book, 1963*; per capita city planning expenditures from *The Municipal Year Book, 1965*; and per capita urban renewal grants requested from *Urban Renewal Directory, December 31, 1969* (Washington: Urban Renewal Administration, 1970).

11. Whenever there was only incomplete or no data for a city, that city was not included in that particular analysis. The 1960 census of the population provided the base number of cities over 50,000. To this total was added a number of cities estimated by the 1966 *Municipal Year Book* to have reached 50,000 by the middle of the decade. Also it should be noted that when size was controlled (by separately examining cities under and over 500,000) the results were not markedly different from those reported in this paper.

the content of the public interest was therefore a technical rather than a political one. . . . The best qualified men would decide "policy" and leave its execution . . . to professionals. . . .[12]

Two mid-western surveys focusing upon these proposed relationships have reported that policy outputs of those "reformed" and "unreformed" cities included in their studies did vary significantly. In general, each author interpreted his findings as being supportive of the reformist hypothesis. Examining three measures of policy outputs (per capita expenditures, debt, and property tax) of 74 Chicago suburbs, Sherbenou concluded that "proponents of the [council-manager] plan argue that council-management tends to develop a public confidence in the efficiency and responsibility of municipal government. Such evidence as the present study affords tends to support this argument."[13] Based upon his survey of 75 cities in Ohio and Michigan, Booms observed, ". . . (1) the form of government has an effect on the level of per capita expenditures and that (2) . . . manager cities might be considered more 'efficient'. . . ."[14] These two studies support the hypothesized relationships among administrative structures and the three measures of policy outputs summarized in Table 1.

TABLE 1   Hypothesized Structural/Policy Relationships

POLICY	STRUCTURE	
	Reformed	Unreformed
Percent of municipal employees covered by civil service	High	Low
Per capita city planning expenditures	High	Low
Per capita urban renewal requests	High	Low

Although they were primarily concerned with the relationships among various socioeconomic measures and political structures, Wolfinger and Field observed that those policy outputs which they examined were largely affected by region of the country. The level of civil service coverage, for example, was found to be much lower in southern and border cities than in other areas of the country. They concluded, in fact, that when area of the country is controlled for, all other relationships tended to disappear. In his analysis of policies in cities over 25,000 population, Froman tended to agree with Wolfinger and Field and stated, "In general, the highest association of the manager-council plan of city government is with region of the country."[15] It should be noted that, regardless of the very powerful arguments presented by Wolfinger and Field and Froman's concurrence with their conclusions, Jacob and Lipsky have somewhat tempered the notion that region is the single most important predictive variable. They state that "While Southern politics con-

12. Banfield and Wilson, *City Politics*, pp. 139–140.
13. Sherbenou, "Class, Participation, and the Council-Manager Plan," p. 134.
14. Booms, "City Governmental Form and Public Expenditure Levels," p. 192.
15. Froman, "An Analysis of Public Policies in Cities," p. 99.

tinues to display unique political configurations . . . , it is by no means clear that other regional configurations are particularly salient."[16]

Based primarily upon these four surveys, in any case, the initial expectation of this study was that form of political structure (Sherbenou, Booms), as well as region (Wolfinger and Field, Froman), would measurably influence local policy outputs. It is possible, of course, that neither structure nor region will be found to be a significant predictor of urban policy. This alternative is evaluated more fully in the concluding section. The purpose of the analysis which follows is to measure precisely the degree of the total inter-city variance of urban policy outputs for all U.S. cities over 50,000 which can be "explained" in terms of political structure and region.

Findings: Government Structures and Policy Outcomes

Table 2, below, presents a comparison of means of all three dependent variables with the independent variable, structure of local government.

TABLE 2 Comparison of Means

	City Manager-Commission (N = 239)	Mayor-Council (N = 142)
Percent of municipal employees covered by civil service	.6687	.6901
Per capita city planning expenditures	.7728	.5320
Per capita urban renewal requests	79.5221	155.4003

Contrary to the reformist expectations, Table 2 indicates that the mayor-council cities have slightly higher proportions of their employees covered by a civil service system and have requested substantially more per capita funds for urban renewal. However, the average per capita spent on city planning does appear to conform to the reformist hypothesis. In order to measure more accurately the difference with respect to revenue spent per capita on city planning between city manager-commission and mayor-council cities, the results of the one-way analysis of variance test are presented in Table 3.

As Table 3 indicates, the difference of mean scores for revenue per capita spent on city planning is significant at the .01 level. In addition, ω^2 indicates the degree of that relationship to be slight. One-way analysis of variance tests measuring the differences of means among the cities for the other two policy variables (each contradicting the reformism prediction) indicated that the apparent difference of mean scores for percent of employees covered by civil service was not significant at the .05 level. The difference of means for per capita urban renewal funds was significant at the .001 level and ω^2 indicated the magnitude of that relationship to be slight.

16. Herbert Jacob and Michael Lipsky, "Outputs, Structure, and Power: An Assessment of Changes in the Study of State and Local Politics," in *Political Science*. ed. by Marian Irish (Englewood Cliffs: Prentice-Hall, 1968), p. 241. See also, Ira Sharkansky, *Regionalism in American Politics* (Indianapolis: Bobbs-Merrill, 1969).

TABLE 3   Effect of Administrative Structure Upon
Per Capita Funds Allocated to City Planning

Sources	D.F.	Mean Squares	F Ratio	P	ω^{2}*
Manager-Commission/Mayor	1	3.6016	10.0342	.01	.030
Residual	288	.3589			
Total	289				

*ω^2 is a statistic used to estimate the magnitude of a relationship once the significance of that relationship is affirmed.[a]

[a]A more complete discussion of the interpretation and use of ω^2 (omega squared) is presented in: William Hays and Robert Winkler, *Statistics: Probability, Influence, and Decision*, II (New York: Holt, Rinehart and Winston, 1970), p. 132.

As a further test of the significance of governmental structures upon the determination of policy outputs, the three variables of form of local government, mode of electing local officials, and the manner of districting were combined into the scale of "reformism" described above. All cities were classified according to the following four categories:

1. Cities with none of the reformed institutions (city manager, nonpartisan elections, at-large districts);
2. Cities with only one of the three reforms;
3. Cities with any two of the reforms;
4. Cities with all three of the reform institutions.

Table 4 presents a comparison of means of all three dependent variables with the independent variable, "institutional reform scale."

As Table 4 indicates, the first two variables (percent of employees covered by civil service and per capita expenditures on planning) do appear to vary in the direction hypothesized.

TABLE 4   Comparison of Means

	1 (least reformed)	2	3	4 (most reformed)
Percent of municipal employees covered by civil service	.5840	.6859	.7302	.6767
Per capita city planning expenditures	$ .4790	$ .5440	$ .7050	$ .7965
Per capita urban renewal requests	$168.3611	$138.4994	$93.5211	$75.4210

Table 5 indicates that what inter-city differences may appear to exist among the mean percentages of employees covered by civil service are not significant at the .05 level. While the mean differences of per capita funds spent for city planning again were significant at the .05 level, the ω^2 score (also Table 5) indicates the magnitude of that relationship to be only .028. Interestingly, the mean sums of per capita funds requested for urban renewal again contradict the reform hypothesis and the differences are significant at the .01 level. In addition, ω^2 indicates the degree or magnitude of that relationship to be only .053.

TABLE 5   Effect of Administrative Structure Upon
Civil Service Coverage and City Planning Expenditures

Dependent Variable	Sources	D.F.	Mean Squares	F Ratio	P	ω^2
Civil Service	Reformism	3	.1920	1.3720	not sig.	----
Coverage	Residual	316	.1400			
Total		319				
City Planning	Reformism	3	1.3975	3.8529	.05	.028
Expenditures	Residual	285	.3622			
Total		288				

The results presented in Tables 2 through 5 clearly indicate that, by itself, political structure is an inadequate predictor of urban policy. For all tests conducted, structure was found to be significantly related (in the direction of the reformist expectation) to policy outputs for only one measure: funds per capita spent for city planning. Furthermore the strongest relationship between political structure and per capita funds for city planning accounts for only 3 percent of the total inter-city variance in that policy. No significant differences are observed concerning percent of employees covered by civil service, and mean differences involving per capita urban renewal funds requested consistently contradict the reform hypothesis at a statistically significant level.

Findings: Political Structure, Region, and Public Policy

It has also been hypothesized that area of the country would prove to be a significant predictor of urban policy outputs. Two-way analysis of variance techniques were employed to test the influence of both structure of local government (utilizing the same scale of reformism constructed above) and region upon policy outputs. Table 6 presents an analysis of the impact of both governmental structure and region of the country upon the percent of employees covered by civil service and upon per capita funds spent for city planning.

Table 6 indicates that, as would be expected, governmental structure remains a non-significant predictor of urban policy pertaining to civil service coverage of

TABLE 6   Effect of Structure and Region Upon Civil
Service Coverage and City Planning Expenditures

Dependent Variable	Sources	D.F.	Mean Squares	F Ratio	P	ω^2
Civil Service	Structure	3	.2948	2.29	not sig.	----
Coverage	Region	3	1.3576	10.54	.01	.081
	Residual	312	.1288			
Total		318				
City Planning	Structure	3	.1852	.58	not sig.	----
Expenditures	Region	3	4.5306	14.25	.001	.121
	Residual	282	.3179			
Total		288				

municipal employees. After structure has been accounted for, however, region does significantly distinguish between the mean percentages of employees covered by civil service. In addition, ω^2 indicates the magnitude of the relationship between region and civil service coverage to be .081.[17]

Previous tables have indicated that the only public policy which appeared to be significantly affected by governmental structure was per capita funds allocated to city planning. As Table 6 indicates, this relationship disappears when region of the country is accounted for. Region, moreover, is not only significantly related to per capita allotments for city planning at the .001 level, the ω^2 score indicates that region "explains" 12.1 percent of the total inter-city variance of this policy.[18]

Previous discussions also have indicated that the relationship between urban renewal funds requested per capita and governmental structure tended to contradict the reformist prediction. The final table analyzes the impact of both governmental structure and region upon urban renewal requests.

Table 7 indicates that structure of local government continues to affect urban renewal funds requested per capita in a manner contradictory to the reformist prediction. However the ω^2 score indicates that, when region is also accounted for, structure explains only slightly more than one percent of the total inter-city variance for such funds requested. Region, on the other hand, remains the stronger predictor of urban policy and, in this instance, accounts for almost 12 percent of the total inter-city variance.[19]

TABLE 7   Effect of Structure and Region Upon Per
Capita Urban Renewal Funds Requested

Sources	D.F.	Mean Squares	F Ratio	P	ω^2
Structure	3	46776.18	2.76	.05	.012
Region	3	301460.49	17.82	.001	.118
Residual	368	16917.62			
Total	374				

Conclusions

As mentioned above, students of state and local politics increasingly are attempting to determine what sorts of variables are most associated with policy outcomes. Utimately it is hoped that causal models relating such variables may be constructed. At the local level, it has been proposed that at least two sorts of phenomena are significant predictors of urban policy. These are local political structures and region. Having analyzed the effect of these variables upon three policy outputs for all cities over 50,000, the following conclusions seem warranted:

---

17. As Wolfinger and Field discovered, civil service coverage is the least in the southern cities (mean of .5162). The highest mean is that of the western cities (.7769). The mean score of the north central cities is .6963, and that of cities in the northeast is .7638.

18. Mean scores for per capita funds spent on city planning are as follows: northeast (.5151); south (.6128); north central (.5187); west (1.1066).

19. Mean scores for urban renewal funds requested per capita are as follows: northeast (206.0199); south (92.9055); north central (66.4438); west (60.3009).

1. Political structure is a very weak predictor of urban policy. Of the three policies examined, structure significantly accounted for inter-city differences (in the direction predicted by the reformist thesis) for only per capita funds spent for urban planning. Even here the strongest such relationship accounted for just three percent of the total variance. Furthermore, when region was accounted for, even this relationship faded to insignificance.[20] Such a conclusion, of course, should be no real surprise. Contemporary students of state political systems have produced a number of studies denying a significant impact of structural differences (such as apportioned vs. malapportioned legislatures) upon policy outputs at the state level.[21]

2. When both political structure and area of the country were examined, region accounted for over 8 percent of the variance in percentage of municipal employees covered by civil service, slightly more than 12 percent of the inter-city variance in per capita funds alloted for city planning, and almost 12 percent of the variance of per capita funds requested for urban renewal. Although it is evident that region is a more significant predictor of urban policy than is political structure, its total impact upon the policy process must also be described as slight and clearly additional factors must be considered in any attempts to construct a complete model of the urban policy process.[22] This study complements the findings of Sharkansky's analsis of the influence of region upon policy outcomes at the state level. In his study, Sharkansky concluded that, "By itself, 'regionalism' is not a satisfying explanation for public policies. Yet when they are viewed along with other information . . . , regional findings provide important clues about the determinants of governmental activity."[23]

3. Finally, the results of this survey have broader implications for the study of urban politics and especially for those attempting to construct models or theories explaining policy outputs. The obvious point is that the policy process is complex and attempts to construct an explanatory model based upon a single gross phenomenon (whether it be called "structure," or "ethos," or "reformism," or whatever) is destined to be a simplistic, inadequate, and, at best, only partial model of such a

---

20. Throughout, it has been noted that structure appears to be significantly related to urban renewal funds requested in a manner contradictory to the reformist expectation. However the magnitude of this association also is reduced significantly (from about five percent to one percent) when region is included in the analysis.

21. Among the most widely cited of these studies are the following: Richard E. Dawson and James A. Robinson, "Inter-Party Competition, Economic Variables, and Welfare Policies in the American States," *Journal of Politics*, 25 (May, 1963), pp. 265–289; Herbert Jacob, "The Consequences of Malapportionment: A Note of Caution," *Social Forces*, 43 (Dec., 1964), pp. 256–261; Richard I. Hofferbert, "The Relation between Public Policy and Some Structural and Environmental Variables in the American States," *American Political Science Review*, 60 (March, 1966), pp. 73–82; and Thomas R. Dye, *Politics, Economics, and the Public: Policy Outcomes in the American States* (Chicago: Rand McNally and Co., 1966).

22. Again, a cautionary note concerning the utility of "region" as a causal variable must be expressed. The reservations of Jacob and Lipsky were mentioned above. Lineberry and Fowler have rather vigorously objected to its use, arguing that regionalism is a composite of a number of "socioeconomic, attitudinal, historical, and cultural variables." Their argument, in part, is based upon that of Hubert M. Blalock, *Causal Inference in Nonexperimental Research* (Chapel Hill: The University of North Carolina Press, 1961), pp. 164–165, who states further that, "Although it may not always be possible to avoid the use of such complex indicator variables, the investigator should be alerted to possible misinterpretations owing to the complexity of the causal situation."

23. Ira Sharkansky, "Regionalism, Economic Status, and the Public Policies of American States," *Social Science Quarterly*, 49 (June, 1968), pp. 9–26.

process.[24] Lineberry and Fowler are correct, it seems to me, in suggesting that such a model must account for a variety of socioeconomic cleavages as well as a variety of political variables. This does not mean that a satisfactory model of the urban policy process is impossible; it simply means that such a model will have to be as intricate as the process it attempts to depict.

---

24. Robert Lineberry and Ira Sharkansky (*Urban Politics and Public Policy*, New York: Harper and Row, 1971) have provided a catalog of a variety of factors which may affect municipal spending levels. Among those "government variables" which they mention are the following: state-local centralization; intergovernmental aid; state debt and expenditure limits; previous expenditures; participation in local politics; and party competition. Hopefully, future research will soon provide precise measurements of the impact of these variables upon the urban policy process.

DONALD MATTHEWS
JAMES PROTHRO

Social and Economic Factors
and Negro Voter Registration
in the South

The Matthews and Prothro article focuses on social and
economic factors accounting for levels of Negro voter registration in
the South. The data include twenty socioeconomic independent variables (derived
from census data and related sources of aggregate data by county) at the
interval level of measurement for a universe of southern counties. After
an overview of the statistical model and its limitations, the authors
present some basic descriptive data and simple product-moment correlations
between independent variables and the registration dependent variable. In
order to further isolate selected independent effects, partial correlation
is employed with controls for several independent variables. Furthermore,
by calculating a multiple correlation coefficient and a corresponding
coefficient of determination, the authors are able to isolate the per-
centage of variance in Negro voter registration caught by the series of
independent variables operating together.

Reprinted from Donald Matthews and James Prothro, "Social and Economic Factors and Negro Voter Registration in the South," *American Political Science Review* 57 (1963): 24–44, by permission of the American Political Science Association and the authors.

This study has been supported by a grant from the Rockefeller Foundation to the Institute for Research in Social Science of the University of North Carolina. The first named author holds a Senior Award for Research on Governmental Affairs from the Social Science Research Council. We wish to express our gratitude to these organizations for providing the resources needed to engage in this analysis. Professors V. O. Key, Jr., Warren E. Miller, and Allan P. Sindler have commented generously upon an earlier version of this paper. Professor Daniel O. Price afforded us the benefit of his counsel on statistical problems throughout the preparation of the article. While we have learned much from these colleagues, neither they nor the organizations named above should be held responsible for the contents of this article.

The vote is widely considered the southern Negro's most important weapon in his struggle for full citizenship and social and economic equality. It is argued that "political rights pave the way to all others."[1] Once Negroes in the South vote in substantial numbers, white politicians will prove responsive to the desires of the Negro community. Also, federal action on voting will be met with less resistance from the white South — and southerners in Congress — than action involving schools, jobs, or housing.

Such, at least, seems to have been the reasoning behind the Civil Rights Acts of 1957 and 1960, both of which deal primarily with the right to vote.[2] Attorney General Robert F. Kennedy and his predecessor, Herbert Brownell, are both reported to believe that the vote provides the southern Negro with his most effective means of advancing toward equality, and recent actions of the Justice Department seem to reflect this view.[3] Many Negro leaders share this belief in the over-riding importance of the vote. Hundreds of Negro registration drives have been held in southern cities and counties since 1957.[4] Martin Luther King, usually considered an advocate of non-violent direct action, recently remarked that the most significant step Negroes can take is in the "direction of the voting booths."[5] The National Association for the Advancement of Colored People, historically identified with courtroom attacks on segregation, is now enthusiastically committed to a "battle of the ballots.''[6] In March, 1962, the Southern Regional Council announced receipt of foundation grants of $325,000 to initiate a major program to increase Negro voter registration in the South.[7] The Congress of Racial Equality, the NAACP, the National Urban League, the Southern Christian Leadership Conference, and the Student Nonviolent Coordinating Committee are among the organizations now participating in the actual registration drives.

While the great importance of the vote to Negroes in the South can hardly be denied, some careful observers are skeptical about the extent to which registration drives can add to the number of Negroes who are already registered. Southern Negroes overwhelmingly possess low social status, relatively small incomes and limited education received in inferior schools. These attributes are associated with low voter turnout among all populations.[8] The low voting rates of Negroes in the South are, to perhaps a large extent, a result of these factors more than a consequence of *direct political* discrimination by the white community. Moreover, the

---

1. *New York Times*, January 7, 1962. See also H. L. Moon, *Balance of Power: the Negro Vote* (Garden City, N.Y., Doubleday, 1949), p. 7 and *passim*.

2. 71 Stat. 635; 74 Stat. 86. *Cf.* U.S. Commission on Civil Rights, *1959 Report* (Washington, 1959); *1961 Report*, Vol. I, "Voting" (Washington, 1961).

3. *New York Times*, January 7, 1962; Louis E. Lomax, "The Kennedys Move in on Dixie," *Harpers Magazine*, May 1962, pp. 27–33.

4. *Wall Street Journal*, November 6, 1961; *New York Times*, July 10, 1961.

5. Baltimore *Afro-American*, October 7, 1961; *New York Times*, August 17, 1961.

6. The 1962 Atlanta, Georgia, national convention of the NAACP had the "Battle of the Ballots"as its theme. Raleigh (N.C.) *News and Observer*, June 24, 1962.

7. *New York Times*, March 29, 1962. Louis E. Lomax, *op. cit.*

8. For useful summaries of the literature see Robert E. Lane, *Political Life* (Glencoe, Ill.: The Free Press, 1959), ch. 16; and Seymour M. Lipset *et al.*, "The Psychology of Voting," in G. Lindzey (ed.), *Handbook of Social Psychology* (Cambridge, Mass.: Addison-Wesley Publishing Company, 1954), Vol. II, pp. 1126-1134.

low status, income, and education of southern whites foster racial prejudice.[9] Thus poverty and ignorance may have a double-barrelled effect on Negro political participation by decreasing the Negroes' desire and ability to participate effectively while increasing white resistance to their doing so. Negro voting in the South is not, according to this line of argument, easily increased by political or legal means. A large, active, and effective Negro electorate in the South may have to await substantial social and economic change.

Despite the current interest in the political participation of southern Negroes, the literature of political science tells us little about the factors which facilitate or impede it. A theoretical concern as old as political science — the relative importance of socio-economic and political factors in determining political behavior — is raised when one addresses this problem. Can registration drives, legal pressures on the region's voter registrars, abolition of poll taxes, revision of literacy tests, and similar legal and political reforms have a significant impact on Negro registration in the former confederate states? Or do these efforts deal merely with "superstructure," while the social and economic realities of the region will continue for generations to frustrate achievement of Negro parity at the ballot box? Social scientists owe such a heavy, if largely unacknowledged, debt to Karl Marx that most would probably assume the second alternative to be more valid. But the tradition of James Madison, recognizing the importance of social and economic factors but also emphasizing the significance of "auxiliary" governmental arrangements, offers theoretical support for the former possibility.

A single article cannot hope to answer such a broad question, but we can attack part of it. In this article we offer a detailed analysis of the relationships between variations in rates of Negro voter registration in southern counties and the social and economic characteristics of those counties. While we shall not be directly concerned with political variables, the analysis has an obvious relevance for their importance. The more successful the explanation of the problem with socio-economic variables, the less imperative the demand to examine political and legal factors. Alternatively, if we can account for only a small part of the variance with socio-economic factors, the stronger the case for abandoning socio-economic determinism and adding political and legal variables to the analysis.[10]

I. The Data and the Approach

While the literature offers no comprehensive effort to account for variations in Negro voter registration in the South, previous studies of southern politics suggest

---

9. Herbert H. Hyman and Paul B. Sheatsley, "Attitudes Toward Desegregation," *Scientific American*, Vol. 195 (1956), pp. 35–39; B. Bettelheim and N. Janowitz, *The Dynamics of Prejudice* (New York; 1950); Melvin M. Tumin, *Desegregation: Resistance and Readinesss* (Princeton University Press, 1958), p. 195 and *passim*. James W. Vander Zanden, "Voting on Segregationist Referenda," *Public Opinion Quarterly*, Vol. 25 (1961), pp. 92–105, finds the evidence in support of the relationship in voting on segregationist referenda in the South "inconsistent and even contradictory . . . this study seems to suggest that the socioeconomic factor may not play as simple or as critical a role as some of us doing research in this field have been prone to assign it" (p. 105).

10. In addition to the problem of the relative importance of political variables, we are postponing consideration of still another possibility — that variations in state systems (social, economic, and political) account for a significant proportion of the variation in Negro registration among southern counties.

a number of specific influences. Drawing upon this literature, we collected data on 20 social and economic characteristics of southern counties (counting Virginia's independent cities as counties). Some of these items, such as per cent of population Negro or per cent of population urban, could be taken directly from the U.S. Census. Others, such as per cent of nonwhite labor force in white collar occupations or white and nonwhite median income, were derived from census figures but required calculations of varying degress of complexity for each county. Still other items, such as per cent of population belonging to a church or the number of Negro colleges in each county, came from noncensus sources.[11] Since our focus is on Negro registration, 108 counties with populations containing less than one per cent Negroes were excluded from the analysis. All other counties for which 1958 registration data were available by race were included.[12] This selection procedure gave us a total of 997 counties for the analysis of Negro registration and 822 for the consideration of white registration.[13]

While this represents the most massive collection of data ever brought to bear upon the problem of political participation by southern Negroes, it is subject to several limitations.

To begin with, the measure of the dependent variable is two steps removed from a direct measure of the voting turnout of individuals. Registration rather than voting figures had to be employed because thcy are available by race whereas the number of Negroes actually voting is not known. This tends to exaggerate the size of the active Negro electorate since, for a number of reasons, some registered Negroes seldom if ever exercise their franchise. Moreover, voting lists in rural areas are often out of date, containing the names of many bonafide residents of New York, Detroit, and Los Angeles, to say nothing of local graveyards. In some states, the payment of a poll tax is the nearest equivalent of voter registration and numerous exemptions from the tax make lists of poll tax payers not strictly comparable to the enfranchised population. Finally, statewide statistics on voter registration (or poll tax payment) by race are collected only in Arkansas, Florida, Georgia, Louisiana, South Carolina and Virginia. In the remaining states, the number of registered Negro voters must be obtained from estimates made by county registrars, newsmen, politicians, and the like. Nonetheless, when analyzed with caution, the sometimes crude data on Negro voter registration can throw considerable light on Negro voting in the South.

The measure of the dependent variable is further removed from the actual behavior of individuals in that it consists of the percentage of all voting age Negroes who are registered to vote in each southern county. This employment of *areal* rather

---

11. A complete list of sources used to obtain county frequencies for the independent variables used in this analysis would be too lengthy to reproduce here. A mimeographed list will be supplied by the authors upon request.

We are indebted to the following research assistants for their help in collecting these data: Lawton Bennett, Lewis Bowman, Barbara Bright, Jack Fleer, Donald Freeman, Douglas Gatlin, and Richard Sutton. All told, the collection and coding of these data took one man-year of work.

12. Voter registration rates, by race, are presented in U.S. Commission on Civil Rights, *1959 Report* and *1961 Report*, Vol. I, "Voting." The 1958 registration data, contained in the *1959 Report*, are more complete and were used for all states except Tennessee. The 1960 figures, printed in the *1961 Report*, are the only ones available for Tennessee.

13. There are 1136 counties in the 11 southern states, 1028 of which have populations containing at least 1 per cent Negroes.

than *individual* analysis narrows the question we can examine. Rather than an unqualified examination of the relationship of social and economic characteristics to Negro registration, the effort must be understood to focus on the relationship of social and economic characteristics of given areas (counties) to variations in Negro registration among those areas. Accordingly, the data furnish no evidence of the sort afforded by opinion surveys directly linking political behavior to individual attributes. But they do permit conclusions linking varying registration rates to county attributes. Compensation for the loss of the former type of evidence is found in the acquisition of the latter type, which cannot be secured from surveys because they are conducted in a small number of counties. Our approach maximizes what we can say about counties, then, at the same time that it minimizes what we can say about individuals.

Another limitation stems from the fact that our measures capture an essentially static picture of both the characteristics of southern counties and of the relationship of their characteristics to variations in Negro registration. If data were available on Negro registration, at the county level, for earlier points in time, the analysis could be geared principally to rates of change. Only since the creation of the Civil Rights Commission, however, have adequate county registration data become available. We are necessarily limited, therefore, to an analysis based on *areal* rather than *temporal* variation.

A final limitation lies in the statistical approach employed here, which is that of correlation and regression analysis.[14] The coefficient of correlation (r) is a measure of the association between different variables when each variable is expressed as a series of measures of a quantitative characteristic. The value of the measure varies from 0 (no association between independent and dependent variables) to 1.0 (one variable perfectly predicts the other). A positive correlation indicates that as one variable increases the other also increases; a negative correlation indicates an inverse relationship — as one variable increases, the other decreases. We shall first consider simple correlations, describing the association between per cent of Negroes registered and each of the social and economic characteristics of southern counties. In order to make a better estimate of the independence of these relationships, we shall also present partial correlations, which measure the remaining association between two variables when the contribution of a third variable has been taken into account. Finally, we shall employ multiple correlation (R) in order to determine the strength of association between all our independent variables and Negro registration.

While these measures are efficient devices for determining the strength and direction of association between the variables with which we are concerned, a caveat is in order. Correlations do not reflect the *absolute level* of the variables. Thus, a given amount and regularity of change in Negro registration will produce the same correlation whether the actual level of Negro registration is high or low. Only for the more important variables will we look beneath the correlations to examine the level of Negro registration.

In the analysis which follows, we shall first consider the development of Negro registration and compare the distribution of white and Negro registration rates. Then we shall examine the correlations between a battery of social and economic

---

14. For a good discussion of correlation analysis see M. J. Hagood and D. O. Price, *Statistics for Sociologists* (New York, 1952), chs. 23 and 25.

variables and Negro voter registration in order to determine the extent to which the former are predictive of the latter for the South as a whole. The same social and economic factors will be correlated with the registration rate of whites to ascertain the extent to which the factors are related to voter registration in general, rather than to Negro registration alone. Finally, the multiple correlation between all the social and economic variables and Negro voter registration will be presented, and conclusions and implications will be drawn from the analysis.

II. Negro Voter Registration: An Overview

Immediately after *Smith* v. *Allwright* declared the white primary unconstitutional in 1944, the number and proportion of Negro adults registered to vote in the southern states increased with startling speed (Table I). Before this historic decision, about

TABLE I   Estimated Number and Per Cent of Voting
Age Negroes Registered to Vote in 11 Southern States,
1940–60

Year	Estimated Number of Negro Registered Voters	% of Voting Age Negroes Registered as Voters
1940	250,000	5%
1947	595,000	12
1952	1,008,614	20
1956	1,238,038	25
1958	1,266,488	25
1960	1,414,052	28

Sources: Derived from U.S. Census data on nonwhite population and Negro registration estimates in G. Mydral, *An American Dilemma* (New York, 1944), p. 488; M. Price, *The Negro Voter in the South* (Atlanta, Georgia: Southern Regional Council, 1957), p. 5; Southern Regional Council, "The Negro Voter in the South — 1958," *Special Report* (mimeo.), p. 3; U.S. Commission on Civil Rights, *1959 Report* and *1961 Report*, Vol. I, "Voting."

250,000 Negroes (5 per cent of the adult nonwhite population) were thought to be registered voters. Three years after the white primary case, both the number and proportion of Negro registered voters had doubled. By 1952, about 20 per cent of the Negro adults were registered to vote. Since then, however, the rate of increase has been less impressive. In 1956, the authoritative Southern Regional Council estimated that about 25 per cent of the Negro adults were registered. Four years, two Civil Rights Acts, and innumerable local registration drives later, the proportion of Negro adults who were registered had risen to only 28 per cent. Of course, the fact that Negroes held their own during this period is a significant accomplishment when one considers such factors as heavy outmigration, increased racial tensions stemming from the school desegregation crisis, the adoption of new voter restrictions in some states, and the stricter application of old requirements in other areas.

Figure 1 shows the 1958 distribution of southern counties according to level of voter registration for Negroes and whites. The point most dramatically demonstrated by the figure is that Negro registration is still much lower than white reg-

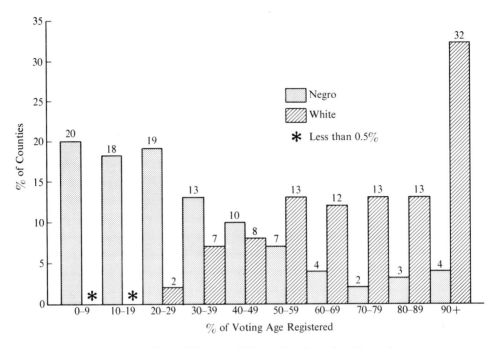

FIGURE 1   White and Negro Registration Rates in
Southern Counties

istration. In 38 per cent of the counties, less than 20 per cent of the adult Negroes
are registered, whereas less than 1 per cent of the counties have so few whites registered. Indeed, the most common (modal) situation for Negroes is a registration
below 10 per cent of the potential; the most common situation for whites is a registration in excess of 90 per cent. Nevertheless, the range of Negro registration
in the South is sizeable; in a significant minority of cases, the level of Negro registration compares favorably with that of white southerners.

III. Social and Economic Correlates of Negro Registration

What accounts for the wide variation in Negro voter registration rates? The simple
correlations between the per cent of the voting age Negroes registered to vote and
20 social and economic characteristics of southern counties are presented in the
first column of Table II.[15]

Negro Concentration

In most political settings, the concentration of an ethnic or occupational group in a
geographical area provides reinforcement of common values sufficient to produce

---

15. All computations were made on the University of North Carolina's UNIVAC 1105 high-speed
digital computer. The inaccuracy of some of the registration figures tends to reduce the magnitude of
all correlations obtained by this analysis. The assumption of linearity underlying the computation of *r*
also reduces the size of the correlations where the relationship between dependent and independent
variables is, in fact, a curvilinear one. It is therefore safe to assume that the *r*'s reported in this article
err in the conservative direction.

TABLE II   Correlations Between County Social and
Economic Characteristics and Per Cent of Voting Age
Negroes Registered to Vote, by County, in 11 Southern
States

County Characteristics	Simple Correlations (r)	Partial Correlations, Controlling for Per Cent Negro, 1950
Per cent of nonwhite labor force in white collar occupations	+.23	+.15
Nonwhite median school years completed	+.22	+.01
Nonwhite median income	+.19	+.02
Per cent of total church membership Roman Catholic	+.15	+.10
Per cent increase in population, 1940–50	+.08	.00
Per cent of labor force in manufacturing	+.08	+.09
White median income	+.08	−.03
Per cent of population urban	+.07	−.02
Percentage point difference in per cent population Negro, 1900–50	+.04	−.02
Per cent of total church membership Jewish	+.004	+.01
Difference in white-nonwhite median school years completed	−.02	−.02
Difference in white-nonwhite median income	−.02	−.05
Number of Negro colleges in county	−.05	+.01
Per cent of total church membership Baptist	−.10	−.07
Per cent of population belonging to a church	−.17	+.01
Per cent of labor force in agriculture	−.20	−.07
White median school years completed	−.26	−.15
Per cent of farms operated by tenants	−.32	−.13
Per cent of population Negro in 1900	−.41	−.01
Per cent of population Negro in 1950	−.46	—

Note: No tests of significance are reported in this paper since the correlations are based upon a complete enumeration rather than a sample.

more active political participation. But southern Negroes are in a peculiarly subordinate position. And the larger the proportion of Negroes in an area, the more intense the vague fears of Negro domination that seem to beset southern whites. Thus in virtually every study of southern politics, the proportion of Negroes in the population has emerged as a primary explanatory variable.[16]

It is not surprising, therefore, that the per cent of Negroes in the county population in 1950 is more strongly associated with the county's rate of Negro registration than any other social and economic attribute on which we have data. The negative value of the simple correlation (−.46) verifies the expectation that smaller proportions of Negroes register in those counties where a large percentage of the population is Negro. This does not mean, however, that the decline in Negro registration associated with increasing Negro concentration occurs at a constant rate. If the relationship between these two variables is examined over the entire range of southern

16. V. O. Key, Jr., *Southern Politics* (New York, 1949) gives little attention to Negro voting since it was of little importance at the time he wrote. His stress upon the overriding importance of Negro concentration for all aspects of southern politics makes his study highly relevant, nonetheless. Other works specifically on Negro voting which stress the importance of Negro concentration include: James F. Barne's *Negro Voting in Mississippi*, M.A. thesis, University of Mississippi, 1955; Margaret Price, *The Negro and the Ballot in the South* (Atlanta, Georgia: Southern Regional Council, 1959); H. D. Price, *The Negro and Southern Politics: A Chapter of Florida History* (New York: New York University Press, 1957); Donald Strong, "The Future of the Negro Voter in the South," *Journal of Negro Education*, Vol. 26 (Summer, 1957), pp. 400–407; United States Commission on Civil Rights, *1961 Report*, Vol. I, "Voting."

counties, we see that increases in the proportion Negro from 1 per cent to about 30 per cent are not accompanied by general and substantial declines in Negro registration rates (Figure 2). As the proportion Negro increases beyond 30 per cent, however, Negro registration rates begin to decline very sharply until they approach zero at about 60 per cent Negro and above. There would seem to be a critical point, at about 30 per cent Negro, where white hostility to Negro political participation becomes severe.

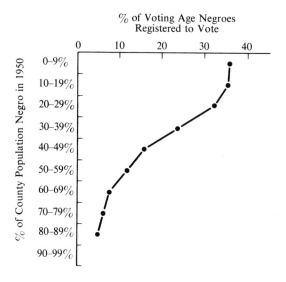

FIGURE 2 Median % of Voting Age Negroes Registered to Vote by % of County Population Negro in 1950: 11 Southern States

One reason Negro concentration is such a powerful explanatory factor in analyzing southern politics may be that it is related to so many other social and economic characteristics of the region's counties. The simple correlation between per cent Negro in 1950 and per cent of farms operated by tenants is $+.49$; the correlation with non-white median income is $-.40$; with non-white school years completed, $-.47$; with per cent of the labor force in agriculture, $+.30$; with per cent of the total population belonging to a church, $+.38$. Such characteristics as these are in turn related to variation in rates of Negro voter registration. It is possible that these related factors rather than Negro concentration, viewed largely as an index of white attitudes, account for the $-.46$ correlation between per cent Negro and per cent registered to vote.

The partial correlations between Negro registration and Negro concentration, controlling separately for the contribution of all other county characteristics, reveals that this is not the case: Negro registration in southern counties goes down as the proportion of Negroes goes up regardless of the other characteristics of the counties. Only one county characteristic is so closely related to both Negro registration in 1958 and Negro concentration in 1950 that the strength of their association drops when its contribution is taken into account — and this characteristic is an earlier measurement of the same independent variable. Controlling for per cent of Negroes in the population in 1900 reduces the correlation between 1950 Negro concentration and registration to $-.21$. Even with this control, the independent tendency of Negro registration to decrease in counties currently containing more Negroes is not eliminated, though it is reduced substantially.

Let us be clear on what a partial correlation does. It is designed to give us, as indicated above, the strength of association between two variables that remains after the contribution of a relevant third variable is taken into account. But when the third variable is introduced into the equation, so are all of the additional hidden variables that are associated with it. The magnitude of the partial correlation will accordingly be reduced not only by any contribution of the third variable to the association between the two original variables, but also by any contribution of factors that are associated with the third variable. This means that, when we attempt to examine the contribution of a third variable by computing partial correlations, we can be certain about its contribution only when the results are negative. That is, if the partial correlation is not much smaller than the simple correlation, we can be sure that the third variable is not responsible for the magnitude of the simple correlation. When the partial correlation is substantially smaller, however, we cannot conclude that the third variable *alone* is responsible for the magnitude of the simple correlation. It happens in the present instance that almost all of the county characteristics are similarly associated with Negro concentration in both 1900 and 1950. As a result, virtually all of the factors that contribute slightly to the correlation of Negro registration with 1950 Negro concentration are added to the contribution that 1900 Negro concentration makes to the correlation. The result is that Negro concentration in 1900 *and the hidden factors related to it* account for about half of the magnitude of the association between 1950 Negro concentration and Negro registration.

Before we conclude that Negro concentration at the turn of the century is as important as mid-century Negro concentration for current variations in Negro registration, we need to consider both the nature of the two measures and the detailed relationships of the variables. The two measures are of the same county characteristic, differing only in the point in time from which they were taken. And the characteristic they reflect cannot reasonably be thought to act directly on Negro registration. Today's lower rates of Negro registration in counties where Negroes constitute a large portion of the population certainly do not stem from any tendency of Negroes to crowd one another out of registration queues! Even more evident is the fact that the percentage of Negroes in a county's population over half a century ago cannot have a direct effect on current rates of Negro registration. Both measures appear to be indexes of county characteristics (most importantly, white practices and attitudes on racial questions) that are of direct consequence for Negro registration.

The 1900 measure was included in the analysis on the assumption that practices and attitudes produced by heavy Negro populations may persist long after the Negroes have died or left for more attractive environs. Earlier research has suggested that Negro concentration around the turn of the century — when southern political practice was crystallizing in its strongly anti-Negro pattern — may be as important as current Negro concentration for rates of Negro political participation.[17]

---

17. On this point see H. D. Price, *op. cit.*, p. 41ff.

Since the proportions of Negroes in different southern counties have not decreased at uniform rates (and have even increased in some counties), the measures at the two points in time afford an opportunity to test this hypothesis. And it seems to be supported by the fact that Negro concentration in 1900 is almost as highly (and negatively) correlated with Negro registration ($-.41$) as is Negro concentration a half century later. This large simple correlation, added to the decrease in the correlation between 1950 Negro concentration and registration where 1900 Negro concentration is controlled, is impressive evidence of the stability of southern racial practices. The virtual absence of correlation ($+.04$) between Negro registration and the percentage point difference in the proportion of population Negro between 1900 and 1950 seems to point to the same conclusion.[18]

It would be a mistake, however, to conclude either that 1900 Negro concentration is as important as 1950 Negro concentration for Negro registration, or that decreases in Negro concentration are not associated with increasing Negro voter registration. When we reverse the partialling process, and control for Negro concentration in 1950, the correlation between current Negro registration and 1900 Negro concentration disappears (it becomes $-.01$). The 1900 simple correlation accordingly seems to come from stable racial practices that in turn reflect a large measure of stability in Negro concentration and related county characteristics. The 1900 Negro concentration in itself has no autonomous relationship to present rates of Negro registration.

Moreover, decreases in Negro concentration are not as inconsequential as they would appear from the small simple correlation obtained from percentage point decreases. The lack of correlation seems to be an artifact of our crude measure. The largest percentage *point* decreases in Negro population have occurred in counties with very high Negro proportions in 1900, and most of these counties still have heavy concentrations of Negro population. When one looks at the relationship between registration and decreases in Negro concentration, holding constant the proportion of the population Negro in 1900, several heretofore hidden relationships emerge (Figure 3). (1) In counties with heavy (over 70 per cent) Negro concentrations in 1900, decreases in the proportion Negro seem to make little difference — their Negro concentration was still relatively high in 1950 and the proportion of Negroes registered is negligible. (2) In counties with relatively few (less than 30 per cent) Negroes in 1900, rates of Negro registration tend to be high whether a decline in the proportion Negro was experienced or not. A decline in Negro concentration in these counties, however, is associated with a somewhat higher rate of Negro registration than in those counties where the division of the two races remained approximately the same between 1900 and 1950. (3) In counties with moderate (30 to 70 per cent) Negro concentrations in 1900, a decline in Negro concentration is clearly related to higher Negro voter registration. Moreover, the larger the decrease in the Negro population percentage, the higher the registration. The average county in this moderate group with a 30 percentage point decrease in Negro proportions has a voter registration rate double or triple that of the average county which did not experience significant change in the numerical balance between colored and white inhabitants.

18. See H. D. Price, *op. cit.*

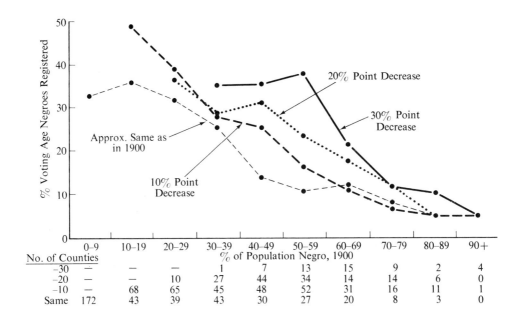

No. of Counties	0–9	10–19	20–29	30–39	40–49	50–59	60–69	70–79	80–89	90+
–30	—	—	—	1	7	13	15	9	2	4
–20	—	—	10	27	44	34	14	14	6	0
–10	—	68	65	45	48	52	31	16	11	1
Same	172	43	39	43	30	27	20	8	3	0

FIGURE 3   Median % of Voting Age Negroes Registered to Vote, by County Negro Concentration in 1900
and % Point Change since 1900

The proportion of the county population which is Negro is the single most important social and economic factor for explaining its rate of Negro voter registration. The −.46 correlation accounts for about 20 per cent (r^2) of the variation in Negro registration rates, an unusually high explanatory power for any variable in the complex world of political and social relationships. But it leaves room for considerable fluctuation in registration rates unrelated to the per cent of Negroes in the population. This "unexplained" fluctuation may be the result of random and idiosyncratic factors, of political variables[19] which have been excluded from this analysis, or the result of the operation of other social and economic factors. In the remainder of this paper we shall examine this last possibility.

Negro Attributes

The higher the educational level, occupation, or income of a person, the more likely he is to participate actively in politics: these are among the more strongly

19. In view of the relatively high associations between Negro concentration and a wide variety of political phenomena (including Negro registration rates), it might be argued that Negro concentration is, in fact, a "political" rather than a "demographic" variable. But Negro concentration is as strongly associated with many social and economic characteristics of southern counties as it is with their political peculiarities. And while the correlations of Negro concentration with political characteristics are relatively large, they fall far short of a 1.0 correlation. As we shall demonstrate in a subsequent article, a number of political variables have an association with Negro registration that is independent of Negro concentration. Under these circumstances, to call Negro concentration a "political" variable would be distinctly misleading.

supported generalizations in contemporary research on political participation.[20] Moreover, these three factors are probably a pretty good index of the size of the county's Negro middle class. It is widely believed by students of Negro politics that the low rate of voter registration by southern Negroes is partly the result of a lack of leadership.[21] Only when there is a pool of educated and skillful leaders whose means of livelihood is not controlled by whites can sufficient leadership and political organization develop to ensure a relatively high rate of Negro registration in the South.

Our data support both lines of argument. The three largest positive correlations with Negro voter registration are per cent of the nonwhite labor force in white collar occupations (+.23), the median number of school years completed by non-whites (+.22), and the median income of nonwhites (+.19). These are simple correlations, however, and fairly small ones at that. It is quite possible that they are largely, if not entirely, the result of some third factor associated both with Negro registration rates and with Negro education, occupation, and income. The large negative correlation of Negro concentration with Negro registration suggests that the percentage of the population Negro in 1950 is the most likely prospect as a key third variable. This expectation is heightened by the fact that it is also substantially correlated with Negro school years completed (−.47), income (−.40), and white collar workers (−.23). When controls are introduced for per cent of Negroes in the population (see the second column of Table II), the positive association of Negro registration with both income and education is reduced almost to the vanishing point. Thus Negro income and education levels are intervening variables, which help to explain why more Negroes are registered in counties with fewer Negroes in their population. But in themselves, they have no independent association with Negro registration; in the few counties with large Negro concentrations but high Negro income and education, no more Negroes are registered than in similar counties with lower Negro income and education.

The explanatory power of our occupational measure — the per cent of the non-white labor force in white collar occupations — is also reduced when per cent of Negroes is taken into account, but to a much lesser degree. It becomes +.15. While this is a small partial correlation, it is one of the higher partials obtained in this study while controlling for the important factor of Negro concentration. The proportion of the employed Negroes in white collar jobs does, therefore, have a small but discernible independent association with Negro voter registration.

Moreover, small increases in the proportion of Negro white collar workers are associated with large increases in Negro voter registration (Figure 4), and these higher rates cannot be simply attributed to the registration of the white collar workers themselves. A very small increase in the size of the Negro middle class seems to result in a substantial increase in the pool of qualified potential leaders.

20. See Lane, *op. cit.;* Lipset *et al., op. cit.;* Angus Campbell, Philip E. Converse, Warren E. Miller and Donald E. Stokes, *The American Voter* (New York, 1960), ch. 13; V. O. Key Jr., *Public Opinion and American Democracy* (New York, 1961), ch. 6. For a study of these variables and political participation among southern Negroes, see Bradbury Seasholes, "Negro Political Participation in Two North Carolina Cities," Ph.D. dissertation, University of North Carolina, 1962.

21. For an extreme statement of this position, see E. Franklin Frazier, *Black Bourgeoisie: The Rise of a New Middle Class in the United States* (Glencoe, Ill.: The Free Press, 1957). Less exaggerated statements to the same effect may be found in the literature cited in *n.* 16, above.

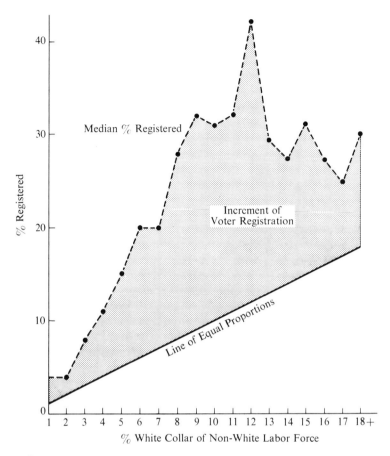

FIGURE 4   Median % of Voting Age Negroes Registered to Vote, by % of Nonwhite Labor Force in White
Collar Occupations

Middle class Negroes are far more likely to register, and they in turn appear to stimulate working class Negroes to follow their example. The average southern county with 1 per cent of its nonwhite labor force in white collar jobs has only 4 per cent of its voting age Negroes registered to vote; at 5 per cent white collar, 15 per cent of the Negroes are registered, and so on, each percentage point increase in white collar occupation being associated with a 3 to 4 percentage point increase in voter registration. This trend continues until 12 per cent of the nonwhites are in white collar jobs and 42 per cent of the potential Negro electorate is registered. After this point, additional increases in the proportion of Negroes in white collar jobs are no longer associated with increases in voter registration; indeed, voter registration actually declines as per cent white collar increases. Perhaps when the Negro middle class becomes fairly large, it tends to become more isolated from other Negroes, more preoccupied with the middle class round of life, less identified with the black masses.[22] A sharpening of class cleavages within the Negro community may lead to some loss of political effectiveness. Even so, this decline in effectiveness is not enough to wipe out the added increment from jobs to registered votes; it merely declines from 3 or 4 votes for every white collar job to about 2.

Despite the independent association of Negro white collar employment with voter registration, the correlations between Negro registration and Negro education, income, and occupation are far smaller than many of the correlations between Negro registration and the characteristics of the white-dominated community. The level of Negro voter registration in southern counties is far less a matter of the attributes of the Negro population than of the characteristics of the white population and of the total community. The rest of our correlations, therefore, are with community and white characteristics rather than with Negro attributes.

The Agrarian Economy

It is widely believed that the South's relatively poor agricultural economy contributes to the low levels of Negro political participation in the region.[23] People living in poverty are unlikely candidates for active citizenship anywhere. The Negroes' economic dependence upon local whites in the rural South serves as a potent inhibition to those few who are not otherwise discouraged from voting. Rural whites are both more hostile to Negro voting and in a better position to do something about it than their urban kin.

Our correlations tend to support this line of reasoning. Two measures included in the analysis reflect the degree to which a county has an agrarian economy — the per cent of labor force in agricultural employment and the per cent of farms operated by tenants.[24] The negative relationship of both these attributes to Negro voter registration ($-.20$ and $-.32$, respectively) indicates that Negro registration is lower in the old-style agrarian counties. But the region's Negro population is still primarily rural: the simple correlation between per cent in agriculture and per cent Negro is $+.30$; between farm tenancy and Negro concentration, $+.49$. Are these two characteristics of the counties still associated with low Negro voter registration when Negro concentration is controlled? The partial correlation between farm tenancy and Negro registration is $-.13$ when Negro concentration is controlled; between per cent in agriculture and registration it is reduced even further to $-.07$. There is, therefore, some tendency for Negro voter registration to decline as agricultural employment and farm tenancy increase which holds true even when differences in Negro concentration from one county to the next are taken into account. Nonetheless, it is a far less important factor than Negro concentration and is no more important than the size of the Negro middle class as a factor explaining Negro participation and non-participation.

22. This is the basic argument of Frazier, *op. cit.* A more mundane explanation would be called for if counties from particular states were clustered at particular points on the curve in Figure 4, but examination of the same relationships for each state reveals no such state-by-state clustering.

23. See especially, U.S. Commission on Civil Rights, *1961 Report*, Vol. I, "Voting," pp. 143–199.

24. This and other measures of county-wide characteristics might better be considered separately for Negroes and whites, but they are not separately reported in the census.

Urbanization and Industrialization

If the South's agrarian economy tends to discourage Negro registration and voting, then industrialization and urbanization should facilitate them. The urban-industrial life is more rational, impersonal, and less tradition-bound; both Negroes and whites enjoy more wealth and education; the Negroes benefit from a concentration of potential leaders and politically relevant organizations in the cities. The urban-ghetto may provide social reinforcement to individual motivations for political action. Many other equally plausible reasons might be suggested why urbanization and industrialization should foster Negro registration.[25] Our southwide correlations, however, cast serious doubt upon the entire line of reasoning.

The simple correlations between the per cent of the county population living in urban areas and Negro registration is a mere +.07; between per cent of the labor force in manufacturing and Negro registration the correlation is +.08. When partial correlations are figured, controlling for Negro concentration, the association between urbanization and Negro registration completely disappears, a fact which suggests that the initial +.07 simple correlation may be largely the result of the low proportion of the urban population which is Negro and associated factors. The partial correlation between per cent in manufacturing and Negro registration goes up slightly to +.09 when controls for Negro concentration are added. Partial correlations figured after controlling for many other social and economic variables do not significantly increase either correlation.

What accounts for these surprising findings? One possible explanation is the imperfections of the statistical measures we have employed. The 1950 census definition of "urban," for example, includes all places of 2,500 plus the densely settled fringe around cities of 50,000 or more. Many "urban" places in the South are therefore exceedingly small. From the potential Negro voter's point of view, it may make little difference whether he lives in a town of 5,000 or in the open country, but one place is classified as "urban" and the other as "rural." Moreover, a county with a relatively small population concentrated in two or three small towns may possess a higher "urban" percentage than a very large county with a medium-sized city in it. A more meaningful classification of counties along an urban-rural dimension might possibly lead to different results.

It seems plausible to assume, however, that if urbanization does facilitate Negro voter registration, the effect should be particularly clear in the region's largest urban complex. If the Negro registration rates of the 70 counties contained in the South's Standard Metropolitan Areas[26] are compared with registration rates for

---

25. On Negro voting in urban settings see Charles D. Farris, "Effects of Negro Voting Upon the Politics of a Southern City: An Intensive Study 1946–48," Ph.D. dissertation, University of Chicago, 1953; George A. Hillery, "The Presence of Community Among Urban Negroes: A Case Study of a Selected Area in New Orleans," M.A. thesis, Louisiana State University, 1951; Leonard Reissman *et al.*, "The New Orleans Voter: Handbook of Political Description," *Tulane Studies in Political Science*, Vol. II (1955), pp. 1–88; Cleo Roberts, "Some Correlates of Registration and Voting Among Negroes in the 1953 Municipal Election of Atlanta," M.A. thesis, Atlanta University, 1954; Harry J. Walker, "Changes in Race Accommodation in a Southern Community," Ph.D. dissertation, University of Chicago, 1945.

26. The Bureau of the Census defines Standard Metropolitan Areas as a county or group of contiguous counties which contains at least one city of 50,000 inhabitants or more. The contiguous counties must be socially and economically integrated with the central city to be included in the SMA.

non-metropolitan counties (Figure 5), we note that the "metropolitan" counties are far more likely to have from 20 to 40 per cent of their voting age Negroes registered than the other counties. Moreover, there is a tendency for counties in larger metropolitan areas to have slightly higher registration rates than counties in less populous SMAs. However, the metropolitan counties have smaller concentrations of Negroes than the rural and small town counties. Do these relationships hold true when comparisons are made between metropolitan and non-metropolitan counties with approximately the same proportion of Negroes within their boundaries? Table III indicates that the answer is no: there is no meaningful difference in the rate of Negro registration between metropolitan and non-metropolitan counties when Negro concentration is controlled. Thus, neither "urbanism" nor "metropolitanism," as crudely defined by the census categories, appears to be independently related to high Negro voter registration.

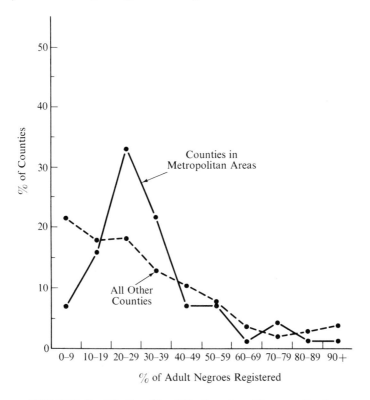

FIGURE 5   Median % of Voting Age Negroes Registered to Vote in Metropolitan and Other Areas

The very low correlation between per cent of the labor force in manufacturing employment and Negro voter registration appears to be the result of other considerations. The word "manufacturing" conjures up images of the "New South" — with belching smokestacks, booming cities, and bulging payrolls. For the South as a whole, this is a quite misleading picture. While manufacturing in 1950 was associated with somewhat higher income for both Negroes and whites (the correlation between per cent in manufacturing and median income was +.19 for both

TABLE III   Median Per Cent of Voting Age Negroes
Registered to Vote in Counties Within Standard
Metropolitan Areas and All Other Counties, by Level of
Negro Concentration

% Negro in pop. 1950	Counties in SMAs of over 200,000 pop.	Counties in SMAs of less than 200,000 pop.	Counties not in SMAs
%	%	%	%
0–9	25.0 (6)	28.8 (11)	37.8 (236)
10–19	45.0 (11)	30.0 (12)	35.7 (133)
20–29	30.0 (6)	35.0 (6)	32.2 (153)
30–39	24.0 (6)	23.8 (7)	23.8 (142)
40–49	—	15.0 (5)	15.9 (110)
50–59	—	—	12.0 (78)
60–69	—	—	8.1 (50)
70–79	—	—	5.8 (22)
80–89	—	—	5.0 (4)
Total Counties	(29)	(41)	(928)

races), it was not primarily an urban phenomenon (the correlation between per cent in manufacturing and per cent urban was +.08), nor was it associated with rapid population growth (the correlation with population increase between 1940 and 1950 is +.05). Manufacturing was negatively correlated with school years completed by both whites and Negroes (−.14 and −.05, respectively). This kind of low-wage manufacturing centered in relatively stable, small towns is not very strongly associated with growing Negro voter registration. It is possible that the recent industrialization of the region — electronics as opposed to home production of chenille bedspreads, for example — may be quite differently related to Negro participation. So few counties have this new type of industry that they tend to be hidden by the bedspreads in a county-by-county correlation.

While our analysis should not be taken as the last word on the subject, it does strongly suggest that urbanization and industrialization are vastly overrated as facilitators of Negro voter registration. Urbanization and industrialization may provide necessary conditions for high levels of Negro political participation but, by themselves, they are not sufficient to insure them.

White Educational Levels

If, as we have argued, Negro registration rates in the South respond far more to the characteristics of the white community than to the attributes of the Negroes themselves, then it seems reasonable to expect Negro voter registration to be positively correlated with white educational levels. Numerous studies have shown that racial prejudice and discrimination tend to be related to low levels of formal education.[27] Where the whites are relatively well educated, there should be less resistance to Negro political participation and, therefore, more Negro voter registration.

Just the opposite is the case for the South as a whole. The correlation between median school years completed by whites and Negro voter registration is −.26,

27. See the literature cited in *n.* 9, above.

one of the largest negative correlations obtained in this study. When the education of whites in a county increases, Negro voter registration in the county tends to decrease.

How can we account for this unexpected finding? In view of the surprising nature of the relationship, the first expectation would be that it is merely a reflection of some third variable which happens to be related both to Negro registration and to white education. If so, it should disappear when other factors are held constant. But the correlation holds up surprisingly well when other variables are controlled: only one of the other social and economic characteristics of southern counties reduces the correlation at all. The third variable is, once again, Negro concentration in the population. With Negro concentration in 1950 controlled, the partial correlation between white educational level and Negro registration is $-.15$; controlling for Negro concentration in 1900 produces a partial correlation of $-.16$. While these are substantial reductions, the partial correlations are among the largest obtained after controlling for the extraordinarily important factor of Negro concentration. The strong correlation ($+.30$) between Negro concentration and median school years completed by whites is almost as unexpected as the correlation between Negro registration and white education. The whites in the black belt counties tend to be better educated — at least quantitatively — than other white southerners. And, regardless of the percentage of Negroes in the population, fewer Negroes are registered in counties where whites have more education.

A second explanation for the negative relationship between white education and Negro registration might be that their relationship is curvilinear: at the lower educational levels, increases in white median school years might be associated with declining rates of Negro registration but, at higher educational levels, the relationship might be reversed. If this were the case, then the overall negative relationship would be a result of the generally low educational levels of the South, concealing the fact that the few counties with high white educational levels had the highest rates of Negro registration. Figure 6 suggests only a moderate tendency in this direction. As the number of school years completed by whites goes up through the primary and secondary grades, the proportion of voting age Negroes registered declines.[28] In the very few counties in which the average white adult has completed high school or received some higher education, the trend reverses and Negro registration rates begin to increase. But the reversal is not sharp enough for the counties with the highest white education to reach as great a Negro registration as the counties with the lowest white education. Southern counties with extremely high white educational levels have only about average rates of Negro registration. The impressive fact revealed by Figure 6 is the near uniformity with which an increase in white school years is associated with a decrease in Negro registration.

Being unable to "explain away" our finding entirely, either by examining the correlation for hidden third variables or by examining the regularity of the association, we must conclude that white education in southern counties is independently and negatively associated with Negro registration. Short of the highest levels, the more educated the whites the more actively and effectively they seem to enforce

---

28. Eleven of the 28 counties in which the average white adult has completed less than seven years of schooling are French-Catholic parishes in Louisiana. Even if those parishes are eliminated, the trend shown in Figure 6 remains the same. The partial correlation between white school years and Negro registration, controlling for per cent Roman Catholic, is $-.25$.

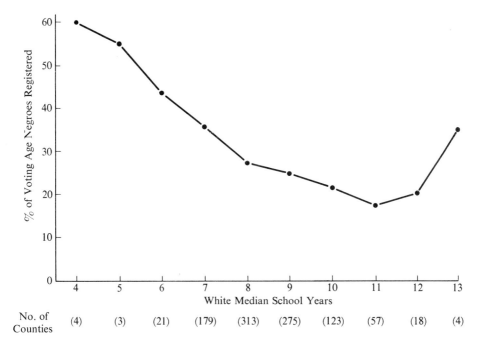

FIGURE 6   Median % of Voting Age Negroes Registered to Vote, by Median School Years Completed by
Whites in County

the traditional mores of the region against Negro participation in elections. The usual effect of an increase in average schooling for whites in the South as a whole appears to be to give the white people more of the skills that are needed to express effectively their anti-Negro sentiment. For example, the correlation between median school years completed by whites and the presence or absence of a White Citizens Council or similar organization is +.32. It seems to take considerably more formal education than the average southern white receives to *alter* his attitude toward the Negro's place in southern politics.

White Religious Affiliation

A variety of studies suggest that religion plays some role — either as independent or intervening variable — in the racial politics of the South. Church-goers have been found to be less tolerant than non-attenders,[29] and the South is a church-going region. Studies of Louisiana politics have found substantial political differences between the Catholic and Protestant sections of the state.[30] It seemed worthwhile, therefore, to examine the correlation between white religious affiliation and Negro registration rates for the South as a whole.

29. Samuel A. Stouffer, *Communism, Conformity, and Civil Liberties* (New York, Doubleday, 1955).
30. Allan P. Sindler, *Huey Long's Louisiana* (Baltimore: The Johns Hopkins Press, 1956); V. O. Key, Jr., *op. cit.*, ch. 8; John H. Fenton and Kenneth N. Vines, "Negro Registration in Louisiana," *American Political Science Review*, Vol. 51 (1957), pp. 704–13.

We find that Negro registration rates are depressed as church membership among whites[31] increases (−.17), despite the fact that white membership in different churches has different functions — Baptist membership is negatively related to Negro registration (−.10) while Catholic membership is positively related (+.15). On a southwide basis, the percentage of Jews in the county's total church membership is not significantly associated with Negro registration.

Granted that Catholicism is positively related to Negro registration, we can partial out the influence of Catholicism in order to determine the correlation between non-Catholic white church membership and Negro registration. This partial correlation is, as expected, slightly greater (−.23) than the simple correlation. But the negative correlation between white church membership and Negro registration disappears when Negro concentration is held constant. (The partial correlation is +.01.) Greater church membership among whites accordingly appears to be a reflection of other county attributes rather than an independent factor in relation to Negro registration. When we examine the correlations between church membership and all of our other measures of county attributes, we find very low correlations with all other variables except Negro concentration (+.38) and Catholicism (+.31). Apparently, then, white church membership *per se* is unimportant for Negro registration. White people in the kinds of counties with more Negroes and in predominantly Catholic counties are more often members of churches. In the former kinds of counties, fewer Negroes will vote regardless of non-Catholic church membership. Most non-Catholic churches presumably take on the racial attitudes of their localities; or, if they do not, they have little effect on those attitudes in so far as the attitudes are reflected in rates of Negro registration.

Per cent of Roman Catholics in the white church population appears to be by far the most important of our religious attributes of southern counties. And the relationship between Catholicism and Negro voter registration does not disappear when Negro concentration is controlled. (The partial correlation is +.10.) The presence of Roman Catholics, then, does seem to facilitate Negro voter registration on a southwide basis. Roman Catholic churches and priests presumably react less directly to other county attributes than most Protestant churches and their ministers; in any case Catholicism is independently and positively related to Negro voter registration.

However, the concentration of Catholic population in Louisiana and the small number of Catholics in most other parts of the South dictate caution in accepting this explanation. For one thing, the distribution of Catholic percentages deviates so far from the assumption of normal distribution underlying correlation analysis that our southwide correlations may have been curiously and unpredictably affected. In the second place, the atypical political patterns of Louisiana — rather than Catholicism *per se* — may account for a large part of the correlation obtained. Only state-by-state analysis of the correlations can indicate if Catholicism is a genuinely independent and significant factor facilitating Negro registration throughout the entire South.

---

31. The most recent attempt to compile county-by-county figures on church membership is reported in a census by the National Council of Churches of Christ, *Churches and Church Membership in the U.S.*, Series C, 1956. Negro churches are not included in this census, and the figures reported for many white churches appear to be incomplete.

IV. Negro Versus White Registration Rates

We have assumed that our analysis is of *Negro* voter registration rather than of voter registration *in general*. But this assumption might be incorrect: while Negroes register to vote in the South at a much lower rate than whites (Figure 1), the registration rates of the two races could be highly correlated with one another, both responding to the same social and economic characteristics of southern counties. The data permit two tests of this possibility: (1) an examination of the relationship between Negro and white registration; (2) a comparison of the relationships between county attributes and white registration with the relationships found between the same attributes and Negro registration.

The Relationship Between Negro and White Registration

To a limited extent, Negro registration does increase as white registration increases; their simple correlation is +.24. Figure 7 presents the relationship of Negro to white registration for every level of white registration. The detailed relationships depicted by the graph reveal that the lowest and the highest levels of white registration contribute most of the small correlation between the registration rates of the two races; if both of the extreme points were eliminated, the curve would be virtually horizontal, indicating that Negro registration had no relationship at all to white registration. Only when white registration is extremely high or extremely low, then, is it associated with the rate of Negro registration. For the broad middle range of counties with from 30 to 89 per cent of the whites registered — a group which contains over 70 per cent of all southern counties — Negro registration appears to be independent of white registration.

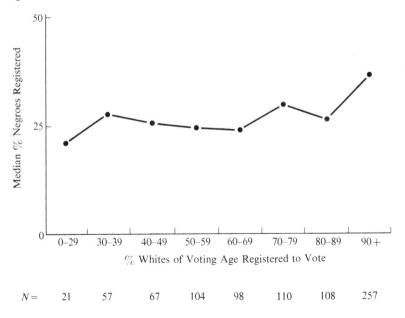

FIGURE 7 Median % of Voting Age Negroes Registered to Vote, by % of Whites Registered in Same County

The Relationships Between Socio-Economic Factors and Negro and White Registration

Table IV presents the correlations between the per cent of eligible whites registered to vote and the same 20 social and economic factors utilized in our effort to explain Negro registration. While these factors were chosen for their presumed relevance for Negro registration, the magnitude of the simple correlations in the first column of the table suggests that they are as strongly related to white as to Negro registration. When these simple correlations for whites are compared with those for Negroes in Table II, however, we see that the direction of the correlation is reversed for 15 of the 20 social and economic factors. Not one of the 20 variables is substantially and consistently related to both Negro and white rates of voter registration.

TABLE IV   Correlations Between County Social and
Economic Characteristics and Per Cent of Voting Age
Whites Registered to Vote, by County, in 11 Southern
States

County Characteristics	Simple Correlations (r)	Partial Correlations, Controlling for:	
		% Negro, 1950	% Urban, 1950
Per cent of nonwhite labor force in white collar occupations	−.26	−.24	−.15
Nonwhite median school years completed	−.34	−.34	−.28
Nonwhite median income	−.19	−.17	−.08
Per cent of total church membership Roman Catholic	−.09	−.08	−.03
Per cent increase in population, 1940–50	−.06	−.04	+.08
Per cent of labor force in manufacturing	+.05	+.05	+.07
White median income	−.19	−.19	−.05
Per cent of population urban	−.25	−.24	
Percentage point difference in per cent population Negro, 1900–50	+.10	+.11	+.05
Per cent of total church membership Jewish	−.03	−.03	+.04
Difference in white-nonwhite median school years completed	+.11	+.07	+.14
Difference in white-nonwhite median income	−.12	−.13	−.03
Number of Negro colleges in county	−.10	−.11	−.04
Per cent of total church membership Baptist	+.20	+.19	+.15
Per cent of population belonging to a church	+.06	+.02	+.07
Per cent of labor force in agriculture	+.21	+.19	+.06
White median school years completed	−.08	−.11	+.03
Per cent of farms operated by tenants	+.09	+.05	+.05
Per cent of population Negro, 1900	+.03	−.12	+.02
Per cent of population Negro, 1950	+.10		+.06

Note: County characteristics are listed above in the same order as in Table II in order to facilitate comparison of Negro and white correlations.

The reversal of relationships is so regular that social and economic attributes might appear to have opposite meanings for Negro and white registration.[32] Closer inspection reveals, however, that the relationships are disparate rather than opposite.

---

32. A simple Kendall tau rank order correlation of the two distributions of correlations in Table II and IV is −.54.

The crucial variable for Negro registration is Negro concentration in the population, which not only furnishes the strongest simple correlation but is also the variable that most consistently accounts for other apparent "influences" on Negro registration. Indeed, Negro concentration has generally been cited as the critical factor in all dimensions of southern political behavior. Hence, one immediately suspects that all of the variables which facilitate white registration must be positively correlated with concentration of Negro population, which would thereby stand as the dominant third factor for both Negro and white registration. While this familiar interpretation would conveniently account for the striking discrepancy between correlates of white and Negro registration, it is not supported by our findings. On the contrary, *Negro concentration has a negligible relationship to white voter registration.* Moreover, the small simple correlation of Negro concentration and white registration (+.10) drops to the vanishing point (+.06) when urbanism is controlled.

No single variable is as important for white registration as Negro concentration is for Negro registration, but urbanism emerges as particularly significant. Per cent of population urban — which proved inconsequential in the analysis of Negro registration — furnishes one of the strongest negative correlations with white voter registration, a correlation that is not affected when Negro concentration is controlled. And the same relationship is found if, instead of per cent of population urban, we use Standard Metropolitan Areas as our index of urban-rural difference; white registration is consistently higher in rural than in urban counties. Other county characteristics associated with urbanization — such as high income and education levels for whites and Negroes — are similarly related to low white registration. Perhaps the rural white resident finds politics more meaningful in a one-party region, where personality plays such an important role in elections.[33] In any event, urban-rural differences are a key factor in variations in white voter registration.

Similar variations are found in the relationships of white and Negro registration rates to the other social and economic characteristics of southern counties. Average white education, for example, manifested a strong negative association with Negro registration — an association that held up under various controls so well that it led to novel conclusions. White education is also negatively related to white registration, but the correlation is extremely small and it is reversed when per cent of population urban is controlled.

Without an extended consideration of white registration, then, we can conclude that our analysis does apply to Negro voter registration in particular rather than to voter registration in general. The social and economic characteristics of southern counties have widely different meanings for Negro and white registration.

V. Conclusions

The proportion of voting age Negroes registered to vote in the former confederate states has increased more than 500 per cent since *Smith* v. *Allwright* was decided in 1944. Today, 28 per cent of the voting age Negroes are registered voters, a rate which is about half that of white adults in the South. In this article we have ex-

---

33. Urban counties in the South undoubtedly purge their registration lists with greater regularity than the more rural ones. How much effect this may have on these correlations cannot be ascertained.

amined the statistical associations between selected social and economic characteristics of southern counties and Negro registration in an effort to ascertain the extent to which variations in Negro registration can be explained by the social and economic realities of the region.

The personal attributes of Negroes — their occupations, income, and education as reflected in county figures — were found to have relatively little to do with Negro registration rates. The size of the Negro middle class does appear to have an independent and positive correlation with Negro registration, but this correlation is small compared to those between Negro registration and the characteristics of the whites and of the total community.

The largest single correlation ($-.46$) was between the per cent of the population Negro in 1950 and Negro registration. Differences in the proportion of the population Negro up to about 30 per cent are not associated with drastic reductions in the per cent of Negroes registered, but increasing Negro concentration above this figure seems to lead to very rapid decreases. Negro concentration in the past seems almost as important as Negro concentration today until one discovers that the close association of past with present Negro concentration accounts for the finding. Indeed, declines in Negro proportions in counties with populations from 30 to 70 per cent Negro in 1900 are associated with substantial registration increases over similar counties which have not experienced such change.

The presence of an agricultural economy and farm tenancy were found to have a small, independent, and depressing effect on Negro registration rates. Neither urbanization nor industrialization, on the other hand, seems to be associated with Negro registration increases when other factors are controlled.

White educational levels were of about equal importance to the size of the Negro middle class and the existence of an agrarian economy. The more highly educated the whites in a county, the lower the rate of Negro registration — until the average white adult was a high school graduate or possessed some higher education. In these few counties, the rate of Negro registration was moderate. Up to the highest levels, increases in white educational levels apparently lead to more effective enforcement of the region's traditional mores against Negro participation in elections.

Another factor of about equal importance to all the others save Negro concentration is Roman Catholicism. The larger the proportion of Roman Catholics in a county, the higher the rate of Negro registration regardless of what other factors are controlled.

When the same social and economic characteristics of southern counties are analyzed for their relationships to white voter registration, a radically different pattern is discovered. The direction of the relationship is reversed for most of the attributes with the shift from Negro to white registration, but more than a simple reversal is involved. The magnitudes of the correlations with white registration (disregarding direction of correlation) are quite different, and a different variable emerges as the most consistent independent correlate. Whereas Negro registration tends to increase in the counties — rural or urban — that have smaller portions of Negroes in their populations, white registration tends to increase in the more rural counties — regardless of the portions of Negroes in their populations. We can accordingly have some confidence that we are dealing with an autonomous set of relationships in our analysis of Negro registration in the South.

In all of the preceding analysis, we have examined the association between selected social and economic factors and Negro registration one at a time. While controls for the impact of one social and economic factor on another have been introduced, we have not yet attempted to estimate the extent of the association between all the social and economic factors taken together and Negro registration. In order to do this, we have computed the multiple correlation coefficient between all 20 social and economic factors (plus the size of the Standard Metropolitan Area, if any, within which the county is contained — a qualitative variable for which simple correlations could not be obtained) and Negro voter registration. The correlation between all of the social and economic variables and county registration rates of Negroes is .53, which explains about 28 per cent (R^2) of the variation in Negro registration.

A multiple correlation of this magnitude demonstrates the great importance of social and economic characteristics for Negro registration.[34] To explain over one-fourth of the variance in Negro registration — or any other significant political phenomenon — is no mean achievement in the current state of political science. But almost three-fourths of the variance remains to be accounted for. This leaves room for significant variation independent of social and economic forces that have been considered here. If political variables were added to the analysis, could still more of the variance in Negro registration be explained? If political variables do emerge as having an autonomous set of relationships to Negro registration, what is the comparative importance of political and demographic variables? Finally, if variations in state systems (social, economic, and political) were taken into account, could still more explanatory power be gained? A social and economic analysis has taken us a long way in our effort to understand Negro registration rates but we still have a lot further to go. The massive bulk and complexity of our data requires that an analysis of political and legal factors, of the relative importance of demographic versus political variables, and of variations in state systems be reported separately. Our expection is that, by an analysis of these addtional factors, we can reduce the range of unexplained variation still further.

The application of our findings to the contemporary policy problem of how best to increase Negro voting in the South must be approached with the utmost caution. Our analysis deals with registration, not voting, and they are not identical forms of political participation. Our data deal with the characteristics of counties, not individuals, and the leap from the areal to the individual level is hazardous. Third, the analysis has been of variations in rates of registration and not of factors which determine its absolute level. To find that an independent variable accounts for some of the variation in the dependent variable gives us no direct information on the size of the dependent variable. Fourth, correlations are not "causes" but merely associations; attributing causal relationships to variables which are correlated with one another is to engage in the drawing of inferences, which sometimes is spectacularly wrong. Finally, the bulk of our analysis has been restricted to one

---

34. Indeed it was on the basis of a roughly equal multiple correlation, based on survey data rather than aggregate county data, that an early voting behavior study concluded that "social characteristics determine political preference." Paul F. Lazarsfeld, Bernard Berelson, and Hazel Gauclet *The People's Choice* (New York: Columbia University Press, 1948), p. 27. This work reports a multiple correlation between voting preference and social factors of "approximately .5"

point in time so that it does not directly produce predictions in which time is a key factor.

If these caveats are not forgotten but merely set aside, our correlations suggest that reformers should not expect miracles[35] in their efforts, through political and legal means, to increase the size and effectiveness of the Negro vote in the South. The Negro registration rate is low, in rather large part, because of the social and economic characteristics of southerners — both Negro and white. These facts are not easily and quickly changed by law or political action. One cannot help but be impressed by the massive indications of stability in the situation — the extremely high negative correlation between per cent Negro in 1900 and Negro registration in 1958, the apparent failure of urbanization and industrialization to provide sufficiently favorable conditions for Negro political participation, the negative correlation between white educational levels and Negro registration, and so on.

At the same time, Negro registration has increased rapidly since 1944 and the social and economic factors we have considered account for only about 28 per cent

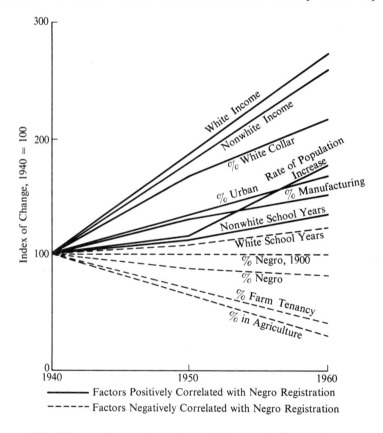

FIGURE 8   Rates of Social and Economic Change in
the South 1940–1960

35. For example, Martin Luther King's statement in a speech to the 1962 NAACP annual convention about southern Negroes being "able to elect at least five Negroes to Congress in the next few years" seems to underestimate wildly the social and economic barriers to Negro political participation. *New York Times*, July 6, 1962. See also the sanguine expectations of Lomax, *op. cit.*

of its 1958 variation. Changes in the southern society and economy strongly argue that Negro registration will continue to increase. In Figure 8, the trend since 1940 is presented for the variables we found to be most strongly related to Negro voter registration.[36] *Every one of the variables positively associated with Negro registration is on the increase* — some have doubled in 20 years and all but one have increased by at least 50 per cent. Only one of the factors associated with low Negro registration — white school years completed — is also increasing, and there is reason to believe that a good many southern counties will soon reach the stage where this factor may tend to facilitate rather than hinder Negro political participation.[37] All the other factors negatively correlated with Negro registration (except, of course, per cent Negro in 1900) are declining rapidly.

The South's social and economic structure may be the reformer's major barrier — but it may also be a long-run cause for hope.

---

36. No trend data were available on religious affiliation. Median income figures, by race, were not available for 1940. In Figure 8, it is assumed that median income for both races increased at the same rate between 1940 and 1950 as between 1950 and 1960.

37. If white school years completed continues to increase at the 1950–60 rate, the average southern white will have completed 11.4 years of schooling by 1970 and many southern counties will have average white school years completed of 12 years or more. Assuming that the relationship presented in Figure 6 continues to hold true, the effect of white education on Negro registration may gradually reverse.

JOHN E. MUELLER

Presidential Popularity
From Truman to Johnson

*In this example we move from previous considerations
using aggregate indicators alone to a statistical model using survey
data as well. The mode of analysis also provides some perspective for
our later treatment of time series (chapter 5). Mueller's goal is to
offer explanatory statements about factors influencing presidential
popularity from the beginning of the Truman administration to the end of
the Johnson administration. The dependent variable is the percentage of
respondents approving the way the president is handling his job (over
time). Four independent predictors then are examined for their association
with the popularity measure: (1) a "coalition of minorities" variable
operationalizing the concept of intensifying minority opposition over
time for any one president (measured as the length of time since each
president was inaugurated or reelected); (2) a "rally round the flag"
variable representing potential boosts in popularity with the occurrence
of international crises (measured as the length of time since the last
rally point, with each point defined on the basis of three a priori
criteria — the event must be international, it must involve the United
States and the president directly, and it must be dramatic); (3) an
"economic slump" variable measured as the unemployment rate at the time of*

Reprinted from John E. Mueller, "Presidential Popularity from Truman to Johnson," *American Political Science Review* 64 (1970): 18–34, by permission of the American Political Science Association and the author.

This investigation was supported by a grant from the National Science Foundation. At various stages helpful comments, criticisms, and complaints were lodged by Richard Fenno, Gerald Kramer, Richard Niemi, Peter Ordeshook, Alvin Rabushka, William Riker, and Andrew Scott.

*the survey minus the rate at the beginning of a presidential term, with
its value set equal to zero if the first rate is lower than the second;
and (4) a war variable measured dichotomously as a value of one during
a war period (Korea and Vietnam) and as a value of zero during other
periods. These independent variables then are examined for their impact
on popularity through various regression analyses, including results with
and without the war variable, equations with the coalition of minorities
variable divided into presidential terms, and equations with dummy variables
for economic slump by term. An additional analysis of residuals (the
equation predictions versus actual levels of the dependent variable)
enables the author to spot particular instances where the variables
interrelate in unusual fashion to produce deviant results.*

I think [my grandchildren] will be proud of two things. What I did for the Negro and
seeing it through in Vietnam for all of Asia. The Negro cost me 15 points in the polls and
Vietnam cost me 20.

Lyndon B. Johnson[1]

With tenacious regularity over the last two and a half decades the Gallup Poll
has posed to its cross-section samples of the American public the following query,
"Do you approve or disapprove of the way (the incumbent) is handling his job
as President?" The responses to this curious question form an index known as
"Presidential popularity." According to Richard Neustadt, the index is "widely
taken to approximate reality" in Washington and reports about its behavior are
"very widely read"[2] there, including, the quotation above would suggest, the
highest circles.

Plotted over time, the index forms probably the longest continuous trend line
in polling history. This study seeks to analyze the behavior of this line for the period
from the beginning of the Truman administration in 1945 to the end of the Johnson
administration in January 1969 during which time the popularity question was asked
some 300 times.[3]

Four variables are used as predictors of a President's popularity. These include a
measure of the length of time the incumbent has been in office as well as variables
which attempt to estimate the influence on his rating of major international events,
economic slump and war. To assess the independent impact of each of these variables as they interact in association with Presidential popularity, multiple regression
analysis is used as the basic analytic technique.

---

1. Quoted, David Wise, "The Twilight of a President," *New York Times Magazine*, November 3,
1968, p. 131.

2. Richard E. Neustadt, *Presidential Power: The Politics of Leadership* (New York: Wiley, 1960),
p. 205n.

3. A general picture of what this line looks like can be gained from the figure in Robert A. Dahl,
Pluralist Democracy in the United States (Chicago: Rand McNally, 1967), p. 107. The Presidential
popularity data for the Johnson administration have been taken from the *Gallup Opinion Index*.
All other poll data, unless otherwise indicated, have come from the archives of the Roper Public
Opinion Research Center at Williams College, Williamstown, Massachusetts.

I. The Dependent Variable: Presidential Popularity

The Presidential popularity question taps a general impression about the way the incumbent seems to be handling his job at the present moment. As Neustadt notes, the response, like the question, is "unfocused,"[4] unrelated to specific issues or electoral outcomes. The respondent is asked to "approve" or "disapprove" and if he has "no opinion," he must volunteer that response himself. He has infrequently been asked *why* he feels that way — and many respondents when asked are able only vaguely to rationalize their position.[5] And only at times has he been asked to register how strongly he approves or disapproves.

A disapproving response might be considered a non-constructive vote of no-confidence: the respondent registers his discontent, but he does not need to state who he would prefer in the Presidency. Thus the index is likely to be a very imperfect indicator of success or failure for a President seeking re-election. While approvers are doubtless more likely than disapprovers to endorse his re-election, on considering the opposition some approvers may be attracted into voting against the incumbent just as some disapprovers may be led grudgingly to vote for him.[6]

Whatever peculiarities there are in the question itself, they are at least constant. Unlike many questions asked by the polling organizations, wording has not varied from time to time by whim or fashion. The stimulus has therefore been essentially fixed; only the response has varied.

And the variation has been considerable. Harry Truman was our most popular President in this period — for a few weeks in 1945 when more than 85 percent of the public expressed approval — and our least popular — from early 1951 until March 1952 when less than 30 percent were usually found to be favorably inclined. Other Presidents have stayed within these limits with Lyndon Johnson most nearly approaching the Truman extremes. President Eisenhower's popularity was never higher than 79 percent, but it never dropped below 49 percent either. President Kennedy also maintained a rather high level of popularity but was in noticeable decline at the time of his death.

The proportion of respondents selecting the "no opinion" option, averaging 14 percent, remained strikingly constant throughout the period.[7] This is a little surprising since it might be expected that when opinion changes, say from approval to disapproval of a President, the move would be seen first in a decrease in the support figure with an increase in the no opinion percentage, followed in a later survey by an increase in the disapproval column with a decrease in the no opinion

---

4. *Op. cit.*, p. 96.

5. See for example the breakdowns in *Gallup Opinion Index*, March, 1966, p. 4.

6. There is also a more technical reason why the popularity index has little direct relevance to the electoral result: Gallup does not ask the question during a President's re-election campaign. Thus for the months between early summer and late fall in 1948, 1956, and 1964 no Gallup data on Presidential popularity exist. One other technicality is worth mention. There is a slight underrepresentation of data points in Truman's first years. By 1950, except for the election year phenomenon, the Gallup organization was asking the question on virtually every survey conducted — some dozen or sixteen per year. Before that time the question was posed on the average only about half as frequently. Neither of these technical problems, however, is likely to bias the results in any important way, especially since so much of the analysis allows each administration a fair amount of distinctiveness.

7. The standard deviation for the no opinion response is 2.93. By contrast the comparable statistic is 14.8 for the approve response and 14.5 for the disapprove response.

portion. There are a few occasions in which the no opinion percentage seems to rise and fall in this manner, one occurring in the early weeks of the Korean War, but by and large it would appear that if movements into the no opinion column do occur they are compensated for by movements out of it.

This means therefore that the trend in approval is largely a mirror image of the trend in disapproval; the correlation between the two is −.98. And, most conveniently, this almost means that the President's popularity at a given moment can be rendered by a single number: the percentage approving his handling of the job. The no opinion percentage is almost always close to 14 percent and the percentage disapproving is, of course, the remainder.

There is, however, one small wrinkle. The no opinion percentage does get a bit out of hand, quite understandably, in the early weeks of the Kennedy and Eisenhower administrations as substantial numbers of respondents felt inclined to withhold judgment on these new men. This inordinate withholding of opinion declined in the first weeks to more "normal" levels with the result that *both* the level of approval *and* disapproval tended to increase.[8]

Since one of the propositions to be tested in this study proposes that there exists a general downward trend in each President's popularity, this initial rating situation causes something of a problem. If the disapproval score is used as the dependent variable there will be a slight bias in favor of the proposition. It seems preferable to load things against the proposition; hence for the purposes of this study *the dependent variable is the percentage approving the way the incumbent is handling his job as President*.[9] The average approval rating for the entire twenty-four year period is 58 percent.

II. The Independent Variables

If one stares at Presidential popularity trend lines long enough, one soon comes to imagine one is seeing things. If the things imagined seem also to be mentioned in the literature about the way Presidential popularity should or does behave, one begins to take the visions seriously and to move to test them.

In this manner were formulated four basic "independent" variables, predictor variables of Presidential popularity. They are: 1) a "coalition of minorities" variable that suggests the overall trend in a President's popularity will be downward; 2) a "rally round the flag" variable which anticipates that international crises and similar phenomena will give a President a short-term boost in popularity; 3) an "economic slump" variable associating recessions with decreased popularity; and 4) a "war" variable predicting a decrease in popularity under the conditions of the Korean and Vietnam wars.

---

8. In the case of President Eisenhower, the no opinion response actually rose a bit before it began to descend, reaching the highest level recorded for any President in the period in March 1953 when 28 percent had no opinion. (President Nixon has proved to be the greatest mystery of all: fully 36 percent registered no opinion after his inauguration.)

9. It is argued by some that percentages should not be used in their pure state as variables, but rather should be transformed into logits: $Y^* = \log_e [Y/(1 - Y)]$. The transformation was tried in the analysis, but it made little difference. Therefore the more easily communicated percentage version has been kept. In any event the dependent variable rarely takes extreme values. It rises to 80 percent only three or four times and never dips below 23 percent.

1. The "Coalition of Minorities" Variable

In a somewhat different context Anthony Downs has suggested the possibility that an administration, even if it always acts with majority support on each issue, can gradually alienate enough minorities to be defeated. This could occur when the minority on each issue feels so intensely about its loss that it is unable to be placated by administration support on other policies it favors. A clever opposition, under appropriate circumstances, could therefore forge a coalition of these intense minorities until it had enough votes to overthrow the incumbent.[10]

Transposed to Presidential popularity, this concept might inspire the expectation that a President's popularity would show a general downward trend as he is forced on a variety of issues to act and thus create intense, unforgiving opponents of former supporters. It is quite easy to point to cases where this may have occurred. President Kennedy's rather dramatic efforts to force back a steel price rise in 1962, while supported by most Americans, tended to alienate many in the business community.[11] Administration enforcement of the Supreme Court's school desegregation order tended to create intense opposition among white Southerners even if the Presidential moves had passive majority support in most of the country.[12]

Realistically, the concept can be extended somewhat. From time to time there arise exquisite dilemmas in which the President must act and in which he will tend to alienate *both* sides no matter what he does, a phenomenon related to what Aaron Wildavsky has called a "minus sum" game.[13] President Truman's seizure of the steel mills in 1952 made neither labor nor management (nor the Supreme Court, for that matter) happy. For the mayor of New York, situations like this seem to arise weekly.

There are other, only vaguely related, reasons to expect an overall decline in popularity. One would be disillusionment. In the process of being elected, the President invariably says or implies he will do more than he can do and some disaffection of once bemused supporters is all but inevitable. A most notable example would be the case of those who supported President Johnson in 1964 because he seemed opposed to escalation in Vietnam. Furthermore initial popularity ratings are puffed up by a variety of weak followers. These might include leering opposition partisans looking for the first excuse to join the aggrieved, excitable types who soon became bored by the humdrum of post-election existence, and bandwagon riders whose fair weather support dissolves with the first sprinkle.[14] As Burns Roper notes, "In a sense, Presidential elections are quadriennial myth builders which every four years make voters believe some man is better than he is. The President takes office with most of the nation on his side, but this artificial 'unity' soon begins to evaporate."[15]

---

10. *An Economic Theory of Democracy* (New York: Harper and Row, 1957), pp. 55–60.

11. See the data in H. G. Erskine, "The Polls," 28 *Public Opinion Quarterly*, 341 and 338 (Summer 1964).

12. See John M. Fenton, *In Your Opinion* (Boston: Little, Brown, 1960), p. 146.

13. "The Empty-head Blues: Black Rebellion and White Reaction," *The Public Interest*, Spring 1968, pp. 3–16.

14. On the bandwagon effect among nonvoters, see Angus Campbell, Philip E. Converse, Warren E. Miller, and Donald E. Stokes, *The American Voter* (New York: Wiley, 1960), pp. 110–115.

15. Burns Roper, "The Public Looks at Presidents," *The Public Pulse*, January 1969.

For these reasons the coalition of minorities variable, as it is dubbed here, predicts decline. "Love," said Machiavelli, "is held by a chain of obligation which, men being selfish, is broken whenever it serves their purpose."[16]

The coalition of minorities variable is measured simply by the length of time, in years, since the incumbent was inaugurated (for first terms) or re-elected (for second terms). It varies then from zero to about four and should be negatively correlated with popularity: the longer the man has been in office, the lower his popularity. It is; the simple r is $-.47$. The decline is assumed to start over again for second terms because the President is expected to have spent the campaign rebuilding his popular coalition by soothing the disaffected, re-deluding the disillusioned, and putting on a show for the bored. If he is unable to do this, he will not be re-elected, something which has not happened in the post-war era although twice Presidents have declined to make the effort.

The analysis will assume a *linear* decline in popularity. That is, a President's popularity is assumed to decline at an even rate for all four years of his term: if a decline of 6 percentage points per year is indicated, he will be down 6 points at the end of his first year, 12 at the end of the second, 18 at the end of the third, and 24 after four years. There is nothing in the justification for the coalition of minorities variable which demands that the decline must occur with such tedious regularity but, when curvilinear variants were experimented with, little or no improvement was found. Hence the reliance in this study on the linear version which has the advantage of simplicity and ease of communication.

2. The "Rally Round the Flag" Variable

This variable seeks to bring into the analysis a phenomenon often noted by students of the Presidency and of public opinion: certain intense international events generate a "rally round the flag" effect which tends to give a boost to the President's popularity rating. As Kenneth Waltz has observed, "In the face of such an event, the people rally behind their chief executive."[17] Tom Wicker: "Simply being President through a great crisis or a big event . . . draws Americans together in his support."[18] Richard Neustadt notes "the correspondence between popularity and happenings,"[19] Burns Roper finds "approval has usually risen during international crises,"[20] and Nelson Polsby observes, "Invariably, the popular response to a President during international crisis is favorable, regardless of the wisdom of the policies he pursues."[21]

The difficulty with this concept is in operationalizing it. There is a terrible temptation to find a bump on a popularity plot, then to scurry to historical records to find an international "rally point" to associate with it. This process all but guarantees that the variable will prove significant.

---

16. *The Prince*, ch. XVII.

17. Kenneth N. Waltz, "Electoral Punishment and Foreign Policy Crisis" in James N. Rosenau, *Domestic Sources of Foreign Policy* (New York: Free Press, 1967), p. 272.

18. Tom Wicker, "In the Nation: Peace, It's Wonderful," *New York Times*, July 4, 1967, p. 18.

19. *Op. cit.*, p. 100.

20. *Op. cit.*

21. *Congress and the Presidency* (Englewood Cliffs, N. J.: Prentice-Hall, 1964), p. 25.

The strategy adopted here to identify rally points was somewhat different and hopefully more objective. A definition of what a rally point should look like was created largely on *a priori* grounds and then a search of historical records was made to find events which fit the definition. Most of the points so identified *are* associated with bumps on the plot — that after all was how the concept was thought of in the first place — but quite a few are not and the bumps associated with some are considerably more obvious than others.

In general, a rally point must be associated with an event which 1) is international and 2) involves the United States and particularly the President directly; and it must be 3) specific, dramatic, and sharply focused.

It must be international because only developments confronting the nation as a whole are likely to generate a rally round the flag effect. Major domestic events — riots, scandals, strikes — are at least as likely to exacerbate internal divisions as they are to soothe them.

To qualify as a rally point an international event is required to involve the United States and the President directly because major conflicts between other powers are likely to engender split loyalties and are less likely to seem relevant to the average American.

Finally the event must be specific, dramatic and sharply focused in order to assure public attention and interest. As part of this, events which transpire gradually, no matter how important, are excluded from consideration because their impact on public attitudes is likely to be diffused. Thus sudden changes in the bombing levels in Vietnam are expected to create a reaction while the gradual increase of American troops is not.

Errors in this process could occur by including events whose importance is only obvious in retrospect or by ignoring events like the Geneva summit of 1955 which may seem minor in historical perspective but were held significant at the time. For this reason more reliance has been put on indexes of newspaper content than on broad, historical accounts of the period.[22] In general if there has been a bias in selecting rally points it has been in the direction of excluding border-line cases. This was done in profound respect for the lack of public interest and knowledge on most items of international affairs.

At that, some 34 rally points were designated. In general they can be said to fall into six categories. First, there are the four instances of sudden American military intervention: Korea, Lebanon, the Bay of Pigs, and the Dominican Republic. A second closely related category encompasses major military developments in ongoing wars: in Korea, the Inchon landing and the Chinese intervention; in Vietnam, the Tonkin Bay episode, the beginning of bombing of North Vietnam, the major extension of this bombing, and the Tet offensive. Third are the major diplomatic developments of the period: crises over Cuban missiles, the U-2 and atomic testing, the enunciation of the "Truman doctrine" with its offer of aid to Greece and Turkey, the beginning of, and major changes in, the peace talks in Korea and Vietnam, and the several crises in Berlin. Fourth are the two dramatic technological

---

22. Especially valuable was Eric V. Nordheim and Pamela B. Wilcox, "Major Events of the Nuclear Age: A Chronology to Assist in the Analysis of American Public Opinion," Oak Ridge National Laboratory, Oak Ridge, Tennessee, August 1967. Other sources often consulted included the *New York Times Index* and the Chronology section of the *World Almanac*.

developments: Sputnik and the announcement of the first Soviet atomic test. The fifth category includes the meetings between the President and the head of the Soviet Union at Potsdam in 1945, Geneva in 1955, Camp David in 1959, Paris in 1960, Vienna in 1961, and Glassboro in 1967. While these events are rarely spectacular they, like crisis, do generate a let's-get-behind-the-President effect. Because they are far less dramatic — even if sometimes more important — Presidential conferences with other powers (e.g., the British at Nassau) are excluded as are American meetings with the Soviet Union at the foreign minister level.

Sixth and finally, as an analytic convenience the start of each Presidential term is rather arbitrarily designated as a rally point. Presidents Truman and Johnson came in under circumstances which could justifiably be classified under the "rally round the flag" rubric although the crisis was a domestic one. The other points all involve elections or re-elections which perhaps might also be viewed as a somewhat unifying and cathartic experience.

These then are the events chosen to be associated with the rally round the flag variable. No listing will satisfy everyone's perspective about what has or has not been important to Americans in this 24 year period. However, in the analysis the variable has proven to be a rather hardy one. Experimentation with it suggests the addition or subtraction of a few rally points is likely to make little difference.

The rally round the flag variable is measured by the length of time, in years, since the last rally point. It varies then from zero to a theoretical maximum of about four or an empirical one of 1.9. Like the coalition of minorities variable, it should be negatively correlated with popularity: the longer it has been since the last rally round the flag event, the lower the popularity of the incumbent. It is; the simple r is $-.11$. Some experiments with curvilinear transformations of the variable were attempted but, since improvement again was marginal at best, the variable has been left in linear form.

Each rally point is given the same weighting in the analysis. One effort to soften this rather crude policy was made. The rally points were separated into two groups: "good" rally points (e.g., the Cuban missile crisis) in which the lasting effect on opinion was likely to be favorable to the President and "bad" ones (e.g., the U-2 crisis, the Bay of Pigs) in which the initial favorable surge could be expected to be rather transitory. Two separate rally round the flag variables were then created with the anticipation that they would generate somewhat different regression coefficients. The differences however were small and inconsistent. The public seems to react to "good" and "bad" international events in about the same way. Thus, to this limited extent, the equal weighting of rally points seems justified.

In tandem, the concepts underlying the coalition of minorities and rally round the flag variables predict that the President's popularity will continually decline over time and that international crises and similar events will explain short term bumps and wiggles in this otherwise inexorable descent.[23]

---

23. Roper notes that President Kennedy's highest point of popularity occurred after the Bay of Pigs invasion and concludes this fact says something special about that crisis event (*op. cit.*) But this phenomenon is due to *two* effects — the rally round the flag effect *and* the fact that the event occurred very early in Kennedy's administration when the value for the coalition of minorities variable was yet very low.

3. The "Economic Slump" Variable

There is a goodly amount of evidence, and an even goodlier amount of speculation, suggesting a relationship between economic conditions and electoral behavior. The extension of such thinking to Presidential popularity is both natural and precedented. Neustadt, for example, concludes the recession in 1958 caused a drop in President Eisenhower's popularity.[24]

The economic indicator used here will be the unemployment rate. The statistic recommends itself because it is available for the entire period and is reported on a monthly basis.[25] It is used as a general indicator of economic health or malaise and is not taken simply as a comment about the employed. It is assumed that the individual respondent, in allowing economic perceptions to influence him, essentially does so by comparing how things are *now* with how they were when the incumbent began his present term of office. If conditions are worse, he is inclined to disapprove the President's handling of his job, if things are better he is inclined to approve. The economic variable therefore becomes the unemployment rate at the time the incumbent's term began subtracted from the rate at the time of the poll.[26] It is positive when things are worse and negative when things are better. It should be negatively correlated with popularity. But it isn't.

Unemployment reached some of its highest points during the recessions under the Eisenhower administration. The problem, to be examined more fully in Section VI below, is that Eisenhower was a *generally* popular President. Thus even though his popularity seemed to dip during the recessions, high unemployment comes to be associated with a relatively popular President. This problem can be handled rather easily within regression analysis by assigning to each of the Presidential administrations a "dummy" variable, the care and feeding of which will be discussed more fully in Section III below.

However, even when this circumstance is taken into account, the correlation coefficient and the regression coefficient for the economic variable remain positive. This seems to be largely due to the fact that *both* unemployment and the popularity of the incumbent President were in general decline between 1961 and 1968. The correlation for the period is .77.

Therefore a final alteration administered to the economic variable was to set it equal to zero whenever the unemployment rate was lower at the time of the survey than it had been at the start of the incumbent's present term. This alteration is a substantive one and is executed as the only way the data can be made to come out "right." In essence it suggests that *an economy in slump harms a President's popularity, but an economy which is improving does not seem to help his rating.* Bust is

---

24. *Op. cit.*, p. 97ff.

25. Data were gathered from Geoffrey H. Moore (ed.), *Business Cycle Indicators*, Vol. II (Princeton: Princeton University Press, 1961), p. 122; and, for more recent data, issues of the *Monthly Labor Review*.

26. One wrinkle, which is intuitively comfortable but makes little difference in the actual results, was to do something about the unemployment rates at the start of the first terms of Presidents Truman and Eisenhower when unemployment was "artificially" depressed due to ongoing wars. Presumably the public would be understanding about the immediate postwar rise in unemployment. Therefore for these two terms the initial unemployment level was taken to be that level which held six months after the war ended while the economic variable for the few months of the war and the six month period was set equal to zero.

bad for him but boom is not particularly good. There is punishment but never reward.

Perhaps this can be seen in a comparison of the 1960 and the 1968 campaigns. In 1960, as Harvey Segal notes, "What was important was the vague but pervasive feeling of dissatisfaction with the performance of the economy, the pain that made the public receptive to JFK's appeals."[27] In 1968, representing administrations that had presided over an unprecedented period of boom, Vice President Humphrey never seemed able to turn this fact to his advantage.

It is important to note that in practice this variable, which will be called the "economic slump" variable because of its inability to credit boom, takes on a non-zero value only during the Eisenhower administration and during the unemployment rise of 1949–50. In symbolic form the variable's peculiarities can be expressed in the following; the units are the percentage of unemployed:

$$E = U_t - U_{t_0} \qquad \text{if } U_t - U_{t_0} > 0$$
$$= 0 \qquad \text{if } U_t - U_{t_0} \leq 0$$

where

$$U_t = \text{Unemployment rate at the time of the survey}$$

and

$$U_{t_0} = \text{Unemployment rate at the beginning of the incumbent's present term}$$

4. The "War" Variable

It is widely held that the unpopular, puzzling, indecisive wars in Korea and Vietnam severely hurt the popularity of Presidents Truman and Johnson.[28] As noted in the quotation that heads this report, President Johnson himself apportions 20 percentage points of his drop in popularity to the Vietnam War.

This notion seems highly plausible. The popularity of Presidents Truman and Johnson was in steady decline as the wars progressed with record lows occurring during each President's last year in office at points when the wars seemed most hopeless and meaningless. The wars unquestionably contributed in a major way to their decisions not to seek third terms and then, when they had stepped aside, the wars proved to be major liabilities for their party's candidates in the next elections. Overall, the correlation between Presidential popularity and the presence of war is −.66.

There are problems with this analysis, however. The coalition of minorities concept argues that decline is a natural phenomenon and, indeed, a glance at a plot of Presidential popularity clearly shows Truman and Johnson in decline *before* the wars started. Furthermore, as will be seen, both men experienced noticeable

---

27. "The Pain Threshold of Economics in an Election Year," *New York Times*, July 15, 1968.
28. Waltz, *op. cit.*, pp. 273ff, 288; Neustadt, *op. cit.*, pp. 97–99; Wicker, *op. cit.*; Roper, *op. cit.*

declines during their *first* terms when they had no war to contend with. The real question is, then, did the war somehow add to the decline of popularity beyond that which might be expected to occur on other grounds?

An answer can be approached through multiple regression analysis. After allowing for a general pattern of decline under the coalition of minorities variable, the additional impact of a variable chosen to represent war can be assessed. It is also possible in this manner to compare the two wars to see if their association with Presidential popularity differed.

The presence of war is incorporated in the analysis simply by a dummy variable that takes on a value of one when a war is on and remains zero otherwise. The beginning of the Vietnam War was taken to be June 1965 with the beginnings of the major US troop involvement. At that point it became an American war for the public; before that ignorance of the war was considerable: as late as mid-1964, 25 percent of the public admitted it had never heard of the fighting in Vietnam.[29]

Other war measures of a more complex nature were experimented with. They increase in magnitude as the war progresses and thus should be able to tap a wearying effect as the years go by and should be negatively associated with popularity. These measures, however, are very highly correlated with the coalition of minorities variable for the two relevant Presidential terms and thus are all but useless in the analysis. The simple dummy variable suffers this defect in lesser measure, although it is far from immune, and thus, despite its crudities, has been used.[30]

5. Other Variables

The analysis of Presidential popularity will apply in various ways only the four variables discussed above — a rather austere representation of a presumably complex process. As will be seen, it is quite possible to get a sound fit with these four variables, but at various stages in the investigation — which involved the examination of hundreds of regression equations — a search was made for other variables which could profitably be added to the predictor set.

International developments are reasonably well incorporated into the analysis with a specific variable included for war and another for major crisis-like activities. Domestically, however, there is only the half-time variable for economic slump and the important but very unspecific coalition of minorities variable.

Accordingly it would be valuable to generate some sort of domestic equivalent to the rally round the flag variable to assess more precisely how major domestic events affect Presidential popularity. Operationally, however, this is a difficult task. First, while it is a justifiable assertion that international crises will rebound in the short term to a President's benefit it is by no means clear how a domestic crisis, whether riot, strike, or scandal, should affect his popularity. Furthermore major domestic concerns have varied quite widely not only in intensity and duration, but also in nature. Labor relations, which rarely made big news in the mid-1960's, were

---

29. A. T. Steele, *The American People and China* (New York: McGraw-Hill, 1966), p. 294. In May 1964 Gallup found almost two-thirds of the population said they paid little or no attention to developments in South Vietnam. Lloyd A. Free and Hadley Cantril, *The Political Beliefs of Americans* (New York: Clarion, 1968), pp. 59–60.

30. Although the Korean War continued into President Eisenhower's administration, he is not "blamed" for the war in the analysis since of course he was elected partly because of discontent over the war. Accordingly the war variable is set at zero for this period.

of profound concern in the middle and late 1940s as a multitude of major strikes threatened to cripple the nation and the adventures of John L. Lewis and the Taft-Hartley bill dominated the headlines. In the 1950s, however, labor broke into the news only with an occasional steel or auto strike or with the labor racketeering scandals in the last years of the decade. On the other hand, race relations, of extreme importance in the 1960s, made, except for the Little Rock crisis of 1957 and an occasional election-time outburst, little claim to public attention before that time. From the late 1940s into the mid-1950s sundry spy and Communist hunts were of concern, but the issue fairly well fizzled after that. Other issues which might be mentioned had even briefer or more erratic days in the sun: the food shortage of 1947, the MacArthur hearing of 1951, various space flights. Similarly, personal crisis for the Presidents such as heart attacks and major surgery for Presidents Eisenhower and Johnson and the attempted assassination of President Truman could not readily be fashioned into a predictor variable. In any event, these events seem to have far more impact on the stock market than on popularity ratings.

Scandal is a recurring feature of public awareness and thus is more promising as a potential variable in the analysis. Besides the scandals associated with alleged spies and Communists in the government during the McCarthy era and those associated with labor in the late 1950s, Americans, with greatly varying degrees of pain, have suffered through the five percenter scandal of 1949–50; charges of corruption in the RFC in 1951, in the Justice Department in 1952, and in the FHA in 1954; and scandals over Sherman Adams in 1958, over television quiz shows in 1959, over industry "payola" in the late 1950s, over Billie Sol Estes in 1962, and over Bobby Baker in 1963. While scandal is never worked into the regression analysis some preliminary suggestions as to its relevance to a "moral crisis" phenomenon which may in turn affect Presidential popularity are developed in Section VI below.

Some thought was given to including a "lame duck" variable when it was observed that the popularity of Presidents Truman and Johnson rose noticeably after they decided not to seek third terms. The trouble is, however, that President Eisenhower was a lame duck for his entire second term and it was found easier to ignore the whole idea than to decide what to do about this uncomfortable fact.

One domestic variable which did show some very minor promise was a dummy variable for the presence of a major strike. The variable takes on a zero value almost everywhere except in parts of President Truman's first term. After that time major strikes were rather unusual and, when they did occur, usually lasted for such a short time that there was barely time to have a public opinion survey conducted to test their effects. Despite these peculiarities, the variable did show statistical significance, though only after the Korean War dummy had been incorporated in the equation to allow for a major peculiarity of President Truman's *second* term. Substantively the variable suggests a popularity drop of less than three percentage points when a major strike is on and, as such a minor contributor, it is not included in the discussion below. Its small success, however, may suggest that further experimentation with the effects of specific domestic events could prove profitable.

III. Results without the War Variable

In summary the expected behavior of Presidential popularity is as follows. It is anticipated 1) that each President will experience in each term a general decline of popu-

larity; 2) that this decline will be interrupted from time to time with temporary upsurges associated with international crises and similar events; 3) that the decline will be accelerated in direct relation to increases in unemployment rates over those prevailing when the President began his term, but that improvement *in unemployment rates will not affect his popularity one way or the other; and 4) that the President will experience an additional loss of popularity if a war is on.*

In this section the relation of the first three variables to Presidential popularity will be assessed. In the next section the war variable will be added to the analysis.

The association between the first three variables and Presidential popularity is given in its baldest form in equation 1 in Table 1.[31] The equation explains a respectable, if not sensational, 22 percent of the variance. The coalition of minorities variable shows, in conformity with the speculation above, a significant negative relationship. The equation suggests that, in general, a President's popularity rating starts at 69 percent and declines at a rate of about six percentage points per year.

However, while the coefficients for the rally round the flag and economic slump variables are in the expected direction, they are not significant either in a statistical or a substantive sense. The trouble with the economic slump variable was anticipated in the discussion about it in Section II: the economic decline occurred during the relatively popular reign of President Eisenhower; while the slump seems to have hurt his popularity, even with the decline he remained popular compared to other Presidents; hence what is needed is a variable to take into account this peculiar "Eisenhower effect."

To account for this phenomenon, equation 2 mixes into the analysis a dummy variable for each of the Presidents. This formulation insists that all Presidents must decline (or increase) in popularity at the same rate but, unlike equation 1, it allows each President to begin at his own particular level. Thus peculiar effects of personality, style, and party and of differences in the conditions under which the President came into office can be taken into account.[32]

The addition improves things considerably. The fit is much better and the rally round the flag and economic slump variables attain respectable magnitudes in the predicted direction, although the rally round the flag variable does not quite reach statistical significance.

The equation suggests that the Presidents have declined at an overall rate of over five percentage points per year but that each has done so at his own particular level. President Truman's decline is measured from a starting point of 54.51 percent (when the dummy variables for the Eisenhower, Kennedy, and Johnson administrations are all zero). President Eisenhower declines from a much higher level, about 79 percent (54.51 + 24.08), President Kennedy from 78 percent, and President Johnson from 65 percent.

---

31. Each equation is displayed vertically. The dependent variable, the percentage approving the way the President is handling his job, has a mean of 57.5 and a standard deviation of 14.8. The number of cases is 292. The figures in parentheses are the standard errors for the respective partial regression coefficients. To be regarded statistically significant a regression coefficient should be, conventionally, at least twice its standard error. All equations reported in this study are significant (F test) at well beyond the .01 level. The Durbin-Watson *d* is an indicator of serial correlation which suggests decreasing positive serial correlation as the statistic approaches the value of 2.0. All equations in this study exhibit a statistically significant amount of positive serial correlation.

32. The dummy variables formalize the sort of discussion found in Neustadt, *op. cit.*, p. 98. They account for what a singer might call tessitura.

TABLE 1 Regression Results Including Administration Effects

	EQUATIONS			
	(1)	(2)	(3)	(4)
Intercept	69.37	54.51	68.15	71.52
Independent variables				
Coalitions of minorities (in years)	−6.14 (0.71)	−5.12 (0.48)		
Rally round the flag (in years)	−0.31 (1.95)	−2.15 (1.35)	−1.87 (1.07)	−2.63 (1.07)
Economic slump (in % unemployed)	−0.09 (0.96)	−3.18 (0.75)	−5.30 (0.60)	−5.86 (0.60)
Dummy variables for administrations				
Eisenhower		24.08 (1.42)	0.51 (2.29)	
Kennedy		23.87 (1.82)	11.33 (2.96)	
Johnson		10.46 (1.54)	4.26 (2.48)	
Coalition of minorities variable for administrations (in years)				
Truman			−11.44 (0.84)	−1.54 (0.50)
Eisenhower			0.83 (0.57)	0.13 (0.47)
Kennedy			−5.96 (1.36)	−1.58 (0.82)
Johnson			−9.12 (0.67)	−8.68 (0.50)
d	.13	.30	.46	.44
Standard error of estimate	13.16	8.88	6.86	7.06
R^2	.22	.65	.79	.78

The importance of these dummy variables clearly demonstrates that *an analysis of Presidential popularity cannot rely entirely on the variables discussed in Section II, but must also incorporate parameters designed to allow for the special character of each administration.* To an extent this is unfortunate. The beauty of equation 1 is that it affords a prediction of a President's popular rating simply by measuring how long he has been in office, how long it has been since the last rally point, and how many people are unemployed. Such predictions, however, would be quite inaccurate because the fit of the equation is rather poor. Instead one must include the administration variables, the magnitudes of which cannot be known until the President's term is over. So much for beauty.

In equation 3 administration effects are incorporated in a different manner, greatly improving fit and reducing serial correlation. In this formulation each

President is allowed to begin at his own level of popularity as in equation 2, but in addition each may decline (or increase) at his own rate: for each administration there is a different coefficient for the coalition of minorities variable. Three of the four values so generated are strongly significant while the magnitudes of the administration dummies drop greatly. When the administration dummies are dropped entirely from consideration, as in equation 4, the regression coefficients mostly remain firm and the fit of the equation is scarcely weakened. It is clear that *the important differences between administrations do not lie so much in different overall levels of popularity, but rather in the widely differing rates at which the coalition of minorities variable takes effect.*

The popular decline of Presidents Truman and Johnson has been almost precipitous. President Truman's rating fell off at some 11 or 12 percentage points per year while President Johnson declined at a rate of around 9 points a year. President Kennedy was noticeably more successful at holding on to his supporters. Then there is the Eisenhower phenomenon: in spite of all the rationalizations for the coalitions of minorities concept tediously arrayed in Section II, President Eisenhower's rating uncooperatively refuses to decline at all.[33]

In equation 3, Presidents who served two terms were required to begin each term at the same level and their rate of decline or increase also had to be the same in each term. Liberation from these restrictions is gained in the rather cluttered equation 5 of Table 2 which is like equation 3 except that it affords a term by term, rather than simply an administration by administration comparison. As can be seen President Eisenhower managed a statistically significant *increase* of popularity of some two and a half percentage points per year in his first term. His second term ratings showed a more human, but very minor and statistically non-significant decline.[34]

No important differences emerge in the Eisenhower phenomenon when the economic slump variable, which functions mainly during the Eisenhower years, is dropped from the equation.

No matter how the data are looked at then the conclusion remains the same. *President Eisenhower's ability to maintain his popularity, especially during his first term, is striking and unparallelled among the postwar Presidents.* An examination of some of the possible reasons for this phenomenon is conducted in Section VI below.

The rally round the flag and the economic slump variables emerge alive and well in equations 3, 4, and 5 (and 6). Both are usually statistically significant but their substantive importance varies as one moves from an administration by administration formulation of the coalition of minorities variable (equations 3 and 4) to the term by term formulation in Table 2. Specifically, the rally round the flag variable gets stronger while the economic slump variable weakens.

---

33. It was noted in Section I that some minor bias in these results is introduced by an embellished rate of "no opinion" in the first weeks of the Kennedy and first Eisenhower terms. As this rate declined, there was some tendency for the Presidents' approval *and* disapproval rates to rise. To see if this peculiarity had any major impact, equations 3 and 4 were recalculated using the percentage *disapproving* as the dependent variable. This manipulation causes no fundamental differences, although President Eisenhower's rating behaves a little less outrageously.

34. If the term dummies are dropped from the equation to attain a version comparable to equation 4, the Eisenhower phenomenon holds except that his first term increase drops to 2.00 (still significant) and his second term decrease is a slightly steeper —0.36 (still not significant).

TABLE 2 Regression Results Including Term
Effects and the War Variables

	EQUATIONS	
	(5)	(6)
Intercept	72.00	72.38
Independent variables		
Rally round the flag (in years)	−4.88 (1.04)	−6.15 (1.05)
Economic slump (in % unemployed)	−2.67 (0.65)	−3.72 (0.65)
Dummy variables for terms		
Truman — second	−15.25 (3.69)	−12.41 (3.57)
Eisenhower — first	−3.17 (3.15)	−2.41 (3.02)
Eisenhower — second	−5.30 (3.07)	−4.35 (2.94)
Kennedy	7.53 (3.29)	7.18 (3.14)
Johnson — first	7.14 (5.50)	6.77 (5.26)
Johnson — second	−1.15 (3.06)	−0.79 (3.25)
Coalition of minorities variable for terms (in years)		
Truman — first	−9.21 (1.41)	−8.93 (1.35)
Truman — second	−7.98 (1.00)	−2.83 (1.37)
Eisenhower — first	2.45 (0.85)	2.58 (0.82)
Eisenhower — second	−0.07 (0.65)	0.22 (0.62)
Kennedy	−5.11 (1.21)	−4.76 (1.16)
Johnson — first	−4.98 (14.01)	−3.71 (13.39)
Johnson — second	−8.15 (0.66)	−8.13 (0.80)
Dummy variables for wars		
Korea		−18.19 (3.43)
Vietnam		−0.28 (2.79)
d	.57	.67
Standard error of estimate	6.07	5.80
R^2	.84	.86

The rally round the flag variable is very much a parasite — it is designed to explain bumps and wiggles on a pattern measured mainly by the other variables. Consequently the rally round the flag variable does very poorly on its own and only begins to shine when the overall trends become well determined by the rest of the equation. In the end, *the rally round the flag variable suggests a popularity decline of around five or six percentage points for every year since the last rally point* — about the same magnitude as the coalition of minorities variable in its general state as in equations 1 and 2.

The declining fortunes of the economic slump variable suggest that the variable in equations 3 and 4 was partly covering for the differences between the two Eisenhower terms: the first term was associated with increasing popularity and a smaller recession, the second with somewhat declining popularity and a larger recession. With the Eisenhower terms more thoroughly differentiated in equation 5, the variable is reduced to a more purely economic function. The magnitude of the coefficient of the *economic slump variable* in this equation *suggests a decline of popularity of about three percentage points for every percentage point rise in the unemployment rate over the level holding when the President began his present term.* Since the unemployment rate has varied in the postwar period only from about 3 to 7 percent, the substantive impact of the economic slump variable on Presidential popularity is somewhat limited.

IV. Results with the War Variable Added

The variable designed to tap the impact on Presidential popularity of the wars in Korea and Vietnam was applied with no great confidence that it would prove to have an independent, added effect when the coalition of minorities had already been incorporated into the equation especially given the problem of multicollinearity. It is obvious from a perusal of a plot that, as noted in Section II and as demonstrated in equation 5, Presidents Truman and Johnson were in popular decline during their warless first terms.[35] Furthermore each was in clear decline in the first part of his second term before the wars started and it is not at all obvious that this trend altered when the wars began.

The equations suggest otherwise, however. When a war dummy was appended to the equations already discussed, it emerged significant and suggested that the presence of war depressed the popularity of Presidents Truman and Johnson by over seven percentage points.

The next step, obviously, was to set up a separate dummy variable for each war. This brought forth the incredible result documented in equation 6: *the Korean War had a large, significant, independent negative impact on President Truman's popularity of some 18 percentage points, but the Vietnam War had no independent impact on President Johnson's popularity at all.*

Confronted with a result like this, one's first impulse is to do something to make it go away. This impulse was fully indulged. Variables were transformed and transmuted, sections of the analysis were reformed or removed, potentially biassing

---

35. Regression statistics relating to President Johnson's first term are very unreliable, as the size of the standard errors suggests, because the popularity question was posed so few times during this brief period.

data were sectioned out. But nothing seemed to work. The relationship persisted. In fact under some manipulations the relationship became stronger.

One's second impulse, then, is to attempt to explain the result. One speculates.

The wars in Korea and Vietnam differed from each other in many respects, of course, but it seems unlikely that these differences can be used in any simple manner to explain the curious regression finding. This is the case because, as one study has indicated, public response to the wars themselves was much the same. Support for each war, high at first, declined as a logarithmic function of American casualties — quickly at first, then more slowly. The functions for each of the wars for comparable periods were quite similar. Furthermore both wars inspired support and opposition from much the same segments of the population.[36]

Therefore it is probably a sounder approach in seeking to explain the regression finding to look specifically at popular attitudes toward *the President's relation to the war*, rather than to perceptions of the war itself. A comment by Richard Neustadt seems strikingly relevant in this respect. "Truman," he observes, "seems to have run afoul of the twin notions that a wartime Chief Executive ought to be 'above politics' and that he ought to help the generals 'win.' "[37]

President Johnson seems to have run considerably less afoul. In seeking to keep the war "above politics," he assiduously cultivated bipartisan support for the war and repeatedly sought to demonstrate that the war effort was simply an extension of the policies and actions of previous Presidents. He was especially successful at generating public expressions of approval from the most popular Republican of them all: General Eisenhower. Vocal opposition to the war in Vietnam came either from groups largely unassociated with either party or from members of the President's own party. Then, when the latter opposition began to move from expressions of misgivings at congressional hearings to explicit challenges in the primaries, President Johnson removed himself from the battle precisely, he said, to keep the war "above politics." And, while there were occasional complaints from the right during Vietnam that President Johnson had adopted a "no win" policy there, these were continually being undercut by public statements from General William Westmoreland — a man highly respected by the right — insisting that he was receiving all the support he needed from the President and was getting it as fast as he needed it.

If these observations are sound, the single event which best differentiates the impact of the Korean and Vietnam wars on Presidential popularity was President Truman's dismissal of General Douglas MacArthur. That move was a major factor in the politicization of the war as Republicans took the General's side and echoed his complaints that it was the President's meddling in policy that was keeping the war from being won.[38]

---

36. John E. Mueller, "Patterns of Popular Support for the Wars in Korea and Vietnam," unpublished paper, Department of Political Science, University of Rochester, 1969.

37. *Op. cit.*, p. 97.

38. See John W. Spanier, *The Truman-MacArthur Controversy and the Korean War* (Cambridge, Mass.: Belknap, 1959); also Neustadt, *op. cit.*, passim; and Trumbull Higgins, *Korea and the Fall of MacArthur* (New York: Oxford, 1960). See also the data in George Belknap and Angus Campbell, "Political Party Identification and Attitudes Toward Foreign Policy," 15 *Public Opinion Quarterly* 601–23 (Winter 1951–52). Note especially the strong party polarization on the issue. That the public was strongly inclined to support General MacArthur in the dispute can be seen from poll data. The first polls, conducted as the General was making his triumphal, "old soldiers never die" return to the United States in April 1951, suggest more than twice as many people supported the General as sup-

The differing impact of the wars on Presidential popularity therefore may be due to the fact that Korea became "Truman's war" while Vietnam never in the same sense really became "Johnson's war."[39]

One other item of speculation might be put forth. Domestically, the war in Vietnam was accompanied by a profoundly important crisis as America confronted its long-ignored racial dilemma head on. There seems to have been nothing comparable during the Korean War. The clamor associated with McCarthyism comes to mind but many analysts feel that, however important to politicians, intellectuals, and journalists, McCarthyism was of rather less than major concern to public opinion.[40] Furthermore its dramatic climax, the Army-McCarthy hearings, took place months after the Korean War had ended and over a year after President Truman left office.

It may be, then, that the discontent associated with the racial crisis was enough by itself to cause much of President Johnson's popular decline and thus that the unhappiness over the Vietnam War could make little additional inroad. In the Truman case, there was no profound independent domestic source of discontent: his second term coalition of minorities decline is usually found as in equation 5 to have been less than his first term decline and when, as in equation 6, a variable has already accounted for the war effect, his decline is quite moderate. Thus in a sense there was "room" for the war to have an independent impact.

It would be wise in concluding this section to emphasize what has and what has not been said. It has *not* been argued that the war in Vietnam had nothing to do with President Johnson's decline in popularity and thus the analysis cannot really be used to refute the President's own estimation of the impact of Vietnam as indicated in the quotation that heads this study. However it is argued that whatever impact the war had was tapped by the other variables in the equation, especially the coalition of minorities variable which is specifically designed to account for general overall decline. When the same sort of analysis is applied in the Korean period it is found that a variable associated with the Korean war does show significance even after other variables have been taken into account. What the regression analysis shows therefore is that, while the Korean War does seem to have had an *independent, additional* impact on President Truman's decline in popularity, the Vietnam War shows no such relation to President Johnson's decline.

---

ported the President. As Neustadt suggests (*op cit.*, p. 97), emotion on the issue faded during the Senate Hearings on the issue which lasted until June and this seems to have been to the benefit of President Truman's position. The Truman point of view received its greatest support in late June and early July as peace talks were being begun. As the talks began to prove unproductive, however, public opinion began to revert to its previous support of General MacArthur, until, by the first days of 1952 (when the polling agencies grew bored with the issue), the MacArthur position was as strongly approved and President Truman's as strongly rejected as ever.

39. There is evidence which suggests that World War II, a much more popular (and much larger) war than either Korea or Vietnam, may have worked to the distinct *benefit* of President Roosevelt. (The National Opinion Research Center in its post-election poll in 1944 asked Roosevelt supporters if they would have voted for Dewey "if the war had been over." Enough answered in the affirmative to suggest that Dewey might well have won in a warless atmosphere. From data supplied by the Inter-University Consortium for Political Research.

40. Samuel A. Stouffer, *Communism, Conformity, and Civil Liberties* (Garden City, N.Y.: Doubleday, 1955), especially ch. 3; Campbell, *et al., op. cit.*, pp. 50–51; Nelson W. Polsby, "Toward an Explanation of McCarthyism," 8 *Political Studies* 250–71 (October 1960); Elmo Roper, *You and Your Leaders* (New York: Morrow, 1957), pp. 250–51.

V. The Residuals

An analysis of the residuals finds that equation 6 predicts worst in President Truman's first term. The President's extremely high initial ratings are not well predicted suggesting that the equation does not adequately account for the trauma of President Roosevelt's death[41] combined as it was with the ending of World War II and with important peace conferences. It was almost as if Americans were afraid to disapprove of President Truman.

From these spectacular highs, President Truman plunged to great lows during the labor turmoil of 1946. These ratings are also badly specified by the equation. The Truman popularity rose in early 1947, as the labor situation eased, and then declined for the rest of the term. Thus while President Truman's first term, like the other Democratic terms, shows an overall decline of popularity, that decline was considerably more erratic than the others. The dummy variable for strikes, discussed briefly in Section II, improved matters only slightly.

Beyond this, the residuals are reasonably well behaved. There are small but noticeable effects from the lame duck phenomenon at the end of the Truman and Johnson administrations and from the "no opinion" peculiarity of the initial weeks of the Eisenhower and Kennedy administrations. And here and there are data points whose magnitudes have somehow managed to escape specification by the variables in the regression equation. One can of course generate a unique explanation for each of these but this procedure clutters the analysis more than it is worth. Besides, the laws of sampling insist that Gallup must have made *some* mistakes.

As the magnitude of the Durbin-Watson d indicates, serial correlation has by no means been eliminated in the regression equations. Allowing the coalition of minorities variable to be specified for each term improved things considerably, but much is left to be desired.

VI. The Eisenhower Phenomenon

Great noise was made in Section II about the coalition of minorities variable with its stern prediction that a President's popularity would decline inexorably over his four year term. The noise was not entirely unjustified since the variable proved to be a hardy and tenacious predictor for the postwar Democratic administrations.

The variable fails for the Eisenhower administration, however, especially for the

---

41. In late November 1945, over six months after President Roosevelt's death, Gallup asked his sample, "In your opinion, who is the greatest person living or dead, in world history?" Fully 28 percent proffered Roosevelt's name. Abraham Lincoln was mentioned by 19 percent, Jesus Christ by 15 percent, and George Washington by 8 percent. No one else received more than 2 percent. And the aura lasted. A survey conducted in June 1949 in the city of Philadelphia (which had voted 59 percent for Roosevelt in 1944 as against a national rate of 55 percent) posed this question: "Could you tell us the name of a great person, living or dead whom you admire the most?" The most commonly mentioned names were Roosevelt with 42 percent, Lincoln with 9 percent, and Washington with 5 percent. (The absence of Jesus Christ on this latter list presumably can be laid to the peculiarities of question wording — or of Philadelphians.) Fillmore H. Sanford, "Public Orientation to Roosevelt," 15 *Public Opinion Quarterly* 190–91, 200 (Summer 1951). In 1948, Roper found 43 percent of a national sample offering Roosevelt's name when queried, "Considering all the men in America who have been prominent in public affairs during the past 50 years, which one or two have you admired the most?" Dwight Eisenhower was second at 17 percent. E. Roper, *op. cit.*, p. 22.

General's first term. The analysis suggests then that if a President wants to leave office a popular man he should either 1) be Dwight David Eisenhower, or 2) resign the day after inauguration.

The Eisenhower phenomenon, noted but left dangling without explanation or rationalization in Section III, deserves special examination. Why didn't President Eisenhower decline in popularity like everybody else? A number of suggestions can be proffered.

1. To begin with, credit must be given to President Eisenhower's *personal appeal:* he was extremely likeable — a quality very beneficial in a popularity contest and one lacked in abundance by, say, Lyndon Johnson. As Fillmore Sanford has observed, "The American people, in reacting to a national leader, put great emphasis on his personal warmth"[42] — a quality projected to an unusual degree by President Eisenhower. As part of this, he was able to project an image of integrity and sincerity which many found to be enormously attractive.[43]

2. Early in his first term President Eisenhower was able to present to the public one sensational achievement: he *ended the Korean War* — or, at any rate, presided over its end. This accomplishment was seen by the public as he left office to be a great one[44] and was used with profit by the Republicans in a Presidential campaign a full 15 years after it happened. From the standpoint of public opinion it may well have been the most favorable achievement turned in by any postwar President. As such it may have tended to overwhelm the negative impact of anything else the President did, at least for the first years of his administration. Some credit for this is given in the regression analysis since the signing of the truce is counted as a rally point, but this may be a totally inadequate recognition.

There is another aspect of President Eisenhower's first term which may not be sufficiently accounted for in the rally round the flag variable: the euphoria of the "spirit of Geneva" period toward the end of the term when the President's popularity should have been at its lowest ebb.

3. President Eisenhower's *amateur status* may also have worked to his benefit, at least for a while. The public may have been more willing to grant him the benefit of a doubt, to extend the "honeymoon" period, than it would for a President who is a political professional. It is also easier under these circumstances for the President to appear "above the battle" and thus to be blamed only belatedly and indirectly for political mishaps, thereby softening their impact.

4. President Eisenhower may have been curiously benefited by the fact that, especially on the domestic front, *he didn't do anything.*[45] Indeed analysts of the

---

42. *Op. cit.*, p. 198.

43. See Philip E. Converse and Georges Dupeux, "De Gaulle and Eisenhower: The Public Image of the Victorious General," in Angus Campbell, *et al.*, *Elections and the Political Order* (New York: Wiley, 1966), pp. 292–345.

44. In December 1960 the public was asked what it felt was Eisenhower's greatest accomplishment. The ending of the Korean War was mentioned by 11 percent and a related comment, "he kept us out of war," was suggested by an additional 32 percent. No other specific accomplishment was mentioned by more than 5 percent; only 3 percent mentioned anything having to do with the domestic scene. See also Neustadt, *op. cit.*, p. 98.

45. As Irving Kristol argues, ". . . when a conservative administration does take office, it pursues no coherent program but merely takes satisfaction in not doing the things that the liberals may be clamoring for. This, in effect, is what happened during the two terms of President Eisenhower . . ." "The Old Politics, the New Politics, and the *New*, New Politics," *New York Times Magazine*, November 24, 1968, p. 167.

Eisenhower administration often argue that its contribution lies in what it *didn't* do. The times called for consolidation, they argue, and President Eisenhower's achievement was that he neither innovated nor repealed, but was content to preside over a period of placidity in which he tacitly gave Republican respectability to major Democratic innovations of earlier years: the programs of the New Deal domestically and the policies of the Truman Doctrine internationally.[46]

In terms of the justification for the coalition of minorities variable as discussed in Section II, such behavior could have a peculiar result. It was assumed in part that the President would enact programs which, while approved by the majority, would alienate intense minorities which would gradually cumulate to his disadvantage. But suppose the President doesn't do anything. Those who want no change are happy while, if things are sufficiently ambiguous, those who support change have not really been denied by an explicit decision and can still patiently wait and hope. At some point of course those who want change begin to see that they are never going to get their desires and may become alienated, but this will be a delayed process. At least in moderate, placid times, a conservative policy may dissipate some of the power of the coalition of minorities phenomenon. Were polls available, one might find that President Warren Harding maintained his popularity as strikingly as President Eisenhower.

5. Although it might be difficult to sort out cause and effect, it is worth noting that President Eisenhower's first term (and most of his second) coincided with a *period of national goodness*. In a brilliant article Meg Greenfield has noted that "moral crises" as appraised and bemoaned by intellectuals seem to follow a cyclic pattern: we go through a period in which the popular journals are filled with articles telling us how bad we are after which there is a period of respite.[47]

Miss Greenfield's main indicator of these ethical cycles is exquisite: the number of items under the heading, "US: Moral Conditions," in the *Readers' Guide to Periodical Literature*. The pattern, elaborated and duly pedantified, is given in Table 3. As she notes, our first moral crisis in the postwar period arose in the early 1950s and was associated with "five percenters, deep freezes, mink coats, the Kefauver hearings and a series of basketball fixes," while "the symbols of our present [1961] decline are Charles Van Doren, payola, cheating in school, and the decision of Frances Gary Powers not to kill himself." We never recovered as thoroughly from that crisis as we did from the earlier one for, as the crisis showed signs of waning (the success of the Peace Corps began to show how good we were at heart), new elements — Billie Sol Estes, Bobby Baker, President Kennedy's assassination, campus revolts, the hippies, and the city riots — proved once again that we have a "sick society." Our moral crises are regenerated every eight years and seem to coincide with the end of Presidential administrations.[48]

Of course objective indicators of public morality have not been careening in this manner. Much of the fluctuation in the Greenfield index is no doubt due to journalistic fad. A sensational fraud, scandal or disruption causes theologians, journalists, and other intellectuals to sociologize: society is sick. Others pick up the idea and it

---

46. See Clinton Rossiter, *The American Presidency* (New York: Harcourt, Brace, 1960), pp. 161–78.

47. Meg Greenfield, "The Great American Morality Play," *The Reporter*, June 8, 1961, pp. 13–18.

48. It may, or then again may not, be worth noting that Presidential elections in which the incumbent party was removed, 1952, 1960, and 1968, occurred during moral crises while the elections in which the President was retained, 1948, 1956, and 1964, all took place during times of relative goodness.

TABLE 3   The Greenfield Index

Number of Items under the Heading, "US: Moral Conditions" in *Readers' Guide to Periodical Literature*, 1945–1968, by year	
1945	1
1946	0
1947	8
1948	1
1949	1
1950	3
1951	35
1952	17
1953	1
1954	4
1955	2
1956	0
1957	7
1958	0
1959	9
1960	32
1961	23
1962	10
1963	11
1964	5
1965	6
1966	7
1967	18
1968	10

blossoms into a full moral crisis. In a year or two the theme no longer sells magazines and the space is filled with other profundities. Fraud, scandal, and disruption continue, but the moral crisis eases.

But — and this is a logical and empirical leap of some magnitude — to the extent that these patterns reflect and influence public attitudes, they may be relevant to Presidential popularity. The early Eisenhower years are notable for their absence of moral anguish and they differ from other between-crisis periods in an important respect: not only were we not demonstrably bad, we were positively good for we were undergoing a religious revival. Miss Greenfield looked at the items under the heading, "US: Religious Institutions." She finds only six items in the 1951–53 period, but 25 in 1953–55 while "in the 1955–57 volume, at the height of our virtue . . . the religious listings reached thirty-four with twenty-eight 'see alsos.' "

If we were so good ourselves, how could we possibly find fault in our leader?

VII. Further Research

This study has been reasonably successful at generating a regression equation based on only four rather simple variables, which fits quite well the erratic behavior over 24 years of the Presidential popularity index. There is, however, much room for improvement and refinement.

Little has been done to separate out from the coalition of minorities variable the specific and divergent influences of domestic events on Presidential popularity. There was one variable designed to account in a general way for changes in the economy, some limited analysis was made of the relevance of major strikes, and comments were interjected about the role of scandal and "moral crisis." But domestic life is considerably more complicated than this and more precise social, political, and economic indicators can be sought.

It would also be of value to get better estimates of the impact of different *kinds* of international events on Presidential popularity — although, as already suggested, such analysis may find that all dramatic international events affect popularity in much the same way no matter how they may differ in historical significance.[49]

The analysis strongly suggests that Presidential style as well as the ideological and political nature of the administration and the times can make a sizeable difference in the way popularity ratings behave. A more precise assessment of these relationships would be most desirable.

The study has dealt entirely with general popular approval of the President. Left unexamined are the ways population groups differ in their approach to the President. Supporters of the President's own party, for example, are more likely to approve the way he handles his job. Presumably they are also relatively hard to alienate, are more likely to be enchanted by his successes, and are more tolerant of his blunders.

It should also be possible to extend the analysis to other bodies of data. Somewhat comparable data from the Roosevelt administration are available. Although the popularity question was posed with far less regularity in those days (and was largely dropped during World War II) and although there are problems with varying question wording, students of President Roosevelt's popularity ratings emerge with findings which fit well with those of this study.[50] The popularity ratings of Governors and Senators in states with active statewide polls can also be analyzed as can data on national leaders from such countries as Britain, Canada, and France.[51]

VIII. Summary

This investigation has applied multiple regression analysis to the behavior of the responses to the Gallup Poll's Presidential popularity question in the 24 year period from the beginning of the Truman administration to the end of the Johnson administration. Predictor variables include a measure of the length of time the incumbent has been in office as well as variables which attempt to assess the influence

49. It may prove valuable to attempt to see how spectacular and cumulative international events and shifts in governmental policy — to use the distinction made by Karl Deutsch and Richard Merritt — differ in impact. "Effects of Events on National and International Images" in Herbert C. Kelman (ed.) *International Behavior* (New York: Holt, 1965), pp. 132–87.

50. Wesley C. Clark has found some relation between the Roosevelt popularity and the state of the economy in the 1937–1940 period. He also notes a general "downward slant" in the rating over time and finds a rise of popularity during international crises. ("Economic Aspects of a President's Popularity," Ph.D. Dissertation, University of Pennsylvania, 1943, pp. 41, 28, 35). See also B. Roper, *op. cit.*, and E. Roper, *op. cit.*, chapters 2 and 3. And V. O. Key has observed that during 1940 "the popularity of Roosevelt rose and fell with European crises." *Politics, Parties and Pressure Groups* (New York: Crowell, 1952, 3rd. ed.), p. 596 (cited in Waltz, *op. cit.*, p. 272.)

51. British observes have noted an apparent relation between unemployment and party preference in their country: rising unemployment seems to have benefited Labor while declining unemployment favors the Tories. Henry Durant, "Indirect Influences on Voting Behavior," 1 *Polls* 7–11 (Spring 1965). Extensive data from France on the popularity of President De Gaulle have been published: for example, *Gallup Opinion Index*, March 1968, pp. 27–28. A study by Howard Rosenthal has investigated regional aspects of the General's popularity. "The Popularity of Charles De Gaulle: Findings from Archive-based Research," 31 *Public Opinion Quarterly* 381–98 (Fall 1967).

on his rating of major international events, economic slump, and war. Depite the austerity of this representation of a presumably complex process, the fit of the resulting equation was very good: it explained 86 percent of the variance in Presidential popularity.

This degree of fit could only be attained, however, by allowing the special character of each Presidential administration to be expressed in the equation. Thus it does not seem possible to predict a given President's popularity well simply by taking into account such general phenomena as the state of the economy or of international affairs.

The first variable, dubbed the "coalition of minorities" variable, found, as expected, the popularity of most Presidents to be in decline during each term. The important differences between administrations do not lie so much in different overall levels of popularity, but rather in the widely differing rates at which this coalition of minorities variable takes effect. Specifically, the popular decline of Presidents Truman and Johnson was quite steep while President Kennedy seems to have been somewhat better at maintaining his popularity. Present Eisehnower's popularity did not significantly decline at all during his second term and actually increased during his first term.

In considering this Eisenhower phenomenon it is suggested that a combination of several causes may be relevant: the President's personal appeal, his ending of the Korean War, his amateur status, his domestic conservatism at a time when such a policy was acceptable, and his fortune in coming to office at a time of national goodness.

The second variable, the "rally round the flag" variable, predicts short term boosts in a President's popularity whenever there occurs an international crisis or a similar event. The variable proves to be a sturdy one and suggests a popular decline of about five or six percentage points for every year since the last "rally point."

Economic effects were estimated in the third variable. The variable could only be made to function if it was assumed that an economy in slump harms a President's popularity, but an economy in boom does not help his rating. A decline of popularity of about three percentage points is suggested for every percentage point rise in the unemployment rate over the level holding when the President began his present term.

The fourth variable attempted to take into account the influence of war on Presidential popularity. It was found that the Korean War had a large, significant independent negative impact on President Truman's popularity of some 18 percentage points, but that the Vietnam War had no independent impact on President Johnson's popularity at all. It is suggested that this difference may be due to the relationship between the Presidents and the wars: President Truman was less able than President Johnson to keep the war "above" partisan politics and he seemed to the public to be interfering and restraining the generals. The absence in the Truman case of a domestic crisis comparable to the racial turmoil of the Johnson era may also be relevant.

CHAPTER 3

Causal Analysis in Political Science

An underlying or implicit motivation in more sophisticated forms of data analysis in political science reflects an ultimate concern for cause. From Aristotle's symbolic logic treatment of the causes of war to the modern political scientist's concern for explanations of mass violence, our discipline has developed a variety of empirical-theoretical explanations of political phenomena. However, the bulk of this theoretical revolution has occurred only recently[1] and that which has developed is largely informal. Despite the inherent relationship between causal thinking and independent-dependent variable analysis, formal-empirical treatment of cause is a relatively recent phenomenon. In general, causal analysis as a body of techniques has been constrained by necessary mathematical assumptions,[2] underdeveloped techniques, untrained political scientists, complexity of political phenomena, measurement problems, a fear of explicit causal statements,[3] and philosophical "hang-ups." The latter two are of particular importance: political scientists have approached real world phenomena from a "variable" perspective, yet a rich philosophical tradition, its merits aside, has constrained our search for causal answers to empirical questions.[4]

---

1. See David Easton, *The Political System* (New York: Alfred A. Knopf, 1953).

2. See Hayward R. Alker, Jr., "Statistics and Politics: The Need for Causal Data Analysis," in *Politics and the Social Sciences*, ed. Seymour M. Lipset (New York: Oxford University Press, 1969), pp. 244–313, for statistical-mathematical problems in causal inference.

3. For a discussion of our reluctance to use causal language see Hayward R. Alker, Jr., "Causal Inference and Political Analysis," in *Mathematical Applications in Political Science II*, ed. Joseph L. Bernd (Dallas: Southern Methodist University Press, 1966), pp. 7–44.

4. See ibid. for Alker's discussion of Hume. Also see Palumbo's discussion of the Humean problem which limits proven causal relationships to specific and physical entities: Dennis J. Palumbo, "Causal Inference and Indeterminacy in Political Behavior: Some Theoretical and Statistical Problems" (Paper presented at the Annual Meeting of the American Political Science Association, New York, September, 1969), pp. 3ff.

Herbert Simon suggests that "cause" can perform a useful function if it is "carefully scrubbed free of any undesirable philosophic adhesions."[5] Even for those who think in theoretic terms, there is frequently a serious gap between theory and research because we test in terms of variations.[6] Although important arguments exist beyond the scope of this chapter, a richer appreciation for causal analysis will enable the researcher to more adequately perform the analytical function, develop more formal theory from verbal statements,[7] and develop deductive theory which assumes an inductive process of variable inclusion.

Concepts of Control

Two necessary conditions for causal statements are temporal ordering and control.[8] The question of time sequence of variables is usually answered by the means of measurement. That is, the use of concrete empirical measures in a multivariate scheme locate the data point along a time dimension as well as a case and variable dimension. The concept of control, although explored briefly in our discussion of partial correlation, is more difficult. The use of controls enables the researcher to make statements about explicit, unconfounded, and nonspurious relationships. The ultimate statistical goal is to measure unique covariance between variables, such that the relationship between X and Y is not changed by the introduction of Z. Both Alker and Lazarsfeld define such controlled and nonspurious relationships as "causal."[9]

The concept of control, however, has a variety of meanings, particularly when we compare experimental and statistical controls.[10] The argument for "scientific" or experimental controls suggests that greater control, precision, and manipulability lead to conclusive answers and the testing of precise theoretical questions. Often the claimed advantages of these controls blind the researcher from the following considerations: there are disadvantages to such a design; certain fields of study find the design inapplicable; research would be retarded if the high goals of experimentation were stressed; and statistical controls are very useful in most fields of endeavor and certainly not a poor substitute for more "scientific" study.

Scientific controls and experimentation involve the creation of a specially suited situation and precision in the control and manipulation of variables. The creation of a specially suited situation is difficult in most social sciences. Such a scheme

---

5. Cited in Hayward R. Alker, Jr., *Mathematics and Politics* (New York: Macmillan, 1965), p. 112.

6. Hubert M. Blalock Jr., *Causal Inferences in Nonexperimental Research* (Chapel Hill: The University of North Carolina Press, 1964), pp. 11ff.

7. See Hubert M. Blalock, Jr., *Theory Construction: From Verbal to Mathematical Formulations* (Englewood Cliffs, N.J.: Prentice-Hall, 1969).

8. Alker, *Mathematics and Politics*, p. 115.

9. Ibid., and Paul Lazarsfeld, "The Algebra of Dichotomous Systems," in *Item Analysis and Prediction*, ed. H. Solomon (Stanford: Stanford University Press, 1959), pp. 145ff.

10. Claire Selltiz et al., *Research Methods in Social Relations*, rev. ed. (New York: Holt, Rinehart and Winston, 1959), chap. 4; Fred N. Kerlinger, *Foundations of Behavioral Research* (New York: Holt, Rinehart and Winston, 1964), pp. 275–375; Hanan C. Selvin, "A Critique of Tests of Significance in Survey Research," *American Sociological Review* 22 (1957): 519–27; Robert McGinnis, "Randomization and Inference in Sociological Research," *American Sociological Review* 23 (1958): 408–14; Leslie Kish, "Some Statistical Problems in Research Design," *American Sociological Review* 24 (1959): 328–38; and Donald T. Campbell and Julian C. Stanley, *Experimental and Quasi-Experimental Designs for Research* (Chicago: Rand McNally, 1963).

has advantages of control and randomization that are not as complete in ex post facto research, yet statistical control and a random sampling can be achieved despite the fact that the investigator rather than the experimenter must take things as they are. In a truly scientific situation (which rarely if ever exists) the probability that X is in reality related to Y is greater than it is in an ex post facto situation, because the control of X and other possible X's is greater. Such claimed precision, however, does not render statistical controls and ex post facto research inadequate. In political science it is difficult, if not impossible, to expose a group to X political variables; the researcher cannot create political variables and "treat" individuals as an agronomist "treats" the soil. Even the laboratory experiment can omit variables; that is, no matter how carefully controlled the study, there is no way to be completely certain of the validity of inferences that may be drawn. This is especially true in the social sciences where there is little knowledge of what factors should be controlled and where many relevant factors are almost impossible to control (e.g., individual characteristics). In an experimental situation the researcher can introduce controls and provisions can be made for testing specific alternative causal factors, but in dealing with political phenomena, manipulation of the independent variable is not feasible. For example, in studying political socialization the political scientist will rarely be able to "scientifically" control for various childrearing conditions. He must locate individuals exposed to different types of socialization and test the outcomes of that process. If correlations exist, there is evidence of concomitant variation. As Hovland suggests, "it is not, for example, feasible to modify voting behavior by manipulation of the issues dicussed by the opposed parties during a particular campaign."[11] The political scientist gets variation by selecting individuals in whom the variable is present, not by direct manipulation of the variable itself.

The control of extraneous variables is of particular concern to sciences which necessitate multiple variable analysis. More scientific controls would include the following: (1) build the extraneous variable into the design as an independent variable, if it can be located and identified. (2) Eliminate the variable as a variable; that is, choose subjects so that they are as homogeneous as possible on the influential independent variable. A serious difficulty is that the researcher can then only generalize to that grouping. (3) A method of controlling all possible variables is through a process of randomization, however, the political scientist cannot always, if ever, assign cases randomly to different conditions. The experimenter in the natural sciences has manipulative control and he can randomize and assign treatments to groups at random. (4) A final general category of control is through the process of matching subjects. When dealing with political data it is difficult to obtain equivalent groups and the underlying assumption of experimental design is that the groups being compared are equivalent before the introduction of treatments.[12] The variable on which matching is based must be substantially related to the dependent variable or matching is useless. It is difficult to know which factors are most important to use in a case by case matching, and with more factors there is a loss of precision. If individuals are to be matched on several factors there must be a large number of cases and all these cases must be measured in the relevant

11. Carl I. Hovland, "Reconciling Conflicting Results Derived from Experimental and Survey Studies of Attitude Change," *American Psychologist* 14 (1959): 15.
12. Selltiz et al., *Research Methods in Social Relations*, chap. 4.

factors. Therefore, in most social science research, matching loses subjects and it is difficult to find matched pairs if that matching must be done on a large number of variables. When those observations for which there are no similar cases have to be eliminated, the randomness assumption is altered: it makes it difficult to determine the nature of the population to which the researcher is generalizing. Practical difficulties and our limited knowledge of the importance of variables makes it impossible to control for all relevant variables in the matching process.

Other problems are created by experimental situations. With "scientific" controls the independent variables lack strength and it is difficult to create forces strong enough to be measurable because the variables operate most strongly in real-life situations. In spite of increased control, it is likely that factors will be so weak that no differences will be apparent between conditions created experimentally. There is also a greater temptation to interpret results incorrectly. Experimenters have been criticized for their attempts to extrapolate beyond the laboratory; that is, experiments suffer from a lack of external validity. At times when statistical tests are weak on controls, they are strong on representation, an important element to all social sciences. Political variables occur in a variety of contexts and therefore one must frequently study a representative sample of situations in which the political variables occur. To achieve this, political scientists must often abandon notions of experimental control and take the interactions among variables as they find them in the particular situations included in the sample.

To reiterate, proponents of experimental controls claim that they enable the simultaneous gathering of various lines of evidence, the manipulation of independent variables, and greater causal certainty. This is not to suggest that such a design is inapplicable to political phenomena; we have avoided the use of such designs too frequently. In this context, popular misconceptions are evident with regard to causality. If the experimenter is more concerned with cause, and he may not be, it does not follow that causal analysis is the only legitimate analysis for political science.[13] Those who demand such controls in the name of cause fail to realize that a prime function of statistics is the discovery of relationships and that the meaning given to data depends on the user rather than an inherent element of the statistical test. Furthermore, statistical controls and important developments in causal modeling assist us in making causal inferences. One type of basic evidence necessary for such inference is concomitant variation: it must be shown that X and Y vary together, and that Y should appear in more cases where X is present than in cases where X is absent. In multiple variable analysis we can speak of X being related to Y with certain controls, and at this level we can begin to speak of cause and apply our substantive knowledge. Complex statistical methods get at sophisticated concepts such as interaction and interrelationship, and they handle a large number of independent variables more successfully than the experimenter who finds it difficult to manipulate several variables simultaneously. Social scientists must aim for more scientific controls, but a more pragmatic goal is the improvement and more rigorous use of applied statistical tools. The realities of political data, as well as factors of speed and economy, necessitate that statistical methods must constitute a good substitute for more scientific procedures. Causal modeling is a quantitative technique which efficiently applies the concepts of statistical control.

13. See the Selvin, McGinnis, and Kish controversy cited in n.10.

Simon-Blalock Technique and Path Analysis

Although there are a number of nonexperimental multivariate data analysis techniques useful in making causal statements, the central logic of causal analysis is built upon the Simon-Blalock technique and its predecessors. In the context of control, however, other techniques can yield causal information:[14] (1) Variance and covariance techniques: the analysis of variance isolates main effects, interaction effects, and random error effects and covariance analysis and variance component models provide relevant information.[15] (2) Regression techniques: multiple regression provides the essential regression coefficients and partial correlation coefficients, and step-wise regression parsimoniously maximizes explanatory power by repeatedly adding variables until the increment in explanatory ability is due only to random effect (i.e., not significant), and interaction-seeking regression models combine step-wise procedures and a means of increasing variance explained by taking into account interaction effects. The best example of the latter is an Automatic Interaction Detector routine which Alker describes as the nearest thing to "automated, interaction-seeking, nonlinear causal modeling."[16] (3) Factor analytic techniques (see chapter 4). (4) Reciprocal causal modeling: this technique attempts to treat complex two-way causation schemes.[17] A related technique which assesses the direction of causality is cross-lagged correlation.[18] It relies upon the temporal sequence assumption and the time lag between cause and effect.[19] For example, the correlation between X_{t_1} and Y_{t_2} must be greater than the correlation between X_{t_2} and Y_{t_1}. (5) Path analysis.[20] This technique involves procedures and assumptions similar to the Simon-Blalock technique. The goal is to assess the relative weight of paths of causal influence through the use of path coefficients which measure the relative influence of one variable on the correlation between two other variables.[21]

---

14. Alker, in *Politics and the Social Sciences*, ed. Lipset, pp. 248–65.

15. Donald Stokes, "A Variance Components Model of Political Effects," in *Mathematical Applications in Political Science I*, ed. John M. Claunch (Dallas: Southern Methodist University Press, 1965), pp. 61–85.

16. In *Politics and the Social Sciences*, ed. Lipset, p. 258.

17. Alker, in *Mathematical Applications in Political Science II*, ed. Bernd, pp. 27–36; Blalock, *Theory Construction*, chap. 6; and Blalock, ed., *Causal Models in the Social Sciences* (Chicago: Aldine-Atherton, 1971), part III.

18. Campbell and Stanley, *Experimental and Quasi-Experimental Designs for Research*, and Blalock, *Causal Inferences in Nonexperimental Research*, pp. 191–93.

19. Herbert Simon, "Spurious Correlation: A Causal Interpretation," in *Models of Man*, ed. Simon (New York: John Wiley, 1957), chap. 2, and Alker, *Mathematics and Politics*, chap. 6.

20. Related distinctions are made for "dependence analysis." For a discussion of Simon-Blalock models as a special case of this general method and its relationship to Sewall Wright's techniques, see Raymond Boudon, "A Method of Linear Causal Analysis: Dependence Analysis," *American Sociological Review* 30 (1965): 365–74, and his "A New Look at Correlation Analysis," in *Methodology in Social Research*, ed. Hubert M. Blalock and Ann B. Blalock (New York: McGraw-Hill, 1968), pp. 199–235. His "dependence coefficients" are extensions of the regression concept and measures of direct influence of one variable on another. When causal equations can be identified, they are regression coefficients.

21. Blalock, *Casual Inferences in Nonexperimental Research*, p. 192–93; Kenneth C. Land, "Principles of Path Analysis," in *Sociological Methodology*, 1969, ed. Edgar F. Borgatta (San Francisco: Jossey-Bass, 1969), pp. 3–37; David R. Heise, "Problems in Path Analysis and Causal Inference," ibid., pp. 38–73; Otis Dudley Duncan, "Contingencies in Constructing Causal Models," ibid., pp. 74–112.

The measures combine features of correlation[22] and regression coefficients.[23] Most of the applications of the technique have occurred in more experimental settings,[24] and Blalock contends that it is most useful in areas which are well developed theoretically and where a dependent variable is highly associated with others in the explicit variable system.[25] Since the derivation of path coefficients is so closely allied to Simon-Blalock procedures, we will treat them later in this chapter.

The Simon-Blalock method and alternative approaches to causal modeling involve several steps in data analysis: model building, model testing, model alteration, and the assignment of numerical weights to possible causal links between variables. The emphasis is on hypothetical models of reality tested for their correspondence with the real world as the political scientist has measured it. In order to overcome the philosophical suggestions of cause and an empirically based contention that no two events are exactly repeated and that no sociopolitical realities remain the same over time, Blalock has emphasized the use of theoretical models of reality.[26] Some researchers, however, are able to contend that an understanding of real world phenomena necessitates certain assumptions which they can readily accept: that events are more than unique and that some phenomena have some constant properties over time. For those unwilling to accept such propositions, the use of theoretical models of reality is an alternative escape.

The concept of causal inference in the social sciences is borrowed from the concept of forcing in physics. The mere covariation of two or more measured political phenomena is insufficient. Our ultimate goal is to make empirical statements of forcing or producing, e.g., X produces changes in Y. Nevertheless, the measurement of covariation is an essential first step. That is, measures of the strength of relationship or the dispersion of data points about a regression line such as the correlation coefficient and its square, the coefficient of determination, provide necessary information about the degree of association between variables. The researcher should always have information about sampling inference and the shape of the data distribution. That is, does the relationship exist in the universe (statistical significance) or was it determined by mere chance? Are the data linear in shape or have they been forced into a linear equation which distorts the underlying distributions? An even more important item is the form of the data, i.e., the slope of the line of least squares (regression) which yields information about the increases in one variable relative to unit increases in another variable. It is the latter, regression coefficients, which give us the "laws of science"[27] whereas the coefficient of determination describes the degree of relationship. The correlation coefficient squared is symmetrical and in a multivariate setting it has cumulative characteristics, i.e., by adding a variety of

22. Sewall Wright, "Path Coefficients and Path Regressions: Alternative or Complementary Concepts," *Biometrics* 16 (1960): 189–202.

23. For an analogy between path coefficients and factor loadings see Malcolm E. Turner and Charles D. Stevens, "The Regression Analysis of Causal Paths," *Biometrics* 15 (1959): 236–58.

24. For a discussion of biological applications see John W. Tukey, "Causation, Regression and Path Analysis," in *Statistics and Mathematics in Biology*, ed. Oscar Kempthorne et al. (Ames: Iowa State College Press, 1954), pp. 35–67. For sociological applications see Otis D. Duncan, "Path Analysis: Sociological Examples," *American Journal of Sociology* 27 (1966): 1–16.

25. *Causal Inferences in Nonexperimental Research*, p. 192. Also see his "Path Coefficients versus Regression Coefficients," *American Journal of Sociology* 72 (1967): 675–76.

26. *Causal Inferences in Nonexperimental Research*, p. 14.

27. Ibid., p. 51.

potentially spurious variables to the variable system we can increase the amount of explained variance. We not only need to know what proportion of the dependent variable is explained by the independent variable(s), but the extent to which the dependent variable changes with changes in the independent variable(s). Assuming that we begin with measured political variables and a theoretical framework that leads to a model of reality, measures must be chosen with this model in mind. Because the researcher wants it to make a difference as to which variables are independent and dependent, he will come to rely upon the use of regression coefficients. That is, $b_{yx} \neq b_{xy}$ while r remains the same. It makes a difference if we are predicting X from Y or Y from X and the choice of regression coefficients should reflect the underlying theoretical model.[28] Yet correlation coefficients have a particular usefulness in this scheme beyond their contribution to sampling inference and measures of association. Their relationships to regression coefficients makes them useful for testing alternative models.

Assumptions

The measurement and analysis of causality requires that we state causal concepts in precise and abstract form applicable to mathematical modeling. The result is a system of equations linking the fundamental relationships between variables. Such equation systems make testable assumptions about basic philosophically related aspects of cause. Alker traces the philosophical linkages and defines causal components to include:[29] (1) asymmetry — cause precedes effect; (2) contiguity — direct links between cause and effect; (3) lawfulness — empirical generalizations; (4) determinativeness — the concept of producing changes; and (5) *ceteris paribus* — tentative conclusions are required because of the "other things being equal" assumption. From the above we can proceed to mathematics and assume that causal laws can be stated as linear and additive equations, that in order to move away from purely deterministic or single cause theories we can approach stochastic or probabilistic theories by making assumptions about inferences outside the variable system (random or error or residual terms), that *ceteris paribus* constraints relate to the error terms, that independent and dependent variables are identifiable, and that the linkages between them can be measured.

Proceeding from these general assumptions which enable quantitative treatment of causal inferences, the Simon-Blalock technique in particular requires certain assumptions which make it operational and relatively easy to interpret. Despite a variety of valid criticisms[30] the assumptions have limited the technique to simpler statistical rather than mathematical analysis and therefore have stimulated its application to political data. These assumptions can be summarized in four categories.[31]

(1) Level of measurement: because the technique is an extension of regression analysis it assumes that variables are measured intervally. In theory, the use of

28. For a defense of regression coefficients see Simon, in *Models of Man*, ed. Simon, chap. 2, and for a critique of correlation see Tukey, in *Statistics and Mathematics in Biology*, ed. Kempthorne et al., pp. 35–67.

29. In *Mathematical Applications in Political Science II*, ed. Bernd, pp. 9–13.

30. For a discussion of alternatives see ibid., pp. 7–41.

31. For extensive treatment see Blalock, *Causal Inferences in Nonexperimental Research*, chap. 2.

nominal categories distorts relationships and the interval level assumption enables the use of built-in statistical controls (partials) and an examination of incremental changes in one variable associated with incremental changes in another (regression coefficients). The use of statistical controls, in turn, assists us in testing for a crucial element — spurious correlation.[32] We want to discover if the relationship between variables persists or disappears when other variables are included in the scheme of analysis. However, the extent to which levels of measurement make a difference is an area clearly in need of specification in the social sciences. Blalock[33] suggests flexibility on this question, i.e., the necessity of comparing the results of different procedures such as tabular controls for nominal data and a variety of ordinal based techniques. Other alternatives suggest the use of dummy variables and related techniques.

(2) Shape of the data: the use of linear regression techniques assumes that the data are distributed along a straight line through a cluster of data points, yet theoretically, there is nothing to prevent us from applying curvilinear techniques to such a scheme. Such applications, however, have been limited.[34] A related assumption is that of additivity or the lack of built-in interactive terms.[35]

(3) Direction of causation: by assuming that causation is hierarchical (one-way or asymmetrical), coefficients of relationships can be estimated relatively easily and different models based on alternative sets of equations can be tested.[36] More complicated techniques for treating reciprocal causation are in their infancy. The one-way assumption enables ease of handling and assumes that each variable after the first independent variable is a dependent variable influenced by prior independent variables. That is, each variable is defined recursively or only in terms of a previous variable. This enables us to write a set of recursive or hierarchical equations which build incrementally toward a final dependent variable. In a three-variable scheme such as the one in figure 3.1, it means that the arrows of causal inference always go forward and never back. If we take a regression coefficient as an example of a measure of influence, this results in a matrix of regression coefficients for three variables, where one side of the diagonal is zero or blank.

	X_1	X_2	X_3
X_1	1	0	0
X_2	b_{21}	1	0
X_3	b_{31}	b_{32}	1

That is, such that X_1 is regressed on X_2 (b_{21}), but X_2 is not regressed on X_1.

(4) Outside influences and error: the basic difficulty in defining causal systems is our inability of knowing what all the relevant variables are and building them

---

32. Simon, in *Models of Man*, ed. Simon, chap. 2.

33. *Causal Inferences in Nonexperimental Research*, pp. 35, 143.

34. Ibid., p. 44, and Blalock, *Theory Construction*, pp. 86, 101.

35. Blalock, "Theory Building and the Statistical Concept of Interaction," *American Sociological Review* 30 (1965): 374–80.

36. Alker, in *Mathematical Applications in Political Science II*, ed. Bernd, pp. 15–16.

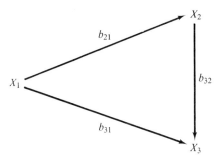

FIGURE 3.1

into the variable system. Because we are never sure of this and because causal laws are applicable to isolated systems, certain "simplifying assumptions"[37] must be made about the variables outside that system. That is, we recognize that there are "error terms" influencing each of the variables in the system. This kind of error is transmitted through the system or passed from one variable to another. For example, in a simple three variable linear scheme, error is accumulated in each variable. That is, each may be influenced by some undetermined outside force plus the accumulated error from other variables.

$$X_1 \quad \rightarrow \quad X_2 \quad \rightarrow \quad X_3$$
$$\uparrow \qquad\quad \uparrow \qquad\quad \uparrow$$
$$e_1 \qquad\quad e_2 \qquad\quad e_3$$

An indication that such error is not present can be estimated from regression coefficients between the variables. For example, a linkage between X_1 and X_2 of b_{21} equals .7, and X_2 and X_3 of b_{32} equals .8, when the total path (b_{31}) is merely the product of the other two paths ($b_{21} \cdot b_{32}$) or .56. The Simon-Blalock model allows for outside error if certain assumptions are made about that error. The basic assumption is that outside influences are independent of each other; that a major outside cause of a variable in the system operates only on one variable in that system.[38] That is, the error terms are uncorrelated and therefore the expected product of error terms is 0 $[E(e_i \cdot e_j) = 0]$. If there are outside influences on a dependent variable (remembering that all but the first variable in the system is dependent on previous variables in the system), ones that produce unexplained variation in this dependent variable, they cannot be related to the independent variables which are built in. Therefore, the error terms which are hypothetically influencing a dependent variable are assumed to be creating variation in that variable which is unrelated to that created by the independent variables.

It is obvious that we can never say anything very exact about error terms which remain unmeasured and unidentified. The goal is to bring in disturbing influences;

---

37. Blalock, *Causal Inferences in Nonexperimental Research*, pp. 13–14.

38. See Alker, in *Mathematical Applications in Political Science II*, ed. Bernd, pp. 16–17, for a discussion of correlated error techniques.

that is, if the variable is known it should be included in the variable system. However, this raises a question about the extent to which independent variables may be related to each other. This is the problem of multicollinearity or high interrelationship between independent variables. The inclusion of many interrelated independent variables, despite the fact that they improve estimation or prediction, should be avoided for conceptual clarity. Sometimes this can be accomplished by reducing variables into an index, assuming that the index is not measuring the same thing as another independent variable.[39] The goal is to isolate the effects of each independent variable and when there is a high interrelationship relative effects are difficult to isolate unless measurement and sampling errors are low.[40] This suggests that conceptual clarity is not the only issue, but that sampling error is crucial. The stronger the relationship between independent variables, the more solutions there are which will fit the data and even small changes caused by sampling error will significantly alter correlation and regression coefficients.[41] The reader also is reminded that causal modeling dependent upon correlation-regression concepts makes the same assumption about measurement error inherent in those concepts: that measurement errors in the dependent variable are permissible, but it is assumed that there are none in the independent variables.

Mathematizing the Relationships

Assuming that the political scientist has developed a particular theoretical framework with a final dependent variable in mind, conceptualized reality in terms of variables that intuitively or by previous analysis make causal "sense," and measured these variables within tolerable error limits, he has reached the stage at which he can begin to test alternative models with different causal linkages between variables. By combining regression analysis and the recursive assumptions, equations can be written for each variable as a dependent variable. That is, there is not just one dependent variable and each variable may be caused by all of the previous variables. Equations are written so as to include variables sequentially and incrementally. If we have a four-variable model with X_4 as the final dependent variable, X_1 stands alone as being influenced by outside and random effects (i.e., exogenous), X_2 is influenced by X_1 plus error, X_3 by X_1 and X_2 plus error, and X_4 by X_1, X_2, and X_3 plus error. You will recall from the previous chapter that a regression equation equals some constant (a) plus an increment (b) times a score (X) plus error (e). That is, $Y = a + bX + e$ and that from this we can determine a line of least squares through the data. The constants are removed through the assumption that each variable is measured as deviations from its mean,[42] however, the regression coefficients, the variable scores, and the error terms (with the uncorrelated assumption) are kept and written into a set of recursive equations using conventional regression notation:

39. Blalock, *Causal Inferences in Nonexperimental Research*, p. 48.
40. Blalock, *Theory Construction*, p. 89.
41. See Robert A. Gordon, "Issues in Multiple Regression," *American Journal of Sociology* 73 (1968): 592–616, and Hubert M. Blalock, Jr., "Correlated Independent Variables: The Problem of Multicollinearity," *Social Forces* 42 (1963): 233–37.
42. Blalock, *Causal Inferences in Nonexperimental Research*, p. 54.

$$X_1 = e_1$$
$$X_2 = b_{21} X_1 + e_2$$
$$X_3 = b_{31.2} X_1 + b_{32.1} X_2 + e_3$$
$$X_4 = b_{41.23} X_1 + b_{42.13} X_2 + b_{43.12} X_3 + e_4$$

This is a set of equations showing causation in one direction, built incrementally through the variable system. That is, regression coefficients going in the opposite direction (e.g., b_{13} predicting variable one from variable three vs. b_{31} predicting variable three from variable one) have been eliminated. These are the coefficients which must be zero as expressed in the earlier regression matrix for three variables. Any higher order partial regression coefficients (e.g., $b_{21.3}$, $b_{31.24}$) are also omitted from the set of equations.

By beginning with a diagram including every causal link, the relative location of regression coefficients becomes evident (see fig. 3.2). The goal, however, is to test alternative models and subsequently choose the best to be expressed with coefficients on each path of influence. In order to accomplish this there must be fewer unknowns than equations, therefore, one or more of the b's must be set $= 0$ (i.e., aside from the b's in the opposite direction). These equations for $b = 0$ then remain as prediction equations to verify or nullify the model with real world data. If our theory suggests that there should be no direct linkage between variable one and three, $b_{31.2}$ is set $= 0$ and the line vanishes for purposes of the model. That is, we hypothesize that when X_2 is controlled for, X_1 has no impact on X_3 but that which "travels

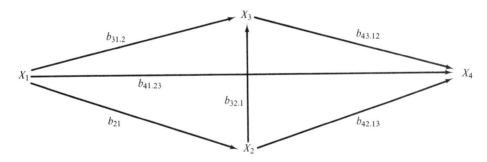

FIGURE 3.2

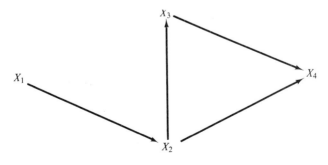

FIGURE 3.3

through" X_2, i.e., X_2 is an intervening variable. If our hypothesis further suggests that X_1 has no direct impact on X_4, that is, that influence must pass through X_2 and X_3, $b_{41.23}$ can be set $= 0$. These eliminated arrows yield the model in figure 3.3 where variable one causes variable two, variable two (and indirectly variable one) causes variable three, variable two directly causes variable four, but it also influences variable four through its impact on variable three which has a direct link with variable four.

Through the use of regression analysis there are two frequently used operational techniques, closely related, which can be used as tests of the hypothesized model and means by which alternative models are derived. Following the testing of models using these methods, weights or numbers are typically assigned to the causal path in the "best" model based upon regression coefficients (unstandardized or standardized, the latter being analogous to the path coefficient).

Both model testing techniques described below are based on the relationship between regression and correlation coefficients. As described above, it is the regression coefficient which enables us to discuss causal inferences, whereas the correlation coefficient provides us with associative information. Yet there is a relationship between r and b which assists us in causal modeling: when $b = 0$, $r = 0$. Therefore, when partial correlation coefficients are $= 0$ we can assume that the corresponding regression coefficients will be zero. The use of partial correlation coefficients for model testing is most evident in Goldberg's analysis of voting behavior.[43] He begins with a model derived deductively from a body of theory and previous findings, hypothesizes which causal links are missing and calculates the partial correlation coefficients for those links following a set of recursive equations. If certain linkages (i.e., partial correlation coefficients) are not equal to zero (or in this example, less than .1), they are added to a later model, variable sequences are changed and partial r's are again calculated for a new model.

If the researcher has only a simple correlation matrix to begin his testing of models, another technique is available. Following a linear model, the simple relationship between two variables can be expressed as the product of simple r's between variables along an alternative path. For example, if we hypothesize that $b_{31.2} = 0$ and therefore $r_{13.2} = 0$, there is a missing link between variable one and variable three, i.e., X_1 affects X_3 indirectly through X_2 (fig. 3.4). By using the first testing technique, $r_{13.2}$ can be calculated from the data to see if, in fact, it should remain missing (if

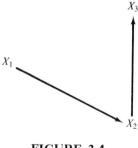

FIGURE 3.4

43. Arthur S. Goldberg, "Discerning a Causal Pattern Among Data on Voting Behavior," *American Political Science Review* 60 (1966): 913–22; see the readings below.

it equals zero). By saying that variable one's impact on variable three is the product of variable one's impact on variable two and variable two's impact on variable three, we see that $r_{13} = r_{12}r_{23}$ and when $r_{13.2}$ is zero this equality will hold. Although Goldberg prefers the first method, he provides us with a simple correlation matrix[44] enabling us to use his data as an example for both methods.

For purposes of simplicity, let us focus on the first three variables in his causal scheme of voting behavior: the respondent's social characteristics, his father's social characteristics, and his father's party identification. For theoretical reasons, this portion of his first model hypothesizes that the father's social characteristics influence the respondent's social characteristics and the father's party identification, but that there is no link between father's party identification and respondent's social characteristics (fig. 3.5.). It is therefore predicted that $r_{32.1} = 0$, but when this is computed it equals .101, indicating at least a weak linkage. Therefore in the second model a line from X_2 to X_3 is added. Although the partial correlation coefficients for $X_1 \rightarrow X_2$ and $X_1 \rightarrow X_3$ are not given, they can be calculated from the simple r's in the correlation matrix ($r_{12.3} = .22$ and $r_{13.2} = .76$).

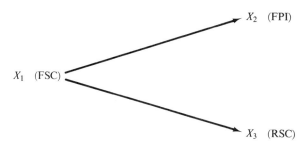

X₂ (FPI)

X₁ (FSC)

X₃ (RSC)

FIGURE 3.5

Following the second method[45] the hypothesized missing link is tested by comparing the simple r along that line to see if it equals the product of the simple r's on the other two lines and, if so, the missing link is confirmed. If not, it is added to the model. For example, using the Goldberg data

	Model	Expected r		Actual r	Difference
A	$r_{23} = r_{12}r_{13}$	(.454)(.808) =	.367	.420	.053
B	$r_{13} = r_{12}r_{23}$	(.454)(.420) =	.191	.808	.617
C	$r_{12} = r_{13}r_{23}$	(.808)(.420) =	.339	.454	.115

we see that the hypothesized missing link is in fact weaker than the others, but that it does not equal zero. In the above context we should note the difficulty in accepting or rejecting a line of causal influence. The original $r_{32.1} = .101$ was on the borderline of acceptance-rejection based on the .1 criterion. Although this criterion

44. Ibid., p. 916, n. 17.
45. For example, Donald J. McCrone and Charles F. Cnudde, "Toward a Communications Theory of Democratic Political Development: A Causal Model," *American Political Science Review* 61 (1967): 72–79; see the readings below.

seems to be prevalent in the literature, there are fewer norms of reference if we use the second method. If we use absolute zero as a criterion, each of the three links should be included in the model, but if we use the criterion of relativity (i.e., one model provides a closer degree of fit than another[46]), model A is the best of the set ABC. If parsimony-conceptual clarity is used as a criterion there is little assistance when we deal with only three variables because each model is about equally parsimonious. Therefore, in a situation like the above, we frequently find a researcher choosing one model over the other because of some assumption about the real world (e.g., that it makes sense to assume a respondent's social characteristics will be caused by his father's party identification). Of course, such criteria are not antithetical to the concept of model building. In a subsequent reading, Forbes and Tufte spend a considerable time discussing these issues in their review of some early causal modeling in political science.[47]

After alternative models have been developed and tested for their degree of fit with the data, numerical meaning must be given to the model. The goal is to assess the direct impact of one variable on another, controlling for others. A frequently used technique, borrowed directly from correlation-regression analysis, is to compare the increases in one variable associated with unit increases in another by means of regression coefficients (standardized or unstandardized). Earlier in this chapter we have shown how unstandarized regression coefficients are manipulated through recursive equations. If standardized measures are preferred, the technique of path analysis can be employed to derive path coefficients — values which are identical to the least squares estimator for the standardized partial regression coefficient. The resultant path coefficients measure the fraction of the standard deviation of the dependent variable for which the independent variable is directly responsible. Therefore, the path coefficient squared measures the amount of variance of the dependent variable directly responsible to the independent variable. The calculation of these coefficients is closely tied to the correlation coefficients in a causal model and to the idea of direct and indirect effects so vital to that model. As an example of these effects, we will return to the initial portion of the Goldberg model. The correlation between father's social characteristics (X_1) and respondent's social characteristics (X_3) can be divided into two parts: (1) the direct effect of X_1 on X_3 (path coefficient p_{31}), plus (2) the indirect effects of X_1 on X_3, reflected in the product of the correlation between X_1 and X_2, and the path coefficient between X_2 and X_3. Therefore,

$$r_{13} = p_{31} + r_{12}p_{32}$$

In order to measure direct effects for all components of the model and thereby place weights on the lines of the model, the relationships between correlation coefficients are utilized. For example,

$$p_{31} = \frac{r_{13} - r_{23}r_{12}}{1 - r_{12}^2}$$

46. Blalock, *Causal Inferences in Nonexperimental Research*, pp. 75ff.
47. Hugh D. Forbes and Edward R. Tufte, "A Note of Caution in Causal Modelling," *American Political Science Review* 62 (1968): 1258–64.

Using Goldberg data, the path between X_1 and X_3 equals

$$p_{31} = \frac{.808 - (.420)(.454)}{1 - .454^2} = .777$$

The linkage between X_1 and X_2 is dependent on no other causally prior variables (except error), and in the bivariate case $p_{21} = r_{12} = \beta_{21}$, therefore $p_{21} = .454$. The remaining and weakest link is that between the father's partisan identification (X_2) and the respondent's social characteristics (X_3), where

$$p_{32} = r_{23} - p_{31}r_{12}$$

or

$$p_{32} = .420 - (.777)(.454) = .067$$

These above coefficients are most useful to determine the actual impact of the variables on each other, yet Blalock suggests that unstandardized regression coefficients are more useful for hypothetical statements regarding causal laws[48] and in this comparison, the basic differences are due to standardized vs. unstandardized measures. Path coefficients are appropriate for generalizations about a specific population whereas unstandardized coefficients are useful for comparing populations with regard to similar causal laws. It has been suggested that standardized measures may be best suited for closed populations.[49] Earlier it was suggested that standardized regression coefficients (beta weights) are advantageous because they usually vary between $+1$ and -1 and enable comparisons of variables despite different underlying units of measurement. Such standardized techniques can measure importance in a specific population (and standardized path coefficients would do this by sorting out the impact of each independent variable), but if the goal is general hypothetical laws, standardized measures are misleading because they "vary from population to population even where the underlying laws are the same"[50] because of the differing characteristics of each population (e.g., standard deviation). Therefore, on the one hand, standardized measures enable easy comparison of variables based on different measures, but if these variables are in comparative populations (vs. a closed population) they will vary according to the characteristics of those populations irrespective of any common underlying causal laws. Note that because unstandardized regression coefficients are tied to the unit of measurement, they are at least interpretable to the researcher as long as he remembers what he is saying. Therefore, unstandardized regression coefficients have an advantage over standardized measures because unstandardized coefficients can compare populations and are interpretable with regard to the unit of measurement, whereas there is no basis for interpretation with regard to the standard deviations used in

---

48. Blalock, "Path Coefficients versus Regression Coefficients," p. 675.

49. A closed population is one isolated from outside influences and one in which no respondents enter or leave. See Hubert M. Blalock, "Causal Inferences, Closed Populations, and Measures of Association," *American Political Science Review* 61 (1967): 130–37.

50. Blalock, "Theory Building and Causal Inferences," in *Methodology in Social Research*, ed. Blalock and Blalock, p. 190.

the standardization procedure.[51] That is, the political scientist can handle the unit of measurement problem empirically and theoretically but when he is dealing with different populations, there are no theoretical bases for determining the standard deviations.

Because the application of causal modeling to political data is in its infancy, many of these small but important questions are in a state of indeterminancy. The alternatives to the Simon-Blalock technique cited at the beginning of this chapter will develop rapidly. For those utilizing the technique, there is an apparent preference for standardized measures to give substantive meaning to the models of best fit. Only the political scientist with a grasp of multivariate statistics, and the assumptions, variations, and issues of causal modeling, will be able to cast light on our historical concern for substantive answers to causes of political phenomena.

Research Examples and Introductory Notes

The following research examples illustrate the application of causal modeling to the study of political phenomena. They utilize a variety of technique options treated above for the isolation of causal influences and they illustrate the stages of analysis necessary for the alternative model testing process. In addition to their clarity in presenting elaborations of the basic techniques, they were selected on the basis of their treatment of various kinds of data: national and subnational survey data, and national, subnational, and cross-national aggregate indicators. They also cover a range of theoretical concerns in political science, from voting behavior to cross-national political development. Different methodological viewpoints and some controversies surrounding causal modeling are treated in an exchange between several authors whose works are reviewed in this chapter.

---

51. For the calculation of standardized regression coefficients see Hubert M. Blalock, *Social Statistics*, 2d ed. (New York: McGraw-Hill, 1972), p. 453, and chapter 2 above.

Selected Bibliography of Applications

Alker, Hayward. "Causal Inference and Political Analysis." In *Mathematical Applications in Political Science II*, ed. Joseph L. Bernd, pp. 7–43. Dallas: Southern Methodist University Press, 1966.

Bell, Roderick. "The Determinants of Psychological Involvement in Politics: A Causal Analysis." *Midwest Journal of Political Science* 13 (1969): 237–53.

Beyle, Thad L. "Contested Elections and Voter Turnout in a Local Community: A Problem in Spurious Correlation." *American Political Science Review* 59 (1965): 111–16.

Blalock, Hubert M., Jr., ed. *Causal Models in the Social Sciences.* Chicago: Aldine-Atherton, 1971.

Capecchi, Vittorio, and Galli, Giorgio. "Determinants of Voting Behavior in Italy: A Linear Causal Model of Analysis." In *Quantitative Ecological Analysis in the Social Sciences*, ed. Mattei Dogan and Stein Rokkan, pp. 235–84. Cambridge: MIT Press, 1969.

Cnudde, Charles F., and McCrone, Donald J. "The Linkage Between Constituency Attitudes and Congressional Voting Behavior: A Causal Model." *American Political Science Review* 60 (1966): 66–72.

Cox, Kevin R. "Voting in the London Suburbs: A Factor Analysis and a Causal Model." In *Quantitative Ecological Analysis in the Social Sciences*, ed. Mattei Dogan and Stein Rokkan, pp. 343–70. Cambridge: MIT Press, 1969.

Gurr, Ted. "A Causal Model of Civil Strife: A Comparative Analysis Using New Indices." *American Political Science Review* 62 (1968): 1104–24.

Kirkpatrick, Samuel A., and Morgan, David R. "Policy Support and Orientations Toward Metropolitan Political Integration Among Urban Officials." *Social Science Quarterly* 52 (1971): 656–71.

Langton, Kenneth P., and Karns, David A. "The Relative Influence of the Family, Peer Group, and School in the Development of Political Efficacy." *Western Political Quarterly* 22 (1969): 813–26.

Miller, Warren E., and Stokes, Donald E. "Constituency Influence in Congress." *American Political Science Review* 57 (1963): 45–56.

Nie, Norman H.; Powell, G. Bingham; and Prewitt, Kenneth. "Social Structure and Political Participation: Developmental Relationships, I, and II." *American Political Science Review* 63 (1969): 361–78, 808–32.

Putnam, Robert D. "Toward Explaining Military Intervention in Latin American Politics." *World Politics* 20 (1967): 83–108.

Sharkansky, Ira, and Turnbull, August B. "Budget-Making in Georgia and Wisconsin: A Test of a Model." *Midwest Journal of Political Science* 13 (1969): 631–45.

Tanter, Raymond. "Toward a Theory of Political Development." *Midwest Journal of Political Science* 11 (1967): 145–72.

Winham, Gilbert R. "Political Development and Lerner's Theory: Further Test of a Causal Model." *American Political Science Review* 64 (1970): 810–18.

ARTHUR S. GOLDBERG*

Discerning a Causal Pattern
Among Data on Voting Behavior

This first article in our set of examples on causal
modeling tests several alternative models for explaining the presidential
vote. The data should not be unfamiliar since a brief explanation and
re-analysis appeared in the text part of this chapter. The final dependent
variable is the respondent's vote for president in 1956 (dichotomized
from the 1956 Survey Research Center Study), and the independent variables
(which are at times dependent on others) in the recursive Simon-Blalock
equation system include: (1) the father's sociological characteristics
measured as an expected value of being Republican derived from the regression
of religion, class, community size, region, and race on the father's
partisan identification; (2) the father's partisan identification (dichotomous);
(3) the respondent's sociological characteristics (an expected value of
being Republican derived from a regression of selected respondent charac-
teristics on his party identification, not unlike the procedure used for
the father's characteristics); (4) the respondent's party identification
(dichotomous); and (5) the respondent's partisan attitudes measured by
an index based upon the regression of selected attitudes on the vote.
These variables are tested for their interrelationships in a series of

Reprinted from Arthur S. Goldberg, "Discerning a Causal Pattern Among Data on Voting Behavior," *American Political Science Review* 60 (1966): 913–22, by permission of The American Political Science Association and the author.

*While I have incurred a great many intellectual debts in the conduct of this inquiry, I am most particularly indebted to Hayward R. Alker, Jr., at Yale University, for so generously making available to me his understanding of causal inference strategies. I also wish to thank the University of Rochester for the research fellowship which enabled me to devote the summer of 1964 to the study of causality and causal inference techniques. Of course, neither mentor nor patron is responsible for such errors as may have been perpetrated herein. For these I alone am culpable.

recursive equations where vanishing causal arrows are based upon zero
values for the theoretically relevant partial correlation coefficients.
By progressing through a series of alternative models tied to modified
or different theoretical expectations, the author is able to derive
a final model which offers a best fit with the data.

1. Causal Explanations: Simon's Model

The present analysis is devoted to making an empirically based choice among alternate causal explanations. This entails making causal inferences from statistical correlations. While this might, at one time, have constituted a heresy, I believe that the procedure to be followed here will soon be a part of statistical orthodoxy.[1]

This is not the place for an extended philosophical discussion of the problem of causality. Yet I would like to make my position on the problem as clear as concise presentation will permit. My basic sympathies are with that school which argues that scientifically relevant causal explanation inheres only in our theories, i.e., that the explained event takes the shape which it does because our postulates and logic preclude any other shape on pain of being themselves incorrect.[2] However, the development of such theory, containing such postulates, is usually the product of an inspired insight on the part of one thoroughly immersed in the manifestations of the empirical phenomonon under consideration. The production and verification of such insight in a systematic and reproducible way is the goal of inductive research. Where controlled experimentation is possible, Mill's canons may apply. Where such experiments are either impossible or impracticable, statistical inference becomes necessary. It is in this situation that the present approach, based upon a model developed by Herbert Simon and others, seems justified.[3]

Simon's model is designed to capture the asymmetry in our notions of causality. When one speaks of A as a cause of B, one usually has in mind a unidirectional forcing, and not merely a covariation, or phased covariation. Thus, if one speaks of rains as a cause of floods, one expects that a variation in rainfall will be accompanied by a variation in flooding, *but* one does *not* expect that variations in flooding deriving from other causes, e.g., faulty dam construction, will be accompanied by variations in rainfall. Again, it should be noted that the concept of

1. Cf. Warren E. Miller and Donald E. Stokes, "Constituency Influence in Congress," *American Political Science Review* (March, 1963), 45–56; Donald C. Pelz and Frank M. Andrews, "Causal Priorities in Panel Study Data," *American Sociological Review*, 24 (December, 1964), 836–847; Hayward R. Alker, Jr., *Mathematics and Politics* (New York: The Macmillan Company, 1965), chap. VI.

2. Cf. Robert Brown, *Explanation in Social Science* (Chicago: Aldine Publishing Company, 1963), chap. XI. See also Norwood Russell Hanson, *Patterns of Discovery* (Cambridge: Cambridge University Press, 1958), chap. III; and William H. Riker, "Causes of Events," *Journal of Philosophy*, 55 (1958), 281–291.

3. See Herbert A. Simon, *Models of Man* (New York: John Wiley & Sons, Inc., 1957), chaps. I–III; and Hubert M. Blalock, Jr., *Causal Inferences in Nonexperimental Research* (Chapel Hill: The University of North Carolina Press, 1964), chaps. I–III. These authors, in turn, have drawn heavily upon the work of econometricians. Among basic sources are, for example, Ragnar Frisch, *Statistical Confluence Analysis by Means of Complete Regression Systems* (Oslo: Universitets Økonomiske Institutt, 1934) and T. C. Koopmans (ed.), *Statistical Inference in Dynamic Economic Models* (New York: John Wiley and Sons, 1950).

alternate causes is alien to deductive theory, which seeks to postulate the most inclusive principles. However, inductive inference is concerned with perceiving an
ever-increasing proportion of the total set of alternate causes in order to facilitate
formulation of a principle of commonality.

Simon suggests that a patterned causal ordering can and should be described as a
recursive set of simultaneous equations dealing sequentially with each of the variables in the causal ordering and describing each in terms of the regression of its
causal antecedents upon it. Thus if one had four variables, $x_1 \cdots x_4$, in which x_1 was
considered causally independent of all of the rest, and x_4 was considered causally
dependent upon all of the rest, and in which x_2 and x_3 were causally intervening,
this could be described as follows:[4]

$$x_1 = c_1$$

$$x_2 = b_{21}x_1 + c_2$$

$$x_3 = b_{31.2}x_1 + b_{32.1}x_2 + c_3$$

$$x_4 = b_{41.23}x_1 + b_{42.13}x_2 + b_{43.12}x_3 + c_4$$

The non-zero regression coefficients describe the impact of each of the causal
antecedents upon a given variable; the pattern of impacts is inferable from the zero
regression coefficients, and asymmetry is accomplished in that manipulation of the
value of a given variable leaves unaltered the relationships among its causal antecedents, and can affect only causally subsequent variables.[5]

Since it is the case that causal impacts should appear as non-zero value regression
coefficients, causal models in which any of the variables contribute directly to less
than the full set of subsequent variables have implied zero value regression cofficients.
Hubert Blalock points out that such regression coefficients imply zero value correlation coefficients. It thus becomes possible with the aid of partial correlation coefficients to make an empirically based decision among alternate causal models
purporting to describe the causal relationships within the same set of variables.
This is the technique which will be used in the present analysis.

It should be noted that there are several assumptions being made which bear
substantially upon the logic of the analysis. These are: that the effects on the dependent variable of variables excluded from the model are not related to effects
produced by any of the independent variables in the model; that all variables which
have a substantial impact on the dependent variable and are correlated with independent variables in the model are also included in the model (i.e., the error
terms are uncorrelated); that the phenomena to be explained entail no reciprocal
causation.[6]

It should also be noted that there is a serious controversy among econometricians
with regard to the uncorrelated error term assumption.[7] Although I do not wish to
indulge in an extended discussion of the subject, it is perhaps only fair that I make

---

4. Simon, *op. cit.*, chap. I.

5. Blalock, *op. cit.*, pp. 52–60.

6. See *ibid.*, pp. 46–54.

7. See, for example, Fritz C. Holte, *Economic Shock-Models* (Oslo: Norwegian Universities Press,
1962), pp. 14–17.

my own position explicit. In general, I believe that this assumption is almost always invalid, and that science proceeds not only in spite of this invalidity, but to a large extent through efforts to cope with it. When the limit of a theory is encountered, in the form of the occurrence of a theoretically precluded phenomenon, the search is begun for some component of the error term which is correlated in the relevant sense, and in conjunction with its discovery, the substance of the theory is revised. This is but one form of the retroductive process.[8]

II. Causal Relations Among Six Variables

The present analysis is concerned with making inferences about the pattern of causal relationships among six variables: father's sociological characteristics (FSC); father's party identification (FPI); respondent's sociological characteristics (RSC); respondent's party identification (RPI); respondent's partisan attitudes (RPA); and respondent's vote for President in 1956 (RV). The assumed causal ordering is the sequence in which the variables are listed above, except when otherwise noted. In each case to be examined, the model will be presented schematically, and the variables will be numbered in accordance with their assumed causal sequence.

Variables were selected for inclusion in the analysis on the bases of their repeated occurrence in the voting literature and their availability in a reliable body of data.[9] The sociological characteristics of the respondent's father and the father's party identification were taken as indicators of the context in which the respondent underwent his early political socialization. The literature is replete with the importance of this early socialization for political behavior in general and for voting behavior in particular.[10] The respondent's sociological characteristics were taken as an indicator of the constraints placed upon him by his current social environs. This variable represents the approach taken by Berelson *et al.* in *Voting*, and thus the general sociological explanation of voting behavior.[11] The respondent's party identification was included because of its well established and substantial correlation with direction of vote in a number of major studies.[12] Finally, the respondent's

---

8. See Hanson, *op. cit.*, chap. IV.

9. The body of data used consisted of that generated in the 1956 election study (#417) by the Survey Research Center at The University of Michigan, and made available to me through the Inter-University Consortium for Political Research. The exact operationalization of the variables is described in the Technical Note at the end of the article. The number of respondents in the present analysis is 645 out of the 1762 provided in the SRC survey. The 645 are those who had full information on the full set of variables. There is thus a slight overrepresentation of Republicans and upper SES respondents. This bias is slight and there appears to be no other systematic bias in the sub-sample. For more detailed discussion, see Arthur S. Goldberg, *The Intergenerational Transmission of Party Identification* (unpublished doctoral dissertation, Yale University, 1966), Appendix B.

10. Surveys of the literature on this point are available in Herbert H. Hyman, *Political Socialization* (Glencoe, Illinois: The Free Press, 1959); and Robert E. Lane and David O. Sears, *Public Opinion* (Englewood Cliffs: Prentice-Hall, Inc., 1964).

11. See, for example, Bernard R. Berelson, Paul F. Lazarsfeld, and William N. McPhee, *Voting* (Chicago: The University of Chicago Press, 1954), chaps. IV–VII. See also Seymour Martin Lipset, *Political Man* (Garden City, New York: Doubleday & Company, Inc., 1960), Part II.

12. See, for example, Angus Campbell, Gerald Gurin, and Warren E. Miller, *The Voter Decides* (Evanston, Illinois: Row, Peterson and Company, 1954), chap. VII. See also Angus Campbell, Philip E. Converse, Warren E. Miller, and Donald E. Stokes, *The American Voter* (New York: John Wiley & Sons, Inc., 1960), chap. VI.

partisan attitudes were included as an indicator of his perceptions of the political arena, on the basis of the argument made in *The American Voter*, and because of the high correlation of these attitudes with voting behavior in that study.[13]

III. Model I

As a point of departure, let us consider one version of an attitude-field theory model, that presented in *The American Voter*.[14] The authors have told us very little about what to expect in such a model, except that in pure Gestalt theory, the attitude field is the final mediator of all causes of the behavior in question. Based upon this requirement, let us consider one plausible model. In this model the attitude field is taken to be the result of two causal streams, one consisting in the sociological conditioning of childhood and adult life,[15] and the other consisting in affective conditioning to the party label.[16] This model is presented in Fig. 1. Let us call

Model I. Attitude as final mediator.

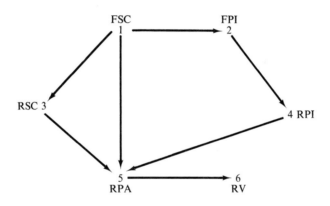

Prediction Equations	Actual Values
$r_{41.23} = 0$	0.017
$r_{61.2345} = 0$	−0.019
$r_{32.1} = 0$	0.101
$r_{52.134} = 0$	0.032
$r_{62.1345} = 0$	0.053
$r_{43.12} = 0$	0.130
$r_{63.1245} = 0$	−0.022
$r_{64.1235} = 0$	0.365

FIGURE 1

13. *The American Voter*, chap. IV. See also Donald E. Stokes, Angus Campbell, and Warren E. Miller, "Components of Electoral Decision," *American Political Science Review*, 52 (June, 1958), 367–87.

14. Cf. *The American Voter*, pp. 24–37.

15. Cf. Berelson, Lazarsfeld, and McPhee, *loc. cit.*

16. Cf. Lane and Sears, *op. cit.*, pp. 18–19.

this Model I, Attitude as Final Mediator. Fig. 1 contains a schematic of the model, the theoretical prediction equations implied by the model, and the empirical values which those equations yielded from the data in the analysis.[17]

Given the assumption of a unidirectional causal ordering, there are fifteen possible causal arrows in a six variable model.[18] In Model I there are seven arrows present. The eight missing arrows mean that the model posits no causal impact in eight of the possible fifteen causal connections. One therefore expects the regression coefficients, and therefore the correlation coefficients associated with the missing arrows to be zero. This yields the set of prediction equations consisting in the list of partial "r's" predicted to be equal to zero in Fig. 1.

While Model I may seem plausible, there are some substantial incongruities between the prediction equations and the actual values. Most notably, these incongruities derive from the omission of causal links between RPI and RV, between RSC and RPI, and between FPI and RSC. Of greatest theoretical importance is the size of $r_{64.1235}$, i.e., 0.365. While this amounts to only 13.3% of the variance, it is sufficient to give one qualms about regarding attitudes, as operationalized by *The American Voter*, as the final mediator. Clearly party identification has an impact not caught in the screen which those researchers drew across their funnel of causality.[19] The need for a link between RSC and RPI, based upon the actual value of $r_{43.12}$ being equal to 0.130 instead of zero, reflects the idea that adult sociological characteristics play a role in party identification. The fact that this role accounts for a miniscule proportion of the variance (1.7%) suggests that the adult sociological environs are supportive of earlier learned behavior, rather than the primary source of this behavior. The need for a link between FPI and RSC is suggested by the value of $r_{32.1} = 0.101$. The size of this value suggests that the link is quite weak, and a more parsimonious model might well do without it. A possible explanation may be in upwardly aspirational parents adopting a party identification normally associated with higher status groups and transmitting their status aspirations to their offspring with sufficient impact to have them realized to some extent. This is, to be sure, a most tentative explanation, but then this particular linkage is also rather tentative.

---

17. Although the aid of a computer was enlisted for the statistical computations in the present article, the lower order partials could be calculated with a slide rule or desk calculator. The appropriate formulae are available in Hubert M. Blalock, *Social Statistics* (New York: McGraw-Hill Book Company, Inc. 1960), pp. 333–336. For those who wish to check the computation of some of the lower order partials, the matrix of simple correlations is provided below:

	FSC	FPI	RSC	RPI	RPA	RV
FSC	1.000					
FPI	0.454	1.000				
RSC	0.808	0.420	1.000			
RPI	0.400	0.603	0.411	1.000		
RPA	0.318	0.453	0.289	0.710	1.000	
RV	0.282	0.466	0.271	0.722	0.742	1.000

18. Assuming that reciprocal causation is not involved, there are always $n!/2(n-2)!$ possible arrows among n variables.

19. *The American Voter*, p. 35. The relative size of this impact is a function of factors which will be dealt with later in the present analysis.

IV. Model II

On the basis of the experience provided by Model I, a second model is proposed. In Model II party identification is taken as the final arbiter. Three arrows have been dropped: those linking FSC and RPA, RSC and RPA, and RPA and RV. The first two were dropped in a search for parsimony, and the third was dropped to implement the central idea of this particular model. Finally the lessons of Model I have been incorporated in Model II presented in Fig. 2. Note that in Model II the time sequence between RPI and RPA is the reverse of what it was in Model I. Thus the subscripts do not necessarily refer to those variables which carried the same subscripts in Model I. Comparisons between models require translation of subscript numbers, which indicate causal ordering, into variable symbols through the use of the schematic diagrams. Each set of subscripts should be used only within its own diagram.

Model II. Party identification as final mediator.

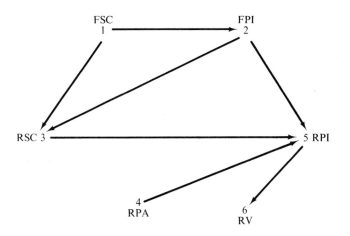

Prediction Equations	Actual Values
$r_{41.23} = 0$	−0.017
$r_{51.234} = 0$	0.037
$r_{61.2345} = 0$	−0.019
$r_{42.13} = 0$	0.357
$r_{62.1345} = 0$	0.053
$r_{43.12} = 0$	0.031
$r_{63.1245} = 0$	−0.022
$r_{64.1235} = 0$	0.470

FIGURE 2

Examination of Fig. 2 indicates two rather gross discrepancies between predicted and actual values. One of these, $r_{64.1235} = 0.470$, simply invalidates the notion of party identification as final arbiter. It suggests the need for a direct causal link between RPA and RV. The other major discrepancy, $r_{42.13} = 0.357$ requires a more complex interpretation. Given the causal ordering in this model, what is implied is the need for a causal link between FPI and RPA. However, if one glances back at Model I, it can be seen that the omission of the causal link between FPI and RPA produced no serious discrepancy (predicted value = 0, actual value = 0.032). It is this pair of findings which enables a choice to be made between the two causal orderings. On the basis of Simon's asymmetric model of causality, the causal link between two variables may be affected by all of the variables antecedent to the dependent variable, but *cannot* be affected by any of the variables subsequent to the dependent variable.[20] Thus, in Model I the antecedents to RPA are FSC, FPI, RSC, and RPI. In describing the impact of FPI upon RPA, it was therefore necessary to control for FSC, RSC, and RPI. However, in Model II, RPA is assumed to be antecedent to RPI. Therefore, in describing the impact of FPI upon RPA in this model, one is prohibited from including RPI as a control. Clearly, the omission of the control yields a poor fit with the data and suggests that to the extent that unidirectionality is assumed and parsimony desired, the RPI ought to be regarded as prior to RPA. Support is thus lent to the positions of Lane and Sears, Greenstein, and others who have urged the importance of the early socialization of political symbols.[21]

V. Model III

Reverting, then, to the causal ordering in Model I, and incorporating the lessons taught by Models I and II, a third model is proposed, that of dual mediation. The schematic, prediction equations, and findings are presented in Fig. 3. Here, in Model III, one has a model which fits the data relatively well. Its distinctive features are: it hypothesizes *both* party identification and partisan attitudes as direct causes of vote direction; it assigns a pivotal position to party identification in denying that any of the antecedents to party identification have a direct bearing on partisan attitudes or vote direction; within the framework of the model, no causes are hypothesized for partisan attitudes other than party identification. The last point, of course, suggests that the framework of the model is too restricted, since party identification in its total impact accounts for only about 50% of the variance in partisan attitudes ($r = .710$, see n. 17, above). This point will be elaborated upon. However, before launching into a serious critique of Model III, one ought to consider that while the model fits the data rather well, it is not a perfect fit. Since it is possible to make perfectly valid direct inferences from correlation coefficients to regression coefficients only where the former are actually zero, and since the inferences here have been based upon correlation coefficients slightly different from zero, a further analytic step seems warranted, i.e., calculation of standardized regression coefficients (beta weights). Based upon the causal ordering of Model III, such coefficients were generated for all of the linkages possible within that ordering. In general, the inferences made from the correlation coefficients are supported. That is, the implied zero impacts prove to be very small and statistically insignificant

20. Blalock, *Causal Inference* . . . , p. 59.
21. Lane and Sears, *loc. cit.* Fred I. Greenstein, "The Benevolent Leader: Children's Images of Political Authority," *American Political Science Review*, 54 (1960), 934–943.

Model III. Dual mediation.

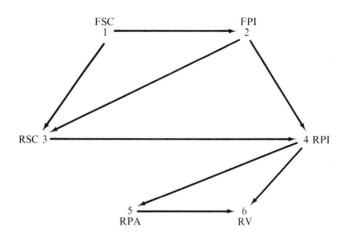

Prediction Equations	Actual Values
$r_{41 \cdot 23} = 0$	-0.017
$r_{51 \cdot 234} = 0$	0.083
$r_{61 \cdot 2345} = 0$	-0.019
$r_{52 \cdot 134} = 0$	0.032
$r_{62 \cdot 1345} = 0$	0.053
$r_{53 \cdot 124} = 0$	-0.073
$r_{63 \cdot 1245} = 0$	-0.022

FIGURE 3

Model IV. Dual mediation, revised.

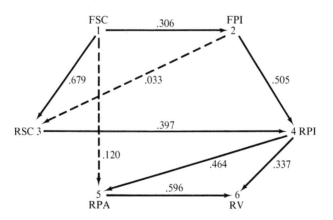

Key: The beta weights of the implied linkages appear either immediately above or immediately to the right of their representational arrows. The beta weights of the linkages represented by solid arrows prove significant at the .001 level. Those represented by broken arrows prove significant at the .05 level but not at the .01 level. None of the possible linkages which have been omitted have beta weights which are significant even at the .05 level.

FIGURE 4

at the .05 level.[22] However, there is one exception: the FSC to RPA linkage, while relatively small, proved to be significant at the .05 level. Thus there is occasioned the revision presented in Model IV, in Fig. 4. Within the assumptions made with regard to unidirectional causality and causal ordering, this is the model which best fits the data, and which requires critical assessment.

VI. Model IV

From the viewpoint of theory, Model IV has both desirable and undesirable features. Let us first look at the happier side of this situation. Certainly the model achieves a certain amount of parsimony. Of fifteen possible causal arrows, six have been eliminated and of the remaining nine, two are clearly of secondary importance, leaving a dominant seven-arrow model. Moreover, the model is theoretically informative, both in terms of what it omits and in terms of its dominant patterns. The omission of direct causal links between sociological characteristics, both childhood (FSC) and adult (RSC), and voting behavior, as well as the omission of such a link between childhood sociological characteristics and adult party identification certainly justify the qualms of the authors of *The American Voter* about the sociological explanations of voting behavior.[23] However, it can also be seen, in this empirically supported model, that sociological characteristics do have a substantial *indirect* impact on voting behavior, exerted primarily through party identification. The mediating role of party identification as described in Model IV suggests that father's sociological characteristics, father's party identification, and respondent's sociological characteristics have almost no impact upon voting behavior save as they act through respondent's party identification. Therefore one expects $r_{65.4} = r_{65.1234}$. The actual values are: $r_{65.4} = 0.472$, $r_{65.1234} = 0.470$.

The fact that party identification rather than partisan attitudes proves to be the pivotal encapsulator of political socialization, substantiates the position that such socialization entails an affective relationship to symbols rather than a conscious evaluative relating of political means to ends. This position is given still further support by the absence of a direct link between childhood sociological characteristics and adult party identification; there is a relationship, but it is dependent upon mediation by paternal party identification. However, this is not to say that there is no rational calculus involved in voting. The fact that partisan attitudes have a substantial impact beyond that of party identification, suggests that such a calculus is operative, but operative against a set of predispositions dominated by party

---

22. The decision to accept or reject linkages on the basis of significance tests poses some problems. The significance test is designed to deal with the type I error (rejection of the null hypothesis when it is true). That is to say, it provides a statement of the probability that a strength of association as great as that found in the sample could have been drawn from a population in which there was in fact no relationship between the variables in question. However, in deciding to omit a link, one is concerned with the risk of a type II error (acceptance of the null hypothesis when it is false). The information desired in this case is the probability that a strength of association as weak as that in the sample could have been drawn from a population in which there was a stronger association. Unless one has an a priori expectation of the strength of association in the population, it is not possible to calculate this probability.

23. *The American Voter*, pp. 32–37.

identification.[24] Thus, the model suggested by this study comports well with the data of other studies and imposes a certain order upon their findings.

Yet certain caveats are in order. One should bear in mind that the present study has dealt, to this point, only with respondents who claimed a Republican or a Democratic party identification for themselves. Those who were classified as Independents or as apolitical have been excluded. This has an important bearing upon the partial correlation between party identification and vote, controlling for partisan attitudes. In the present study, this partial correlation is 0.415, amounting to 17.2% of the variance. It has been pointed out to me by Professor Donald Stokes of the Michigan Survey Research Center that in the full sample, which, of course, includes Independents and those classed as apolitical (together amounting to 12.6% of the sample), this partial correlation drops to 0.238, thus accounting for less than 5.7% of the variance.

To one interested primarily in mapping a particular population, the figures based upon the full sample ought to be more salient. However, for one interested in the logic of the explanatory theory, both sets of figures are of interest. Taken together they suggest that the impact of party identification on voting behavior in a given population will depend upon the ratio of partisans to non-partisans in that society. In those instances in which, for whatever reasons, individuals have not developed a party identification, the impact of partisan attitudes would be substantially increased, if the logic of Model IV is correct. As the proportion of such instances in a population increased, the net impact of party identification on vote would be expected to diminish.[25] Essentially this is the obverse of the argument made in *The American Voter* about the efficacy of partisan attitudes as a guide to voting behavior.[26]

At this point attention is directed to certain unsatisfactory features of the model itself. While it leaves room for a rational calculus prior to the voting act, it does not permit party identification to benefit from this calculus. This prohibition derives from the requirements of the mathematical model of causality used in the analysis. A major requirement of that model, it will be recalled, was unidirectionality. Yet this is a limitation which, in the long run, must be circumvented, if theory is to be relevant to events. As this model stands, party identification is nearly immutable. There is very little if any variation over time in its antecedents, nor is there any provision for what V. O. Key calls a critical election.[27] This derives from two factors. First the model does not permit partisan attitudes to have an impact upon party identification. Second, the model does not include among its components the political events in the environment in which it is assumed to operate. The failure of partisan attitudes to feed back upon party identification would mean that even if the correlation between partisan attitudes and party identification were substantially reduced, voting behavior would be influenced, but party identification would be

24. Cf. Berelson, Lazarsfeld, and McPhee, *op. cit.*, pp. 227–233. See also *The American Voter*, pp. 128–131; and Lane and Sears, *op. cit.*, pp. 81–82.

25. Note that this "net impact" refers to a population parameter, or statistic thereof, rather than to the impact of party identification on the vote of any single individual in the population. While the latter would doubtless be of interest, it would be extremely difficult to come by in non-experimental data.

26. See *The American Voter*, pp. 139–142.

27. V. O. Key, Jr., "A Theory of Critical Elections," *Journal of Politics*, 18 (1955), 3–18.

unaffected. Clearly the model needs revision on this point. Moreover, unless one includes an additional variable there is no source within the model for variation of partisan attitudes. Thus, the model is itself a partial description of the impact of the past upon the present, but its connection with the future rests almost entirely in the error factors of the recursive equations which define the model — a situation both undesirable and unnecessary.

Let us first consider amending the model to permit partisan attitudes to have an impact upon party identification. This could be done within a recursive set of equations by "lagging" some of the variables, as Blalock suggests.[28] This entails treating a single variable through time as a set of discrete variables, and treating two interacting variables as two sets of discrete variables. Thus in the time interval $t_0 \cdots t_n$, an interaction between X and Y could be schematized as follows: $X_{t_0} \rightarrow Y_{t_1} \rightarrow X_{t_2} \rightarrow Y_{t_3} \rightarrow X_{t_4} \cdots$. This technique, of course, requires data through time, and will not be utilized with the data of the present study, but is presented for future research purposes.

Introjection of political events into the model presents rather more difficult problems. All of the variables in the model are, in some sense, attributes or activities of the actors. Political events, on the other hand, are external to the actors and cannot be brought into the model directly. They can however, be brought in through his perceptions. Now to some extent these perceptions are measured in partisan attitudes. These attitudes are, however, assessed only immediately prior to the election itself. What would have to be done in a more dynamic and adaptive model would be to sample perceptions of political events as they arise in the political arena, probing in each case for evaluation of the party's handling of the event. The adequacy of the series of events selected would depend upon the astuteness of the analyst and could be tested by the amount of variance in partisan attitudes immediately prior to the election which is accounted for by the attitudes on the full set of events. Moreover, selected probing techniques, such as factor analysis, could be applied to draw inferences about the factors underlying shifts in partisanship over time.

A model incorporating these modifications is presented in Fig. 5 below. The model exploits the mediating roles of partisan attitudes and party identification in order to avoid reincorporation of political socialization characteristics over time. This is not to say that these are not operative. On the contrary, they form the background, encapsulated largely in party identification, against which partisan attitudes are formed and operate. The model represents a continual reality-testing and adjustment process. To the extent that party identification exceeds the impact of partisan attitudes, little learning is taking place. To the extent that partisan attitudes exceed and have the same directional impact as party identifications, reinforcement is taking place. Finally, to the extent partisan attitudes operate in a direction opposite to party identification, that identification is being eroded. There are several other points in the proposed model that bear discussion, e.g., the requirement that partisan attitudes operate on party identification through vote (or vote intention). However, this and other excluded arrows had best wait upon the systematic analysis of data in future studies.

---

28. Blalock, *Causal Inferences . . .* , pp. 53–57.

Model V. A proposed dynamic.

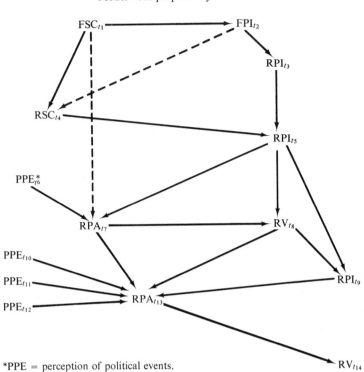

*PPE = perception of political events.

FIGURE 5

VII. Conclusion

In concluding the present analysis, it is important to bear in mind that we are as yet very far from concluding the inquiry into causality in voting behavior. First, it should be noted that the full set of independent variables accounts for only 50% of the variance in voting. This suggests, of course, that one or more important variables have been excluded from the model. In itself, this is only an indication of the need for a broader searching effort. However, there is a distinct possibility that the omitted variable(s) may be correlated with both the dependent variable and one or more of the independent variables in the present model. In such a case the regression coefficients in the model might be substantially affected, even to the extent of reducing to zero some of the now nonzero coefficients, and of reasserting causal linkages estimated as zero in the present model.[29] The present model is thus tentative, an initial approximation to be continually retested not only with the same variables in different populations at different times, but against the impact of the inclusion of new variables.

---

29. *Ibid.*, pp. 46–47. See also Herman Wold and Lars Jurcen, *Demand Analysis* (New York: John Wiley & Sons 1953) pp. 37–38, and Fritz C. Holte, *loc. cit.*

Technical Note

The variables were operationalized from the source decks of the 1956 election study (Project 417) of the Survey Research Center at the University of Michigan in the following manner:

1. Father's Sociological Characteristics (FSC)

This variable consists in an index generated by running five sociological characteristics of the father against the father's party identification in order to generate an expected value of his being Republican. This value constituted the index. The variables utilized, their sources, and their categorizations are presented in table 1.

TABLE 1

Variable (Source Deck: Column)	Categories	(Rows)
Religion (5:27)	Protestant Catholic Jewish	(1) (2) (3)
Class (8:11)	Working Middle	(1,2,3) (4,5,6)
Size of community (6:34)	Farm Town Metropolis	(1) (2,3,4,5,6,8) (7,9)
Region (6:31–32)	South (1 in col. 31, 4 or 5 in col. 32) Non-South	 (all others)
Race (6:10)	White Negro	(1) (2)

2. Father's Party Identification (FPI)

This was established on the basis of data gathered in a later wave with the same panel, i.e., the 1958 election study, project 431. Within that study, the information was taken from Deck CO4: column 23, and the only categories used were Democrat (Row 1) and Republican (Row 2).

3. Respondent's Sociological Characteristics (RSC)

The procedure here was the same as that entailed in building the index of father's sociological characteristics, except that the variables used in the regression were characteristics of the respondent rather than of the father (table 2).

TABLE 2

Variable (Source Deck: Column)	Categories	(Rows)
Religion (5:27)	Protestant Catholic Jewish	(1) (2) (3)
Class (8:10)	Working Middle	(1,2,3) (4,5,6)
Size of community (1:17)	Farm Town Metropolis	(6, — , &) (3,4,5,8,9,0) (1,2,7)
Region (1:15)	South Non-South	(8,9,0) (1–7)
Race (6:10)	White Negro	(1) (2)

4. Respondent's Party Identification (RPI)

This information was taken from Deck 4, column 9. It was dichotomized as follows: Democrat (Rows 1–3), Republican (Rows 5–7).

5. Respondent's Partisan Attitudes (RPA)

This variable was received directly from the Survey Research Center at the University of Michigan as an index, drawn from their analysis deck number 86, columns 3–9, and based upon their regression of six dimensions of partisan attitudes against reported vote in 1956.

6. Respondent's Vote

Deck 7: Column 26   Democrat (Row 1), Republican (Row 2)

ANNE H. HOPKINS

Right-to-Work Legislation in the States: A Causal Analysis

*The following article by Anne Hopkins is based on
an unpublished paper revised especially for this volume. It involves a
variety of analysis techniques, but the primary focus is on causal
modeling. It is a rather straightforward example of alternative model
building utilizing the Simon-Blalock technique and the host of decisions
facing a researcher using this method. The purpose of the analysis is
to isolate influences on passage of right-to-work laws in the American
states. The data include a mixture of attitudinal and system-level
variables across the states, whereas our preceding examples have utilized
either data gathered from survey research or aggregate measures of
political phenomena. The final dependent variable for the various models
is a dichotomous measure indicating the presence or absence of right-to-
work laws in each state. The predictor variables in the models include:
(1) five political system variables reduced by a factor analysis (see
chapter 4) from fourteen original variables; (2) measures of each state's
attitudinal preferences on right to work (derived from transformations of
national surveys) for each of four electorates — the total eligible*

This reading was written especially for this volume on the basis of a previously unpublished paper
delivered at the annual meeting of The Southwestern Political Science Association, 1969.

The research reported in this paper was conducted at Syracuse University under National Science
Foundation Grant GS-1573, "Two-Party Competition and Policy Making in the American States,"
Frank J. Munger, Principal Investigator, and at Hobart and William Smith Colleges under National
Science Foundation Grant GS-2617, "Causal Modeling and Explanations of Policy Enactments."
I wish to express thanks to Frank J. Munger and Ronald E. Weber for their helpful comments and
assistance. Computations for this paper were performed at the Syracuse University Computing
Center under National Science Foundation Grant GP-1137 and at the Hobart and William Smith
Colleges Computing Center.

electorate, the voting or participating electorate, and the attentive
and active electorates; and (3) two factors representing the environment
of state political systems (derived from six variables). These variables
represent the various components of a systems model — the environment,
opinion inputs, the political system, and policy outputs.
The models being tested through a causal inference approach employ
varying measures of the predictor variable: state factor scores on the
economically developed and economically developing environmental factors,
factor scores on the elections factor from the political system variables,
plus the opinion input and right-to-work output measures. The opinion
measure varies since each model is tested for each of four types of
electorates in the states. The author follows a consistent procedure
for reporting results: simple correlations between variables in each
model, prediction equations based on correlation coefficients with
expected zero values compared to actual values from the data, and
standardized regression coefficients (betas) applied to the causal paths.

Explaining the reasons why political units enact the public policies they do remains a major unanswered problem for political science. The purpose of this paper is to provide a partial explanation for one kind of political unit — the American states — and for one kind of policy output — right-to-work laws. This study differs from previous efforts in two ways. First, the opinions of the various state electorates will be considered as a potentially significant independent variable. Secondly, the use of causal modeling will permit the making of causal inferences in explaining policy variations among the states. Hopefully, the technique described can be and will be subsequently applied to other areas of public policy.

One of the earliest and most suggestive works dealing with the question of differential state policy enactments was V. O. Key's *Southern Politics*.[1] Key suggested that different kinds of party organization and competitive structures within the states tended to produce divergent policy outcomes. In the years since Key formulated this hypothesis, numerous studies have been conducted to measure the impact of party competition and other independent variables on variations in policy outputs, defining the variation most frequently in fiscal terms.[2] Of these studies, only two, those by Lockard and Fenton, conclude that party competition has a significant independent effect on policy. The general findings of the other studies were that socioeconomic or environmental factors were the most significant variables in explaining policy variations and that political factors such as competition played either a secondary or fairly insignificant explanatory role.

1. V. O. Key, Jr. *Southern Politics in State and Nation* (New York: Alfred A. Knopf, 1949).

2. Of the studies seeking to provide explanations of policy outputs at the states level, the most notable works are: Richard E. Dawson and James A. Robinson, "Inter-Party Competition, Economic Variables and Welfare Policies in the American States," *Journal of Politics* XXV (May 1963): 265–87; Dawson and Robinson, "The Politics of Welfare," *Politics in the American States: A Comparative Analysis*, ed. Herbert Jacob and Kenneth N. Vines (Boston: Little, Brown, 1965), pp. 371–10; Thomas Dye, *Politics, Economics and the Public: Policy Outcomes in the American States* (Chicago: Rand McNally, 1966); John Fenton, *People and Parties in Politics* (Glenview, Ill.: Scott, Foresman, 1966); Duane Lockard, *New England State Politics* (Princeton, N.J.: Princeton University Press, 1959); and Ira Sharkansky, *Spending in the American States* (Chicago: Rand McNally, 1968).

Measurement of Systems Model Components

A systems model has been selected to analyze differential enactments of right-to-work laws in the American states. While most of the previous research on state policy outputs has either implicitly or explicitly utilized a systems model, "the theory rarely guides the research."[3] It *is* an explicit guide to the research reported here and the model provides a framework within which to test the causal determinants of one policy area.

Before proceeding to a causal analysis of the differential enactment of right-to-work laws, it is first necessary to outline the systems model to be employed and to provide a brief description of the components of the model and the linkages involved. Figure 1 illustrates this systems model. It will be noted that all feedback has been eliminated from the model. This was done to permit the use of the Simon-Blalock technique of causal modeling which assumes one-way, hierarchical causation.[4] The model presented in figure 1 is in broad outline comparable to Easton's model of the political system,[5] but in order to utilize this model to explain differential state enactments of right-to-work laws (a task considerably less complex than that posed by Easton), the original model has been simplified substantially.

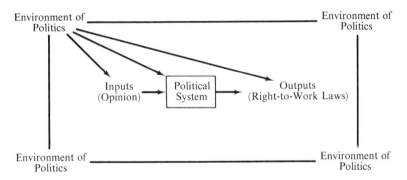

FIGURE 1   A Systems Model of the Policy Process

The central structure within the model is the political system within which most decision making takes place. The primary function of the political system in this model is to act as an arbiter among the various demands made upon the political system by its citizenry. Although delineation of the factors to be included within the system is difficult, clearly both formal governmental structures as well as formal and informal arrangements must be included in defining its bounds.

---

3. Herbert Jacob and Michael Lipsky, "Outputs, Structure, and Power: An Assessment of Changes in the Study of State and Local Politics," *Political Science: Advance of the Discipline*, ed. Marian Irish (Englewood Cliffs, N.J.: Prentice-Hall, 1968), p. 224.

4. See Herbert Simon, *Models of Man* (New York: John Wiley, 1957), chapters I–III, and Hubert Blalock, Jr., *Causal Inferences in Nonexperimental Research* (Chapel Hill: University of North Carolina, 1961) for an explanation of the causal modeling employed in this paper. The elimination of feedback is no doubt a substantial deviation from reality. It is necessary, however, in light of the assumptions required to permit this form of causal modeling. See the discussion of these assumptions in footnote 16.

5. See David Easton, *The Political System* (New York: Knopf, 1953); *A Framework for Political Analysis* (New York: Prentice-Hall, 1965); and *A Systems Analysis of Political Life* (New York: John Wiley, 1965).

Innumerable specific factors might be interpreted as influencing action within the system. With the findings of previous research as a guide, fourteen variables were selected to represent the characteristics of the political system. Eight of these factors are generally termed nonstructural or process variables: competition, participation, partisanship, four measures of conflict within the legislature, and the extent of divided control. The remaining six factors selected are structural variables: apportionment, the power of the governor, a somewhat analogous measure of centralization, the length of state constitutions, initiative and referendum, and the length of legislative terms.[6] It should be noted that these variables are "representative" of the system and not fully descriptive of it. In addition, several of the variables act as inputs and linkages to the system as well as affecting operations within the system itself.

Both the large number of system variables and the high intercorrelations among these variables necessitated the development of an index to represent these characteristics of the political system. Thus the fourteen system variables were subjected to principal components factor analysis with orthogonal (varimax) rotation. Standardized factor score indices for the fifty states were computed on each rotated factor. Employing this technique, five factors were derived accounting for 75.3 percent of the total variance among the fourteen variables. Table I presents the rotated factor loadings for these variables. The first and strongest factor clearly emerges as an electoral dimension with high loadings for competition, turnout, partisanship, divided control, and partisan conflict. The second factor is reflective of its two principle loadings of the related measures of gubernatorial influence

---

6. Measurement of the system variables is as follows:
  (1) Competition, 1946–1967: computation based on method developed by John Fenton, *People and Parties in Politics* (Glenview, Ill.: Scott, Foresman, 1966).
  (2) Participation, 1946–1967: average turnout for presidential, gubernatorial, and congressional elections.
  (3) Partisanship, 1946–1967: 1-average percent of seats held by Democrats in the upper and lower houses and percent democratic vote for governor.
  (4) Legislative conflict (partisan, factional, regional, and pressure group conflict): from Wayne L. Francis, *Legislative Issues in the Fifty States: A Comparative Analysis* (Chicago: Rand McNally, 1967).
  (5) Divided control, 1946–1967: percent of the time that control of state offices (governor and state legislature) have been divided between parties.
  (6) Appointment: factor score index derived from the malapportionment measures of Glendon Schubert and Charles Press, "Measuring Malapportionment," *American Political Science Review* 58 (1964): 302 and corrections 966–70; Manning J. Dauer and Robert G. Kelsay, "Unrepresentative States," *National Municipal Review* 44 (1955): 571–75 as corrected in 45 (1956): 198; and Paul T. David and Rolph Eisenberg, *Devaluation of the Urban and Suburban Vote: A Statistical Investigation of Long Term Trends in State Legislative Representation* (Charlottesville: University of Virginia, Bureau of Public Administration, 1961).
  (7) Power of the governor: from Joseph Schlesinger, "The Politics of the Executive," *Politics in the American States: A Comparative Analysis* ed. Herbert Jacob and Kenneth N. Vines (Boston: Little, Brown, 1965), pp. 207–37.
  (8) Centralization: from Wayne L. Francis, *Legislative Issues in the Fifty States: A Comparative Analysis* (Chicago: Rand McNally, 1967).
  (9) Legislative terms, 1965: summation of terms provided in both houses of the state legislature from *Book of the States, 1966–67.*
  (10) Length of state constitution, 1965: in words from *Book of the States, 1966–67.*
  (11) Initiative and referendum: categories based on legal provision, from *Book of the States, 1966–67.*
For a more complete description of these variables see Anne H. Hopkins, "Variations in the Enactment of Right-to-Work Laws: A Causal Explanation" (Ph.D. dissertation, Syracuse University, Syracuse, N.Y., 1969).

TABLE I   Rotated Factor Loadings: The Political
System

Variables	Elections	Governor	Formal Limits on Legislature	Leg I	Leg II
Competition	−.953	−.086	−.065	−.021	−.089
Turnout	−.916	.055	−.149	−.088	−.119
Partisanship	.842	−.097	.209	.134	.119
Divided control	−.831	.071	.137	.151	−.012
Partisan conflict	−.775	−.351	−.196	−.190	−.006
Centralization	.246	−.892	−.084	.014	.025
Governor power	−.440	−.666	.265	−.011	−.046
Legislative terms	.136	.014	.827	.115	.163
Constitution	482	−.206	.579	−.162	−.150
Apportionment	−.302	−.098	−.032	−.749	−.260
Factional conflict	.275	.147	−.071	−.650	.353
Regional conflict	−.058	.190	.379	.009	.761
Initiative and referendum	−.314	.140	.200	−.035	−.694
Pressure Group conflict	−.195	−.358	.306	−.403	.465
TOTAL VARIANCE	32.5	11.8	10.7	9.1	11.1

— Francis' centralization and Schlesinger's index of the power of the governor. The third factor is again composed of two major elements — the length of legislative terms — both of which represent potential limitations on the exercise of power by the legislature. The fourth and fifth factors are both characterized by high loadings for variables related to the setting within which legislative decisions are made.

The second major component of the model is the input into the system which directly influences the allocations of values and resources made within the system. Although Easton considers both supports and demands as inputs into the system, only the demand structure is directly considered in this paper.[7] Supports were a major element in Easton's theory because of this concern with the ability of the system to maintain itself within an environment comprehending both stability and change. Although there most certainly are differentials in terms of system supports among the fifty states, in general the states are insulated by the federal government from the kinds of instability and uncertainties which play a major role in national political systems.

Demands made upon the political system by the individuals who compose it vary widely. People have certain goals which they believe can be satisfied in the political arena and make demands upon the system in order to achieve these goals. Different people and groups have more influence on the actors in the political arena than others. Some desires are fully articulated while others remain latent. All this makes the identification of demands an enormously complex task.

No one will deny, however, that a major portion of the demand structure is composed of the opinions or attitudes of those seeking to influence the decision-

---

7. Several of the variables which have been included as within the political system also generate supports for the entire political system (e.g., competition, participation, and partisanship).

making process.[8] For this paper, the demand structure of a state will be defined by the attitudes and opinions of the citizens in regard to right-to-work legislation.

Measurements of a state's attitudinal preferences on right-to-work laws was accomplished by transforming national survey results into state-by-state preference patterns.[9] The methodology derived to estimate state policy preferences is based on a voter-type methodology analogous to the procedures employed by the MIT Simulmatics Project.[10]

The national survey data employed to estimate state-by-state preferences on right-to-work legislation was derived from four American Institute of Public Opinion surveys.[11] In each of the four surveys employed, the following question was asked: "Do you think a person should be required to join a union if he works in a unionized factory or business?" Negative responses to this question were viewed as attitudes favorable to the enactment of right-to-work legislation. Because these four surveys were executed within less than one year, the four surveys were combined to provide a larger N and thus increase the reliability of the estimating process.

Implementation of the model becomes especially difficult at this point because of the gap between the attitudes and opinions of a given state's general population and the actual demands made upon the state systems. In order at least partially to account for this problem, estimates were made of the policy preferences of four different electorates within each state. The four electorates include the eligible, participating, attentive, and active electorates. The eligible electorate is composed of all those persons technically able to vote because of age and citizenry. Lack of data prohibited a definition taking into account other limiting factors such as residence requirements. The participating electorate is defined for these purposes to include all those who participate in the political process by voting and more specifically those who participated by casting a ballot in the 1964 presidential election. The attentive electorate is characterized by those individuals who care greatly about the outcome of elections, follow campaigns closely, have high levels of interest in campaigns and politics generally and who almost always vote. Finally, the active electorate is composed of those who lend financial support to candidates

8. See Easton's discussion of public opinion as one of the elements of the demand structure in *A Systems Analysis of Political Life*, p. 42.

9. No data is available on a state by state basis relating to policy preferences. Several reliable state polls do exist, however, because almost no comparable questions are asked about political opinions directly related to areas of state policy concern, these polls were of little use. The problem of comparable questions does not arise with national surveys and they do contain numerous questions directly related to areas of state policy concern, including, of course, right-to-work legislation. The individual state components of national surveys, however, although identifiable, are ordinarily unrepresentative in character and too small in size to permit use.

10. See Ithiel de Sola Pool, Robert P. Abelson, and Samuel L. Popkin, *Candidates, Issues and Strategies: A Computer Simulation of the 1960 and 1964 Presidential Elections* (Cambridge, Mass.: The MIT Press, 1964). The methodology utilized to estimate policy preferences in this paper was developed at Syracuse University. A description of this methodology is available in Ronald E. Weber and Anne H. Hopkins, "A Methodology for Synthesizing State Policy Preferences" (mimeographed), Paper delivered at Conference on the Measurement of Public Policies in the American States, Ann Arbor, Michigan, University of Michigan, July 30–August 3, 1968, and Michael L. Mezey, "A Method for Estimating Voter Types in the 50 States" (mimeographed) available through Professor Frank J. Munger, Department of Political Science, University of North Carolina.

11. The four surveys employed were: AIPO 711, 5/11/65; AIPO 717, 9/14/65; AIPO 718, 10/6/65; and AIPO 723, 1/19/66. These surveys were made available through the Roper Center for Public Opinion Research, Williams College, Williamstown, Massachusetts.

or parties, those who attend political meetings, rallies or dinners, and those who belong to political clubs or organizations. An examination of the impact of the preference of these four electorates will permit testing whether preferences have a greater impact on the variation in enactment of right-to-work laws as one moves from the eligible, to the participating, to the attentive, to the active electorates. In other words, whether the preferences of those who actually do participate or those who are attentive to or active in politics are of greater significance in explaining policy outcomes than the preferences of the public at large.

The third major element in the systems model of the policy process is called the environment of politics. By definition, the environment of politics includes all factors external to the political system, its demand structure and outputs, which are relevant to the state policy-making process. In operationalizing this definition, certain arbitrary decisions had to be made as to what is and is not relevant to the state policy-making process. To limit the number of factors which might be included within the environment of politics, it was decided to use only those factors which through previous investigation had been found to be related to differential policy outcomes.

On this basis, six factors were selected as indicators of the nature of the environment of politics: measures of race, level of wealth, education, urbanization, ethnicity, and industrialization. As was the case with measuring the variables used to represent the political system, the number of variables and the high intercorrelations required development of factor score indices (again utilizing principal components factor analysis with varimax rotation) to represent the environment of politics. Table II presents the rotated factor loadings for the environmental factors. Two principle factors emerged from the analysis which together accounted for 86 percent of the total variance among the six variables. The first of the two principle factors has very high positive loadings for the measures of industrialization, urbanization, and income and a moderate loading for ethnicity. The index derived from these loadings has high scores for such economically developed states as New York, California, and Illinois and low scores for both rural farm states such as the Dakotas and the less developed southern states such as Mississippi and Arkansas. The second factor has a high positive loading for nonwhite and substantial negative loadings for education and ethnicity. The second factor score index for the environmental variables allots the highest scores to states such as Mississippi and South Carolina which have high proportions of nonwhites and low levels of education and ethnicity. States receiving the lowest scores on this index include states

TABLE II Rotated Factor Loadings: The Environment

Variables	Economically Developed	Economically Developing
Industrialization	.883	.575
Urbanization	.872	−.070
Income	.703	−.233
Nonwhite	.153	.818
Education	.316	−.771
Ethnicity	.476	−.621
TOTAL VARIANCE	48.6	37.4

such as Wyoming and Nebraska which have low levels of nonwhite population and high educational levels as well as states such as Massachusetts with low nonwhite, high ethnicity and industrialization and moderately high educational levels.

The fourth and final major component of the systems model is the output emanating from the political system. Right-to-work legislation was selected for this study because of its importance as a substantive policy concern within the reach of state authority. Since the enactment of the Taft-Hartley Act in 1947, all of the states have considered the adoption of right-to-work laws.[12] Twenty-five states have adopted some form of right-to-work law since 1947 and of these laws, nineteen remain in effect.[13]

In order to utilize data on the enactment of right-to-work laws by the states as outputs, it was necessary to assign numerical values to the kinds of policies enacted. To this end, states which had either never enacted right-to-work legislation or which had enacted but repealed such legislation were assigned a "1"; states which had a right-to-work law in effect were assigned a "2." This categorization was applied as of January 1, 1968, to permit a two-year lapse between the timing of the questions utilized to measure the opinion structure in the states and the existence of right-to-work laws.

Returning to the presentation of the model in figure 1, five linkages between the major components of the model are evident. The environment of politics is linked to inputs, the political system and outputs. Inputs are linked to the system and system is linked to outputs. The logic of the first of these linkages, between the environment and the demand structure, has been fairly well substantiated. Research on opinion formation has shown that the kinds of attitudes and opinions held by individuals are directly related to such factors as social status, ethnicity, and race, elements of which have been incorporated in the measures of the environment used in this study. In effect, previous research on variations in state policy outputs has seemed to rely entirely on environmental or socioeconomic factors as proxies for the demand structure.

The environment of politics also exerts an independent influence on the nature of the political system itself. Previous investigations have found that the socioeconomic environments of political units are highly related to such political system characteristics as competition, participation, and partisanship.[14] Some researchers have held that certain levels of social and economic conditions are prerequisites to the development of certain kinds of political system characteristics.[15] In the context of this study, it is apparent that in certain cases, the environment may affect the character of the political system and, at times, conditions within the environment

---

12. The Wagner Act (1935) contained a provision which permitted unions to negotiate union contracts requiring union membership as a condition of employment in a company. Section 14(b) of the Taft-Hartley Act forbade the closed shop and permitted states to adopt right-to-work laws which would forbid employers and unions from signing union shop contracts.

13. The nineteen states which presently have such laws include: Alabama, Arizona, Arkansas, Florida, Georgia, Iowa, Kansas, Maine, Mississippi, Nebraska, Nevada, North Carolina, South Carolina, South Dakota, Tennessee, Texas, Utah, Virginia, and Wyoming. Six additional states have adopted and later repealed right-to-work laws: Delaware, Hawaii, Indiana, Maine, New Hampshire, and Louisiana.

14. For example, see the presentation of Dye, *Politics, Economics and the Public*, pp. 46–73.

15. See, for example, Seymour Martin Lipset, *Political Man: The Social Bases of Politics* (Garden City, N.Y.: Doubleday, 1960), pp. 27-63.

of politics are taken into account by actors within the political system. An example of this latter kind of an impact in regard to right-to-work laws would be an assessment by actors in the system of the level of industrialization and thus of the potential strength of unions within the environment. Since unions have been strongly opposed to the enactment of right-to-work laws, the existence of an environment in which the level of industrialization is high might tend to limit or condition the range of politically feasible alternatives to the actor.

The remaining two linkages in the model are between the demand structure and the political system and outputs or policies. Demands are at times directed toward the political system: the political system decides whether and how to act on these demands and policy decisions emanate from the system. Actors in the political system often seek to maximize their position by responding to these demands through enacting the desired policies. Other factors such as type and clarity of communication enter into the process of decision making. However, demands appear to be one of the central elements which account for variations in the enactment of policies. At most points in time, demands are so numerous and conflicting that the political system must act as eliminator, consolidator, and arbiter before decisions can be reached. According to the definition of the model provided above, policies emerge from the political system, although the environment of politics may limit or condition the kinds of decisions reached.

Methodology

Before proceeding to a testing of the model, a few words of caution and explanation in regard to causal modeling are necessary. Whether or not the determination of causality is a possibility in the natural, physical, or social sciences has been argued extensively. Given the nature of the data available to social scientists and the nature of the social world, the answer must surely be that it is not possible to establish causality. However, it is possible to gain considerable understanding of a given set of interrelationships by making causal inferences on the basis of knowledge about which model best fits a given set of empirical data. The leap from causality to causal inference is a significant one in terms of diminishing the theoretical problems associated with the determination of causality.

The technique of causal modeling utilized in this research was suggested and developed by Herbert Simon and Hubert Blalock. Several important assumptions must be accepted for this technique of analysis to be utilized.[16]

---

16. First of all, the model to be tested must be hierarchical in form. One-way causation within the variables of the model must be assumed. It is for this reason that the feedback loops in the system's model were eliminated earlier. This assumption is, no doubt, contrary to reality in which two-way causation, feedback, and reciprocal interaction are continuing processes.

In testing any given model, a finite set of explicitly defined variables must be utilized. Given the fact that no system can be completely isolated that one would never know that all relevant variables had been located, certain assumptions must be made about the operation of unknowns. At some point in the analysis, one must assume, as Blalock has stated, that "outside variables while operating, do not have confounding influences that disturb the causal patterning of the variables explicitly being considered." In addition to assuming that variables outside the system do not have confounding effects, the Simon-Blalock technique requires that the ordering of the variables and the direction of the causal relationships between them must be determined prior to testing the fit of a given model. The nature of the systems model being tested in this paper is such that both the ordering of the variables and the direction of the relationships are predetermined by the nature of the model.

Causal modeling does permit, within the limitation of assumption, the inferring of causal relationships. One is never able to establish the validity of a given model within the confines of the data, but one is able to establish which models do not fit the data and thus, by inference, suggest possible explanatory models.

Having outlined the systems model and the techniques which will be utilized to test the model, it is now appropriate to examine the data. It will be remembered that five factor score indices were developed to characterize different aspects of the political system. In addition, two factor score indices were created to represent the environment of politics. Although it is theoretically possible to execute causal modeling given eight independent variables (the seven noted above plus demands), the computations for such an analysis would be exceedingly complex. As an alternative, it was decided to make use of one variable to measure each of the three categories of independent variables: the political system, the environment, and public opinion.[17] As a criterion to select among the five system variables and the two environment of politics variables, the factors accounting for the largest proportion of the total variance were selected. The largest political system factor was "elections" and for the environment the factor entitled "economically developed." Utilizing this criterion, four models are developed and tested using the "elections" political system factor, the "economically developed" environmental factor, and alternating the four opinion variables. Four additional models also are developed comparable to those described above except for the substitution of the second environmental factor "economically developing." These second four models are presented because the components of this environmental factor are substantially different than those employed in previous research.

Findings: Models I-IV

The first model to be examined incorporates the opinions of the eligible electorate, the "elections" political system factor, the "economically developed" environmental factor, and right-to-work laws. Simple correlations were calculated for each of the interrelationships involved and are shown in figure 2.

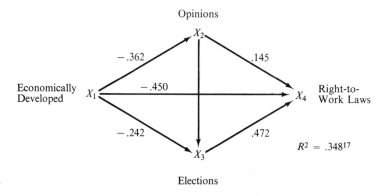

FIGURE 2   Correlations: Model I, the Eligible Electorate

---

17. With each model that is presented, the square of the multiple correlation coefficient (R^2) for the three independent variables will be given. This will permit the reader to evaluate the proportion of the variation in the dependent variable that is explained by the three independent variables acting together.

In order to test to see if the model including all possible relationships among the four variables is the best representation of the data, a series of prediction equations were utilized. With a four variable model, such as model I, there are six possible causal relationships. Five of the six relationships (excluding $X_1 \rightarrow X_2$) can be predicted from other data in the model. The prediction equations proceed by the ordering of the variables in the model. Each prediction equation takes the form of predicting a partial correlation of zero. If the actual values of the partial correlations approximate zero,[18] the correlation is judged to be spurious and the given causal arrow is eliminated from the model. The prediction equations and partial correlations for each of the testable interrelationships are shown in table III. In only one instance does the partial correlation approximate zero. In this one case, the linkage between opinion and right-to-work-laws was eliminated from the model.

TABLE III   Predictions: Model I, the Eligible Electorate

Prediction Equations	Actual Values	Judgment
$r_{31.2} = 0$	−.122	Keep
$r_{32.1} = 0$	−.252	Keep
$r_{41.23} = 0$	−.335	Keep
$r_{42.13} = 0$	.089	Erase
$r_{43.12} = 0$	.427	Keep

In order to evaluate the relative importance of the various causal paths in model I the betas were calculated for each linkage in the model. The beta measurements indicates the amount of change in the dependent variable produced by standardized changes in the independent variable controlling for all prior independent variables.[19] Figure 3 represents the betas for all causal arrows which are maintained within the

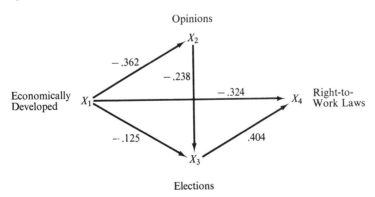

FIGURE 3   Betas: Model I, The Eligible Electorate

18. Although establishing a cutting point is always to some extent an arbitrary decision, it is necessary for the purposes at hand. As has been done in previous research employing causal modeling, a partial correlation of 0.1 or less will be considered to approximate zero and thus be eliminated from a best fitting model.

19. Hubert Blalock, *Social Statistics* (New York: McGraw-Hill, 1960), p. 343. For a discussion of this statistic, see pp. 343–46.

model. An examination of the betas indicates that there are three paths of influence in determining variation in the enactment of right-to-work legislation.[20] The first path of influence and that most clearly approximating the systems model runs from the environment to opinion to system to laws. Of comparable strength is the direct linkage between environment and laws. The third and final linkage in the model is substantially weaker, running from the environment to system and from system to policy.

The second model to be examined is similar to model I in including the "elections" system factor, the "economically developed" environmental factor, and right-to-work laws. In model II, however, the opinions of the participating electorate are substituted for those of the eligible electorate. The simple correlations for model II are shown in figure 4. Comparison of figures 2 and 4 indicates that alternation of the opinion factor substantially strengthened the correlations between opinions and laws and opinions and system.

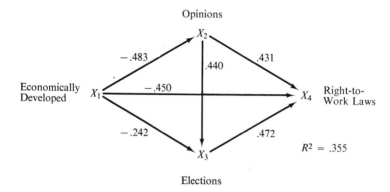

FIGURE 4   Correlations: Model II, the Participating
Electorate

Comparable prediction equations were again utilized and the appropriate partials and judgments are shown in table IV. Most of the increased correlation between

TABLE IV   Predictions: Model II, the Participating
Electorate

Prediction Equations	Actual Values	Judgment
$r_{31.2} = 0$	.078	Erase
$r_{32.1} = 0$	.305	Keep
$r_{41.23} = 0$	−.314	Keep
$r_{42.13} = 0$	.135	Keep
$r_{43.12} = 0$	.355	Keep

20. Although it was not executed for this paper, note should be made of the availability of a technique to measure the influence coefficients of each causal path in the model. Examples of the use of path analysis may be found in Warren E. Miller and Donald E. Stokes, "Constituency Influence in Congress," *American Political Science Review* 57 (1963): 45–56, and Charles F. Cnudde and Donald J. McCrone, "The Linkages Between Constituency Attitudes and Congressional Voting Behavior: A Causal Model," *American Politcal Science Review* 60 (1966): 66–72.

opinions and laws has been partialled out but the relationship between opinions and system remains stronger and in a positive direction. Figure 5 presents the betas for model II.

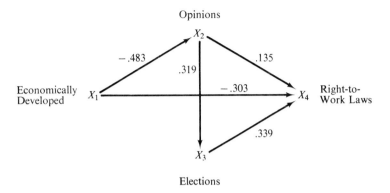

FIGURE 5   Betas: Model II, The Participating Electorate

Comparison of the betas for models I and II reveal both similarities and differences. Two of the three paths of influence in model I also appear in model II: the direct linkage from environment to policy and the path from environment to opinion to system to law. The principle difference between the models involves the elimination of the linkage from environment to system in model II and its maintainence in model I and the maintainence of the weak linkage from opinions to laws in model II and its elimination in model I.

The third of the four models utilizing the "economically developed" environmental factor incorporates the opinions of the attentive electorate. Examination of the intercorrelations in figure 6 indicates that the two relationships, which increased when the opinions of the participating electorate were utilized, were again increased, although less dramatically. The predication equations for model III are shown in table V. The results indicate that the best fitting model for this set of data is comparable to that for model II with only slight alterations in the strength of the relationships maintained.

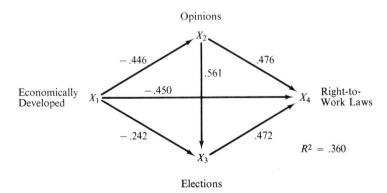

FIGURE 6   Correlations: Model III, the Attentive
Electorate

TABLE V   Predictions: Model III, the Attentive
Electorate

Prediction Equations	Actual Values	Judgment
$r_{31.2} = 0$	.106	Keep
$r_{32.1} = 0$	.443	Keep
$r_{41.23} = 0$	−.319	Keep
$r_{42.13} = 0$	.162	Keep
$r_{43.12} = 0$	.300	Keep

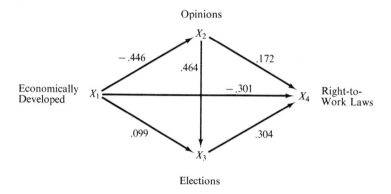

FIGURE 7   Betas: Model III, the Attentive Electorate

The fourth model to be examined incorporates the opinions of the active electorate. Although the model which best fits this set of data is the same as that for
models II and III, the opinions of the active electorate are much less important as
linkages within this model. The simple and partial correlations in figure 8 and
table VI indicate that reduction of strength occurs both with the direct link from
opinion to policy but more substantially with the linkage from opinion to system.
Figure 9 presents the betas for model IV.

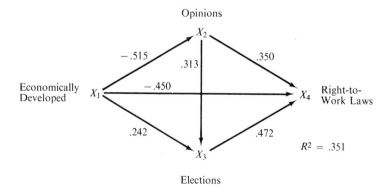

FIGURE 8   Correlations: Model IV, the Active Electorate

TABLE VI   Predictions; Model IV, the Active
Electorate

Prediction Equations	Actual Values	Judgment
$r_{31.2} = 0$	.035	Erase
$r_{32.1} = 0$	.163	Keep
$r_{41.23} = 0$	−.309	Keep
$r_{42.13} = 0$	.112	Keep
$r_{43.12} = 0$	.393	Keep

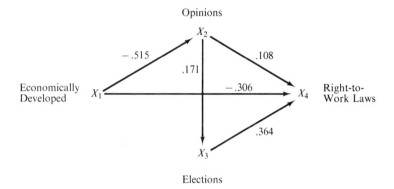

FIGURE 9   Betas: Model IV, the Active Electorate

Findings: Models V-VIII

The second set of four models to be tested differ from the first in the substitution of
the "economically developing" environmental factor for "economically developed."
The first of these models (model V) incorporates the opinions of the eligible electorate. The simple correlations for all possible interrelationships within the model
are shown in figure 10.

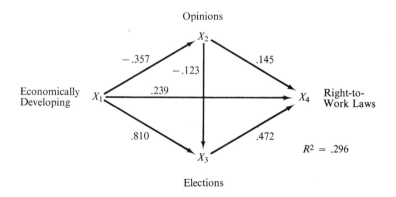

FIGURE 10   Correlations: Model V, the Eligible
Electorate

The predictions relative to model V are shown in table VI and indicate that all possible relationships are maintained within the model. The strength of these linkages can be assessed by examining figure 11 which presents the betas. Clearly the strongest linkage in this model runs from "economically developing" to system and from system to policy. The path of second influence is the direct link from environment to policy. Of lesser significance is the longest path (which was the most important with the first set of models) from environment to opinion to system to policy. The final path of influence is from environment to opinions to policy.

TABLE VI   Predictions: Model V, the Eligible
Electorate

Prediction Equations	Actual Values	Judgment
$r_{31.2} = 0$	.812	Keep
$r_{32.1} = 0$	.202	Keep
$r_{41.23} = 0$	−.200	Keep
$r_{42.13} = 0$	.131	Keep
$r_{43.12} = 0$	.448	Keep

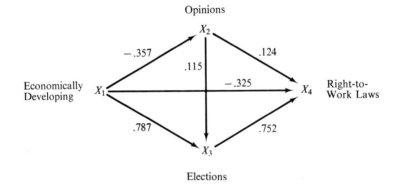

FIGURE 11   Betas: Model V, the Eligible Electorate

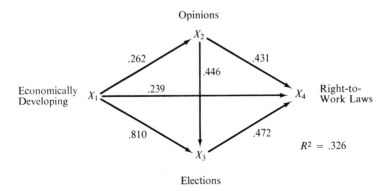

FIGURE 12   Correlations: Model VI, the Participating
Electorate

The second in this set of models is model VI, which substitutes the opinions of the participating electorate for those of the eligible electorate. The simple correlations and predictions for model VI are shown in figure 12 and table VII respectively. Comparison of the correlations for models V and VI reveal several differences. These variations are, however, reduced to one, when the betas are compared (see figs. 13 and 11). This one difference relates to the linkage between economically developing and opinions. In model VI, this linkage is reversed to the expected direction. The reversal of this linkage with the substitution of the participating for the eligible electorate also occurred with the first set of models.

TABLE VII   Predictions: Model VI, the Participating
Electorate

Prediction Equations	Actual Values	Judgment
$r_{31.2} = 0$	.810	Keep
$r_{32.1} = 0$	.262	Keep
$r_{41.23} = 0$	−.241	Keep
$r_{42.13} = 0$	.246	Keep
$r_{43.12} = 0$	.394	Keep

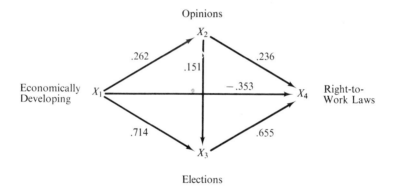

FIGURE 13   Betas: Model VI, the Participating
Electorate

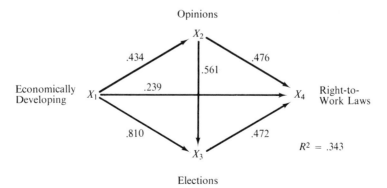

FIGURE 14   Correlations: Model VII, the Attentive
Electorate

Model VII which incorporates the opinions of the attentive electorate is shown in figure 14. The correlations for models VI and VII are similar with moderate increases in the size of the relationships involving the opinion variable. The prediction equations for the seventh model are presented in table VIII.

TABLE VIII   Predictions: Model VII, the Attentive
Electorate

Prediction Equations	Actual Values	Judgment
$r_{13.2} = 0$	.780	Keep
$r_{32.1} = 0$	.239	Keep
$r_{41.23} = 0$	−.278	Keep
$r_{42.13} = 0$	.289	Keep
$r_{43.12} = 0$	.386	Keep

All of the possible relationships among the variables in the model are maintained. The betas for this model (see fig. 15) are essentially comparable to those for model VI except that the strength of the relationship between economically developing and opinions has been increased over the same relationship when the participating opinions were utilized in model VI.

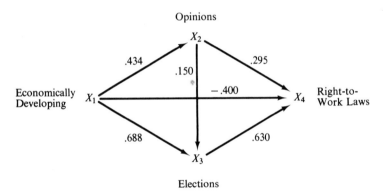

FIGURE 15   Betas: Model VII, the Attentive Electorate

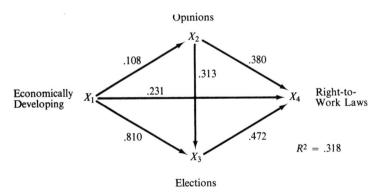

FIGURE 16   Correlations: Model VIII, the Active
Electorate

The last of the eight models examined in this paper substitutes the opinions of the active electorate in the model (see fig. 16). Substantial reductions in the strength of the correlation coefficients occurs with this model as compared to model VII, although these correlations are much closer to the ones for the eligible and participating electorates. The prediction equations for this model are shown in table IX, and like model VII all relationships are maintained within the model.

TABLE IX   Predictions: Model VIII, the Active
Electorate

Prediction Equations	Actual Values	Judgment
$r_{13.2} = 0$	.823	Keep
$r_{32.1} = 0$	.255	Keep
$r_{41.23} = 0$	−.221	Keep
$r_{42.13} = 0$	.221	Keep
$r_{43.12} = 0$	.405	Keep

The betas for model VIII (see fig. 17) are, despite differences in correlation coefficients, similar between models VII and VIII with the exception of the strength of the relationship between the environment and opinions.

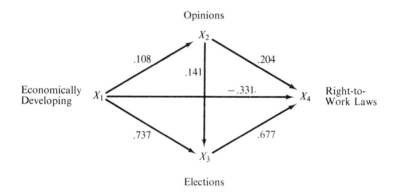

FIGURE 17   Betas: Model VIII, the Active Electorate

Conclusion

Each of the eight models of the political system have been examined. One general kind of model emerged from each of the sets of analysi. In the first set of models (economically developed) there was some variation, but in general the findings approximate figure 18. There are two principle linkages in the model: the direct path from environment to law and from environment to law by way of opinions and system. The path indicated in dotted lines in figure 18 appeared in three of the four models but was weak in all cases. The fairly strong linkage via opinions and system is of particular interest because it contradicts the findings of much previous

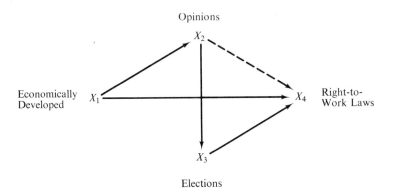

FIGURE 18   General Model I: Economically
Developed

research that systemic variables did not have importance as intervening variables.[21]
It is also suggestive of the problems associated with using environmental factors as
proxies for the demand structure.

The first general model differs from the systems model posited in figure 1 in two
ways. First, there is no linkage between environment and systems indicating an
independence of the environmental and system factors utilized in these models.
Second, the dotted line in general model I is not posited in the systems model.
The general thrust of this model, however, coincides with the systems model in that
the principle linkages maintained within the model indicate, at least in part, an
intervening role for both opinions and the political system.

The second general model also departs at least slightly from the systems model
(see fig. 19). However, this model more closely approximates the posited model than
does the first. Deviation from the model exists only in the maintenance of the

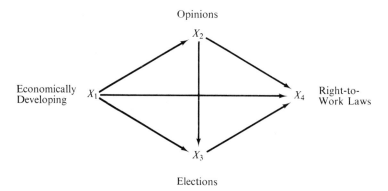

FIGURE 19   General Model II: Economically
Developing

21. See Dawson and Robinson, "Inter-Party Competition, Economic Variables and Welfare Policies"
and "The Politics of Welfare"; Dye, *Politics, Economics and the Public;* Fenton, *People and Parties in
Politics;* and Sharkansky, *Spending in the American States.*

linkage between opinions and laws. There are three major and one minor linkages in this model. Of principle importance is the path from environment to system to policy. Of somewhat lesser significance are the direct link between environment and policy and the path between environment and policy mediated by opinions. The fourth and least important causal linkage runs from environment to opinions, opinions to system (very weak), and from system to policy.

Perhaps of more interest, however, is the contrast between the two general models. The second general model departs from the first in two principle ways. First, when the "economically developed" environmental factor was used, opinions were a very important part of the linkage process. In contrast, when the "economically developing" factor was employed, the role of opinions in the linkage process was small as is indicated by the dotted line in figure 19. The second contrast between the two general models is in the very strong linkage between environment and system in general model II and the absence of that link in general model I.

Note has not yet been taken of the different explanatory levels of the models. The multiple correlation coefficients squared (R^2) were noted in tables III and IV. The overall explanatory power of the two general models is only slightly different with the first general model explaining a somewhat larger proportion of the variation in the enactment of right-to-work laws.[22] In addition, examination of the R^2's reveals that there is little variation with the two general models when different opinion electorates are substituted. Since opinions were found to be an important linkage in the first general model it is interesting to note that there is some indication of a stronger role for opinions when either the participating or more particularly the attentive electorate is used. Enough variation does exist, however, so that the question raised of the impact of different opinion structures on the enactment of policy will have to await further investigation in a broad range of policy areas.

Two different general models emerged from the analysis as best fitting the given sets of data. The first model has a primary role for opinions, the second does not. Both models have direct links between environment and policy and both maintain in varying degrees a path from opinions to policy. Environment is independent of system in the first model and strongly dependent in the second. Perhaps of greatest importance is not the particular linkages kept or eliminated, but the fact that altering environmental factors changes the causal interrelationships and further illustrates the complexity of the process by which decisions are made.

The limitations of the findings outlined above must be reviewed. Several assumptions were made in regard to the model being tested. One-way causation, hierarchical structure, and a lack of confounding effects on the model by the operation of unknowns was assumed. The results of the causal modeling in no way confirm these assumptions; rather, causal inferences may only be made with the acceptance of these assumptions. In addition, it is important to note that the inferences made apply only to one area of public policy — right-to-work laws — and to one point in time. It is probably erroneous, as Jacob and Lipsky have suggested, "to expect that

---

22. Some may contend that the use of causal modeling with R^2's at such a level is of questionable utility. Indeed, when more than half of the variance in the dependent variable is left unexplained there may be some difficulty in assuming the random operation of unknowns. However, the *present* status of our understanding of the operation of state political systems does not indicate any compounding effects among measurable variables.

inputs and process variables are associated in the same way to each policy output."[23] Validation of this point is possible only through the investigation of other areas of state policy concern.[24]

23. Jacob and Lipsky, in *Political Science*, ed. Irish, p. 228.
24. The author is presently engaged in a comparative analysis of seven state policy areas in which the systems model will form the basis of the study.

DONALD J. McCRONE
CHARLES F. CNUDDE

Toward a Communications Theory
of Democratic Political Development:
A Causal Model

In an analysis of cross-national data, McCrone and
Cnudde attempt to develop an empirical model of democratic political
development with reference to previous theoretical and empirical works by
Lipset and Cutright. Political democracy as the final dependent variable
is measured by Cutright's continuous variable denoting complexity and
specialization of institutions. It is based upon sets of officials in
office, political leaders out of office and reliance on political parties
and free elections. In order to move beyond studies of the correlates
of democratic political development, such as the previous works by Lipset
and Cutright, the authors propose causal modeling as a technique useful for
developing theoretical formulations. On the basis of previous research
and normative considerations, communications development is examined as
a primary linkage in a political development model including urbanization
and education measures as well. Their technique of alternative model
testing is based upon prediction equations suggested by theoretical
linkages in each four-variable model compared to the actual fit of the
data. In order to assess the weight of relationships remaining in
the models, path coefficients are derived to measure changes in the
political development variable produced by standardized changes in an
independent variable.

Reprinted from Donald J. McCrone and Charles F. Cnudde, "Toward a Communications Theory of
Democratic Political Development: A Causal Model," *American Political Science Review* 61 (1967):
72–79, by permission of the American Political Science Association and the authors.

The construction of an empirical theory of democratic political development is dependent on the formulation of causal propositions which are generalizations of the developmental process. To date, several essential steps in the process of constructing such a theory have been taken. First, concept formation and clarification by students of political development has led to an emphasis upon political democracy as one of the dependent variables for the field.[1] Second, the gathering and publication of quantitative indicators of social, economic, cultural, and political phenomena provide a firm basis for subsequent empirical inquiry.[2] Finally, correlational analysis has identified numerous variables which are closely associated with the development of democratic political institutions.[3]

The next major task is the formulation and testing of empirical models of democratic political development which provide a basis for inferring causal relationships by distinguishing between spurious correlations and indirect and direct effects.[4] The accomplishment of this task would enable us to derive explanatory propositions concerning the process of democratic political development.

The purpose of this essay is to suggest the combined utility of two similar theory-building techniques in the accomplishment of this task and to take a modest step in the direction of constructing an empirical model of democratic political development.

I. Concepts of Political Development

Seymour Martin Lipset explicitly adopts democratic political development as his dependent variable. He defines political democracy as:

> a political system which supplies regular constitutional opportunities for changing the governing officials. It is a social mechanism for the resolution of the problems of societal decision-making among conflicting interest groups which permits the largest to choose among alternative contenders for political office.[5]

For Lispset, this definition of democracy implies three key specific conditions: first, one set of political leaders who occupy official governing positions; second, one or more sets of competing leaders who do not occupy governing positions, but who act as a loyal opposition; third, widespread acceptance of a "political formula" which specifies the legitimate political institutions for the society (political parties, free press, etc.) and legitimizes democratic political competition.[6] European and English-speaking nations are classified as stable democracies or unstable democracies

---

1. For an interesting discussion of this material as well as important findings on factors which relate to democracy, see Seymour Martin Lipset, "Some Social Requisites of Democracy: Economic Development and Political Legitimacy," *American Political Science Review*, 53 (1959), pp. 69–105.

2. Bruce M. Russett, *et al.*, *World Handbook of Political and Social Indicators* (New Haven: Yale University Press, 1964).

3. Phillips Cutright, "National Political Development," in Nelson Polsby, *et al.* (eds.), *Politics and Social Life* (Boston: Houghton Mifflin, 1963), pp. 569–82.

4. For an example of this type of model testing in political science, see Charles F. Cnudde and Donald J. McCrone, "The Linkage Between Constituency Attitudes and Congressional Voting Behavior: A Causal Model," *American Political Science Review*, LX (1966), pp. 66–72.

5. Lipset, *op. cit.*, p. 71.

6. *Loc. cit.*

and dictatorships on the basis of whether they fulfilled these specific conditions in the period since World War I. Lipset also adds the condition that there be an absence of Communist or Fascist parties (i.e., political movements opposed to the democratic "political formula") garnering more than twenty percent of the vote in the last twenty-five years.[7]

Lipset's measurement of political democracy unfortunately has severe limitations. His "all-or-nothing" requirement transforms political democracy from a continuous variable into an attribute. Theoretically, democracy may be most usefully conceived of as a continuum. A political system is not democratic or nondemocratic — democracy is not present or absent — rather a political system is more or less democratic. Moreover, even if democracy were best conceived to be an attribute, the problem of selecting nonarbitrary cutpoints would still present severe problems.[8] Finally, a dichotomous dependent variable places strains on the power of the statistical techniques that may be applied.

Philips Cutright, on the other hand, attempts to define political development in terms which do not rely explicitly on liberal democratic standards.

> The degree of political development of a nation can be defined by the degree of complexity and specialization of its national political institutions.[9]

Nevertheless, a careful examination of Cutright's political development scoring procedure indicates a reliance on the same standards utilized by Lipset. In fact, Cutright's measurement procedure is an excellent operationalization of Lipset's concept of political democracy. Points are assigned to a political system on the basis of one set of officials in office, one or more sets of political leaders out of office, and reliance on political parties and free elections as the legitimate political institutions for the society.[10] The virtue of the Cutright measure is that it transforms Lipset's democratic attribute into a continuous variable, thereby avoiding the problems cited above. Pending further refinements in this field, democratic political development may best be conceptualized in Lipset's terms and measured by Cutright's procedures.[11]

---

7. *Ibid.*, pp. 73–74. Latin American political systems are classified somewhat differently, but still dichotomously.

8. For the pitfalls involved in choosing cutpoints, see Hubert M. Blalock, Jr., *Causal Inferences in Nonexperimental Research* (Chapel Hill: University of North Carolina Press, 1964).

9. Cutright, *op. cit.*, p. 571.

10. *Ibid.*, p. 574. Scores may vary from 0 to 66 based on a total of three for each of twenty-two years (1940–1961).

11. Of course political scientists' interest in democracy includes more than the existence and maintenance of democratic institutions. Two lines of further refinements have relied upon system-level democratic "behaviors" to make additional distinctions among political systems with democratic institutions. One of these developments deals with Dahl's concept of polyarchy, the other with political equality. While extremely meaningful, these concepts require much ingenuity to operationalize, especially on a cross-national level. For the concept of polyarchy see Robert A. Dahl, *A Preface to Democratic Theory*, (Chicago: The University of Chicago Press, 1956), p. 84. For operational measures of the concept see Deane E. Neubauer, "Some Conditions of Democracy" (forthcoming), and Haywood R. Alker, Jr., "Causal Inference and Political Analysis" (forthcoming). For an operational measure of political equality within the United States, see Charles F. Cnudde, "Consensus, 'Rules of the Game' and Democratic Politics: The Case of Race Politics in the South" (unpublished Ph.D. dissertation, Department of Political Science, University of North Carolina, 1966).

Both Lipset and Cutright have established correlations between socio-economic factors and democratic political development. Lipset finds that indices of *wealth* (per capita income, thousands of persons per doctor, and persons per motor vehicle), *communication* (telephones, radios, and newspaper copies per thousand persons), *industrialization* (percentages of males in agriculture and per capita energy consumed), *education* (percentage literate, and primary, post-primary, and higher education enrollment per thousand persons), and *urbanization* (per cent in cities over 20,000, 100,000, and in metropolitan areas) are all strongly related to political democracy.[12]

Cutright, using product-moment correlation analysis, identifies indices of *communication* (summed T scores of newspaper readers, newsprint consumption, volume of domestic mail, and number of telephones per capita), *urbanization* (T score of the proportion of the population in cities over 100,000), *education* (combined T scores of literacy and number of students per 100,000 in institutions of higher education), *agriculture* (T score of the proportion of the economically active labor force employed in agriculture) as being closely associated with political development.[13]

Regardless of the imaginativeness and utility of these studies, they do not constitute theoretical formulations of the process of democratic political development. They remain studies of the correlates of democratic political development.

II. A Communications Development Model

Communications development suggests itself as a variable around which a theory of the process of democratic political development might be constructed for several reasons.[14] First, both normative and empirical theory point to communications as a prerequisite to a successfully operating political democracy. Normative thinking gives communications networks the role of providing an informed citizenry, while more empirical scholarship sees communications as integrative, producing the social cohesion necessary to prevent disintegration in the face of democratic policy conflict.[15] Second, Cutright finds that communications development is by far the strongest socioeconomic correlate of political development.[16] Third, the most ambitious attempt at a theoretical formulation of the process of democratic political development views communications development as the final prerequisite for a successfully functioning democratic political system.[17]

---

12. Lipset, *op. cit.*, pp. 76–77. He relies on means and ranges to establish the relationships.

13. Cutright, *op. cit.*, p. 577.

14. For theoretical contributions which indicate the central role of communications systems in more general types of political development, see Lucian W. Pye, (ed.), *Communications and Political Development* (Princeton, N. J.: Princeton University Press, 1963).

15. Karl W. Deutsch, *The Nerves of Government* (New York: The Free Press of Glencoe, 1963); Karl W. Deutsch "Communication Theory and Political Integration " in Phillip E. Jacob and James V. Toscano (eds.) *The Integration of Political Communities* (Philadelphia and New York: J. B. Lippincott Co., 1964), pp. 46–74. For the relationship between communication and civic cooperation at the individual level in nations which vary in the degree to which democracy is successfully institutionalized, see Gabriel A. Almond and Sidney Verba, *The Civic Culture: Political Attitudes and Democracy in Five Nations* (Princeton: Princeton University Press, 1963), pp. 378–81.

16. Cutright, *op. cit.*, p. 577.

17. Daniel Lerner, *The Passing of Traditional Society* (Glencoe: The Free Press, 1958).

Daniel Lerner theorizes that the process of democratic political development (which he defines as the "crowning institution of the participant society") is the consequence of a developmental sequence beginning with urbanization.

The secular evolution of a participant society appears to involve a regular sequence of three phases. Urbanization comes first, for cities alone have developed the complex of skills and resources which characterize the modern industrial economy. Within this urban matrix develop both of the attributes which distinguish the next two phases — literacy and media growth. There is a close reciprocal relationship between these, for the literate develop the media which in turn spread literacy. But, literacy performs the key function in the second phase. The capacity to read, at first acquired by relatively few people, equips them to perform the varied tasks required in the modernizing society. Not until the third phase, when the elaborate technology of industrial development is fairly well advanced, does a society begin to produce newspapers, radio networks, and motion pictures on a massive scale. This, in turn, accelerates the spread of literacy. Out of this interaction develop those institutions of participation (e.g. voting) which we find in all advanced modern societies.[18]

Lerner's thesis is not satisfactorily confirmed by his data, but his conceptualization of political development as a developmental sequence provides a basis for a causal formulation of the process of democratic political development.

Figure 1 represents our initial causal model based on the conception of democratic political development as a developmental sequence. This four-variable causal model is, of course, only one of a whole family of logically alternative models utilizing the same four variables. A means for testing the adequacy of this particular causal model and for eliminating alternative models is clearly needed.

U ⟶ E ⟶ C ⟶ D

FIGURE 1   Initial Conception of Democratic Political Development as a Developmental Sequence (U —Urbanization, E — Education, C — Communications, D — Democratic political development)

III. Testing the Model

Two interrelated theory-building techniques are applied in this study in an effort to eliminate logical alternative models and to provide a basis for inferring the adequacy of the postulated model of democratic political development. First, Simon-Blalock causal model analysis is utilized because it enables us

to make causal *inferences* concerning the adequacy of causal models, at least in the sense that we can proceed by eliminating inadequate models that make predictions that are not consistent with the data. [19]

18. *Ibid.*, p. 60.
19. Blalock, *op. cit.*, p. 62. Also see Herbert A. Simon, "Spurious Correlations: A Causal Interpretation," *Journal of the American Statistical Association*, 49 (1954), pp. 467–479.

Prediction equations based on the correlation coefficients between variables are computed for each alternative model. Models that make prediction equations inconsistent with the actual relationships between the variables in the system are rejected.[20]

Second, path coefficients are computed for the causal model that is inferred by use of the Simon-Blalock technique. In causal analysis, we are primarily concerned with changes in the dependent variable(s) which are produced by changes in the independent variable(s). The correlation coefficients used in the Simon-Blalock prediction equations only measure the goodness of fit around the regression line. Path coefficients which may be viewed as being analogous to beta weight(s), are used because they measure changes in the dependent variable produced by standardized changes in the independent variable.[21]

The data to be utilized in this study consist of Cutright's previously published intercorrelations computed from four aggregate indicators for seventy-six nations. The four variables are urbanization, education, communication, and political development.[22]

Prior to the analysis of alternative causal models, several fundamental assumptions on which this analysis is based must be explicitly set forth. First, political development is assumed to be the dependent variable and urbanization is conceived not to be dependent on any other variable in the system. Second, relationships between the variables in the system are assumed to be additive and linear. Third, other causes of each of the four variables are assumed to be uncorrelated with the other variables in the system. And fourth, it is necessary to assume uni-directional causation.

Unfortunately, assumptions of this nature are usually left implicit. Yet whenever correlational analysis is attempted with the assumption of which are independent and dependent variables these other assumptions logically follow. The techniques to be applied in this paper merely make the assumptions more explicit. However, this state of affairs should not obscure the basic similarity between making causal inferences from a variety of techniques, whether they be correlation coefficients, regression coefficients, path ceofficients, or the Simon-Blalock technique.[23]

Perhaps the least satisfying of these assumptions is that of uni-directional causation. While several respectable hypotheses involving reciprocal effects could be constructed, they would considerably complicate the analysis. We will therefore tentatively exclude such possibilities here. In a subsequent analysis we will attempt to evaluate these possible reciprocal relationships with a technique devised by one of the authors.[24]

---

20. Blalock, *op. cit.*, pp. 60–94.

21. Sewall Wright, "Correlation and Causation," *Journal of Agricultural Research*, 20 (1921), pp. 557–85.

22. Cutright, *op. cit.*, p. 577.

23. Social scientists are becoming increasingly aware of the similarities in the logic of these techniques. Boudon, for example, subsumes them all under a more general formulation which he calls "dependence analysis": Raymond Boudon, "A Method of Linear Causal Analysis: Dependence Analysis," *American Sociological Review*, 30 (1965), pp. 365–374.

24. See Charles F. Cnudde, "Legislative Behavior and Citizen Characteristics: Problems in Theory and Method," (a paper delivered at the Midwest Conference of Political Scientists, Chicago, Ill., April 29, 1966).

Figure 2 shows the seven logically possible causal relationships between the four variables in the model under the assumptions as set forth above.

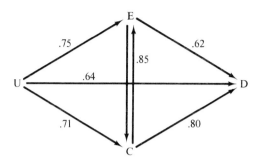

FIGURE 2   Seven Logically Possible Causal Paths Between the Four Variables, Including Correlation Coefficients

IV. Alternative Causal Models

Restricting our attention to the first half of the democratic political development model (the relationships between U, E, and C), Figure 3 notes three logically alternative causal relationships. Model Ia predicts that the relationship between E and C is spurious due to the causal effects of U on both variables. If Model Ia were to fit the data, both educational and communications development would be inferred to be the common consequence of the rise of urbanization with no causal link between

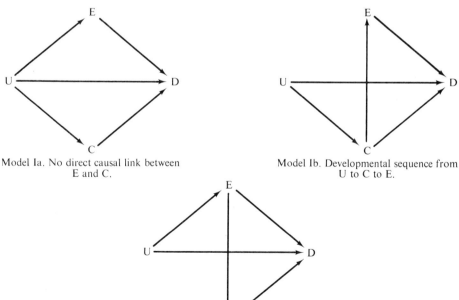

FIGURE 3   Alternative Causal Models — First Half

education and communication. Model Ib, on the other hand, predicts that the developmental sequence from U to C to E interprets the relationship between U and E. If the prediction equations for Model Ib were correct, urbanization would be seen as producing the spread of communications which would, in turn, produce widespread growth in literacy and education levels. The spread of mass media would be inferred to be a prerequisite to the spread of mass education, rather than the reverse. Model Ic, based on our original model, predicts that the causal links proceed from U to E to C and account for the original relationship between U and C. The success of Model Ic in predicting the actual relationships between these three variables would confirm the notion that urbanization is the prerequisite to the widespread growth of literacy and education. The consequent educational development would then provide the mass public neccessary for the growth of the mass media of communication.

The prediction equations for Ia, Ib, and Ic in Table 1 show the Simon-Blalock test of each of these alternative models. Clearly, the excellence of the fit between the predicted and actual correlations for Model Ic, as opposed to the results for Ia and Ib, provides a basis for eliminating the latter two alternatives and inferring that the direction of causation is indeed from urbanization to education to communication.

TABLE 1 Prediction Equations and Degree of Fit for
Models of Democratic Political Development —
First Half

		PREDICTIONS		DEGREE OF FIT	
	Models	Predicted		Actual	Difference
Ia.	rUErUC = rEC	(.75) (.71) = .53		.85	.32
Ib.	rUCrCE = rUE	(.71) (.85) = .60		.75	.15
Ic.	rUErEC = rUC	(.75) (.85) = .64		.71	.07

Turning our attention to the second half of the democratic political development model (the relationships between E, C, and D), Figure 4 indicates that only two logically alternative causal models can be posited. This is due to the fact that we

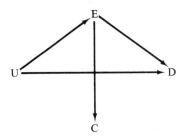

Model IIa. No direct causal link
between C and D.

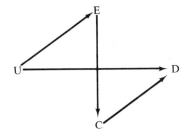

Model IIb. Developmental sequence
from E to C to D.

FIGURE 4 Alternative Causal Models — Second Half

have already inferred the direction of causation between E and C from Model Ic. Model IIa predicts that the relationship between C and D is spurious due to common causation by E. If this model were to fit the data, education, not communication, would be confirmed as the final prerequisite to a successfully functioning political democracy. Model IIb posits a developmental sequence from E to C to D as interpreting the original correlation between E and D. If this model is confirmed, communications development will be seen to be the final link in the chain of causation. The spread of mass education creates an informed public that supports the growth of a system of mass communication which penetrates and integrates the society thereby laying the basis for democratic political competition.

Table 2 shows the prediction equations for Models IIa and IIb. These prediction equations confirm the inference that the relationship between education and democratic political development is an indirect one through communications.

TABLE 2   Prediction Equations and Degree of Fit for
Models of Democratic Political Development —
Second Half

	PREDICTIONS	DEGREE OF FIT	
Models	Predicted	Actual	Difference
IIa. rECrED = rCD	(.85) (.62) = .53	.80	.27
IIb. rECrCD = rED	(.85) (.80) = .68	.62	.06

One final link, the direct original relationship between U and D, remains to be tested. A final logically possible model would postulate that the developmental sequence from U to E to C to D accounts for the entire relationship between U and D. If Model III were to be confirmed, the inference would be that there is no direct relationship between U and D. Figure 5 and Table 3 illustrate and test this possible alternative respectively. The relatively poor fit (over .10 difference) indicates that Model III can be rejected and the direct link between U and D should be maintained.

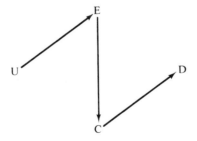

FIGURE 5   Model III — Developmental Sequence
from U to E to C to D

Before settling on the final system of causal relationships indicated by use of the Simon-Blalock technique, let us briefly evaluate the direct effects of each of the remaining paths through the computation of path coefficients. The correlation

TABLE 3 Prediction Equation and Degree of Fit for
a Model of Democratic Political Development —
Final Link

PREDICTIONS		DEGREE OF FIT	
Model	Predicted	Actual	Difference
III. rUErECrCD = rUD	(.75) (.85) (.80) = .51	.64	.13

coefficients utilized in the Simon-Blalock analysis, it should be recalled, only measure the degree of association between variables. We found above, for example, that
the association between U and D is maintained even when the effect of the path
from U to E to C to D was taken into account. Correlation coefficients, however,
do not measure the amount of change in the dependent variable which is associated
with changes in the independent variable. Our primary concern at this stage is with
the measurement of changes in the dependent variable produced by changes in the
independent variable, path coefficients, therefore, are utilized because they measure
the amount of *change* in the dependent variable produced by *standardized changes*
in the independent variable.

Figure 6 shows two paths from U to D remain in associational terms. First,
there is the developmental sequence from U to D with three links — U to E, E to
C, and C to D. Second, there is the direct link between U and D. Path coefficients
for each of these links in the causal model of democratic political development are
computed in Table 4.

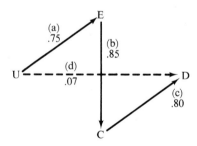

FIGURE 6 A Causal Model of Democratic Political
Development Including Path Coefficients

TABLE 4 Simultaneous Equations and Path
Coefficients for the Causal Model in Figure 6

Path	Equation	Path Coefficient
a	bUE + rUE = 0	.75
b	bEC + rEC = 0	.85
c	bCD + rCD = 0	.80
d	bUD + (bCD × rUC) + rUD = 0	.07

An examination of the path coefficients placed on each link in Figure 6 indicates that the overwhelmingly important causal links in the process of democratic political development are contained in the developmental sequence from U to E to C to D. The direct effect of urbanization on democratic political development (as indicated by the use of a broken line) is negligible.

The remarkable correspondence between this empirically derived causal model of democratic political development and the original causal model postulated in Figure 1 is clear.

V. Conclusion

This causal model, because it represents the beginnings of a parsimonious theory of, rather than mere correlates of, the process of democratic political development enables us to derive a series of empirical propositions concerning this crucial process.

1. Democratic political development occurs when mass communications permeates society.
    Education affects democratic political development by contributing to the growth of mass communications, therefore:
2. Mass communications occurs when literacy and educational levels rise in society.
    Urbanization affects democratic political development primarily by increasing educational levels, which then increase mass communciations, therefore:
3. Education and literacy development occur in urbanizing societies.

This causal model, then, is a series of interrelated causal propositions which link urbanization through a developmental sequence to democratic political development.

Since the causal relationships specified in the model are not perfect, the model and the propositions derived therefrom are probabilistic in nature. The r^2 between U and E (.56), E and C (.72), and C and D (.64) leave a significant proportion of the variance unexplained. For this reason, deviant cases (in terms of the model) can be found. Basically, there are two kinds of deviant cases. First, there are those cases where the nation is "overdeveloped" in one of the variables included in the model. For example, Cutright discusses nations with a relatively low level of communications development which are defined as being relatively highly developed politically.[25] In this case, the democratic political system does not have sufficient communications development to maintain the regime. In terms of our model, this nation is likely to experience severe difficulty in maintaining democratic political competition and may even collapse. The dangers of attempting to impose a democratic regime on socio-economically underdeveloped nations in the post-World War II world are indicated by this type of analysis.

Stepping further back in the chain of causation, we may also find nations which are experiencing communications revolutions, but without prior developments in urbanization and education. In this case, disruption of the regime may occur because the citizenry has not been prepared for the sudden exposure and communications development may bring social disintegration, rather than social cohesion. The

25. Cutright, *op. cit.*, pp. 577–581.

examination of such deviant cases may give us insight into other factors that produce changes in these four variables and bring such disruptions. Moreover, we may also ascertain the explanatory power of the model by examining the reliability of predictions about disruption based on these discontinuities.

The second type of deviant case is the nation that has fulfilled the requirements for development, in terms of the model, yet fails to maintain a democratic regime. Germany, for example, would seem to have fulfilled the prerequisites for a democratic regime long before the present Federal Republic. Nevertheless, Germany has experienced severe difficulty in establishing and maintaining a democratic regime in the twentieth century. Apparently, the developmental sequence can be disrupted by influences outside the model. Cutright, for example, examines the impact of foreign invasion and war on political development. He finds that such events seem to intervene to upset the normal sequence of events.[26] The examination of this type of deviant case and of time series data may subject our propositions to further tests. For example, the effect of urban growth over time may be quite different from that of variations in urbanization at one point in time. In general, additional research should shed light on other variables that might be included in a more complete model of the process of political development.[27]

A major virtue of this form of causal model analysis is its capacity to elaborate and extend the model by the inclusion of new variables. This type of elaboration may take two forms. First, when variables outside the system are identified and hypothesized to be causal variables in the process of democratic political development, they can be explicitly introduced into the model. The introduction and testing of such variables provides a test of both the causal nature of the specified variable and the adequacy of the existing model. As additional causal variables are identified and included, the model of democratic political development will begin to match the complexity of the phenomenon it seeks to explain.

A second form of elaboration is the introduction and testing of new dependent variables. In this manner, we can gauge the effects of democratic political development. By the introduction of measures of welfare, education; and military expenditures into the model, we can measure the effects of both democratic political systems and the causal factors in development on public policy. More specifically, answers might be obtained to these questions: what is the independent effect of democratic politics on welfare expenditures? What are the effects of education on welfare expenditures? Are the effects of education interpreted through political development? Answers to questions such as these require the testing of several alternative models including welfare expenditures as a new variable.

In a previous study, on an unrelated substantive matter, the authors have expressed the belief that

> in regard to the subject of theory building in political science, the cumulative nature of empirical model building needs to be stressed. By explicit articulation of the model of

---

26. *Ibid.*, p. 580.

27. Clearly, there is no incompatibility between Cutright's technique of using the prediction equation based on the regression line and this type of causal analysis. In fact, Cutright's technique applied at each stage of the developmental process would effectively isolate the deviant cases at each stage. His present research on historical trends in political development should also shed light on the adequacy of this causal model. See *ibid.*, pp. 577–581 for a discussion of Cutright's techniques and research.

constituency influence and emphasis on establishing empirical relationships, the Miller-Stokes study provides a basis for further development. The application of new techniques and the possible inclusion of new variables is thereby facilitated.[28]

We can only hope that this particular causal model of the process of democratic political development may also facilitate the elaboration and testing of models of development by the application of new techniques and the inclusion of new variables. In this manner, a cumulative body of development theory may arise.

---

28. Cnudde and McCrone, *op. cit.*, p. 72.

HUGH D. FORBES
EDWARD R. TUFTE

A Note of Caution in Causal Modelling

*The following article and the accompanying exchange of
comments by the authors involved raises a number of methodological issues
in causal modeling. The Forbes and Tufte essay is a methodological
critique of two previous studies utilizing the Simon-Blalock technique:
a reanalysis of Miller-Stokes data on consistency influence on congressional
roll call behavior by Cnudde and McCrone, and a causal analysis of Negro
political participation offered by Matthews and Prothro. Space did not
enable us to include these earlier pieces, particularly in light of the
rather detailed overview of previous findings by Forbes and Tufte. The
authors are critical of these previous applications of causal modeling
on two general grounds: they fail to distinguish between conclusions and
assumptions, and they fail to link assumptions used in the model with
prior knowledge of the phenomena being studied.*

*The authors focus their critique of the Cnudde-McCrone constituency
influence model on the need to examine the causal processes within subgroups
of the data. They illustrate how three different models (not one) can
fit the basic correlations in the data set. A choice between these models
then rests on either (1) parsimony (but if model parsimony is used as
a criterion, it may be meaningless), or (2) the researcher's assumptions
about the causal mechanisms most likely present in the real world (an
assumption, not a finding). Forbes and Tufte suggest that one way to
approach this problem is to examine whether the hypothesized relationships*

Reprinted from Hugh D. Forbes and Edward R. Tufte, "A Note of Caution in Causal Modelling,"
American Political Science Review 62 (1968): 1258–64, by permission of the American Political Science
Association and the authors.

within the model hold for various subgroups within the population of individuals being studied (e.g., congressmen from competitive and noncompetitive districts; roll call behavior in different policy areas). Using one policy area, the authors point to different causal models operating for competitive and noncompetitive districts.

Forbes and Tufte are also critical of the Matthews-Prothro Negro participation model particularly with regard to the difficulty in isolating effects of highly correlated independent variables (i.e., the presence of multicollinearity). They suggest that the separate effects of two highly related variables — community structure and characteristics of the political system — cannot be isolated due to this multicollinearity.

In a reply, Cnudde and McCrone suggest the difficulty in applying standardized coefficients to this data set, point out the mounting sampling error involved by subgrouping the data, and suggest that even without these problems, the Forbes and Tufte example is a refinement rather than a rejection of the earlier model. In addition, they agree with the inherent difficulty of linking conclusions and assumptions. The subsequent comment by Forbes and Tufte attempts to justify the subgroup analysis and the use of standardized coefficients on variables with different metrics or underlying units of measurement.

Many empirical investigations in the behavioral sciences today aim at tracing the causes of variations in some key dependent variable. The search for satisfying causal explanations is difficult because of the complexity of social phenomena, the crudeness of the measures of many important variables, and the prevalence of simultaneous cause and effect relations among variables. Although these difficulties remain, a number of important methodological contributions have clarified the conditions under which causal inferences can be made from non-experimental data.[1] In particular the Simon-Blalock technique has recently gained considerable attention, and has been profitably used by a number of political scientists in their research.[2] Examination of some of these applications does, however, reveal the need for a better understanding of the purposes and limitations of the technique. This paper reviews two studies: (1) the reanalysis of the Miller-Stokes data by Cnudde

1. See Herbert A. Simon, "Causal Ordering and Identifiability," and "Spurious Correlation: A Causal Interpretation," reprinted in *Models of Man* (New York: Wiley, 1957), chs. 1–2; and Paul F. Lazarsfeld, "Evidence and Inference in Social Research," *Daedalus*, 87 (Fall, 1958), 99–130. Blalock's work is reported in Hubert M. Blalock, Jr., *Causal Inferences in Nonexperimental Research* (Chapel Hill: University of North Carolina Press, 1964).

2. Political science applications of causal modelling approaches include Warren E. Miller and Donald E. Stokes, "Constituency Influence in Congress," *American Political Science Review*, 57 (March, 1963), 45–56; Hayward R. Alker, Jr., "Causal Inferences and Political Analysis," in Joseph Bernd (ed.), *Mathematical Applications in Political Science* (Dallas: Southern Methodist University Press, 1966); and Arthur S. Goldberg, "Discerning a Causal Pattern Among Data on Voting Behavior," *American Political Science Review*, 60 (December, 1966), 913–22. Causal modelling ideas have also been used to clarify the study of power; for example, Herbert A. Simon, "Notes on the Observation and Measurement of Political Power," *op. cit.*, ch. 4; and Robert A. Dahl, "Power," *International Encyclopedia of the Social Sciences* (Macmillan, 1968), vol. 12, pp. 405–415.

and McCrone,[3] and (2) the analysis of the determinants of Negro political participation in the South by Matthews and Prothro.[4] We shall argue that both these applications have two faults: (1) a failure to distinguish conclusions from assumptions, and (2) an inadequate correspondence between the assumptions made in constructing the mathematical models and our prior knowledge about the phenomena being studied. In addition, we shall use the first study to illustrate a principle of general importance in causal analysis: the investigator should check the possibility that different causal mechanisms occur in different subgroups of his data. And we shall use the second study to illustrate the difficulty of separating the effects of two highly correlated independent variables.

The purpose of these criticisms is not to suggest that causal modelling is an inherently misleading technique. On the contrary, this note should be seen as a defense of the technique against some of its proponents. Causal modelling formalizes and extends the common practice of social scientists in much of their work. Potentially, by making the logic of causal inference clearer and by introducing more powerful procedures, causal modelling can lead to great improvements in data analysis. Misguided applications of the technique, however, not only lend a spurious air of certainty to false conclusions; such misapplications can also lead to an unwarranted distrust of the methods which seem to have produced the conclusions.

I. Assumptions and Conclusions

In any kind of statistical analysis, conclusions about the nature of the world are the result of both the investigator's data and his prior assumptions. A change in assumptions in data analysis may lead to a change in conclusions. For example, a given collection of data may be used to estimate the parameters of many different causal models — models that incorporate different assumptions about the nature of the causal mechanisms that produced the data. The Simon-Blalock technique uses correlation and regression coefficients to test hypotheses about the presence or absence of particular causal links in a given hierarchical model. (Hierarchical models are those in which it is assumed that there is only one-way causation within the whole set of variables being analyzed; simultaneous cause and effect relationships are assumed not to exist, as are feedback loops around several variables.[5]) The structure of the hierarchical model — including the *direction* of all possible causal links between variables — must be decided before a test of the existence or nonexistence of any particular link is possible. Given a fair number of variables, a great many different initial assumptions are logically possible, and a large number

3. Charles F. Cnudde and Donald J. McCrone, "The Linkage Between Constituency Attitudes and Congressional Voting Behavior: A Causal Model," *American Political Science Review*, 60 (March, 1966), 66–72. More recently the same authors have published an analysis of the causes of democratic political development that suffers from the same faults as their earlier paper. See Donald J. McCrone and Charles F. Cnudde, "Toward a Communcations Theory of Democratic Political Development: A Causal Model," *American Political Science Review*, 61 (March, 1967), 72–79.

4. Donald R. Matthews and James W. Prothro, *Negroes and the New Southern Politics* (New York: Harcourt, Brace and World, 1966), ch. 11.

5. These models are called "hierarchical" because they assume that all the variables in the analysis can be ordered *a priori* in a hierarchy of causes and effects. Variables in a model are said to form a causal hierarchy if they can be ranked so that those "higher" in the ranking appear in the equations of the model only as causes, and never as effects, of those variables which are "lower" in the ranking.

may often be equally plausible. To choose any one of these possible hierarchical orderings is, in effect, to decide the directions of causal impact among all of the variables. If several initial assumptions about the ordering of the variables are equally plausible, then the Simon-Blalock technique provides no means for deciding between them.[6] Both the applications of causal modelling examined in this paper ignore this important fact.

In their reanalysis of the Miller-Stokes data Cnudde and McCrone fit a hierarchical causal model to a pattern of six correlations and then make a number of inferences about the relationship between Congressmen and their constituents. Their most important conclusions, seemingly disconfirming the results of other research on Congressmen, are (for civil rights issues): "1. The lack of a direct link between Congressmen's attitudes and district attitudes indicates that elite recruitment is not the basis for constituency control. 2. Unlike the private citizen, the Congressmen does not distort his perceptions to coincide with his own attitudes. Because the costs of misperceiving are so high for an elected official, his perceptions are likely to cause him to modify his attitudes to fit his reasonably accurate perceptions."[7] Their report suggests that these conclusions are empirical findings in the ordinary sense: the Miller-Stokes data imply these conclusions and no others (they are said to "emerge" from the analysis of the data). Using the Simon-Blalock technique, however, the second conclusion — about the direction of causation between Congressmen's attitudes and their perceptions of district opinion — can never be more than a (perhaps justified) prior assumption. The first conclusion — about the existence of a causal link between constituency attitudes and Congressmen's attitudes — is contingent upon the assumption that they present as their second conclusion; change the assumption and the opposite conclusion results. In neither case do their manipulations of correlation coefficients constitute empirical tests of their conclusions.

---

6. Moreover it is not true, in general, that we can "infer the most likely [model]" if we "resort to the use of regression coefficients": Cnudde and McCrone, *op. cit.*, p. 68. A given set of data may be used to estimate the parameters of many different models. The basic logic of model building and testing is especially clearly set out in Stefan Valavanis, *Econometrics: An Introduction to Maximum Likelihood Methods* (New York: McGraw-Hill, 1959), ch. 1.

7. *Ibid.*, pp. 71–72. Compare the second proposition with Lewis Anthony Dexter's description of the representative: "A congressman's conception of his district confirms itself, to a considerable extent, and may constitute a sort of self-fulfilling prophecy . . . . A congressman hears most often from those who agree with him . . . . Some men automatically interpret what they hear to support their own viewpoints." See "The Representative and His District," in Robert L. Peabody and Nelson W. Polsby (eds.), *New Perspectives on the House of Representatives* (Chicago: Rand McNally, 1963), pp. 9f. See also Raymond A. Bauer, Ithiel de Sola Pool, and Lewis Anthony Dexter, *American Business and Public Policy* (New York: Atherton, 1963), part V. Donald R. Matthews makes the same point with reference to Senators: "Without the most stubborn and conscientious efforts, a senator is almost certain to see and talk mostly with friends and supporters on such a trip [to his constituency]. Since both categories are likely to be in general agreement with him, the image of constituency opinion he brings back to Washington is usually distorted in favor of his own views": Donald R. Matthews, *U.S. Senators and Their World* (New York: Vintage Books, 1960), p. 229.

The first proposition seems inconsistent with the frequent emphasis on the "localism" of Congressmen; see Samuel P. Huntington, "Congressional Responses to the Twentieth Century," in David B. Truman (ed.), *The Congress and America's Future* (Englewood Cliffs, N.J.: Prentice-Hall, 1965), pp. 5–31, especially Table II, p. 13; also David B. Truman, "Federalism and the Party System," in Arthur W. Macmahon (ed.), *Federalism: Mature and Emergent* (Garden City, N.Y.: Doubleday, 1955), pp. 115–136. Even though restricted to the civil rights issue area (in 1958), Cnudde and McCrone's findings, if valid, would be of considerable substantive importance in view of the above literature.

To illustrate this argument, we shall examine three causal models connecting district attitudes with Congressmen's roll call votes. All three models fit the pattern of correlations. Moreover all three models satisfy two additional restrictions: they treat district attitudes as purely an independent variable and they do not require any direct link between district attitudes and roll call votes.

Figure 1 shows the basic pattern of correlations used in this analysis.

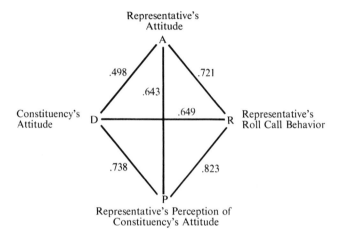

aData are Miller-Stokes correlations reported in Cnudde and McCrone, *op. cit.*, p. 67.

FIGURE 1   Intercorrelations of Variables Pertaining
to Civil Rights — Whole District[9]

Figure 2 shows three different causal models linking district opinion and the votes of Congressmen. Cnudde and McCrone have shown that Model 2(a) fits the data. Model 2(b) also fits: the addition of the link between district opinion and Congressmen's attitudes generates no new prediction equations that distinguish model 2(b) from 2(a). And model 2(c) also fits as Table 1 shows.

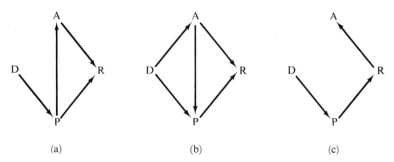

FIGURE 2   Three Causal Models That Fit the Intercorrelations of Variables Pertaining to Civil Rights

How do we choose between these three different models, each of which suggests a different conclusion about the relationship between attitudes and perceptions? It should be apparent that the choice between them must rest (in the absence of additional data) on the investigator's hunch (or assumption) about what causal

TABLE 1   Prediction Equations and Degree of Fit for
Model 2 (c) of Constituency Influence[a]

Prediction Equations	Predicted	Actual	Difference
$r_{DP}r_{PR}r_{RA} = r_{DA}$	$(.738)(.823)(.721) = .438$	.498	.060
$r_{DP}r_{PR} = r_{DR}$	$(.738)(.823) = .607$	.649	.042
$r_{PR}r_{RA} = r_{PA}$	$(.823)(.721) = .493$	.543	.050

[a]Data are Miller-Stokes correlations reported in Cnudde and McCrone, *op. cit.*, p. 67.

mechanisms are likely to exist in the real world. The only other imaginable basis for choice is the criterion of parsimony: the fewer the links (or causal paths) in a model, the better. Model 2(a), suggesting that perceptions cause attitudes, might be accepted over 2(b) (which suggests the opposite) since the former contains one less causal link.[8] But if we were to take parsimony seriously, then Model 2(c) would seem most acceptable: it has the minimum number of links possible between four variables. Thus this criterion of parsimony leads to the surprising conclusion that there is a correspondence between Congressmen's own attitudes and their perceptions of their district's attitudes only because of their participation in roll call voting.[9] One need not accept this conclusion; the criterion of parsimony that leads to it is really irrelevant. There is no reason to believe that parsimony in this sense (a relatively small number of unidirectional causal linkages) is a distinguishing characteristic of valid models of social phenomena.

In this case, then, the choice between the three models is, in itself, a decision about the relationship between the attitudes, perceptions, and votes of Congressmen; it is a decision that is logically prior to looking at the data, and one for which the prescription of parsimony provides no guidance. Similarly it is clear that the first proposition (which suggests that elite recruitment is not relevant to district control of Congressmen) rests on the postulated relationship between attitudes and perceptions.[10] Neither of the assertions made by Cnudde and McCrone are "findings."[11]

---

8. This seems to be the approach of Cnudde and McCrone; see the reasoning leading to their model III (p. 69) and the comment about parsimony (p. 72).

9. Model 2(c) is actually somewhat plausible; it implies that the representative's perceptions of constituent attitudes have an impact only when mediated by voting in accordance with district opinion, that is, playing the role of agent of the constituency.

10. In addition, the absence of a direct link between district opinion and Congressmen's attitudes *in a single issue area* would not seem to be an adequate basis for inferences about "elite recruitment.'•

11. The three models just discussed are *hierarchical* models; they force the investigator to decide at the outset, for example, whether attitudes cause perceptions or the other way around. Yet both these alternatives seem excessively strong in the light of research revealing the significant interaction between attitudes and perceptions. Miller and Stokes (*op. cit.*, p. 51) observe: "Out of respect for the processes by which the human actor achieves cognitive congruence we have also drawn arrows between the two intervening factors, since the Congressman probably tends to see his district as having the same opinion as his own and also tends, over time, to bring his own opinion into line with the district's." Lacking adequate theory to justify temporal or psychological priority of one variable over another, one will be unable to select between a number of hierarchical models that fit the data.

The assumptions made in a *reciprocal* model, in contrast to a hierarchical model, allow some variables to be both the cause and effect of each other. Such a model would, in theory at least, help disentangle attitudes and perceptions. Estimation of links in such models is a difficult empirical matter, however. On the problems and requirements in estimating the parameters of reciprocal models, see Valavanis, *op. cit.*, chs. 4 and 6; and J. Johnston, *Econometric Methods* (New York: McGraw Hill, 1963), ch. 9.

II. Interaction Effects

Applying a single causal model to all the data that an investigator has collected is not always the best way of revealing the structure of the data. To fit a single causal model to a collection of data means, in effect, to assume that the data have been generated by an underlying causal mechanism that is roughly the same for all the units being studied. The structure of the mechanism is represented by the mathematical model, and the data are used to estimate its parameters. But different units can have different causal processes.[12] In any case, the validity of the mechanism hypothesized for all units in the population is not established by using all the data at once for a single estimation. Rather the general validity of the model is established by showing that the hypothesized set of relationships holds for various relevant subgroups within the population. This is the familiar notion of controlling for a variable applied to causal modelling; a model ought to be tested within different subgroups of the sample. This method may, indeed, yield interesting results even if a single causal model is inappropriate, since it may be possible to show that different causal processes are operating in different parts of the population. The importance of examining subgroups of the data to establish the wider validity of a causal model is not merely a methodologist's maxim; in this section we shall show the consequences of the failure to test a model among relevant subgroups of the study population.

Miller, in a paper using the Miller-Stokes data on Congressmen, shows that the correlation patterns between district opinion and Congressmen's perceptions, attitudes, and votes vary widely across different types of districts (competitive and noncompetitive) and across three issue areas (social welfare, civil rights, and foreign policy).[13] There are, in short, many different types of representation. The model proposed by Cnudde and McCrone would have been more plausible if it had been tested among various subgroups of Congressmen, and in different issue areas — if they had, in effect, controlled for some of the prominent variables suggested by other studies of Congress.

Additional analysis of the Miller-Stokes data sharply illustrates the dangers of accepting a causal model tested only by reference to correlations across the entire sample. Using the data in Miller's paper, we tested the two major propositions for Congressmen from competitive and noncompetitive districts in the civil rights issue area. The basic Cnudde-McCrone model under consideration holds that there is no relationship between district opinion and the attitudes of the Congressmen when perceptions of district opinion by the Congressman are held constant: " ... perceptions are likely to cause him [the Congressman] to modify his attitudes to fit his reasonably accurate perceptions."[14]

---

12. Alker has drawn attention to the importance of this point in inter-nation comparisons. See Hayward R. Alker, Jr., "Regionalism Versus Universalism in Comparing Nations," in Bruce Russett et al., World Handbook of Political and Social Indicators (New Haven: Yale University Press, 1964) pp. 322–40; and also Hubert M. Blalock, Jr., "Theory Building and the Statistical Concept of Interaction," American Sociological Review, 30 (June, 1965), 374–80. In many cases it may be useful to transform the variables to eliminate nonadditive effects. See Joseph B. Kruskal, "Transformations of Data," International Encyclopedia of the Social Sciences (Macmillan, 1968), vol. 16, pp. 182–93.

13. Warren E. Miller, "Majority Rule and the Representative System of Government," in Erik Allardt and Yrjo Littunen (eds.), Cleavages, Ideologies, and Party Systems: Contributions to Comparative Political Sociology (Helsinki: Proceedings of the Westermarck Society, 1964), pp. 343–376.

14. Cnudde and McCrone, op. cit., p. 72.

Analysis of the data shows that the model fits for one-party districts but does not fit for competitive districts (Table 2). Furthermore, as we saw earlier, there are many other possible models which would fit the data from one-party districts.[15]

TABLE 2   Test of the District Opinion — Perceptions
— Attitudes Model for Competitive and Noncompetitive Districts[a]

Civil Rights	Predicted Correlation	Fit Model?[b]
One-party districts	$\dfrac{.54}{.78} = .69$	yes
Competitive districts	$\dfrac{-.16}{.23} = -.70$	no

[a]Data are for majority district opinion from Miller, *op. cit.*, pp. 362–363.
[b]The Cnudde-McCrone model implies that $r_{DA} = r_{DP}r_{PA}$. This in turn implies that the ratio r_{DA}/r_{DP} is positive.

III. Multicollinearity

In *Negroes and the New Southern Politics*, Matthews and Prothro propose a causal model to account for variations in Negro political participation. Figure 3 shows the model which leads to the conclusion that:

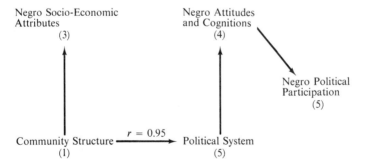

Source: Matthews and Prothro, *op. cit.*, pp. 322–323.

FIGURE 3   Causal Model of Negro Political
Participation

Community structure . . . is thus seen to have *direct* effects on social and economic attributes of individual southern Negroes and on the community political system, but *not* on Negro attitudes and cognitions *or* on Negro political participation. Individual socio-

15. Although Cnudde and McCrone restrict themselves to the civil rights issue area, their hypotheses would, if true, have more general significance. We tested their model for welfare and foreign policy issues in competitive and noncompetitive districts (based on the data in Miller, *op. cit.*). The model failed to fit in all four of these tests.

economic attributes and the political system have direct effects *only* on attitudes and cognitions. *All effects on political participation are interpreted by Negro attitudes and cognitions.*[16]

There are two major difficulties in this use of causal modelling that point to more general problems in multivariate analysis. First is a difficulty we have already discussed: the reporting of assumptions as conclusions. The causal model of Negro political participation makes dubious assumptions about the relationships between the variables in the model (a good example is the one-way relationship postulated between characteristics of the political system and political participation by individuals), and, in the end, these assumptions are presented as if they were findings based on the analysis of the data.[17]

The second problem, deserving the attention of political scientists using multivariate models, is that of separating out the independent effects of highly correlated independent variables. In the study of Negro political participation, for example, the correlation between the "community structure" variable and the "political system" variable is 0.95. The extremely high correlation immediately raises the question of whether it is possible to disentangle the effects of these two variables, as the model requires, since they are virtually identical. It is, in fact, impossible to assess the independent effects of the "community structure" and the "political system" on Negro political participation in any reliable fashion.[18] This is the problem of "multicollinearity": when two or more independent variables are highly correlated, it is difficult to make reliable inferences about their relative contribution to the determination of the dependent variable. As the correlation between two independent variables approaches unity, it becomes literally impossible to tell one variable from the other. As Blalock puts it:

> Stated in most simple terms, whenever the correlation between two or more independent variables is high, the sampling error of the partial slopes and partial correlations will be quite large. As a result there will be a number of different combinations of regression coefficients, and hence partial correlations, which give almost equally good fittings to the empirical data. In any given case the method of least squares will usually yield unique solutions, but with slight modifications of the magnitude that could easily be due to sampling or measurement error, one might obtain estimates which differ considerably from the original set.[19]

Finally, as a matter of general interest, it should be noted that the difficulties arising from multicollinearity persist regardless of the method of data analysis. In short, multicollinearity not only affects estimates in multiple regression procedures; it also weakens inferences based on cross-tabulations. While occasionally the use of additional information may alleviate the problem, it often happens that when the social scientist must rely on "experiments" performed by nature, he

---

16. Matthews and Prothro, *op, cit.*, pp. 323–324, emphasis in the original.
17. See the reasoning about "direction of causation," *ibid.*, pp. 321–323.
18. The beta weights included in the analysis (*ibid.*, p. 321) also run contrary to the model.
19. Hubert M. Blalock, Jr., "Correlated Independent Variables: The Problem of Multicollinearity," *Social Forces*, 62 (December, 1963), p. 233. For more detailed discussions of the problem, see Donald E. Farrar and Robert R. Glauber, "Multicollinearity in Regression Analysis: The Problem Revisited," *Review of Economics and Statistics*, 49 (February, 1967), 92–107; and Johnston, *op. cit.*, pp. 201–207.

will be unable to obtain the independent variation necessary to assess the independent effects of his explanatory variables.

IV. Conclusions

This review of two recent applications of causal models to political data suggests the need to stress certain elementary principles of data analysis. As models grow more complex, basic principles may often be lost in the maze of elaborate analyses. We can suggest a number of specific points growing out of the preceding discussion:

1. In complicated multivariate models, there are a number of inherent problems of estimation. These often arise in attempts to distinguish the relative impact of different variables that are themselves highly intercorrelated. The accuracy of the estimates degenerates as the intercorrelation between independent variables approaches unity. Indeed, in the case of perfect correlation between two variables, the variance of the estimates of the relative impact is infinite!

2. Any investigator, and especially those aiming to give a causal interpretation of their findings, should consider the possibility that different causal processes operate in different subgroups of their data. This may be formally incorporated into the model by using statistical procedures that take interaction effects into account.

3. Complex multivariate models require a good many assumptions in order to estimate the parameters of the model. These assumptions are often not testable and they do not, of course, "emerge" from the analysis of the data, and should not be reported as empirically grounded conclusions.

The Simon-Blalock technique does not eliminate these problems. The investigator, regardless of his particular data analysis strategy, must face them and avoid the unthinking manipulation of correlation coefficients in an attempt to "eliminate" causal links.

CHARLES F. CNUDDE
DONALD J. McCRONE

Reply

Forbes and Tufte level three charges against our linkage article. They are: (1) that our model is somehow suspect because underlying the nationwide data are different patterns of linkage for competitive and non-competitive districts; (2) that our assumptions are not reasonable given other literature on representation; and (3) that we state one of our assumptions as a conclusion.

The hypothesis that different models are appropriate for competitive and non-competitive constituencies is an attractive one and worth investigating properly. If the hypothesis were supported by appropriate testing, it would be an important and welcome addition to the literature on representation. Unfortunately, Forbes and Tufte utilize an unsound and misleading methodology in their test.

The magnitude of correlation coefficients depends in part upon the variance which is measured in a variable. When we divide a body of data into subgroups, say into competitive and non-competitive districts, we may differentially affect the variance in variables and, therefore, the correlation coefficients. Since the values of those correlation coefficients depend in part on how we divided the data, they are descriptive of the divided data only and should not be used as comparisons with those from the originally undivided set or from the set divided in other ways. It is not surprising, then, that these writers find a model other than ours in one of their subgroups since their analysis utilized correlation coefficients. (Note that our analysis also uses correlation coefficients and therefore describes our data set only, but we do not attempt comparisons with other sets or subsets.) We suggest that if Forbes and Tufte are serious in the testing of their hypothesis, they should use unstandardized regression coefficients in the future. The procedure they utilize was specifically

Reprinted from Charles F. Cnudde and Donald J. McCrone, "Communications to the Editor," *American Political Science Review* 62 (1968): 1269–70, by permission of the authors and the American Political Science Association.

warned against and reliance on unstandardized coefficients was suggested nearly two years ago in this REVIEW (March, 1967) by Blalock. Ironically, Blalock used the Miller-Stokes data as his case study in warning against reliance on correlation coefficients for this type of model analysis.

We should also note, however, that for Forbes and Tufte to utilize unstandardized regression coefficients for subgroup analysis, they will still have to face the major problem of sampling error in the Miller-Stokes data. To use even regression coefficients for subgroup analysis, we must be able to ignore sampling error. With only 116 districts to be divided into competitive and non-competitive districts and very few (average of 15–20) interviews per district, sampling error might produce disparate results even utilizing regression coefficients.

Finally, we would also like to make clear that even if the model were different for competitive and non-competitive districts, this would constitute a specification of the conditions under which our model was operative or inoperative. It would not constitute grounds for rejecting it.

Their second charge that there is "an inadequate correspondence between the assumptions made in constructing the mathematical models and prior knowledge about the phenomena being studied . . ." is indeed weak. Despite their manipulations of the roll-call behavior in their model 2c, we assume that there is no quarrel over considering district attitudes as independent and roll-call vote as the dependent variable. The objection seems to be that it is unreasonable to think that a congressman's attitudes are affected by his perceptions of district attitudes.

What, then, are their grounds for objection? They cite two studies in which the authors stress misperception as descriptive of congressmen. Dexter, in his article and in *American Business and Public Policy*, for example, sees misperception on fair trade legislation. But is fair trade legislation civil rights legislation? Miller and Stokes find considerable misperception on foreign policy and social welfare, but on civil rights the correlation between perception and district attitude is .74, which is higher than that between his own attitude and his perception (.46). One would expect that if attitudes were causing perceptual distortions the latter correlation would be higher than that between perception and district attitude.

More importantly, however, they fail to make clear, as we did, that two specifying conditions need to be set for accepting the notion that this attitude can be affected by his perceptions. "Because the *costs of misperceiving are so high* for an elected official, his perceptions are likely to cause him to modify his attitudes to fit his *reasonably accurate perceptions*." (Italics added). We feel that .74 correlation is reasonably accurate perception. The Hays-Alford case demonstrates the costs of "error" in civil rights.

As to the third criticism, it has some merit. A pitfall of causal modeling is the ease with which assumptions become conclusions. Their "note of caution" is in order for us and several other practitioners of the art.

In conclusion, we would like to take this opportunity to clear up several misconceptions about our article which we found in Forbes and Tufte and in conversations with colleagues. Our model was *solely* devised as a model of constituency influence on civil rights. We were quite certain that it was not a general model and at no point did we seek to call it one.

Second, when we stated that we accounted for the 88% of the original relationship between district attitude and roll-call vote, many failed to recognize that this original relationship accounts for only 42% of roll-call behavior. In other words, like Miller and Stokes, we dealt only with constituency influence models.

Third, though we argue that perceptions are influential on congressmen's attitudes, we do not mean that they are the sole, or even primary determinant of his attitudes. The magnitude of the correlations leave considerable room for the operation of other influences on Congressmen's attitudes.

HUGH D. FORBES
EDWARD R. TUFTE

Comment

Near the end of their communication, Cnudde and McCrone agree with our main criticism of their paper, that they reported their assumptions as conclusions. Their other points, however, suggest a few additional cautionary remarks.

First, their discussion of subgroup analysis should not discourage anyone from controlling for key variables and testing explanatory models within regions of the data. Subgroup analysis is an essential tool for discovery in the detective kit of the data analyst. In such analysis one will face obvious difficulties when the variability within subgroups is small. These difficulties weaken all inferences, not merely those based on comparisons of correlation coefficients across subgroups. In the case of the Miller-Stokes data, Cnudde and McCrone provide no evidence that the variability is severely reduced in the comparison between competitive and non-competitive districts. Miller, of course, has reported a wide range of results for such subgroups of Congressional districts.

Second, their comments about unstandardized regression coefficients are quite misleading. Regression coefficients generally provide a better summary of a linear relationship than a correlation coefficient, although for some data this general rule does not apply. For the Miller-Stokes data, unstandardized regression coefficients are inappropriate because their metrics do not possess the substantive meaning required for the sensible use of such coefficients. Here we would recommend the paper that Blalock somewhat inaccurately cites in his justification of unstandardized coefficients. John Tukey wrote that "correlation coefficients are justified in two and only two circumstances, when they are regression coefficients,

Reprinted from Hugh Donald Forbes and Edward R. Tufte, "Communications to the Editor," *American Political Science Review* 62 (1968): 1270–71 by permission of the authors and the American Political Science Association.

or when the measurement of one or both variables on a determinate scale is hopeless
. . . .[An] area in which correlation coefficients are prominent includes psychometrics and educational testing in general. This is surely a situation where determinate scales are hopeless." Since that is also the situation for the Miller-Stokes
data, the advice of Blalock (seconded by Cnudde and McCrone) is inappropriate.

Data Analysis in the Scaling Tradition

The political scientist, as a social and behavioral scientist, quickly discovers that the concepts of measurement and analysis are inextricably related. What we are calling a scaling tradition represents attempts at analysis as well as measurement. Scaling techniques as measurement devices facilitate analysis which, in turn, makes the efforts of hypothesis testing and generalization possible. Measuring with even simple scales effectuates comparison of people, things, and objects, and to this extent, making distinctions about degrees is as much a function of analysis as it is a function of data collection.[1] As the scientific scholar progresses through his well-ordered research design he invariably recognizes the necessity of feedback within that design. This process of anticipatory analysis is necessary because the modes of analysis available influence the form of the data collected. Furthermore, scales are measures of dimensions and these must be an integral part of the researcher's framework.[2] The point at which this process becomes numerical suggests that the degree and validity of quantification must be decided by the scholar on the basis of evidence which suggests a particular numerical set. We suggested earlier that data may be viewed as "that which is analyzed," implying that the same observa-

---

1. See Claire Selltiz et al., *Research Methods in Social Relations*, rev. ed. (New York: Holt, Rinehart and Winston, 1959), chap. 10.

2. An inventory of the availability and usefulness of tested scales for the researcher's conceptual dimensions can be found in John P. Robinson, Jerrold G. Rusk, and Kendra B. Head, *Measures of Political Attitudes* (Ann Arbor: Survey Research Center, Institute for Social Research, The University of Michigan, 1968); John P. Robinson and Phillip R. Shaver, *Measures of Social Psychological Attitudes* (Ann Arbor: Survey Research Center, Institute for Social Research, The University of Michigan, 1969); Delbert C. Miller, *Handbook of Research Design and Social Measurement*, 2d ed. (New York: David McKay, 1970); Charles M. Bonjean, Richard A. Hill, and S. Dale McLemore, *Sociological Measurement: An Inventory of Scales and Indices* (San Francisco: Chandler, 1967); and M. Shaw and J. Wright, *Scales for the Measurement of Attitudes* (New York: McGraw-Hill, 1967).

tions may be interpreted as different kinds of data. The kind of data, therefore, depends on the meaning given by the observer. The political scientist must first select one or a few things to record, but these recorded observations must be translated into data, i.e., individuals and objects must be classified, identified or labeled. This preliminary structuring process suggests the necessity of mental frameworks. Once these observations are mapped, the analytical process can proceed with the discovery of relations, order, and structure which follows as a consequence of the data. The rigorous scientist quickly discovers that anticipatory analysis is not only necessary and desirable but that the scientist's decisions in the research design process determine the results of this analysis.[3]

The scientific enterprise of political research demands a set of constructs ordered in relation to each other and an observable set of data. Science involves both schematics and empirics, that is, it involves a necessary linkage between a set of abstractions on the one hand and a series of real world observations on the other. Measurement plays a vital role in the "schemapiric enterprise by which the schematic model is made to map the empirical observation."[4] The concept of data theory has been used to refer to the translation of the empirical into the abstract, whereas measurement theory focuses on defining the correspondences between elements in empirical and abstract systems.[5] Rules of correspondence link the theoretical to the empirical and assist in defining the theoretical in terms of the empirical. A formal set of constructs forms a model, and when linked with the real world, theory emerges. An operationally defined construct (e.g., political attitude, interaction, status) is an index or a measure of the empirical side of scientific inquiry. Measurement therefore refers to the properties of empirical systems rather than the systems themselves.[6] When measurement of a political property is possible, performance of the descriptive and analytical functions is also possible. Measurement is the assignment of numbers to objects according to specific rules[7] and these numbers are susceptible to mathematical and statistical manipulation. Once numbers have been assigned defining the relations between objects, the property has been measured and a scale of measurement has been established. These levels of measurement have been described previously as criteria for the selection of modes of statistical analysis applied to political data.

Simple Scales

The sections to follow examine a selected set of quantitative techniques applicable to political data which have evolved from the scaling tradition. This tradition has been closely associated with concepts of measurement suggested above, and therefore, it has been based on a large body of simple scaling techniques too complex and numerous for discussion in the analytical context. The primary goal of these

3. See Clyde H. Coombs, *A Theory of Data* (New York: John Wiley, 1964), p. 5.

4. S. S. Stevens, "Measurement, Statistics, and the Schemapiric View," *Science* 161 (1968): 856.

5. Coombs, *A Theory of Data*, chap. 1.

6. For an extension see Warren S. Torgerson, *Theory and Methods of Scaling* (New York: John Wiley, 1958), chap. 1.

7. See S. S. Stevens, "Mathematics, Measurement and Psychophysics," in *Handbook of Experimental Psychology*, ed. S. S. Stevens (New York: John Wiley, 1951), pp. 1–49.

scales is an ordering along a dimension so that qualitative data can be converted into quantitative data. We often judge the usefulness of these tools according to some basic concepts of measurement. For example, a scale serves its purpose best if it is a measure of one latent attribute, object, or thing. This is the criterion of unidimensionality. In addition, it might follow a straight line model with a scoring system that denotes order, equal appearing intervals, or equal intervals. The property of reproducibility is frequently applied to scales representing degrees of feeling or other characteristics so that a scale position automatically provides information about the individual's response to a whole series of items. Finally, two basic criteria are uniformly applied in measurement with simple scales: reliability or consistency demands that the scale yield similar results time after time, and the test of validity tells us whether the scale measures what it is supposed to measure.[8]

These concepts have been applied to a wide variety of scales used in the social sciences to measure a number of dimensions. Many of the early developments led to basic sociological scales measuring social distance applied to groups and values (Bogardus scale); group structure, interaction, and communication (sociometric technique); the alignment of subjects along a scale by judges (rating scales); and measures of social status and occupational prestige.[9] Attitude scales measure cognitive and affective components (e.g., Thurstone and Likert scales), and a wide variety of political measures have evolved using concepts of conservatism, liberalism, authoritarianism, alienation, efficacy and others, accompanied by behavioral measures of such things as political participation and voter turnout.[10] Although we are not treating them in detail here, evidence of the political scientist's concern for measurement and scaling pervades the detailed reading presented throughout the book.

Guttman Scaling

Although the scaling tradition is replete with methodological techniques necessary for data analysis, the remainder of this chapter focuses on those techniques which are most applicable to, and widely used in, the analysis stage of the research process. An underlying theme for the scaling tradition applied to the analytical function is dimensionality — the alignment of persons, attributes, or objects along a continuum or scale which assists in describing and analyzing those persons, attributes, or objects. Indirectly, the techniques perform the lower level function of classification or taxonomy which enables a parsimonious analysis of vastly complex and sometimes apparently randomly distributed political phenomena. The range of techniques to be discussed are most useful for the reader capable of conceptualizing the real world as a model fashioned in multidimensional space: a space that by definition includes all possible politically relevant variables. The goals of analysis include

---

8. For elaboration see A. N. Oppenheim, *Questionnaire Design and Attitude Measurement* (New York: Basic Books, 1966), chap. 6, and William J. Goode and Paul K. Hatt, *Methods in Social Research* (New York: McGraw-Hill, 1952), chap. 15.

9. See Selltiz et al., *Research Methods in Social Relations*, chap. 10; Goode and Hatt, *Methods in Social Research*, chaps. 16 and 17; and John P. Robinson, Robert Athanasiou, and Kendra B. Head, *Measures of Occupational Attitudes and Occupational Characteristics* (Ann Arbor: Survey Research Center, Institute for Social Research, The University of Michigan, 1969).

10. Robinson, *Measures of Political Attitudes*, and Harry S. Upshaw, "Attitude Measurement," in *Methodology in Social Research*, ed. Hubert M. Blalock and Ann B. Blalock (New York: McGraw-Hill, 1968), pp. 60–111.

the theoretical and operational isolation of the boundaries or dimensions of that space so that the model of real world effects is defined by dimensions along which persons, attributes, or objects relate. A basic distinction between the techniques used here is also one of dimensionality: the researcher's political model and relevant data may be basically unidimensional (e.g., Guttman scaling, unfolding analysis) analyzed by comparisons along one continuum, or multidimensional (e.g., factor analysis, multidimensional scaling) analyzed by comparisons between dimensions as well as along dimensions.

Guttman scaling, sometimes referred to as the scalogram method, is an attempt to measure and analyze attitudinal response patterns along one dimension. As a measure of unidimensionality it assists us in judging whether a group of attitudes describe one latent attribute or underlying factor. An important criterion is the concept of reproducibility, that is, the proportion of responses which fit a unidimensional pattern. It is therefore basically an ordinal technique which provides a measure of consistency in a cumulative set of responses. The cumulative characteristic implies that knowledge of an individuals' ranking along the continuum identifies his entire response set for a variety of attitude items.

As an example, let us focus on a small set of four attitude items referring to government involvement in the economy as a cluster which attempts to measure that particular kind of liberalism-conservatism. For a random sample with inferential linkages to a universe, or for an entire universe, the hypothetical example taps attitudes on four basic items: (1) government regulation of the economy; (2) government ownership of power plants; (3) government ownership of industry; and (4) government ownership of private sources. If these items are scalable according to Guttman criteria (although our hypothetical example is too small for meaningful analysis), knowledge of a respondent's most liberal (i.e., toward greater control of private sources) answer implies his stand on the other items. In a perfect scale, an individual who agrees with a particular item also agrees with those below it. He then is assigned a scale position based on his pattern of responses. For example, using the most popular dichotomous form with favorable attitudes scored as + and unfavorable attitudes scored as −, a perfect scale would display only five scale types ($0 \rightarrow 4$) as shown in table 4.1. If all of our respondents fell into one of these five response patterns, we could judge our items as measuring one continuum (i.e., economic-political liberalism or conservatism) and by knowing an individual's scale score, we would know his entire response set and therefore, his ordered degree of liberalism-conservatism.

TABLE 4.1 Response Pattern for a Perfect Guttman Scale

Scale Score	Response to Item:			
	#1	#2	#3	#4
4	+	+	+	+
3	+	+	+	−
2	+	+	−	−
1	+	−	−	−
0	−	−	−	−

Because of the complex nature of political attitudes and the political world, and because of the inevitability of measurement error and response uncertainty, such attitude items will rarely fit a perfect scale. Furthermore, it may be important for the researcher's hypothesis if they do not scale. As we will see, the extent to which a set of items fit such an ordered and cumulative scale pattern is determined by a measure of error within that pattern known as a coefficient of reproducibility. In order to keep our example manageable, let us assume that a sample of ten respondents answered the four questions with the patterns shown in table 4.2. In order to

TABLE 4.2 Response Pattern for a Guttman Scale

Respondents	Item: #1	#2	#3	#4	Score
R_1	+	+	−	−	2
R_2	−	−	+	−	1
R_3	+	+	+	+	4
R_4	+	+	−	+	3
R_5	−	−	−	−	0
R_6	+	+	+	−	3
R_7	+	−	−	−	1
R_8	+	+	+	−	3
R_9	+	+	−	+	3
R_{10}	+	−	+	−	2

measure the reproducibility of these patterns, the number of errors or inconsistencies must be calculated. This is easiest to accomplish if the array is reordered so that it begins to approximate the perfect scale pattern. The usual criterion is a reordering based on a descending order of scale scores calculated by summing the number of positive responses. This reordered array appears in table 4.3. The errors in this pattern are indicated by values in parentheses. In each instance, if the array would fit perfect Guttman criteria, the positive values in parentheses would be negative values. However, Guttman's criteria for a scalable pattern permits a less than perfect array, that is, a minimal number of errors (10 percent) is permitted and we can still conclude that the response pattern is cumulative or unidimensional. This

TABLE 4.3 Reordered Response Array for a Guttman Scale

Respondents	Item: #1	#2	#3	#4	Score
R_3	+	+	+	+	4
R_8	+	+	+	−	3
R_6	+	+	+	−	3
R_9	+	+	−	(+)	3
R_4	+	+	−	(+)	3
R_1	+	+	−	−	2
R_{10}	+	−	(+)	−	2
R_7	+	−	−	−	1
R_2	−	−	(+)	−	1
R_5	−	−	−	−	0

error variance is measured by the coefficient of reproducibility which is the number of errors divided by the total number of responses subtracted from one.

$$CR = 1 - \frac{e}{r}$$

With 10 percent errors or less permissible, the minimum CR value necessary for a scalable pattern is .90. In our example there were four errors out of a possible forty (four items times ten respondents):

$$CR = 1 - \frac{4}{40} = .90$$

Since the coefficient is within the limits of acceptability we can conclude that the pattern is a unidimensional representation of economic-political liberalism or conservatism. By knowing particular scale scores, we can "reproduce" responses to each item. Since our measure is less than perfect, however, we cannot reproduce the array perfectly. For example, scale score 3 may be one of two patterns in the above array: $(+ + + -)$ or $(+ + - +)$. This deviation is tolerable according to Guttman criteria and the usual practice is, as above, to add the number of positive responses for dichotomous items in order to determine a scale position. In a sense, these are best-fitting scale types. Other options are available, such as assigning error patterns to the most popular scale type.[11]

   Several remaining issues assist in placing constraints on the usefulness of the Guttman technique. Some of these issues are basically theoretical, while others are operational. It is crucial that the researcher keep the purpose of scalogram analysis in mind: it is a measure of unidimensionality. In the complex realm of interacting and interrelated political variables, a single scale may not be an effective basis for attitude measurement. A clue to this complexity is the inherent difficulty of scaling political attitudes and responses (e.g., legislative roll calls) in such a pattern. Again, the failure of the items to scale in such a way may be important for suggesting other dimensions or variables involved in determining the responses. Furthermore, the degree of unidimensionality may vary across populations. If our hypothetical example had not met Guttman criteria, we might find that a sociological dimension is also important. For example, the response pattern may vary for different social status groupings of respondents.

   There are also issues surrounding the selection of scale items and the criteria necessary to prevent a spuriously high coefficient of reproducibility. The proper selection of items may utilize a set of judges to evaluate the questions; the ultimate coefficient of reproducibility is partially dependent on the researcher's arrangement of responses. Although it is common for the researcher to consciously seek out a scalable set of items, the Guttman procedure, aside from permitting inferences to a population of individuals through sampling techniques, assumes that the items are a sample from the population of items. This constraint is usually avoided; nevertheless, the researcher should become familiar with these assumptions.[12] Further-

---

11. Torgerson, *Theory and Methods of Scaling*, p. 329.
12. Ibid., pp. 332–36.

more, in an operational sense, the coefficient of reproducibility is dependent on the number of items, the proportion of respondents in the most popular category, and the number of categories per item. With a small number of items (as in our example) the coefficient of reproducibility is likely to be higher, therefore, it is usually suggested that ten items are minimal for a set of dichotomous questions. If a sample is used in place of a universe, a larger number of items also means that there will be greater confidence that a particular scalable pattern can be inferred to the population.[13] Furthermore, a spuriously high coefficient of reproducibility can be prevented if there are few extreme values (e.g., 80 percent of the respondents should not be positive or negative on all but a few questions) and if responses are more uniform (e.g., some items should split 50–50 and at least 5 percentage point differences between proportions responding positively on consecutive items helps to assure a valid coefficient).[14] The researcher also might consider eliminating an item with many errors, yet he should remember that other variables are likely to be operating if many subjects have many similar error patterns.[15]

Whether attempts to measure and analyze data along one dimension are computed by hand[16] or by use of cards and a counter-sorter,[17] or by computer routine, they all involve several basic steps: the selection of measurement items, judgements by the researcher about necessary distributions and the number of items in order to prevent a spuriously high coefficient of reproducibility, the assignment of scale scores, a reordering of scores and the array to determine the number of errors, and the comparison of errors to total responses to yield a coefficient of reproducibility. As we will see from the readings to follow, the Guttman technique is an adequate device for analyzing patterns of political attitude responses and patterns of legislative roll call voting.

Factor Analysis

In the multivariate context of political research it is often unsatisfactory to relate variables along a single explanatory dimension without consideration of other variables and dimensions which are potentially useful explanatory tools for political phenomena. Unlike Guttman scaling, factor analysis is a multivariate statistical technique which has evolved from the scaling tradition, enabling us to conceptualize

---

13. Upshaw, in *Methodology in Social Research,* ed. Blalock and Blalock, pp. 104–5, discusses these issues and describes procedures for determining chance distributions.

14. For a discussion of tests of significance for the Guttman coefficient of reproducibility see Roland J. Chilton, "A Review and Comparison of Sample Statistical Tests for Scalogram Analysis," *American Sociological Review* 34 (1969): 238–45. It also should be noted that many researchers would prefer to rely on a coefficient of reproduciblity significantly higher than 0.90 in the light of recent evidence suggesting that a minimum coefficient can occur by chance. See Carmi Schooler, "A Note of Extreme Caution on the Use of Guttman Scales," *American Journal of Sociology* 73 (1968): 296–301.

15. For elaboration see Selltiz et al., *Research Methods in Social Relations,* pp. 373–77; Goode and Hatt, *Methods in Social Research,* pp. 285–95; Upshaw, in *Methodology in Social Research,* ed. Blalock and Blalock, pp. 98–106; Oppenheim, *Questionnaire Design and Attitude Measurement,* pp. 143–51; and Torgerson, *Theory and Methods of Scaling,* pp. 307–45. Extensions to legislative roll-call analysis are found in Lee F. Anderson, Meredith W. Watts, and Allen R. Wilcox, *Legislative Roll-Call Analysis* (Evanston: Northwestern University Press, 1966), pp. 89–121, and Oliver Benson, *Political Science Laboratory* (Columbus, Ohio: Charles E. Merrill, 1969), pp. 240–45.

16. Details appear in Goode and Hatt, *Methods in Social Research,* pp. 289–95.

17. For details see Oppenheim, *Questionnaire Design and Attitude Measurement,* pp. 149–50.

political phenomena in a multidimensional space composed of many potentially important variables. As we have suggested previously, it is frequently difficult to scale attitudes or objects along a single cumulative dimension and even if this can be accomplished, there is a remaining vast and complex political universe of influences which may be underlying such a continuum. Factor analysis attempts to isolate a variety of underlying dimensions which account for similarity in a large group of political variables. On the one hand, it is a higher order measurement device, while on the other, it is a means for finding particular interrelationships among variables. These variables are often those characterized as independent in our research design, yet independent-dependent variables analysis is not impossible with factor analysis.[18]

Functions

Although factor analysis performs a variety of functions for the political scientist, the most important is parsimony. When dealing with numerous and complex "real world" data, the technique enables the parsimonious reduction of masses of data into manageable, and hopefully, theoretically meaningful form. At the same time that it limits the number of variables for analysis, it attempts to represent underlying factors or fundamental properties of the larger set of variables. By creating classificatory units and a smaller number of hypothetical dimensions from a large number of variables, it performs a parsimony function by explaining observed relations among variables in terms of simpler relations.[19] It therefore performs the essential function of taxonomy or classification, which is a crucial task enabling a discussion of order, structure, and relationships between political phenomena. The economy of description which results is necessary for the researcher faced with many interrelated measures. In statistical terms, factor analysis satisfies parsimony and taxonomic functions by taking advantage of shared statistical relationships. That is, it takes advantage of shared variations between a large set of variables in order to determine a smaller set of reference variables or factors. By classifying variables into sets of variables (factors) it enables the researcher to make judgements about what types of variations these sets are measuring. By grouping variables by the observed clusters of correlations among them, it enables statements about underlying sources of variation. Factor analysis, therefore, uses correlational techniques to measure what pairs of variables have in common in order to determine more pervasive patterns of shared variance.[20] In general, the most important factor analytic technique (principal components) determines the "minimum number of independent

---

18. For example, two sets of variables can be factor analyzed and correlated through canonical correlation techniques. See Harold Hotelling, "Relations Between Two Sets of Variates," *Biometrika* 28 (1936): 321–77.

19. G. A. Ferguson, "The Concept of Parsimony in Factor Analysis," *Psychometrika* 19 (1954): 281–90, and Raymond B. Cattell, "Factor Analysis: An Introduction to Essentials," *Biometrics* 21 (1965): 190.

20. For interval data Pearson's r is most frequently used; however, there is disagreement over the applicability of particular techniques best suited to lower levels of measurement, e.g., phi. See Carl D. McMurray, "Some Problems in the Application of Factor Analytic Techniques to Roll Call Votes, Judicial Decisions, and Survey Responses" (Paper presented at the Annual Meeting of the American Political Science Association, Chicago, September, 1964).

dimensions needed to account for most of the variance in the original set of variables."[21]

Aside from assisting us in classifying, describing, and reducing data, factor analysis is most closely related to the scaling tradition through its scale properties. If a large number of variables have been reduced and classified into a few basic factors, each factor can represent a scale based upon common interrelationships of variables in that particular factor. For example, if all of these variables are attitudinal, we may find several underlying attitude dimensions (e.g., conservatism, alienation) which represent unique scales along which individuals are scored. These scores then may be used in later analysis of basic dimensions.[22] Therefore, factor analysis performs a data transformation function by translating the data into forms suitable for other analysis techniques.[23] This is particularly useful when a large number of variables are interrelated (multicollinearity) and we wish to reduce them to one independent dimension.

Finally, factor analysis demands attention to theory. The factors themselves are constructs which underlie relationships between variables and, although they are concretely based on shared statistical variance, identification of the substantive meaning of this sharing involves the theoretical process of explaining factors. Although factor analysis appears to be a means for making invisible influences visible, there is considerable room for the researcher to interpret the meaning of what is visible. More specifically, the technique performs inductive functions by posing hypotheses, i.e., testing for the existence of certain dimensions, relating data and exploring concepts. Deductively, dimensions can be hypothesized and then tested for their presence and the factor analysis model itself can be used to construct theory and arrive at deductions about political relationships.[24] Although it is sometimes difficult to judge at what stage the research process is inductive or deductive, such distinctions can be very important in factor analysis. While it is a very efficient technique for reducing data, it also permits considerable flexibility in interpretation. Furthermore, both approaches to theory are susceptible to criticism. For example, it has been suggested that

> factor analysis may provide a means for evaluating theory or of suggesting revisions in theory. This requires, however, that the theory be explicitly specified prior to the analysis of the data. Otherwise, there will be insufficient criteria for the evaluation of the results.[25]

On the other hand, "by the application of higher mathematics to wishful thinking, he [the factor analyst] always proves that his original fixed idea or compulsion was right or necessary."[26] Although the rewards of factor analysis far outweigh the de-

---

21. William W. Cooley and Paul R. Lohnes, *Multivariate Procedures for the Behavioral Sciences* (New York: John Wiley, 1962), p. 151.

22. Subsequent analysis also may include higher order factor analysis; that is, the correlation of factors to obtain patterns among factors.

23. R. J. Rummel, "Understanding Factor Analysis," *Journal of Conflict Resolution* 11 (1967): 450.

24. For an elaboration of inductive-deductive aspects see ibid., pp. 451–52.

25. J. Scott Armstrong, "Derivation of Theory by Means of Factor Analysis or Tom Swift and His Electric Factor Analysis Machine," *The American Statistician* 21 (1967): 21.

26. Edward E. Cureton, "The Principal Compulsions of Factor Analysts," *Harvard Educational Review* 9 (1939): 287.

privations, it is perhaps the least circumscribed area of political analysis; an area in which that delicate balance between scientist, theory, and data is crucial.

General Factor Methods

Factor analysis is described above as a technique for the parsimonious reduction of political variables into some substantively and theoretically meaningful set of patterns. Nevertheless, the word "variable" may be misleading; we can speak more accurately of "data points." That is, a data point is defined by a particular case and its characteristic (as well as a point in time). The cases are often individuals or geographical units in political analysis and the characteristics are numerous, e.g., attitudes, social characteristics, economic characteristics, and so on. At the lowest level, without any economy of description or parsimony, we can refer to, for example, a particular person's attitudes at one point in time. This concept of data point suggests two general factor analytic methods: one which treats variations of cases across characteristics (Q factor analysis) and one which treats variations of characteristics across cases (R factor analysis). Whereas Q factor analysis results in groupings of cases (e.g., groups of individuals or nations), R factor analysis results in groupings of characteristics (e.g., similar attitudes or economic and social characteristics). As we shall see in the readings to follow, both general perspectives have been applied to the study of politics.

Aside from these two general methods, there are two general models for each. The first, often called common factor analysis, is frequently used and often a general reference to factor analysis implies common factor analysis. The terminology, however, is not derived from its usefulness and acceptance. Instead, "common" refers to the fact that it treats common variation among a set of variables (i.e., data points). That is, it isolates patterns of shared variance. This shared or common variance, however, is only part of the total variance in any variable. Total variance is a composite of common variance (or that shared with other variables), plus variation which is unique to a variable (or that which does not vary with any other measure) and error variance (that contributed by sampling, measurement and other errors). Using h^2 to represent variance which a variable has in common with other variables, S^2 to represent unique variance, and e^2 to represent the remaining variance due to error, total variance = $h^2 + S^2 + e^2$. You will recall that variance is the standard deviation squared, therefore the total variance for variable j is equal to the sum of all shared variances with other variables, plus unique and error variance, represented below for the four-variable case:

$$\sigma_j^2 = \sigma_{j^1}^2 + \sigma_{j^2}^2 + \sigma_{j^3}^2 + \sigma_{js}^2 + \sigma_{je}^2$$

Whereas the common model treats shared variation only, component factor analysis treats all the variations, i.e., that which is unique to a variable as well as that which is shared with others.[27] Nevertheless, the results of both types of analysis are often similar.

---

27. Other models such as alpha and image analysis are beyond our scope; see Rummel, "Understanding Factor Analysis," p. 455.

One of the most common types of factor solutions, i.e., the type of technique used to extract patterns from a larger set of variables, is a multifactor procedure known as principal components, principal factors, or principal axes factor analysis. This technique extracts the maximum amount of variance from a correlation matrix as each factor is determined, so that the correlation matrix is reduced to the smallest number of factors accounting for variance between the larger set of variables. That is, each factor sequentially reduces or accounts for variance. Related techniques include Spearman's two-factor theory, the earliest means used to isolate common variances by examining a correlation matrix; Holzinger's bi-factor theory, a variation of the Spearman technique; the centroid solution, which is easier to calculate than principal components, yet it yields similar results; and cluster methods, which involve the derivation of factors from an inspection of the correlation matrix between variables, accompanied by more advanced techniques for obtaining coefficients of belonging for the intercorrelations.[28] These related techniques have been an important component in the historical development of factor analysis, and cluster analysis in particular remains as a useful preliminary step to the principal components solution. For the most part, the discussion to follow relates to components. As a complex solution, it is nearly impossible to compute by hand and generally requires a higher level of mathematical knowlege than that assumed here. Therefore, our description of factor analysis will emphasize an intuitive understanding based largely upon geometric analogies and the availability of computer routines for factor extraction.

Understanding the Factor Technique

The reduction of a larger number of variables into a smaller set of patterns, factors, or dimensions utilizes the shared relationships between pairs of variables (simple correlation coefficients). A factor maximizes the variance between variables on that factor and attempts to represent an underlying commonality between those variables. Each variable then "loads" on the factors, assisting in the interpretation of their meaning, the establishment of an underlying scale, or in the general analysis of relationships. By thinking spatially, the geometric analogy would involve a large set of variables as points in space with the more highly correlated variables closer to each other. These clusters of points represent variables which have some element in common (e.g., a variety of social characteristics). That is, they have some degree of shared variance. By inserting an axis through each cluster so that each is representative of cluster variances, we have a measuring device for this shared variance when each point is projected on the axis. Each axis represents an underlying factor and as axes are thrust through points we have a means for depicting data along a series of dimensions which are fewer in number than the variables.

In order to depict this procedure geometrically, we will begin with a simple hypothetical example of relationships between two politically relevant independent

---

28. For a general overview see Benjamin Fruchter, *Introduction to Factor Analysis* (New York: D. Van Nostrand, 1954), chaps. 1 and 2; Dennis J. Palumbo, *Statistics in Political and Behavioral Science* (New York: Appleton-Century-Crofts, 1969), pp. 285–89; and Fred N. Kerlinger, *Foundations of Behavioral Research* (New York: Holt, Rinehart and Winston, 1964), pp. 658–61. For issues of immediate interest to political scientists as well as a generally comprehensive treatment of factor analysis, see R. J. Rummel, *Applied Factor Analysis* (Evanston: Northwestern University Press, 1970).

variables: education and income. Many social scientists have used such measures to represent, in part, a basic socioeconomic status dimension. Irrespective of the means of correlation, these two measures usually share a considerable amount of variance. That is, as education levels increase, income levels also increase. If the relationship between education and income were plotted in two-dimensional space, which is all that is necessary for a simple two-variable example, the scatter diagram of points would resemble an ellipse. That is, we have taken each individual's education level (X) and plotted it against that individual's income level (Y). A group of individuals with a positive relationship between these variables would yield a scatter diagram not unlike that used previously in the description of correlation-regression. Figure 4.1 depicts this relationship without data points. In order to measure what the variables have in common, all points are projected perpendicularly onto the principal axis of the ellipse (A), in a fashion similar to regression. If we had more than two variables several principal axes of an ellipsoid would be necessary to account for a variety of basic dimensions or patterns of shared variance. The principal axis has been inserted through the data so as to maximize the variance of the variables accounted for by that axis. A second axis (B), perpendicular to the first (A), maximizes the remaining variance. In the two-variable example, axis A defines the factor or dimension which education and income are measuring in common. Since variance is shared, the number of dimensions needed to account for most of the variance is less than the number of variables. Depending on our theory and the means of measurement, we might call this a socioeconomic factor. Both education and income would load (or project) high on it. That is, education and income would correlate highly with this factor. The variance which remains would be loaded on axis B. However, in our example, most of the shared variance between education and income would be accounted for by axis A. Conceptually, we are beginning with an N-dimensional space, finding the direction along which the variance of

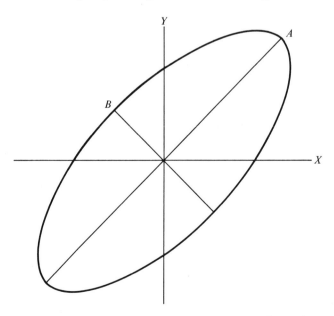

FIGURE 4.1 Two-Dimensional Data Configuration

points is maximized, and another dimension orthogonal to it (right angles) so that the remaining variance is maximized. If there are more than two variables, it is likely that one factor or axis will not account for as much of the shared variance (unless all the variables are highly interrelated), therefore, additional axes are added with each maximizing the amount of variance not explained by the previous axes. We may find several major factors along which groups of variables project or relate.

The above example suggests that factor analysis can reduce the dimensionality of a set of variables by considering their intercorrelations. Operationally, a correlation matrix is analyzed to extract factors. Sometimes these factors are suggested by clusters of high correlation coefficients, thereby giving a clue to factors possibly extracted by principal components analysis. The researcher, however, begins with a raw data matrix where each case or unit has a particular characteristic. As we have suggested earlier, this characteristic is a variable and when linked to a case it becomes a data point. In popular terminology, the resulting data point is often called a variable and, for ease of description, we will adhere to this rhetoric. Therefore, a data matrix is bounded by cases and characteristics which yield the variables shown in table 4.4. Variable X_{11} may be the first respondent's education, X_{12} the

TABLE 4.4   Data Matrix

		Characteristics				
		1	2	3	. . .	j
Cases	1	X_{11}	X_{12}	X_{13}	. . .	X_{1j}
	2	X_{21}	X_{22}	X_{23}	. . .	X_{2j}
	3	X_{31}	X_{32}	X_{33}	. . .	X_{3j}
	.	.	.	.		.
	.	.	.	.		.
	i	X_{i1}	X_{i2}	X_{i3}	. . .	X_{ij}

first respondent's income, and so on. In later analysis, the case reference is usually dropped and we speak of variable 1 (X_1), variable 2 (X_2), and the like. When this group of variables is intercorrelated (e.g., by the frequently used Pearsonian technique for interval data), the result is a correlation matrix such as table 4.5. Therefore,

TABLE 4.5   Correlation Matrix

		Variable				
		1	2	3	. . .	j
Variable	1	r_{11}	r_{12}	r_{13}	. . .	r_{1j}
	2	r_{21}	r_{22}	r_{23}	. . .	r_{2j}
	3	r_{31}	r_{32}	r_{33}	. . .	r_{3j}
	.	.	.	.		.
	.	.	.	.		.
	i	r_{i1}	r_{i2}	r_{i3}	. . .	r_{ij}

r_{21} might be the correlation coefficient between income and education across the entire group of individuals or cases. Since a correlation coefficient is symmetrical, r_{21} and r_{12} will be the same values. Also, the correlation of a variable with itself is usually assumed to be unity, i.e., r_{11}, r_{22}, $r_{33} = 1$. Shared variance between any two variables is measured by squaring the respective correlation coefficient to derive a coefficient of determination.

Geometrically, each variable can be represented by a vector, i.e., a line with length and direction. For the moment, the correlation between variables can be represented by the angle between variable vectors. For example, a zero correlation between variables suggests that the variable vectors are perpendicular, orthogonal, or at 90° to each other. With a correlation of $r = 1$, the variable vectors are coterminous (0°) or perfectly related, and with $r = -1$ they are 180° apart. An example of relationships appears in figure 4.2. By factorial definition,[29] the correlation between two variables is equal to the product of the length of their vectors times the cosine of the angle between variable vectors. Therefore, $r_{ij} = h_i h_j \cos \phi_{ij}$. If for the moment we assume variable vectors of unit length, the correlation coefficient equals the cosine of the angle between variable vectors. That is, the cosine of 90° = 0, the

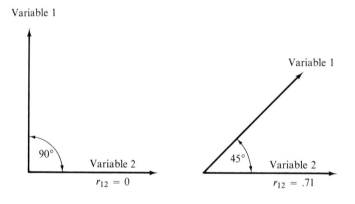

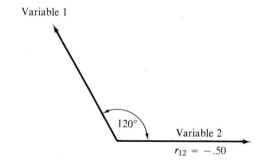

FIGURE 4.2 Relationships Between Variable Vectors and Correlation Coefficients

29. Developed by L. L. Thurstone, *Multiple Factor Analysis* (Chicago: University of Chicago Press, 1947).

cosine of 45° = .71, and the cosine of 120° = −.50. If the angle is greater than 90°, the correlation coefficient will be negative, i.e., a perfect negative correlation of −1 = 180° between vectors. The extent to which variables exist in one or more dimensions depends upon the angular relationship between them. Several simple examples will assist in clarifying this pattern.

Let us assume a simple three-variable design where the correlations between variables are represented in the correlation matrix of table 4.6. As usual in correlational analysis, we focus on either side of the matrix diagonal. Since there is no relationship ($r = 0$) between variable one and two, the respective variable vectors are orthogonal to each other. Furthermore, a correlation of +.76 equals the cosine of 40°; therefore, vectors two and three must be 40° apart in space. Since the correlation between vectors one and three is negative (−.76) it is equal to 130°. The vectors can be depicted as in figure 4.3. Since the relationship between three and one can be angularly represented by the sum of degrees of separation between three and two, and two and one, the data can be represented in two dimensions. That is, the rank of the correlation matrix is two.[30] If the relationship between vectors three and one had equaled only 120°, the correlation between three and one is less negative ($r = −.50$), but if the other relationships were constant, the data would have to be represented in three dimensions. That is, vector three would swing

TABLE 4.6 Correlation Coefficients Between Pairs of
Three Variables

	X_1	X_2	X_3
X_1	1	0	−.76
X_2	0	1	+.76
X_3	−.76	+.76	1

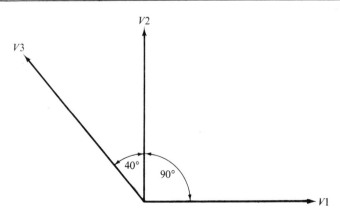

FIGURE 4.3 Correlation Coefficients Represented as
Angles Between Variable Vectors

30. For the mathematical derivation of matrix ranks see Fruchter, *Introduction to Factor Analysis*, chap. 3, and Paul Horst, *Matrix Algebra for Social Scientists* (New York: Holt, Rinehart and Winston, 1963), chaps. 15 and 16.

outward toward the reader so that it is 40° from vector two yet only 120° from vector one. We will need another dimension to express the data, and the rank of the correlation matrix would be three.[31]

Factors are characterized by the way in which sets of variables relate to them. In our most simple example, we found a primary factor representing a socioeconomic dimension. This was because one factor accounted for most of the variance between education and income, i.e., these two variables loaded high on this factor. With the introduction of more variables, the factor identification process becomes more complex. We may find that the factors are difficult to identify theoretically. Although these factors represent shared variances, the attribution of substantive meaning to the factors remains a difficult task, particularly if they represent unusual clusters of variables. In order to attribute such meaning, however, the meaning of a factor loading must be explored. Technically, it is the projection of a variable vector onto a factor vector. Continuing with a two-dimensional example, we will take the correlation matrix of table 4.7 as a given. With these four variables (e.g., attitudes,

TABLE 4.7   Correlation Matrix for Four Variables

	X_1	X_2	X_3	X_4
X_1	1.0	.91	.57	.00
X_2	.91	1.0	.87	.42
X_3	.57	.87	1.0	.82
X_4	.00	.42	.82	1.0

roll call data) the three highest relationships exist between variable one and two, two and three, and three and four (in that order). Furthermore, the rank of the matrix is two because it can be represented in two dimensions. Therefore, all four variable vectors can be represented in a space of two dimensions. For ease of description, variable vectors one and four also can be used as factor vectors since they are orthogonal to each other ($r_{14} = .00 = 90°$). Variable vectors one and three also can be plotted by translating the correlation coefficients into degrees based upon their cosines. For example, .91 is the cosine of 25°, .87 is the cosine of 30°, and so on. Geometrically, the data appear as follows in figure 4.4. The higher the correlation coefficient between variables, the smaller the angle between variable vectors. The correlation coefficients also are used to plot relationships between vectors as projections. For example, the correlation between variable three and variable four is .82, which is the cosine of angle 35°, and variable vector three (V_3) projects at .82 on variable vector four (V_4). Treating the unrelated variables (four and one) as orthogonal factor vectors or axes, we can project the other variables onto them and, therefore, obtain a set of factor loadings. These projections are indicated by broken lines in figure 4.4. Therefore, variable vector three is equal to .82 of variable vector four (which we treat as factor vector I), plus .57 of variable vector one (which

---

31. A visual representation is easy to accomplish with a set of pick-up sticks or knitting needles and a Styrofoam ball.

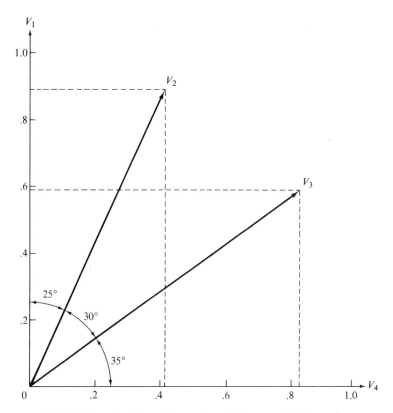

FIGURE 4.4 Two-Dimensional Representation of Variable Vectors

we treat as factor II). The entire set of projections can be represented by the following equations:

$$V_1 = .0V_4 + 1.0V_1$$
$$V_2 = .42V_4 + .91V_1$$
$$V_3 = .82V_4 + .57V_1$$
$$V_4 = 1.0V_4 + .0V_1$$

Since vectors four and one are our reference axes, each is represented by its own value. The above values then can be used for the most important output of factor analysis, the factor matrix of table 4.8. This table represents the loadings of each variable on two underlying factors. These factors are identifiable by their high loadings. For example, if variable three and four were basically economic, and variables one and two were basically social, their respectively high loadings on factor one and two would suggest that factor one is measuring an economic dimension whereas factor two represents a social dimension. Furthermore, the original correlation coefficient can be reproduced by summing cross-products of factor loadings, e.g., $r_{23} = (.42)(.82) + (.91)(.57) = .87$.

TABLE 4.8 Factor Matrix

	Factor	
Variable	I	II
1	.0	1.0
2	.42	.91
3	.82	.57
4	1.0	.0

In order to determine the extent to which the factors account for the variance in each variable, the factor loadings can be squared and summed by row. This procedure yields communality values (h^2) for each variable, and in the above case, all h^2 values equal unity. All of the variance in each variable is accounted for by factors one and two. In effect, we are saying that each vector is of unit length because the Pythagorean theorem maintains that the square of the hypotenuse of a right triangle is equal to the sum of the squares of its sides. For example, from the geometric representation in figure 4.4, the squared length of vector three equals the sum of the squares of the triangle formed by its projections. From another perspective, each h^2 value can be interpreted as the amount of the variance in each variable which is correlated with the other variables. Therefore, these values rarely attain unity. In such instances, a vector's correlation with other variables is lower since the correlation coefficient equals the product of the two respective vector lengths times the cosine of their angle of separation.

If we wish to determine the amount of variance accounted for by each factor, each factor loading is squared and summed by columns. The sum of squared loadings for factor I $= .0^2 + .42^2 + .82^2 + 1.0^2 = 1.85$. The comparable value for factor II $= 2.15$. These values are called eigenvalues, or sometimes, algebraic or characteristic roots. When each is divided by the number of variables and standardized, we derive the percentage of total variance between all variables accounted for by each factor. In the above example, factors one and two account for 46 percent and 54 percent of the total variance. The total of these figures is the percentage of variation among all the variables in all the factors (100 percent).

Although the above example serves our illustrative purposes well, its simplicity must not confuse the reader or hide the rich complexities of factor analysis. Such a hypothetical example could misrepresent a number of points: (1) In political research designs factor analysis is most useful and most frequently used in a more complex multivariate situation. The purposes of parsimonious reduction of data are best fulfilled with a larger set of variables. Furthermore, such a set of variables usually contains a larger number of factors than those shown above. That is, complex political data are usually multidimensional in character. (2) As we have suggested previously, 100 percent of the variance is rarely accounted for by a number of factors smaller than the number of variables. In principal components analysis the number of factors is almost always equal to the number of variables; therefore, reduction is achieved by ignoring the last factors to be extracted since they account for trivial variance. (3) In the above example, two variable vectors at right angles were chosen to represent the two underlying factor vectors. However, the principal axes or principal components method of factoring, with calculations too involved to present here, inserts a unique set of orthogonal reference axes through the data or variable vectors such that each extracts the maximum amount of variance. In other words, the first reference axis finds the major thrust of the variable vectors and others are placed at right angles to it until the amount of unexplained variance is successfully decreased. Sometimes called eigenvectors, these factors ensure that the sum of the squared factor loadings will be at a maximum.

Alternative Factor Analytic Procedures

As factor analytic techniques have developed over the years a variety of alternative technical procedures have been offered for the reduction of data into underlying dimensions. These specific procedures are usually distinct from the more general methods and models discussed previously. The researcher's utilization of factor analysis therefore depends upon his ability to select the proper set of alternatives available to him. This is particularly an asset if pre-programmed computer routines are used by those who are not well versed in the mathematics of factor extraction. The issues to be explored below include diagonal values in the correlation matrix, the number of factors to be extracted, factor scores, and factor rotation.

One of the earliest decisions which the factor analyst must make does relate to the basic models previously considered. This decision focuses on the issue of what values to place in the diagonal of the correlation matrix. Generally, factor analysis can be based on either the total variance (common plus specific variance) within the correlation matrix or the common variance within that matrix. The component factor analysis model extracts all the variation by placing unities in the principal diagonal, whereas common factor analysis only treats common variation among the set of variables. By placing ones in the diagonal the analyst forces the common variance (h^2) to equal the total variance and, therefore, the real common variance is not separated from other variances. If this option is chosen, the resultant factor matrix can account for the complete variance of each variable. Even with the use of unities, however, the researcher will frequently fail to calculate all of the principal components, i.e., the factoring is stopped at a certain point. The central advantages of this decision are twofold: it enables the data to be most completely described by calculating all or most of the principal components,[32] and factor scores, the correlation of a case or individual with a particular factor, can be precisely calculated.

On the other hand, if common factor analysis is the goal, estimates (since one rarely has precise values) of common variance or communalities are placed in the principal diagonal of the correlation matrix. If this decision is chosen, only a fraction of each variable's variance will be accounted for by the factors, i.e., the factor matrix will only explain common variance. Another decision then must be made to determine which of several methods will be used to estimate these communalities. For example, it has been suggested that the communalities should equal the highest correlation of each particular variable with any other variable in the correlation matrix.[33] The most preferred method, however, utilizes the squared multiple corre-

---

32. See Jack E. Vincent, "Factor Analysis as a Research Tool in International Relations: Some Problem Areas, Some Suggestions and an Application" (Paper presented at the Annual Meeting of the American Political Science Association, New York, September, 1969), p. 6.

33. Fruchter, *Introduction to Factor Analysis*, p. 61 and other alternatives on p. 88. Also see Palumbo, *Statistics in Political and Behavioral Science*, p. 285, and Harry H. Harman, *Modern Factor Analysis*, rev. ed. (Chicago: The University of Chicago Press, 1967), chap. 5.

lation coefficient for each variable against all others. For example, if the correlation matrix is four by four, we want to know how much of the variance in variable one can be explained by variables two, three, and four together. Therefore, each variable is treated as a dependent variable in a multiple correlation scheme and the respective values are placed in the diagonal. The larger the correlation matrix, the larger the number of variables, and the multiple correlation coefficient begins to approach unity. Therefore, with a large data set, the use of unities or communalities will produce similar results.[34] The central advantage of the communality approach relates to cause rather than description: the researcher most interested in cause wishes to compare common factors which generate a particular set of intercorrelations, i.e., he wishes to identify factors producing similarities between variables.[35]

A second important decision in factor analysis relates to the number of factors to be extracted from a correlation matrix. Several classes of criteria are available such as statistical tests, specific criteria, and rules of thumb. If survey data are utilized in the factor analysis, individual measurements and their intercorrelations are subject to sampling fluctuation. Likewise, the resultant factor matrix contains some degree of sampling variation. Since some of the extracted factors may result from random variation, a variety of statistical tests of significance have been devised to provide probability level cutoff points for factor derivation.[36]

The other criteria available relate to the idea of practical significance rather than statistical significance. We may frequently find that the utilization of tests of significance permits the extraction of some factors which have little practical meaning. That is, a statistically significant factor may be a nonsense factor substantively. Therefore, some specific criteria may be employed to determine levels of factor extraction. A frequently used recommendation is called Kaiser's criterion[37] which limits the number of factors to those with eigenvalues greater than one (with diagonal unities). This ensures that even the least explanatory factor will account for one variable's variance. In more practical terms, the number of factors extracted under Kaiser's constraint will usually be equal to 1/6 or 1/3 of the number of variables.

The remaining set of criteria are even less exact; they are crude guides and rules of thumb. Crude judgements about the number of factors are abstractly determined, yet they may be remarkably close to the number produced under the constraint of statistical significance. It should be remembered that if too few factors are specified, some variables will be hardly accounted for by the extracted factors. On the other hand, the rules of thumb have developed from years of practical experience with factor analytic techniques. For example, factor derivation should be stopped after 75 percent of the total variance is explained, so long as no additional factors account for 5 percent or more of the total variation.

---

34. Harman, *Modern Factor Analysis*, chap. 5.

35. See Fruchter, *Introduction to Factor Analysis*, pp. 51–52; Vincent, "Factor Analysis as a Research Tool," p. 6; and Cooley and Lohnes, *Multivariate Procedures for the Behavioral Sciences*, p. 159 for their discussion of "construct seeking."

36. Harman, *Modern Factor Analysis*, pp. 196–99.

37. Henry T. Kaiser, "The Application of Electronic Computers to Factor Analysis," *Educational and Psychological Measurement* 20 (1961): 41–51; Cooley and Lohnes, *Multivariate Procedures for the Behavioral Sciences*, p. 160; and Harman, *Modern Factor Analysis*, p. 198. For other factor analytic criteria see Fruchter, *Introduction to Factor Analysis*, pp. 77–84.

Although the above criteria are complex, requiring the theoretical and substantive involvement of the scientist in his data, it has been suggested that there are few variations between factor patterns extracted by a variety of criteria.[38] Nevertheless, the political scientist's role becomes important when we remember that one of the primary goals of factor analysis is the derivation of the number of *substantively* meaningful factors representing patterns of relationship among a set of variables.

A third set of decisions facing the factor analyst relates to the calculation of factor scores: he must decide whether or not to use such scores, and, if they are desired, he must decide the means of calculation. Although we will briefly discuss factor scores, the final technical decision about means of calculation is too involved for presentation here.[39] Furthermore, if the researcher is using preprogrammed computer routines, this technical decision is beyond his reach. The mathematical goal is to find a weighted combination of variables which predict a particular factor.

Following the usual R technique of factor analysis, a factor score is a value which relates a particular case or unit to each factor. For example, a legislator will have a score for each dimension of roll call voting, a nation will have a score for each dimension of national characteristics or an individual will have a score for every attitude factor. By examining these factor scores the researcher can identify each case's contribution to a factor and, therefore, assist him in interpreting that factor. These scores also are used as scale positions along each dimension to be utilized in later analysis. Such a combination of techniques permits the reduction of many interrelated variables into a smaller set of uncorrelated factors along which a particular case has a score, thereby avoiding more serious problems of unmanageable data and multicollinearity. A set of factor scores along underlying dimensions then can be used in later analysis, such as causal modeling or the correlation of individual scores with other variables. It also can be plotted graphically to depict an individual's or a nation's relationship to a set of factor axes, and, in turn, the relationships between individuals or nations in a space defined by underlying factors. Since the R technique of factor analysis yields dimensions of characteristics (e.g., attitudes, social and economic characteristics), the case's factor scores along these dimensions are rough representations of groupings of cases or units (individuals, nations) resulting from the Q technique.[40] Similarly, when the Q technique is pursued, the resultant factor scores represent a characteristic's score along a factor of similar cases.

A fourth set of alternatives which must be approached by the factor analyst involves the issue of rotation.[41] One of the basic theoretical problems of factor analysis is that there is no unique location for factor vectors. That is, any set of factor vectors can describe data in space because each variable vector projects on the factor vectors. This is basically a problem of relativity and can be controlled;

38. Rummel, "Understanding Factor Analysis," pp. 462-66.

39. Ibid., pp. 469–70; Harman, *Modern Factor Analysis*, chap. 16; and Vincent, "Factor Analysis as a Research Tool," pp. 8–10.

40. Anderson, Watts, and Wilcox, *Legislative Roll-Call Analysis*, pp. 142–43, 165–67, refer to this analogy and the oversimplification involved.

41. For a general discussion see ibid., pp. 137–39; Rummel, "Understanding Factor Analysis," pp. 466–68, 471–77; Fruchter, *Introduction to Factor Analysis*, pp. 38–41, 106–48; and Palumbo, *Statistics in Political and Behavioral Science*, pp. 301–5.

e.g., a principal axis solution is unique for any correlation matrix. However, there are options with regard to the location of factors, i.e., they can be rotated[42] to yield the most meaningful factors from the researcher's theoretical perspective. Once the rotation option is chosen, then there are decisions to be made about the particular type of rotation.

Unrotated principal components analysis, as described previously, maximizes loadings on factors so that variables have high loadings for several factors. Geometrically, the first factor or eigenvector, in accounting for the largest percent of shared variance, will fall between clusters of correlated variables. Therefore, many variables tend to load high or alike on the first factor and it may be difficult to actually distinguish clusters. For example, if the data are represented by two clusters of three variables, the first factor, in order to maximize variances, will be thrust between the clusters, and the second will be placed orthogonal to it, as shown in figure 4.5. The primary purpose of rotation is to bring the factors more in line with the clusters of variables in order to examine the extent to which these clusters exist. That is, we rotate so that factors have more predictive power for some variables rather than distributing their loadings over many factors. The most common form of rotation is simple structure, where factors are rotated to find distinct clusters. The basic criteria were developed by L.L. Thurstone:[43] (1) each variable should have at least one loading near zero; (2) each factor should have as many zero loadings as there are factors; (3) only a few variables should have high loadings on any pair of factors; but also, (4) for every pair of factors several variables that load on one should not load on the other. In practical terms this means that factors will be

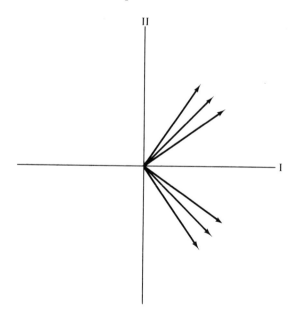

FIGURE 4.5 Unrotated Factor Vectors

---

42. By mathematical criteria for orthogonal rotation such as varimax or quartimax criteria, or for oblique rotation, such criteria as covarimin, quartimin, biquartimin, binormin, promax or maxplane.
43. *Multiple Factor Analysis*, p. 335.

cleaner, i.e., a few variables will load high on the first factor, a few different variables will load high on the second, and so on. Therefore, rotation is closely related to the goal of parsimony.

There are two basic types of rotation within the simple structure context. The first is orthogonal rotation where factor vectors are rotated at right angles to each other. This process will most accurately isolate unrelated clusters. The effect of variables on the first factor is removed so that independent factors are produced. If we have variable vectors similar to those in figure 4.5, the orthogonal rotation of factor vectors will place each factor in closer proximity to the actual variable cluster, thereby enabling the identification of distinct groups as shown in figure 4.6. The second type of rotation, oblique solution, permits the factors to be correlated, i.e., they are not at right angles to each other. If the variable clusters are closer together

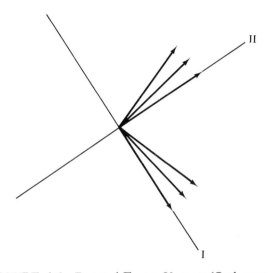

FIGURE 4.6   Rotated Factor Vectors (Orthogonal)

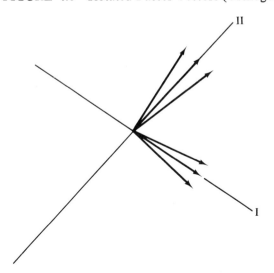

FIGURE 4.7   Rotated Factor Vectors (Oblique)

(correlated) in the real world, the oblique rotation permits the identification of these clusters by rotating axes to fit the clusters (see fig. 4.7.) An unrotated or an orthogonally rotated solution would have difficulty discriminating these related clusters. If the clusters are in fact uncorrelated, oblique factors will be orthogonal.

Although many analyses will produce similar patterns by either method of rotation, there are important differences and advantages to each method. A basic argument in favor of the oblique solution is that real world political processes make it difficult to treat political phenomena as unrelated — between clusters as well as within clusters. If clusters of variable vectors are too correlated, an orthogonal solution will not be able to distinquish them clearly, and, despite their cluster patterns, it will produce uncorrelated factors or patterns. On the other hand, independent (orthogonal) factors are often theoretically preferable. Operationally, if factor analysis is being used as a preliminary step to later analysis, the oblique method does not yield independent factor scores and thereby does not assist us in the problem of multicollinearity. In such an operation, factor scores are correlated, confounding later analysis. Of course, this is not a problem unless the correlation between oblique axes is very large (e.g., .7 or .8), which is rarely the case. While the oblique technique provides an extra piece of information — the proximity of clusters and the correlations of factors — the solution varies from analysis to analysis, making research comparisons and theory building difficult. Also, the oblique angular separations between clusters are particularly susceptible to sampling variation. If parsimony is the goal, however, the oblique case may make factors more parsimonious by reducing the number of moderate loadings on each factor. This solution is generally more difficult to interpret (but not theoretically useless) because oblique rotation involves one of two systems of axes. These are primary axes or reference axes, and for each set of axes there are two possible factor matrices — factor structure and factor pattern. The primary factor pattern and the reference structure matrices have loadings which best distinguish clusters of interrelated variables, whereas the primary factor structure and reference factor pattern matrices are characterized by loadings which measure the actual correlation between each variable and each factor.[44] Finally, the preferences of social scientists reflect the usefulness of either rotation technique: those searching for cause most commonly use oblique rotations (using communalities) whereas those performing a descriptive function commonly use orthogonal rotation (with unities).[45]

In addition to the above issues of factor rotations, diagonal values in the correlation matrix, factor scores and the number of factors, factor analysis is dependent upon skills of measurement. Although the focus for this book is data analysis, the researcher must realize that factor analysis is not unlike other analytical techniques in its dependence upon reliability and validity criteria of measurement. We have previously suggested that levels of measurement influence the selection of correlational methods necessary for factor extraction.[46] The type of variables selected to represent a linkage between the theoretical and empirical elements of the research design are also important for the isolation of subsequently meaningful dimensions. For operational purposes, the empirical measurement of these variables may

44. For elaboration see Rummel, "Understanding Factor Analysis," pp. 467-68.
45. Vincent, "Factor Analysis as a Research Tool," p. 8.
46. For example, see Fruchter, *Introduction to Factor Analysis*, p. 201.

necessitate data transformation (e.g., to reduce extreme values) and the prevalence of missing data in social science designs may necessitate decisions about the means for treating such cases. Finally, if sampling is involved in data collection, it must be performed with high levels of sophistication in order to prevent error and misinterpretation of particular aspects of factor analysis which are sensitive to sampling fluctuation. The high level of sophistication involved with factor analysis should not encourage us to overlook accuracy at early measurement stages. Indeed, we may find a linear relationship between technical sophistication of methods and one's capacity for error and distortion of real world effects. Hopefully, a richer understanding of method will encourage more precise and accurate statements of description and cause in political science.

A Model of Factor Analysis Output

The basic empirical consequences of a factor analysis have been explained in the simple example given above (table 4.8) and real world applications appear in the readings to follow. Nevertheless, there is a need for consistency in reporting factor results in all their details.[47] The model in table 4.9 is an attempt to represent these necessary components in factor analysis output and to summarize results common to most factor analyses. The suggested factor matrix is generally appropriate for both unrotated and rotated matrices with exceptions noted below.[48]

TABLE 4.9 Model Factor Matrix

	Factors			
Variables	1	2	3	
1	a_{11}	a_{12}	a_{13}	h^2
2	a_{21}	a_{22}	a_{23}	h^2
3	a_{31}	a_{32}	a_{33}	h^2
4	a_{41}	a_{42}	a_{43}	h^2
5	a_{51}	a_{52}	a_{53}	h^2
	PTV	PTV	PTV	H
	PCV	PCV	PCV	
	EV	EV	EV	

The matrix represents a small number of variables loaded on a fewer number of factors, but of course these vary from one analysis to another. The loadings, a_{ij}, indicate each variable's relationship to a factor and they are used for a variety of purposes such as descriptive or causal. The sum of loading cross-products for any pair of variables reproduces the correlation coefficient between those variables. For example:

$$a_{11}a_{21} + a_{12}a_{22} + a_{13}a_{23} = r_{12}$$

---

47. Rummel, "Understanding Factor Analysis," pp. 462–66.
48. Technically, eigenvalues are produced by unrotated solutions, therefore, they are not given for rotations.

The sum of squared loadings by row or variable indicates the amount of variance which the factors account for in each variable. For example:

$$a_{11}^2 + a_{12}^2 + a_{13}^2 = h^2$$

If unities are inserted in the principal diagonal of the original correlation matrix each h^2 value will equal one (if *all* factors are extracted). When h^2 is multiplied by 100, the result is the percent of variation accounted for by the factors. With unities this is 100 percent (if all factors are kept in the analysis) and with communality estimates in the correlation matrix it is a percent less than 100, the remainder being uniqueness. The amount of variation explained by each factor across the variables equals the sum of squared factor loadings by column. For example:

$$a_{11}^2 + a_{21}^2 + a_{31}^2 + a_{41}^2 + a_{51}^2 = EV$$

The result for each factor is an eigenvalue (EV) which can be divided by the number of variables and multiplied by 100 to yield the percent of total variance (PTV) explained by each factor:[49]

$$PTV = \frac{EV}{5} \cdot 100$$

The percent of total variation in the data explained by all the factors (H) equals the sum of variances explained for each variable by the factors ($\Sigma\, h^2$) divided by the number of variables and multiplied by 100:

$$H = \frac{\Sigma\, h^2}{5} \cdot 100$$

This is equivalent to the sum of total variances explained by each factor across variables. That is, $H = \Sigma\, PTV$. The percent of common variance (PCV) is that percent of variation in all factors involved in each factor. That is, out of all the variation caught it indicates what percent is accounted for by each factor. It is therefore a standardized measure which always sums to 100 percent.

$$PCV = \frac{EV}{H}$$

Although all factor analyses do not present this range of figures, the interrelationships indicated above provide a basis for calculation by the reader. The readings to follow, representing varying degrees of this model, will provide additional insights into the purposes and operations of factor analysis, as well as the substance and theory emerging from political research.

---

49. PTV and PCV are not given for oblique rotations.

Unfolding Analysis

Introduction

To this point in our discussion we have focused on two widely used quantitative techniques which evolved from the scaling tradition. From a dimensionality perspective, one of these was unidimensional (Guttman scaling) and the other was multidimensional (factor analysis). Two less prevalent techniques are points for further discussion: unfolding analysis and multidimensional scaling. Although unfolding analysis has multidimensional extensions which are not unlike multidimensional scaling,[50] our focus is on unfolding analysis in one dimension. In addition, while Guttman scaling and unfolding analysis are essentially unidimensional approaches, there are important distinctions between them.[51] Guttman scaling is a procedure by which we rank-order attitudinal or behavior variables for a number of individuals along a cumulative dimension in order to examine the aggregate patterns of cumulative distribution, thereby testing for unidimensionality and establishing scale types for sets of individuals. Unfolding analysis also begins at the ordinal level of measurement; however, it treats stimulus data. That is, the individual orders his preferences (e.g., for a candidate). If certain criteria are met, any individual then can be placed along a dimension with these preferences to indicate his relative position. In unfolding, stimulus objects and the individual's ranking of them in terms of his own position are located along a continuum, but in Guttman scaling the cutting points of questions are located on a continuum.[52] The most pervasive difference (and this analogy holds for the relationship between factor analysis and multidimensional scaling) is unfolding analysis' concern for relative interpoint distances. From a measurement perspective, each individual can be located and ordered in relation to the order of stimulus preferences. From an analysis perspective, an aggregate of individuals' preference orderings can be used to define relationships between variables (preferences) along one dimension.

Unfolding is basically a measurement and scaling technique, yet its analysis potential for political data remains largely unexplored. As we shall examine later, the consequences of unfolding in one dimension are similar to the data configurations obtained when multidimensional scaling is constrained in one dimension. Therefore, it could be argued that most aspects of the technique are irrelevant with the availability of high speed computer routines associated with multidimensional scaling. However, an appreciation of unfolding analysis is necessary for a conceptual understanding of other techniques, such as multidimensional scaling.

An important aspect of unfolding is its emphasis on and treatment of measurement. Specifically, it offers an appreciation for the extent to which ordered data have higher measurement levels of information inherent in them. From a measurement perspective it seeks to extract more than mere order from ordered data, and

---

50. Coombs, *A Theory of Data*, chap. 7.

51. See ibid, chap. 1, for Coombs' comparative typology. See Clyde H. Coombs, Robyn M. Dawes, and Amos Tversky, *Mathematical Psychology: An Elementary Introduction* (Englewood Cliffs, N.J.: Prentice-Hall, 1970), for a treatment of Guttman scaling, unfolding analysis, and multidimensional scaling.

52. James S. Coleman, *Introduction to Mathematical Sociology* (New York: The Free Press of Glencoe, 1964), p. 19. Also see pp. 16–21 for a general discussion of the relationships between Guttman scaling, unfolding analysis, latent structure analysis, and factor analysis.

from an analysis perspective, it enables judgements about relative distances on the basis of orders. Our previous levels of measurement distinctions were based on S.S. Stevens' levels:[53] nominal, ordinal, interval, and ratio. However, unfolding brings a fifth level to our attention — ordered metric information. From an original ordering of points (e.g., preferences for, or perceptions of, political candidates), it enables a judgement about relative distances between pairs of points, i.e., the ordering of interpoint distances. Ordered metric information therefore lies between ordinal and interval levels of measurement. For example, from a series of preference orders for political candidates we can provide information about relative perceptual closeness of candidates to each other. This is more than a mere ordering but less than interval data with equal distances between points. In this respect, the immediate measurement consequences of unfolding provide more information than an obvious ordering. Although it provides more information, the technique is often rendered limited in the face of newly developed mathematical techniques for the extraction of numerical information. Although it may be important to determine that two points are further apart than others, research efforts have focused on attempts to answer: "how far apart?"[54] The final derivation of this information is mathematical. For example, Abelson and Tukey[55] suggest a method for quantification based on correlation coefficients, and similar metric results can be obtained by hand with a procedure developed by Goode and described by Coombs.[56] Shepard extends these attempts to a larger number of variables or points.[57]

Technique

The two basic components of unfolding theory as developed by Coombs[58] include the individual and a set of stimuli or variables. The fundamental conceptual framework is spatial or dimensional, with a focus on psychological space. This space includes "both stimuli and individuals mapped into points in such a way that the mutual relations among the points in the space reflect, by some rule, the observed preference ordering of the various individuals."[59] This space therefore includes the individuals and a set of perceived or evaluated variables with an underlying assumption that one's order of preferences for variables or points reflects the distances between these variables and the individual's ideal position. Unlike Guttman scaling or factor analysis, sets of individual's perceptions are conceptualized in space, accompanied by a configuration of variables or stimuli.

---

53. In *Handbook of Experimental Psychology*, ed. Stevens, pp. 1–49.

54. The conceptual underpinning of these attempts suggests that with more points along a continuum, there is less room for movement and a closer approximation of numerical intervals. If there are only a few points they can be moved without violating the ordered metric.

55. Robert P. Abelson and John W. Tukey, "Efficient Conversion of Nonmetric Information Into Metric Information," in *The Quantitative Analysis of Social Problems*, ed. Edward R. Tufte (Reading, Mass.: Addison-Wesley, 1970), pp. 407–17.

56. *A Theory of Data*, pp. 96ff.

57. Roger N. Shepard, "Metric Structures in Ordinal Data," *Journal of Mathematical Psychology* 3 (1966): 287–315. His conceptual underpinning is one of the easiest to understand, e.g., "If nonmetric constraints are imposed in sufficient number, they begin to act like metric constraints," p. 288.

58. This section relies heavily on Coombs, *A Theory of Data*, chap. 5.

59. Ibid., p. 9.

This focus on individuals or stimuli suggests two continua basic to unfolding. The first, called an *I* scale, is the individual's preference ordering of the variables (i.e., stimuli). Let us assume that the set of variables represents four political candidates *A*, *B*, *C*, and *D* and that an individual's preference ordering is *BCAD*. That is, his first preference is candidate *B*, his second choice is candidate *C*, and so on. The second scale, called a *J* scale, is a continuum of points representing a series of stimuli and the location of an individual along that series. This *J* scale is an unfolded *I* scale, or in the opposite sense, the *I* scale is a folded *J* scale. The diagram in figure 4.8 depicts these relationships for an individual with a preference ordering of *BCAD*.

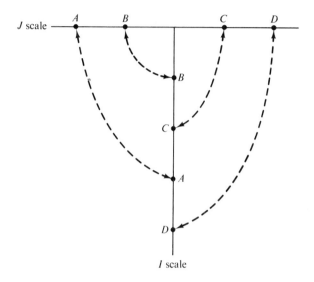

FIGURE 4.8   Relationship Between *I* and *J* Scales

The arrows point in two directions to indicate folding or unfolding. Operationally, we begin with a set of preference orderings (*BCAD*) and unfold them into a *J* scale. Conceptually, it is frequently easier to view this process from the opposite direction; the *I* scale is a *J* scale folded at the location of the individual (ideal point). This ideal point can be obtained through an unfolding process and, by doing so, the order information on an *I* scale is translated into ordered metric information which indicates relative distances between variables in space. If unfolding criteria are met, these variables can be located along one dimension or common attribute. These criteria or assumptions include the following:[60] (1) The number of *I* scales or preference ordering combinations across a series of individuals must be less than or equal to $(N(N - 1)/2) + 1$, where *N* is the number of stimuli. Our four-candidate example therefore permits no more than $(4(4 - 1)/2) + 1 = 7$ sets of *I* scales. (2) A set of mirror image *I* scales must exist such that one begins with the first stimuli and ends with the last, and the other begins with the last stimuli and ends with the first. One individual's preference ordering must therefore be the exact opposite of another's. (3) All the preference orderings must end in either the first or the last stimuli letters. The unidimensional model assumes that a *J* scale is an unfolded *I* scale,

---

60. Ibid., p. 87.

therefore a four-variable I scale must end in either A or D. (4) Finally, the sets of preferences must be ordered so that movement from one I scale to another involves a reversal in an adjacent pair of preferences, e.g., in I scale $ABCD$ pair AB becomes pair BA in the next adjacent I scale, $BACD$.

If we assume that the following set of I scales or preference orderings for candidates A, B, C, and D were obtained across a set of individuals,

$CDBA$

$ABCD$

$BCAD$

$CBAD$

$CBDA$

$DCBA$

$BACD$

an inspection of the preference orderings indicates that the first three criteria are met: the number of I scales $= 7$, there is a set (only one set) of mirror images ($ABCD$, $DCBA$), and each I scale ends in either A or D. In order to meet the fourth criterion the I scales must be ranked such that adjacent pairs of preferences are reversed. This can often be determined visually with a small number of stimuli and, consequently, a small number of I scales. The mirror image preference orderings provide guidance in this process. The first mirror image, the one with sequential stimuli ($ABCD$), is I scale number one, and the other mirror image, its opposite ($DCBA$), is the last I scale (rank 7). The rankings of preference orderings between the first and last I scale then can be determined by using midpoints. In effect, each pair of points (candidate locations) on a final J scale has a midpoint and an individual's choice between a pair of stimuli indicates his location on either side of it. For example, we might begin with a hypothetical J scale which contains the sequential ordering of equidistant points A, B, C, and D and their respective midpoints (see fig. 4.9). With temporarily equidistant points, the midpoint between A and C (AC)

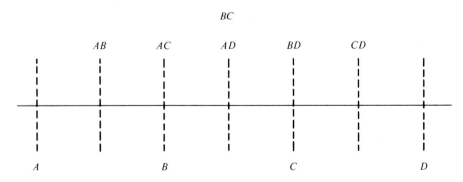

FIGURE 4.9 A Four-Variable J Scale with Equidistant
Points

falls on point B, the midpoint BD falls at point C, and midpoints BC and AD coincide. As you will see, the final midpoint ordering which we derive will indicate the relative distances between points or candidates. Since we begin with a set of I scales and we want to derive a J scale, the I scales must be ordered so that they reflect midpoint orderings. By mirror image definition, I scale number one is preference ordering $ABCD$. That is, an individual with this ordering will be on the A side of midpoint AB (he is closest to candidate A, next closest to B, and so on; i.e., his first choice is A, his second choice is B, his third choice C and his fourth choice is D). When that midpoint is crossed, I scale number two should reverse the midpoint order, i.e., an individual is on the B side of midpoint AB. This is preference ordering $BACD$. This trial process also can be pursued from the opposite end of a hypothetical J scale since the mirror image criterion places $DCBA$ as I scale number seven, i.e., on the D side of midpoint CD. If other pairs of I scales are mirror images, the J scale will not be unidimensional.

The easiest formula for ranking I scales involves counting the number of midpoints crossed and adding one.[61] The ranking of I scales is as follows: (1) $ABCD$: no midpoints are crossed, plus one; (2) $BACD$: C and D are in the proper order, but A has crossed one of its midpoints, i.e., one stimuli is to its left, plus one; (3) $BCAD$: A has crossed two of its midpoints, plus one; (4) $CBAD$: A has crossed two midpoints and B has crossed one, plus one; (5) $CBDA$: A has crossed three, D none, and B has crossed one, plus one; (6) $CDBA$: A crossed three, B crossed two, plus one; (7) $DCBA$: A crossed three, B crossed two, and C crossed one, plus one.

The midpoint ordering on a J scale derived from the I scales will provide the necessary information to determine relative distances between candidates. The crucial midpoints are BC and AD. Although our hypothetical equidistant J scale made them coterminous, if midpoint BC were to the left of midpoint AD, point C would be closer to point B and the distance between C and D would be greater than the distance between A and B. If midpoint AD precedes BC, the distance between points A and B will be greater than the distance between C and D ($\overline{AB} > \overline{CD}$). That is, given four candidates, the particular mirror images and the previously mentioned criteria, there are two possible sets of midpoint orders: AB, AC, BC, AD, BD, CD or AB, AC, AD, BC, BD, CD. The proper order of midpoints can be determined by examining the rank order of I scales and looking for a pair of stimuli which reverse. The I scales and midpoint rankings are given in table 4.10.

TABLE 4.10 I Scale and Midpoint Rankings

I Scales		Midpoints
I_1	$ABCD$	
I_2	$BACD$	AB
I_3	$BCAD$	AC
I_4	$CBAD$	BC
I_5	$CBDA$	AD
I_6	$CDBA$	BD
I_7	$DCBA$	CD

61. Ibid., p. 90.

You will notice that the *I* scales which we have derived meet all of the criteria and can be tested for their accuracy of order by the following criterion: going down the *I* scales, any one stimuli moves completely to the left before it moves to the right (e.g., follow *B* to the left and then to the right). Again, the midpoint ordering is based on reversals in adjacent stimuli. For example, in I_2, the *AB* pair in I_1 is reversed; in I_3, the *AC* pair in I_2 is reversed. This rank order of midpoints on a *J* scale now provides us with ordered metric information. Midpoint *BC* occurs before midpoint *AD*, therefore $\overline{CD} > \overline{AB}$ and points *B* and *C* in our hypothetical *J* scale should be moved closer together (fig. 4.10). Therefore, the psychological space for our aggregate of individuals is unidimensional (previously determined) and their preference orderings for four political candidates indicate the relative perceived distances between candidates along this evaluative dimension.

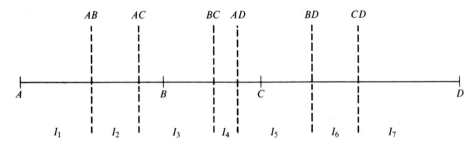

FIGURE 4.10   Final *J* Scale Representing Relative
Perceived Distances Between Four Candidates

The tedium inherent in the above procedure, particularly with a large number of stimuli or points,[62] has necessitated a reliance on high speed computer routines. The most frequently used means available involves aspects of theoretically analogous procedures developed by Kruskal, where data point configurations are constrained into one dimension.[63] Hopefully, our discussion of unfolding will provide an intuitive understanding which is fundamental to an appreciation of multidimensional scaling discussed below. Unfolding analysis can therefore serve a variety of purposes: it can extract ordered metric information from ordered information; as described here, it is a test of unidimensionality; and it assists us in the analysis of distances between data points.

Although all of the above consequences can be of assistance to the political scientist, our immediate concern is an understanding of dimensionality as a prerequisite for understanding concepts of multidimensional scaling. If the researcher's data do not meet the necessary criteria for unidimensionality as described above, it suggests that individuals do not arrive at their preferences on the basis of one common attribute. Past theory and research suggest that in the complex realm of social and political phenomena, preferences for, or perceptions of, politically relevant stimuli are best explained along a variety of dimensions. In the section to follow we will focus on multidimensional configurations of data and our examples will suggest the inadequacy of a model which treats candidate evaluations on the basis of one underlying dimension.

62. See ibid., chaps. 5 and 6, for more involved examples.
63. For Coombs' extension of unfolding analysis to more dimensions see ibid., chap. 7.

Multidimensional Scaling

Functions

The general purpose of multidimensional scaling is not unlike that of factor analysis: the mapping of relationships between variables in space along a number of dimensions. Given a set of potentially relevant variables (e.g., attitudes, roll calls) we wish to align them in N-dimensional space so that the most similar variables are closer together, hoping to define a theoretical dimension explaining these variables. Often the results from a factor analysis will lead to conclusions similar to those derived from multidimensional scaling, yet factor analysis is likely to yield more dimensions and produce results in less visualizable form. The analogy between multidimensional scaling and unfolding analysis in one dimension is not unlike the analogy between Guttman scaling and factor analysis. In our discussion of unfolding analysis we suggested that if the relationships between variables do not meet unfolding criteria, i.e., their ability to unfold along one dimension, the relationships may need to be explained by a variety of underlying dimensions. For example, it is reasonable to assume that an electorate's perception of candidates is based upon evaluations of candidates in terms of more than one underlying criterion (such as ideology).[64] Researchers also have been interested in spatial distances between political parties[65] and congressional roll call votes.[66] The basic assumption is inherent to many multivariate procedures, yet most effectively measured by dimensional techniques: individuals arrive at preferences by using more than one common attribute or dimension. This assumption is common to a variety of multidimensional procedures[67] which follow similar methodological patterns:

> Given a set of stimuli which vary with respect to an unknown number of dimensions, determine (a) the minimum dimensionality of the set, and (b) projections of the stimuli (scale values) on each of the dimensions involved.[68]

Therefore, multidimensional scaling assists us in scaling values, reducing data, and analyzing distances.

Although the purposes are similar to those of factor analysis, we need have only an initial ordinal level of measurement in order to analyze interpoint distances between variables in space. Multidimensional scaling can therefore be viewed as a nonparametric version of the factor analysis concept. The model which we will examine in greatest detail was developed by Kruskal[69] and relies heavily on re-

---

64. See Herbert F. Weisburg and Jerrold Rusk, "Dimensions of Candidate Evaluation," *American Political Science Review* 64 (1970): 1167-85. This article is included in the readings which follow.

65. Philip E. Converse, "The Problem of Party Distances in Models of Voting Change," in *The Electoral Process*, ed. M. Kent Jennings and L. Harmon Zeigler (Englewood Cliffs, N.J.: Prentice-Hall, 1966), pp. 175-208.

66. Duncan MacRae, Jr., and Susan Borker Schwarz, "Identifying Congressional Issues by Multidimensional Models," *Midwest Journal of Political Science* 12 (1968): 181-202.

67. These procedures stem from a class of psychological scaling techniques traced by Torgerson, *Theory and Methods of Scaling*, chap. 11, and Coombs, *A Theory of Data*, chaps. 21 and 22.

68. Torgerson, *Theory and Methods of Scaling*, pp. 247-48.

69. J. B. Kruskal, "Multidimensional Scaling by Optimizing Goodness of Fit to a Nonmetric Hypothesis," *Psychometrika* 29 (March 1964): 1-27, and "Nonmetric Multidimensional Scaling: A Numerical Method," *Psychometrika* 29 (June 1964): 115-29.

search by Shepard.[70] It requires no assumptions beyond the ordered metric level because it compares a rank ordering of interpoint distances with rank-order measures of data. Furthermore, multidimensional scaling focuses directly on interpoint distances and, whereas factor analysis establishes dimensions and indicates the projections of variables, multidimensional scaling takes the relationships between variables and uses them to derive dimensionality. That is, "one seeks from the relations of variables to one another to derive the dimensionality into which they fit."[71] Although the metric coordinates of variables are like factor loadings in concept, often leading to similar findings, there are no preferred coordinates in multidimensional scaling such that a large proportion of variance is explained first and subsequently reduced. That is, there is no absolute origin for coordinates except a center of gravity of all points. Squared distances from this origin are not unlike factor analysis communalities.

The more specific goal of multidimensional scaling is the location of patterns of points in a specified number of dimensions where distances between points coincide with measures of similarity or dissimilarity between objects or things. Distances are derived through the use of geometric projections. The most commonly used measures of similarity cover a range of ordinal and interval measures of association, e.g., Pearson's *r*, Spearman's rho. As a structuring and ordering technique, multidimensional scaling finds an order on the basis of similarities or dissimilarities between things (e.g., attitudes, roll calls) and these objects or variables are represented by points in space so that distances between points fit the measures of similarity (association). Therefore, the results of multidimensional scaling can be used to plot interpoint distances between variables and analyze the data dimensionally. For example, it can be used for locating dimensions running through variables which were not immediately evident in the data, describing the positioning of variables along dimensions, and analyzing variable scores on dimensions.

Procedures

The final configuration of points in space which results from multidimensional scaling is based upon matching similarities (or dissimilarities) to distances. The earliest techniques first estimated tentative interpoint distances from the data and calculated spatial coordinates without referring to the original data. The newer

---

70. Roger N. Shepard, "Stimulus and Response Generalization: A Stochastic Model Relating Generalization to Distance in Psychological Space," *Psychometrika* 22 (1957): 325–45, and "The Analysis of Proximities: Multidimensional Scaling with an Unknown Distance Function," *Psychometrika* 27 (1962): 125–39, 219–46. Also see Roger N. Shepard, A. Kimball Romney, and Sara Beth Nerlove, eds., *Multidimensional Scaling: Theory and Applications in the Behavioral Sciences* (New York: Seminar Press, 1972), vol. 1 and 2. The technique is similar to Guttman-Lingoes smallest space analysis; see J. C. Lingoes, "An IBM-7090 Program for Guttman-Lingoes Smallest Space Analysis," *Behavioral Science* 10 (1965): 183–84, and Louis Guttman, "A General Nonmetric Technique for Finding the Smallest Coordinate Space for a Configuration of Points," *Psychometrika* 33 (1968): 496–506. An application to political science appears in Glendon Schubert, "Academic Ideology and the Study of Adjudication," *American Political Science Review* 61 (1967): 106–30. The Kruskal technique also is similar to one developed by Coombs, *A Theory of Data*, chaps. 21 and 22, but the latter does not attempt to yield metric information. The Coombs technique starts with an ordering of interpoint distances and it results in only an ordering of points on axes, whereas the final multidimensional scaling output by the Kruskal method yields a configuration containing metric information.
71. Cattell, "Factor Analysis: Introduction to Essentials," p. 414. Also see his discussion of the relationship of canonical correlation and nonlinear factor analysis to these techniques.

techniques (Shepard-Kruskal) use iterative procedures to provide a closer fit to the data. The Kruskal technique matches an array of distances to an array of similarities, such that the greatest similarities are associated with the smallest distances. The procedure begins with a matrix of similarities or dissimilarities generally known as delta's (δ). These can be a variety of measures of association, however, the technique only uses a ranking of data based on the coefficients of association, preserving only the order even if these measures are Pearson correlation coefficients. For example, we might have a correlation matrix between attitudes or between roll calls such as table 4.11, for which we obtain ranked information:

TABLE 4.11 Correlation Matrix Input for Multidimensional Scaling

		Variables			
		1	2	3	4
Variables	1				
	2	.7			
	3	.5	.6		
	4	.25	.4	.45	

$$r_{41} < r_{42} < r_{43} < r_{31} < r_{32} < r_{21}$$

or

$$\delta_{41} < \delta_{42} < \delta_{43} < \delta_{31} < \delta_{32} < \delta_{21}$$

The extremes range from the greatest similarity between variables ($r_{21} = .7$) to the smallest similarity (or greatest dissimilarity, $r_{41} = .25$).

As in our discussion of factor analysis, our immediate goal is an intuitive understanding of procedures. Beyond the very simple first step of obtaining similarities, these procedures rely on a variety of higher mathematical functions and techniques which must be avoided for our present purposes. Generally, multidimensional scaling requires the assistance of computer routines and the Kruskal technique is available in this form. Hopefully, an intuitive understanding will ease the burden of application to political phenomena and lead to further substantive and methodological research.

After similarity measures are derived (as an input to multidimensional scaling) distances between pairs of variables (or points) are calculated (d_{ij}) by projecting the points on orthogonal axes so that the distance equals the square root of the sum of squared differences in projections. That is, if the space is treated as Euclidean, the most frequently used model,[72] we can utilize the Pythagorean theorem and treat projections as right triangle sides and the distance as the hypotenuse.[73] By using

---

72. The algorithm can employ other distance functions, such as Minkowski's r-metric or the Manhattan metric. See Kruskal, "Nonmetric Multidimensional Scaling," pp. 116–17, 125–26. Other distance-measuring options could utilize Coombs' techniques, *A Theory of Data*, chaps. 21 and 22, yet Kruskal is critical of the latter and relies on the other models following Shepard, "The Analysis of Proximities."

73. Torgerson, *Theory and Methods of Scaling*, pp. 51–54.

axes to describe positions, the distance between points or variables is invariant over different axes so long as these axes are orthogonal to each other in Euclidean space. This technique enables the distance between points to be a function of the degree of similarity. The final configuration of interpoint distances then is based upon comparison of similarity (δ) with distances (d).

The step following derivation of similarities and distances is the most important and complex aspect of multidimensional scaling. This process involves the plotting of distances against similarities (or dissimilarities), where the criterion for matching is monotonicity. This criterion implies that the measures of similarity increase in the same order as the distances decrease. If there is a perfect relationship, the order of similarities/ dissimilarities is the same as the order of distances. Following our hypothetical ordering of similarities (δ) a perfect monotonic relationship would indicate that the distance between variables four and one (d_{41}) is the largest of all distances and the corresponding similarity (δ_{41}) is the smallest similarity. If this holds for all corresponding distance values, the distance and similarity rankings are opposite:

$$d_{41} > d_{42} > d_{43} > d_{31} > d_{32} > d_{21}$$

If this ordering exists in the data (δ), a perfect monotonic curve could be applied to the plotting of distances and similarities/dissimilarities. If we plot distances and dissimilarities we have an ascending curve moving to the right and never going down or to the left, or if similarities are used, we have a descending curve never going

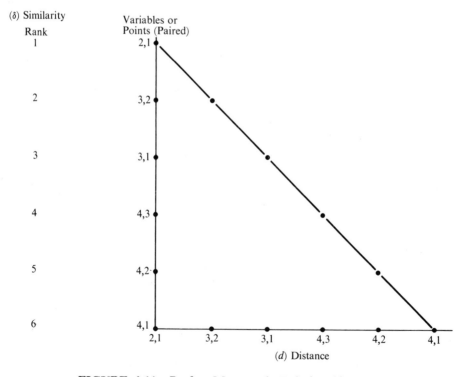

FIGURE 4.11   Perfect Monotonic Relationship Between Similarities and Distances

up or to the left. Using similar sets of orderings, such a monotonic curve can be depicted as in figure 4.11.

If the measures of distance are not of the same order as the measures of similarity/dissimilarity (the usual case) the goal is to find a function to best fit the scatter plotting so that the curve approaches monotonicity. The measure of fit, i.e., the degree to which δ and d do not match, is called stress (S). This process involves fitting a curved line to the scatter diagram and calculating deviations from the curve measured along the distance axis. This is a line of least squares, but at the monotonic level. Similarities are given and we find the configuration whose distances best fit the similarities. Each original point (points in figure 4.11 are really pairs of points) has a value of d and a corresponding δ value, but when the points are moved to create a monotonic curve, this new distance is called $\hat{d}_{ij}$, i.e., we fit the d-hat values to the curve. These are not actual distances, but ones which are as nearly equal to the actual measured (original) distances as possible. Therefore, the $(\hat{d} - d)$'s are measures of d's deviation from monotonicity so that each point (pairs of points) on the curve now has an original similarity coordinate (δ) and a new distance coordinate ($\hat{d}$). These $\hat{d}$'s or deviations are ordered so that each is greater than or equal to the immediately preceding $\hat{d}$ value, i.e., monotonic.

Let us assume the same ordering of similarities as we presented previously, but with the distances in a different order. The most similar variables are two and one ($r_{21} = .7$) and the smallest distance between any two variables is that distance between variables two and one. Therefore, the sequential orders begin properly. The next highest similarity (or the next to lowest dissimilarity) exists between variables three and two ($r_{32} = .6$), but the next smallest distance is between variables three and one rather than three and two. The other different distance orderings appear on the following distance axis and they can be compared to those presented previously (see fig. 4.12).

The $\hat{d}$'s represent the monotone regression distance values ($\hat{d}$'s represent the average of the corresponding d's) which are fitted to the curve. The curve which is placed through the points is like the line of least squares described in chapter 2, but it is monotonic and nonparametric. In order to measure deviation from the curve of best fit we utilize the differences between d and $\hat{d}$, and to obtain a total measure of deviation we use a procedure familiar to many statistical tests: sum of squares. Each deviation is squared and summed across the scatter diagram; $\Sigma (d_{ij} - \hat{d}_{ij})^2$. Since this measure varies for different configurations it is standardized and the square root is taken. It can be standardized either by dividing the sum of squared deviations by the sum of squared deviations from the mean distance, or by dividing by the sum of squared distances. This value measures degree of monotonic fit, and using the latter denominator, the formula is:

$$S = \sqrt{\frac{\Sigma (d_{ij} - \hat{d}_{ij})^2}{\Sigma d_{ij}^2}}$$

This stress value measures the disparity between ranked information on data (δ) and a corresponding ranking of interpoint distances. Technically, "for any given configuration we perform a monotone regression of distance upon dissimilarity, and use the residual variance, suitably normalized, as our quantitative measure."[74]

---

74. Kruskal, "Multidimensional Scaling by Optimizing Goodness of Fit," p. 3.

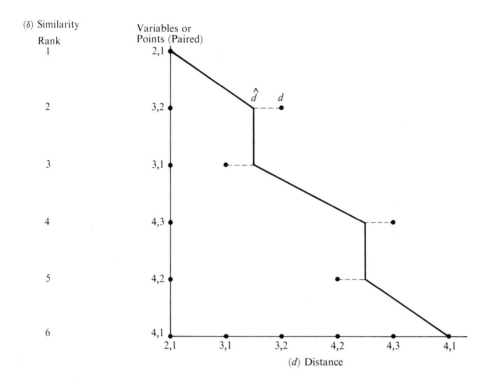

FIGURE 4.12   Fitting Distances to Similarities

The lower the residual sum of squares, the lower the stress, and the better the resultant configuration represents the data.[75] When the configuration exactly reproduces the ranking of data, the stress is zero.

  The process of stress reduction usually involves a complex series of iterations,
i.e., trials. Through an iterative procedure the coordinates of points are moved to
reduce stress. This entire process occurs in any number of dimensions (usually less
than ten) which the researcher specifies and, generally, the greater the number of
dimensions, the less the stress. The larger the number of dimensions, the less difficult
it is to fit the data to dimensions. It is easier to make the δ's and the d's monotonic
with one another, i.e., stretching and shrinking ($\hat{d}$) is easier. The researcher usually
begins this iterative process with an initial arbitrary configuration of points (or with
a specified configuration, particularly if the input is a configuration resulting from
a previous multidimensional procedure), specifying the number of dimensions in
which the process occurs. The number of dimensions might partially depend on the
researcher's purposes and the degree of forcing he wants. As in factor analysis, we
are looking for the number of dimensions which are substantively and theoretically
interpretable. Different configurations derived in different dimensions and the
changes that occur from one dimension to another set of dimensions can provide
the basis for theory building. Generally, through a series of trials, the researcher

75. The $\hat{d}$ values are those values which minimize stress. For the algorithm see Kruskal, "Nonmetric
Multidimensional Scaling," pp. 126–28.

should choose a number of dimensions which make stress "acceptably small,"[76] i.e., so that an increase in the number of dimensions does not greatly reduce the stress. The perfect stress value is zero and Kruskal contends that 2 1/2 percent is excellent, 5 percent is good, 10 percent is fair and 20 percent is poor.[77]

The iterative process involves the moving of points in a specified number of dimensions until the configuration cannot be improved, i.e., the stress value cannot be reduced and we are approaching monotonicity (d and $\hat{d}$ are becoming more alike). In effect, the computer is shifting interpoint distances until they best fit the measures of similarity and it continues to do so until the ordering of the distances is as monotonic as possible with the ordering (similarity) in the data. The Kruskal technique utilizes a form of numerical analysis known as the method of gradients.[78] In the iteration process we go in the direction where stress is reduced most quickly. This direction is called the (negative) gradient. Each time we arrive at a better point in space, the gradient is determined and we move along it (from an original arbitrary starting point). When the gradient equals zero, stress equals zero. When we are at a "point in configuration space from which no small movement is an improvement,"[79] we have encountered a global minimum of the stress. Yet the stress might be reduced if much bigger steps were employed. The most difficult problem is judging whether this minimum is an overall minimum or merely a local minimum, i.e., a false stopping point. A rational starting configuration (such as that yielded by a preliminary factor analysis) helps to avoid the problem of local minima, as well as reduce the number of iterations necessary.

If this iterative procedure does not reach the desired goal of zero stress, it can be stopped when a satisfactory stress value is obtained. The entire process then can be calculated in a successively lower number of dimensions so that the data configuration is forced to fit a smaller number of dimensions. This is in line with our goal of parsimony. Generally, we have "pushed" the data too far if the stress coefficient is above .15. The general goal is to keep the dimensions low enough to be parsimonious and to facilitate interpretation, yet at the same time capture the complexity of the relationships in the data.

Results

Unlike factor analysis, multidimensional scaling is such a new and relatively unused quantitative technique that a standard model for its presentation has failed to emerge. Unfortunately, it is not such an easy task to present the various consequences of multidimensional scaling in a research article as it is to present a summary of computations involved in factor analysis. Since many aspects of the computational output do not appear in the readings to follow, we will briefly examine a substantive example which resembles the research report by Weisberg and Rusk.

The broad focus of our attention is the evaluative space of the American electorate. Recent research and various multivariate approaches have suggested the usefulness of a dimensional view of electoral politics. The assumption is that individuals'

76. Kruskal, "Multidimensional Scaling by Optimizing Goodness of Fit," p. 16.
77. Ibid., p. 3.
78. Kruskal, "Nonmetric Multidimensional Scaling," pp. 118–19.
79. Ibid., p. 118.

TABLE 4.12 Correlation Matrix Between Selected Issues and Candidate Evaluations in 1968

Variables	1	2	3	4	5	6	7	8	9	10	11	12	13	14
(1) CR Speed														
(2) Housing	.26													
(3) Urban	−.32	−.20												
(4) Party	−.15	−.05	.15											
(5) Southerners	−.14	−.21	.14	.02										
(6) Blacks	.34	.32	−.23	−.12	.05									
(7) Humphrey	.24	.20	−.32	−.45	−.18	.28								
(8) Johnson	.20	.13	−.24	−.41	−.11	.28	.70							
(9) Kennedy	.19	.15	−.27	−.34	−.19	.28	.53	.47						
(10) Muskie	.21	.24	−.21	−.29	−.19	.25	.58	.46	.43					
(11) Nixon	−.12	−.03	.08	.42	.07	.02	−.18	−.09	−.13	−.09				
(12) Reagan	−.16	−.05	.18	.28	.13	−.02	−.19	−.09	−.10	−.07	.41			
(13) Agnew	−.13	−.09	.06	.27	.16	−.02	−.10	−.04	−.01	−.03	.60	.44		
(14) Wallace	−.29	−.31	.37	.02	.31	−.27	−.32	−.23	−.22	−.26	−.03	.20	.13	

perceptions of political objects (e.g., candidates and issues) and the resultant electoral competition space are multidimensional. At least, there is reason to suspect
that individual evaluations are not unidimensional (e.g., only ideological). For
simplicity, a successful two-dimensional solution is presented here.

Our immediate purpose was to find a dimensional solution which indicates interpoint distances between a selected set of civil rights issues and evaluations of presidential candidates in 1968. By using structured issue questions and feeling thermometer scales from the Survey Research Center's 1968 Election Study,[80] we begin
with an intercorrelation matrix (Pearson r) presented in table 4.12.

The variables include the respondent's attitudes toward the speed of the civil
rights movement, Black rights to housing, the solution to urban unrest, his party
identification, and his rating of candidates in terms of degrees of favorableness
along a "feeling thermometer" and his ratings of southerners and Blacks. Briefly,
the correlation matrix suggests a clustering of Democratic and Republican candidates, plus certain clusterings of issues. Although the reader can analyze these
relationships in extensive detail, the matrix lacks sufficient descriptive information
with regard to the location of each variable to one another. Generally, our goal
is a more parsimonious configuration, accompanied by guidelines for delineating
dimensions of evaluation of these political objects.

In order to derive a configuration, the Kruskal computer routine utilizes ranked
information in the matrix and derives distances between points to plot a scatter
diagram of the relationship between the data (δ from r) and new (i.e., best-fitting
monotonic) distances ($\hat{d}$). The final configuration of data relationships (interpoint

TABLE 4.13   History of Multidimensional Scaling
Computations

Iteration	Stress	Stress Ratio	Gradient
0	0.112	0.800	0.0289
1	0.078	0.696	0.0262
2	0.081	1.036	0.0324
3	0.065	0.810	0.0106
4	0.066	1.016	0.0192
5	0.063	0.946	0.0067
6	0.063	0.997	0.0086
7	0.062	0.989	0.0030
8	0.062	0.998	0.0033
9	0.062	0.998	0.0015
10	0.062	0.999	0.0012
11	0.061	0.999	0.0013
12	0.061	1.000	0.0021
13	0.061	0.999	0.0009
14	0.061	1.000	0.0006
15	0.061	1.000	0.0003
16	0.061	1.000	0.0003
17	0.061	1.000	0.0002
18	0.061	1.000	0.0012
19	0.061	1.000	0.0004

80. I wish to acknowledge the assistance of Mary Ann Armour of the Department of Political Science
at Southern Illinois University. The data utilized were made available by the Inter-University Consortium for Political Research and were collected originally by the Survey Research Center of the
University of Michigan. Neither source bears responsibility for the analysis or interpretation.

distances) is a consequence of this plotting and the monotonic curve fitting process inherent in it. As described previously, we begin with an arbitrary starting point and make adjustments in the distances ($\hat{d}$) over a variety of iterations until stress is sufficiently reduced. Using our data as an example of output, the iterative process stopped after nineteen iterations, i.e., the stress values were no longer decreasing, the stress ratio (the ratio between the stress value at any one iteration and the stress value at the immediately preceding iteration) was equal to one over a number of iterations and the gradient was approaching zero. This history of computations is presented in table 4.13. The stress value of 0.06 indicates a quite satisfactory solution (less than 0.15), particularly since the data were constrained into two dimensions (assuming an unsatisfactory one-dimensional solution). We also will note that the size of the gradient is successfully reduced over the nineteen iterations.

We will recall that stress is a measure of deviation from a perfectly monotonic curve. This curve depends on ranked information in the data (δ) and distance adjustments along a distance axis. The relationships between the data (δ), the original distance (d), and the best-fitting monotonic distances ($\hat{d}$) are presented in the sum-

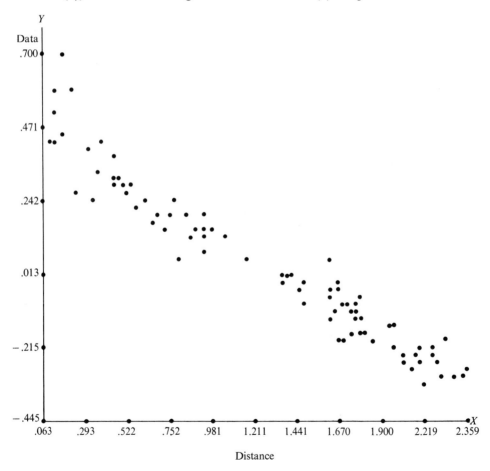

FIGURE 4.13 Plotting of Distances (d)
Against Data (δ)

mary of relationships in table 4.14. The data correlation coefficients are ranked from high positive values to high negative values and the relationships between the data, distance, and $\hat{d}$'s can be seen. Note that for several groups of distances, the $\hat{d}$ values are equal. This means that similar distance adjustments were made in pairs of variables in order to derive a monotonic curve. This monotonicity is evident from a comparison of the ranked data measures and their corresponding $\hat{d}$'s, e.g., as the relationships in the data decrease in similarity (i.e., correlation coefficients decrease), the corresponding new (i.e., best-fitting monotonic) distances ($\hat{d}$) increase.

Figure 4.13 presents the plotting of the similarities in the data against the original distances. Since we are using measures of similarity, monotonic relationships move down and to the right. An examination of the graph suggests a general monotonic tendency, yet many points deviate from monotonicity.

Figure 4.14 presents a plotting of similarities against new adjusted distances that resulted after the nineteen iterations in two dimensions. There is a smaller number of points because many $\hat{d}$ values are equal. The graph represents a monotonic relationship with a stress value equal to 0.06. That is, the variables in two-dimensional space have now been arranged in their most parsimonious structure.

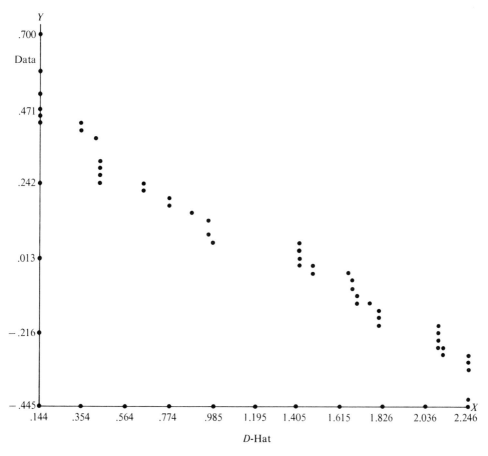

FIGURE 4.14   Plotting of Adjusted Distances ($\hat{d}$)
Against Data (δ)

TABLE 4.14 Multidimensional Scaling Summary of Similarity, Distance, and Adjusted Distance Relationships Between Pairs of Points

I Point	8	13	10	9	9	10	13	10	11	12	14	6	6
J Point	7	11	7	7	8	8	12	9	4	11	3	1	2
Data (δ)	0.700	0.595	0.580	0.528	0.473	0.459	0.436	0.429	0.419	0.413	0.371	0.336	0.320
Dist. (d)	0.181	0.223	0.128	0.126	0.063	0.173	0.141	0.141	0.375	0.315	0.445	0.368	0.487
D-Hat ($\hat{d}$)	0.144	0.144	0.144	0.144	0.144	0.144	0.144	0.144	0.345	0.345	0.407	0.407	0.445

I Point	14	8	9	7	12	13	2	10	11	7	10	7	8
J Point	5	6	6	6	4	4	1	6	1	1	1	2	1
Data (δ)	0.305	0.282	0.281	0.280	0.280	0.266	0.258	0.245	0.242	0.236	0.210	0.201	0.200
Dist. (d)	0.446	0.499	0.454	0.452	0.534	0.534	0.250	0.346	0.775	0.611	0.571	0.836	0.743
D-Hat ($\hat{d}$)	0.445	0.445	0.445	0.445	0.445	0.445	0.445	0.445	0.652	0.652	0.652	0.770	0.770

I Point	12	9	12	13	3	9	3	13	8	12	11	11	13
J Point	14	1	3	5	4	2	5	14	2	5	3	5	3
Data (δ)	0.200	0.191	0.181	0.157	0.148	0.147	0.142	0.134	0.132	0.127	0.075	0.069	0.063
Dist. (d)	0.935	0.682	0.655	0.938	0.976	0.889	0.718	1.050	0.946	0.872	0.947	1.160	0.793
D-Hat ($\hat{d}$)	0.770	0.770	0.770	0.880	0.880	0.880	0.880	0.954	0.954	0.954	0.954	0.977	0.977

I Point	6	5	14	11	13	13	12	11	13	11	13	4	12
J Point	5	4	4	6	6	9	6	2	10	14	8	2	2
Data (δ)	0.050	0.023	0.016	0.016	-0.014	-0.014	-0.015	-0.028	-0.028	-0.030	-0.036	-0.052	-0.054
Dist. (d)	1.627	1.393	1.368	1.417	1.374	1.666	1.493	1.466	1.613	1.250	1.667	1.775	1.634
D-Hat ($\hat{d}$)	1.436	1.436	1.436	1.436	1.436	1.498	1.498	1.498	1.498	1.498	1.667	1.679	1.679

I Point	10	10	8	13	8	13	9	8	11	6	13	9	5
J Point	12	11	11	2	12	7	12	5	1	4	1	11	1
Data (δ)	-0.070	-0.086	-0.086	-0.087	-0.094	-0.102	-0.103	-0.111	-0.115	-0.120	-0.129	-0.131	-0.138
Dist. (d)	1.717	1.689	1.763	1.498	1.762	1.741	1.764	1.641	1.613	1.775	1.614	1.754	1.977
D-Hat ($\hat{d}$)	1.679	1.679	1.679	1.679	1.701	1.701	1.701	1.701	1.701	1.701	1.701	1.754	1.809

I Point	4	12	7	11	10	12	9	3	10	5	9	8	3
J Point	1	1	5	7	5	7	5	2	3	2	14	14	6
Data (δ)	-0.149	-0.159	-0.175	-0.176	-0.187	-0.187	-0.193	-0.197	-0.205	-0.208	-0.225	-0.231	-0.234
Dist. (d)	1.944	1.744	1.791	1.816	1.684	1.845	1.674	2.239	2.175	2.977	2.108	2.078	2.018
D-Hat ($\hat{d}$)	1.809	1.809	1.809	1.809	1.809	1.809	1.809	2.099	2.099	2.099	2.099	2.099	2.099

I Point	8	10	14	7	10	14	14	7	7	3	9	8	7
J Point	3	14	6	3	4	1	2	3	14	1	4	4	4
Dat (δ)	-0.239	-0.258	-0.272	-0.273	-0.287	-0.290	-0.313	-0.315	-0.316	-0.318	-0.338	-0.411	-0.445
Dist. (d)	2.176	2.111	2.023	2.194	2.058	2.359	2.329	2.296	2.222	2.316	2.126	2.136	2.185
D-Hat ($\hat{d}$)	2.104	2.104	2.104	2.126	2.246	2.246	2.246	2.246	2.246	2.246	2.246	2.246	2.246

When these adjustments made in the scatter diagram are translated into two-dimensional configuration space,[81] the final configuration of interpoint distances results. Whereas the scatter diagrams indicate a plotting of similarities against distances, the final configuration indicates a final set of interpoint distances between variables. That is, figures 4.13 and 4.14 are plottings of all possible pairs of variables and figure 4.15 shows intervariable distances between all variables.

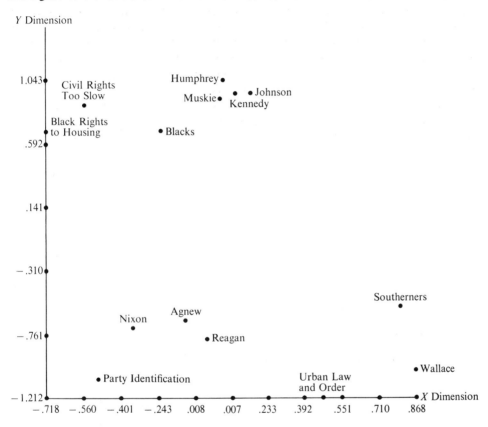

FIGURE 4.15   Final Configuration of Points in Two
Dimensions

Each variable point in this configuration is defined by its coordinates on two arbitrary axes. For example, variable one (civil rights speed) is defined by its coordinate on the X axis (-0.55) and its location on the Y axis (0.87). These coordinates are analogous to loadings in a factor analytic procedure. Each variable's coordinates on the two axes could be given, however, these coordinates would have little substantive meaning. Points in two-dimensional Euclidean space can be defined by any set of orthogonal axes and the set generated in multidimensional scaling is arbitrary. In order to provide an accurate rotation based upon mathematical criteria, the coordinates of the points in the final configuration (fig. 4.15) were

---

81. The relationships also were constrained into one-dimensional space, however, a stress value of 0.42 suggested that too much forcing occurred in order to speak of these variables in one dimension.

treated as factor loadings and rotated to a varimax orthogonal solution. This rotated configuration appears in figure 4.16 with the origin shifted to the centroid of the configuration space in order to facilitate description of the data.[82] Our findings in both figures indicate that the electorate perceives the Democratic candidates and the Republican candidates each clustering together based upon evaluations of or feelings toward candidates, with party nearby. An emphasis upon more housing rights for Blacks and a feeling that the civil rights movement is progressing too slowly cluster together, with positive feelings toward Blacks occurring nearby in space. On the other hand, a favorable evaluation of Wallace, southerners, and an issue position favoring more "law and order" in the urban context have small interpoint distances at the other extreme. Our rotated axes therefore suggest a partisan dimension with favorable evaluations of Nixon, Agnew, Reagan, and Republican party identification; at the other end, a clustering of attitudes favorable to Muskie, Kennedy, Johnson, and Humphrey. The other dimension suggests that the electorate evaluated Wallace in terms of the civil rights issue dimension, with

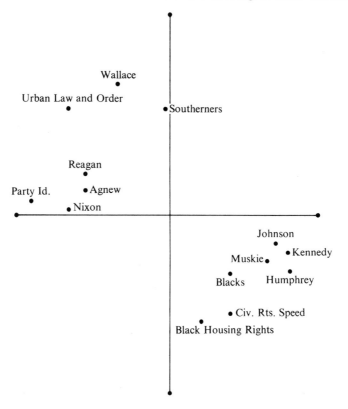

FIGURE 4.16   Rotated Configuration with Centered
Orgin

82. These are hypothetical axes which can be confirmed using mathematical criteria similar to factor analysis rotation. That is, coordinates on each axis can be treated as factor loadings and subject to, for example, varimax orthogonal rotation criteria. This was accomplished through the use of the Configuration Analysis Package available through the OSIRIS computer package of the Inter-University Consortium for Political Research.

favorable feelings toward Wallace, southerners, and law and order at one extreme, and favorable attitudes toward Blacks, housing for Blacks, and a civil rights movement at the other extreme. Although a detailed analysis cannot be presented here, an extension of similar research can be seen in the reading by Weisberg and Rusk. Our configuration at least confirms the failure of the American electorate to evaluate George Wallace in terms of candidate and party orientation; instead, he was evaluated along a civil rights issue dimension.

Research Examples and Introductory Notes

The following political science research examples highlight the application of techniques discussed in this chapter. In addition to simple descriptive statistics necessary for most research efforts, the applications include the use of Guttman scaling, factor analysis, and multidimensional scaling. The factor analysis articles depict the use of both Q and R methods of factoring, and the forms of data to which dimensioning is applied include roll calls, environmental and aggregate political data on the American states, and cross-national characteristics. The multidimensional scaling example is applied to political attitudes in the mass public. In reading these articles, one should recall the various technique options available to the researcher and offer critical judgements about the choice of variables, measurement sophistication, validity, reliability, and the theoretical explanations employed.

Selected Bibliography of Applications

Guttman Scaling

Anderson, Lee. "Variability in the Unidimensionality of Legislative Voting." *Journal of Politics* 26 (1964): 568-85.

Andrain, Charles F. "A Scale Analysis of Senators' Attitudes Towards Civil Rights." *Western Political Quarterly* 17 (1964): 488-503.

Farris, Charles D. "Prohibition as a Political Issue." *Journal of Politics* 23 (1961): 507-25.

Fishel, Jeff. "Party, Ideology, and the Congressional Challenger." *American Political Science Review* 63 (1969): 1213-32.

Kuroda, Yasumasa. "A Cross-Cultural Analysis of the Desire for Political Power." *Western Political Quarterly* 20 (1967): 51-64.

———. "Sociability and Political Involvement." *Midwest Journal of Political Science* 9 (1965): 133-48.

Lipsitz, Lewis. "Work Life and Political Attitudes: A Study of Manual Workers." *American Political Science Review* 58 (1964): 951-62.

MacRae, Duncan, Jr. "A Method for Identifying Issues and Factions From Legislative Votes." *American Political Science Review* 59 (1965): 909-26.

Munger, Frank, and Blackhurst, James. "Factionalism in the National Conventions." *Journal of Politics* 27 (1965): 375-94.

Patterson, Samuel C. "Dimensions of Voting Behavior in a One-Party State Legislature." *Public Opinion Quarterly* 26 (1962): 185-200.

Price, Hugh D. "Are Southern Democrats Different? An Application of Scale Analysis to Senate Voting Patterns." In *Politics and Social Life*, ed. Nelson Polsby, Robert Dentler, and Paul Smith, pp. 740-50. Boston: Houghton Mifflin, 1963.

Rieselbach, Leroy N. "The Basis of Isolationist Behavior." *Public Opinion Quarterly* 24 (1960): 645-57.

———. "Quantitative Techniques for Studying Voting Behavior in the U.N. General Assembly." *International Organization* 14 (1960): 291-306.

Schubert, Glendon. "The 1960 Term of the Supreme Court: A Psychological Analysis." *American Political Science Review* 56 (1962): 90-107.

Swinerton, E. Nelson. "Administrative-Political Role Consensus Among American State Executives." *Social Science Quarterly* 50 (1969): 264-71.

Ulmer, S. Sidney. "The Dimensionality of Judicial Voting Behavior." *Midwest Journal of Political Science* 13 (1969): 471-83.

———. "Supreme Court Behavior and Civil Rights." *Western Political Quarterly* 13 (1960): 288-311.

Factor Analysis

Aberbach, Joel D. "Alienation and Political Behavior." *American Political Science Review* 63 (1969): 86-99.

Alker, Hayward R., Jr. "Dimensions of Conflict in the General Assembly." *American Political Science Review* 58 (1964): 642-57.

Banks, Arthur S., and Gregg, Philip M. "Dimensions of Political Systems: A Factor Analysis of 'A Cross-Polity Survey'." *American Political Science Review* 59 (1965): 602-14.

Bobrow, Davis B. "Organization of American National Security Opinions." *Public Opinion Quarterly* 33 (1969): 223-39.

Burgess, Philip M., and Hofstetter, C. Richard. "The 'Student Movement': Ideology and Reality." *Midwest Journal of Political Science* 15 (1971): 687-702.

Crew, Robert E., Jr. "Dimensions of Public Policy: A Factor Analysis of State Expenditures." *Social Science Quarterly* 50 (1969): 381-88.

Crittenden, John. "Dimensions of Modernization in the American States." *American Political Science Review* 61 (1967): 989-1002.

Easton, David, and Dennis, Jack. "The Child's Acquisition of Regime Norms: Political Efficacy." *American Political Science Review* 61 (1967): 25-38.

Grumm, John G. "A Factor Analysis of Legislative Behavior." *Midwest Journal of Political Science* 7 (1963): 336–56.

Hofferbert, Richard I. "Socioeconomic Dimensions of the American States: 1890–1960." *Midwest Journal of Political Science* 12 (1968): 401–19.

Hofstetter, C. Richard. "The Amateur Politician: A Problem in Construct Validation." *Midwest Journal of Political Science* 15 (1971): 31–56.

Hopkins, Raymond F. "Aggregate Data and the Study of Political Development." *Journal of Politics* 31 (1969): 71–94.

Luttbeg, Norman R. "The Structure of Beliefs Among Leaders and the Public." *Public Opinion Quarterly* 32 (1968): 398–410.

MacRae, Duncan, Jr., and Meldrum, James A. "Factor Analysis of Aggregate Voting Statistics." In *Quantitative Ecological Analysis in the Social Sciences*, ed. Mattei Dogan and Stein Rokkan, pp. 487–506. Cambridge: MIT Press, 1969.

Marwell, Gerald. "Party, Region and the Dimensions of Conflict in the House of Representatives: 1949–54." *American Political Science Review* 61 (1967): 380–99.

McMurray, Carl D., and Parsons, Malcolm B. "Public Attitudes Toward the Representational Role of Legislators and Judges." *Midwest Journal of Political Science* 9 (1965): 167–85.

Patterson, Samuel C., and Boynton, G. R. "Legislative Recruitment in a Civic Culture." *Social Science Quarterly* 50 (1969): 243–63.

Rummel, R. J. "Indicators of Cross-National and International Patterns." *American Political Science Review* 63 (1969): 127–47.

Russett, Bruce. "Delineating International Regions." In *Quantitative International Politics*, ed. J. David Singer, pp. 317–52. New York: Free Press, 1968.

———. "An Empirical Typology of International Military Alliances." *Midwest Journal of Political Science* 15 (1971): 262–89.

Schubert, Glendon. "Jackson's Judicial Philosophy: An Exploration in Value Analysis." *American Political Science Review* 59 (1965): 940–63.

Shapiro, Michael J. "Rational Political Man: A Synthesis of Economic and Social-Psychological Perspectives." *American Political Science Review* 63 (1969): 1106–19.

Strong, Donald S. "Further Reflections on Southern Politics." *Journal of Politics* 33 (1971): 239–56.

Tanter, Raymond. "Dimensions of Conflict Behavior Within and Between Nations." *Journal of Conflict Resolution* 10 (1966): 41–64.

Vincent, Jack E. "National Attributes as Predictors of Delegate Attitudes at the U.N." *American Political Science Review* 62 (1968): 916–31.

Walker, Jack L. "The Diffusion of Innovations Among the American States." *American Political Science Review* 63 (1969): 880–99.

Unfolding Analysis, Multidimensional Scaling, and Smallest Space Analysis

Bloombaum, Milton. "The Conditions Underlying Race Riots as Portrayed by Multidimensional Scalogram Analysis." *American Sociological Review* 33 (1968): 76–92.

Butler, David, and Stokes, Donald E. *Political Change in Britain*, pp. 200ff. New York: St. Martin's Press, 1969.

Converse, Philip E. "The Problem of Party Distances in Models of Voting Change." In *The Electoral Process*, ed. M. Kent Jennings and L. Harmon Zeigler, pp. 175–207. Englewood Cliffs: Prentice-Hall, 1966.

Jennings, M. Kent. "Pre-Adult Orientations to Multiple Systems of Government." *Midwest Journal of Political Science* 11 (1967): 291–317.

MacRae, Duncan, Jr. *Issues and Parties in Legislative Voting*. New York: Harper and Row, 1970.

Niemi, Richard G. "Majority Decision-Making With Partial Unidimensionality." *American Political Science Review* 63 (1969): 488–97.

Schubert, Glendon. "Academic Ideology and the Study of Adjudication." *American Political Science Review* 61 (1967): 106–29.

Spaeth, Harold J., and Peterson, David J. "The Analysis and Interpretation of Dimensionality: The Case of Civil Liberties Decision-Making." *Midwest Journal of Political Science* 15 (1971): 415–41.

*IRA SHARKANSKY**

Voting Behavior of Metropolitan Congressmen: Prospects for Changes with Reapportionment

*This study analyzes roll call voting by 180 metro-
politan congressmen, with a focus on their significance during an era
in which legislative reapportionment will increase "urban presence" in
the United States House of Representatives. After suggesting several
reasons why urban representatives may or may not follow a consistently pro-
urban policy stance, the author elaborates his choice of metropolitan
congressmen based on districts within SMSA's, i.e., areas where reapportionment benefits will have the greatest impact. The major research
questions investigate the issue differences between these metropolitan
congressmen and other congressmen, as well as differences between
metropolitan congressmen with regard to metropolitan policy issues.*

*A series of roll call dependent variables fall into three categories
represented by simple indices: greater federal role, support for the
conservative coalition, and municipal support. Spearman's rho rank-order
correlation coefficient then is used to test relationships between these
indices as an indication of ideological similarity. An explanation for
variations in the roll call dependent variables is sought through six
independent variables which are hypothesized as affecting legislative
behavior for the urban congressman, where pro-metro and liberal voting is*

Reprinted from Ira Sharkansky, "Voting Behavior of Metropolitan Congressmen: Prospects for
Changes with Reapportionment," *Journal of Politics* 28(1966): 774–93, by permission of the journal
and the author.

*My thanks to Geoffrey Scott for help in gathering the data for this study, to Professor Malcolm B.
Parsons, of Florida State University, for his comments on an early draft, and to Richard Eiswirth and
the Computer Center of Florida State University for technical assistance.

hypothetically linked to Democratic party identification, high Democratic support in the most recent congressional election, high population density, high nonwhite population, low median income, and a central city constituency.

In order to test the above hypotheses, Sharkansky relies on descriptive statistics, correlation coefficients, and Guttman scaling. After the mean percentages of support for the dependent variables are differentiated for metropolitan and nonmetropolitan congressmen, the author examines the extent to which the roll calls comprising the simple municipal support index adhere to a unidimensional pattern by Guttman criteria. An array for the voting pattern is presented, facilitating visual inspection of the predominant groups and errors in the ideal Guttman model. This array meets the Guttman criteria of reproducibility with only 5 percent errors (CR = 95 percent) and it enables the assignment of scale scores where a zero value represents the most anti-metro positions and where a six value (assigned by groups) represents the highest metro support. When individuals do not fit perfectly with a group pattern, they are assigned to the group (and to the relevant scale score) that is most representative of this voting pattern. Characteristics of each group of congressmen then are examined by presenting mean values of several independent and nonmetropolitan dependent variables for each scale score. The strength of these relationships then is tested by intercorrelating (Spearman's rho) the set of independent and dependent variables. For the district location, party affiliation, and region variables, each level of the variable is described in relation to mean scale scores on the municipal support measures and the mean number of votes on the two other dependent variable measures (accompanied by standard deviations). District location and party are subsequently held constant through tabular controls, and more descriptive data on SMSA's are presented to support findings congruent with the author's hypotheses.

This is an analysis of the choices made on roll calls by 180 members of the U.S. House of Representatives during the 88th Congress. These Congressmen came from 48 of the largest metropolitan areas in the country. The "metropolitan Congressmen" warrant attention because they comprise a large proportion of the House membership, and this proportion is likely to increase with the combined effects of continued urbanization and Congressional reapportionment. Despite their significance during the current concern with legislative apportionment, however, metropolitan Congressmen have not been the subjects of intensive bloc analysis.

There are several unresolved controversies about the orientations of urban and rural legislators. Much of the dispute surrounding reapportionment assumes distinct urban or rural inclinations among legislators who are from markedly urban or rural constituencies. Although studies of *state legislatures* do not have direct relevance for this study of the United States Congress, three of them have cast doubt on the assumptions about urban and rural legislators. Derge finds no pronounced urban-rural antagonisms in the voting records of metropolitan and out-

state representatives in the legislatures of Illinois and Missouri.[1] Jacob, and Dye —
in separate studies — conclude that the degree of equity in the apportionment
scheme (with respect to urban and rural voters) shows no significant relationship
with the nature of policies enacted by state legislatures.[2] Yet it is possible that the
research methods of Derge, Jacob, and Dye have not revealed the extent of pro and
anti urban orientations that exist among the types of state legislators whose numbers
will be increased or decreased as a result of reapportionment. Derge lumps together all "contested" roll calls cast within a period of time. By doing this, he may
hide whatever antagonisms exist between metropolitan and outstate legislators on
issues that are especially relevant to urban or rural affairs.[3] Jacob and Dye focus
on coefficients of correlation between certain policy outcomes that represent legislative decisions, and measures of malapportionment. Their coefficients are generally
low. However, their data do not identify the behavior of legislators from the types
of districts that seem likely to be affected by reapportionment. As a result, their
findings do not indicate the results to be expected from reapportionment.

The existing literature does not clearly indicate whether the effects of Congressional malapportionment are more or less pronounced than the effects of state
legislative malapportionment. In size and population, Congressional districts are
larger than those of state legislatures, and Congressional districts are likely to be
more heterogeneous in their social, economic, and political elements.[4] Because of
this heterogeneity, Congressmen may be more likely to receive a variety of stimuli
from their constituents, and less likely to follow a consistently pro-urban or pro-rural
policy than state legislators.[5]

In contrast, there are also reasons to expect that urban and rural Congressmen
will have more consistently pro-urban or pro-rural records than state legislators
from similar districts. Compared to state legislators, Congressmen are more experienced politically when they reach office, and they retain their seats for a longer
period of time. Their experience may permit Congressmen to perceive their constituents' interests more accurately than is the case with state legislators. Furthermore, Congressmen's seats are more prized — in terms of social and political
status, as well as salary — than those of state legislators. As a result, urban and
rural Congressmen may have more incentive to vote consistent pro-urban or pro-
rural positions in order to retain their seats.[6]

Turner, MacRae, and Havens have found differences in the voting records of
urban and rural Congressmen, but their classifications of legislators are too gross
to illuminate the apportionment controversy. Turner and Havens define metropolitan districts as those in which more than 50 per cent of the population lives,

---

1. David R. Derge, "Metropolitan and Outstate Alignments in Illinois and Missouri Legislative
Delegations," *American Political Science Review*, 52 (1958), pp. 1051–65.

2. Herbert Jacob, "The Consequences of Malapportionment: A Note of Caution," *Social Forces*, 43
(1964), pp. 256–61; and Thomas R. Dye, "Malapportionment and Public Policy in the States,"
Journal of Politics, 27 (1965), pp. 586–601.

3. R. T. Frost, "On Derge's Metropolitan and Outstate Legislative Delegations," *American Political
Science Review*, 53 (1959), pp. 792–95.

4. Malcolm Jewell, *The Politics of Reapportionment* (New York, 1962), p. 22

5. *Ibid.*, p. 21 ff.

6. See Thomas R. Dye, "State Legislative Politics," in Herbert Jacob and Kenneth N. Vines, *Politics in
the American States* (Boston, 1965), pp. 151–206.

respectively, in "metropolitan areas," and in "urbanized districts."[7] MacRae defines urban districts and rural districts by the percentage of farmers, farm laborers, professionals, and managers among the working males in the population.[8]

In order to relate a roll call study to the question of reapportionment, it seems necessary to identify the legislators as coming from districts that are more likely or less likely to benefit from reapportionment. In this way, it may be feasible to conclude that a certain type of legislative voting will show an increase or decline as a result of reapportionment. The present techniques — explained below — identify legislators according to the location of their districts in and around the cores of metropolitan areas. Moreover, this study concentrates on urban-relevant roll calls (indices of municipal support, support for a larger Federal role, and support for the conservative coalition) that — unlike Derge's — seem likely to reveal whatever pro or anti urban orientations exist among the legislators.

Procedures

The "metropolitan Congressmen" considered here are those members of the 88th Congress whose districts include parts of the Standard Metropolitan Statistical Areas that surround 48 cities having populations of at least 250,000 in 1960.[9] These metropolitan areas included 72 million people in 1960, comprising 40 per cent of the total population. Between 1950 and 1960, the population of these metropolitan areas grew by 14.9 million. This accounted for 53 per cent of the Nation's population growth. Fully 82 per cent of the growth within the large metropolitan areas occurred *outside* of the central cities.

The 180 Representatives from the 48 metropolitan areas were 41 per cent of the House membership. The almost perfect correspondence between the metropolitan areas' proportion of the population (40 per cent) and their Congressmen's proportion of the House indicates a lack of severe malapportionment with respect to large urban areas. Democrats and Republicans were represented among the metropolitan Congressmen within two per cent of their parties' proportions in the House. Democrats held 61 per cent of the metropolitan seats, and 59 per cent of the total seats.

Two major questions are considered:

1) To what extent do Congressmen from large metropolitan areas differ from other Congressmen on issues that are relevant to metropolitan areas?

2) How do Congressmen from large metropolitan areas differ among themselves on issues that are relevant to metropolitan areas?

It is no simple task to define a set of dependent variables that will measure important differences among metropolitan and nonmetropolitan Congressmen. This study employs three voting indices that seem likely to measure facets of the differences: 1) support for a set of 15 issues during the first and second sessions of the

---

7. Julius Turner, *Party and Constituency: Pressures on Congress* (Baltimore, 1951), p. 74; Murray Clark Havens, "Metropolitan Areas and Congress: Foreign Policy and National Security," *Journal of Politics,* 26 (1964), pp. 758–74.

8. Duncan MacRae, Jr., *Dimensions of Congressional Voting* (Berkeley and Los Angeles, 1958), pp. 257–58.

9. Three metropolitan areas having central cities of 250,000 are absent from the sample: Birmingham and Honolulu (because Alabama and Hawaii selected all of their Congressmen at large in 1962), and Washington, D.C.

88th Congress identified by *Congressional Quarterly* as signifying a willingness to increase the role of the Federal Government; 2) support for 24 issues during the first and second sessions of the 88th Congress identified by *Congressional Quarterly* as signifying support for the "conservative coalition" of Republicans and southern Democrats; and 3) support for the "pro-metro" positions on six roll calls during the first and second session of the 88th Congress that presented pro and anti metropolitan alternatives to the Congressmen.[10] These six roll calls in my "index of municipal support" include five votes on proposals for direct Federal grants-in-aid to local governments that have special interest for large urban areas, plus one vote on the question of Federal court involvement in state legislative apportionment. The pro-metro positions are:

1) S 2265: "nay" on an amendment to delete aid to urban areas from a proposal to amend the Library Services Act to extend Federal aid for library services to urban areas[11]

2) S 1153: "nay" on a motion to recommit the 1965–67 authorization of the Airport Construction Program, and to reduce the proposed $75 million annual authorization to $60 million annually[12]

3) HR 3881: "yea" for passage of the Urban Mass Transportation Act of 1964, providing grants for acquiring, constructing, and improving facilities and equipment for mass transportation (highways excepted)[13]

4) HR 11926: "nay" on the proposal to deny the Supreme Court and lower Federal Courts jurisdiction over matters dealing with state legislative apportionment[14]

5) HR 6518: "yea" on the conference report for the Clean Air Act, providing for the initiation and strengthening of programs for the prevention and abatement of air pollution[15]

6) S 3049: "yea" on the conference report for the Housing Act of 1964, providing for continuation and expansions of Federal activities in public housing and urban renewal[16]

The six votes on the index of municipal support qualify as items on a Guttman scale, and thereby appear to have more than merely intuitive resemblance. Metropolitan Congressmen voted on these roll calls in a manner to suggest that the issues cluster around a common meaning. There were only 54 "non-scale" votes out of 1,068 possible votes, for an "index of reproducibility" of 95 per cent.[17]

The Federal role index and the conservative coalition index include votes on domestic and international issues that other studies have found to be of dispro-

---

10. The Federal role and municipal support indices are calculated on the basis of votes, announced pairs and responses to polls of *Congressional Quarterly*. Following the style of the *Congressional Quarterly*, the conservative coalition index is calculated solely on the basis of votes cast.

11. *Congressional Quarterly Almanac, 1964*, p. 602, column 3.

12. *Ibid.*, p. 600, column 1.

13. *Ibid.*, p. 634, column 59.

14. *Ibid.*, p. 654, column 101.

15. *Congressional Quarterly Almanac, 1963*, p. 648, column 104.

16. *Congressional Quarterly Almanac, 1964*, p. 654, column 99.

17. See George M. Belknap, "A Method for Analyzing Legislative Behavior," *Midwest Journal of Political Science*, 2 (1958), pp. 377–402; and H. Douglas Price, "Are Southern Democrats Different? An Application of Scale Analysis to Senate Voting Patterns," in Nelson W. Polsby *et al*, *Politics and Social Life: An Introduction to Political Behavior* (Boston, 1963), pp. 740–57.

portionate interest to urbanites, even though not of clear benefit to municipalities.[18] Presumably, a generally increased Federal role would result in increased U.S. services for urbanites and local governments in metropolitan areas,[19] while the conservative coalition would seek to limit these types of Federal activity. The Federal role and conservative coalition indices also serve to rank Congressmen on a liberal-conservative spectrum. It was a preliminary hypothesis of this study that Congressmen scoring *high* on the index of municipal support would also score *high* as supporters of a larger Federal role, and *low* as supporters of the conservative coalition. The following rank order correlation coefficients (Spearman's *r*), calculated from the records of metropolitan Congressmen, suggest the extent of the ideological similarity among the indices:[20]

municipal support index and Federal role index	.88
municipal support index and conservative coalition index	−.61
Federal role index and conservative coalition index	−.69

In order to explain variations among metropolitan Congressmen's records on the three voting indices, this study employs six independent variables. Each of these variables measures a facet of the Congressmen's environment that seems likely to affect their behavior with respect to metropolitan interests. Five of the measures are from the *Congressional District Data Book:* 1) the Congressman's party affiliation; 2) the percentage of the vote received by the Democratic candidate in the 1962 Congressional election; 3) the population per square mile; 4) median family income; and 5) the percentage of the population that was nonwhite in 1960. The sixth variable represents the location of the district *vis a vis* the central city.[21] After map comparisons of Congressional district boundaries and local government boundaries, each metropolitan district was placed in one of four categories: a) entirely within the central city; b) partly in the central city and partly in the surrounding suburban or rural areas; c) entirely in the suburbs (i.e., no part in the central city, but entirely within the SMSA); d) partly in suburbs and partly in the rural area outside of the SMSA.

Preliminary hypotheses maintained that the following factors would accompany a high degree of pro-metro and liberal voting among metropolitan Congressmen: Democratic party affiliation; high Democratic percentage of the vote in the recent Congressional election; high population density; high percentage nonwhite; low median family income; constituency location entirely within, or partly within the

---

18. See Turner, *op. cit.*, p. 91; and MacRae, *op. cit.*, p. 260 ff. For the data relating to the Federal role and conservative coalition indices, see *Congressional Quarterly Almanac, 1964*, pp. 752, 764.

19. See Roscoe Martin, *The Cities and the Federal System* (New York: 1965), especially Chapter 5.

20. The Federal role and conservative coalition indices found in the *Congressional Quarterly Almanac, 1964* include three items in common, and each includes some items from the municipal support index. For purposes of this analysis, the votes on the Mass Transportation Act and Federal Court participation in state legislative apportionment were deleted from the Federal role and conservative coalition indices, the vote on the Clean Air Act was also deleted from the Federal role index, and the vote on Mine Safety was deleted from the conservative coalition index. In each instance where one item appeared in more than one index, it was deleted from the indices having the largest number of items.

21. Central cities in the case of Standard Metropolitan Statistical Areas with more than one major core: Long Beach-Los Angeles, Oakland-San Francisco, Minneapolis-St. Paul. For a discussion of the importance shown by constituency location, see Leo M. Snowiss, "The Cities and Congress," unpublished paper delivered at the 1965 Meeting of the American Political Science Association, Washington, D.C.

central city. In environments of population congestion, poverty, high incidence of nonwhites, and widespread Democratic orientations, Congressmen seem more likely to perceive a need for pro-metro and liberal voting.[22] Moreover, it seems likely that municipal officials of the central city — more than those of outlying communities — will make sophisticated appeals for the support of their Representatives. Compared to officials of outlying towns, central city officials are more likely to work full time at their jobs, they are more likely to have skilled staff assistants, plus travel funds to pay for Washington visits. Moreover, central city officials may receive more demands from organized groups that lead to the request for a Congressman's help.

By analysis of means and standard deviations, coefficients of rank order correlation (Spearman's r) and scaling techniques, it will be possible to assess the relationships between the voting behavior of metropolitan Congressmen, and the variables of district location, political, economic, and racial composition.

Findings

The 180 Congressmen from large metropolitan areas differ from the rest of Congress — and in the expected directions — on the indices of municipal support, Federal role, and conservative coalition. The data of Table I show that metropolitan Congressmen are more likely than their colleagues to have chosen the pro-metro position on the six issues, to have supported an increase in the Federal role, and to have voted in opposition to the conservative coalition. However, the data of Table I do not show pervasive antagonisms between metropolitan and nonmetropolitan Congressmen. A majority of both groups sided together in support of a larger Federal role, and in support of three items on the municipal support index. On the Housing, Clean Air, and Airport bills, majorities of metropolitan and non-metropolitan Congressmen supported the pro-metro positions.

TABLE I Voting on Three Indices: Metropolitan Congressmen and Others

	Metropolitan Congressmen	Nonmetropolitan Congressmen	Total Congress
Average percentage of Congressmen supporting:			
Items of municipal support index	64%	54%	58%
Individual items of index:			
a. Housing vote	83	75	78
b. Clean Air vote	77	65	70
c. State apportionment vote	68	25	43
d. Mass Transportation vote	66	39	50
e. Airport Construction vote	59	60	60
f. Library Services vote	56	42	48
Fifteen items of CQ's Federal role index	65	54	61
Twenty-four items of CQ's conservation coalition index	34	59	48

22. See Lewis A. Froman, *Congressmen and Their Constituencies* (Chicago, 1963).

There are prominent differences among metropolitan Congressmen in the nature of their metropolitan and liberal orientations. One hundred and six metropolitan Congressmen scored most pro-metro on the index of municipal support. On the average, these Congressmen supported all six of the municipal support items, 13 of the 15 items on the Federal role index, and only four of the 24 items on the conservative coalition index. In contrast, a group of 17 metropolitan Congressmen averaged zero pro-metro positions on the municipal support index, only three liberal positions on the Federal role index, and 18 conservative positions on the conservative coalition index.

By applying Guttman scaling techniques to the votes of metropolitan Congressmen on the six roll calls of the municipal support index, it is possible to array both the men and the issues in ascending order of pro-metropolitan orientation. The scale that follows places each of 178 metropolitan Congressmen into one of seven cumulative groups that differ according to the degree of their members' support for pro-metro positions.[23] Group #6 includes the Representatives whose voting patterns most nearly reflect a pro-metro position on each of the six items. Group #5 includes the Representatives whose voting patterns most nearly amount to support for the five pro-metro positions most commonly supported by metropolitan Congressmen, and an anti-metro position on the roll call that was least frequently supported by metropolitan Congressmen. Groups #4, #3, #2, #1, and #0 include those Representatives whose voting patterns show decreasing support for pro-metro positions, and increasing support for anti-metro positions. Where a Member's votes do not fit perfectly the pattern of any one group, he is placed in the one that most nearly corresponds to his pattern. Where a Member has provided no indication of his position (shown by a "o" on the scale), this counts as a neutral vote and does not detract from his placement in a particular group. Announced pairs, and responses to polls of the *Congressional Quarterly* are counted as votes. Two Representatives who failed to indicate a position on any of the six votes are omitted from the scale analysis.

The scale shows that items of the municipal support index range from the Housing act of 1964 (most likely to attract support from metropolitan Congressmen) to the Library Services Act (likely to attract support only from metropolitan Congressmen who are thoroughly in favor of metropolitan interests). In conjunction with other tests, the scale also identifies the characteristics that are associated with different levels of pro-metro orientation. Table II shows how metropolitan Congressmen in each of the scale groups average on several measures.

The data of Table II confirm several of the preliminary hypotheses: pro-metro voting tends to increase along with population density and Democratic strength. Also, increasing scores on the municipal support scale tend to go along with increasing support for a larger Federal role and decreasing support for the conservative coalition. Table II does not show a clear relationship between pro-metro voting and median family income or percentage nonwhite.

---

23. The scale is composed of "cumulative groups" in the sense that it arrays the roll calls to indicate those votes that elicit pro-metro expressions from most metropolitan Congressmen, and those votes that are likely to elicit support only from the more committed pro-metro Congressmen. Vote "d", for example, attracts Representatives who supported the cumulation of more popular pro-metro positions in "f" and "e", plus another group that is more pro-metro in their orientation. At the same time, members supporting only "d", "e", and "f" do not support the pro-metro positions on issues that attract fewer, apparently more thoroughly committed pro-metro Congressmen.

Scale Analysis of Municipal Support Index

Member and metropolitan area	Pro-metro votes						Anti-metro votes					
	Library	Airport	Mass Tr.	Reappor.	Cl. Air	Housing	Library	Airport	Mass Tr.	Reappor.	Cl. Air	Housing
	a	b	c	d	e	f	a	b	c	d	e	f
Group #6:												
Holifield, Long Beach-Los Angeles	x	x	x	x	x	x						
Roosevelt, Long Beach-Los Angeles	x	x	x	x	x	x						
Burkhalter, Long Beach-Los Angeles	x	x	x	x	x	x						
Corman, Long Beach-Los Angeles	x	x	x	x	x	x						
Hanna, Long Beach-Los Angeles	x	x	x	x	x	x						
King, Long Beach-Los Angeles	x	x	x	x	x	x						
Brown, Long Beach-Los Angeles	x	x	x	x	x	x						
Wilson, Long Beach-Los Angeles	x	x	x	x	x	x						
Roybal, Long Beach-Los Angeles	o	o	x	x	x	x	o	o				
Cameron, Long Beach-Los Angeles	x	x		x	x	x			x			
Leggett, Oakland-San Francisco	x	x	x	x	x	x						
Edwards, Oakland-San Francisco	x	x	x	x	x	x						
Cohelan, Oakland-San Francisco	x	o	x	x	x	x		o				
Miller, Oakland-San Francisco	x	x	x	x	x	x						
Burton, Oakland-San Francisco	o	o	x	x	x	x	o	o				
VanDeerlin, San Diego	x	x	x	x	x	x						
Rogers, Denver	x	x	x	x	x	x						
Weltner, Atlanta	x	x	x	x	x	x						
Flynt, Atlanta	x	x	x		x					x		
Davis, Atlanta	x	x	x		x	x				x		x
Landrum, Atlanta	x	x	x		x	x				x		
Finnegan, Chicago	x	x	x	x	x	x						
O'Hara, Chicago	x	x	x	x	x	x						
Murphy, Chicago	x	x	x	x	x	x						
Rostenkowski, Chicago	x	x	x	x	x	x						
Dawson, Chicago	x	o	x	x	x	o		o				o
Kluczynski, Chicago	x	o	x	x	x	x		o				
Libonati, Chicago	x	x	x	x	x	x						
Pucinski, Chicago	x	o	x	x	x	x		o				
Boggs, New Orleans	x	x	x	x	x	x						
Garmatz, Baltimore	x	x	x	x	x	x						
Fallon, Baltimore	x	x	x	x	x	x						
Friedel, Baltimore	x	x	x	x	x	x						
Lankford, Baltimore	o	o	x	x	x	o	o	o				o
Donohue, Boston	x	x	x	x	x	x						
O'Neill, Boston	x	x	x	x	x	x						
Burke, Boston	x	x	x	x	x	x						
MacDonald, Boston	o	o	x	x	x	x	o	o				
Keith, Boston	x		x		x	x		x	x			
Ryan, Detroit	x	x	x	x	x	x						
Griffiths, Detroit	x	x	x	x	x	x						
Nedzi, Detroit	x	x	x	x	x	x						
Dingell, Detroit	x	x	x	x	o	x					o	
O'Hara, Detroit	x	o		x	x	x		o	x			
Diggs, Detroit	x	o	x	x	x	x		o				
Lesinski, Detroit	x	x	x	x	x	x						
Broomfield, Detroit	x	x		x		x			x		x	
Karth, Minneapolis-St. Paul	x	x	x	x	x	x						
Fraser, Minneapolis-St. Paul	x	x	x	x	x	x						
Bolling, Kansas City	x	x	x	x	x	x						
Randall, Kansas City	x	x	x	x	x	x						
Karsten, St. Louis	x	x	x	x	x	x						
Sullivan, St. Louis	x	x	x	x	x	x						
Gallager, Jersey City	x	x	x	x	x	x						
Osmers, Jersey City	x	x	x		x	x				x		

Scale Analysis of Municipal Support Index (*continued*)

	Pro-metro votes						Anti-metro votes					
	a	b	c	d	e	f	a	b	c	d	e	f
Daniels, Jersey City	x	x	x	x	x	x						
Rodino, Newark	x	x	x	x	x	x						
Dwyer, Newark	x	x	x	x	x	x						
Minish, Newark	x	x	x	x	x	x						
Wallhauser, Newark	x	x	x		x	x				x		
Dulski, Buffalo	x	x	x	x	x	x						
Halpern, New York	x	x	x	x	x	x						
Pike, New York	x	x	x	x	x	x						
Addabbo, New York	x	x	x	x	x	x						
Delaney, New York	x	x	x	x	x	x						
Celler, New York	x	x	x	x	x	x						
Keogh, New York	x	x	x	x	x	x						
Multer, New York	x	x	x	x	x	x						
Rooney, New York	x	x	x	x	x	x						
Farbstein, New York	x	x	x	x	x	x						
Ryan, New York	x	x	x	x	x	x						
Healey, New York	x	x	x	x	x	x						
Gilbert, New York	x	x	x	x	x	x						
Murphy, New York	x	x	x	x		x					x	
Rosenthal, New York	x	x	x	x	x	x						
Kelley, New York	x	o	x	x	x	x		o				
Carey, New York	x	o	x	x	x	x		o				
Powell, New York	x	o	x	x	x	x		o				
Buckley, New York	x	x	x	x	x	o						o
Feighan, Cleveland	x	x	x	x	x	x						
Vanik, Cleveland	x	x	x	x	x	x						
Ashley, Toledo	x	x	x	x	x	x						
Jarman, Oklahoma City	x	x		x	x	x			x			
Green, Portland	x	x		x	x	x			x			
Toll, Philadelphia	x	x	x	x	x	x						
Barrett, Philadelphia	x	x	x	x	x	x						
Nix, Philadelphia	x	x	x	x	x	x						
Byrne, Philadelphia	x	x	x	x	x	x						
Green, Philadelphia	o	o	x	x	x	x	o	o				
Millikan, Philadelphia	o	o	x		o	x	o	o		x	o	
Fulton, Pittsburgh	o	o	x	x	x	x	o	o				
Moorhead, Pittsburgh	x	x	x	x	x	x						
Dent, Pittsburgh	x	o	x	x	x	x		o				
Clark, Pittsburgh	x	x	x	x	x	x						
Morgan, Pittsburgh	x	x	x	x	x	x						
Roberts, Dallas	x	x			x	x			x	x		
Purcell, Dallas	x	x		x	x	x			x			
Thomas, Houston	x	x		x	o	x			x		o	
Gonzalez, San Antonio	x	x	x	x	x	x						
Zablocki, Milwaukee	x	x	x	x	x	x						
Reuss, Milwaukee	x	x	x	x	x							x
Pepper, Miami	x	x	x	x	x	x						
Fascell, Miami	x	x	x	x	x	x						
Gibbons, Tampa	x	x		x	x	x			x			
Hebert, New Orleans	x	x			o	x	x	x	o			
Group #5:												
Morse, Boston		x	x	x	x	x	x					
Cannon, St. Louis		x	o	o	x	o	x		o	o		o
Frelinghusen, Newark		x	x	x	x	x	x					
Grover, New York		x	x	x		x	x				x	
Reid, New York		x	x	x	x	x	x					
Lindsay, New York		o	x	x	x	x	x	o				
Horton, Rochester		x	x	x	x	x	x					
Schweiker, Philadelphia		x	x	x	x	x	x					
Holland, Pittsburgh		x	x	x	x	x	x					

Scale Analysis of Municipal Support Index (*continued*)

	Pro-metro votes						Anti-metro votes					
	a	b	c	d	e	f	a	b	c	d	e	f
Davis, Memphis	o	x		x	x	x	o	x				
Casey, Houston		x		x			x	x			x	x
Hardy, Norfolk		x		x		x	x	x		x		
Group #4:												
Mailliard, Oakland-San Francisco			x	x	o	x	x	x			o	
Younger, Oakland-San Francisco			x		x	x	x	x		x		
Bates, Boston			x		x	x	x	x		x		
Miller, Buffalo			o	o	x		x	x	o	o		x
Derounian, New York			x	o	x	o	x	x		o		o
Wydler, New York			x	x	x	x	x	x				
Fino, New York			x		x	x	x	x		x		
Barry, New York			x		x	x	x	x		x		
Minshall, Cleveland			x	x	x		x	x				x
Curtin, Philadelphia			x	x		x	x	x			x	
Corbett, Pittsburgh			x	x	x	x	x	x				
Group #3:												
Bell, Long Beach-Los Angeles		o		x	x	x	x	o	x			
Hosmer, Long Beach-Los Angeles				x	x	x	x	x	x			
Martin, Boston	o	o		x	o	x	o	o	x		o	
MacGregor, Minneapolis-St. Paul	x			x	x	x		x	x			
Ayers, Akron				x	x	x	x	x	x			
Bolton, F.P., Cleveland			o	x	o		x	x	x	o		o
Wright, Ft. Worth	x			x	x	x		x	x			
Group #2:												
Clauson, Long Beach-Los Angeles					x		x	x	x	x		x
Lipscomb, Long Beach-Los Angeles					x	x	x	x	x	x		
Baldwin, Oakland-San Francisco	x				x	x			x	x		
Wilson, San Diego		x			x	x	x		x	x		
Brotzman, Denver					x	x	x	x	x	x		
Rumsfeld, Chicago					x	x	x	x	x	x		
Hull, Kansas City		x			x	x	x		x	x		
Ichord, St. Louis		x			x	x	x		x	x		
Ostertag, Rochester					x	x	x	x	x	x		
Rich, Cincinnati					x	x	x	x	x	x		
Bolton, O.P., Cleveland					x	x	x	x	x	x		
Schenk, Dayton					x	x	x	x	x	x		
Teague, Dallas		x			x		x		x	x		x
Downing, Norfolk		x			x	x	x		x	x		
Group #1:												
Clausen, Oakland-San Francisco		x					x	x		x	x	x
Reid, Chicago							x	x	x	x	x	
Derwinski, Chicago							x	x	x	x	x	
Collier, Chicago							x	x	x	x	x	
Shriver, Witchita		o					x	x	o	x	x	x
Quie, Minneapolis-St. Paul							x	x	x	x	x	
Cunningham, Omaha			x				x	x	x		x	x
Clancy, Cincinnati							x	x	x	x	x	
Norblad, Portland							x	x	x	x	x	
May, Seattle							x	x	x	x	x	
Stinson, Seattle							x	x	x	x	x	
Westland, Seattle							x	x	x	x	x	
Group #0:												
Rhodes, Phoenix							x	x	x	x	x	x
Smith, Long Beach-Los Angeles							x	x	x	x	x	x

Scale Analysis of Municipal Support Index (*continued*)

	Pro-metro votes						Anti-metro votes					
	a	b	c	d	e	f	a	b	c	d	e	f
Utt, Long Beach-Los Angeles							x	x	x	x	x	x
McClory, Chicago							x	x	x	x	x	x
Hoffman, Chicago			o	o			x	x	o	o	x	x
Bruce, Indianapolis							x	x	x	x	x	x
Snyder, Louisville				x			x	x	x		x	x
Curtis, St. Louis				x			x	x	x		x	x
Pillion, Buffalo							x	x	x	x	x	x
Becker, New York							x	x	x	x	x	x
St. George, New York							x	x	x	x	x	x
Devine, Columbus							x	x	x	x	x	x
Belcher, Tulsa				x			x	x	x		x	x
Dague, Philadelphia		x					x	x		x	x	x
Alger, Dallas				o			x	x	x	o	x	x
Foreman, El Paso							x	x	x	x	x	x

x = vote, announced pair, or response to *Congressional Quarterly* poll
o = no indication of sentiment

The data of Table III, showing coefficients of rank order correlation, provide some indication of the relative strength of relationships between the voting behavior of metropolitan Congressmen and four independent variables. All of the relationships are in the expected direction: population density, per cent nonwhite, and Democratic percentage of the recent vote relate positively with the municipal support support index (shown on Table III both as the number of pro-metro votes and scale score) and the Federal role index, and negatively with the conservative coalition index; median family income relates negatively with the municipal support index and the Federal role index, and positively with the conservative coalition index. All of the relationships except those between median family income and the municipal support index are strong enough to pass a common test for "statistical significance."[24] Among the four independent variables considered here, the party variable and population density show the strongest relationships with the voting behavior of metropolitan Congressmen.

It is apparent that the factor of constituency location *vis a vis* the central city is also important in explaining the voting behavior of metropolitan Congressmen. In particular, the group of 41 Congressmen whose constituencies are entirely within the limits of central cities are markedly more pro-metro and liberal than Congressmen from any of the other metropolitan districts. This is clear from Table IV, showing the mean scores and standard deviations of metropolitan Congressmen's votes — according to the location of their district, their party affiliation, and their section — on the indices of municipal support, Federal role, and conservative coalition. Congressmen from the central cities show the most extreme pro-metro and liberal positions on each of the indices, and their voting on the indices varies

24. This test for statistical significance actually does not apply to the data, insofar as the subjects represent a universe (Congressmen from certain large metropolitan areas) rather than a sample chosen to represent a larger population. Nevertheless, the test for significance is useful for the purpose of denoting coefficients of rank order correlation that are "sizeable." See Hubert M. Blalock, *Social Statistics* (New York, 1960), p. 319.

TABLE II Municipal Support Scale Scores of Metropolitan Congressmen, and Means of Several Characteristics

Scale score	Population per sq. mi.	Percentage nonwhite	Median family income	Democratic percentage of vote	Number of pro-Fed'l role votes	Pro-conservative coalition voting percentage	Number of pro-municipal support votes	Number of Congressmen in each scale group
0	1145	6.4%	$6747	38.4%	2.6	74.6	0.3	17
1	897	3.0	6502	37.5	5.2	69.6	1.3	11
2	1035	7.5	6271	51.6	6.5	74.9	2.3	14
3	2145	5.1	7021	39.5	7.6	48.4	2.7	7
4	4466	2.5	7469	39.8	7.5	50.9	2.9	11
5	6427	9.5	6664	47.7	8.7	36.2	4.3	12
6	12608	14.5	6110	64.1	12.6	15.2	5.5	106

TABLE III   Coefficients of Rank Order Correlation,
for 180 Metropolitan Congressmen

Independent variables:	INDEX			
	Municipal support		Federal role	Conservative coalition
	Number of support votes	Scale score		
Democratic percentage of vote in recent Congressional election	.58*	.71*	.52*	−.55*
Population per square mile	.47*	.53*	.49*	−.60*
Percentage nonwhite	.26*	.38*	.19*	−.19*
Median family income	−.14	−.12	−.15*	.17*
*significant at the .05 level				

least among themselves. As Congressional districts become further removed from the central city, the incumbents show decreasing support for pro-metro and liberal positions. The sharpest break in this regression occurs between constituencies that are entirely within the central city and all other metropolitan constituencies.[25]

It is also apparent from the data of Table IV that metropolitan Democrats are — as expected — considerably more pro-metro and liberal than metropolitan Republicans. According to the sectional breakdown included in Table IV, southern metropolitan Congressmen appear more conservative than their nonsouthern counterparts, but the southerners are not less pro-metro on the municipal support index.[26]

District location and party affiliation both are able to distinguish among Congressmen from metropolitan areas. This is evident from Table V, showing the voting behavior of metropolitan Congressmen, with both party and district location held constant. Although some of the differences among metropolitan Democrats are small, and although the small number of central city Republicans requires a tenuous acceptance of the findings, central city Congressmen of both parties are more pro-metro and liberal than fellow metropolitan partisans. Also, the expected party differences are evident when district location is constant. The most pro-metro and liberal Congressmen portrayed in Table V are central city Democrats, while the least pro-metro and most conservative metropolitan Congressmen are non-central city Republicans. Indeed, this latter group of metropolitan Republicans were less pro-metro and more conservative than the non metropolitan Members of the 88th Congress.

The available data do not indicate clearly what it is about a central city district that brings about pro-metro and liberal voting records among Congressmen. However, it is likely that the social, economic, and political composition of the central city affects Congressional voting records. Table VI reveals that central city constituencies — especially those of Democrats — have the characteristics that previous

---

25. Havens reports that no such differences exist with respect to foreign policy and national security issues. However, he provides no data to support his claim about the lack of differences in the voting records of central city and suburban Congressmen, and it is difficult to discern how his definition of metropolitan constituencies would support such a finding.

26. "Southern" metropolitan Congressmen are those from Miami and Tampa, Florida; Atlanta, Georgia; Louisville, Kentucky; New Orleans, Louisiana; Baltimore, Maryland; Oklahoma City and Tulsa, Oklahoma; Memphis, Tennessee; Dallas, El Paso, Ft. Worth, Houston, and San Antonio, Texas; and Norfolk, Virginia.

TABLE IV Mean Scores and Standard Deviations (in Parentheses) of Voting on Three Indices: by Location of Constituency, Party and Section

		INDEX			
		Municipal support			
Congressmen's characteristic	[Number of Congressmen in group]	Number of pro-municipal votes	Scale score	Number of pro-Federal role votes	Percentage pro-conservative coalition
By location of district:					
Entirely within central city	[41]	5.4 (1.2)	5.9 (0.5)	12.7 (2.9)	7.0% (8.8)
Partly in central city	[78]	3.9 (2.2)	4.2 (2.4)	9.4 (4.6)	38.3 (32.7)
Entirely in suburban SMSA	[24]	3.5 (1.9)	4.3 (2.0)	8.5 (4.1)	43.9 (23.5)
Partly in suburban SMSA and partly outside SMSA	[37]	3.4 (2.0)	3.8 (2.3)	8.2 (4.2)	45.9 (29.0)
By Party:					
Metropolitan Democrats	[110]	5.3 (1.2)	5.8 (0.8)	12.1 (3.3)	16.0 (21.2)
Metropolitan Republicans	[69]	2.2 (1.7)	2.5 (2.1)	6.1 (3.4)	61.3 (21.4)
By section:					
South	[29]	4.1 (1.9)	4.7 (2.2)	8.8 (4.4)	48.1 (26.1)
nonSouth	[151]	4.1 (2.1)	4.5 (2.1)	10.0 (4.4)	30.7 (30.6)

TABLE V Mean Scores of Voting on Three Indices, with Party and District Location Held Constant

	DEMOCRATS INDEX				REPUBLICANS INDEX			
	Municipal support		Number of pro-Fed'l role votes	Percentage pro-conserv. coalition	Municipal support		Number of pro-Fed'l role votes	Percentage pro-conserv. coalition
	Number of votes	Scale score			Number of votes	Scale score		
Entirely within central city	5.6	6.0	12.8	5.4%	4.0	4.8	11.8	22.3%
Other metropolitan Congressmen	5.2	5.7	11.8	21.3	2.1	2.3	5.8	63.7

The number of Congressmen in each cell are:

	Democrats	Republicans
Entirely within central city	37	4
Other metropolitan Congressmen	73	65

The mean scores of nonmetropolitan Congressmen are:

INDEX			
Municipal support		Number of pro-Fed'l role votes	Percentage pro-conservative coalition
Number of votes	Scale score		
3.2	#	8.0	58.5%

not available

analysis has shown to be associated with pro-metro and liberal voting: high congestion, a high incidence of Democratic voting, a high percentage of nonwhites and lower than average income. Although this study has no relevant data, it may also be a part of the central city environment that municipal officials and interest groups are more likely than in outlying areas to make sophisticated presentations to their Representatives.

TABLE VI   Means of Several Characteristics, by District Location

	Population per sq. mi.	Percentage nonwhite	Median family income	Democratic percentage of vote	
Entirely within central city*	28,122	21.8%	$5976	65.4%	N = 41
Partly in central city	4,114	9.9	6503	54.1	N = 78
Entirely in suburban SMSA	2,597	5.7	7350	47.0	N = 24
Partly in suburban SMSA and partly outside SMSA	583	4.7	5837	54.6	N = 37
*Central city Democrats	28,167	23.7	5793	68.5	N = 37
Central city Republicans	27,708	3.9	7672	36.3	N = 4

Summary and Conclusions

The data of Tables I–V provide evidence for the following propositions:

1) Congressmen from large metropolitan areas differ from other Congressmen on roll calls that are relevant to metropolitan interests and more broadly defined liberalism.

2) Metropolitan Congressmen from districts with the following characteristics are most likely to vote for pro-metro and liberal points of view: location entirely within the central city; high Democratic percentage among the electorate; high population density; high percentage of nonwhites; low median family income.

These findings may serve to refine some widespread assumptions about urban-rural conflict within the U.S. House of Representatives. During the 88th Congress, the Congressmen from 48 of the largest metropolitan areas gave more support to pro-metro and liberal positions than their colleagues. Among the Congressmen from large metropolitan areas, it was the Democrats, and Republicans from central city constituencies who were most consistent in their support of municipal and liberal interests. As a result of reapportionment and continued urbanization, certain types of decisions in the U.S. House of Representatives may change. However, the changes will be minimized if the suburbs of metropolitan areas live up to expectations and benefit more than central cities from reapportionment and continued urbanization.[27] Insofar as Republican-oriented suburbs benefit most from reapportionment, there are not likely to be significant changes in policy.

Because of differences in technique and subject-matter, it is not feasible to equate these findings with those of Derge, Jacob, and Dye pertaining to state legislatures. Like their findings, however, these suggest temperance in estimating the changes in public policy that will result from legislative reapportionment.

27. Jewell, *op. cit.*, p. 23; and *Congressional Quarterly Weekly Report*, XX (1962), pp. 153–69.

BRUCE M. RUSSETT*

Discovering Voting Groups
in the United Nations

*The following article, its substantial rejoinder,
and the exchange between the respective authors focuses on theoretical
and methodological problems associated with factor analysis applied to
the study of roll call voting. Russett's goal is the identification of
voting groups in the United Nations through the use of a Q factor analysis
technique. We will recall that a Q analysis utilizes a correlation
matrix where cases (countries) become variables so that each correlation
represents the relationship between pairs of countries across a set of
roll call observations. The Q technique therefore yields dimensions or
groups of nations similar in their voting behavior in the United Nations.
This procedure yields fifteen factors or groups through a varimax rotation
maximizing high and low loadings, with the factoring process terminated
when eigenvalues drop below unity. The analysis focuses on six factors
which had more than one loading above .50. Factors are named by the
groups of countries loading highest on them and they are presented in
the order of decreasing percentages of total explained variance where
countries are organized in groups on the factors (in descending order of
their primary loadings). Because the solution yielded two factors on
which several countries "jointly loaded," Russett utilizes a scattergram
plotting the positions of these countries on the two factors. Through*

Reprinted from Bruce M. Russett, "Discovering Voting Groups in the United Nations," *American
Political Science Review* 60 (1966): 327–39, by permission of the American Political Science Association
and the author.

*This research was begun under a Junior Faculty Fellowship from Yale University. It has also been
supported by the Yale Political Data Program under a grant from the National Science Foundation,
and by the Mental Health Research Institute of the University of Michigan.

*this procedure, he is able to identify a third grouping of nations (Latin
American) which fall between (in terms of variance explained) the other two.*

*In order to isolate influences affecting the grouping of nations,
Russett turns to an explanation relying on substantive issues. From a
previous R factor analysis of roll calls, he was able to isolate several
major issue dimensions which again appeared for the session being analyzed
in the present study. In order to discover the basic issue dimension
distinguishing the grouping of countries derived from Q analysis, the
nations' factor scores on the R issue dimension were correlated with
their factor loadings from the Q analysis grouping of nations.*

*The Mueller article is critical of Russett's procedures on a number
of grounds and it suggests constructive comments which point to some
problems in many factor analysis designs. First, Mueller raises questions
about the ability of factor analysis to yield satisfactory ("true")
results in the study of complex phenomena when, in effect, a number of
factor solutions may yield contradictory results. Although Mueller
probably overstates the whimsical nature of solutions (particularly when
uniform criteria are employed across the same data set), the point is
well taken that subjective interpretation plays a primary role in factor
analysis which is otherwise billed as a mathematically objective routine.*

*In moving beyond the above criticisms, Mueller is unhappy with the
tools as applied to U.N. bloc voting. For example, he points out that
if two nations have a similar loading on a factor, it does not insure
that these two nations' voting preferences will be highly correlated with
each other. Rather, factor analysis addresses itself to broader patterns
among groupings of nations. This criticism holds for all factor analyses —
dimensioning and parsimony are arrived at with some cost in individual
variable interpretation. He is also critical of the Pearson product-moment
correlation coefficient's inability to treat middle cell responses in a
three by three table in a consistent fashion. He suggests an index
which solves this problem, yet many other researchers have found it
useful to address the issue through proper missing data correlation routines
or through the use of phi coefficients. Indeed, many computer program
routines are now constructed to properly handle roll call data.*

*Finally, Mueller addresses the problem of choice in factor analysis —
the generation of oblique vs. orthogonal solutions in rotating the factors.
He suggests that both types of solutions should be employed, particularly
in light of the fact that an orthogonal solution will only make sense if
the factors are in fact uncorrelated.*

*In response to Mueller's comments, Russett defends his position by
claiming that he took all the precautions necessary and suggested by
Mueller, and thanking him for the general warnings about factor analysis.
Specifically, he defends his presentation of only the factor matrix
without the total original correlation matrix; suggests that Mueller's
example of Pearson correlation problems is not appropriate to the actual
distributions in U.N. voting data; and he claims to have analyzed
oblique solutions which were not reported because of their similarity
to orthogonally rotated results.*

I. An Inductive Approach to Voting Patterns

The discussion of voting groups or blocs within the United Nations General Assembly has long been a popular pastime. It is, of course, merely a special case of a wider concern with groups and coalitions in all aspects of international politics. With the apparent loosening of the early postwar bipolarity it is increasingly important to discern the number, composition, and relative strength of whatever coalitions of nations may emerge from the present seemingly transitional period.

Voting groups in the General Assembly provide a relevant datum, though hardly the only one, for an effort to identify these groups. The United Nations gives no perfect image of broader international politics; due to the one-nation one-vote principle and to the fact that it is not a world government with authority to enforce its decisions, power relationships within the Assembly are not the same as in other arenas, such as functional or geographic ones. It might well be argued that because of the majority-rule principle the smaller and poorer states have an incentive to band together in the UN that they do not have elsewhere. Thus the discovery of a "bloc" of underdeveloped countries in the UN proves nothing about the cohesion of that "bloc" in other contexts. Yet votes in the General Assembly do provide a unique set of data where many national governments commit themselves simultaneously and publicly plan wide variety of major issues. The range of issues includes almost everything of major worldwide concern; even policy positions on parochial or regional questions (the intrabloc relations of Communist states, for instance) can often be inferred from the nations' votes on other issues. However warped or distorted an image of general world politics the General Assembly may convey, it remains one of our best sources of replicable information policy positions for its 100-plus members.

An interest in voting groups may have a number of payoffs. From a frankly manipulative point of view, it may give information which can assist American policy-makers to increase their gains in the UN political process. Of more scientific interest, it can tell us about blocs and coalitions in ways that can be related to broader theories about parliamentary behavior. And finally it can indeed give some, admittedly imperfect, information about the nature — such as bipolar or multipolar, etc. — of the emerging international system.

The last concern must proceed from an inductive approach to the identification of voting groups, and so, for most purposes, should the second. That is, if one is asking how many such groups there are, the advance specification of certain aggregates, such as caucusing groups (Commonwealth, Communist, Afro-Asian) is a very roundabout way to get the answer. True, there is a tendency for caucusing groups to be more cohesive than any set of states picked purely at random, but the association between caucusing group membership and voting identity is very rough, as Thomas Hovet has so compellingly demonstrated.[1] Furthermore, by dealing only with pre-selected groups one could easily conclude, for example, that disagreement and conflict within the Afro-Asian group is extremely high, but not even notice some subgroups, including some which do not formally caucus together, that nevertheless show very high agreement. Or one might ignore the cohesion of an aggregate of states (such as those of the North Atlantic area) which includes both

---

1. *Bloc Politics in the United Nations* (Cambridge: Harvard University Press, 1960).

one or more caucusing groups and a number of countries that are not in any caucusing group.

Most of the published studies to date have been directed to measuring the cohesion of caucusing, geographic, or other pre-selected groups.[2] One major exception is Leroy Rieselbach's article, which introduces an inductive method of bloc analysis.[3] He constructs a table showing the percentage of votes on which each of a large number of pairs of countries agree, and arranges the table in such a way as to indicate cohesion, with lines drawn around any group of countries achieving a given level of agreement. In the article he illustrates this method for selected countries, those in Latin America, but it becomes extremely awkward for a body as large as the entire Assembly in recent years (over 110 members). In such a large table (each of 100 countries' scores with every other nation) it is very difficult to be sure one has found all the "blocs" that meet one's criterion.[4] Rieselbach also illustrates an approach using Guttman scaling, but it can only find groups who vote together on a particular set of issues (cold war, colonial self-determination, etc.). We shall discuss this aspect below. In many ways it is a major improvement over studies which attempt to find groups when lumping all issues together, for coalitions on cold war issues are *not* identical with those on self-determination. Yet the inability to employ it simultaneously, when one wishes, to more than one issue is a limitation.

Arend Lijphart has with great force pointed out the overwhelming concentration of interest in the previous literature on analyzing preselected groups, and to counter it offers an ingenious inductive method which he illustrates for states in the 11th through 13th Sessions.[5] It again depends upon a version of an index of the percentage of times two states' voting positions agree, modified to account for the abstentions which are rather common in the General Assembly. He employs a graphic method of presentation (vaguely reminiscent of spider webs) that is superior to the tabular one but nevertheless becomes quite difficult to interpret for a body the size of the current Assembly. Furthermore, it can only identify those pairs or groups of states which achieve or exceed a particular *level* of agreement (in his illustration, 87.5 per cent), and is not an economical method for showing the *degrees* of agreement which may exist among all states.

Thus no fully satisfactory method for the identification of voting groups has yet appeared in the international organization literature. What is required is a technique which is *inductive*, given to a means of presentation which is readily *interpretable*, which shows *gradations* in agreement among nations (not just whether or not they exceed a particular level of agreement), which reliably *identifies all the groupings*, and which can be applied either to a *selected* set of issues or to *all* roll-call votes of a Session.

2. *Ibid.*, and Thomas Hovet, *Africa in the United Nations* (Evanston, Illinois: Northwestern University Press, 1963). See also M. Margaret Ball, "Bloc Voting in the General Assembly," *International Organization*, 5 (1951), 3–31; Robert E. Riggs, *Politics in the United Nations* (Champaign: University of Illinois Press, 1958); and Hayward R. Alker, Jr., and Bruce M. Russett, *World Politics in the General Assembly* (New Haven, Conn.: Yale University Press, 1965), ch. 12.
3. "Quantitative Techniques for Studying Voting Behavior in the UN General Assembly," *International Organization*, 14 (1960), 291–306.
4. Even in Rieselbach's Table 2 of Latin American countries there would seem to be one other group (Uruguay, Costa Rica, Paraguay, Honduras, Peru) that meets his criteria (five countries, 80 per cent agreement) for a bloc.
5. "The Analysis of Bloc Voting in the General Assembly," *American Political Science Review*, 57 (1963), 902–17.

I believe that factor analysis, and more specifically a particular application of factor analysis, the so-called "Q-technique," is such a method. Originally developed by psychologists, during the past several years factor analysis has been employed sufficiently widely by political scientists that it probably requires no detailed introduction or justification to most readers, though its application to the United Nations has so far been limited.[6] In the most common employment of factor analysis every variable is correlated with every other variable, using the product-moment correlation coefficient. Factor analysis is then a data-reduction technique, as those variables which show high correlations among themselves and very low correlation with other variables are interpreted as pointing to a single underlying dimension, or *factor*. The factors themselves are uncorrelated with each other. Thus in Alker's initial application of the technique to UN voting patterns it was found that certain roll-calls (e.g. in 1961 on South Africa, Angola, Rhodesia, Ruanda-Urundi, trade, and economic aid) had similar voting alignments that pointed to an underlying "self-determination" issue. These voting alignments were unrelated to those on such issues as Cuba, Hungary, Tibet, and disarmament, which were like each other and pointed to a different underlying issue (the cold war).[7] In this application each roll-call vote was a variable, with each "actor" (country) serving as an item or observation.

The versatility of factor analysis, however, suggests an alternative use. It can just as readily be used to find similar *actors* (test takers, legislators, nations) as similar *variables* (questions on a psychological test, roll-call votes). If, for example, one began with a table (matrix) where each country was a row and each column a roll-call, one could simply turn the table 90 degrees so that, in effect, the countries became variables and the roll-calls became observations. When the matrix is then factor-analyzed in this fashion the correlations identify *countries* with similar voting patterns and the factors point to voting groups or blocs. This procedure is usually designated "Q-analysis" to distinguish it from the somewhat more common technique mentioned first (R-analysis).[8] To repeat, the procedure is inductive in that it involves no prior specification of the groups to be looked for, nor is even the number of such groups specified in advance.

II. Cohesive Voting Groups: A Q-Analysis of the 18th Session

We shall illustrate the technique with an analysis of roll-call votes in the 18th Session, beginning in the autumn of 1963, and in the process be able to make some useful

---

6. Hayward R. Alker, Jr., "Dimensions of Conflict in the General Assembly," *American Political Science Review*, 58 (1964), 642–57 and Alker and Russett, *op. cit.* A much more detailed discussion of how factor analysis is employed can be found in chapter 2 of the latter. As yet unpublished analyses of UN votes have been performed by Goerge Chacko, Rudolph Rummel, Raymond Tanter, Charles Wrigley, and others.

7. Alker, *op. cit.*

8. Although it has been used rather frequently in other disciplines, to my knowledge the only application in comparative or international politics is a paper by Arthur S. Banks and Phillip Gregg, "Grouping Political Systems: Q-Factor Analysis of *A Cross-Polity Survey*," *American Behavioral Scientist*, 9, 3 (November, 1965), 3–6. An application to the Kansas state legislature can be found in John Grumm, "A Factor Analysis of Legislative Behavior," *Midwest Journal of Political Science*, 7 (1963), 336–56. It is worth noting that in his pioneer study of voting blocs in the United States Congress David Truman discusses the difficulty of finding blocs in a large matrix and suggests factor analysis as a method possibly superior to his own; *The Congressional Party* (New York: John Wiley and Sons, 1959), p. 329.

substantive points about the nature of politics in the Assembly. Because of the United States vs. Russia and France controversy over dues there was only a single recorded vote in the 19th (1964) Session, so these are the most recent data available or likely to become so until the *Official Records* of the 20th (1965) Session are published sometime in 1967.

Our data consist of all 66 roll-call votes, both plenary and committee, except those which are virtually unanimous (defined here as more than 90 per cent of those voting taking one side — usually in favor).[9] This restriction is necessary because the product-moment correlation coefficient is seriously distorted by a distribution more lopsided than 90–10. The omission might result in the hiding of any very small group that was consistently in the minority, but is not likely to be important because typically such very lopsided votes account for less than 10 per cent of all those in a session. In practice the only real possibility of a group whose cohesion and isolation might be understated is the handful of states (Portugal, Spain, South Africa, France, Belgium, sometimes the United Kingdom) which are so out of step with the Assembly majority on African colonial issues. As we shall see below Portugal and Spain do actually cluster together anyway, and South Africa is not even included in the analysis because of high absenteeism. This example, however, constitutes a warning against processing the data too mechanically without a careful inspection of the *Records*.

On every vote each state was coded either 2 (affirmative) 1 (abstain) or 0 (negative) Absenteeism is rather frequent in the Assembly, however, and posed something of a problem. In a few cases a country, though absent, later officially recorded its position. I listed it as if it had so voted. Also, in some cases an absence is clearly intended to demonstrate opposition to the resolution, or a conviction that the Assembly is overstepping the bounds of its authority in considering the issue. The United Kingdom found itself in such a position over several votes on Southern Rhodesia in the 18th Session. In those cases I recorded the absence as a negative vote. Both of these procedures are in conformity with the practice of earlier researches.[10]

The remaining absences are in general concentrated on a few countries, often those with small delegations. While it would sometimes be possible to estimate an absent nation's voting position from the votes of other states in its geographical area or caucusing group, in our inductive search for voting groups such a procedure would prejudice the results and would not be admissible. Instead I chose to equate an absence with abstention. In many instances an absence does in fact mean abstention, but by no means always, and when it does not the result is to incorporate a degree of imprecision in the analysis. The average absenteeism for the Assembly is about 12 per cent, and for the vast majority of states less than 25 per cent. Since the equation of absence with abstention actually assigns a state to a middle position on our three-point scale, and since it is sometimes the correct interpretation anyway, this treatment of absences will not seriously distort the voting position of all countries with 25 per cent for fewer absences — their scores on the factors below are not affected by more than about 8 per cent. For those countries (11 in the 18th Session)

9. Committee votes often preview later plenary ones, but more frequently there is no plenary roll call vote repeating one in committee. Even when the same paragraph or resolution does come up again the alignments usually shift somewhat; there are no duplicates in the following analysis.
10. Lijphart, *op. cit.*, and Alker and Russett, *op. cit.*

with greater absenteeism the distortion is potentially more serious, and they are marked with a † symbol to indicate that their positions should be treated with some caution. Four other states (Dominican Republic, Honduras, Luxembourg, and South Africa) were absent more than 40 per cent of the time and so were excluded entirely from the analysis. Kenya and Zanzibar, admitted well after the Session was under way, were also omitted.

Table 1 presents the factor "loadings" of every country on each of the six meaningful factors which emerge from the analysis. Each factor identifies a group of countries whose voting patterns are very similar, and the loadings are product-moment correlation coefficients of a country's voting pattern with the underlying factor. The highest loadings or correlations identify those countries with the "purest' pattern, those whose voting is most fully described by the factor. Labelling the factors is always somewhat arbitrary, but in most cases the descriptive label should be appropriate. The percentages at the head of each column indicate the percentage of the total variation (variance) among all 107 countries that is explained (accounted for) by the factor. All loadings of .50 or greater have been underlined for emphasis, as loadings in the .40's are underscored with dashed lines. Squaring the correlation coefficient provides a means of discovering the amount of the country's total variance which is accounted for by the underlying factor. Thus it is reasonable largely to ignore correlations below .40 since the factor in question accounts for less than a sixth of the variance. The countries are listed in descending order of their loadings on the factor which best "explains" their voting pattern. Countries with no loading above .49 (and thus for whom no one factor "explains" as much as one-fourth of their voting variance) seemed best left "unclassifiable." In factor analytic terms the table presents the orthogonal solution, which means that the factors are uncorrelated with each other.[11]

I have labelled the first factor "Western Community" in an attempt to indicate the predominance of European and European-settled states among those with high loadings. "Western Community" in this context must be interpreted as a cultural and not just a geographical phenomenon, including the white Commonwealth. This relationship is indicated by the fact that of 35 UN members either physically located in Europe or whose population is predominantly of European origin (Argentina, Australia, Canada, Costa Rica, Cyprus, New Zealand, Uruguay, and United States), 22 have loadings of .50 or greater on the second factor. This works out to a fairly low correlation coefficient of .35. Each of the top 15 loadings, however, is held by such a country.

Note also the high loadings of Japan and (nationalist) China on this factor. Japan's basic foreign policy has become quite well integrated with those of her North Atlantic associates in recent years, and is so perceived by Afro-Asian observers.[12] Nationalist China is of course heavily dependent upon United States

---

11. In Tables 1 and 2 I present the factors as rotated according to the varimax technique. Unities were inserted in the principal diagonal of the correlation matrix. "Rotating" the original factors to "simple structure" maximizes the number of both very high and very low loadings, thus making interpretation easier. Each factor has an "eigen value" which expresses the amount of variance in the entire table that it accounts for. The eigen value, when divided by the total number of variables (countries), gives the *percentage* of variance accounted for by the factor. All 15 factors with eigen values greater than one were rotated. Nine factors which had no more than one loading as high as .50 are omitted from the table.

12. Cf. Saburo Okita, "Japan and the Developing Nations," *Contemporary Japan*, 28, 2 (1965), 1–14.

military and diplomatic support. This leads to another observation about the factor: among those with .50 or higher loadings are 33 of the 38 UN members who have a formal military alliance with the United States (including the United States itself and counting Iran). Such a close association produces a correlation of .79. France is by far the lowest of all NATO allies on this factor, with also a strong *negative* loading on the Afro-Asian factor (number three).

The second factor is named "Brazzaville Africans," though the name is far from perfect and a number of non-African states also correlate with it. The six highest loadings, and 14 above .50 in all, are possessed by countries which were members of the former Brazzaville caucusing group, of whom all but the Congo (Leopoldville) were ex-French colonies. Both the Brazzaville and Casablanca groupings had been formally dissolved by the 18th (1963) Session, ostensibly in the interest of promoting African unity, but the essential differences in voting patterns seem still to persist. Note also the high loadings of Haiti (Negro, very underdeveloped) and of several Asian and Latin American states. Previous studies have noted that the Brazzaville states tend to be less anti-Western on cold war issues than the Afro-Asian "neutralists," but more so, and especially on colonial questions, than the typical Latin American state. This second factor then picks out, in addition to the Brazzaville Africans, both several of the more pro-Western Asians (Philippines and Pakistan, plus Israel) and a number of Latin Americans who are rather to the "east" of their caucusing group (Uruguay and Bolivia, for example). The first two factors together account for 40 per cent of the total roll-call variance, and indicate most of the states which can generally be expected to take the Western position on most cold war issues.

TABLE 1   United Nations Groupings in 1963

Nation	Factor 1 "Western Community" 23%	Factor 2 "Brazzaville Africans" 17%	Factor 3 "Afro-Asians" 16%	Factor 4 "Communist Bloc" 11%	Factor 5 "Conservative Aabs" 4%	Factor 6 "Iberia" 2%
		"Western Community"				
Denmark	.90	.12	−.02	−.27	−.01	−.17
Norway	.89	.10	−.03	−.23	−.11	−.04
Sweden	.89	.09	−.03	−.25	−.12	−.09
Finland	.88	.06	.03	−.22	−.04	−.10
Austria	.87	.20	.00	−.17	−.10	−.01
Ireland	.86	.15	−.08	−.25	.16	−.03
Turkey	.83	.18	−.10	−.33	−.04	.23
Australia	.82	.10	−.15	−.38	.01	.10
Belgium	.82	.13	−.15	−.44	−.07	.15
New Zealand	.82	.17	−.14	−.27	.07	.05
Iceland	.82	.14	−.05	−.22	.14	−.20
United States	.81	.07	.23	.−27	.09	.23
Italy	.81	.12	−.12	−.37	.14	.11
Canada	.80	.09	−.15	−.44	−.02	.17
Netherlands	.80	.05	−.11	−.46	.03	.09
Japan	.76	.23	−.11	−.33	.31	.06
China	.75	.40	−.01	−.11	.07	.09
United Kingdom	.72	−.16	−.22	−.46	.07	.09
Greece	.71	.23	−.21	−.29	−.03	.15
*Venezuela	.70	.52	−.01	−.07	.13	−.02

TABLE 1 (*continued*)

Nation	Factor 1 "Western Community" 23%	Factor 2 "Brazzaville Africans" 17%	Factor 3 "Afro-Asians" 16%	Factor 4 "Communist Bloc" 11%	Factor 5 "Conservative Arabs" 4%	Factor 6 "Iberia" 2%
*Argentina	.70	.49	−.04	−.10	.12	.09
*Guatemala	.65	.52	.07	−.17	.09	−.05
*Panama	.63	.51	.05	.08	.09	.05
*Colombia	.62	.52	.15	.08	.16	.09
*Ecuador	.62	.50	−.05	−.06	.32	.05
Iran	.61	.38	−.01	−.04	.33	−.04
*Costa Rica	.61	.61	.09	.11	.11	.05
*Mexico	.61	.52	.11	.01	.39	−.07
*Thailand	.60	.52	.05	−.02	.15	.14
*Jamaica	.59	.51	.03	.06	.32	−.19
†El Salvador	.59	.36	.00	−.29	.29	.34
France	.59	.01	−.48	−.02	−.23	.27
*Chile	.58	.52	.28	−.08	.18	.05
*Brazil	.56	.43	.01	−.04	.10	.05
*Peru	.56	.49	.03	.02	.17	.34
*Malaysia	.55	.55	.21	.06	.43	.03
†Nicaragua	.55	.38	.09	−.32	.02	.17
*Paraguay	.53	.47	.00	−.20	.19	.18

"Brazzaville Africans"

Nation	Factor 1	Factor 2	Factor 3	Factor 4	Factor 5	Factor 6
Chad	.12	.87	.17	.01	−.03	.06
Cameroun	.20	.79	.29	−.08	−.08	−.06
†Gabon	.20	.79	.23	.08	.06	.04
Cen. African Rep.	.17	.78	.03	.01	−.09	.10
Niger	.02	.78	.34	−.03	.04	.14
Congo (B)	.07	.77	.28	.08	−.09	−.00
Rwanda	.23	.76	.16	−.09	.05	−.20
†Haiti	.16	.74	−.06	.00	.01	.10
Ivory Coast	.08	.73	.35	−.04	.27	−.04
Upper Volta	−.09	.73	.37	.05	−.12	−.06
Congo (L)	.22	.72	.22	.01	.01	−.17
*Cyprus	.52	.71	.04	−.06	.08	.01
Dahomey	.07	.70	.32	−.03	.05	−.11
†Bolivia	.37	.68	.10	−.15	.14	.01
Senegal	.12	.68	.26	.19	.19	.15
Uruguay	.35	.68	.11	.08	.23	.04
*Philippines	.49	.63	.09	−.05	.26	.03
Madagascar	.39	.62	.05	−.14	.32	−.09
Sierra Leone	.05	.62	.41	−.01	−.02	−.09
Liberia	.41	.62	.09	−.14	.32	−.17
Togo	.09	.62	.49	−.02	.23	−.01
*Israel	.43	.53	−.04	−.18	.04	−.31
Mauretania	.08	.53	.38	.18	.49	.00
*Pakistan	.50	.51	.21	.01	.09	−.09

"Afro-Asians"

Nation	Factor 1	Factor 2	Factor 3	Factor 4	Factor 5	Factor 6
Ghana	−.09	.14	.88	.17	−.11	−.04
Afghanistan	−.15	.15	.84	.23	−.00	.06
Indonesia	−.17	.08	.82	.13	−.19	.12
Egypt	−.09	.07	.82	.30	.06	.06

TABLE 1 (*continued*)

Nation	Factor 1 "Western Community" 23%	Factor 2 "Brazzaville Africans" 17%	Factor 3 "Afro-Asians" 16%	Factor 4 "Communist Bloc" 11%	Factor 5 "Conserva-tive Arabs" 4%	Factor 6 "Iberia" 2%
Syria	−.05	.09	.82	.30	.04	.07
Ethiopia	−.02	.11	.82	.18	.00	−.14
Yugoslavia	−.18	.15	.80	.29	−.03	.02
India	.12	.19	.75	.02	.31	−.07
Algeria	−.22	.16	.74	.40	.09	.02
Nigeria	.01	.26	.74	−.13	.04	.25
Iraq	−.24	.15	.73	.30	.25	−.04
Tunisia	−.02	.25	.73	.13	−.01	−.07
†Burma	.05	.13	.72	.24	−.06	.08
Cambodia	−.13	.13	.72	.31	.03	−.03
Tanganyika	−.18	.33	.67	.22	.10	−.16
Guinea	−.13	.29	.67	.32	.09	.05
Mali	−.25	.09	.65	.42	.27	−.11
Ceylon	.02	.19	.65	.21	.05	−.02
Sudan	.00	.24	.60	.24	.05	−.09
Kuwait	.14	.29	.58	.24	.47	−.06
Morocco	−.15	.13	.58	.35	.40	−.06
†Somalia	−.04	.22	.55	.11	.08	−.27
†Uganda	−.02	.32	.55	.27	.06	.03
†Yemen	−.02	.24	.53	.32	.04	−.13

"Communist Bloc"

Nation	Factor 1	Factor 2	Factor 3	Factor 4	Factor 5	Factor 6
Czechoslovakia	−.42	−.04	.28	.85	−.02	−.02
U.S.S.R	−.42	−.04	.28	.85	−.02	−.02
Bulgaria	−.41	−.05	.29	.85	−.03	−.02
Byelorussia	−.42	−.05	.29	.85	.07	−.06
Poland	−.42	−.05	.29	.85	.07	−.06
Cuba	−.36	.00	.28	.85	−.07	−.02
Romania	−.39	−.05	.32	.84	−.02	.02
Ukraine	−.45	−.02	.28	.83	−.04	−.03
Hungary	−.40	−.07	.27	.83	.16	−.08
Mongolia	−.42	−.06	.29	.82	.16	−.10
Albania	−.27	.01	.49	.59	−.05	−.07

"Conservative Arabs"

Nation	Factor 1	Factor 2	Factor 3	Factor 4	Factor 5	Factor 6
Lebanon	.09	.16	.46	.08	.66	.10
Jordan	.17	.34	.46	.25	.58	−.03
Libya	.21	.44	.45	.01	.54	−.05

"Iberia"

Nation	Factor 1	Factor 2	Factor 3	Factor 4	Factor 5	Factor 6
Portugal	.23	−.25	−.06	−.44	−.08	.68
Spain	.52	.13	−.11	−.26	.09	.66

Unclassifiable

Nation	Factor 1	Factor 2	Factor 3	Factor 4	Factor 5	Factor 6
Burundi	.14	.30	.48	.19	−.09	−.17
†Laos	.26	.19	.40	.07	.27	.04
Nepal	.14	.36	.47	−.06	.04	−.01
†Saudi Arabia	.22	.14	.39	.32	.18	.15
Trinidad & Tobago	.42	.41	.18	.06	.07	−.03

*Moderately high loadings on Factors 1 and 2.
†More than 25% absenteeism (but less than 40%); absent equated with abstain.

The third factor quite clearly picks out those Asians and Africans sometimes identified by the term Afro-Asian neutralists. More often than not they vote with the Soviet Union on both cold war and colonial questions. They include such long-time leaders of this group as Egypt, India, and Indonesia, most of the Arab countries, Yugoslavia, and a number of African states, especially (but not only) those with rather leftist governments which belonged to the former "Casablanca" caucusing group. And while these are (except for Yugoslavia) non-Communist governments, of 24 UN members outside of the Sino-Soviet bloc known to have received economic and/or military aid from China, the U.S.S.R., or Eastern Europe by mid-1962, 19 have loadings of at least .50 with this third factor. Using all 96 non-Soviet bloc governments in this table, and simple receipt or non-receipt of Sino-Soviet aid as the variable, this produces a correlation (r) of .72. All of the top nine countries on this factor received such aid.

Not surprisingly, the Soviet bloc accounts for the other major factor. Only Communist states load heavily on this factor — though Yugoslavia emphatically does not and belongs with Factor 3. Cuba and Mongolia are virtually indistinguishable from the European members of the bloc. But one important evidence of the crack in what had in previous years been a solid voting alignment is the behavior of Albania. Since the defection of Yugoslavia in 1948 this is the first time that any study of the United Nations has shown a noticeable deviation by a Communist nation. Albania's loading on the factor is a mere .59, and if we return to the original votes from which the factor analysis is derived. Albania's voting pattern correlates but .75 with those of other Soviet "bloc" states. That is, voting by the U.S.S.R. "accounts for" little more than half the variance in Albania's behavior in the Assembly.

Finally, there are two minor factors, each accounting for but four and two per cent of the total variance. Factor five has three countries loading highly on it: Lebanon, Jordan, and Libya. The name "Conservative Arabs" seems appropriate, for all are non-revolutionary regimes, in cold-war politics these states vote relatively often with the Western powers, and each has received substantial foreign aid from the United States. Factor six picks out Portugal and Spain only; the label "Iberia" is obvious.

Most commonly in a factor analysis of this sort the factors can with relative ease be used to identify "groups" of variables (in this case nations). This is true for four of our six factors, but not for two others. Many of the countries loading either on Factors 1 or 2 (called "Western Community" and "Brazzaville Africans") actually show fairly high loadings on *both* factors, so that they cannot unequivocally be identified with either. The majority of states with loadings between .50 and .70 on either factor share this property. In such circumstances it is often useful to make a scattergram and plot the positions of the countries in question on the two competing factors. Figure 1 is a graph where the vertical axis represents the percentage of variance (simply 100 times the factor loading squared) accounted for by Factor 2, and the horizontal axis the percentage explained by Factor 1. All countries with loadings of .40 or higher on *both* factors are represented, as well as a couple of others for reference.

In some instances one factor accounts for three or more times as much of a country's variance as does the other, and when this happened there is little question as to where the nation should be grouped. This applies, for example, to Uruguay

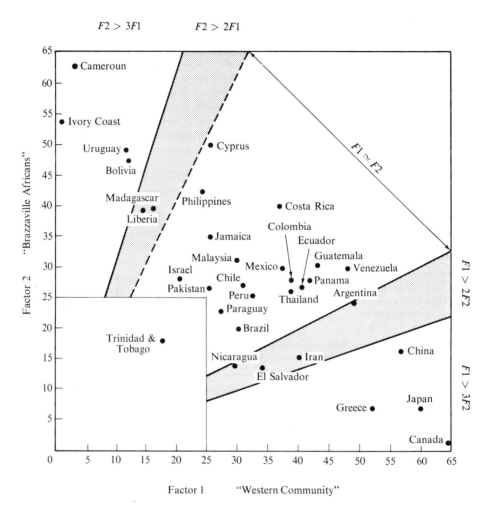

FIGURE 1 "Latin American" Grouping as Identified
by Moderate Loadings on Factors 1 and 2

and Bolivia, for whom Factor 2 accounts for almost 50 per cent of the variance and
Factor 1 less than 15 per cent. Any country which occupies a position either between the vertical axis and the sloping solid line to its right, or between the horizontal
axis and the sloping solid line above it, has this variance ratio of more than three
to one. The sloping dashed lines to the right and above the solid ones respectively
mark the gray area where the variance ratio is over two to one. Although the countries occupying this space are distinctly more marginal than one lying closer to the
axes, it is probably not unreasonable still to assign them as weak members of the
group whose factor accounts for more than twice as much variance as any other.
Most clearly it seems appropriate to think of Liberia and Madagascar with the
"Brazzaville" countries. And for any state which has less than 25 per cent of its
variance accounted for by any factor (e.g. Trinidad & Tobago) we have little choice
but to term it "unclassifiable." The square in the lower left marks out this area of
the diagram.

But for the countries where the percentage of variance explained by the most powerful factor is less than twice that of the next most important factor, it may be misleading to label them as belonging with either of the groups for which the factor is named. This is especially so in the situation illustrated in the above figure, where no less than 18 states occupy the area between the two dashed lines. Here we must speak of yet a sixth voting group, which we can label "Latin America." Twelve of these nations are physically located in the Western Hemisphere. With Honduras and the Dominican Republic excluded from our analysis for excessive absenteeism, only Haiti, Bolivia, Uruguay, Cuba, Trinidad & Tobago (in the lower left box) Salvador, Argentina, and Nicaragua do not fall into this area. And the latter two are extremely marginal. Those 20 countries (including Argentina and Nicaragua) have been marked with an asterisk in Table 1 and should be considered as comprising a separate group. A number of pro-Western Asian states — Malaysia, Thailand, Pakistan, Philippines and Israel — have quite similar voting patterns.

III. Groups and Super-Issues

The influences affecting these groupings are not unique or substantially peculiar to the 18th Session. By and large the issues voted upon in the Assembly during the Session closely resemble those that prevailed earlier. It has been shown through factor analyses with *issues as variables* (*R*-analysis) that three major issue dimensions or "super-issues" can be identified in each of four different Sessions spread over virtually the entire history of the United Nations.[13] They have been characterized as "cold war," "colonial self-determination," and "supranationalism" issues, and among them they regularly accounted for more than half the total variance in all roll-call voting. Two other super-issues, concerned with problems of intervention in southern Africa and of Palestine, were found in three of the four Sessions. The four or five factors appearing in any Session always accounted for between 59 and 70 per cent of the total variance in that Session.

A similar analysis of the 18th (1963) Session (using the roll-call data described earlier in this paper) showed these same five factors appearing and accounting for two-thirds of all the roll-call variance. Most prominent was the cold war issue, accounting for 21 per cent of the variance and characterized by votes on such specific matters as the seating of Communist China and the role of the United Nations in Korea — both topics which have long exemplified the cold war issue in the Assembly. A new matter, in form at least, concerned a resolution about extended participation in general multilateral treaties concluded under the League of Nations. Disagreement arose over whether all nations should be eligible, or merely those which were members of the United Nations and its specialized agencies. Since the latter formula would exclude mainland China and East Germany but include West Germany (which is a member of several specialized agencies), it is not surprising that the issue was perceived and voted upon in much the same way as the more familiar cold war issues. Another set of roll-calls loading highly on this super-issue came from discussing item A/5671, a resolution on "Consideration of Principles of International Law Concerning Friendly Relations and Cooperation Among States." One section which called for the establishment of an international

---

13. Alker and Russett, *op. cit.*

center of inquiry and fact-finding for the peaceful settlement of disputes was opposed by the Soviet Union and its allies.[14]

A second super-issue, accounting for 19 per cent of the variance, concerned such familiar problems as Southern Rhodesia, South West Africa, and "territories under Portugese administration." These issues formerly turned up on the self-determination factor or on the southern Africa one; here the super-issue can quite clearly be identified as southern Africa. With the dismemberment of the great overseas empires there are hardly any other concrete colonialism questions. A similar though less thorough convergence occurred in 1961.[15] What remains of any separate self-determination issue may perhaps be found in a small factor identified in only two roll-calls and accounting for but four per cent of the variance. A section on granting independence to colonial peoples and countries was inserted in the "Draft Declaration on the Elimination of all Forms of Racial Discrimination." The United Kingdom and some Western Europeans tried to have the section deleted, with the argument that it was irrelevant to the Declaration.

The other major super-issue, accounting for 18 per cent of the variance, is related to what has for previous years been called "supranationalism," composed of votes affecting the retention or expansion of the Organization's powers, especially its peacekeeping forces. As in earlier years votes on the United Nations' role in the Congo and UNEF in the Middle East loaded highly on it, as did a number of roll-calls about the proposed expansion and new composition of ECOSOC and the Security Council. While nations' votes on this dimension surely are not solely the product of their preference for or opposition to a stronger and more effective UN, this question is nevertheless a common thread through all these roll-calls. Finally, there was a factor composed primarily of two votes on the status of Palestine refugees and accounting for four per cent of the variance.

Thus the basic issues and alignments underlying the groupings in the 18th Session are familiar ones. But in the process of identifying them we are reminded of the distinct and uncorrelated nature of these super-issues; knowing a nation's position on one dimension provides no information by which we can predict its position on another. Because no two of these issue-dimensions or issue-areas[16] together account for more than 40 per cent of all members' voting variance we must reject one- or two-dimensional representations as *general* interpretations of group voting, for which we used the Q-analysis approach instead. Nevertheless we return to the point raised by Lijphart and Rieselbach: for many purposes we want to distinguish behavior on one super-issue from that on another, and to see how voting on a particular issue-dimension is related to other behavioral or environmental influences.

One procedure has been to compute countries' factor scores on each of the major factors or super-issues from the R-analysis, and then to correlate those factor scores

---

14. In all there were nine factors with eigen values greater than one, accounting for 75 per cent of the total variance. I list here only those roll calls which correlated at least .71 with the underlying factor, and thus more than half of whose variance can be accounted for by the factor. More detailed information on the resolutions can be found in the "Summary of Activities" of the General Assembly in *International Organization*, 18, 2 (1964), 313–467 and of course in the *Official Records* themselves. *International Conciliation*, No. 544 (September 1963) discusses the issues before their consideration by the Assembly.

15. See Table 2 in Alker, *op. cit.*

16. Cf. James Rosenau, "The Functioning of International Systems," *Background*, 7, 3, (1963), 111–17, for an illuminating discussion of issue-areas in national politics.

with caucusing or other group memberships and with ecological variables such as national per capita income, foreign aid receipts, or racial composition.[17] The factor score summarizes a nation's voting behavior, especially on those roll-calls which load heavily on the factor in question. It is computed according to an equation which weights each roll-call roughly according to its correlation with the factor, so that the roll-calls which are best accounted for by the factor make the greatest contribution to the factor score. Thus a country which voted affirmatively (coded as two) on virtually all successful roll-calls that loaded heavily on, say, the cold war factor would have a high factor score and a state regularly voting negatively (coded zero) would have a very low one. Because the original factors are uncorrelated with each other the consequent factor scores will also be uncorrelated. These factor scores, serving as summary indices of national behavior on the major super-issues before the Assembly, can then be correlated with national factor loadings from the Q-analysis. Thus we can discover the basic issue-dimensions which distinguish our inductively identified "groupings" of countries. Table 2 gives the correlation of nations' factor scores on each of the three important super-issues (cold war, southern Africa, and supranationalism) with their factor loadings on each of the six factors from the Q-analysis.

TABLE 2   Correlation of Grouping Loadings with
Super-Issue Factor Scores

National Groupings	"Cold War"	"Intervention in Africa"	"Supra- nationalism"
"Western Community"	.79	−.13	.38
"Brazzaville Africans"	.47	.45	.36
"Afro-Asians"	−.82	.43	.17
"Communists"	−.56	.45	−.64
"Conservative Arabs"	.11	.26	.16
"Iberia"	.10	−.74	−.06

From this we can quickly obtain a thumbnail sketch to characterize the behavior of each inductively derived "group" of countries. The Afro-Asians, for example, are pro-Soviet on cold war issues, or at least they share with the Soviets an opposition to Western use of the UN for cold-war purposes, and are quite anti-colonial about the problems of southern Africa.[18] But they generally favor initiatives, such as those concerning the role of ONUC in the Congo and expanding the Security Council and ECOSOC, which comprise the "supranationalism" dimension and which the Soviet Union vigorously opposed in 1963. It is on these issues that they oppose the Communists and on which Yugoslavia (rather favorable to strengthening the UN in these contexts) is distinguishable from the other Communist states

---

17. As was done in Alker, *op. cit.*, and Alker and Russett, *op. cit.*

18. The fact that the Afro-Asians correlate more highly than do the Communists with the "cold war" factor indicates that the latter is a slightly misleading label. There are some roll-call votes, such as those about the role of the UN in reunifying and rehabilitating Korea, or establishing a fact-finding commission for the peaceful settlement of disputes, which have substantial "supranational" loadings and overtones. On these votes the Afro-Asians and Communists often part company, at least to the degree of an abstention. Putting a descriptive label on a factor is always a somewhat tentative exercise, which is why I have here enclosed the labels in quotation marks.

of Eastern Europe. Similarly, the Brazzaville countries more or less share the Afro-Asians' position on southern Africa and supranationalism but are fairly pro-Western on cold-war questions. The Western Community countries generally vote in favor of those supranationalist initiatives that actually come to a roll call, and while moderately unsympathetic with the Assembly's basic position on intervention in Africa are nowhere nearly as isolated as are the lonely Iberians.

It is tempting to refer to some of our groups by more explicitly political labels. The "Brazzaville Africans," for instance, are not well named since they include Latin Americans, Asians, and other Africans as well. Possibly one might want to call them simply "pro-Western underdeveloped states." But we must ascetically refrain from plucking that apple. A word like "pro-Western" demands a uni-dimensional set of issues which does not exist. Each group's substantive position can be spotted only with reference to all *three* of the major issue dimensions. Imagine a cube defined by three axes — left to right: cold war, with the "West" at the left and the Communists on the right; vertical: intervention in Africa, with the colonial powers at the top and the ex-colonies at the bottom; depth: surpanationalism, with those favoring a stronger UN at the front and their opponents behind. These three axes can be thought of as dividing the whole cube into eight subcubes and each of the major groups falls into a different subcube. The Western Community states belong in the upper left front cube, and the Communists are more or less polar opposites in the lower right rear segment. But the other two groups do *not* fall between the two poles; rather they are off to one side or the other of the shortest-distance-between-two-points lines. The Afro-Asians are lower right but front, and the Brazzaville nations lower front but left. Such a picture implies a multipolar pattern of cross-pressures and shifting coalitions that can mitigate international conflict.

In describing the correlations of the issue factor scores with the "grouping" loadings we of course are only ascertaining the typical voting positions of a group, especially those countries loading heavily on the R-factor. Any individual member may differ from the group pattern, as for example the United States is more "supra-nationalist" than are most states with equally high loadings on the Western Community factor. Except for establishing very general limits from the group, the behavior of a particular country can be determined only by a check of its own factor scores.

IV. Voting Groups and General Assembly Politics

In the Q-analysis we found that an inductive procedure identified six factors, and through them seven voting groups, in the Assembly. The six factors together accounted for 73 per cent of all the countries' variance. Thus the political process is relatively structured and subject to description by a small number of alignments. Yet the groups resembled only to a limited degree those which would be discovered from a list of geographical or caucusing groups alone. While geographical labels have sometimes been used they are very approximate and neither inclusive nor exclusive (e.g., "Brazzaville Africans"). Of our inductively-derived groups only the "Communists" closely resembled a caucusing group in terms both of who was included and who excluded.

In contrast to the mere evidence of caucusing groups the Q-analysis reveals other politically based groupings as follows:

1. The members of the Scandinavian caucusing group do indeed agree almost entirely among themselves in this Session, but Ireland and Austria differ from them in no significant way.

2. Analysis of the Latin American caucusing group would find a moderate element of cohesion, but entirely miss the very high similarity of Israel and several pro-Western Asians to the Latin voting pattern.

3. If the examination were based on caucusing groups extant in 1963 it would also not uncover the great consensus remaining within the officially disbanded Brazzaville and Casablanca groups.

4. The convergence of interest among the North Atlantic countries would not be found by examining any formal caucusing group.

The use of an inductive procedure also permits us to make some more general statements about politics in the Assembly. A simplified East-West-Neutral categorization which has characterized so much journalistic and even scholarly analysis of the world organization is utterly misleading. In terms of the states' behavior, five major groups (on four factors) emerge, in addition to two small groups and a few marginal countries. It should be emphasized that the identification of these groups depends upon their final behavior in the vote, not upon tacit or explicit bargaining among diverse log-rolling coalitions which may exchange promises of support before the vote. It might be supposed, for instance that one set of countries might offer its support to another set on cold war issues, in response to the other's votes on a self-determination roll-call. While this kind of bargaining undoubtedly does occur, an analysis of voting patterns alone would not find it since both sets of countries would *vote* identically, whatever their reasons for doing so. But a number of groups in the General Assembly retain their distinctiveness in the actual balloting. Two or more groups must combine to make a majority, and majorities on each of the different super-issues are composed differently. Comparisons with politics within national parliamentary assemblies may provide many fruitful insights and hypotheses, but the multiparty pattern of shifting coalitions that was approximated in the French Third and Fourth Republic may provide a closer analogy than will the aggregation of multiple interests within two stable parties as in Britain or even the United States.

Finally, there is reason to believe that this multi-group phenomenon is not especially new. It existed both before the well-known conflicts within NATO and the communist countries became evident, and largely before the admission of most of the new states. I conducted a similar Q-analysis of voters in the 1952 and 1957 sessions, to be reported upon more fully elsewhere.[19] By the same criteria employed here the 1952 analysis found four groups, and the 1957 analysis uncovered eight, though four were quite small. Therefore the discovery of but five large groups and two small ones in 1963 comes as something of a surprise, especially since the 1952 and 1957 analyses were performed on only 57 and 81 countries respectively. The expansion of Assembly membership (to 107 for purposes of this analysis) has in

19. Bruce M. Russett, *International Regions and International Integration* (Chicago: Rand McNally, 1967).

fact outpaced the differentiation of new voting groups. Nor has their composition altered radically. Except for the emergence of the "Brazzaville" group and a certain greater differentiation between most other Afro-Asians and a somewhat pro-Western minority, the changes over the three sessions have not been great. Recent discoveries of a complex pattern of relationships in the General Assembly not only identify new reality but also show some lag between reality and our perception of it.

JOHN E. MUELLER

Some Comments on Russett's "Discovering Voting Groups in the United Nations"

Factor analysis, a statistical technique of growing popularity in political science, has recently found application in the June, 1966 issue of *American Political Science Review* in an attempt to identify U.N. voting blocs. The hand is that of Professor Bruce M. Russett, the author of a number of outstanding contributions toward the systematic and quantitative study of international relations. The following paragraphs are designed to be cautionary in nature, not destructive and endeavor to suggest: 1) that factor analysis has questionable value as a tool for the study of complex phenomena; 2) that even if acceptable as a tool, it has peculiar faults when applied to U.N. bloc voting; and 3) that even if acceptable as a tool for the study of bloc voting in the U.N., an application somewhat different from the one chosen by Professor Russett might have been more profitable. In the process it will be argued that the procedures of the sort proffered by Professor Arend Lijphart for determining U.N. voting blocs are preferable.[1]

1. If appealing in its seeming promise to make order of disorder and sense of nonsense, factor analysis proves to be exasperating in practice. For while it is true, that, as Professor Russett has noted elsewhere, "the method is completely *objective*"[2] in the sense that the decision as to which variables are to "load" on which factors is made entirely by the impartial machinery, the criteria which the machinery applies in arriving at this decision are manipulated by the operator and depending on these criteria, the outcome can vary widely. Thus factor analysis can generate not

Reprinted from John E. Mueller, "Some Comments on Russett's 'Discovering Voting Groups in the United Nations,'" *American Political Science Review* 61 (1967): 146–48, by permission of the American Political Science Association and the author.

1. "The Analysis of Bloc Voting in the General Assembly: A Critique and a Proposal," *American Political Science Review*, 57 (1963), pp. 902–17.
2. *Trends in World Politics* (New York: Macmillan, 1965), p. 68. Emphasis in the original.

one, but a number — in fact an infinite number — of solutions to the same prob-lem. In choosing among these solutions the one most likely to represent truth (if that is what one is interested in), the analyst is commonly urged to select the solution which makes the most "sense" — in other words to embrace the objective solution which is most subjectively appealing. Therefore, one can get out of factor analysis almost whatever one wants to get. For example, in an argument a few years ago over such central psychological concerns as agreement response set, anal ex-pression, social desirability, and (of course) the Minnesota Multiphasic Personality Inventory, two teams of psychologists factor analyzed the same sort of data, select-ed different solutions, and came to precisely opposite conclusions.[3]

Claims that factor analysis is an "economical" procedure (e.g., Russett, p. 328) therefore should best be cautiously weighed. For the process of sorting through several exasperatingly different factor matrices is a tedious and frustrating process and at the same time one which is likely to be less conclusive than a form of cluster analysis of the sort Lijphart advocates.

Of course it is possible to assign a single set of criteria, based on grounds of mathematical and statistical elegance and parsimony, and to seize upon the first factor solution that pops out of the machinery as the most likely approximation to truth. This ploy, widely adopted by political scientists including, apparently, Pro-fessor Russett, has the advantage of reducing the paper work. The profound ar-bitrariness of this approach however must be duly appreciated.

The problems of interpreting the factor solution even after one has been decided upon have often been noted. Professor Russett for example brings forth a U.N. voting alignment dubbed "Brazzaville Africans" in which Haiti and Bolivia are important members and Israel is a fellow traveler. In another equally valid factor solution these nations might well appear allied with an entirely different group of associates and contribute therefore to a strikingly different interpretation of the data.

Faced with dilemmas of this sort Lijphart's approach, which keeps the investigator much closer to the data, seems far less elusive and far more interpretable: one is confronted simply by a set of descriptive statistics giving the degree of cohesiveness of a series of inductively-located voting blocs.

Professor Russett's claim then that factor analysis is a technique which is "given to a means of presentation which is readily *interpretable*" and which "reliably *identifies all the groupings*" (p. 328) is surely overly sanguine.

2. If one shrugs aside these objections on the grounds perhaps that the gain in mathematical elegance is worth the cost in decisiveness of result (after all, no method is completely free from arbitrariness), there are still certain special problems which attend the application of factor analysis to bloc voting patterns in the United Nations.

First, because the voting choices of two nations correlate reasonably well with a particular factor, it does not follow that the voting preferences of the two countries correlate well *with each other*. In fact the correlation between two voting units which have loadings of .50 on a single factor could be anywhere between 0.00 and +1.00.

---

3. Arthur Couch and Kenneth Keniston, "Agreeing Response Set and Social Desirability," *Journal of Abnormal and Social Psychology*, 62 (1961), pp. 175–79; and Allen L. Edwards, and Jerald N. Walker, "Social Desirability and Agreement Response Set," *ibid.*, 62 (1961), pp. 180–83.

Professor Russett finds that Madagascar, Togo, and Liberia all load .62 on the "Brazzaville African" factor. Using some data that is at hand I find that at the same session, on plenary session votes at least (Professor Russett also includes committee votes in his analysis), Madagascar correlates .84 with Liberia but only .35 with Togo. Or, to order the problem in reverse, I find that Algeria and Burundi correlate .85 on plenary votes — they vote in complete agreement 90 per cent of the time; yet Algeria is disclosed to be an enthusiastic member of the "Afro-Asian" bloc while Burundi is not. Since the definition of a voting bloc insists that all members of the group agree with all other members at a specifically designated level, factor analysis would appear to be faulty as a selection device.

To sort out those pairs within a factor "bloc" which correlate well with each other from those which do not, the analyst must deal with the mammoth correlation matrix, something factor analysis was specifically adopted to avoid — but which Lijphart's method embraces from the beginning.

A second special problem in applying factor analysis to U.N. voting arises from the use of the Pearson product-moment correlation coefficient as a measure of agreement. Because abstention is a meaningful voting option in the United Nations (unlike the U.S. Congress), the voting relationship between each pair of states can be represented in a 3×3 table of the sort exemplified in Tables 1–3. Lijphart's proposed index of agreement (IA) is based on the idea that any entries on the principal diagonal of the table represent cases of agreement between the states — they agree either in affirming the resolution, in opposing it, or in adopting a middle position by abstaining. Entries in the upper right and lower left cells are treated as instances of utter disagreement — in each case one state favors while the other opposes. (Entries in the four non-diagonal cells are regarded as cases of half-agreement.)

TABLE 1

		STATE A		
		Yes	Abst	No
STATE B	Yes	10		
	Abst		80	
	No			10
		$r = 1.00$		
		IA $= 100\%$		

TABLE 2

		STATE A		
		Yes	Abst	No
STATE B	Yes			10
	Abst		80	
	No	10		
		$r = -1.00$		
		IA $= 80\%$		

TABLE 3

		STATE A		
		Yes	Abst	No
	Yes	5		5
STATE B	Abst		80	
	No	5		5

r = 0.00
IA = 90%

However, the Pearson coefficient when applied to the Tables does *not* treat the middle cell in a consistent manner. To make the point with a somewhat extreme example, consider Tables 1, 2, and 3. In each case 80 per cent of the time the states agree to cast joint abstentions. Nevertheless, depending on the distributions of the remaining twenty votes, the value for the Pearson r varies wildly: the entries in the middle cell are treated in Table 1 as cases of utter agreement, in Table 2 as cases of utter disagreement, and in Table 3 as cases neither of agreement nor of disagreement. At the same time Lijphart's index remains relatively unperturbed.

To be sure, all summary measures will at times distort and muddle information. One might question whether the Lijphart index is justified in treating entries in the middle cell as instances of as strong agreement as those in the two corner cells of the principal diagonal. But the flaws of the Pearson coefficient in application to the 3 × 3 table seem far greater.

3. One of the numerous mysterious decisions one must muddle through in applying factor analysis (assuming one is not dissuaded by the arguments above from using it at all), is whether to demand that the final factors be correlated or uncorrelated with one another, that is, whether to demand an oblique or an orthogonal solution. When in doubt it is probably safest to do both, although of course this leads to yet more factor matrices to ponder over and choose among.

Professor Russett has apparently chosen to ask for and adhere to a single orthogonal solution. There are good reasons to believe that this is not a wise choice. While in some applications of factor analysis it may be argued from the nature of things that factor solutions only make sense if the factors are uncorrelated, in the analysis of voting blocs such reasoning seems distinctly invalid. In searching for blocs, the analyst expects to be able to pick out a number of clusters of like-minded voters and he expects each cluster to possess a certain unity and meaning, but he does *not* demand that each bloc be utterly unrelated to all of the others. Indeed most analyses of U.N. voting find hierarchies of blocs, some quite closely linked to each other, some only remotely associated. Indications that this is the case can be seen in Professor Russett's data. He finds that there are a number of states, mostly Latin American, which load on his first factor above the level arbitrarily chosen to be significant, .50, while at the same time they load rather well on the second factor. From this it is argued that these states have "similar voting patterns" and comprise a "separate group" distinct from those states which only load on either factor one or factor two. But the arguments of the previous section are especially relevant here, for while these states do seem to be distinctive in that they load (at relatively low levels) on two factors, it cannot be argued from the data presented that they have high correlations among themselves and thus are a separate group. What the data *do* suggest is that some (or perhaps all) of these nations will line up rather neatly on a factor which is somewhere in between the first two factors determined by the orthogonal solution. Thus, if one wishes to use factor analysis to ferret out blocs in United Nations voting, it would seem on both intuitive and empirical grounds that an oblique solution is more likely than an orthogonal one to prove satisfying.

Other problems arise from the use of the Pearson r and its well-known tendency to do peculiar things when the marginals are extreme. In many sessions of the U.N. it is simply the case that the vast majority of votes taken are strongly affirmative and thus there are a fair number of states which have extremely affirmative voting patterns — of the African states in 1963, for example, ten did not vote negatively on a single measure in plenary session. It would seem wise to eliminate such cases from consideration or at least to watch carefully over them (or else adopt another method for roll call analysis). Professor Russett does eliminate all unanimous or near-unanimous *votes* from consideration, but in a bloc analysis the important distorting component will be "unanimous" or near-"unanimous" *voters*.

It is doubtful that the actual impact of these comments, even if the whole array were applied in series, would radically alter some of the bloc patterns uncovered by Professor Russett: Poland and Czechoslovakia for example will doubtless always emerge in the same bloc. On some of the more subtle levels of investigation, however, where the most interesting and non-obvious distinctions lie, the application of factor analytic procedures does appear to have caused distortions which might well alter the interpretation of bloc voting in the United Nations significantly.

BRUCE M. RUSSETT

Reply

It is useful to be reminded of the limitations of factor analysis and that one must never mechanically report computer output as an immutable substantive finding. But in this instance the conclusion is derived not from a rigorous evaluation, but merely from numerical examples that are inappropriate and often purely hypothetical.

Certainly one should not conclude that because two variables have the same loading on *one* factor they are very highly correlated with each other. That is why I reproduced the entire factor matrix for all *six* major factors. While Madagascar and Togo indeed both load .62 on Factor 2, they load .39 and .09 respectively on Factor 1, and .05 and .49 respectively on Factor 3. Thus by looking at factors other than the one with the highest loading, it is possible to discriminate differing variables *without* having to go back to the mammoth correlation matrix.

When making a methodological comparison of two indices it is necessary to examine the same data in each case. Professor Mueller cites only plenary votes, whereas my analysis employed both plenary and committee roll-calls. Although Algeria and Burundi do vote in complete agreement on about 90 per cent of the 24 *plenary* roll-calls, they differ on fully one-third of the 42 *committee* ballots. Hence it is not surprising that in the factor analysis their loadings differ.

His rejection of the product-moment correlation coefficient (r) depends upon an essentially irrelevant numerical example. The dramatic differences between the Pearson r and the Lijphart index of agreement in Tables 1–3 rely on what he himself calls an extreme case; namely on having the great bulk (*80 per cent* in the example) of the votes concentrated in the *middle*, or abstain, category. In real UN voting

Reprinted from Bruce M. Russett, "Communications to the Editor," *American Political Science Review* 61 (1967): 149–50, by permission of the American Political Science Association and the author.

data the distortion is very much less; absences and abstentions together were well *under 30 per cent* of my total. Later he talks about the distortion caused by countries which nearly always cast *affirmative* votes. Even this would be much less damaging than the kind of thing in his numerical example, and in fact there are in the data of my article *no* countries which vote affirmatively as much as 85 per cent of the time — absences and abstentions are more common in committee than in plenary session, as are initiatives which fail of majority support. Finally, there is some literature on the essential toughness and resistance of factor analytic procedures to whatever distortion in the *correlation matrix* is produced by the Pearson r. Mueller's point, however, is technically correct and warns us all that it is essential to know what one's data look like before deciding what statistical manipulations will or will not be tolerable. One should be especially careful with a collection composed exclusively of plenary roll-calls.

The caution against accepting any one analytic solution as completely satis-factory before seeing others, including various oblique rotations, is perhaps the best-grounded. To discuss the matter experientially rather than hypothetically, I did also perform some oblique rotations, but they did not change the basic pattern nor affect the grouping decisions in more than a half dozen of the most marginal countries, and were not reported in the article. This has usually been my experience, yet I agree that before staking too much on the conclusions it is still wise to try not just oblique rotations, but actually quite different grouping or clustering techniques. The longer study from which the article was drawn, my *International Regions and the International System* (Chicago: Rand McNally, 1967) considers this problem at some length.

IRA SHARKANSKY
RICHARD I. HOFFERBERT

Dimensions of State Politics, Economics and Public Policy*

*The Sharkansky and Hofferbert article is an investi-
gation of the linkages between political characteristics, socioeconomic
variables, and measures of public policy in the American states. Expressing
dissatisfaction with previous operationalizations of political, economic,
and policy variables, the authors approach the problem of delineating and
interrelating variables through factor analysis in order to speak of
broader dimensions of politics, economics, and policy. In an attempt to
overcome previous criticisms and to offer a theoretically meaningful
analysis, the authors follow several procedures in their factor analysis.
To avoid problems of bias and overly loaded factors representing variables
which are merely surrogates for one another, they eliminate individual
variables which are highly correlated with another variable. This procedure
was particularly relevant to measures of party competition employed in a
set of political variables. Second, the first results of a factor
analysis on the largest set of variables in each category are used to
selectively eliminate variables that load on two or more principal factors.
The surviving variables then are factor analyzed to yield the most
parsimonious and distinguishing factors in each of the three areas.
Each state's factor scores on the resulting dimensions then are calculated
and intercorrelated to test for relationships between dimensions. Factor
analysis is therefore used to (1) reduce a large number of variables in*

Reprinted from Ira Sharkansky and Richard I. Hofferbert, "Dimensions of State Politics, Economics
and Public Policy," *American Political Science Review* 63 (1969): 867–79, by permission of the
American Political Science Association and the authors.

*Separate grants to each of the authors from the Social Science Research Council Committee on
Governmental and Legal Processes provided financial support for the work that is reported here.

each category to a smaller number of dimensions, which are named on the basis of content, and (2) to create indices of economic, political, and policy measures along which states are arrayed. The results of this process (factor scores, intervally measured) then are intercorrelated through simple, partial, and multiple techniques to isolate inter-relationships and independent influences.

I. Introduction

A question often posed by students of American state politics is: "Do state political systems leave a distinctive imprint on patterns of public policy?" Prior to recent years the nearly automatic response of political scientists was an unqualified "yes." More recent research has led to a qualified but increasingly confident "no."[1]

Several recent publications have explored relationships between various indices of state politics, socio-economic characteristics, and public policy. The general conclusion has been that central features of the political system such as electoral and institutional circumstances do not explain much of the variation in policy. There are occasionally high correlations between individual measures of voter turnout, party competitiveness, or the character of state legislatures and some aspects of governmental spending. But these political-policy correlations seem to disappear when the effect of socioeconomic development is controlled.

These are disturbing findings. They have not gone unchallenged.[2] But the challenges, rather than reassuring those who have asserted the relevance of parties, voting patterns, and government structures, have demonstrated that the burden of proof now rests on those who hypothesize a politics-policy relationship. The problem has not been resolved.

Part of the problem may rest on the conceptualization and measurement of the central variables. Electoral balance or alternation in office is not "inter-party competition," except in the most mechanical sense. Compare Massachusetts' loose-knit party structure to the centralization of Connecticut's. "Party competition" is not the same as "party organization." And party competition, voting habits, and patterns of apportionment fall far short of being equivalents of "political systems." We have been too simple-minded in our measurement of "politics" and "policy." Concepts are, hopefully, ever more closely approximated by the things we use to denote them. We propose to advance further in the approximation of "politics," "economics," and "policy" as they are used in comparative state research. As an added payoff, we offer some clarification of their interrelationships.

1. Richard E. Dawson and James A. Robinson, "Interparty Competition, Economic Variables, and Welfare Policies in the American States," *Journal of Politics*, 25 (May, 1963), 265–89; Thomas R. Dye, *Politics, Economics, and the Public: Policy Outcomes in the American States* (Chicago: Rand McNally, 1966); Richard I. Hofferbert, "The Relation Between Public Policy and Some Structural and Environmental Variables in the American States," *American Political Science Review*, 60 (March, 1966), 73–82. One of the present authors has employed a different conception of "political" characteristics and his results qualify those of the authors listed above. See Ira Sharkansky, *Spending in the American States* (Chicago: Rand MacNally, 1968).

2. See Sharkansky, *op. cit.*, plus James A. Wilson, *City Politics and Public Policy* (New York: Wiley, 1968), Chapter 1; and Duane Lockard, "State Party Systems and Policy Outputs," in Oliver Garceau (ed.), *Political Research and Political Theory* (Cambridge: Harvard University Press, 1968), pp. 190–220.

Our results confirm some and challenge other findings of recent research. Because we deal with factors and not isolated variables, we can speak with improved precision of which *dimensions* of policy respond to what *dimensions* of politics and economics. Our findings show that different social and economic characteristics have different relevance for policies, and their relevance varies between substantive areas of policy. Furthermore, central features of state politics are important for some policies, even when socioeconomic variation is controlled.

II. Methods of Index Construction

The conceptualization of state policy making into three sectors — social, political-governmental, and policy — has proven sufficiently fruitful to warrant its continued use. We have followed the guidance of previous studies in separating the objects of our study in this manner. Within each sector, however, there is no *a priori* reason to assume that the component variables are unidimensional or of equal weight. For that reason, we wish to employ techniques which test for dimensionality and which assess the relative contribution of specific variables to the patterns of relationship.

In any situation where one seeks to pin numbers on a concept, a wise stratagem is to employ multiple measures in the hope that they will, in a sense, triangulate on the conceptual target more accurately than any single item.[3] Multiple measurement, however, still leaves one guessing what is the common element of the many variables used. Averaging scores or ranks and constructing composite indices of unweighted items runs the risk of making several unwarranted and unnecessary assumptions.[4] It allows for no indication of the relative impact of the items included. Multiple regression analysis runs a similar risk. It provides no means for handling the multiple measures of dependent variables. A strong case can be made for a lengthy list of indicators, but one also needs a mechanism for sorting out their commonality and diversity. If used with some sensitivity, factor analysis serves this need.[5]

---

3. For a lucid critique of single indicator analysis and a discussion of the methodological justification for multiple indicators see Eugene J. Webb, Donald T. Campbell, Richard D. Schwartz, and Lee Sechrest, *Unobtrusive Measures: Nonreactive Research in the Social Sciences* (Chicago: Rand McNally, 1966), pp. 3ff.

4. For an example of such an index, see Hofferbert, "The Relation . . . ," *op. cit.*

5. The technique of factor analysis starts from the basic assumption that interrelations among separate variables signal the existence of underlying traits — or "factors" — that they share in common. A factor analysis manipulates a collection of variables in order to discern the various patterns of relationships among them. The groups of variables that relate closely to one another, but only loosely (or not at all) to variables in other groups are extracted as the principal factors. The individual variables that show the strongest relationships with other members of their factor have, in the language of factor analysis, the higest *loadings*. A variable's *loading* is, in effect, the coefficient of correlation between that variable and the underlying factor. By knowing the variables with the highest loadings on each factor, it is possible to infer something about the underlying traits that the factor represents. The variables with the highest loadings come closest to representing the underlying trait, although it is unlikely that any single variable represents that trait perfectly. The factoring technique used with the political and service variables employs orthogonal rotation. The device examines the correlation matrix of the individual variables and extracts factors whose members show maximum correlations among themselves and minimum correlations with the members of other factors. The program used is "Image," by Walter Stoly, Mass Communications Center, University of Wisconsin, Madison, version of July 2, 1968. For an explanation of techniques used in the socioeconomic factor, see Hofferbert, "Socioeconomic Dimensions . . . ," *op. cit.* Although Hofferbert employed oblique rotation in the extraction of his factors, the comparability to our political and service factors is not appreciably affected. The intercorrelation of the two socio-economic factors for 1960 is .023.

Some writers have been critical of some uses to which factor analysis has been put, particularly with the increased availablity of pre-packaged programs and sophisticated computing facilities. Two major criticisms are relevant in the present context. First, it is charged that factor analysis has been used in lieu of theory.[6] If one simply plugs into the machine all of the data at his command, some kind of factors will emerge. Factor analysis is not a substitute for theory. There must be some prior rationale which justifies the particular variables fed into the computer. Secondly, the technique has been criticized because the factors which emerge often seem to make little sense in terms of the theory with which one is working.[7] Theory is juggled to accommodate the machinery.

This is not the appropriate context in which to explore the intracacies of factor analysis. But we do recognize the necessity to account for some of the major criticisms and to point out how we have tried to minimize the difficulties in our inquiry. We have attempted to avoid these pitfalls in two ways. First, the variables we include have been employed because of their widespread currency in analyses by other scholars and the appealing theoretical rationale which these analysts have offered.[8] Second, as will be apparent, the factors we obtain *do* make sense and we have employed a number of checks to insure that the apparent sense they make is not an artifact of the technique.[9] In order to use the results of factor analysis to test relationships among various dimensions of politics, economics, and public policy we derived "factor scores" for each state from the combination of its value on the individual variables and the loading of each variable on each factor. The derivation of state scores on the socioeconomic factors is discussed elsewhere.[10] With factor

---

6. J. Scott Armstrong, "Derivation of Theory of Means of Factor Analysis or Tom Swift and His Electric Factor Analysis Machine," *American Statistician* (December, 1967), 17–21.

7. See, for example, John E. Mueller, "Some Comments on Russett's 'Discovering Voting Groups in the United Nations,'" *American Political Science Review*, 61 (March, 1967), 146–48. [Reprinted earlier in this volume — ED.]

8. But we have been sensitive to the possibility of biased results. Certain initial steps have been taken to reduce this bias. Factor analysis cannot be relied upon to define the dimensions of a complex phenomenon (e.g., the state political system), particularly if the collection of variables subject to factor analysis is pre-loaded with many measures of the same phenomenon, each of which is highly correlated with others. Thus our first task was to insure that we did not "stack" our deck of variables with highly intercorrelated measures ($r > .70$) of the same phenomenon. This problem was particularly acute in the case of measures of party competition. Similar screening of the policy variables we examined did not reveal comparable redundancies.

9. To maintain *prima facie* relevance, we use factor analysis in "stages" first to select from among a large collection those variables that load highly on principal factors and then to define the loadings of these variables on factors that contain only those highly-loaded components. In this way, the factor technique produces relatively "pure" factors, devoid of large numbers of variables that contribute only weakly to the principal factors. In both the political and policy analyses, a large number of variables load low on two principal factors, and several variables load about equally on each principal factor. In order to simplify these factors for the purposes of clarity and further analysis, we eliminated all variables loading below .5 on both principal factors and those loading at least .5 on one but above .4 on the other factor in each sector. (The variables surviving this elimination are noted as such on Tables 1 and 3.) We then made separate factor analyses of the variables that remained after this culling procedure. (The results in Tables 2 and 4.) The values derived from this final set of analyses constitute the bases for constructing indices of the political and policy sectors of our model.

10. Hofferbert, "Socioeconomic Dimensions of the American States: 1890–1960," *Midwest Journal of Political Science*, 12 (August, 1968), 401–18. The factor scoring program used for the political and policy factors is "FACTSCR2" by Keith R. Billingsley, Department of Political Science, University of Wisconsin, Madison, version of July 20, 1968. The scoring technique is described in Henry F. Kaiser, "Formulas for Component Scores," *Psychometrika*, 27 (March, 1962), 83–87.

scores as our independent and dependent variables, we use simple, partial and multiple correlation techniques to assess relationships between dimensions of state economics, politics, and public policy.

Political Factors

In choosing the items for construction of the political indices an effort was made to include a comprehensive list of characteristics that have long been of concern to political scientists. We chose measures of participation and party competition, the character of the legislative, judicial and executive branches of state government, and the individual and mutual aspects of state, local and intergovernmental fiscal structures.

The measures of turnout and competition assess prominent aspects of the electoral process, involving contests for both governor and United States Representative. The measures of party competition include both the spread of the vote received in recent elections and the distribution of legislative and gubernatorial control between parties and over time.

The variables indicating government structures, personnel and revenues tap several aspects of state and local government that may affect perception of and responsiveness to citizen interests. The variables pertaining to the legislature include three separate indices of apportionment equity, plus the number of legislators, the length of the legislature's session, the number of committees, the salary of members and total expenditures for legislative services, and the number of bills introduced and passed at a recent session. Other scholars have used these variables to assess the representativeness of state legislatures, their "professionalism" and their activism.[11] Several of the variables pertaining to the executive branch assess the magnitude and professionalism of the civil service, and the formal nature of leadership in the executive branch. They show the relative number of employees and their conditions of work. Two variables relative to executive leadership are the score of each state's governor on an index of formal authority,[12] and the number of administrative officials who are directly elected. The age and length of the state constitution and the number of its amendments have been used by one scholar to assess the activism of state interest groups and their orientation toward constitution-building.[13] Also examined are terms, official qualifications, compensation and pension opportunities of the state judiciaries; these should denote some central aspects of judicial professionalism.

We measure state and local tax systems by the proportion of revenues raised from the major taxes. Each tax has a distinctive impact upon a particular segment of the population;[14] thus, the composition of state and local revenue systems may reflect the political strength of different economic groups, and affect the relationship between each group of taxpayers and state and local governments.

---

11. Dye, *op. cit.*, and John G. Grumm, "Structure and Policy in the Legislature," a paper presented at the Southwestern Social Science Association annual meeting, Dallas, March, 1967.

12. Joseph A. Schlesinger, "The Politics of the Executive," in Herbert Jacob and Kenneth N. Vines (eds.), *Politics in the American States* (Boston: Little, Brown, 1965), pp. 207–238.

13. Lewis A. Froman, Jr., "Some Effects of Interest Group Strength in State Politics," *American Political Science Review*, 60 (December, 1966), 952–962.

14. See George A. Bishop, "The Tax Burden by Income Class, 1958," *National Tax Journal*, 14 (March, 1961), 41–58.

Several measures of intergovernmental relationships assess the mutual dependence of state and local governments and the role of federal agencies in financing public services. These variables permit an answer to the question: "Which government pays the bills?" Federal, state and local taxes vary in their progressivity-regressivity.

TABLE 1   Political Variables Subject to Analysis †

(Participation and Party)

**1. Percent voting age population voting for Governor
2. Percent voting age population voting for U.S. Representative
**3. Number of items on Milbrath's list of suffrage regulations on which a state scores as a "facilitator"
**4. Percent of gubernatorial vote won by major party
5. Percent of congressional vote won by major party
**6. Percent of seats in lower house of state legislature held by major party
7. Percent of seats in upper house of state legislature held by major party
*8. Number of years during 1952–62 when major party controlled Governor's office
**9. Number of years during 1954–62 when major party controlled lower house of legislature
*10. Number of years during 1954–62 when major party controlled upper house of legislature

(Institutions and Personnel)

*11. Dauer-Kelsay index of legislative apportionment
*12. David-Eisenberg index of legislative apportionment
*13. Shubert-Press index of legislative apportionment
*14. Number of state legislators
**15. Legislators' compensation
**16. Total expenditures on legislative services per legislator (minus compensation)
*17. Number of legislative committees
**18. Number of bills introduced into the legislature
19. Number of bills passed by the legislature
*20. Proportion of bills introduced that were passed
*21. Number of days in the legislative session
*22. Term of judges on state court of last resort
*23. Minimum age requirement for judges on appeals courts
*24. Minimum age requirement for judges on trial courts
**25. Compensation of judges on court of last resort
*26. Minimum term that will make state judges eligible for pension
27. Number of state employees per 10,000 population
28. Average salary of state employees

*29. Percent of state employees covered by state personnel system
*30. Schlesinger index of gubernatorial formal power
*31. Number of separately elected executive officials in the state government
*32. Number of state plus local government employees per 10,000 population
*33. Average salary of state plus local government employees
*34. Percent of state and local government employees covered by government supported health and hospital insurance
*35. Percent of state and local government employees covered by government supported life insurance
36. Number of words in state constitution
*37. Number of amendments in state constitution
*38. Date of state constitution's ratification
*39. Population per local governmental unit

(Fiscal Structure)

*40. Percent of state and local government revenues collected from real property taxes
*41. Percent of state and local government revenues collected from individual income taxes
*42. Percent of state and local government revenues collected from general sales taxes
43. Percent of state and local government revenues collected from excise taxes
*44. Percent of state and local government revenues collected from current service charges
45. Percent of state government revenue received as federal aid
**46. Percent of state and local government revenue received as federal aid
47. Percent of state and local government revenue raised by state government
**48. Percent of state and local government revenue spent by state agencies
49. Percent of state and local government revenue raised by local governments
50. Percent of local revenue received from the state government
*51. Percent of state aid to localities allocated on the basis of fixed criteria of population or the amount of certain taxes collected locally
52. Percent of state aid to localities allocated on the basis of need
*53. State aid to localities per capita

†Unless indicated otherwise, the data pertain to 1962.
*Variables surviving test for high intercorrelations among substantively similar variables.
**Variables surviving test for high loading on a single factor. (All ** variables also meet the test of those being noted with * only.)

A state that relies heavily on locally financed services may generate a different type of response among taxpayers than one that relies on state or federal revenues. It is also likely that each level of government differs in its responsiveness to demands. Thus a state that emphasizes services financed by federal or state agencies may present a different complexion of need-gratifications than one which is localist in orientation. Finally, the supervision of "avoided" programs is likely to differ from that of programs financed locally. A heavy reliance on federal and state revenues, therefore, may have administrative implications that influence other dimensions of state politics.

No two of our political variables measures the same phenomena in exactly the same manner. It is possible, however, that our penchant for a comprehensive list of indicators will overload the factor analysis in favor of phenomena (e.g., party competition) that have been the subject of several earlier measurements. In order to guard against this kind of overloading, we computed a matrix of simple correlation coefficients between all of our political variables. In those cases where variables measuring similar phenomena showed high coefficients of correlation ($r > .7$), we eliminated one of the highly intercorrelated pair from the factor analysis. The 41 variables that survived this first screening process are indicated in Table 1 and were entered into a preliminary factor analysis. This analysis was used to identify those variables which loaded high on two or more factors or loaded high in no factor. (See notes 8 and 9) A second factor analysis was performed without these ambiguities and irrelevancies, and produced the two principal factors reported in Table 2.

TABLE 2   Loadings of Political Variables on Two
Principal Factors

Variables*	Professionalism — Local Reliance	Competition — Turnout
Compensation of judges (25)	.897	.045
Compensation of legislators (15)	.865	.142
Legislative Service expenditures (16)	.821	.025
Number of bills introduced (18)	.812	−.130
State and local revenue from federal government (46)	−.763	−.293
State and local revenue spent by state agencies (48)	−.732	−.330
Lower house seats of major party (6)	−.280	−.861
Gubernatorial election turnout (1)	.033	.827
Gubernatorial vote for major party (4)	−.077	−.755
Liberal suffrage laws (3)	−.006	.717
Lower house tenure of major party (9)	−.061	−.623
Percent of Total Variance	36.7	28.8

*The parenthesized numbers correspond to the variable numbers in Table 1.

The first principal factor is labeled "Professionalism-Local Reliance." It draws its name from the *positively-loaded* measures of judicial and legislative compensation, expenditures on legislative services, and legislative activity; and from the *negatively-loaded* measures of reliance upon *state* government expenditures and *federal* aids. States scoring high on this factor show high salaries for judges and legislators, well-financed legislative staffs, and primary reliance on locally raised and spent revenues. The inverse juxtaposition in factor #1 of professionalism in government and the use of state and federal aids makes sense in terms of functions that intergovernmental payments are reputed to serve. They are often defended as devices that are used most by governments which redistribute resources from *have* to *have not* jurisdictions. And in fact, the recipients have apparent needs for assistance. Factor #1 suggests that states making heavy use of intergovernmental assistance have judicial and legislative institutions that are less well-developed than average.

The second factor — "Competition-Turnout" — has as its highest-loaded variables the measures of turnout in a gubernatorial election, an index of suffrage liberality, and (negatively) one-party dominance in the state legislature and in recent elections for governor.[15] The Competition-Turnout dimension provides some post hoc justification for the many studies of state politics that have focused almost entirely on electoral processes and inter-party struggles. Books and articles by V. O. Key, Duane Lockard, and John Fenton, among others, view party competition and electoral behavior as the primary stuff of politics.[16] Our factor analyses suggest that an electoral-party dimension has indeed some importance as a distinct component of state politics.

Public Policy Factors

Our list of policy measures is limited in conception to the expenditures for and outputs of major public services. It is not designed to measure "everything government does." Some measures of government activity seem better conceived as measures of state politics than as measures of policy.[17] In the factor analysis of state public policies, the variables were chosen to represent both current expenditures for major services and approximations of results from service operations.[18] The non-expenditure variables measure "outputs" expressed as service actually rendered. Table 3 lists the variables entered into the factor analyses of policy outputs.

The measures of educational output show the capacity of secondary schools to entice students to remain until graduation and the success of each state's residents on a nation-wide examination. Presumably, the first measure assesses the schools'

---

15. In interpreting the results of the factor analysis, a loading of .700 will be considered to be high.

16. V. O. Key, *Southern Politics* (New York: Alfred A. Knopf, 1949); Key, *American State Politics: An Introduction* (New York: Alfred A. Knopf, 1956); Duane Lockard, *New England State Politics* (Princeton: Princeton University Press, 1959); John H. Fenton, *Politics in the Border States* (New Orleans: Hauser Press, 1957); and Fenton, *Midwest Politics* (New York: Holt, Rinehart and Winston, 1966).

17. We have described above our justifications for including measures pertaining to government personnel, structure, and revenue among our political variables. In brief, they represent features of revenue inputs and governmental structures that may affect response to citizens' needs and demands. Our policy measures are more narrow in representing the benefits which governments actually provide to their citizens within the prominent categories of service.

18. Although some research has relied almost exclusively on expenditures as indicators of public policy, a recent study shows the risk in assuming an expenditure-service relationship. The current expenditures of state and local governments may not be uniformly reliable indicators of the service that is actually provided to the population. But on the other hand spending may represent the effort that state and local governments are making in order to improve or maintain their services. Therefore it deserves a place on our list of policy variables. See Sharkansky, "Government Expenditures and Public Services in the American States," *American Political Science Review*, 61 (December, 1967), 1066–1077.

TABLE 3   Policy Variables Subject to Analysis†

(Education)
*1.   Percent of ninth grade students (1959) graduating three years later
*2.   Percent of candidates passing selective service mental examination
 3.   State and local government expenditures for education per capita

(Highways)
 4.   Total road mileage per capita
*5.   Rural road mileage per rural resident
 6.   Municipal road mileage per urban resident
 7.   Percent of designated Interstate mileage completed
 8.   Population per highway fatality
*9.   State and local government expenditures for highways per capita

(Welfare)
*10.   Average payment, Aid to Families of Dependent Children
*11.   Average payment, Old Age Assistance
*12.   Average payment, Aid to the Blind
*13.   Average payment, Aid to the Permanently and Totally Disabled
 14.   Incidende of AFDC recipients among population with incomes of less than $2,000
*15.   Incidence of OAA recipients among population with incomes of less than $2,000 and over 65
        years of age
 16.   Incidence of AB recipients among population with incomes of less than $2,000
 17.   Incidence of APTD recipients among population with incomes of less than $2,000
 18.   State and local government expenditures for public welfare per capita

(Health)
 19.   Proportion of white infants surviving their first year of life
 20.   Proportion of non-white infants surviving their first year of life
 21.   State and local government expenditures for health, hospitals, and sanitation per capita

(Natural Resources)
 22.   Visits per 10,000 population to state parks
*23.   Fishing licenses sold per 10,000 population
*24.   Hunting licenses sold per 10,000 population
*25.   State and local government expenditures for natural resources per capita

(General)
 26.   Total state and local government general expenditures per capita

†The data all pertain to 1962.
*Variables surviving test for high loading on a single factor.

ability to serve the needs of the students, whether they are inclined toward college preparation or immediate placement in business or the trades. The incidence of examination passes should reflect the quality of information and the intellectual skills that state residents possess by the time they finish secondary school.

The highway output measures record the mileage of various types of state roads in relation to population. Population seems to be the best measure of traffic needs that is readily available.[19] Therefore, the measures show the incidence of various roads in relation to the demands of traffic. Admittedly, road location is not considered. Some states may build many miles of roads but place them unwisely with respect to centers of population, commercial needs, etc. The completion rate of the interstate system provides some indication of state highway department administrative skills and capacity to respond quickly in the face of a major opportunity. The inverted death rate provides a measure of road safety. Where a state scores high

19. See Philip H. Burch, Jr., *Highway Revenue and Expenditure Policy in the United States* (New Brunswick: Rutgers University Press, 1962), p. 23.

on the latter measure, it should indicate high standards of road design and maintenance and/or an adequate system of highway patrol.

Output measures in the public welfare field reflect both the generosity of payments and the coverage of each major public assistance program. These specific programs have been in operation generally for several years. They represent much of the work carried out by state departments of public welfare. However, the indicators do not assess such things as quality or quantity of counselling services, cost of living differences, or activities under the newer programs sponsored by the federal Office of Economic Opportunity.

Measures of health policies assess the likelihood of white and non-white children surviving their first year. Admittedly, these variables cover only a small portion of health-relevant services within each state. And they show the influence of many social and economic processes. Nevertheless, we assume that high scores on these scales reflect the presence of health and hospital facilities that are adequate in the face of cultural and medical needs.

Natural resources policies are reflected in measures of the tendency of state residents to use the programs and facilities offered by state departments of parks and wildlife. High scores on these variables should signal attractive programs. The basic assumption is that an attractive program stimulates usage by state residents.[20]

Examination of the simple correlations among the policy measures revealed no redundancies comparable to those found in the list of political variables. A preliminary factor analysis of the policy variables led us to eliminate ambiguities and irrelevancies which loaded high on two factors or on no factors. (See notes 8 and 9). Then a second factor analysis was performed with the remaining variables. The variables retained and their loadings are shown in Table 4. The first factor — "Welfare-Education" — emphasizes generous welfare payments, the tendency of high school pupils to remain until graduation, and the success of state residents on the national examination.

The second principal policy factor is "Highway-Natural Resources." Its major components are measures of rural highway mileage and highway expenditures, plus measures of fish and wildlife services and expenditures for natural resources. A curious variable that is loaded highly on this factor is Old Age Assistance recipients. At first glance, it seems out of its proper place in the Welfare-Education factor. Aid to the aged, however, is the product of a policy process that is distinct from that of other welfare and education programs. A number of rural states that

20. In collecting the data for the measures of outputs and services, the assumption was made that recorded information is a reasonably accurate reflection of fact. The authors recognize considerable controversy about the reliability of the data. Yet the data chosen appear to be the best available, and they enjoy wide use among social scientists. For comments about each item the reader is referred to the sources. The sources for the political variables include: *Census of Governments, 1962; The Book of the States 1964–1965; Statistical Abstract of the United States, 1964;* the index of gubernatorial power comes from Schlesinger's article cited in note #12; the index of suffrage regulations comes from Lester Milbrath, "Political Participation in the States," in Jacob and Vines, *op. cit.,* pp. 25–60; the indices of legislative apportionment comes from Paul T. David and Ralph Eisenberg, *Devaluation of the Urban and Suburban Vote* (Charlottesville: Bureau of Public Administration, University of Virginia, 1961), p. 5, 15, and Glendon Shubert and Charles Press, "Measuring Malapportionment," *American Political Science Review,* 58 (1964), 969. The sources for policy variables include: National Education Association, *Rankings of the States, 1963;* U.S. Bureau of Public Road, *Annual Report 1963;* Social Security Administration, Social Security Bulletin: *Annual Statistical Supplement 1963; The Book of the States, 1964–1965; Statistical Abstract of the United States, 1964.*

TABLE 4   Loadings of Policy Variables on Two
Principal Factors

Variables*	Welfare — Education	Highways — Natural Resources
AFDC payments (10)	.911	.049
OAA payments (11)	.864	.170
High school graduates (1)	.848	.113
AB payments (12)	.834	.042
Examination success (2)	.779	.414
APTD payments (13)	.719	−.274
Rural road mileage (5)	.109	.869
Hunting licenses (24)	−.058	.860
Highway expenditures (9)	.118	.857
Fishing licenses (23)	.040	.800
Natural resource expenditures (25)	.310	.719
OAA recipients (15)	.041	.709
Percent of Total Variance	35.4	34.9

*The parenthesized numbers correspond to the variable numbers in Table 3.

have paid little attention to the average level of welfare benefits have shown considerable concern for their aged and have made the program available to a large number of beneficiaries. Some of this concern may be related to the political strategy of state governmental decision makers. Aside from welfare mothers (who are tainted with a stigma of illegitimacy), the aged are the largest groups of potential welfare recipients who are eligible to vote.[21] The lines of reasoning suggested by this instance will be more carefully explored in Section III below.

Socioeconomic Factors

The factor analysis of socioeconomic characteristics is discussed in detail elsewhere.[22] It includes measures of income, urbanization, industrialization, ethnicity, education and other likely components of "economic development." The variables included are listed in Table 5 in the order in which they load on two principal factors. The factors are here labelled "Industrialization" and "Affluence" according to the variables that load highest on each one.[23] In this article, these factors are used to assess the socioeconomic conditions that support various aspects of state politics and public service and to test the interaction between the major dimensions of state economics, politics, and policy.

21. For a discussion of the politics of old age assistance in Alabama, see Sharkansky, *Spending in the American States*, pp. 138–41.

22. Hofferbert, "Socioeconomic Dimensions . . . ," *op. cit.*

23. *Ibid.* The label given to one of the socioeconomic factors is new with this article. In the original article "Affluence" was labelled "Cultural Enrichment," the present term seems more appropriate as a description of the contents of this factor.

TABLE 5 Loadings of Socioeconomic Variables on
Two Principal Factors: 1960*

Industrialization		Affluence	
value added by manufacture/capita	+.907	median school years completed	+.909
percentage employed in manufacturing	.877	estimated value of real property/capita	.792
value/acre of farm land and buildings	.831	personal income/capita	.730
population/square mile	.775	motor vehicle registration/1,000	
		population	.703
percent foreign	.703	telephones/1,000 population	.675
total population	.672	percent increase in population	.551
percent urban	.657	percent urban	.522
telphones/1,000 population	.650	acreage per farm	.488
average no. of employees per		divorce rate	.430
manufacturing establishment	.638	percent failures business + commercial	
personal income/capitia	.573	establishments	.287
percent failures business + commercial		percent housing owner occupied	.240
establishments	.421	percent foreign	.230
estimated value real property/capita	.132	total population	.045
percent Negro	.066	value per acre of farm land and buildings	.024
percent illiterate	.039	value added by manufacture/capita	
		population/square mile	.008
percent increase in population	.006	percentage employed in manufacturing	.132
median school years completed	.026	average no. of employees per	
percent farms operated by tenants	.266	manufacturing establishment	.351
percent housing owner occupied	.316	percent farms operated by tenants	.468
divorce rate	.325	percent illiterate	.737
acreage per farm	.503	percent Negro	−.752
motor vehicle registration/1,000			
population	−.568		
percent of total variance	32.4		25.3

*Source: Hofferbert, "Socioeconomic Dimensions of the American States," *Midwest Journal of Political Science*, August, 1968.

III. Economic-Political-Policy Relationships:
A Comparison of Factor Versus
Individual Variable Relationships

One controversy that is clarified by the use of factor score concerns relationships among political and economic characteristics of the states that are alleged to influence the nature of public policies. Several publications employ individual variables to answer the question raised in our introduction, i.e., how do political and economic elements relate with each other and with the nature of public policies? Although most authors use comparable measurements and attempt to make their research additive with respect to each others', the interpretation of their findings is made difficult by the discreteness of the variables examined. The correlations reported by Dye, for example, often show differing policy relationships with "industrialization" and "urbanization" than with "income" and "education."[24] The findings claimed when the "political" measures assess a certain type of voter turnout or party competition differ from the findings derived from "political" measures

24. See, for example, Dye, *op. cit.*, p. 125 and p. 162.

that assess the equity of apportionment or the centralization of state-local financial relationships. Likewise, findings vary with the use of expenditures or other variables that purport to measure public policy.[25]

At this point it is possible to face the issue of political or economic influences on public policies with some important new tools. The six factors measure prominent

TABLE 6   Factor Scores for the States on Two
Political and Two Policy Factors

State	Profes-sionalism — local-reliance	Compe-tition — turnout	Welfare — educa-tion	Highway — natural resources
Alabama	−.399	−2.504	−1.753	−.405
Arizona	−.005	−.141	−.266	.175
Arkansas	−.827	−1.360	−1.263	.056
California	2.140	.363	1.849	−.345
Colorado	−.255	.679	.711	.473
Connecticut	.200	.431	.846	−.845
Delaware	.116	.192	−.390	−.779
Florida	.260	−.560	−.875	−.589
Georgia	.087	−2.516	−.1452	−.535
Idaho	−1.052	1.266	−.045	1.583
Illinois	1.154	1.034	1.258	−.877
Indiana	.036	1.152	.155	−.399
Iowa	−.163	.326	.845	−.059
Kansas	−.159	.359	.852	−.082
Kentucky	−.661	−.351	−1.041	−.420
Louisiana	.031	−1.152	−.729	−.361
Maine	−.619	.045	−.465	.344
Maryland	.500	−.377	−.155	−.787
Massachusetts	1.651	.071	1.446	−1.363
Michigan	1.354	.627	.761	−.578
Minnesota	.417	1.339	1.316	.594
Mississippi	−.210	−1.770	−2.432	−.191
Missouri	.126	.305	−.378	−.298
Montana	−1.095	1.235	−.063	1.847
Nebraska	−.297	1.494	.705	.337
Nevada	−.221	−.170	−.535	2.866
New Hampshire	−.752	.191	1.035	.183
New Jersey	1.010	.843	1.035	−1.115
New Mexico	−.734	−.615	.184	.269
New York	4.230	−.643	1.152	−1.079
North Carolina	−.161	−.198	−1.079	−.857
North Dakota	−.869	.780	.901	.614
Ohio	.619	.226	.284	−.756
Oklahoma	−.799	−.293	.785	−.262
Oregon	−.207	.913	.735	.656
Pennsylvania	1.648	.192	.085	−.769
Rhode Island	−.328	.166	.640	−1.144
South Carolina	−.013	−2.838	−1.580	−.808
South Dakota	−.976	−.138	−.072	1.546
Tennessee	−.582	−.556	−1.738	−.169
Texas	.289	−.566	−.808	−.493
Utah	−1.032	1.629	.124	.688
Vermont	−1.546	−.483	−.615	1.313
Virginia	−.243	−.964	−1.062	−.645
Washington	−.160	6.94	.789	.063
West Virginia	−.739	.281	−1.360	−.422
Wisconsin	.558	.949	1.445	.095
Wyoming	−1.421	.413	.220	3.728

25. See Sharkansky, *Spending in the American States*, Chapters 4 and 7.

dimensions of state economics, politics and public policies. They should enable us to see which types of economic and political phenomena are most relevant for which types of public policy. The statistics employed in this section are commonly used in the analysis of policy determinants: coefficients of simple, partial, and multiple correlation. The innovation here is in the variables. Instead of individual measures, the variables are represented by the factor scores reported in Table 6.

There is a strong association between Competition-Turnout and the Affluence dimension of state economics. (See Table 7.) Evidently, citizens are more likely to participate in politics and parties are most likely to compete with one another where the residents are well-educated and relatively wealthy. Of course, this finding is not new. However, it is a very important relationship in the political and economic systems of American states that is highlighted by the use of factor analysis.[26]

TABLE 7   Coefficients of Simple Correlation Between
Socioeconomic and Political Factors

Political Factors	SOCIOECONOMIC FACTORS	
	Industrial-ization	Affluence
Professionalism-Local Reliance	.73	.14
Competition-Turnout	.11	.66

Another strong relationship is that between the Professionalism-Local Reliance dimension of state politics and the Industrialization dimension of state economics. It is apparently the value of industrial output and the incidence of industrial employment — instead of education, wealth, or ethnicity — that has the most to do with the development of legislative and judicial professionalization and the tendency of local authorities to rely on their own economic resources. It may be that a large industrial tax base and an urbanized population permits governments to rely on locally-raised revenues. An industrial economy may also encourage states to develop professional, active policy making institutions in response to comparable models in the private sector.

The Welfare-Education dimension of state policy shows positive relationships with each of the political and economic factors. (See Table 8.) The coefficients of partial correlation reveal that this policy factor is associated most closely with high scores on Competition-Turnout and Affluence, with neither being significantly more important than the other. The elements of interparty competition, high voter participation, high levels of educational attainment, and wealth seem to provide the impetus — independently from other governmental and economic

26. The strength of relationships between the political and economic factors is stronger than that customarily obtained with individual variables. The correlations that we have described are .73 and .66. Only two out of the forty-eight simple correlations between economic and political variables that Dye reports in his study reach the level of .66 and none reach .73 (see his Chapter 3). The underlying dimensions that are tapped by factor analysis appear to be more salient representations of the economic-political nexus than are apparent in studies using single variables.

TABLE 8 Coefficients of Simple, Partial, and Multiple
Correlation, and Multiple Determination Between
Socioeconomic, Political, and Policy Factors

	SIMPLE CORRELATION		PARTIAL CORRELATION*	
	Welfare — Education	Highways — Natural Resources	Welfare — Education	Highways — Natural Resources
Professionalism — Local Reliance	.39	−.54	.26	−.24
Competition — Turnout	.68	.25	.47	−.02
Industrialization	.37	−.69	.17	−.55
Affluence	.69	.43	.43	.53
	Multiple Correlation		Multiple Determination	
Socioeconomic Factors	.77	.82	.59	.68
Political Factors	.78	.60	.61	.36
Socioeconomic + Political Factors	.83	.84	.69	.70

*Controlling for the other factors.

conditions — for public officials to provide generous welfare payments and successful educational services.[27]

This finding of importance for the Competition-Turnout factor with respect to welfare and education services provides some latter-day support for hypotheses derived from Key and others that electoral and party characteristics of state politics have something to do with the nature of services that are provided.[28] Our findings do not, however, fit the neat, linear, single determinant structure of causality suggested by some of Key's followers. Rather, the data suggest that it is not any one element of state politics, but an underlying factor that is only partly measured by individual variables which exerts an independent influence on public services. The prominence of this finding is increased by the importance of the policy factor involved. Welfare and education services consume a substantial proportion of state and local government resources: 49 percent of general expenditures and 51 percent

27. The political and economic factors are more successful in accounting for interstate variance in the policy factors than are most individual measures of these phenomena. Table 8 shows simple, partial, and multiple correlation coefficients between policy factors as dependent variables and the political and economic factors as independent variables. It shows that both political factors together account for 61 and 36 percent of the variance in the policy factors. In contrast, the multiple correlation coefficients that Dye reports show that his collection of individual political variables account for 36 percent of the variance in only fifteen out of fifty-four dependent variables, and they account for 61 percent of the variance in only two out of the fifty-four instances. (See Dye, *op. cit.*, pp. 286–287.) Both of our socioeconomic factors account for 59 and 68 percent of the variance in the policy factors. In contrast Dye's collection of individual social and economic variables account for 59 percent of the variance in only fourteen of fifty-four dependent variables, and they account for 68 percent of the variance in only eight of fifty-four dependent variables. A similar finding appears when we compare with his data the success of our economic and political factors together in explaining variance in our policy factors. We explain 69 and 70 percent of the variance in the policy factors by means of all political and socioeconomic variables: Dye explains 69 percent of the variance for only thirteen of fifty-four dependent variables.

28. See their works cited in note #16, *supra.*

of government employment in 1965–66. Policy making in welfare and education are characterized by sharp controversies; this may explain their relation with electoral and partisan processes in a manner quite different from other areas of public policy.

The Highway-Natural Resources dimension of public policy shows its primary dependence on economic factors. It is inversely and strongly related to Industrialization and directly related to Affluence. Thus it appears that *low* levels of industrial output and employment, population density and urbanization together with *high* levels of personal wealth and education incline a state toward heavy investments in roads (especially in rural areas) and active fish and wildlife programs. Wide-open spaces present an abundance of recreational opportunities, the need for highway facilities, and the rural interests that have concentrated their political efforts in behalf of these services. Highway-Natural Resource policy also is inversely dependent on the Professionalism-Local Reliance dimension of state politics, but this is secondary to its dependence on socioeconomic characteristics.

Why the lack of dependence on political factors for highway and natural resource policies? Despite conflicting interests, the particular programmatic activities involved in these policies do not fall neatly along the symbolic continua which are most commonly the objects of partisan controversy. There seem to be few issues, for example, which array taxpayers and the economic *haves* against recipients of services and the *have nots* (in contrast to the case in education and welfare). This may be a function of highways, parks, wildlife, and conservation programs being "self-financed" by means of earmarked taxes, licenses and user fees. The recipients pay for much of the benefits received, and do not generate a great deal of conflict across the lines of different social classes or ethnic groups.

IV. Summary and Conclusions

This article reports two separate factor analyses of state politics and public policies. And together with two socioeconomic factors, it employs the political and policy factors to clarify relationships among three sectors of a widely used model of the state policy process. The major findings are:

1) The factor analysis of political variables reveals two underlying dimensions of state politics. These are Professionalism-Local Reliance and Competition-Turnout. The distinctiveness of the Competition-Turnout factor testifies to the importance of this dimension in distinguishing the politics of each state from the others. And it credits the perception of Key, Lockard, Fenton and other political scientists who took aspects of electoral and party behavior as the focus of their own work.
2) The factor analysis of policy variables reveals two principal dimensions of Welfare-Education and Highway-Natural Resources.
3) The examination of political and economic factors shows strong associations between Competition-Turnout and Affluence, and between Professionalism-Local Reliance and Industrialization.
4) The relationships among political, economic, and policy factors show that the Welfare-Education dimension of state policy is significantly dependent upon the Competition-Turnout dimension of state politics and the Affluence dimension of the state economy. Where a state is wealthy and shows high turnout and intense interparty competition, it is likely to score high on the level of welfare and educational services.

The Highway-Natural Resources dimension of policy appears most dependent upon the Industrialization dimension of the states' economies. The relationship is inverse, indicating that well-developed highways and fish-game programs accompany low levels of industrialization and population concentration.

5) The relationships among economic, political, and policy factors are generally stronger than the relationships between individual variables that have previously been used. Thus the underlying dimensions tapped by factor analysis strengthen as well assimplify our explanations of policy making in the American states.

The single most important finding of this article may be its emphasis upon multi-dimensionality in state economics, politics and public policy. There is no single answer to the question: "Is it politics or economics that has the greatest impact on public policy?" The answer (contrary to the thrust of much recent research) varies with the dimensions of each phenomena that are at issue.[29] Welfare-Education policies relate most closely with the Competition-Turnout dimension of state politics *and* with the Affluence dimension of the economy. Highway-Natural Resource policies show their closest (inverse) relationships with the Industrialization dimension of the state economy.[30]

While these findings add to the inquiry into political and economic determinants of public policies, they offer little encouragement to those who would seek to expand the level and scope of public services by manipulating one political or structural characteristic of state government (e.g., voter turnout, party competition, or apportionment). It is apparent only that certain aspects of politics having to do with voter turnout and interparty competition are related to certain public policies. But this does not terminate the inquiry. Factor analyses depend on the nature of the variables included in them. Although this study has included a wide range of political, economic, and policy variables in its factor analyses, it is likely that further analysis

---

29. Charles F. Cnudde and Donald J. McCrone, "Party Competition and Welfare Policies in the American States," *American Political Science Review*, 63 (September, 1969).

30. One limitation of the data employed throughout this article is their lack of historical perspective. A separate study of the two socioeconomic factors and their relationship with individual policy and electoral variables has shown that the strength of relationship is, in some cases, quite fluid over time. (See Hofferbert, "Socioeconomic Dimensions . . . ," *op. cit.*) This fluidity, however, may be a result of simple changes in the value of isolated dependent variables and not an accurate picture of the more analytically interesting dimensions of policy and political life which we have been considering here. Hofferbert found that the relative contribution of individual variables maintained a high degree of consistency in their loadings on the principal factors from one decade to the next, although individual variable-by-variable correlations shifted considerably. If it were possible to analyze the full component of political and service variables over extended time, the same type of configuration could probably be expected. Consequently, the strength of relationship of *factors* could be fairly constant over time even though the individual variable correlations changed considerably. Because of limited availability of the political and policy data for previous years, however, this must remain a matter for speculation.

For a useful discussion of the methodological problems of theory construction employing measures standardized for a specific population and time, such as the correlation coefficients used here, versus unstandardized regression coefficients see Hubert Blalock "Causal Inferences, Closed Populations and Measures of Association," *American Political Science Review*, 61 (March, 1967), 130–136. Blalock argues that in building theoretical statements of more general application, the regression is the most use since it is not as sensitive as the correlation coefficient to specific population values at a given time. However, in an investigation such as ours, where possibility of longitudinal analysis is limited due to the availability of relevant data, it seemed advisable to retain the greater precision of standardized measures. Furthermore, in the case of the states, the relative magnitudes of most of the variables is not particularly fluid as might be the case with some other types of indicators, such as the congressional roll call votes discovered by Blalock.

— with more measures of political, economic, and policy traits — will permit the extraction of additional dimensions from the sectors of state policy systems.

The present factors leave unexplained much of the variance in state politics and policy.[31] This unplumbed variance might be reduced by adding more variables to the factor programs. However, it may be inherent in the nature of the phenomena that much variance will remain unexplained by factor analysis. This unexplained variance may reflect the importance of particularistic, unpatterned happenings that fashion and lend excitement to political institutions. The effort to explain why politics and policies differ from one state to the next may be helped considerably by examining the dimensions lying beneath readily measured variables. But no amount of archival search and factor analysis will account for the contributions made to the institutions of policies of individual states by dynamic personalities or the force of strong traditions. The study of elite and organizational behavior, plus exploration of the values that prevail in the cultural environments of the individual states may be essential for a thorough understanding of inter-state differences in politics and public policy.

---

31. Although the figures in Table 2 report that the political factors account for 66 percent of the variance, this pertains to the variance in the eleven variables that were subject to this factor analysis. These factors do not account for this much of the variance in the total collection of fifty-three variables that are presented in Table 1.

JONATHAN WILKENFELD

Conflict Linkages in the Domestic and Foreign Spheres

*In an original essay written specifically for this
chapter, Professor Wilkenfeld brings together findings from several
related research efforts. The mode of analysis encompasses several
techniques: factor analysis, a correlation analysis based on the factor
solution (including lagged correlations), and an application of the
Markov model to time series data. This research serves to reopen the
scholarly issue regarding relationships between domestic and foreign
conflict across nations. While previous research has found only very
weak relationships, the author hypothesizes that certain salient relationships will be found when three discriminating considerations are taken
into account: (1) the type of nation involved; (2) the type of conflict;
and (3) the type of temporal relationship.*

*In order to assess the effect of these three considerations, the
author begins by delineating basic dimensions of foreign and domestic
conflict derived from a correlational analysis of aggregate conflict
measures across seventy-four nations during a six-year period. Each set of domestic
and foreign conflict dimensions then serves as indices along which nations
are aligned through the use of factor scores. The intercorrelation of
these factor scores enables an assessment of relationships between
domestic and foreign conflict, with the author taking a temporal
dimension into account through the use of cross-lagged correlation
coefficients applied to the factor scores. The type of nation (by*

This paper was written especially for this volume. It serves the function of pulling together findings
reported in four earlier studies by this author (Wilkenfeld, 1968, 1969a, 1969b, Zinnes and Wilkenfeld,
1971). Thus, while most of the findings have been reported elsewhere, this is the first time that the
diverse findings will be confronted simultaneously.

*political characteristics) is measured through a Q factor analysis of
the universe. This procedure yields three groupings of nations used by
the author — personalist, centrist, and polyarchic — which serve as
controls in his investigation of relationships between types of domestic
and foreign conflict.*

*To further analyze the temporal relationships, in a final stage
Wilkenfeld applies a Markov chain model to the data showing the extent
to which foreign conflict in one year is dependent upon the previous
year's level of domestic and foreign conflict. This last analysis,
as well as his use of time-lagged relationships, should serve as a
useful introduction to several time series techniques discussed in
chapter 5. The reader will find it helpful to return to these sections
of the Wilkenfeld article after reading the text material in the next chapter.*

The notion that conflict behavior in one sphere of human activity has a spillover effect in other spheres is one which has seen a good deal of attention in the scholarly literature of the social sciences. Among social psychologists, there is a great deal of attention devoted to the idea that groups experiencing internal dissension may become embroiled in conflict with other groups in order to bring about internal unification (Simmel, 1955, Coser, 1956, Blau, 1964). In the realm of political science, we are confronted with the conception that nations experiencing internal unrest and disorders tend to engage in foreign conflict behavior in order to divert the attention of the population from domestic affairs. This is the notion of uniting a divided people behind the banner of a common cause (Farrell, 1966, Wright, 1942, Rosecrance, 1963, Denton, 1965, Haas and Whiting, 1956, Rosenau, 1969).

In recent years, several data-based studies have turned up evidence which serves to cast doubt upon the popular conceptions discussed above. Thus, R.J. Rummel, in a study based on seventy-seven nations, came to the conclusion that "foreign conflict behavior is generally completely unrelated to domestic conflict behavior" (Rummel, 1963a). This initial finding was further substantiated in two subsequent studies. Utilizing slightly different methods of analysis, Rummel found that there was "a positive association, albeit small, between domestic conflict behavior and the more belligerent forms of foreign conflict behavior on the part of a country" (Rummel, 1963b). Raymond Tanter, in a work which essentially replicated the first Rummel study for a later period, concluded "there is a small relationship between ... domestic and foreign conflict behavior which increases with a time lag" (Tanter, 1966).

The apparent contradiction between the findings of Rummel and Tanter and the commonly accepted theory provided the original stimulus for the present study. Whether linkages exist between conflict behavior in the domestic and foreign spheres is too important a question to be relegated to this limbo. If Rummel and Tanter are correct, then we can finally put to rest the whole notion that foreign conflict behavior is related to domestic conflict behavior. On the other hand, if it can be established that Rummel's and Tanter's conclusions were incomplete because their analyses did not account for certain relevant factors, then we will have significantly advanced knowledge in this area. In either case, it is important that the question of the relationship between domestic and foreign conflict be reopened.

The first premise will be that the Rummel and Tanter approach may have tended to obscure more specific trends evident in their data in the interests of reaching conclusions which could be generalized to all nations. It is these trends in the relationship between the domestic and foreign conflict behavior of nations which are of primary importance in the present study. The purpose here is to demonstrate that the relationship between domestic and foreign conflict behavior does in fact exist and that it takes on various forms, depending upon (1) the type of nation under consideration, (2) the type of conflict behavior involved, and (3) the type of temporal relationship. The crucial supposition of this study is that taking into consideration the type of nation, as measured by differences in governmental structures, will enable us to isolate relationships between various types of conflict behavior. Furthermore, these relationships will be dependent upon specific time lags.

Type of Nation

There is evidence in the literature that the governmental structure of a nation is crucial to an understanding of both the process and the nature of domestic and foreign policy decision making. Some types of governmental structures may be able to withstand large amounts of domestic disorders without resorting to attention-diverting devices such as foreign violence. Under some conditions, nations may be unable to resort to foreign violence, due to the severity of the domestic conflict behavior.

Several recent studies have attempted to show that the supposed differences between democractic and totalitarian systems are not as great as would be imagined. R. Barry Farrell (1966) observes that in constitutional democracies, it is fairly common for decision makers seeking reelection to espouse foreign policy decisions with an eye to the ballot box rather than in accordance with environmental realities. He indicates that in a totalitarian system, while the circumstances are not quite the same, it is nevertheless the case that decision makers perceive international policy as one which can be manipulated to serve domestic interests. Milton J. Rosenberg (1967) contends that given the general anti-Communist trend of public opinion in the United States, conciliatory moves on the part of the government would be considered gross violations of the public trust. These dynamics are present in the Soviet Union as well. With its lack of institutions guaranteeing high office for fixed terms, the leadership must remain sensitive to public opinion among the sub-elite, the military, and provincial functionaries in the party system.

The more conventionally expressed view is that differences in nation type do influence the extent to which the domestic and foreign spheres are related. This is particularly true with regard to conflict linkages. Farrell (1966) again observes that the use of international crises to divert attention away from internal problems is a device most commonly found in the totalitarian system. However, he warns against assuming that the democratic system is completely immune from this type of linkage. Differentiation of nations according to level of economic development also has been cited in this connection. James N. Rosenau (1966) contends that the literature on economic and political development often refers to the ways in which foreign policies of modernizing societies are shaped by their internal needs, such as the sustaining of charismatic leadership, the need for elite identity and prestige, and the needs of in-groups to divert the attention away from domestic problems and thereby to placate their opposition. Elsewhere, Rosenau has stated the following:

> The leaders of underdeveloped countries . . . often seem to be better able to overcome domestic strife and inertia by citing the hostility of the external environment than by stressing the need for hard work and patience at home. In effect, they attempt to solve domestic issues by redefining them as falling in the foreign policy area (Rosenau, 1967, p. 25).

Type of Conflict Behavior

A second major assumption of this study is that the relationship between domestic and foreign conflict behavior differs, depending upon the type of conflict behavior under consideration. It is the contention here that certain types of conflict occurring within a nation may provoke foreign conflict reactions, while the pressures of other types of conflict do not necessitate a foreign conflict response. It also is assumed that nations differ in the extent to which certain types of conflict provoke conflict responses.

Temporal Relationships

The third element which will be introduced into the present analysis is a temporal, or lagged, relationship. In this sense, we are introducing the notion of a directed relationship, which heretofore has been treated merely as an association. Thus, we can investigate the possibility that the occurrence of one type of conflict behavior systematically precedes the occurrence of the other. If, in fact, conflict in one sphere is viewed as a reaction to conflict in the other, then we can note and differentiate those types of conflict which engender immediate reactions from those which involve a delayed response.

The data for the present study were collected by Rummel and Tanter in connection with the Dimensionality of Nations Project (DON). Specifically, the data are for seventy-four nations for the period between 1955 and 1960. There are nine domestic conflict behavior variables and thirteen foreign conflict behavior variables. The exact nature of these data has been adequately described elsewhere (Rummel, 1963a, Tanter, 1966).

Once the data set had been determined, the study proceeded in three distinct stages. In Stage 1, factor analysis was employed as a technique by which indices of domestic and foreign conflict behavior could be constructed. By reducing the number of measures of conflict behavior to a more parsimonious arrangement, it was felt that the subsequent analyses would better isolate the important trends in the relationship between domestic and foreign conflict behavior.

Stage 2 of the study involves the computation of correlations between domestic and foreign conflict factors. Using the factor scores as data, it is possible to investigate lagged relationships between the two types of variables. Relationships between prior domestic conflict and subsequent foreign conflict, as well as prior foreign conflict and subsequent domestic conflict, will be investigated.

Finally, Stage 3 involves the use of Markov chains to reanalyze, from a slightly different perspective, the relationships between the two types of conflict behavior.

Specifically, interest here will focus upon the extent to which the level of foreign conflict behavior in a given year is determined by the prior year's levels of domestic and foreign conflict.

Stage 1 — Factor Analyses

Factor analysis will serve three primary functions here. First, it will enable us to reduce the number of domestic and foreign conflict variables with which we are dealing. In addition, the factors which emerge will be used as descriptive categories, or as indices of domestic and foreign conflict behavior. Finally, the technique will be used as a method of scaling in order to determine the relative weight to be assigned to each of the original variables on a given factor.

The measures of domestic and foreign conflict behavior were separately factor analyzed, using a principal component solution and an orthogonal rotation, in order to determine the patterns of conflict for the six-year period.[1] The results of these analyses are presented in tables 1 and 2. Table 1, reporting domestic conflict behavior, indicates that two factors are extracted, accounting for 52 percent of the total variance. The first domestic factor, internal war, includes revolutions, number killed in domestic conflict, guerrilla warfare, purges, and major government crises. This represents an organized, violent type of domestic conflict behavior. The internal war factor accounts for 50.6 percent of the common variance.

TABLE 1   Factor Analysis of Domestic Conflict
Behavior Variables, 1955–1960

	ORGANIZED ROTATION		
Variables	Factor 1 Internal War	Factor 2 Turmoil	h^2
Assassinations	.30	.47	.31
Guerrilla warfare	(.72)	.09	.52
Government crises	(.53)	.35	.40
Revolutions	(.80)	.12	.65
Strikes	.25	(.62)	.44
Purges	(.53)	.15	.30
Riots	.23	(.81)	.71
Demonstrations	.02	(.85)	.72
Domestic killed	(.67)	.42	.63
% Common variance	50.6	49.4	100.0
% Total variance	26.3	25.7	52.0

Parenthesis indicates loadings ≥.50

The second factor, denoted turmoil, contains demonstrations, riots, strikes, and assassinations. The turmoil factor represents a nonorganized, spontaneous type of conflict behavior. In general, these are the least violent of the domestic conflict variables. This factor accounts for 49.4 percent of the common variance.

1. The factor analyses performed in this study were done using the Biomedical Computer Program BMD03M. In order to maintain a parallel between this and the earlier Rummel and Tanter analyses, communalities of 1.00 were used as the diagonal elements in the correlation matrix.

Table 2 presents the factor analysis of the foreign conflict variables. Three factors were extracted, accounting for 51.6 percent of the total variance. The first factor, denoted war, and accounting for 38.8 percent of the common variance, groups those variables which represent the most violent and warlike forms of foreign conflict behavior, such as wars, military actions, mobilizations, and number killed in foreign conflict.

TABLE 2   Factor Analysis of Foreign Conflict
Behavior Variables, 1955–1960

	ORTHOGONAL ROTATION			
Variables	Factor 1 War	Factor 2 Belligerency	Factor 3 Diplomatic	h^2
Severence of diplomatic relations	.14	(.64)	−.32	.54
Expulsions and recalls — ambassadors	.09	−.03	(.55)	.31
Military actions	(.62)	.17	.18	.45
Wars	(.80)	−.04	.16	.67
Troop movements	.08	.09	(.62)	.40
Mobilizations	(.56)	.25	−.05	.38
Anti-foreign demonstrations	.21	(.56)	.13	.38
Negative sanctions	.16	(.64)	.21	.48
Protests	.34	.26	(.66)	.62
Expulsions and recalls — lesser officials	−.23	(.56)	.38	.51
Threats	.40	.48	(.51)	.66
Accusations	.47	.42	(.50)	.65
Foreign killed	(.77)	.09	.21	.65
% Common variance	38.8	30.4	30.8	100.0
% Total variance	20.0	15.7	15.9	51.6

Parenthesis indicates loadings ≥.50

The second factor, belligerency, accounts for 30.4 percent of the common variance and represents an actively hostile mood. This factor includes severance of diplomatic relations, negative sanctions, anti-foreign demonstrations, and expulsions and recalls of lesser officials.

Finally, the third foreign conflict factor, diplomatic, accounts for 30.8 percent of the common variance. This factor represents a nonviolent form of foreign conflict behavior. These are diplomatic moves, short of the use of force, which are intended to influence the behavior of other nations. The factor includes accusations, threats, protests, expulsions and recalls of ambassadors, and troop movements.

The results of these factor analyses will serve as the basis for the analyses conducted in Stages 2 and 3. Thus, we will be working with turmoil and internal war as the underlying domestic conflict behavior factors, and with war, belligerency, and diplomatic as the underlying foreign conflict behavior factors. Factor scores are computed on the basis of the factor analytic results. Each nation, for each of the six years involved in the study, has a score on each of the five conflict behavior factors. These scores constitute composite indices of the variables underlying each factor.

Stage 2 — Correlation Analysis

In this stage of the investigation, correlation techniques will be employed in order to isolate possible relationships between domestic and foreign conflict behavior factors. Through the use of time lags, we will be able to investigate directed relationships. Not only will the case of co-occurrence of the two types of conflict be investigated, but we will also be interested in one-and two-year time lags to be imposed between the two types of conflict.

As indicated earlier, the intervening factor of nation type is included in this analysis. For this purpose, a classificatory scheme developed by Banks and Gregg (1965) is employed. Banks and Gregg performed a Q-factor analysis of the political variables included in *A Cross-Polity Survey* (1963). This technique of factor analysis

TABLE 3 Groupings of Nations

Personalist	Loadings	Polyarchic	Loadings
Guatemala	.78	Norway	−.92
El Salvador	.68	Ireland	−.92
Panama	.68	W. Germany	−.92
Peru	.68	Sweden	−.92
Honduras	.67	Australia	−.92
Argentina	.66	Netherlands	−.91
Korea Rep.	.65	Denmark	−.91
Nicaragua	.64	New Zealand	−.91
Ecuador	.59	Finland	−.90
Lebanon	.59	Switzerland	−.87
Paraguay	.58	Italy	−.86
Iraq	.57	UK	−.86
Haiti	.53	US	−.86
Thailand	.50	Canada	−.85
Indonesia	.35	Belgium	−.84
		Costa Rica	−.81
		Uruguay	−.81
Centrist		Japan	−.79
		Greece	−.77
Bulgaria	.90	Israel	−.75
Albania	.89	France	−.75
E. Germany	.88	Chile	−.74
Hungary	.86	Dom. Rep.	−.74
Mongolia	.86	Philippines	−.73
Czechoslovakia	.86	Turkey	−.72
N. Korea	.85	Columbia	−.66
USSR	.85	Mexico	−.65
Rumania	.84	Venezuela	−.63
Poland	.83	India	−.62
Yugoslavia	.82	Brazil	−.62
Spain	.80	Bolivia	−.57
Portugal	.77	S. Africa	−.55
China	.76	Ceylon	−.50
Cuba	.69		
Afghanistan	.64		
Saudi Arabia	.63		
UAR	.62		
Liberia	.58		
Jordan	.58		
Nepal	.53		
Ethiopia	.52		
Iran	.48		
Pakistan	.48		
Cambodia	.47		
Burma	.41		

results in the grouping of nations according to similarities across certain political variables. Of the five groupings of nations which emerged from that analysis, the three labelled personalist, centrist, and polyarchic were found to be useful in the present context. These groupings, along with their factor loadings, are presented in table 3.

The personalist group is composed of fifteen nations and is by far the smallest of the three. Ten of the fifteen nations are Latin American, three are Asian, and two are Middle Eastern. To a large degree, the nations which make up this group are dictatorships of one sort or another but differ from the centrist group in degree of centralization.

The centrist group is composed of twenty-six nations. Twelve of these nations were communist regimes during the period under consideration, and these nations generally have the highest loadings. An additional four centrist nations are Middle Eastern. These nations, in general, exhibit both dictatorial and highly centralized leadership patterns.

The polyarchic group is composed of thirty-three nations. Virtually all of the nations correlating above 0.80 with this factor are economically developed western nations. Furthermore, those nations with lower loadings (below 0.80) usually exhibit at least one of the above characteristics.

Correlations between all possible pairs of domestic and foreign conflict behavior factors are computed for the total undifferentiated groups of nations, as well as within each of the three groups. These results are presented in tables 4 and 5. *Negative lags* (lag = -1, lag = -2) are the cases in which foreign conflict preceded domestic conflict by one or two years, respectively. *Positive lags* (lag = $+1$, lag = $+2$) are cases in which domestic conflict preceded foreign conflict by one or two years, respectively. The lag = 0 case is one in which the correlation is computed between domestic and foreign conflict measured for the same year.

The results for the total group, reported in table 4, indicate that the belligerency type of foreign conflict is most highly associated with domestic conflict behavior. This result is in line with those found by Rummel, to the effect that there was a small positive association between domestic conflict and the more belligerent forms

TABLE 4 Correlations Between Pairs of Domestic and Foreign Conflict Behavior Factors

	TOTAL — ALL 74 NATIONS				
	lag = -2	lag = -1	lag = 0	lag = $+1$	lag = $+2$
Int-War	.03	.01	.08	.08	.12*
Int-Bel	$-.02$	.10	.12*	.15**	.14*
Int-Dip	$-.10$	$-.14**$	$-.11$	$-.07$	$-.07$
Tur-War	.05	.02	.07	$-.02$	.07
Tur-Bel	.09	.11*	.16**	.18***	.12*
Tur-Dip	.11	.17***	.16**	.06	.10
	N = 296	N = 370	N = 444	N = 370	N = 296

Negative lags indicate the occurrence of foreign before domestic, and positive lags indicate the occurrence of domestic before foreign. Lag = 0 measures both indicators for the same year.

*   p < .05
**   p < .01
*** p < .001

TABLE 5   Correlations Between Pairs of Domestic
and Foreign Conflict Behavior Factors

PERSONALIST

	lag = −2	lag = −1	lag = 0	lag = +1	lag = +2
Int-War	.15	−.08	−.08	−.15	−.30*
Int-Bel	.29*	.37**	.16	.28*	.29*
Int-Dip	.00	−.14	.18	.10	.00
Tur-War	.17	−.14	−.18	−.03	−.02
Tur-Bel	.11	.14	.11	.05	.17
Tur-Dip	−.05	.26*	.24*	−.02	−.05
	N = 60	N = 75	N = 90	N = 75	N = 60

CENTRIST

	lag = −2	lag = −1	lag = 0	lag = +1	lag = +2
Int-War	.11	.15	.31***	.32***	.43***
Int-Bel	−.11	.02	.12	.09	.15
Int-Dip	−.07	−.17	−.13	−.01	.00
Tur-War	−.08	.02	.05	−.16	−.14
Tur-Bel	.06	.03	.12	.28**	.15
Tur-Dip	−.05	.08	.03	.03	.04
	N = 104	N = 130	N = 156	N = 130	N = 104

POLYARCHIC

	lag = −2	lag = −1	lag = 0	lag = +1	lag = +2
Int-War	.00	−.05	−.04	.00	.00
Int-Bel	−.15	−.03	.02	.00	−.09
Int-Dip	−.11	−.08	−.16*	−.13	−.08
Tur-War	.17	.12	.21**	.13	.32***
Tur-Bel	.16	.18*	.23**	.19*	.07
Tur-Dip	.19*	.21**	.23**	.13	.19*
	N = 132	N = 165	N = 198	N = 165	N = 132

Negative lags indicate the occurrence of foreign before domestic, and positive lags indicate the occurrence of domestic before foreign. Lag = 0 measures both indicators for the same year.

* p < .05
** p < .01
*** p < .001

of foreign conflict behavior (Rummel, 1963b). The belligerency factor exhibits an additional pattern of note. In its relationship with the turmoil type of domestic conflict, both positive and negative lags produce significant correlations. Thus, belligerency not only precedes turmoil but also follows turmoil. This pattern of mutual reinforcement reappears for some of the individual groups and may be an instance of what Rosenau, in his work on linkage politics, had referred to as a "fused relationship" (Rosenau, 1969). Domestic conflict may lead to foreign conflict, and foreign conflict may lead to domestic conflict, in such a way that the two phenomena cannot be clearly distinguished from each other.

In regard to the total results, we can note some interesting relationships. However, the small size of the correlation coefficients indicates that these observed relationships are not particularly strong. We will now analyze separately the data for the three individual groups of nations, in order to ascertain whether the relationship between domestic and foreign conflict behavior varies among the three groups.

It will be useful to approach the group results from a perspective of pointing up the differences which can be noted between the three groups of nations, as well as pointing up the differences between the grouped and ungrouped results. For the personalist group, there are two characteristics which stand out and which are unique to it. First, the type of foreign conflict classified as war produces no positive relationships with either type of domestic conflict behavior. Both the centrist and the polyarchic groups exhibit various types of relationships between war and the domestic conflict factors. It is interesting to note, however, that for none of the three groups does the occurrence of war, the most violent foreign conflict factor, systematically precede the occurrence of any type of domestic conflict behavior.

A second result of note for the personalist group is that internal war and belligerency are related for both positive and negative lags. Thus, it was found that belligerency may both precede and follow the occurrence of internal war. Not only is this pattern of mutual reinforcement not found in the other two groups, but these two variables are totally unrelated for the centrist and polyarchic nations.

In general, the personalist group exhibits fewer relationships between domestic and foreign conflict than were apparent in the total group. However, the magnitude of these results has increased sharply over those for the total case. In particular, three results stand out as being different from the total case. First, the personalist nations exhibit a fairly strong negative relationship between the prior occurrence of internal war and the subsequent occurrence of war. The personalist nations, being generally the smallest and perhaps the weakest of the three groups, cannot react in a violent manner externally to a violent type of domestic conflict. Thus, the occurrence of violent domestic conflict may necessitate the pulling back from any violent foreign aggressiveness. Second, the fused relationship between internal war and belligerency is not apparent in the total group. Finally, there was one case, for internal war and belligerency, which exhibited a significant correlation for a two-year negative lag, whereas none appeared for the total group.

The centrist group also exhibits certain unique characteristics. There is a positive relationship between the occurrence of internal war and war for both the lag = 0 and for the two positive lags. While these two factors are completely unrelated in the case of the polyarchic nations, they produce a negative correlation for the personalist group. This relationship is also missing from the total results. Thus, the centrist nations exhibit a tendency for the most violent form of domestic conflict to be associated with the co-occurrence of the most violent form of foreign conflict.

Regarding the relationship between internal war and war, it is interesting to note that the strength of the relationship increases with an increase in the time lag. If what we are observing here is a propensity for centrist nations to react externally to internal problems, then there appears to be both an immediate and delayed response. Thus, the war type of foreign conflict behavior may be a tool in the hands of the leadership of a centrist nation for diverting the attention of the population from domestic disorders.

The above contention is additionally supported by the results for the negative lags, which indicate that prior foreign conflict is never systematically associated with subsequent domestic conflict. The leadership groups of centrist nations need not necessarily fear any domestic conflict repercussions resulting from their foreign conflict behavior. This result is unique to the centrist nations and is apparently an attribute of the type of governmental structures with which they operate.

For the polyarchic group, two interesting and unique characteristics are noted. First, the internal war type of domestic conflict behavior, which is the more violent of the two factors, has no positive relationships with any of the foreign conflict factors. This may indicate that in a democratic type regime, when internal disorders become severe, any attention which might have been devoted to the external sphere must be redirected internally.

A second finding for the polyarchic group is that the turmoil-war pair produces significant positive correlations. These two factors are completely unrelated in both the personalist and centrist groups.

With these findings, we conclude Stage 2 of the study. We have noted that whereas the undifferentiated total group of nations exhibited very weak relationships between domestic and foreign conflict behavior, these results were substantially strengthened when the control was introduced for type of nation. Furthermore, there was a great deal of variation between the individual groups of nations, pointing up the fact that governmental type may in fact influence the conflict behavior process. The generally small magnitude of the correlation coefficients, however, indicates that we have not yet explained a great deal of the variance in the conflict behavior in one sphere on the basis of conflict behavior in the other. Stage 3, which concentrates on the Markov properties of domestic and foreign conflict behavior, will add additional clarification to the relationships we have already observed.

Stage 3 — Markov Chain Analysis

In Stage 3, a Markov chain analysis is performed in order to investigate more carefully the nature of certain of the relationships between domestic and foreign conflict behavior which were observed in the correlation analysis. The primary assumption involved in this analysis is that a nation's level of foreign conflict behavior in a given year is determined in part by the operation of two factors: (1) the level of domestic conflict experienced by that nation in the prior year, and (2) the previous year's level of foreign conflict behavior. As was the case earlier, we will continue to control for type of nation.

The underlying assumption is that while foreign conflict levels may be dependent upon previous levels of domestic conflict, foreign conflict is engaged in within the context of the previous levels of foreign conflict. The model for this analysis, then, can be represented as follows:

$$F_n, D_n \rightarrow F_{n+1}$$

where F_n represents the nation's previous level of foreign conflict, D_n represents the previous level of domestic conflict, and F_{n+1} represents the subsequent level of foreign conflict, presumably revised on the basis of F_n and D_n.[2]

---

2. It is of course possible to postulate a similar model for domestic conflict, i.e.,

$$D_n, F_n, \rightarrow D_{n+1}$$

This model was explored in an earlier study (Wilkenfeld, 1969a), but its inclusion here would unduly lengthen the discussion.

The question which can be answered through the use of Markov chain analysis is the relative weight which should be assigned to each of these two factors in the final determination of a nation's level of foreign conflict behavior. This will be accomplished by holding one of the two factors constant, and observing the effect of the remaining one upon the subsequent level of foreign conflict. First, the model implies that for a given level of domestic conflict behavior, the nation's subsequent level of foreign conflict behavior is only a function of its previous level of foreign conflict. Thus, when D_n is held constant, it is postulated that F_n is a first order Markov chain. That is, when D_n is fixed, it is assumed that the probability of F_{n+1} depends upon F_n and only on F_n. The set of analyses which investigate the effects of F_n on F_{n+1}, when D_n is held constant, is called the *order test*.

The second aspect of the model deals with the effects of domestic conflict on subsequent foreign conflict. It is assumed that the transitions of foreign conflict levels from one year to the next are solely dependent upon the level of domestic conflict involved. In assuming that the probability of changing from one level of foreign conflict to another depends upon the prior level of domestic conflict, the analysis is similar to the positive lags investigated in the correlation analysis. The major difference here is that the effect of domestic conflict levels on foreign conflict levels is investigated while holding the prior level of foreign conflict constant. The set of analyses which investigates the effect of D_n on F_{n+1}, when F_n is held constant, is called the *equality test*.

The data for the Markov portion of the study will once again be the factor scores which emerged from the factor analysis of the 1955–1960 domestic and foreign conflict behavior variables. For purposes of testing the model, it is necessary to convert these factor scores into levels of intensity of conflict behavior. The $D = 0$ (domestic) and $F = 0$ (foreign) levels are those levels in which, for a given year, the factor scores indicate that there is either no domestic or no foreign conflict of the type grouped by the particular factor being considered. It was less easy to define levels one and two of intensity. The factor scores were plotted for each factor, using the smallest reasonable interval. An inspection of these plots indicates an appropriate point at which the intensity of conflict becomes quite high, while at the same time, the number of cases at this level drops sharply. It is this point which is chosen to differentiate between levels one and two, for each particular factor.

The definition of levels of intensity enables us to investigate the transitions in conflict behavior from one year to the next. These transitions are investigated by arranging the data in three-by-three transition matrices. These matrices allow us to ascertain the probability associated with moving from one level of foreign conflict to another under several different circumstances.

As an example, let us take the polyarchic group and examine the transition matrices for the situation in which the domestic conflict factor is internal war and the foreign conflict factor is diplomatic. In terms of the model, this is equivalent to the statement:

$$\text{Diplomatic}_n, \text{ Internal War}_n \rightarrow \text{Diplomatic}_{n+1}$$

The transition matrices for the polyarchic group for this case are as shown in table 6.

Internal War$_n$ = 0 Diplomatic$_{n+1}$	Internal War$_n$ = 1 Diplomatic$_{n+1}$	Internal War$_n$ = 2 Diplomatic$_{n+1}$

TABLE 6

		0	1	2			0	1	2			0	1	2	
	0	.63 / 33	.37 / 19	.00 / 0	52	0	.55 / 12	.41 / 9	.05 / 1	22	0	.40 / 2	.60 / 3	.00 / 0	5
Dip_n	1	.23 / 11	.69 / 33	.08 / 4	48	1	.20 / 4	.65 / 13	.15 / 3	20	1	.50 / 2	.50 / 2	.00 / 0	4
	2	.25 / 3	.25 / 3	.50 / 6	12	2	.50 / 1	.00 / 0	.50 / 1	2	2	.00 / 0	.00 / 0	.00 / 0	0
		$N = 112$					$N = 44$					$N = 9$			

The number in the upper left hand corner of a cell is the proportion of cases in that cell, summing to 1.00 across the rows. The number in the lower right hand corner of a cell is the actual frequency. The first matrix contains the transitions in the diplomatic type of foreign conflict behavior from year n to year $n + 1$ when the level of internal war in year n is held constant at level zero. The second matrix again shows the transitions in diplomatic, when internal war in year n is held constant at level one. Finally, the last matrix holds internal war in year n constant at level two.

Moving back to the first matrix, we can now note that the proportion in a cell can be interpreted as the probability of a particular transition in foreign conflict from year n to year $n + 1$. Thus, there is a probability of 0.63 that if the level of diplomatic was zero in year n, it will remain at level zero in year $n + 1$ in those cases where internal war in year n is also zero. There is a probability of 0.37 that the nation will move up to level one of diplomatic, and a probability of 0.00 that it will move up to level two.

(1) Order Test

It will be recalled that the order test is designed to test the null hypothesis that the rows of the transition matrix come from the same distribution. In the present situation, this is equivalent to saying that if domestic conflict in year n is held constant, the level of foreign conflict in year n has no systematic effect on the level of foreign conflict in year $n + 1$.

In order to test this null hypothesis, chi square tests were performed on the six sets of transition matrices for each of the three groups of nations. The results of these tests are presented in tables 7 and 8. The rows of these tables represent the

TABLE 7   Chi Square Test of the Order Properties of the Total Transition Matrices

	$D = 0$				$D = 1$				$D = 2$				Total			
	χ^2	p	df	N	χ^2	p	df	N	χ^2	p	df	N	χ^2	p	df	N
Int-War	43.720	.000	4	232	28.392	.000	4	95	29.664	.000	4	43	101.776	.000	12	370
Int-Bel	30.949	.000	4	232	21.281	.000	4	95	10.728	.029	4	43	62.958	.000	12	370
Int-Dip	75.893	.000	4	232	19.164	.001	4	95	2.602	.630	4	43	97.659	.000	12	370
Tur-War	84.978	.000	4	198	37.200	.000	4	122	7.453	.113	4	50	129.631	.000	12	370
Tur-Bel	13.241	.010	4	198	26.107	.000	4	122	11.893	.018	4	50	51.241	.000	12	370
Tur-Dip	43.434	.000	4	198	37.746	.000	4	122	9.166	.056	4	50	90.346	.000	12	370

six different tests of the model with the various possible pairings of the two domestic and three foreign conflict factors. The first three columns give the results of the chi square test of each of the individual transition matrices. The total column gives the total chi square as summed over all three individual matrices.

Table 7 presents the results of the order test performed on the total transition matrices. The first thing to be noted is that when the level of domestic conflict is zero or one, all the matrices produce statistically significant results. Furthermore, when domestic conflict is at level two, three of the six chi squares are significant, while an additional two are approaching significance at the .05 level.

These results indicate a rather strong relationship between foreign conflict behavior in one year and foreign conflict behavior in the next. Thus, we can reject the null hypothesis that the rows of the transition matrices are the same. What we are finding is that it may be possible to predict the level of foreign conflict behavior of a nation if we have knowledge of its prior level of foreign conflict. This finding is a rather interesting addition to the earlier correlation results between domestic and foreign conflict, where only a very small relationship was noted.

Turning now to table 8, and taking the results in the reverse order, we can note that for the polyarchic group, when prior domestic conflict is held constant at levels zero or one, there is a strong relationship between prior and subsequent levels of foreign conflict behavior. We might speculate that in these predominantly large, economically developed, and for the most part open societies, changes in the level of foreign conflict from year to year do not occur with a great deal of ease. Once a nation of this type becomes committed to a certain level of conflict behavior, it tends to remain at that level in the following year.

It is interesting to note that the above generalization does not hold equally well for all three levels at which domestic conflict is held constant. When domestic conflict is at level two, there is an apparent lessening of the relationship between prior and subsequent levels of foreign conflict. It would appear that when these nations are experiencing a high level of domestic violence, they are unable to sustain previously high levels of foreign violence.

For the centrist group, we find that when the level of domestic conflict is held constant at level zero, there is a pronounced relationship between prior and subsequent levels of foreign conflict. This relationship does not hold when domestic conflict is at levels one and two. Thus, when the centrist type of political system is experiencing domestic unrest of some sort, at any level, they may be unable to sustain prior levels of foreign conflict behavior. This was the case with the polyarchic nations only when domestic conflict was at its highest level.

The results for the personalist group indicate that there is no apparent relationship between the level of foreign conflict in year n and the level of foreign conflict in year $n + 1$. Thus, none of the individual transition matrices produces significant chi squares. One is led to speculate that there is something in the makeup of the personalist nations which allows them a relatively higher degree of freedom in the exercise of foreign policy than is apparent among the centrist and polyarchic nations. Perhaps the outstanding feature of this table is that it indicates that in the polyarchic case, and to a certain extent in the centrist case, there is a tendency to perpetuate policies from one year to the next, at least in the area of foreign conflict behavior. Since we have examples here of both open and closed political systems, it would appear that at least in this one area, the two types of nations are similar.

TABLE 8 Chi Square Test of the Order Properties of the Personalist Transition Matrices

	$D = 0$				$D = 1$				$D = 2$				Total			
	χ^2	p	df	N	χ^2	p	df	N	χ^2	p	df	N	χ^2	p	df	N
Int-War	1.392	.846	4	33	5.137	.272	4	22	1.319	.249	1	20	7.848	.550	9	75
Int-Bel	4.875	.300	4	33	2.187	.705	4	22	7.446	.113	4	20	14.509	.269	12	75
Int-Dip	0.029	.842	1	33	1.523	.529	2	22	0.381	.826	2	20	1.933	.859	5	75
Tur-War	0.688	.714	2	23	5.431	.245	4	40	0.000	1.000	1	12	6.119	.527	7	75
Tur-Bel	5.951	.202	4	23	6.909	.140	4	40	1.500	.828	4	12	14.360	.278	12	75
Tur-Dip	3.486	.058	1	23	1.001	.612	2	40	5.467	.063	2	12	9.954	.076	5	75

Chi Square Test of the Order Properties of the Centrist Transition Matrices

	$D = 0$				$D = 1$				$D = 2$				Total			
	χ^2	p	df	N	χ^2	p	df	N	χ^2	p	df	N	χ^2	p	df	N
Int-War	16.656	.003	4	87	5.220	.264	4	29	8.585	.071	4	14	30.462	.003	12	130
Int-Bel	25.106	.000	4	87	5.674	.224	4	29	2.794	.596	4	14	33.574	.001	12	130
Int-Dip	25.845	.000	4	87	9.247	.054	4	29	3.194	.528	4	14	38.286	.000	12	130
Tur-War	37.351	.000	4	88	12.768	.012	4	30	3.429	.509	4	12	53.548	.000	12	130
Tur-Bel	11.315	.023	4	88	5.871	.208	4	30	12.300	.015	4	12	29.487	.004	12	130
Tur-Dip	16.014	.003	4	88	9.061	.059	4	30	12.018	.017	4	12	37.093	.000	12	130

Chi Square Test of the Order Properties of the Polyarchic Transition Matrices

	$D = 0$				$D = 1$				$D = 2$				Total			
	χ^2	p	df	N	χ^2	p	df	N	χ^2	p	df	N	χ^2	p	df	N
Int-War	34.530	.000	4	112	33.671	.000	4	44	0.735	.604	1	9	68.936	.000	9	165
Int-Bel	24.319	.000	4	112	22.456	.000	4	44	9.562	.048	4	9	56.337	.000	12	165
Int-Dip	44.897	.000	4	112	9.330	.052	4	44	0.090	.758	1	9	54.317	.000	9	165
Tur-War	59.052	.000	4	87	23.869	.000	4	52	9.425	.050	4	26	92.346	.000	12	165
Tur-Bel	6.304	.041	2	87	31.055	.000	4	52	4.090	.395	4	26	41.448	.000	10	165
Tur-Dip	17.050	.002	4	87	22.381	.000	4	52	7.525	.109	4	26	46.955	.000	12	165

On the other hand, the personalist nations, being somewhat in between the ideal types of open and closed systems, while at the the same time being less economically developed and generally smaller in size, tend not to be under as many constraints concerning the perpetuation of policy from year to year.[3]

---

3. Extensions of the chi square analysis involve a thorough examination of the probabilities involved in transitions from one level of conflict behavior to another. These analyses allow us to examine the directions of the postulated relationships, whereas the chi square can only indicate strength of relationships. Once again, due to their length, these analyses cannot be presented here. The interested reader is referred to Wilkenfeld (1969a) and Zinnes and Wilkenfeld (1971).

(2) Equality Test

The equality test is designed to examine more closely the relationship between prior domestic conflict and subsequent foreign conflict. In holding the level of prior foreign conflict constant, we will be able to observe the effect of prior domestic conflict on subsequent foreign conflict. The matrices which are analyzed are constructed by pulling off the $F = 0$ rows from the $D_n = 0$, $D_n = 1$, and $D_n = 2$ matrices, thereby forming a new three-by-three matrix. This same procedure is followed for the $F = 1$ and the $F = 2$ rows. The null hypothesis being tested is that there is no difference between the three rows of the equality matrix. In other words, prior domestic conflict has no influence upon the subsequent level of foreign conflict behavior. The results of the equality test are presented in tables 9 and 10.

Table 9 presents the results of the equality test for the total group. In contra-

TABLE 9   Chi Square Test of the Equality Properties
of the Total Transition Matrices

	$F = 0$				$F = 1$				$F = 2$				Total			
	χ^2	p	df	N	χ^2	p	df	N	χ^2	p	df	N	χ^2	p	df	N
Int-War	7.024	.113	4	207	2.611	.628	4	132	4.987	.288	4	31	14.622	.262	12	370
Int-Bel	5.137	.273	4	161	10.931	.027	4	180	4.117	.391	4	29	20.184	.063	12	370
Int-Dip	6.961	.137	4	166	3.017	.557	4	177	7.508	.110	4	27	17.486	.132	12	370
Tur-War	2.776	.599	4	207	4.992	.287	4	132	6.851	.143	4	31	14.619	.262	12	370
Tur-Bel	16.153	.003	4	161	2.399	.666	4	180	8.725	.067	4	29	27.277	.007	12	370
Tur-Dip	4.025	.404	4	166	5.001	.286	4	177	2.191	.704	4	27	11.216	.511	12	370

distinction to the results for the order test, here only two of the chi squares for individual matrices are significant. The obvious conclusion to be drawn is that when the level of prior foreign conflict is held constant, domestic conflict has little if any effect upon the subsequent level of foreign conflict.

Despite the general finding of no relationship, there are two pairs of domestic and foreign factors which indicate a tendency in this direction. These cases are turmoil-belligerency and internal war-belligerency. Of the three types of foreign conflict behavior, belligerency appears to be affected by both types of domestic conflict behavior. This finding is entirely consistent with the correlation results obtained earlier for the total group. There we found that for the lag $= +1$ case, which is roughly equivalent to the present analysis, the belligerency factor was the only one which produced significant relationships with prior domestic conflict. Whereas the correlation results indicated only a general relationship, that relationship is further refined in the Markov analysis. These results indicate that turmoil at level zero or level two affects the subsequent level of belligerency. Furthermore, internal war at level one affects subsequent belligerency. In all other cases, both the correlation and Markov analysis indicate no additional relationships.

The results for the polyarchic group reported in table 10 indicate only one significant chi square, between internal war and belligerency, for the case in which the level of foreign conflict is held constant at level one. The evidence in the rest of the table for the polyarchic group indicates that the level of foreign conflict behavior

TABLE 10   Chi Square Test of the Equality Properties of the Transition Matrices

PERSONALIST

	$F = 0$				$F = 1$				$F = 2$				Total			
	χ^2	p	df	N	χ^2	p	df	N	χ^2	p	df	N	χ^2	p	df	N
Int-War	4.755	.313	4	46	3.201	.527	4	26	0.750	.609	1	3	8.706	.534	9	75
Int-Bel	6.285	.178	4	28	5.570	.232	4	37	2.222	.330	2	10	14.077	.169	10	75
Int-Dip	2.593	.273	2	35	5.785	.214	4	39	0.000	—	0	1	8.378	.211	6	75
Tur-War	2.400	.666	4	46	2.366	.672	4	26	0.750	.609	1	3	5.516	.788	9	75
Tur-Bel	7.200	.124	4	28	1.330	.857	4	37	1.667	.562	2	10	10.197	.424	10	75
Tur-Dip	4.998	.080	2	35	5.191	.267	4	39	0.000	—	0	1	10.188	.116	6	75

CENTRIST

	$F = 0$				$F = 1$				$F = 2$				Total			
	χ^2	p	df	N	χ^2	p	df	N	χ^2	p	df	N	χ^2	p	df	N
Int-War	9.735	.044	4	56	3.646	.542	4	57	2.590	.632	4	17	15.972	.192	12	130
Int-Bel	2.491	.650	4	58	4.593	.331	4	60	5.900	.206	4	12	12.984	.370	12	130
Int-Dip	4.460	.347	4	52	1.986	.742	4	66	4.222	.377	4	12	10.668	.558	12	130
Tur-War	2.643	.622	4	56	6.563	.160	4	57	7.910	.094	4	17	17.116	.145	12	130
Tur-Bel	12.584	.014	4	58	6.865	.142	4	60	8.670	.069	4	12	28.119	.006	12	130
Tur-Dip	2.827	.590	4	52	1.519	.825	4	66	1.792	.777	4	12	6.137	.909	12	130

POLYARCHIC

	$F = 0$				$F = 1$				$F = 2$				Total			
	χ^2	p	df	N	χ^2	p	df	N	χ^2	p	df	N	χ^2	p	df	N
Int-War	1.687	.566	2	105	4.174	.383	4	49	2.357	.121	1	11	8.218	.313	7	165
Int-Bel	6.544	.161	4	75	24.078	.000	4	83	0.875	.652	2	7	31.497	.001	10	165
Int-Dip	3.800	.565	4	79	2.563	.637	4	72	0.875	.652	2	14	7.238	.704	10	165
Tur-War	4.806	.088	2	105	3.494	.519	4	49	4.302	.114	2	11	12.602	.126	8	165
Tur-Bel	6.663	.154	4	75	5.091	.277	4	83	0.194	.663	1	7	11.949	.216	9	165
Tur-Dip	6.671	.153	4	79	7.997	.091	4	72	4.475	.345	4	14	19.143	.085	12	165

is unrelated to the prior level of domestic conflict behavior. It is interesting to note that the correlation results for the lag $= +1$ case produced only one significant result also, but not the same one as reported here.

For the centrist group, when prior foreign conflict is held constant at level zero, there are significant chi squares between internal war and war and between turmoil and belligerency. These findings match those obtained earlier in the correlation analysis for the centrist group. The Markov results, in this instance, further refine the correlation results. From this, it is possible to note the levels of conflict behavior which affect conflict in the other sphere.

Finally, the results for the personalist group indicate no significant relationships between prior domestic and subsequent foreign conflict behavior. Once again, the correlation results, which produced one significant relationship for the comparable stage of the analysis, do not match the Markov results.

It would be worthwhile at this point to attempt to summarize the results which were obtained in Stage 3 of the analysis. In the order test, we found that for the centrist and polyarchic nations, there was a very strong tendency for foreign conflict levels to be related to each other from year to year. That is, the level of foreign conflict in which a nation engages must always be viewed within the context of prior foreign conflict levels. As we have already noted, this finding has important implications for students of foreign policy decision making. The indication would seem to be that these types of nations may not be able to make sudden and extreme changes in the level of foreign violence from year to year.

The Markov results for the personalist group indicate that prior and subsequent levels of foreign conflict behavior are virtually unrelated to each other. This result is in sharp contrast to the other two groups of nations and may indicate a much different decision-making structure in these nations.

Conclusion

One is struck initially with the wide variety of results which have been presented here. It seems that many of the results are conflicting, and yet they come from the same data base. In this concluding section, I will attempt to resolve some of these problems and indicate the importance of the results.

We can note initially that there are some very real differences between the three types of nations. While all three types of nations exhibit relationships between domestic and foreign conflict behavior in the correlation analysis, different types of conflict behavior are involved. While both the personalist and polyarchic nations indicated conflict relationships in both directions, the centrist nations indicated that prior foreign conflict was never related to subsequent domestic conflict. Thus, the first important finding is that relationships between domestic and foreign conflict behavior do exist, and that they are at least in part a function of the type of nation under consideration. This finding is in contrast to the original Rummel and Tanter findings, based on an undifferentiated group of nations.

A second important finding relates to the relative weight to be assigned to prior levels of domestic and foreign conflict in determining the subsequent level of foreign conflict behavior. Here we have noted that for the centrist and polyarchic nations, the crucial variable in determining the subsequent level of foreign conflict is in fact the prior level of foreign conflict. All three groups exhibited very few instances in which prior domestic conflict levels were related to subsequent foreign conflict levels.

The question arises as to how the apparent conflict between the correlation and Markov results might be resolved. The Markov results might be viewed as a further refinement of the original correlation results. The fact that the results from the two analyses are not completely in line with each other is at least partially a product of the different levels of measurement involved in the two different statistics. The combined findings clearly point to the fact that conflict behavior in one sphere does not occur in a vacuum completely isolated from either conflict in the other sphere or prior conflict levels.

References

Banks, Arthur S., and Gregg, Phillip M. "Grouping Political Systems: Q-Factor Analysis of *A Cross-Polity Survey.*" *The American Behavioral Scientist* 9 (November 1965).

Banks, Arthur S., and Textor, Robert B. *A Cross-Polity Survey.* Cambridge: M.I.T. Press, 1963.

Blau, Peter M. *Exchange and Power in Social Life.* New York: John Wiley, 1964.

Coser, Lewis. *The Functions of Social Conflict.* New York: The Free Press, 1956.

Denton, Frank H. "Some Regularities in International Conflict, 1820–1949." *Background*, February 1966.

Farrell, R. Barry. "Foreign Politics of Open and Closed Political Systems." In *Approaches to Comparative and International Politics*, ed. R. Barry Farrell. Evanston, Ill.: Northwestern University Press, 1966.

Haas, Ernst B., and Whiting, Allen S. *Dynamics of International Relations.* New York: McGraw-Hill, 1956.

Rosecrance, Richard. *Action and Reaction in World Politics.* Boston: Little, Brown, 1963.

Rosenau, James N. "Compatibility, Consensus, and an Emerging Political Science of Adaptation." *American Political Science Review*, December 1967.

———. "Pre-Theories and Theories of Foreign Policy." In *Approaches to Comparative and International Politics*, ed. R. Barry Farrell. Evanston, Ill.: Northwestern University Press, 1966.

———. "Toward the Study of National-International Linkages." In *Linkage Politics*, ed. James N. Rosenau. New York: The Free Press, 1969.

Rosenberg, Milton J. "Attitude Change and Foreign Policy in the Cold War Era." In *Domestic Sources of Foreign Policy*, ed. James N. Rosenau. New York: The Free Press, 1967.

Rummel, R. J. "Dimensions of Conflict Behavior Within and Between Nations." *General Systems Yearbook* VII (1963a).

———. "Testing Some Possible Predictors of Conflict Behavior Within and Between Nations." *Peace Research Society Papers*, 1963b.

Simmel, Georg. *Conflict and the Web of Group-Affiliation.* Glencoe, Ill.: The Free Press, 1955.

Tanter, Raymond. "Dimensions of Conflict Behavior Within and Between Nations, 1958–1960." *Journal of Conflict Resolution*, March 1966.

Wilkenfeld, Jonathan. "The Determinants of Domestic and Foreign Conflict Behavior of Nations." Doctoral dissertation, Indiana University, 1969a.

———. "Domestic and Foreign Conflict Behavior of Nations." *Journal of Peace Research* 1 (1968).

———. "Some Further Findings Regarding the Domestic and Foreign Conflict Behavior of Nations." *Journal of Peace Research* 2 (1969b).

Wright, Quincy. *A Study of War.* Chicago: University of Chicago Press, 1942.

Zinnes, Dina A., and Wilkenfeld, Jonathan. "An Analysis of Foreign Conflict Behavior of Nations." In *Comparative Foreign Policy: Theoretical Essays*, ed. Wolfram Hanrieder. New York: David McKay, 1971.

HERBERT F. WEISBERG
JERROLD RUSK

Dimensions of Candidate Evaluation*

*The following article is one of the few political
science research examples utilizing multidimensional scaling as an
analysis technique. In the text portion of this chapter we have elaborated
the details of this technique by tying it closely to an example of original
data analysis not unlike that presented by Weisberg and Rusk. Although
the text example presents more tables representing relationships between
variables, thereby showing the reader the complexity of computer solutions
in multidimensional scaling, this article presents findings in a
total research context where theory and previous findings are brought
to bear on the analysis.*

*The authors' basic purpose is to analyze the dimensional space of
candidate evaluations in the 1968 presidential election contest. Following
a correlational analysis of feelings toward the presidential candidates,
a unidimensional solution is presented (analogous to unfolding in one
dimension) and this is followed by a two-dimensional solution based on
stress criteria. This conceptual space then is enlarged by including*

Reprinted from Herbert F. Weisberg and Jerrold G. Rusk, "Dimensions of Candidate Evaluation,"
American Political Science Review 64 (1970): 1167–85, by permission of the American Political
Science Association and the authors.

*This is a revised version of a paper presented at the Annual Meeting of the American Political
Science Association, New York City, September, 1969. We are grateful to Warren E. Miller, George B.
Rabinowitz, and Stuart Rabinowitz for their valuable advice and comments. Professor Weisberg ac-
knowledges the fellowship support of the Horace H. Rackham School of Graduate Studies of The
University of Michigan during the preparation of this article. Professor Rusk was affiliated with the
University of Michigan's Survey Research Center as co-director of its 1968 election study at the time
this article was written. This paper is based on the Survey Research Center's 1968 election study which
was made possible by a grant from the Ford Foundation.

*measures of partisan identification and attitudes toward selected issues,
and a second two-dimensional solution depicts spatial relationships
between candidates, issues, and parties. The attribution of substantive
meaning is assisted through the use of mean scores for selected variables
compared to candidate evaluations and the correlations (eta) between
candidate evaluations, issues, and partisanship.*

The story of a presidential election year is in many ways the story of the actions and interactions of those considered as possible candidates for their nation's highest office. If this is true in the abstract, it certainly was true in the election of 1968. The political headlines of 1968 were captured by those who ran for the nominations of their parties, those who pondered over whether or not to run, those who chose to pull out of the race or were struck down during the campaign, those who raised a third party banner, and those who resisted suggestions to run outside the two-party structure. While 1968 may have been unusual in the extent to which many prospective candidates dominated the political scene, every presidential election is, in its own way, highlighted by those considered for the office of President.

The political scientist has shown scholarly interest in the candidates. His interest, however, has been selective in its focus — mainly concentrating on the two actual party nominees and not the larger set of possible presidential candidates. Research in electoral behavior has detailed the popular image of the nominees in terms of the public's reactions to their record and experience, personal qualities, and party affiliation. Furthermore, attitudes toward the nominees have been shown to constitute a major short-term influence on the vote.[1] Yet attitudes toward other candidates have been surveyed only to ascertain the behavior of those people who favored someone other than the ultimate nominees. The focus in the discipline remains on the nominees — feelings toward them and willingness to accept them.

As research moves from an exclusive concern with explanation of the election outcomes, more scholarly attention should be given to popular attitudes toward the full spectrum of possible candidates. Much remains to be learned about voters' perceptions of the candidates. We still know very little about the psychological dimensions of meaning involved in how an individual perceives, reacts to, and evaluates a set of candidates. We know little about the more general organizing concepts a person uses in developing the specific perceptions and reactions described in contemporary voting and public opinion surveys. In this paper, we shall seek a dimensional interpretation of the individual's perceptions of and preferences for candidates. Extending the set of candidates beyond the bounds of the two nominees allows us to search out broader meanings of candidate evaluation.

While little is known about the factors leading to differing patterns of candidate evaluation, the voting behavior literature suggests a variety of factors as relevant guidelines in any initial inquiries. The most obvious long-term factor is partisan

---

1. See, for example, A. Campbell, G. Gurin, and W. E. Miller, *The Voter Decides* (Evanston, Ill.: Row, Peterson, 1954); A. Campbell, P. E. Converse, W. E. Miller, and D. E. Stokes, *The American Voter* (New York: John Wiley and Sons, 1960); D. E. Stokes, "Some Dynamic Elements of Contests for the Presidency," *American Political Science Review*, 60 (March 1966), 19–28.

identification. This psychological attachment to party has been treated as a major influence on the vote and research has shown that it can color voters' perceptions of the nominees. The various twists such a factor can take with a larger set of candidates will be a continuing theme of this paper.

Additional factors which may affect candidate evaluation include a person's ideology, the issues of the day, and the personality of the candidates. The crucial task is to distinguish which of these factors are important. A related theoretical question is the number of dimensions used as bases for candidate evaluation.

The pioneering work on the modelling of party competition by Anthony Downs was based on a unidimensional ideological continuum.[2] As Stokes has pointed out, Downs's notion of a unidimensional political space is only an assumption, since party competition could instead easily roam over a multidimensional space.[3] The problem of the number of dimensions should be seen as an empirical question. Evidence from surveys indicates that the American public often sees issues in multidimensional terms. Most researchers using dimensional analysis techniques on European multi-party systems have also found the assumption of a single ideological dimension to be inadequate. A prime example is Converse's skillful analysis of the French political scene which found two dimensions being used for the evaluation of that country's many parties.[4] Exploration of the dimensionality of perceptions of candidates in the United States may be one means of testing the dimensionality of the competition space within which national choices of leadership are made.

I. The Thermometer Question

The specific focus of this study will be on individual reactions to a set of twelve candidates for national office. Data will be taken from the interviews of over one thousand respondents in the 1968 election study of the University of Michigan's Survey Research Center. A measure was needed to obtain the feelings of the respondents toward the several candidates. We felt that the respondent should be allowed to use those dimensions which come naturally to him, which are his normal guidelines for thinking about candidates. By obtaining such responses without imposing a frame of reference, it becomes possible in the analysis to deduce the dimensions of importance in the thought of individuals. We have employed a measuring device called the "feeling thermometer" which provides one such neutrally worded means of eliciting responses to a wide variety of candidates.

Basically a "feeling thermometer" is a question asking respondents to indicate on a 0-to-100-degree temperature scale how warm or cold they feel toward a set of objects — in this case, candidates.[5] If a person feels particularly warm or favorable

2. A. Downs, *An Economic Theory of Democracy* (New York: Harper and Brothers, 1957).

3. D. E. Stokes, "Spatial Models of Party Competition," *American Political Science Review*, 57 (June 1963), 368–377.

4. P. E. Converse, "The Problem of Party Distances in Models of Voting Change," in M. K. Jennings and L. H. Zeigler (eds.), *The Electoral Process* (Englewood Cliffs, N.J.: Prentice-Hall, 1966).

5. The thermometer question followed the basic format devised by A. R. Clausen for previous Survey Research Center studies, but was revised by the authors to apply to candidates rather than groups and to screen out "don't know" responses. The full wording of the question is given in the appendix at the end of this paper. For other analysis involving this question in the 1968 election study, see P. E. Converse, W. E. Miller, J. G. Rusk, and A. C. Wolfe, "Continuity and Change in American Politics," *American Political Science Review*, 63 (December 1969), 1083–1105.

toward a political figure, he would give that candidate a score somewhere between 50 and 100, depending on how warm his feeling was toward that candidate. If he felt cold or unfavorable toward that candidate, 0 to 50 degrees would be the appropriate scoring range. The actual score of 50 degrees was explained to the respondent to be for candidates about whom he felt neither particularly warm nor cold, a neutral point on the scale. To make the thermometer scale more concrete, a card listing nine temperatures throughout the scale range and their corresponding verbal meanings as to intensity of "hot" or "cold" feelings was handed to the respondent. A separate statement in the question wording attempted to elicit "don't know" responses to individual candidates when appropriate.

The twelve people the respondents were asked to rate on the feeling thermometer covered a wide range of possible presidential hopefuls and ideological streams. The names listed included the actual presidential nominees themselves — Nixon, Humphrey, and Wallace — and their vice-presidential running mates. Lyndon Johnson was included, being the incumbent President and considered at one time to be a candidate for reelection. The other five mentioned were the main presidential hopefuls discussed at length in the media who failed to get their parties' nominations — Eugene McCarthy, Ronald Reagan, Nelson Rockefeller, George Romney, and the late Robert Kennedy. This list is somewhat arbitrary, as any list of presidential hopefuls must be. Having the respondents rate twelve candidates is a reasonable task in a survey setting and yet provides enough information for a dimensional analysis of the candidate space. The vice-presidential nominees were included on a basically presidential-oriented list because of the use of the vice-presidential candidates as an issue in the 1968 campaign and the fact that they are increasingly considered to be an integral part of the presidential race.

The responses to the twelve candidates can initially be conceived of as indicating each individual's feelings toward each given candidate. Additionally, we shall interpret the relative scores given to the candidates as indicating a person's preference order for these twelve candidates. A respondent is assumed to prefer most the candidate to whom he gives the highest score, and so on. While it must be admitted that there may not be a perfect correspondence between an individuals' relative scores and his preference order, the use of the thermometer question constitutes one of the simplest means of obtaining preference orders over a large number of alternatives in a survey of the mass public. More conventional ranking of a dozen candidates would constitute a very difficult task for many respondents, whereas scoring the candidates on the thermometer scale was generally painless.

It should be pointed out that the thermometer question was asked *after* the election. This timing is likely to have affected the ratings of the candidates. A "bandwagon effect" in favor of president-elect Nixon must be considered likely. Humphrey was also probably evaluated much more favorably at this point of time than he would have been during the early part of the campaign, due to a combination of the increased party unity on his behalf and sympathy for his defeat. The tragedy of the assassination of Robert Kennedy could be expected to yield a more favorable rating for him than would have been obtained from a measurement during the period in which he was actively campaigning. Finally the vice-presidental candidates were probably near their peak of saliency at the moment of this study. The timing of the question will influence our measure of the relative appeal of the candidates, but we shall be able to minimize its effect on the dimensional analysis.

The first thing to explore about the data obtained from the thermometer question is their basic statistical parameters. By statistical parameters we mean the level of salience of the candidates and the differences in assessments of them as reflected in their central tendency and dispersion figures. Table 1 summarizes such descriptive features for the candidates included in the 1968 study.

TABLE 1   Summary of Candidate Thermometers

Candidate	Don't Know	50°	Standard Deviation	Mean	First Choice Mentions*	Last Choice Mentions*
Kennedy	1%	13%	26	70.1	43%	8%
Nixon	1	16	23	66.5	36	8
Humphrey	1	14	27	61.7	25	13
Muskie	8	31	22	61.4	16	10
Johnson	1	15	26	58.4	17	14
McCarthy	5	32	23	54.8	11	14
Rockefeller	4	30	22	53.8	9	15
Agnew	7	41	21	50.4	4	13
Reagan	5	34	22	49.1	5	17
Romney	8	46	19	49.0	3	15
LeMay	7	29	26	35.2	3	40
Wallace	2	13	31	31.4	11	62
N's	1315–1326	1210–1311	1210–1311	1210–1311	1304	1304

*These columns add up to more than 100 percent because a respondent could give the same highest or lowest score to several candidates.

An initial glance at the percentage of "don't know" replies in Table 1 comments to some extent on the salience of each candidate. The names of the candidates in 1968 were generally recognized by the public. The question was deliberately worded to invite "don't know" replies to the candidates when relevant, but very few were given. The greatest proportion of "don't know" responses was only 8 percent for Romney and Muskie. The only other candidates receiving more than 6 percent "don't know's" were the remaining vice-presidential candidates. In particular, Humphrey, Nixon, Wallace, Johnson, and Kennedy were nearly universally recognized.

Although the surface level of salience was high, a substantial number of the thermometer scores did not indicate whether the respondent felt particularly warm or cold toward a given candidate. A score of 50 degrees could indicate either ambivalent feelings or no opinion. The proportions of 50's for the presidental nominees, the incumbent President, and the late Senator Kennedy were all quite small, but the other candidates showed a sizable concentration of such scores. The large number of 50 scores reflects a substantial lack of affective feeling toward some of the candidates and, in turn, qualifies our earlier discussion of their saliency. Some of the candidates are perceived in the most superficial terms while others have a more central place in the respondents' cognitive structures. There appears to be a major threshold for public evaluation of the candidates which can be passed only through an event of great importance such as the actual nomination. This threshold has implications for the subsequent analysis in that the differences in evaluations of the candidates could be related to their differences in saliency.

In general, the candidates were favorably perceived. The mean values in Table 1 show that most of the twelve political figures were given thermometer scores greater than 50, the breakeven or neutral point on the scale.[6] Only George Wallace and his running mate Curtis LeMay scored significantly below 50. In fact over 60 percent of the sample gave George Wallace the lowest score that they gave to any of the candidates, a strong indication that he never succeeded in making a serious appeal to a majority of the electorate. On the popular side of the ledger, the late Robert Kennedy led the field. The two major presidential candidates also ranked high as did Humphrey's running mate. Lyndon Johnson was also seen in fairly postive terms.

The reasons for the generally positive perceptions are not completely clear and cannot be directly ascertained from the thermometer data. One necessary condition for a very favorable rating is the salience of the candidate. The candidates with the most favorable images were particularly well-known. A closely related argument is that the presidential race draws the better men in politics — men with a good image, record, and qualifications and the media publicity and coverage associated with these attributes. A third explanation might be the prestige and dignity associated with seeking the highest office in the land, though some deviant cases exist to question the generality of such a conclusion. Because the thermometer readings were taken after the election, it is difficult to know what explanation might best fit the major party nominees. They may have been nominated because of their public popularity or they may have achieved public popularity because of their nominations and the ensuing campaign and election.

As much as candidates were perceived favorably, individuals still were able to discriminate among those placed before them. Two types of discrimination resulted — variation of scores within candidates across all individuals and variation of an individual's scores across candidates. The standard deviation figures in Table 1 attest to the first type of discrimination. These figures show the considerable fluctuation in "feeling" recorded for each candidate across the set of respondents; such values range from 19 degrees for Romney to 31 degrees for Wallace. A case-by-case inspection reveals the second type of discrimination; the set of twelve candidates was invariably perceived differently by any given individual. The average extent of the range of scores given by a respondent was 73 degrees out of the possible 100. The standard deviation of the values given by the same respondent was 23 degrees, compared to a theoretical maximum of 50 degrees. These two types of discrimination provide the ingredients necessary to justify any analysis of candidate evaluations.

In general, the statistical parameters of the thermometer question point to the recognition and positive evaluation of the candidates along with considerable discrimination among them. A notion of those liked and disliked was gained — a popularity scale was indeed in evidence and it showed the critical position of the presidential nominees. But the basis of these evaluations is yet to be explored. A

---

6. Mean values of all the candidates were drawn closer to the break-even point of 50 on the scale because of use by some respondents of the score of 50 degrees to indicate no feeling about the candidates, a meaning which was other than the intended meaning of neutral feelings. The differential in means between Wallace and LeMay would be all but erased if this factor were corrected by removing all 50 responses while the Muskie-Humphrey difference would be dramatically reversed. If the candidates given large numbers of 50's were better known, it is possible that they would have been received in much more favorable or unfavorable terms as the public would have been better able to judge them.

search beyond the descriptive parameters of the thermometer scores to their underlying dimensions is needed in order to detect the antecedents of candidate evaluation.

II. The Candidate Space

We shall begin a consideration of the dimensional properties of candidate evaluation with an analysis of the three actual presidential nominees by themselves. It is reasonable to expect that their central position in the campaign would accord them critical positions in the overall candidate space which we seek to describe. Then we shall turn our attention to the full set of candidates as a means of noting the relative positions they are assigned in that space.

Table 2 indicates the relative frequencies for the various preference orders for the three nominees.[7] A basic question is whether a single dimension can account for these preferences. A necessary condition for unidimensionality is that all the preference orders end with only two of the alternatives. If the respondents do employ only a single dimension, then their last place choice must be one of the two extreme alternatives on that dimension.[8] If, on the other hand, more than two alternatives receive substantial numbers of last place choices, then multidimensionality of preferences is indicated. Inspection of Table 2 indicates that Nixon received only 8 percent of the last place scores compared to more than twice as many for Humphrey

TABLE 2   Preference Orders for Nominees*

1st Choice	2nd Choice	3rd Choice	Total	Blacks	White Democrats	White Independents	White Republicans
Humphrey	Nixon	Wallace	37%	93%	51%	25%	6%
Nixon	Humphrey	Wallace	37	4	19	42	70
Nixon	Wallace	Humphrey	9	0	7	12	13
Wallace	Nixon	Humphrey	9	0	8	15	8
Humphrey	Wallace	Nixon	5	3	10	3	1
Wallace	Humphrey	Nixon	3	0	5	3	2
			100%	100%	100%	100%	100%
		N =	997	112	344	265	251

*Only the respondents giving different scores to the three nominees are included.

7. The relationship between these preference orders and the vote may be of some interest. Of those voters giving different scores to the three nominees, about 94 percent voted for the candidate they ranked highest while less than one percent voted for the candidate they ranked lowest. About 97 percent of those giving the two major party nominees their highest two rankings voted for their first choice, compared to only 82 percent of those giving Wallace one of their top two scores.

8. These notions are based on C. H. Coombs's "unfolding analysis" discussed in his book, *A Theory of Data* (New York: John Wiley and Sons, 1964), pp. 80–121. The assumption is that an individual choosing among alternative stimuli orders them in terms of their distance from his point of maximum preference. As a result, on a continuum from left to right ordered A, B, C, people may give only the preference orders ABC, BAC, BCA, and CBA. Preference orders with the middle scale item, B, in the third choice position would violate this model so the ACB and CAB patterns would be nonexistent under the condition of perfect unidimensionality.

and many times more for Wallace. These results are basically consistent with a single dimension ranging from Humphrey at one end to Wallace at the other end with Nixon in the middle. This pattern would fit quite well with the journalistic left-right interpretation of the 1968 election. Given the known low level of ideological thought among the mass public, we would assume that this dimension is based more on specific issues than on a general liberal-conservative ideology. We shall consider later the nature of the issues leading to this left-right dimension.

The evidence, however, is not unanimously in favor of a unidimensional left-right interpretation. The two bottom rows of Table 2 run counter to the dimensional model which predicts that Nixon would receive no last place choices. Five percent of the respondents gave Humphrey their first choice and reached across the continuum to allot Wallace their second rather than last choice, although this involved bypassing the middle position on the scale. Also a full quarter of the 117 Wallace supporters in the sample gave Humphrey as their second choice, again violating the left-right dimension. While the overall level of fit is acceptable, we shall consider one further factor which may explain these deviations.

A model of partisan identification and its effects provides the additional explanatory power which is necessary. Party identifiers should give the lowest number of last place scores to the nominee of their party. Thus Democratic identifiers should give fewest last place choices to Humphrey, a prediction opposite to that of the left-right model. The two bottom rows of Table 2 are consistent with this notion of party identification for Democratic respondents but the two middle rows do not fit such an explanation. That fairly equal numbers of Democrats fall into each of these categories suggests that neither model is sufficient in itself.[9] In particular the 15 percent in each category would be a sizable level of error under any model. Predictions from party identification and the left-right theory postulated here are the same in the case of Republican identifiers, so no new information is gleaned from this source. The combined impact of party identification and the left-right model indeed yields a very good fit for Republican identifiers with only 3 percent giving Nixon their last choice. The correspondence of the choice patterns of Independent identifiers to left-right ideas is significant since party identification theory makes no particular predictions for their behavior. Given these results, the left-right dimension is a better ideological discriminator for Republicans and Independents than for Democratic identifiers. The purity of the dimension as an ideological discriminator is lessened for Democratc identifiers because of the conflict for some of them between their party identification and the left-right model. The overall story is basically a reading of two important factors at work — ideology and party, with the former having more weight in the interpretation but with the latter retaining considerable residual explanatory power.

---

9. An alternate explanation of the behavior of Democratic identifiers is that support for Wallace would not be considered defection from the Democratic party in the South given the peculiarities of Southern politics. This hypothesis yields the same prediction we have specified for the party identification model among Democrats. However, the evidence in favor of the prediction of the party identification model is even stronger among the Democratic North than the Democratic South, which suggests that the effects of party identification are more fundamental than are those of Southern politics. While some respondents may have viewed Wallace as a Democratic candidate because of his background, we choose, partly for ease of exposition, to regard his candidacy as separate from either major party. At a minimum there is no evidence that he was viewed together with the remaining Democratic candidates.

Now that we have considered the preferences for the nominees, we wish to turn to the full spectrum of candidates. The mapping of the full candidate space necessitates a shift in analysis procedure. Analysis of the raw preference orders for the twelve candidates is beyond the reasonable limitations of simple inspection and hand analysis — there being 1306 respondents giving meaningful preference orders (different scores to at least two candidates) with a total of 1301 distinct preference orders being given. The alternative which we shall adopt is to analyze the intercorrelations of candidate ratings.[10] Candidates perceived in a similar fashion should have substantial positive correlations; those seen as quite dissimilar from one another should have sizable negative values. Correlation scores close to zero indicate an absence of shared perceptions of the candidates. The correlations among the three nominees, for example, are as follows: −.03 between Nixon and Wallace; −.18 between Humphrey and Nixon; and −.32 between Humphrey and Wallace. The relative magnitudes of these values indicate the very same locations for the nominees on the dimension as revealed in the preference orders of Table 2; the largest negative value, between Humphrey and Wallace, points to the basic opposition of

TABLE 3 Correlations of Candidate Thermometers*

	H	M	K	J	Mc	Rk	Rm	A	N	Rg	L	W
Humphrey (H)	x											
Muskie (M)	.58	x										
Kennedy (K)	.53	.43	x									
Johnson (J)	.70	.46	.47	x								
McCarthy (Mc)	.25	.29	.36	.13	x							
Rockefeller (Rk)	.17	.27	.24	.16	.33	x						
Romney (Rm)	.17	.24	.26	.24	.33	.33	x					
Agnew (A)	−.10	−.03	−.01	−.04	.12	.14	.34	x				
Nixon (N)	−.18	−.09	−.13	−.09	.08	.13	.33	.60	x			
Reagan (Rg)	−.19	−.07	−.10	−.09	.09	.19	.31	.44	.41	x		
Lemay (L)	−.21	−.16	−.09	−.09	−.02	−.04	.10	.30	.11	.28	x	
Wallace (W)	−.32	−.26	−.22	−.23	−.13	−.14	−.06	.13	−.03	.20	.68	x

*All correlations are Pearson r's.

10. The correlations measure the covariation in the ratings of candidate pairs. The average level of popularity of a candidate does not affect such covariation nor does the degree of dispersion in the scores given to a candidate. In particular, the covariation would not be altered by a linear transformation of the scores for a given candidate, such as a "bandwagon effect" which adds five degrees to every respondent's score for Nixon. All temporal effects need not involve simple linear transformations, but the covariation is less affected by such matters than the preference orders would be. Additionally, the use of the covariation measure may affect the distance between a pair of candidates in a spatial representation. A standard unfolding analysis would locate Nixon and Humphrey, for example, very near one another in a geometric space since large numbers of respondents rated both high. However, their correlation is actually a negative value, −.18. This indicates that the higher a respondent rated one of them, the lower he tended to rate the other; thus, the two belong in opposite parts of the space.

the two and hence their placement at opposite ends of the continuum. Inspection of the correlation matrix of Table 3 provides a similar indication of the dimensions underlying the full set of data.

One pattern of interest in the matrix is the relationship of Wallace and LeMay to other candidates. Their correlations are low and often negative. In particular, the two are viewed in opposition to the Democratic candidates, and the generality of this statement could extend to most of the other political figures as well. This suggests the possibility of a Wallace-non-Wallace dimension, though such a dimension could also have partisan and/or issue overtones.

Another pattern in the correlation matrix stands out quite vividly. Candidates belonging to the same party generally have high positive correlations which implies that they are perceived in a similar vein. The four highest correlations involve presidential-vice-presidential teams (including Johnson and Humphrey) and the next eight highest also involve pairs of candidates from the same party. All the intra-party correlations are positive.

Conversely, candidates from different parties are usually viewed as dissimilar or unlike each other. The correlations between Republicans and Democrats tend to be negative, though lower in absolute value than the intra-party correlations. These results buttress the earlier notion of party identification as an important variable affecting the processes of political perception. However, an exception to this patterning stands out. McCarthy, Rockefeller, and Romney, those outside of their parties' "mainstreams," are somewhat correlated with each other — about as much so as with members of their own party. A common bond of popular perceptions may link these three men together. Kennedy is also associated with them, but he has much higher correlations with the members of his party.

A "left-right" ideological dimension or some specific issue manifestation of it might be underlying these patterns and might be intermixed with the partisan factor. The Democratic candidates tending to be more liberal than the Republicans might explain part of the patterning in the matrix as might the extreme position taken by Wallace. A left-right dimension within each party might also explain the relative correlation values for the separate parties. The bipartisan correlations of McCarthy, Rockefeller, and Romney (and, to some extent, Kennedy with them) also suggest an ideological or issue interpretation.

The final comment to be made about the structure of the correlation matrix is that four clusters of candidates are evident. The two American Independent Party candidates form one cluster. Three of the five Republicans — Agnew, Nixon, and Reagan — have their highest intercorrelations with one another as do four of the five Democrats — Humphrey, Muskie, Kennedy, and Johnson. There also appears to be a weak bipartisan cluster involving McCarthy, Rockefeller, and Romney.

In general, the existence of discernible clusters within the correlation matrix indicates an important degree of structuring in this body of data. The relations within and between clusters, however, are difficult to gauge from inspection of the matrix. The fundamental role of party in organizing the correlations is evident from even the most general look at the matrix and there is further evidence of a left-right dimension. However, the interrelationships between these dimensions cannot be found by simple inspection of the matrix. Closer inspection of the candidate space requires the use of a more sophisticated procedure for dimensional analysis.

We shall employ nonmetric multidimensional scaling[11] to obtain the dimensional solution which best explains the correlation patterns of Table 3. A nonmetric technique makes weaker assumptions than does factor analysis; it requires that only the ordering of the correlation values be considered as meaningful data and not the exact values themselves.[12] While making less stringent assumptions, such nonmetric techniques have been shown to yield fairly unique solutions. Multidimensional scaling interprets the correlations as monotonic with distances — the closer to $+1.00$ the correlation between two items (candidates), the closer together should be their corresponding points in a geometric representation. A "goodness-of-fit" measure, called "stress," is calculated to indicate the extent to which the best solution achieved in a given number of dimensions satisfies a monotonic fit with the data. This stress value is at a minimum for the correct solution and increases sharply in value as the number of dimensions being used is cut too far below the correct number. The analysis of the correlation matrix of Table 3 yields a "fair" solution in one dimension with a stress of .108 and a "good" solution in two dimensions with

---

11. See J. B. Kruskal, "Multidimensional Scaling by Optimizing Goodness of Fit to a Nonmetric Hypothesis," *Psychometrika*, 29 (March 1964), 1–27; J. B. Kruskal, "Nonmetric Multidimensional Scaling: A Numerical Method," *Psychometrika*, 29 (June 1964), 115–130. Also, L. Guttman, "A General Nonmetric Technique for Finding the Smallest Coordinate Space for a Configuration of Points," *Psychometrika*, 33 (December 1968), 469–506; J. C. Lingoes, "An IBM-7090 Program for Guttman-Lingoes Smallest Space Analysis — I," *Behavioral Science*, 10 (April 1965), 183–184; R. N. Shepard, "Metric Structures in Ordinal Data," *Journal of Mathematical Psychology*, 3 (July 1966), 287–315.

12. There are several reasons why we have more faith in the order of the correlation values than in their exact magnitudes. First, individuals tended to restrict their responses to the nine scores cited on the thermometer card rather than using the full range provided by the thermometer analogy. Ordinal correlation values on such a nine point scale did not equal the correlation values earlier obtained, but the crucial point is that the order of such values was virtually identical for the two types of coefficients (Spearman's rho = .99). Second, some respondents may have given low scores to two candidates for opposite reasons — such as one candidate being too far to the left and the other too far to the right to satisfy the respondent. Giving similar low ratings to a pair of candidates adds to their correlation, even when the respondents involved actually saw the two candidates as quite distant from one another. This has little effect on correlations of candidates near one another in the space, but it may artificially increase the correlations between distant candidates. As a result, the negative correlations and some of the low positive correlations may be higher (in the direction of $+1.0$) than they should be, though the order of the correlations should be substantially unaffected. Third, all respondents did not necessarily translate the same feelings toward the candidates into the same thermometer values. Individuals could have different response set tendencies — some preferring to give candidates high scores and others tending to give them low scores, a result which would give an artificial positive boost to the correlation of any particular pair of candidates. Such slippage between a person's actual feelings and his verbal scoring of the candidates makes our correlations more positive (or less negative) than they should be. (A detailed proof of this regularity is beyond the scope of this paper.) One way to correct for this effect would be to compute correlations based on each individual's deviation scores from his mean; this, however, would destroy the entire meaningfulness of the thermometer scale and its "anchors" of 0, 50, and 100 degrees. The values obtained from such an operation would be different from our correlation values, but again the order of the two sets of correlations would be essentially similar. (In fact, the Spearman rho coefficient between the original correlations and those obtained by use of such deviation scores is .96, a value which is very high but which does permit some mismatch in the ordering of correlation values for given pairings of candidates.)

An additional consideration motivating the use of a nonmetric technique over factor analysis has to do with the proven tendency of the latter to overestimate the dimensionality of data of the type used here (C. H. Coombs, *A Theory of Data*, Ch. 8). Indeed some exploration with factor analysis on the thermometer data showed that it was supplying one more dimension than was uncovered by our use of a multidimensional scaling algorithm.

a stress of .050.[13] We shall look at these two solutions, one at a time, in order to see what explanatory power each offers.

Figure 1 shows the best unidimensional solution which could be obtained.[14] Note first the partisan separation it provides. The Democratic candidates are at one end of the dimension, the American Independent Party candidates are at the other end, and the Republicans in between. Thus the partisan separation does not correspond to the usual party identification scale with Democrats and Republicans at opposite ends but rather parallels the order of the three nominees on a left-right dimension. The dimension of Figure 1 also distinguishes the clusters found in the correlation matrix. Humphrey, Johnson, Kennedy, and Muskie form one tight cluster and Agnew, Nixon, and Reagan form a second. McCarthy, Rockefeller, and Romney constitute an intermediate cluster between the two major presidential sets, similar to the pattern displayed in the correlation matrix of Table 3. McCarthy is closest to the Democrats, Romney to the Republicans, and Rockefeller midway between them. Ideologically these candidates are as liberal as the Democratic cluster in some respects though less liberal in others. The reasons for the central location of these candidates will be formulated more precisely when we expand the scope of this analysis to include various political attitude measures.

H J K M   Mc Rk Rm   A N Rg   L   W

FIGURE 1   A Unidimensional View of the Candidate
Space

While Figure 1 provides the best fitting unidimensional ordering, we do not regard the candidate space as essentially unidimensional. The unidimensional solution distorts several of the relationships between the candidates. In particular the rule of monotonicity between the correlations and the corresponding interpoint distances demands even greater separation between Nixon and Wallace. It is useful to consider the ordering of the candidates on different possible continua. Nixon would be at the opposite end from the Democrats on a party identification dimension whereas Wallace alone would be at the opposite end from the Democrats on an issue continuum such as civil rights. Further separation between Nixon and Wallace is needed if both of these orderings are to co-exist.

The solution in two dimensions is shown in Figure 2. The four clusters of candidates are again evident and one can still separate the various parties in the space. The added dimension resolves some of the discrepancies in the one dimensional solution. The axes chosen for Figure 2 are intended to simplify the interpretation of

---

13. The terms used are those suggested by Kruskal for the evaluation of various stress values.

14. The exact details of such a solution should not be overinterpreted. Adjacent points, such as Johnson, Kennedy, and Muskie, might switch positions with one another if alternative assumptions had been made in the analysis. Thus small differences in the solution space should not be given too much credence. However, the gross features of the structure of the space — particularly clusters of points in that space — are generally invariant under the uncertainties governing this analysis.

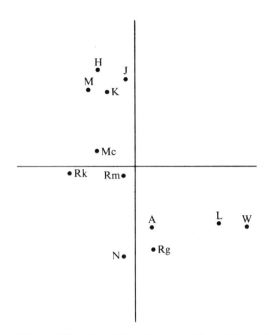

FIGURE 2 The Candidate Space in Two Dimensions

this solution.[15] The horizontal dimension runs from the Democrats and Rockefeller to Wallace. This ordering seems to correspond roughly to a left-right pattern or even to a Wallace-non-Wallace dimension. The vertical dimension runs from the Democratic candidates to the American Independent and Republican Party candidates. The ordering here might correspond roughly with party identification and attitudes on social welfare policy or government power more generally. We shall not justify the exact ordering on these axes but will further explore this question in the next section.[16]

The solutions we have seen do no great damage to our intuitive views of the candidates, but looking at the candidates by themselves provides us with precious few handles by which to interpret the dimensions of the space. Therefore we shall

15. In technical terms, we have employed a varimax rotation around the centroid of the space in order to approximate a simple structure solution. Multidimensional scaling solutions can be rotated freely because the choice of axes in the multidimensional space is arbitrary. The arbitrary determination of the axes suggests that the overall structure of the space should be given the most emphasis or, alternatively, the relation of the candidate items to validating attitude items located in the same space should be stressed.

16. The solution in Figure 2 still portrays the relationships between the parties more accurately than it portrays those within the parties. In particular it understates the distance between McCarthy and Johnson. The three dimensional solution resolves these remaining discrepancies, with the third dimension providing separation within each party. This dimension divides Johnson from Kennedy and McCarthy among the Democrats and divides Nixon and Agnew from Rockefeller, Romney, and Reagan. In each case it separates the "middle-of-the-road" candidates in the party from the more liberal and conservative candidates. Those controlling their parties' organizations are divided from those who opposed their parties' establishments. While the three dimensional solution provides an "excellent" fit to the data (stress = .018), this third dimension yields very little explanatory power so we shall not consider it further.

consider the relations of attitudes toward the candidates to attitudes on issues and parties as a means of further explaining the candidate dimensions. This will allow us to note the similarities in the ways in which respondents view candidates, issues, and parties and will simplify the interpretation of the dimensions of the candidate space itself.

III. Candidates, Issues, and Parties

Political attitudes were important in the 1968 election and, in addition, seemed to stress other issues than those emphasized in earlier decades. The electorate of the 1960's was concerned with problems of the cities, civil rights, Vietnam, protest, and law and order.[17] Civil rights was not a new concern, but it now became associated with urgent new problems of domestic life and foreign affairs. The correlations in Table 4 show that this new issue cluster has a cohesive character of its own and is little related to partisan identification or to the classic social welfare and foreign policy areas. Past voting studies have highlighted the issues of social welfare and foreign policy, showing the two to be independent of each other and the former to be related to party identification.[18] Respondents still mentioned them in 1968 but they, by no means, had the salience and priority of the more contemporary focused issues. The other political orientation of concern, party identification, remained stable in

TABLE 4   Correlations Between Political Attitudes

	Party	Full Employ-ment	Gov't Power	Urban Unrest	Civil Rights	Chicago	Vietnam	Foreign Aid
Party identification — Democratic*	x							
Favor government guarantee of full employment	.20	x						
Federal government is not powerful enough	.29	.26	x					
Solve urban unrest by social solutions rather than force	.15	.24	.15	x				
Favor desegregation	.05	.17	.16	.26	x			
Too much force was used in Chicago	.05	.20	.06	.36	.34	x		
Favor withdrawal from Vietnam rather than escalation	.02	.16	.11	.29	.13	.24	x	
Favor foreign aid	.04	.13	.08	.12	.22	.22	.00	x

*Labels for the issue items indicate the direction of their scoring.

17. Approximately three-quarters of the electorate listed one of these as the major problem facing the government when asked just before the 1968 election. See also Converse, et. al., "Continuity and Change in American Politics."

18. Campbell, Converse, Miller, and Stokes, *The American Voter*, Ch. 9.

1968 compared to earlier years, but its lack of association with the new issue cluster may have dimmed its relevance in this election.

We shall now relate these attitudes directly to the full candidate space. We have chosen four items for closer analysis as being representative of the traditional party and social welfare areas and the new domestic and foreign concerns — the items being party identification and attitudes on full employment, solutions to urban unrest, and Vietnam, respectively.[19] Multidimensional scaling of these attitude items in both their original and reflected forms together with the candidate evaluations yields the solution shown in Figure 3.[20]

The vertical dimension of Figure 3 is basically partisan. The classic party identification item is associated with this dimension. Also the two partisan clusters have their highest loadings on it. The social welfare issue is quite close to this dimension

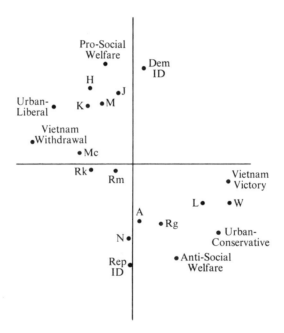

FIGURE 3   Candidates and Attitudes in Two Dimensional Space

19. The questions on urban unrest and Vietnam analyzed here and in Tables 6 and 7 below were devised by R. A. Brody, B. I. Page, S. Verba, and J. Laulicht.

20. The associated stress value is .106, indicating some difficulty in satisfying the monotonic constraints. The need to satisfy the additional relationships between the attitude items and the candidate ratings has affected somewhat the structure of the candidate space embedded in Figure 3, though we would regard this candidate space as being essentially similar to that of Figure 2. The attitude items were included in both their original and reflected forms in order to facilitate comparisons of their locations with respect to both liberal and conservative candidates. While the candidate ratings have a natural direction, the scoring of these attitude items is arbitrary. Therefore it makes sense to consider both possible directions for each item. Unlike some other analysis procedures, the multidimensional scaling model does not force the two poles of an item to be exactly opposite one another in the space, though we find this to be approximately true. If an item is related to a given axis, its alternative scorings would be at opposite ends of that axis. Both poles of an item unrelated to a dimension would project on approximately the same place on that dimension.

— a result which fits well with the fact that party identification and social welfare concerns both grew out of the economic problems of the 1930's. Nixon is nearest to Republican identification while Reagan is closest to the conservative pole of social welfare, indicating that social welfare is tied to party though they are not completely identical.

The horizontal dimension involves the more immediate problems of 1968. Vietnam attitudes are associated most strongly with this dimension and the urban unrest attitudes are also related to it. The American Independent Party candidates and McCarthy, Rockefeller, and Romney have their highest loadings here. The conservative ends of the Vietnam and urban unrest items are near Wallace and LeMay. The liberal end of Vietnam is nearest to McCarthy and Kennedy while the liberal end of urban unrest is closest to Kennedy and Humphrey. Respondents thus did differentiate within this set of issues, though overall perceptions of candidates on urban unrest and Vietnam are quite similar. Differentiation in respondents' perceptions was also evident in their contrasts of Wallace and LeMay with the rest of the candidates. While there have been previous indications of a Wallace-non-Wallace dimension, it is now apparent that such a dimension has issue bases and that some liberal candidates are also linked with this issue continuum.

The two dimensional space also comments on the relative positioning of the major party nominees. The basic opposition of Humphrey and Nixon along the vertical dimension points to the importance of party identification in molding evaluations of the candidates. Differences between them on the issue dimension were not considerable, but the bonds of traditional party identification kept them from moving toward a "tweedledee-tweedledum" position in the space. Even the intrusion of an issue dimension in 1968 did not eliminate the differences due to partisanship. In fact the partisan dimension is of somewhat greater importance than the issue dimension even in the full candidate space, though this should not be given too much emphasis since the measure of importance is considerably affected by the somewhat arbitrary selection of candidates included in the thermometer question.

The two dimensions of Figure 3 represent two basic political continua. The vertical axis corresponds to the partisan issues which divided the old left and the old right. The horizontal axis corresponds to the issues which divide the new left and the new right, issues which are not linked closely to the partisan attachments of an earlier generation. It is true that a very broad left-right dimension divides the issues and candidates in the upper-left corner of the diagram from those in the lower-right. Indeed such a continuum would correspond to the ordering of the candidates in Figure 1. However, the complexities of 1968 were too great for a good fit with a single left-right dimension. Equally important, issues apart from traditional partisan identification were critical in the determination of attitudes toward several of the candidates. The electorate did adapt to changing circumstances in its evaluation of the candidates. Indeed, the mapping of Figure 3 suggests considerable flexibility and sensitivity on the part of the electorate.

Nevertheless the data cannot indicate whether these dimensions are unique to the 1968 election or would have been found in a similar analysis of other recent presidential elections. The "new issues" dimension is most likely to be a recent development while the dimension similar to party identification probably has had a longer existence. Whether there is always a continuum relating to the issues of the day in addition to a long-term party identification dimension cannot be answered by the analysis of a single election. The closeness of the social welfare and party identification items might mean that an "issues of the day" factor would not appear when an election is fought along traditional social welfare lines. The issues of the day might form the basis of candidacies in any election, though we would regard the sharp dichotomization of the dimensions in this election as indicating that more fundamental concerns were at work in 1968.

The dimensional analysis has shown the critical roles of parties and issues in molding popular perceptions of the candidates in 1968. The impact of these factors on the specific candidates must be detailed as must the conditions governing their impact. The two factors could work together or separately, depending on the circumstances of the election year and its cast of leading characters. We shall now concentrate on how these factors operate on each of our twelve candidates and how they interrelate in their effects. We shall later specify the probable conditions under which the different dimensions of candidate evaluation are used, leading to a working knowledge of the formation of candidate evaluations.

The first factor of importance is party. Our suggestion that it is a crucial variable is not exactly novel. Past voting studies have shown that specific perceptions of the nominees are often expressed in terms of party ties. The authors of *The American Voter* have particularly detailed the respondents' likes and dislikes of the nominees in these terms, most notably in the Eisenhower-Stevenson elections of 1952 and 1956. They found that party provided an important basis for the evaluations of these two men — perhaps initially in 1952 because it was one of the few cues available to evaluate such new personalities on the national political scene. They also traced the impact of party on reactions to the personal characteristics of the two nominees and found the expected partisan slope, adherents of each party evaluating their party's candidate more favorably than did adherents of the opposite party.[21]

The theme of party influence was carried further in the literature by Converse and Dupeux as they probed the complexities of the Eisenhower case.[22] They point out that Eisenhower was long seen apart from the party system and that Democratic leaders, at least at one time, hoped he would run for office as the candidate of their party. Reaction to him in the 1952 campaign was influenced by his eventual choice of the Republican banner. Yet Converse and Dupeux argue that there was no reason to feel that admiration for him had previously followed partisan lines and if Eisenhower had chosen the Democratic party, "we may assume the relationship would have rotated in the opposite direction: strong Republicans would have decided they disliked Eisenhower."[23] Party was thus seen as a strong and inexorable influence on the perceptions of the candidates.

Given such research, one should expect that party would be a major orientation to the candidates in 1968. After all, most of the candidates had long backgrounds in partisan politics and were known as national political figures prior to the 1968 campaign. People like Humphrey, Nixon, and Johnson were considered leaders of

21. Campbell, Converse, Miller, and Stokes, *The American Voter*, pp. 128–131.
22. P. E. Converse and G. Dupeux, "De Gaulle and Eisenhower: The Public Image of the Victorious General," translated in A. Campbell, P. E. Converse, W. E. Miller, and D. E. Stokes, *Elections and the Political Order* (New York: John Wiley and Sons, 1966), pp. 292–345.
23. *Ibid.*, p. 325.

their parties and had all held national elective office. Kennedy was well-known as a key participant in his brother's Democratic administration, for being a prominent Democratic senator, and for taking his campaign in 1968 directly to the people. McCarthy, too, was a Democratic office-holder and conducted a quite visible campaign in his party's primaries. On the Republican side, Rockefeller had participated in national campaigns for his party's nomination since 1960 and Romney, also a governor of a large state, was considered by many to be the front-runner for his party's top prize until the start of the 1968 primary season. Reagan did not mount a national campaign but received considerable publicity as a result of his political success in California. Muskie and Agnew were less well-known nationally but were naturally tied to and identified with their party's presidential ticket, awareness of them increasing as the campaign progressed. Only Wallace and LeMay provided a contrast to this general theme in publicly disavowing the two party system and running a third party campaign. With that exception, the candidates of 1968 had direct partisan connections and were generally familiar in that guise. In a very real sense, the party cue was available longer to these men than to either Eisenhower or Stevenson in 1952. Whether they actually were so perceived, however, is a question to which we now turn our attention.

Table 5 suggests the effects of party identification on the candidate evaluations. Partisan slopes are clearly evident for several of the candidates. Strong Democrats gave the highest mean scores to Humphrey, Muskie, Kennedy, and Johnson while strong Republicans gave them the lowest mean scores. This pattern is exactly reversed for Agnew, Nixon, and Reagan. The difference in means between the strong identifier groups for these candidates is 18–37 percent, indicating an effect of considerable magnitude. These seven partisan candidates represent a mixture of those who have been on the national scene the longest and shortest times. In some instances the candidates have long been identified with the parties while in other cases party is one of the few available cues for candidate evaulation. The patterns shown

TABLE 5   Mean Scores of Candidates by Party Identification

	Strong Democrats	Weak Democrats	Independents	Weak Republicans	Strong Republicans	Eta*
Humphrey	81.1	66.0	54.5	50.8	43.6	.46
Muskie	73.8	60.8	58.4	55.5	51.8	.46
Kennedy	81.9	72.7	65.8	61.2	55.5	.32
Johnson	75.7	63.3	51.5	48.0	42.3	.43
McCarthy	55.7	53.8	55.2	56.9	50.6	.08
Rockefeller	54.5	51.7	52.6	58.0	54.0	.09
Romney	49.5	47.4	48.3	49.1	53.8	.10
Agnew	43.8	48.3	50.3	56.0	61.6	.25
Nixon	54.9	61.3	66.8	77.1	84.2	.40
Reagan	41.2	46.9	50.2	53.7	60.2	.25
LeMay	28.4	37.6	38.5	34.6	35.0	.14
Wallace	24.3	35.2	35.5	32.1	23.6	.16
N's	238– 267	298– 331	356– 381	163– 180	125– 132	1192– 1291

*The eta statistic indicates the degree of relationship between the independent variable (party identification) and the candidate's ratings.

for the latter type of candidate are to those found for Eisenhower and Stevenson. But while all seven of these political personalities had sizable party slopes, there is a marked tendency in Table 5 for candidates having been on the national scene the longer time and candidates associated with higher partisan office to have the larger partisan slopes in the group.

A marked departure from partisan guidelines appears for the remaining candidates. Wallace and LeMay, in particular, were seen in relatively non-partisan terms. Their levels of strength, when weak and strong identifiers of each party are combined, are about the same among Democrats and Republicans, indicating that on balance they were not seen as Democrats regardless of Wallace's past partisan ties. Being their party candidates, it is also not surprising that support for them varied inversely with strength of party identification and that, as a result, their greatest backing came from among those not identifying with either major party. There may even have been a shift of Wallace supporters into the ranks of the Independents, although the small differences observed in Table 5 suggest that only a few members of the electorate probably made such a change. The other candidates — McCarthy, Rockefeller, and Romney — received approximately equal backing from all classes of identifiers. This means that their appeal was not strongly partisan and consequently did not reap the usual advantages of partisan support. This finding is more unusual than the Wallace-LeMay pattern since the three had definite partisan background and were identified with the race for their parties' nominations. What remains to be considered is the bases of support which these five candidates employed instead of the usual partisan appeal. Conversely, it will also be important to clarify why the other candidates were seen as "party people" and to determine in what other ways they were viewed.

To explore these questions further, we have examined the relationships between the scores given to the candidates and two of the new issue items. The first item had the respondent indicate on a seven point scale what he considered to be "the best way to deal with the problem of urban unrest and rioting." The scale ranged from solving the underlying problems of poverty and unemployment at one end to using all available force at the other. This "urban unrest" question evoked some of the respondent's basic feelings toward the subjects of law and order, militancy, civil rights, and social welfare. Table 6 shows the mean scores given the candidates by attitudes on urban unrest and enables us to look for "issue slopes" in the same manner that we looked for partisan slopes in the previous table.[24]

The data in Table 6 indicate that some of the more partisan candidates were also seen in issue terms. For instance, Humphrey, Kennedy, and Johnson were evaluated more highly by those in favor of solving the problems of our domestic life by social justice instead of law and order. Muskie also followed suit, but not as much so as his Democratic colleagues. Of the partisan Republicans, Reagan was liked most by those advocating the use of all available force, though the difference is not a sizable one. Feelings toward Nixon and Agnew also tended to be more favorable on the "law and order" side, but their strength is nearly constant across the continuum. Such slopes show that the strength of the issue factor varied for the partisan candidates, although each candidate was evaluated higher on one side of the continuum

---

24. The seven point scales on this and the next issue were collapsed into five point scales by combining the two extreme positions at each end.

TABLE 6   Mean Scores of Candidates by Attitudes
on Urban Unrest

	Solve problems of poverty and unemployment			Use all available force		Eta
Humphrey	71.5	67.7	59.1	51.7	50.2	.32
Muskie	66.2	66.8	60.4	55.6	54.2	.22
Kennedy	78.6	72.3	67.5	59.3	61.0	.28
Johnson	64.8	62.3	58.7	49.8	48.9	.24
McCarthy	60.0	58.3	52.3	52.0	50.2	.18
Rockefeller	56.0	56.6	54.7	50.6	49.6	.12
Romney	48.9	52.6	51.6	48.3	43.9	.16
Agnew	48.6	48.5	51.3	52.6	51.4	.07
Nixon	63.2	63.9	68.8	69.9	66.8	.11
Reagan	43.2	47.4	51.3	51.4	54.3	.19
LeMay	26.3	30.5	35.1	37.9	47.7	.29
Wallace	18.2	24.4	28.9	38.5	51.1	.39
N's	358– 389	124– 129	343– 369	115– 126	224– 249	1173– 1261

than the other. A comparison of these results with Table 5 reveals that the urban unrest issue is not as important as party in its effects on this set of candidate ratings.[25]

Perhaps the most interesting patterns in the table concern the candidates lacking partisan ties. Issue colorations were evident for most of these individuals. Wallace and LeMay, in particular, were supported by those wanting all available force with a strong slope toward the opposite end. The difference in means for Wallace between the two extreme categories was 33 percent, the largest such difference in the table. McCarthy, by contrast, was seen as a liberal with a definite tendency existing for people to evaluate him, as Humphrey, Kennedy, and Johnson, on the social justice end of the urban continuum. Rockefeller and Romney also did best on the social justice side, though the differences are not large which may be due, in part, to their lower level of saliency among the public. The scores given to these five candidates have a greater relation to this dimension than to party identification. The overall public ranking of these and the other candidates along this dimension fits very well with the interpretations given by political commentators. In some cases we are not dealing with large effects, but there is evidence that this dimension was quite salient to the public and that they could accurately locate the candidates on it.

The other overriding issue in 1968 was certainly the Vietnam war. Following a format similar to the urban unrest question, respondents were asked what action they felt the United States should take in Vietnam. The choices ranged from immediate withdrawal at one end to winning a complete military victory at the other. Table 7 shows the mean scores given the candidates by attitudes on Vietnam. The war generally affected ratings of the partisan candidates less than did either party

---

25. In order to gauge the relative importance of these effects, it is necessary to consider the slopes, the distribution of cases on the issue and party variables, and the curvilinear tendencies for some of the candidates. The eta coefficient takes all of these matters into account and, hence, forms the basis for our judgments of relative importance. When squared, it relates the proportion of variance in a candidate's ratings explained by a given factor. Eta values for two variables can be compared to ascertain which factor, issue or party is the more important for the candidate of concern.

TABLE 7   Mean Scores of Candidates by Attitudes
on Vietnam

	Immediate Withdrawal				Complete Military Victory	Eta
Humphrey	64.4	65.8	64.8	63.1	53.3	.19
Muskie	62.5	63.5	63.0	63.0	57.0	.12
Kennedy	76.3	73.2	70.6	67.2	62.6	.20
Johnson	57.0	60.8	62.6	58.8	53.3	.14
McCarthy	61.5	58.9	55.6	52.5	49.6	.20
Rockefeller	54.0	59.1	55.2	55.8	50.3	.12
Romney	46.7	50.2	51.5	51.3	47.0	.12
Agnew	46.8	49.1	50.8	51.6	52.4	.10
Nixon	61.9	69.1	67.1	68.5	67.0	.11
Reagan	43.0	47.6	49.4	51.8	52.4	.16
LeMay	26.4	28.4	31.8	33.9	45.0	.27
Wallace	21.8	20.5	25.7	30.8	45.1	.31
N's	246– 275	95– 101	346– 369	125– 133	336– 357	1152– 1234

or urban issues. Still, some differences on Vietnam did appear among the partisans with higher ratings for Kennedy among the "doves" and somewhat higher scores for Reagan and Agnew among the "hawks." Humphrey and, to a lesser extent, Muskie fared better on the dove side, but their ratings fell off at the extreme. Johnson manifested another pattern — those in the middle of the scale liked him most and then his support trailed off as one moves to the more extreme categories. This fits well with Johnson's "middle-of-the-road" handling of the war and indeed the two extremes of this scale were intended as alternatives to his policies. Nixon's level of support varied little with Vietnam policy except among strong doves who tended to rate him lower. His announcement of a "plan to end the war" without indicating the nature of that plan appears to have hurt him only among doves.

Vietnam attitudes tend to have more impact on the ratings of the remaining candidates than party and are almost on a par with those on the urban issue. Leading off this parade of effects are Wallace and LeMay who are once again found at one of the extremities of the continuum. The two definitely show the strongest issue slopes on the "hawkish" side of the Vietnam question, pointing up the way in which they embodied the issue scene of 1968. Evaluations of McCarthy were also affected by attitudes on the war with the Senator receiving his greatest support among those wishing immediate withdrawal from Vietnam. There is every indication here that his candidacy was visible and that he did succeed in tying it to the war issue. Rockefeller's and Romney's patterns are more ambiguous, again possibly due to their lower level of saliency. Romney's best standing was among those favoring "middle-of-the-road" policies toward the war, possibly suggesting that he experienced difficulty in communicating his war position to the public. Rockefeller's virtual silence on the war may explain the irregularities in his pattern of support, though he definitely did garner greater backing among doves. Basically the data fit usual statements of the twelve candidates' policies quite well. The effects of Vietnam attitudes tend to be smaller than those associated with urban problems, but this may well be explained by smaller differences between the candidates and less clarity on their part in the statement of exact positions on the war.

The data presented here show that some of the candidates not seen in partisan terms are instead associated with the issues of the times. In order for a candidate to become strongly identified with an issue position, it is necessary for him to be salient to the public and for him to take a definite stand on the issue. Wallace and LeMay provide the strongest contrasts in data patternings since they were not partisan candidates and did become strongly identified with the important issues. McCarthy, Rockefeller, and Romney also were differentiated on issue bases, though not as strongly so as Wallace and LeMay because of their lower salience and their less definite positions on some issues. While an elite audience would generally recognize sharper issue positions for these three candidates, their limited salience to the mass public dampened public perceptions of these positions so that only relatively mild reverberations of their issue stand are evident in the data.

Among the partisan candidates, issues were not always relevant, but some contrasts do appear. The Democratic hard core — Kennedy, Johnson, Humphrey, and Muskie — registered moderate issue effects, particularly on solutions to urban problems. Reagan alone among the Republican candidates was seen in fairly distinct issue terms. But generally assessments of the partisan candidates were not necessarily based on current issues whereas the evaluations of the non-party candidates were related to such issues. That issues can be of the same order of importance as party in determining attitudes toward candidates, even candidates for the nominations of the major parties, is significant.

The impact of party and issue factors on perceptions of the candidates has been noted and detailed. The next step is to suggest conditions under which these two factors operate in the molding of candidate orientation. Party seems to be a useful cue for candidate evaluation when the individual is a new candidate without well-known policy stands, as in the case of Eisenhower, Stevenson, Agnew, and Muskie. Party will also loom important as a determinant of ratings when the candidate is a well-known national leader of his party, e.g., Humphrey, Nixon, Johnson, and Kennedy. The candidates of the major parties may still be perceived in issue as well as party terms; Kennedy and Reagan provide examples, though we find them viewed significantly more in the latter than in the former vein. Candidacies based mainly on issues are also possible, even in the major parties. A candidate without a decidedly partisan national reputation may distinguish himself on an issue basis, with little regard to conventional party lines. Wallace and LeMay demonstrate this possibility as third party candidates. McCarthy and, to a lesser extent, Rockefeller and Romney also tend to exhibit the patterning of an issue-based candidate. The conditions making such issue candidacies viable remain to be considered.

IV. An Era of Increasing Ideological Focus

Two ideal types of "ideological focus" have been distinguished by Donald E. Stokes. Some periods of time can be characterized by "strong ideological focus" with political controversy "focused on a single, stable issue domain which presents an ordered-dimension that is perceived in common terms by leaders and followers." By contrast, a period of "weak ideological focus" would be one in which political conflict is "diffused over a number of changing issue concerns which rarely present position-dimensions and which are perceived in different ways by different political actors.[26] The nature of candidacies is basically dependent on the degree of ideological focus; viable issue candidacies require the sharp issue conflicts of periods of strong ideological focus. This election must be viewed in the broader perspective of the nature of party conflict in the last generation in order to determine the impetus for issue candidacies in 1968. This will lead us to an ultimate consideration of the future shape of party competition.

The contemporary period has been typified by the conditions of weak ideological focus and this is particularly true of the 1950's. While there were "issues" of a sort in that decade, they tended not to be position issues. One doubts whether the public perceived the Taft-Eisenhower contest in 1952, the Stevenson, Kefauver, Russell, Harriman, and Barkley contests of 1952 and 1956, or the Eisenhower-Stevenson elections in strong issue terms. In particular Eisenhower and Stevenson did not emerge on the national political scene as the embodiments of strong issue positions. In periods of weak ideological focus, one expects that the candidates will be more party-based than issue-based. The candidates, particularly the new candidates without a partisan reputation, will be more positively evaluated by the identifiers of their own party since there are few competitive cues available.

The degree of ideological focus of American politics has been low since the period of the New Deal. "Then, more than now, the intervention of government in the domestic economy and related social problems provided a position-dimension that could organize the competition of parties and the motivation of electors."[27] What is remarkable is that the social welfare questions which realigned the parties in the 1930's still constitute the basis of party identification regardless of the many changes in our life since then. The stability of partisan loyalties is such that it does not change until the circumstances of the day force such a change.

The stability of partisanship at the mass level has a parallel among the party leaders. The electorate maintains its loyalties, in part, because the party leaders keep their doctrines relatively fixed. The parties originally became differentiated with respect to certain issues, such as social welfare. The differences on these issues are maintained by the parties in order to keep their underlying group support, though these differences may be muted in order to gain electoral advantage.

It is in periods of strong ideological focus that this stability is most seriously threatened. A set of issues may accumulate with little regard to conventional party lines. The parties tend to avoid involvement with new position issues for fear of losing their base of support, instead maneuvering to establish somewhat similar positions on these issues. This allows minor parties to take advantage of the new issues, at least for the short run. If the new position issues permit the minor parties to make a noticeable dent into the normal vote of the major parties and if furthermore these issues do not show signs of receding, the major parties shift their stand on these issues. The resulting changes in group loyalties betoken a realignment of the parties.[28] Those first joining the electorate during a period of strong ideological focus are less tied to traditional party lines and are often most affected by the new issues;

---

26. D. E. Stokes, "Spatial Models of Party Competition," p. 376. "Position-dimensions" involve dimensions of conflict on which political actors — voters and parties — can and do take different policy stands.

27. *Ibid.*

28. A classification of elections in terms of maintaining, deviating, and realigning elections is given in Campbell, Converse, Miller, and Stokes, *The American Voter*, pp. 531–538.

thus the addition of young voters to the system can help provide the momentum needed for a realignment. Issue-based candidacies are more likely in a period of strong ideological focus; the actual nomination of an issue-based candidate by a major party can provide the final spur needed for the realignment to take place. Our political system is stable because few issues are of the magnitude necessary to cause a realignment, but they are not totally absent from the political scene.

Civil rights is one issue which could cause a realignment. It formed the basis of a regional third-party movement in 1948, but no lasting change resulted. The Supreme Court opinions of the 1950's increased the immediacy of the issue. The major parties first became actively involved in the issue in the 1964 election, but the basic problem could still be geographically isolated. By the 1968 election, however, civil rights was a national problem. Furthermore, the civil rights problem fit into a more general syndrome which also included riots in the urban ghetto, campus unrest, protests against the Vietnam war, disorders on the streets of Chicago during the Democratic convention, and the general "law and order" theme. The establishment candidates in the major parties did not take sharply different positions on these issues, basing their appeals instead on conventional issues and party ties. Neither the Republicans nor the Democrats moved to a position on the new issues which would satisfy the extremists on either side, though their differences on the core civil rights problem were sufficient for black Americans to have no doubt as to their direction.

The echoes of these developments are evident in our data. We have found that a new set of issues has emerged, quite distinct from both social welfare and party identification. The civil rights issue of the previous decade provides the core of this new issue cluster, but further domestic and foreign problems are now associated with it. The independence of this new set of issues from the traditional concerns was particularly evident in the candidate/attitude space of Figure 3. Since a new position-dimension emerged at the mass level without the nominees of the major parties taking very different stands on it, a minor party emerged at one end of the dimension. Candidates associated with the liberal end of this dimension unsuccessfully contested for their parties' nominations, but chose not to take their fight to the electorate with a fourth party movement, at least not in 1968.

If our statement of the development of a new issue area independent of conventional party lines is correct, we are left speculating as to the shape of the political future. The new issues could recede in urgency by 1972. This could occur with reference to Vietnam, but seems less probable with regard to the other issues. It is always possible that the civil rights problem will become less urgent for a short period of time, but the long-term trend seems to be one of greater urgency. Protest, the complaints of youth, and the law and order theme are likely to become familiar parts of the political landscape. If indeed the issues do maintain their level of urgency, we may see some efforts toward party realignment by the 1972 election. Efforts toward reform of Democratic party procedures are already suggesting the feasibility of such a realignment.

The changes in the political horizon have a particularly important effect on the youth. Many have been directly affected by the new issues and all have witnessed a more vigorous political climate than that of the previous generation. Not having long participated in the political system, they tend to be less firmly identified with a party and less firmly committed to the parties than are their elders. The three party race of 1968 along with the new issue dimension and the issue candidacies may have further delayed the first real commitment to the party system for many young adults. As a result the pool of young voters who may enter the political system for the first time in the 1972 election includes more than the usual number of delayed entries. Additionally that pool will be larger than in most recent years because of the effects of the post-war "baby boom." That many of the new young voters will be veterans of the Vietnam conflict introduces another note of uncertainty. Taken together these elements point to a potential increase in the fluidity in the electoral system in 1972.

Thus the 1964 and 1968 elections could well constitute the prelude for a series of changes of a scope more vast than those to which voting studies have become accustomed. A deviating election such as 1968 may mark the end of a political era, though it would be too early to suggest the outline of a new one. In particular, the seeming stability of party identification may just mask an increasing irrelevance of traditional party ties during a period of growing ideological focus when some of those ties are becoming unhinged. This election was marked by events having theoretical importance — a new issue dimension developed, issue candidates emerged in the major parties, and a third party made a sizable showing. The voting patterns of significant groups in the electorate, particularly blacks, seem destined for a meaningful change from their patterns in the 1950's. Only time will tell whether a lasting reorientation of American politics occurs along these lines, but a considerable change in the panorama of American politics seems likely even if a full realignment is avoided.

There are two major dimensional antecedents of candidate evaluation. Party provides a basic dimensional antecedent, especially during periods of weak ideological focus when people unknown on the national political scene are nominated by their parties and also when the party leaders fight a rear-guard action against a realignment of the parties along the lines of the issues of the day. However, there is also room for issue dimensions, particularly in periods of strong ideological focus. Minor parties may grow up at the poles of such issue dimensions, though one would expect realignment of the major parties if those issue dimensions remain vigorous for any period of time. Party and issues thus provide two basic mechanisms of candidate evaluation. In 1968 we had both party-based candidates and issue-based candidates, a fact which in itself may be quite suggestive of the future of American politics.

Appendix

As you know, there were many people mentioned this past year as possible candidates for President by the political parties. We would like to get your feelings toward some of these people.

I have here a card (INTERVIEWER HANDS OVER CARD #5) on which there is something that looks like a thermometer. We call it a "feeling thermometer" because it measures your feelings toward these people. You probably remember that we used something like this in our earlier interview with you.

Here's how it works. If you don't feel particularly warm or cold toward a person, then you should place him in the middle of the thermometer, at the 50 degree mark.

If you have a warm feeling toward a person, or feel favorably toward him, you would give him a score somewhere between 50° and 100°, depending on how warm your feeling is toward that person.

On the other hand, if you don't feel very favorably toward a person — that is, if you don't care too much for him — then you would place him somewhere between 0° and 50°.

Of course, if you don't know too much about a person, just tell me and we'll go on to the next name.

Our first person is George Wallace. Where would you put him on the thermometer?

INTERVIEWER   TAKE SOME TIME TO EXPLAIN HOW THE THERMOMETER
              WORKS, SHOWING R THE WAY IN WHICH THE DEGREE
              LABELS CAN HELP HIM LOCATE AN INDIVIDUAL, SUCH AS
              GEORGE WALLACE.

	Rating			*Rating*
a. George Wallace	————	g. Lyndon Johnson	————
b. Hubert Humphrey	————	h. George Romney	————
c. Richard Nixon	————	i. Robert Kennedy	————
d. Eugene McCarthy	————	j. Edmund Muskie	————
e. Ronald Reagan	————	k. Spiro Agnew	————
f. Nelson Rockefeller	————	l. Curtis LeMay	————

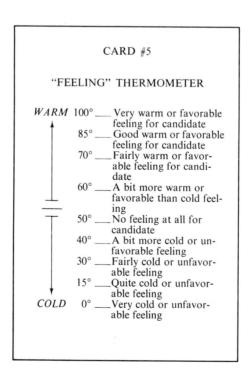

CARD #5

"FEELING" THERMOMETER

WARM 100° ___ Very warm or favorable
                feeling for candidate
       85° ___ Good warm or favorable
                feeling for candidate
       70° ___ Fairly warm or favor-
                able feeling for candi-
                date
       60° ___ A bit more warm or
                favorable than cold feel-
                ing
       50° ___ No feeling at all for
                candidate
       40° ___ A bit more cold or un-
                favorable feeling
       30° ___ Fairly cold or unfavor-
                able feeling
       15° ___ Quite cold or unfavor-
                able feeling
COLD   0° ___ Very cold or unfavor-
                able feeling

The Analysis of
Political Dynamics

It was suggested earlier that the basic dimensions defining any data include the case (individual, nation, event), the values of the characteristics on each case (at various levels of measurement), and the location of the case and its values at a point in time. To this stage in our presentation of quantitative techniques we have generally avoided references to the time dimension. Instead, we have focused on the relationships between variables at one point in time. The focus now shifts to a consideration of the basic statistical properties of observations over time and the relationships between variables which have been measured longitudinally.

The advantages of treating observations over time appear obvious to many social scientists. Explanatory rhetoric and political theories are rich with references to time. Time as a variable itself can help to explain political phenomena and the study of observations over time enables predictions of future values for those observations. Furthermore, our language of causal inferences assumes a temporal ordering in order to make valid statements about causal relationships between variables. The treatment of time observations also facilitates the use of mathematical probability models so that we may reject (or accept) either a single proposition or a set of interrelated propositions in a formalistic and parsimonious manner. Finally, the time dimension bears directly on the concern for social and political change. We could document such advantages, but the more subtle ones will appear throughout this chapter. The basic point at this stage involves a comparison between the frequently espoused advantages and the political scientist's tardiness in utilizing techniques to achieve these advantages.

The lack of widespread applications or methodological elegance in the study of political data over time has been influenced by a number of factors. First, there are some basic philosophical problems in treating time that have endured without solutions.[1] Time is relational and given meaning by events occurring within it, yet time also may have an absoluteness apart from these events. Time may be viewed in at least three ways: as an interval — for example, the time between events or observations of attitudes or behavior; as duration (of an event or series of events); or as a discrete moment of one event's occurrence (or co-occurrence with another event). Furthermore, in the most abstract sense, time is theoretically both continuous and endless, whether we think in terms of its beginning or end, yet we must, by definition, measure it discretely by "stopping the clock" or selecting an arbitrary beginning point. These necessary conditions of measuring time do not normally represent any particular empirical difficulty. We work, as does the layman or the astronomer, in terms of measurements of time *duration* (cases one and two), from nanoseconds to millenia, or of *occurrence* in time (case three) by as accurate a stopping of the clock as is feasible.

An operationalization of time is often easy and the result is a basic unit of measurement at the interval level. However, we do not treat time for time's sake; rather, we examine one variable over time or the relationships between two or more variables over time. The measurement problem is therefore not with time itself, but with developing comparable units of analysis over time. Although political science deals with many units which meet this criterion of comparability (e.g., popular voting, roll calls, budgetary data), important variables such as attitudes and behavior might be measured by a host of different units that change or that are culture-bound. For example, the social scientist's sophistication in measuring attitudes and behavior is a relatively recent phenomena precluding important studies of past actions or attitudes. In addition, our perspective on these variables may be blinded by cultural values (especially in the study of politics over time[2]) or by values of a particular generation. Many of these problems cannot be overcome (such as unavailable attitudinal data for past periods), but most researchers adopt a philosophy of proceeding as best they can. For example, we classify events assuming they repeat themselves and that there is enough similarity in the events to warrant generalizations about the class of events.[3]

In addition to philosophical and measurement problems a variety of analysis problems also appear. These will become evident as techniques are discussed later in the chapter. But the root of these problems is a point to consider now. Despite technical issues in time analysis, many of the most rudimentary techniques have not pervaded the political scientist's research. The methodology of longitudinal analysis was not developed in political science. Indeed, as with so many other classes of techniques, the procedures were borrowed from other areas of study, e.g., economics, demography, psychology, physics, and chemistry. These disciplinary boundaries and the different languages, procedures, and substantive concerns in each have inhibited applications to political science. Finally, in addition to technique differences between disciplines, some basic theoretical differences have made the waters of time rather

---

1. See Robert F. Berkhofer, Jr., *A Behavioral Approach to Historical Analysis* (New York: The Free Press, 1969), pp. 214ff.

2. Robert Burrowes, "Multiple Time-Series Analysis of Nation-Level Data," *Comparative Political Studies* 2 (1970): 465–80.

3. See John E. Mueller, "Systematic History," in *Approaches to Measurement in International Relations,* ed. Mueller (New York: Appleton-Century-Crofts, 1969), chapter 2.

murky. In the formative period of political science many researchers adopted the paradigms of our sister discipline at that time — history. Yet historians have been careless in their empirical treatment of time, dividing it by eras or periods without concern for underlying processes.[4] Furthermore, it has been difficult for political science to look to other social sciences for a useful time model. The social theorists tend to treat time as either an independent variable (concluding that it is important for their frameworks or theories) or in so abstract a fashion that its meaning for empirical research becomes obscure. Economists have been more helpful in adding conceptual clarifications to longitudinal processes, largely through their concern for equilibrium, its static and dynamic states, their concern with cycles, and the impact of long- and short-term forces. These concepts are now prevalent in contemporary empirical theory about politics but a retarding difficulty remains: concepts such as equilibrium are used to refer to the state of a theoretical system rather than to any empirical entity. Unfortunately for most social scientists, time has been merely a theoretical device.

Although many of the considerations outlined above have imposed constraints on the theory and substance of political research, several unifying themes have grown from this diversity across disciplines. Political scientists have adopted a process perspective common to attempts at generalization in other social sciences.[5] This perspective assumes that sequences of events or phenomena recur, either in the long or short run. On the other hand, historians have been traditionally concerned with nonrepetitive sequences, but that exception to unity now appears to be changing. Historians are dubious of such historical cyclists as Marx, Spengler, or Sorokin, and probably with good reason. Toynbee, one of their own, may be a different sort of scholarly explainer of regularities in time, and to that the traditional historian's skepticism may now be changing. The contemporary mood for each of these disciplines reflects a desire to capture the recurrent and general, as well as the unique and particular. Furthermore, the social sciences and history share a common methodology with regard to time. Each discipline acknowledges the importance of comparisons and the comparative method pervades most of this research.

A focus on recurring sequences of observations or events suggests a number of questions that are usually attended to by the political researcher. When did the sequences begin and/or end? What is the order of the sequence or series in relationship to time? Why did the sequence occur when it did? How do several theories compare with one another? What is the duration of sequences, the rate of change, and the regularity of the repetitive process? These questions suggest that at least two basic things are necessary to begin a time series analysis: (1) a definition of the events or phenomena (or their classes), and (2) a delimitation of the time period.[6] Both of these factors are, in turn, shaped by the substantive questions directed at the data and our working hypotheses. Does an election or an event refer to United States presidential elections, local elections, or voting patterns in another country? Which election do we begin and end with? Answering questions like these is obviously

4. See Berkhofer, *A Behavioral Approach to Historical Analysis*, passim.

5. See Michael Haas, "The Rise of a Science of Politics," in *Approaches to the Study of Political Science*, ed. Michael Haas and Henry S. Kariel (Scranton: Chandler, 1970), pp. 3–48.

6. See Mueller, in *Approaches to Measurement*, ed. Mueller.

necessary for the validity of generalizations. Hopefully, a guiding theory or a set of hypotheses will provide assistance in answering them and avoiding an arbitrary or opportunistic selection of cases (or too few cases).

The remainder of this chapter presents a variety of techniques for analyzing time series data and several examples of substantive applications in political science. A series refers to a data set ordered in time with observations normally made at regular intervals. These observations pertain to a host of political variables, whether aggregate or individual. Any one or a number of functions can be performed with time data, including description, explanation and prediction.[7] Although prediction (or forecasting) is most uniquely suited to time data, the operations we perform, some of the questions we ask, the logic employed, and even many of the statistics are comparable to the analysis of data at only one point in time. Furthermore, a concern for variations is common to most data analysis whether at one or more points in time. This notion of variation is, of course, a key element in statistical analysis. When we treated data at one point in time we were primarily interested in variations about a spatial mean; now we are concerned with temporal variations as well. The first sections to follow deal directly with statistical techniques for the analysis of (1) any one series or (2) the relationships between series. After treating these types of temporally observed data, the third part considers procedures for the analysis of quasi-panels (or cohorts) and the fourth moves directly to the individual level for the analysis of panel data with simple probability models.

Statistical Analysis of Univariate Time Series

The means by which we describe a time series representing one variable with successive observations involves procedures not unlike description at one point in time. That is, depending on the type and measurement level of the data, we could present frequencies, percentages, proportions, or means. The most frequently used form of presentation is the graph, with time intervals on the X axis and levels or amounts of the variable on the Y axis. The basic consideration governing graphic form is ease of presentation and interpretability. In most instances the time values on the X axis will have equal intervals. This also may be true for the values of the variables being studied, but sometimes the scale of the graph will be fixed to highlight the characteristics in question.[8] The basic purpose in such plotting is to present a clear picture of variations over time. If there is no variation in a time series it could be plotted in a straight horizontal line and in that case there would be little to explain and probably no need for such analysis. For example, if the proportion of people voting Democratic in presidential elections since the turn of the century was static, we would seek an explanation of aggregate behavior in a variable other than time (or we might not be interested in it at all). But few things are static in political analysis — there are variations, peaks and valley, ups and downs — which are in need of explanation.

---

7. See Paul F. Lazarsfeld and Morris Rosenberg, eds., *The Language of Social Research* (New York: The Free Press, 1955), section III for an overview of types of time series research, including prediction studies.
8. For the basics of graphic presentation see Oliver Benson, *Political Science Laboratory* (Columbus: Charles E. Merrill, 1969), chapter 3.

An explanation of variations depends on a thorough understanding of the forces at work in any one time series.[9] The definition and decomposition of these forces may vary by theoretical approaches taken by the researcher and by the type of data being analyzed (especially in terms of the time intervals between observations). Since one basic approach to these forces is predominant in the quantitative foundations for time series analysis, namely, the economic analysis approach, the beginning of this chapter will attempt to overview these forces from that perspective. In addition to the predominance of this model and the fact that so many varieties of statistical analysis evolve from it, it is most useful for developing the logic necessary for understanding variations in time series. This should not imply that the model is sacred, for it more frequently has theoretical utility for economic series than for some political series. The point is that the parts into which a time series is decomposed are largely a function of the theory one has about the types of change processes which are at work. Unfortunately, political scientists have not been sufficiently attentive to time series to offer elaborate quantitative alternatives to basic models tied to a business cycle analogy. Developments are certain to occur in the near future; but these developments are not likely to emerge if political scientists fail to grasp and apply the basics overviewed in this chapter. As a simple extension, there is already evidence that social scientists may prefer to focus on the durability of time series effects, i.e., whether it is long term, short term, cyclical, or random.

The forces considered in the economic model are reflected in four basic types of variation or types of change in a series. These components may be found separately or in combination in any one series and they include the following: (1) trend (T) representing a long-term tendency; (2) seasonal variation (S) representing a peak of variations at one month or season within a year; (3) cyclical variation (C) representing variation in ups and downs recurring through time with little regularity; and (4) irregular (I) representing random variation or disturbances in the relationship over time. For purposes of analysis, each component may be important in itself, or we may seek to eliminate any particular component(s) so that we can better identify a remaining element or source of variation. Any time series of raw data (TS) may be decomposed into these forces. Two common ways by which a time series is decomposed are (1) the additive model, where $TS = T + S + C + I$, and (2) the multiplicative model, where $TS = T \cdot S \cdot C \cdot I$. The removal of each of these effects is also dependent upon the theoretical approach of the researcher. Generally, the multiplicative model has been found to be more useful to economists and forecasters, and its facility in yielding standardized measures (e.g., ratios which are multiplied by 100) is advantageous for many forms of analysis. The examples

9. A discussion of components and other basics about time series can be found in Carl F. Christ, *Econometric Models and Methods* (New York: John Wiley, 1966); Edward E. Lewis, *Methods of Statistical Analysis in Economics and Business*, 2d ed. (Boston: Houghton Mifflin, 1963); John Johnston, *Econometric Methods* (New York: McGraw-Hill, 1963); Edmond Malinvaud, *Statistical Methods in Econometrics* (Chicago: Rand McNally, 1966); Gerhard Tintner, *Econometrics* (New York: John Wiley, 1952); and M. H. Quenouille, *Associated Measurements* (New York: Academic Press, 1952). For more extensive treatment see Edward J. Hannan, *Time Series Analysis* (New York: John Wiley, 1962); T. C. Koopmans, ed., *Statistical Inference in Dynamic Economic Models* (New York: John Wiley, 1950); and M. H. Quenouille, *The Analysis of Multiple Time Series* (New York: Hafner, 1957). For an introduction to political science applications see V. O. Key, Jr., *A Primer of Statistics for Political Scientists* (New York: Thomas Y. Crowell, 1966).

developed below rely upon division as a means for removing effects rather than subtraction.

In relying on the above forces to describe time series, we should be alert to other components which may be inherent in the data. For example, there may be forces of a regular or periodic variety, such as interim election depressions in voter turnout. Furthermore, we should be aware of the extent to which defined sources are dependent upon the length of time between observations. Seasonal variation, for example, does not exist if we have only one observation per year. Hopefully, the researcher's involvement in data analysis will assume theoretical perspectives, and these may yield different forces useful for analysis.

Trend Variation

Perhaps the most theoretically relevant variation for political data analysis is trend (sometimes referred to as secular trend). It is a long-term tendency for a variable to change its values over time. It represents a regular progression in one direction or the other over time. For example, the size of the potential American electorate has increased regularly (except for small irregularities caused by events such as war), reflecting an underlying upward trend in the population.

In describing trend, there are two basic characteristics which should be examined: (1) the duration of the trend and (2) the amount of decrease or increase. If the direction is always the same for a set of points on a graph, a straight line may be drawn on the points. This trend may be important in itself to describe the progression of values or to compare with another trend. Yet in order to study other factors influencing the series (e.g., seasonal, cyclical, or irregular effects), the trend would have to be eliminated. By measuring trend we are able to describe and remove it, leaving the series composed of seasonal, cyclical, and random variations.

After the series is graphed with a line or curve joining all points across time, there is an opportunity to estimate trend visually. For example, a trend line can be fitted by inspection or by linking typical points representing the increase or decrease. Such a procedure is not harmful at the outset, since it gives a rough idea of the empirical lay of the land; yet it can be highly subjective and there is no reason to rely on it since quantification is possible and relatively easy. Several computation procedures address this question.[10]

One procedure involves the calculation of *semi-averages* as a way of locating "typical" points on an empirical basis. A basic measure of typicality or central tendency is, of course, the mean. Just as the mean is representative of a set of observations at one point in time, it can be representative of a series of observations over time. The "averaging of halves" procedure involves separating the graph line for the raw data into two equal parts and after an average is taken within each part, there are two points to draw a trend line between. This is an easy, but rarely an adequate, solution for two reasons: mean values are easily distorted by extremes, and it does not provide a parsimonious measure of trend useful for its elimination.

---

10. These procedures utilize interval data on the variable; for an example of a nonparametric test for trend in ranked observations of a series, not unlike Kendall's tau, see Gerhard Tintner, "Time Series," in *International Encyclopedia of the Social Sciences*, ed. David L. Sills (New York: Crowell, Collier and Macmillan, 1968), vol. 16, p. 50.

A second procedure enables us to depict trend by "smoothing out" fluctuations in the raw data: *moving averages*. It involves the calculation of a mean for a particular time span and moving it to the center of that period. The first observation in the time span then is dropped and a new average is calculated for a new time period of the same length as the first. This means we have picked up (moved on to) an additional observation in the future to cancel out the omission of the first observation. In effect, the center of the time span moves ahead by one time unit with averages calculated throughout the series. The value of these averages is determined by the number of time points in each period. We therefore speak of these averages as three-year moving averages, four-year moving averages, and so on, depending on the length of the time span chosen for analysis.

As an example consider hypothetical observations of the Democratic percentage of the two-party vote for president in a particular state for a series of presidential election years. The left half of table 5.1 presents the raw data and various computations necessary for a three-year moving average. Since the chosen time span is three years, the first step is to derive a mean for the first three election years. To calculate the second moving average, the first year is dropped (1932) and the next one is added (1944). This process continues until the series is exhausted. These moving averages then are superimposed on, or fitted to, the raw data in the form of a trend line (fig. 5.1).

TABLE 5.1 Computation of the Moving Average

Year	% Dem.	3 Year Moving Total	3 Year Moving Average	4 Year Moving Total	4 Year Moving Average	2 Year Moving Total of 4 Year Moving Average	2 Year Moving Average of 4 Year Moving Total
1932	30						
1936	32	93	31.0				
				126	31.5		
1940	31	96	32.0			64.3	32.2
				131	32.8		
1944	33	99	33.0			67.1	33.6
				137	34.3		
1948	35	106	35.3			70.1	35.1
				143	35.8		
1952	38	110	36.7			73.3	36.7
				150	37.5		
1956	37	115	38.3			77.3	38.7
				159	39.8		
1960	40	121	40.3			80.6	40.3
				163	40.8		
1964	44	126	42.0			84.3	42.2
				174	43.5		
1968	42	134	44.7				
1972	48						

If the time span is an even number of years, the moving average calculated as above would fall at the center of a time period. In the above example the first four-year moving average would fall between 1936 and 1940. This is rarely a meaningful value; therefore, it is realigned with a time period by calculating a moving average of the moving averages. These calculations also are presented in table 5.1.

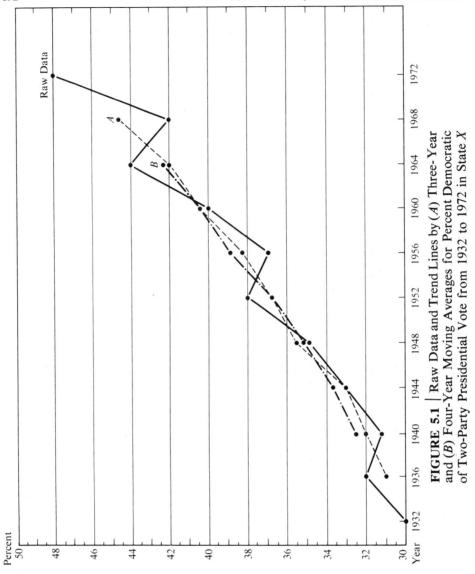

FIGURE 5.1 | Raw Data and Trend Lines by (A) Three-Year and (B) Four-Year Moving Averages for Percent Democratic of Two-Party Presidential Vote from 1932 to 1972 in State X

For adjusting (or centering) a four-year moving average the first two four-year averages are added and divided by two. The second centered value is obtained by averaging the second and third four-year averages and this procedure is followed successively throughout the series. The final result is a set of averages coinciding with measured points in time. These final values then can be plotted, as in figure 5.1.

The above procedure enables the plotting of a trend line and the smoothing out of data fluctuations; yet there is one major disadvantage and one consideration to keep in mind. The disadvantage is that the procedure does not yield a measure of change or prediction because it is not susceptible to mathematical treatment. The major consideration involved is that of choosing a proper time span to govern the calcula-tion of the averages. In some instances we might have an underlying theoretical reason related to the actual empirical distribution. For example, if we were examin-ing political participation rates over time, we might expect them to peak at presidential election years, thereby encouraging a four-year moving average. From a related perspective, we might be trying to smooth out fluctuations and we therefore choose a time span equal to the length of that fluctuation we seek to eliminate. In this example, the average duration of a fluctuation would be four years. Finally, the choice of a time span is also dependent on our willingness to lose relevant information. Since we are calculating averages of periods, we lose data at the beginning and end of the series (see table 5.1). With a larger time span, more of these data are lost. For example, for a seven-year moving average, three years are lost at the beginning and three years at the end of the series. If the values are plotted, the trend line fitting them will be considerably shorter than the raw data line.

Another solution to the trend problem and one that is usually more satisfactory involves the use of *regression* analysis. The procedure is similar to that presented in chapter 2, except that one variable is the values at different observations, and the other variable is time. That is, time (as an independent variable) is regressed against the value of the variable being studied. By following the straight line equation, $Y = a + bX$, where a = the Y value (e.g., percent Democratic votes) at the X origin (t_0), and where b = the rate of change (regression coefficient), any pair of X or Y values can be substituted in the equation once a and b are estimated. The result is a set of points (extremes are usually chosen) necessary for drawing a straight line.

Table 5.2 presents the percentage Democratic data utilized in the calculation of moving averages (above) plus the basic calculation necessary for solving a linear

TABLE 5.2 Computation of Regression Line for Percent Democratic of Two-Party Presidential Vote from 1932 to 1972 in State X

Y (% Dem.)	X (time)	X^2	XY
30	0	0	0
32	1	1	32
31	2	4	62
33	3	9	99
35	4	16	140
38	5	25	190
37	6	36	222
40	7	49	280
44	8	64	352
42	9	81	378
48	10	100	480
$\Sigma Y = 410$	$\Sigma X = 55$	$\Sigma X^2 = 385$	$\Sigma XY = 2235$ $N = 11$

equation. The technique is identical to that employed in chapter 2, where $Y = a + bX$ and

$$b_{yx} = \frac{N(\Sigma XY) - (\Sigma X)(\Sigma Y)}{N(\Sigma X^2) - (\Sigma X)^2}$$

$$- \frac{11(2235) - (55)(410)}{11(385) - (55)^2}$$

$$= 1.682$$

and where

$$a_{yx} = \frac{\Sigma Y - b_{yx}\Sigma X}{N}$$

$$= \frac{410 - 1.682(55)}{11}$$

$$= 28.9$$

By substituting the most extreme X values (time in the linear equation), we derive coordinates for a straight line representing linear trend (fig. 5.2):

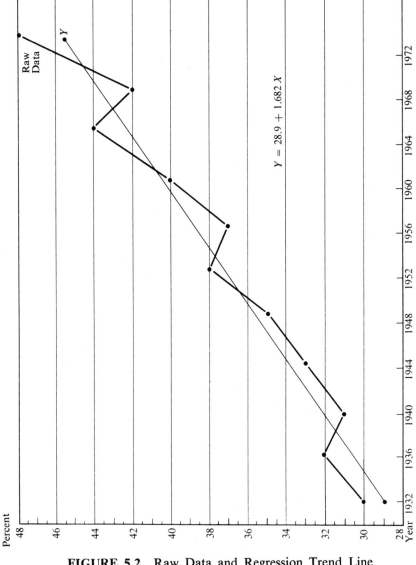

FIGURE 5.2 Raw Data and Regression Trend Line
(Y) for Democratic Percent of Two-Party Presidential
Vote from 1932 to 1972 in State X

$$Y = 28.9 + (1.682)(0) = 28.9$$
$$Y = 28.9 + (1.682)(10) = 45.7$$

The coordinates of the first point are t_0 or 1932 and 28.9, and the coordinates of the second point are t_{10} or 1972 and 45.7. Therefore, the Democratic percentage begins at a (Y intercept) and increases steadily by a factor of b (1.682) per election.

Since trend is a long-term regularity, it will often resemble this linear function, yet if the raw data do not fit a linear pattern, curvilinear regression procedures could be applied.[11] The major advantage of regression applied to trend analysis is that with one procedure we can measure direction of the slope (the sign of the regression coefficient), rate of change (magnitude of the regression coefficient), and derive values to plot a line for graphic presentation. Furthermore, knowledge of the regression coefficient facilitates prediction or forecasting when new time values are substituted in the trend equation.

After plotting a trend line by any one of several procedures, it may be necessary to eliminate the trend variations in order to study other time series effects. That is, through adjustment procedures we can smooth the raw data and then control for this ironing-out tendency. Examples of such adjustments are evident in the research by Smoker and Crittenden at the end of this chapter. As an illustration, one of Smoker's goals is to examine the extent to which later observations in a series are dependent upon immediately preceding observations (Sino-Indian communications). In order to accurately judge this phenomenon, he finds it necessary to remove a general trend in the data apparently caused by the influencing forces at work in economic and political growth. Also consider a hypothetical example, where, if we were to construct a graph of raw numbers showing that election turnout is increasing over time, the trend may be due primarily to population increases. We would therefore control or adjust for the population increase trend and the remaining detrended line would represent other types of variation (e.g., cyclical, seasonal, irregular) or perhaps no variation at all (a horizontal line). This idea is analogous to multiple and partial correlation techniques where the total variance in a dependent variable is explained by one variable controlling for others (partials). In time series total variation is composed of the four major sources of fluctuation (as independent variables), and by explaining one (e.g., trend) and then removing it, we are left with a residual variation due to the three remaining forces. Since this analogy holds, trend may be eliminated by dividing the original or raw data at each point in time by the corresponding trend value for that time. If regression analysis is employed each X value (time) would have a corresponding Y value (e.g., percent turnout, proportion Democratic) on the regression line. This point on the regression line then is divided into the raw data value at that point in time. If the method of moving averages is employed, each moving average value is divided into the raw data at a corresponding period. The values resulting from either division then are plotted to present a new line or curve representing the raw data with trend variation eliminated.

Seasonal Variation

A second type of variation found in time series is a periodic movement recurring at regular time intervals with one peak each year. Such variation is the least frequently

---

11. See descriptions in Lewis, *Methods of Statistical Analysis in Economics and Business*, pp. 608–15; Dennis J. Palumbo, *Statistics in Political and Behavioral Science* (New York: Appleton-Century-Crofts, 1969), pp. 217–22; and Hubert M. Blalock, *Social Statistics* (New York: McGraw-Hill, 1960), pp. 311–17.

occurring force in political data time series since many of these series are sets of yearly observations. Furthermore, seasonal variation is primarily due to either climate or customs. Yet, these factors should not be negated as political influences; for example, civil disturbances might peak once each year during the summer months, or, by the customs analogy, we might find that campaign contributions peak in October immediately preceding the customary general election month in the United States. In dealing with this seasonal variation, we might be interested in a number of things: the seasonal variation in itself can be meaningful, a comparison of two or more seasonal curves can provide comparative information about underlying processes, or we may seek to eliminate this variation in order to study other types of variation.

In order to study this variation a generalized measure for expressing it is necessary. One method would involve averaging observations at similar time periods. For example, if the raw data in a graph of monthly campaign contributions over several years peaked each year during the month of October, we would average October contributions to derive a typical October (or any other month). This would provide a typical annual distribution of the series. We do this because seasonal variation occurs only once each year and is therefore studied on a month by month basis. Yet before a typical annual can be constructed, other forms of variation should be eliminated. For example, campaign contributions may not only be associated with a seasonal high in October, they also may be part of a larger upward *trend;* or any one-time observation may represent an upward phase of a *cycle;* or economic fluctuations or events might add *irregularity* to the data. A hypothetical distribution displaying all of these forces is presented in figure 5.3 where the jagged points represent monthly irregularity (e.g., economic shocks), the yearly peaks represent seasonal variation (October highs), the midyear presidential election slumps and election year highs represent cycles (related to a seasonal pattern, and albeit, a bit too regular for usual cyclical definitions), and the general upward movement signals a trend.

If seasonal variation is the primary focus for studying these hypothetical data, it must be measured and other types of variation removed. Only after this is completed can the time observations be averaged into a typical annual with some control over nonseasonal elements. One of the most frequently used measuring techniques is the *ratio to moving average.* The procedure is very similar to the method of moving averages for measuring trend. The primary difference is that since seasonal implies a span of twelve calendar months, we employ a twelve-month moving average. That is, a series of months for several years are arrayed as in table 5.1, a twelve-month moving average is computed as we move month by month through the series, and since we are treating an even number of time periods, the moving averages are themselves averaged or centered to correspond with measured points in time (similar to the four-year moving average computation in table 5.1).

The calculated moving average values represent trend and cycle effects, so they can be eliminated (as in our discussion of trend) by dividing each corresponding value of the raw data by the respective moving average. For example, the moving average for July is divided into the original July value for campaign contributions, and this is done for each month until the moving averages are exhausted. These new values are usually called "seasonal relatives." When they are graphed with the time period we have a plotting of seasonal and irregular variations with trend and cycle effects eliminated.

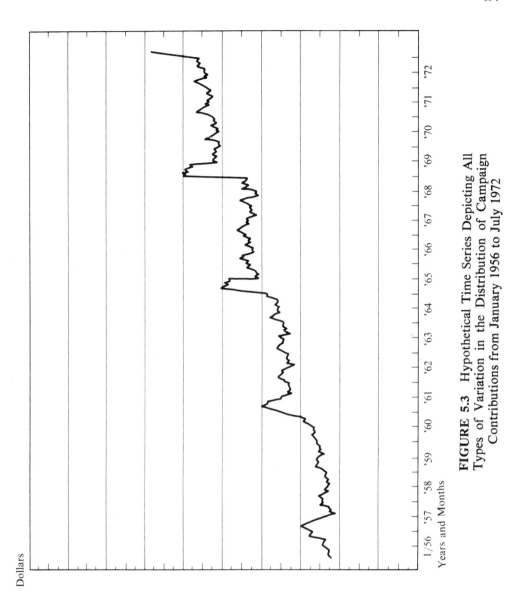

FIGURE 5.3 Hypothetical Time Series Depicting All Types of Variation in the Distribution of Campaign Contributions from January 1956 to July 1972

Another step involves the removal of irregular and random fluctuations from the seasonal relatives. Since the most extreme seasonal relatives are caused by random shocks on the time series, we may exclude these extreme values and thereby reduce the effect of shocks. However, instead of excluding relevant information we can take advantage of a measure of central tendency which is not affected by extreme values — the median. This measure is therefore employed as we construct a typical annual graph and typical seasonal relatives (usually expressed as a percent) for each month. The percentage value means that the value for each is a certain percentage above the trend/cycle value. That is, in averaging all of the Julys, all of the Augusts, and so on, we choose the median July value, the median August value. These median values then can be plotted to derive a graph representing typical seasonal relatives for each month of a hypothetical or average year. The resultant curve on the graph therefore depicts the seasonal variation in the data, with other effects removed. But now that we have displayed a generalized measure, it will often be instructive to return to the original data over the entire period in question. This can now be plotted in its entirety with adjustments for seasonality by dividing the original data by the seasonal index (seasonal relatives for each month, which are the same for every year) for the corresponding month.[12]

Cyclical Variation

A third type of fluctuation present in time series is a cyclical movement with periodic ups and downs, peaks and valleys. These patterns lie somewhere between the regularity of seasonal variation and the irregularity of random fluctuations. When cyclical effects are present they are exemplified by broad patterns varying in duration and intensity and recurring with little regularity. Because of these characteristics, the causes of cyclical variation are more difficult to explain than other variations. Nevertheless, political scientists have attempted to adopt the language of cycles for various forms of data. In studies of the American electorate we might find that new cycles of partisan support begin with certain critical elections, representing a deviation from the base line or normal vote.

In order to isolate cyclical effects, the trend, seasonal, and random variations must be removed. This is an approximation procedure (since we can rarely eliminate other effects completely) which leaves us with the cycle component, i.e., a residual. When dealing with yearly observations, the estimation of this residual is relatively easy. Such annual data do not have seasonal variation, and irregular variation will be minimal or averaged out. Therefore, we often focus on the removal of trend variation alone. This process involves the comparison of original data with the statistical normal or trend. This is accomplished by dividing the raw data by calculated trend values (e.g., from regression analysis or moving averages) to derive "cyclical relatives." These relatives then are plotted to represent cyclical variation in the time series with other variations controlled.

If a particular time series is measured at monthly intervals, the isolation of cycles becomes more involved. With this type of series all four effects are likely to be present (if the period is sufficiently long to capture trend). Therefore, we must eliminate trend, seasonality, and irregularity. In this case, the original monthly data would be divided by each trend value for that month, and this adjusted data would in turn be divided by the seasonal index for each month. The residual is then cyclical and irregular variation. The final step would remove random fluctuation by applying moving averages to smooth out the irregularity in the de-trended and de-seasoned data. As a rule of thumb, the time span for calculating these moving averages should equal the average length of irregular variations in the data.

Irregular Variation

The final type of variation has been referred to at various points in the discussion above. It is fluctuation which is irregular, random, or haphazard, and it may be

---

12. For an overview of other procedures for treating seasonality and cycles, such as periodogram and spectral analysis, see Tintner, in *Encyclopedia of the Social Sciences*, ed. Sills, pp. 50–51.

evident at any point in time throughout a series. It is often associated with the occasional occurrence of events or other phenomena which have a temporary, but jarring, impact on the variable being studied. The impact of certain events on the stock market is a good example of this effect. If we want to isolate it for study, the trend, seasonal and cyclical variations are computed and removed from the original data by division. An alternative means is to use seasonal relatives which are calculated before the median averaging process discussed above for seasonal variation, i.e., seasonal relatives contain irregularity. Therefore, we can eliminate the seasonal index (seasonal alone, after median averaging) by dividing it into the seasonal relatives. The result is a residual representing irregular variations.

Interrelationships Within a Series

Our basic task to this point has been a description of time series data, variations in them, and a concern for processes underlying them. Before moving on in the next section to examine relationships between two or more series, thereby expanding the comparative method across space as well as time, our attention will focus on the nature of interrelationships within a time series. Information about these interrelationships enables judgment about the independence of successive observations over time and the stability of those interrelationships. To perform this function, we rely here on simple correlation between sets of observations and the serial correlation coefficient.

Simple Correlation

When we have a time series with multiple observations at the same point (i.e., a set of aggregated time series), we can rely on usual correlation procedures for estimating shared relationships between sets of observations. As an example, consider data resembling that utilized by Pomper in the readings following this chapter. In order to examine the interdependence of voting in successive presidential elections, he has gathered data on the Democratic percentage of each state's total vote. At each point in time he has a set of observations (percent Democratic) for each state which can be correlated with a similar set of observations at another point in time. The procedure utilizes the regular Pearson product-moment correlation coefficient as described in chapter 2. These coefficients then are plotted to derive a graph expressing the nature of interrelationships between successive elections. Furthermore, these coefficients may be lagged in time (between sets of observations more than one time interval apart) to represent the interrelationship between values at the first point in time (t_1) and at the third point in time (t_3), representing a lag of one, between t_1 and t_4 (lag of two), and so on. Through this technique we can make judgements about stability/instability in the change process over time and the dependence/independence of later observations on previous ones.

Serial Correlation

In the usual time series case, where only one observation is made at each point in time, independence is measured by the serial correlation (or autocorrelation).[13]

---

13. Related tests include the Wald and Wolfowitz R test — see A. Wald and J. Wolfowitz, "An Exact Test for Randomness in the Non-Parametric Case Based on Serial Correlation," *Annals of Mathematical Statistics* 14 (1943): 378–88; the von Neumann Ratio — see John von Neumann, "Distribution

Autocorrelation effects are present in a series when the consecutive items of a series are not independent. This effect is complicated by the fact that many kinds of time series data are not derived from random samples, while most of the theory of statistical estimation and inference assumes statistical independence. That is, in some instances, observations are not independent of one another and therefore they fail to satisfy the assumption of independence in many forms of statistical analysis.[14] Yet this is a more serious problem for econometrics than for political science. Survey data are prevalent in political science (albeit relatively short periods) and, furthermore, autocorrelation tends to increase with a decrease in time intervals between observations. That is, with smaller intervals, observations are closer to each other in a series and we are more likely to obtain a reading of a particular moment of *one* underlying phenomenon or dimension rather than a reading of *separate* events or values.[15] Most data relevant to political observations are not recorded with such frequency.

The null hypotheses being tested through the use of a serial correlation coefficient is that items of a series are independent of each other. The test relies on procedures similar to other methods of correlation, but we get at variation by shifting observations by one time period at a time, i.e., it measures covariation of successive values in a series. For example, let us examine data for ten presidential years, 1932–1968, with the variable measuring the percentage Democratic of the popular vote. The correlation coefficient would examine the relationship between values at these years compared to the values at years lagged by one point in time:

	1932 ─┐
1932	1936
1936	1940
1940	1944
1944	1948
1948	1952
1952	1956
1956	1960
1960	1964
1964	1968
1968	◄──┘

The first values entered into the correlation scheme reflect the relationship between the first observation and the second, then the second and the third, until the last term

of the Ratio of the Mean Square Successive Difference to the Variance," *Annals of Mathematical Statistics* 12 (1941): 367–95; a stochastic process called the linear autoregressive process — see Leonard Hurwicz, "Least-Squares Bias in Time Series," in *Statistical Inference in Dynamic Economic Models*, ed. T. C. Koopmans (New York: John Wiley, 1950), pp. 365–83; and M. H. Quenouille, "A Large Sample Test for the Goodness of Fit of Autoregressive Schemes," *Journal of the Royal Statistical Society* 110 (1947): 123–29. In addition, there are tests for autocorrelation in regression residuals, such as the Durbin and Watson *d* statistic — see J. R. Durbin and G. S. Watson, "Testing for Serial Correlation in Least Squares Regression," *Biometrika* 37–38 (1950–51): 409–28, 159–78. Residual analysis is beyond our scope, but it is discussed extensively in Mordecai Ezekiel and Karl A. Fox, *Methods of Correlation and Regression Analysis*, 3d ed. (New York: John Wiley, 1959), chapter 20.

14. A related problem is that universes from which observations are drawn change over time. See Ezekiel and Fox, *Methods of Correlation and Regression Analysis*, chapter 2.

15. A correction for the serial correlation in light of this problem is presented in Quenouille, *Associated Measurements*, p. 168.

of the series is approached, at which time it is related to the first term. Because of the juxtaposition of the first and last terms, the serial coefficient derived is circular. The generalized formula is:

$$r_L^* = \frac{\Sigma X_t X_{t+1} - (\Sigma X_t)^2/N}{\Sigma X_t^2 - (\Sigma X_t)^2/N}$$

where $t = n$ and $t + 1 = 1$ representing a lag of one. Table 5.3 is a computation

TABLE 5.3 Computation of the Serial Correlation Coefficient for Percent Democratic of the Popular Presidential Vote, 1932–68

Time Periods	Values at Original Time Periods (% Dem.)	Values Shifted by One Point in Time (% Dem.)	Original Observation Values Squared	Product of Original Observation Values and Juxtaposed Values
t	X_t	X_{t+1}	X_t^2	$X_t X_{t+1}$
1932	54.7	54.7 / 60.8	2992.09	3325.76
1936	60.8	54.7	3696.64	3325.76
1940	54.7	53.4	2992.09	2920.98
1944	53.4	49.6	2851.56	2648.64
1948	49.6	44.4	2460.16	2202.24
1952	44.4	42.0	1971.36	1864.80
1956	42.0	49.5	1764.00	2079.00
1960	49.5	61.1	2450.25	3024.45
1964	61.1	42.7	3733.21	2608.97
1968	42.7		1823.29	2335.69
	$\Sigma X_t = 512.9$		$\Sigma X_t^2 = 26734.65$	$\Sigma X_t X_{t+1} = 26336.29$

table for popular vote data showing the derivation of values according to the serial formula.

$$r_L^* = \frac{26336.29 - 512.9^2/10}{26734.65 - 512.9^2/10} = .069$$

A small sample distribution of r_L^* has been derived so that its level of significance can be determined.[16] If it is not significant at the .05 level (as above), the distribution of the series is random, i.e., the values are independent of one another over time. If the r_L^* value had achieved a sufficient significance level, the null hypothesis of independence would have been rejected, and we would have concluded that successive observations (Democratic popular vote) are dependent upon or related to the immediately preceding observation (Democratic popular vote) in a series. Whether or not this value reaches significance, our theory and hypothesis could lead to an examination of serial relationships using more than one time lag. In this case, higher

---

16. A table is available in R. L. Anderson, "Distribution of the Serial Correlation Coefficient," *Annals of Mathematical Statistics* 13 (1942): 1–13.

order serial correlation coefficients would be computed by juxtaposing observations two or more time points apart. In addition, our hypothesis also might encourage us to remove particular variations in the data so that autocorrelation is measured after raw data are adjusted for trend, cycle, seasons, and/or randomness. This can be accomplished by following procedures described earlier in this chapter. In the case of trend, where the first and last observations in the data are of very different magnitude, a correction for trend can be applied through the noncircular serial correlation coefficient (r_L).[17]

Once these simple serial relationships are isolated, it is possible to introduce statistical control procedures, i.e., partial serial correlation coefficients.[18] For example, we might obtain a partial coefficient for a series of observations juxtaposed to two time periods apart, controlling for or eliminating the effect of the intermediate time period observations. This would help us judge the extent to which a particular term was valuable for explaining later observations (i.e., if it contains all the relevant information for a future term). In some time series each observation will be solely dependent upon the immediately preceding observation, rather than one in the past (e.g., population estimates). When this previous information beyond the immediately preceding observation is not helpful in predicting a later term, the observations form a *first order Markov chain*. If no *one* observation is sufficient for predicting a future observation, more than one past observation might be used. This would represent a Markov process of the second or higher order, depending on how many previous observations are needed to explain a later one. In effect, the partial serial correlation coefficients can help us estimate the order of the Markov process.

To obtain these partials, we must calculate at least three separate serials. For example, with a series of 20 observations, the data would be divided into three groups: observations 1 through 18, 2–19, and 3–20. Notice that sets 1–18 and 2–19 are those used for a simple serial coefficient. The next step is to serially correlate these groups with each other to obtain r_{12} (for groups 1–18 and 2–19), r_{23} (2–19 and 3–20), and r_{13} (1–18 and 3–20). These three r values then can be substituted in the usual formula for partial correlation coefficients (see chapter 2). In this example, $r_{13.2}$ represents a control for the intermediate observation. This value may be useful in and of itself, but it also is considered a "rough" test of Markovity. More exact measures of Markov processes are presented later in this chapter.

Interrelationships Between Time Series

In the preceding sections we have discussed means for describing a simple time series, isolating and measuring variations and underlying processes, and examining serial relationships *within* a series. Political analysts are not only interested in the relationship between values of a variable through time, but in the interrelationship between variables and values of another (or more) variables over time. In other words, we extend the comparative method over time *and* space in analyzing relationships *between* series.

---

17. For the formula see Palumbo, *Statistics in Political and Behavioral Science*, p. 270. The distribution of r_L is not known, making considerable guesswork out of significance.

18. See Quenouille, *Associated Measurements*, chapter 11.

At the descriptive level, two series can be plotted on the same graph and visually inspected for relationships. We are most interested in how they vary together, i.e., whether one variable (e.g., the economy) is associated with upward or downward shifts in another (e.g., the reelection of incumbents). In addition, major departures from uniform relationships should be inspected to isolate possible effects on those gaps, as well as reasons for two lines varying together at only certain points in time. Yet these visual procedures, as well as correlational analysis, may lead to errors in interpretation. For example, two variables may peak simultaneously, yet this does not necessarily imply that one causes the other; instead, both variables may be influenced by a third factor or a common event. Furthermore, we should be particularly cautious when comparing relationships between series if different units of measurement are used. It is possible to construct such a graph by measuring one variable up the left-hand side (e.g., apples, economic data) and another up the right-hand side (e.g., oranges, reelection of incumbents), with time arrayed along the X axis. Without employing any means of standardizing these variables (e.g., percentages), interpretation is difficult and frequently erroneous.

In addition to graphic inspection — which at best indicates direction and a feel for covariance — there are some common statistics available to assist us in making comparisons. The most useful are measures of dispersion enabling a quantitative comparison of swings (homogeneity/heterogeneity) in one line vis-à-vis the other. For example, the *ranges* could be compared as well as measures of *standard deviation*. These would assist us in isolating the scatter around a central tendency and in measuring the amplitude of the two series.[19]

Before proceeding to more sophisticated techniques for comparing series, there are two important factors to keep in mind. Standard deviations and other techniques such as correlation hide or cover up some basic components or forces in a time series. Since the time series may be composed of several component forces (T, C, S, I), if correlation techniques are employed the series being compared should be decomposed into their component parts. For example, two trends could have a high positive correlation while their irregularities or cycles are negatively related. Therefore, one or a number of components would be removed. The choice regarding which to remove is guided by our underlying theory and specific research hypotheses. For example, we might want to compare only the seasonality components of each period. If we wish to relate campaign contributions which peak in the fall with a measure of campaign visibility for particular candidates (e.g., by content analysis), covariance will be meaningful so long as cycles, trends, and random effects are removed.

A second factor is also important as a warning. Most correlation coefficients between series assume that neither variables are autocorrelated. Although certain political data are probably less susceptible to autocorrelation than economic data (for which most time series techniques were developed), if the serial coefficients are found to be significant, then there are tests to intercorrelate autocorrelated series.[20] Yet the above assumption is often treated as too constraining. For example, Quenouille claims that correlation and regression is valid so long as only one of two

---

19. For a presentation of simple graphic techniques see Key, *A Primer of Statistics for Political Scientists*, chapters 2 and 3.
20. See Tintner, *Econometrics*, pp. 247ff.

variables is serially correlated and if the deviations from the regression line are serially independent (measured by the Durbin-Watson d). If these conditions are not met, the regression technique must be modified.[21]

Given the above discussion, it should be obvious that the primary statistical comparisons between time series rely on correlation and regression techniques. The methods of analysis for two variables are similar to bivariate regression and correlation between variables measured at only one point in time. Regression analysis may be used to plot linear or curvilinear lines for each series against the time dimension as mentioned earlier. In addition, a regression of one variable against another (with both measured over time) provides information about the direction of relationships (sign of the regression coefficient) and the unit increases/decreases in one variable or series associated with unit increases/decreases in the other (magnitude of the regression coefficients). The correlation coefficients would measure the degree of association between the variables.

Yet one need not stop with two separate serials, the elimination of some component variation, or with a correlation between series — there are further steps possible for the location of covariance between series. Indeed, simple correlation between series might hide some important effects. Furthermore, analysis is complicated by attempting to treat relationships between one serially correlated series (X) and a random series (Y). This autocorrelated series (X) can be viewed as composed of two parts: (1) that which is predicted from previous information, plus (2) a random portion. If the first or explained portion was correlated with the second variable (Y), it would imply that Y was also serially correlated, and this may not be so. Therefore, in testing relationships between series the random part of the serially correlated observations should be used against variable Y. This is achieved by calculating a partial correlation coefficient to eliminate the effect of previous observations on variable X. In effect, this is the test of the correlation between simultaneous random parts of the two series. Although this is a necessary step which provides useful information, it cannot address itself to the relationship between the non-simultaneous random elements of two series. Conceptually, we want to "line up" covariation between two series and seek it out over time. This is accomplished through time-lagged partial correlation coefficients which tell whether random variation in X is reflected in Y a year later (or more, depending on the lag).[22] That is, we correlate Y and X for the previous year and eliminate the effects of X for all previous years.

Let us first consider the partial without time lag. The procedure is analogous to that for calculating partial serial coefficients. For example, X may be divided into three subsets where $X_1 = t_1$ through t_{n-2}, where n equals the total number of time points in the series; $X_2 = t_2$ through t_{n-1}; and $X_3 = t_3$ through t_n. Variable Y is similarly divided into three subsets. These subsets may be intercorrelated in a variety of ways, e.g., $r_{X_3Y_3}$ equals the correlation between X and Y for the third subset of each. Also, $r_{X_3Y_3 \cdot X_2}$ represents the partial coefficient between X_3 and Y_3 with a control for the previous year's value of X. If we want to take the previous two years of X into account — or eliminate them — the higher order partial would equal $r_{X_3Y_3 \cdot X_1Y_2}$. If

---

21. See Quenouille, *Associated Measurements*, pp. 173–77.
22. Ibid., chapter 11.

the latter is statistically significant we would conclude that variation in Y and simultaneous unpredictable variation in X are correlated. If none of these coefficients are significant, then we would find no direct relationship between X and Y.

When the above coefficients are lagged, we build in more pieces of information about shared variances. For example, using the same hypothetical variables (one serially correlated and the other independent), the coefficient $r_{X_3Y_2 \cdot X_1X_2}$ would indicate whether the activity of Y precedes unpredictable changes in X. Similarly, $r_{X_2Y_3 \cdot X_1}$ would show if changes in X's value precede Y.

In instances where *both* X and Y are serially correlated, similar procedures may be used to eliminate previous effects of either or both series. When the partial eliminates previous effects of both series, it tests whether random variation in the two series is correlated. For example, if the coefficient $r_{X_3Y_3 \cdot X_1X_2Y_2}$ is lower than the less complex coefficients, e.g., $r_{X_3Y_3}$, it suggests that the elimination of the effects of previous observations has reduced the coefficient. If the value of the partial is low enough (significance tests are only approximate since both series are autocorrelated), we would conclude that there is no relationship between the residual variation in X and Y for any year.

The presence of autocorrelation in both series should not pose serious constraints on the examination of time-lagged relationships. If we have a simple lagged coefficient, e.g., $r_{X_3Y_2}$ with a high value, we might conclude that the frequency of occurrence of Y is related to X in the following year. Yet this higher relationship also might be due to the serial character of each set of observations. For example, X in any year would be related to X in the previous year, which is in turn related to Y in that year. In effect, autocorrelation is confounding the nature of the relationship, leading to spurious findings. One way of measuring this would rely on cross-lagged (between variables at different time points) partial correlation coefficients. For example, if $r_{X_3Y_2 \cdot X_1X_2Y_1}$ is not significant, then variation in Y for any year is not related to X in the following year (or the lag could go in the other direction as well).

Because of the time dimension built into the above coefficients, it is possible to make them compatible with causal analysis techniques. Indeed, these techniques (see chapter 3) assume a temporal ordering — an assumption which is met too infrequently. In attempting to isolate causal effects, we are generally interested in comparing the relationship between X at time 1 and Y at time 2 versus the relationship between X at time 2 and Y at time 1. If the coefficient for the first set is high and exceeds that for the second, there is evidence for causal inference. However, we have previously noted how autocorrelation can confound these relationships, necessitating cross-lagged correlation coefficients (or regression coefficients or path coefficients, depending on the causal technique).[23]

In summary, information about relationships between time series depends on a variety of processes: (1) eliminating any undesirable, empirically confounding, or theoretically irrelevant variations within the series; (2) testing for serial correlation within each series; (3) plotting the data to visually inspect the relationships between

---

23. See George W. Bohrnstedt, "Observations on the Measurement of Change," in *Sociological Methodology, 1969*, ed. Edgar F. Borgatta (San Francisco: Jossey-Bass, 1969), pp. 113–33; David R. Heise, "Problems in Path Analysis and Causal Inference," ibid., pp. 38–73; and D. C. Pelz and F. M. Andrews, "Detecting Causal Priorities in Panel Data," *American Sociological Review* 29 (1964): 836–48.

variables and the nature of a time lag necessary for linking up peaks and valleys; (4) describing homogeneity and heterogeneity in the data through measures of dispersion; (5) calculating partial serial correlation coefficients for each series to find out which observations contain the most relevant information for later observations (the nature of the Markov order); and (6) testing correlations and causal inferences. These procedures are a healthy order for a discipline where time is a useful explanatory device, where time data are available, and where so few thorough applications are present in research. Hopefully, familiarization with analysis possibilities will encourage the pursuit of time effects.

Cohort Analysis

In the preceding sections we have been treating time data as a set of observations repeated over time. In survey research, for example, a series of random samples usually draws different (yet representative) groups of people from the universe; we therefore have a cross section of individuals at t_1, another cross section at t_2, and so on, through a series. When these data are available, they enable us to generalize about net change only. For example, the series of cross-section data might show that the population is becoming more "dovish" in foreign affairs, yet we cannot generalize to individual behavior to claim that respondent A has changed *his* attitudes nor can we isolate factors influencing that change. Individual generalization can only be accomplished through panel surveys, where the same respondents are reinterviewed in waves over several time periods. But cross-section data contain more information regarding time and change than ordinarily meets the eye. Such information is extracted through cohort analysis, which, in effect, lies somewhere between usual cross-section analysis and panel data, i.e., a quasi-panel procedure.[24]

A cohort is a group of individuals each of which experienced common events during the same time period. Developing from demographic research on time series of fertility and stimulated by the notion of generations prevalent in less quantitative research,[25] it commonly focuses on a group of people born at a particular time whose characteristics are followed through time. Although age or birth date are usual bases for cohort definition, the cohorts could be based on other criteria, e.g., those entering the electorate at a particular election or mothers having their first child at a particular time. Cohort analysis therefore treats changing characteristics of a group or aggregate over time. The change which is measured is net change occurring to an aggregate rather than to individuals within the aggregate. It is therefore a method by which we build the time dimension into cross-section studies so that net change in smaller aggregates is examined. Our reliance on usual cross-section analysis has not only meant that change is often missed or not discussed,

---

24. For development of the concept see William M. Evan, "Cohort Analysis of Survey Data: A Procedure for Studying Long-Term Opinion Change," *Public Opinion Quarterly* 23 (1959): 63–72; Norman B. Ryder, "Notes on the Concept of a Population," *American Journal of Sociology* 59 (1964): 447–63; Ryder, "The Cohort as a Concept in the Study of Social Change," *American Sociological Review* 30 (1965): 843–61; Ryder, "Cohort Analysis," in *Encyclopedia of the Social Sciences*, ed. Sills, vol. 2, pp. 546–50; and Neal E. Cutler, *The Alternative Effects of Generations and Aging Upon Political Behavior: A Cohort Analysis of American Attitudes Toward Foreign Policy, 1946–1966* (Oak Ridge: Oak Ridge National Laboratory, 1968).

25. For example, see Karl Mannheim, "The Problem of Generations," in *Essays on the Sociology of Knowledge*, ed. Paul K. Kecskemeti (London: Routledge and Kegan Paul, 1952), pp. 278ff.

thereby limiting our substantive knowledge, but that a body of change theory was slow in developing throughout the social sciences. Although panel studies are more suited to the study of change, the availability of panel data is usually quite limited and often for relatively short time durations. As a consquence, political science has witnessed a growing interest in cohort analysis in the very recent past.

Cohort analysis uses a group as the analogue of a set of panel respondents over time. These are people who experience relevant events or stimuli at a common point in time, e.g., going to school or war. The cohort is identified by age breakdowns adjusted to the interval between a series of cross-section studies. This interval governing the span of each cohort is not only shaped by the available data (i.e., how far apart observations are), but by our hypotheses. In treating electoral behavior, for example, the four-year span between presidential elections and the age limit on voting would be factors taken into consideration. If we had three cross-section studies ten years apart, the first cohort might consist of people who were 21–30 years old at the t_1 cross section, those who were 31–40 at t_2, and those 41–50 at t_3. A second cohort would include respondents who are, in effect, a generation older: those 51–60 at t_1, 61–70 at t_2, and those 71–80 at t_3. The unit of analysis is the age group, which is the focus for study over time. These are different individuals each time, but by grouping them into a cohort we know, e.g., that they have shared similar events.

As an example, let us assume the availability of three cross sections ten years apart which contain comparable questions for the variable or characteristic under study. Table 5.4 depicts the responses of cohorts on a partisan identification question. If we had cross-section data only, i.e., without cohorts, we would cite the trend for the population to identify more with the Democratic party over the thirty-year period. This information is available in the first column of table 5.4. But when

TABLE 5.4 Hypothetical Distribution of Partisan Self-Identification (Major Party) by Total Samples and Age Cohorts Measured at Three Points in Time, Ten Years Apart

Time Period	% For Total Cross Section	PARTISAN IDENTIFICATION % for Cohorts			
t_1	Dem. 50% Rep. 50	Cohort 1 (21–30) 45% 55			Cohort 2 (50–60) 55% 45
t_2	Dem. 60 Rep. 40		Cohort 1 (31–40) 40 60		Cohort 2 (61–70) 60 40
t_3	Dem. 70 Rep. 30	Cohort 3 (21–30) 80 20	Cohort 1 (41–50) 35 65	Cohort 4 (51–60) 65 35	Cohort 2 (71–80) 65 35

the cohorts are examined we see that the older cohort (#2) at t_1 was more Democratic than the younger cohort (#1) at t_1. It might be suggested that this difference is due to the older cohort's exposure to an event (e.g., economic depression) which is not common to the younger cohort. Furthermore, at t_2 the younger cohort has become more Republican than it was at t_1, while cohort #2 has become more Democratic. At the third point in time both cohorts tended to polarize to a greater extent. Normal cross-section analysis (column 1) will hide these trends and shifts. Also note that at t_3 we can begin to pick up two new cohorts which then could be extended into time with cross-section data.

In analyzing cohorts, there are two basic effects to examine — the effect of aging (*life cycle* or maturation effects) and the effect of common exposure to events (*generational*). In the above example, we see that age relationships are inverse — as one cohort ages it becomes more Republican and as the other follows through a life cycle it becomes more Democratic. We could therefore suggest that a common event in the more Democratic cohort (e.g., depression) had a lasting effect that was also influenced by a Democratic trend in the total population. To analyze this a step further, we could decompose or stratify each cohort by some relevant variable(s) influencing the time series trend. For example, if we divided each cohort into high and low education categories, we might find that the younger group is not only more Republican due to the lack of depression memories, but that it is more highly educated. That is, education tempers the relationship because it is related to partisan identification. By controlling for another variable we can isolate effects that were previously hidden. This is especially important when age itself is not a good self-explanatory variable; as above, where the impact of aging on one cohort is the inverse of the impact on the other cohort. In this example life cycle effects tend to cancel each other out, but this might not be the case if we were studying political participation, which generally (albeit curvilinearly) decreases for age. Similarly, in treating political issues, older respondents tend to become more conservative (life cycle) but this may be "canceled out" by a generation effect, such as New Deal ties influencing one's socialization in favor of liberal causes.

Consequently, in treating cohorts there are several things to look for. We can generalize for each year and cite a trend for the total population. Yet this is not sufficient to show change — we must also examine the trend down the diagonal through one cohort. If the age effect is at work, it should be present in a rather monotonic increase in one value (e.g., proportion Democratic) over time. Incidentally, these values in a cohort matrix can be measured in a variety of ways, e.g., percentages, frequencies, proportions, means, or even correlation coefficients between variables. The typical cohort matrix derived from data as presented in table 5.3 would display age groupings along one dimension and points in time along another dimension (see examples in the readings to follow, especially table 1 in the Cutler article).

One of the more difficult tasks in analyzing cohorts refers to the isolation of generational and life cycle effects. When the matrix is constructed in the usual format, where the row variable is age or birth year and the column variable is the time points at which observations are recorded, one would read down the diagonals to assess life cycle effects, in a sense controlling for generational effects. To make judgements about generational changes we read across the rows, controlling for the effects of life cycle. We also might make attempts at a rough quantification of effects through the following procedure. For generational effects, we would read across each row (in this case, the age variable) comparing all pairs of observations in the row, noting any pair where the second value is larger and tallying a "+" value, and noting any pair in which the second score is less than the first tallying a "−". The number of minuses then can be compared to the number of plusses and the more they are out of balance (e.g., considerably more plusses than minuses or vice versa), the more there is a generational change. A chi square test of significance can aid in this judgement. The same method can be followed up and down the diagonals to test for the presence of life cycle effects.[26]

After solving the problem of isolating generational and life cycle effects it is necessary to keep other complications in mind. It should be clear by now that the presence of trend in a series examined by the cohort technique could confound results. It can be corrected when the values in the matrix are means by measuring each score's deviation from the mean for each year and entering the deviation in the matrix. Similarly, data for each year can be converted into a set of standardized Z scores so that data values have the same mean and standard deviation, thereby making age groups more comparable. Another complication of cohort analysis involves the accumulation of sampling error across cross sections, but most contemporary samples are able to keep this to a minimum. Finally, we have the problem of cohort mortality and change, i.e., the disappearance of some respondents in the cohort due to death, and an influx of new respondents due to migration. The latter is generally not a problem in studies of the entire United States population, but more regionalized universes (e.g., South versus non-South) are particularly susceptible to in and out migration effects.

Simple Probability Models and Panel Analysis

In the discussion of cohort analysis comparisons were made with data-gathering methods focusing on the individual level. By constructing cohorts for analysis purposes we were able to generalize about effects on groupings of individuals by age over a series of cross-section samples. With panel data, the same individual is actually interviewed more than once, thereby enabling an analysis of individual change over time. However, this method of gathering data is not without fault. There are potential contamination effects in the data once the individual realizes he is part of a panel and therefore will be reinterviewed. Furthermore, any study of change involves measurement processes which are not totally reliable. Indeed, the manifest change which we observe in data is composed of some error change (such as response uncertainty) plus some real change. This real change may be unsystematic or it may be rendered systematic by our ability to explain it using specific models. The problem of distinguishing real and error change is always with us, but there are procedures for isolating these effects which we need not discuss here.[27] In addition, panel mortality in a variety of forms can be serious, e.g., there will be deaths and because of mobility some individuals may not be located again.

---

26. See William R. Klecka, "Applying Political Generations to the Study of Political Behavior: A Cohort Analysis," *Public Opinion Quarterly* 35 (1971): 358–73 for a more sophisticated variation to this procedure utilizing the grand average deviation proportion.

27. See James S. Coleman, *Models of Change and Response Uncertainty* (Englewood Cliffs, N.J.: Prentice-Hall, 1964).

Nevertheless, panel data offer a distinct advantage over cross-section data because they encompass a closed rather than an open system. In a cross section, various people are in and out over time. If we study change with usual aggregating measures we cannot tell whether people are changing their minds over time (maturation). Furthermore, if a new generation of people is now in the universe (generational effect) or have migrated there, when net attitudes appear to be changing, it may be an effect due to in or out migration rather than to individual change. On the other hand, panel data provide us with information on more than net change observed in the distribution of marginal frequencies. Consider a two by two table comparing observations at two points in time with the following marginals as shown in table 5.5. With cross-section data we can only derive the marginal or net change (at least without sophisticated estimation procedures based upon regression). Fifty-two people were in state X at the first point in time, but sixty were in state X at time 2. But this does not mean that eight people from state Y at t_1 changed to X at t_2. Some X's might become Y's over time and some Y's might become X's and some of each may remain the same. In order to know something about individual change, we need the cell entries to this table, i.e., gross change. As it is now presented, a variety of different cell entries could satisfactorily sum to the given marginal frequencies. Panel data provide these individual cell entries.

TABLE 5.5

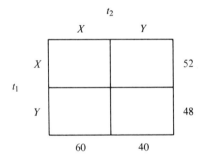

Given these advantages of panel data, it is possible to analyze change in a variety of ways. Aside from the description of tables and the use of correlations and cross-lagged correlations, one of the most fundamental methods involves comparing data over time with a model governing that change process. A host of such models is available for political data[28] that generally belong to a class of *stochastic process* models representing the process of change. These models are governed by the laws of probability, thereby specifying some degree of regularity in the probability of certain answers over time. For example, time dimensions can be separated into a tree of logical possibilities representing attitude or behavior change. A tree for three time periods or waves of a panel measuring Republican and Democratic votes would

---

28. See ibid.; Lee M. Wiggins, "Mathematical Models for the Interpretation of Attitude and Behavior Change: The Analysis of Multi-Wave Panels" (Ph.D. dissertation, Columbia University, 1955); Paul F. Lazarsfeld, "The Logical and Mathematical Foundation of Latent Structure Analysis," in *Measurement and Prediction*, ed. Samuel A. Stouffer et al. (Princeton: Princeton University Press, 1950), pp. 364–412; and Leo Goodman, "Statistical Methods for the Mover-Stayer Model," *Journal of the American Statistical Association* 56 (1961): 841–68.

resemble the diagram in figure 5.4 (with sample probabilities inserted). By using this device, any individual's voting record across time is represented by a particular path. With three waves in a panel, we can fill in the proportion or probability of individuals moving from R to D or D to R through time. That is, each branch of the tree has a probability of transition to another branch or state. This *transition probability* of moving from one response to another is conditional or dependent upon a previous response. The sum of the transition probabilities for each trial or experiment (each pair of R and D) equals unity. In the above tree: at t_1, $R = .4, D = .6$, and $.4 + .6 = 1$; at t_2, $R = (.4)(.8) + (.6)(.1) = .38, D = (.4)(.2) + (.6)(.9) = .62$, and $.38 + .62 = 1$; at t_3, $R = .288 + .008 + .048 + .054 = .398$, $D = .032 + .072 + .012 + .486 = .602$, and $.398 + .602 = 1$.

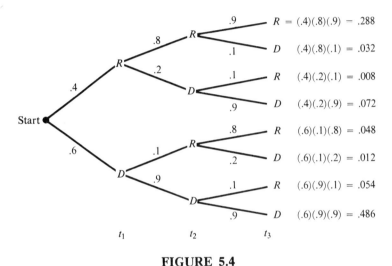

FIGURE 5.4

Generally, "a stochastic process is a series of experiments the outcome of which depends on the relevant transition probabilities."[29] Each transition probability designates the conditional probability (i.e., one that holds true if only certain prior values have occurred) that the response at time 2 will be one value (e.g., Republican), when the outcome of time 1 was one or the other value (Republican, Democratic). The transition probability is therefore the probability of change over time, e.g., Republican to Democratic votes. If 80 percent (0.8) of the Republican voters again cast their ballot for a Republican at time 2, with 20 percent (0.2) switching to a Democratic vote, the process is the result of a large number of voters exposed to random forces (stochastic) over time.

While there is a variety of stochastic processes, only one of them will be considered here. The classification of models depends on three characteristics: (1) the nature of the state space, i.e., the nature of the values of the random variables — this may be either discrete (i.e., qualitative, nominal) or continuous (equal intervals through infinity); (2) the nature of the time domain — this may be discrete (e.g., a set of blocks, trials, or experiments) or continuous; and (3) the nature of the time variance

---

29. Otomar J. Bartos, *Simple Models of Group Behavior* (New York: Columbia University Press, 1967), p. 24.

or homogeneity — where the model is either stationary (the probabilities of change remain the same over time) or nonstationary (an evolving process where variables are no longer identically distributed).[30]

Various models and procedures represent combinations of these characteristics. For example, continuous states and discrete time may be treated with the random walk model in stochastic theory;[31] continuous variables and continuous time are treated with differential equations; and discrete state and continuous time with step functions.[32]

One of the most prevalent and comprehensible class of models are *Markov models*.[33] A process is Markovian if "the future state at any time depends only upon aspects of the process leading up to the present state."[34] The most well-known Markovian model is the *Markov chain*. This represents a Markovian process with discrete state space, a continuous or discrete time domain, and stationarity in the probability laws governing change.

As an example, let us assume panel data on voting behavior at three points in time across 100 panel responses. By discovering whether the transition probabilities from t_1 to t_2 hold for t_3, we can assess how well the data fit a Markov chain model. Furthermore, with stationarity in the transition probabilities, we can predict a future state at t_4. We begin with a contingency table comparing responses at t_1 and t_2 (see table 5.6). By dividing each cell entry by the respective row total, we enter probabilities into the cells (see table 5.7).

TABLE 5.6

t_2

		D	R	
	D	50	2	52
t_1	R	10	38	48
		60	40	100

---

30. See Thomas J. Fararo, "Stochastic Processes," in *Sociological Methodology, 1969*, ed. Borgatta, pp. 245–60, and for a review of areas of application to political data see S. Sidney Ulmer, "Stochastic Process Models in Political Analysis," in *Mathematical Applications in Political Science*, vol. 1, ed. John M. Claunch (Dallas: Arnold Foundation Monographs: Southern Methodist University, 1965), pp. 1–20.

31. See Donald E. Stokes and Gudmund R. Iversen, "On the Existence of Forces Restoring Party Competition," in *Elections and the Political Order*, ed. Angus Campbell et al. (New York: John Wiley, 1966), pp. 180–93.

32. See James S. Coleman, "The Mathematical Study of Change," in *Methodology in Social Research*, ed. Hubert M. Blalock and Ann B. Blalock (New York: McGraw-Hill, 1968), pp. 428–78.

33. Developed by the Russian mathematician, A. A. Markov (1856–1922). For an overview see John G. Kemeny and J. Laurie Snell, *Finite Markov Chains* (Princeton: Van Nostrand, 1963), and Kemeny and Snell, "A Markov Chain Model in Sociology," in *Readings in Mathematical Social Science*, ed. Paul F. Lazarsfeld and Neil W. Henry (Chicago: Science Research Associates, 1966), pp. 148–58.

34. Fararo, in *Sociological Methodology*, ed. Borgatta, p. 254.

TABLE 5.7

		t_2		
		D	R	
t_1	D	.96	.04	1.0
	R	.21	.79	1.0

These represent the probability of making a transition from D at t_1 to D at t_2, and so on. The probability of a respondent remaining Democratic is a high .96. On the other hand, Republicans are less likely to remain Republican (.79). The quality of prediction in successive time periods depends on whether the transition probability matrix remains the same over time. In the Markov model, time relationships fit the model if only a certain amount of past history affects the last or predicted matrix. In effect, a first order chain exists when each link is only dependent on the link immediately preceding it. In its most constraining form (first order) the model assumes (or tests) that the probability of movement of individuals from t_2 to t_3 is independent of what states the individual was in at t_1. By relaxation of the independence assumption, a second order chain would show that values at t_1 could add to the prediction as well (but t_0 would not), i.e., that knowledge about responses in the *two* immediately preceding periods is necessary to understand change in the third period.

The assumption of independence in a first order chain can be viewed in terms not unlike those discussed for causal models, and we have seen previously how serial correlation coefficients provide a rough test for Markovity. By the independence assumption the correlation between t_1 and t_2 times that between t_2 and t_3 should equal the correlation between t_1 and t_3. That is, there would be two independent paths, r_{12} and r_{23}, where $r_{13} = r_{12}r_{23}$ and $r_{13.2} = 0$.

In order to test for independence or predict future values, the matrix of transition probabilities can be converted into algebraic form:

$$D_{t_2} = .96D_{t_1} + .21R_{t_1}$$
$$R_{t_2} = .04D_{t_1} + .79R_{t_1}$$

The first equation tells us that the number of Democratic votes at t_2 equals .96 times the number of Democratic votes at t_1 plus .21 times the number of Republican votes at t_1 (i.e., in our example, sixty Democratic votes at t_2). When these relationships are translated into matrix algebra form:

$$(D_{t_2}, R_{t_2}) = (D_{t_1}, R_{t_1})\begin{pmatrix} .96 & .04 \\ .21 & .79 \end{pmatrix}$$

and substituting the values we have:

$$(60, 40) = (52, 48)\begin{pmatrix} .96 & .04 \\ .21 & .79 \end{pmatrix}$$
$$= (.52)(.96) + (.48)(.21), (.52)(.04) + (.48)(.79)$$

This decomposition of existing data at t_1 and t_2 displays a set of relationships necessary for understanding the next step. Since the Markov model assumes that the matrix of probabilities is constant, if this condition holds we should be able to find the distribution at t_3 or to explain previously collected data at t_3 in terms of its fit to a particular model or process. Using matrix algebra[35] the general formula is:

$$p^{(3)} = p^{(2)}P$$

where p's are row vectors and P is the matrix of transition probabilities. Therefore,

$$p^{(3)} = (60, 40)\begin{pmatrix} .96 & .04 \\ .21 & .79 \end{pmatrix}$$

We then multiply the row vector (marginals at t_2) by the matrix and

$$p^{(3)} = 60(.96) + 40(.21), 60(.04) + (.79)$$
$$p^{(3)} = 66, 34$$

This gives the row vector or marginals at time 3. If the formula is translated into symbolic terms representing cells of a table, then

$$p^{(3)} = DD + RD, DR + RR$$

That is, the DD cell of a table comparing t_2 and $t_3 = 60(.96) = 58$. Each of these values represent the cell observations necessary for Markovity (see table 5.8). If the actual data for t_3 is not reproduced or predicted exactly (or nearly so by χ^2 criterion), then we must conclude that the data do not fit the first order Markov chain. This process tells us the responses in successive time periods are independent of previous responses and whether transition probabilities are constant. It is also possible to break the sample into strata to test for different processes within those strata. For example, we might control for education by following this procedure for

TABLE 5.8

t_3

		D	R	
	D	58	2	60
t_2				
	R	8	32	40
		66	34	

35. For a good description of matrix manipulation see Paul Horst, *Matrix Algebra for Social Scientists* (New York: Holt, Rinehart and Winston, 1963).

high and then low educated respondents to see if the strata are characterized by the same process of change (see the Goodman article to follow).

Usefulness of the Markov model for prediction from data which fit its conditions is shown most clearly by the *fixed point probability vector* associated with all "regular" Markov matrices (a "regular" matrix is one with no zero entries). This vector, when used as a multiplier for the matrix, yields itself — the same vector — as a product. Since in our model of change for Democrats and Republicans, the Democrats gained from t_1 to t_2 and again from t_2 to t_3, we may well be interested in knowing whether this process will continue indefinitely (until there are no Republicans at all), or whether it will taper off at some fixed point in the future. We know that for the matrix $\begin{pmatrix} .96 & .04 \\ .21 & .79 \end{pmatrix}$, the eventual distribution of Democrats and Republicans will be .84, .16. Notice that when the matrix is multiplied by this vector, the product is the vector itself:

$$(.84, .16) \begin{pmatrix} .96 & .04 \\ .21 & .79 \end{pmatrix} = (.84)(.96) + (.16)(.21), (.84)(.04) + (.16)(.79)$$

$$= (.84, .16)$$

Since the model asserts that the fixed point vector is a unique multiplier which yields itself as a product, the vector may be calculated by an elementary solution of simultaneous equations. For our example there will be two unknowns:

$$(a, b) = (a, b) \begin{pmatrix} .96 & .04 \\ .21 & .79 \end{pmatrix}$$

and since $a + b = 1$, we need only solve for a since b is its complement:

$$a = .96a + .21b$$

$$.04\, a = .21b$$

$$b = \frac{.04}{.21} a$$

and,

$$a + \frac{.04}{.21}a = 1$$

$$1.19a = 1$$

therefore,

$$a = \frac{1}{1.19} = .84$$

$$b = 1.00 - .84 = .16$$

A verbal interpretation of this result is that, assuming the data on party change are indeed Markovian (which they probably are not), the Democrats will stop gaining at the fixed point vector percentages of 84 percent, 16 percent.

The Markov model does not tell us how long it will take to reach the transition point (the point at which the process becomes stationary), because the transition matrix is actually a limiting matrix, which is never quite reached. The basic Markov theorem assures us, however, that on the assumption of unchanged probabilities at successive changes in time, there will eventually come a point in time at which the matrix itself will closely approach one consisting of identical rows of the fixed point probability vector. In our example, the limiting matrix will be $\begin{pmatrix} .84 & .16 \\ .84 & .16 \end{pmatrix}$.

How this interesting result occurs requires a further note on the Markov process. Given the probabilities of change indicated in the original matrix P for t_1, successive probabilities for $t_2 \ldots n$ (time intervals) are derived by multiplying the matrix by itself (first squaring it) for each successive stage. A standard procedure for determining whether a given social process is Markovian is to compare the theoretical succession of matrix multiplications with the actual time series.[36] Were the data in our example Markovian, some of the successive matrix multiplications would be, for the initial matrix, $P = \begin{pmatrix} .96 & .04 \\ .21 & .79 \end{pmatrix}$:

$$P^2 = \begin{pmatrix} .93 & .07 \\ .37 & .63 \end{pmatrix}, P^4 = \begin{pmatrix} .89 & .11 \\ .58 & .42 \end{pmatrix}, P^8 = \begin{pmatrix} .86 & .14 \\ .76 & .24 \end{pmatrix}, P^{16} = \begin{pmatrix} .85 & .15 \\ .84 & .16 \end{pmatrix}$$

The last matrix (P^{16}) closely approaches the limiting matrix $\begin{pmatrix} .84 & .16 \\ .84 & .16 \end{pmatrix}$. At this point, the matrix, multiplied by itself, yields itself as a product — that is, the Markovian process has become stationary. It is also true that the fixed point probability vector (.84, .16), used as a multiplier for *any* of the successive matrices in this series of multiplications, yields itself as a product.

This powerful theorem depends of course on the condition of unvarying probabilities through successive time stages, so that it is often inappropriate to political opinion or political behavior data, which are strongly related to factors which change the probabilities. If the changes are not too great, or their effects not too strong, or especially if they show some regularity, the Markov model may be used with appropriate weightings to modify the strict theoretical probabilites at successive stages. Kemeny and Snell have shown how to introduce such modifications in a sociological problem on conformity.[37]

The above Markov model is the most comprehensible of a larger group of stochastic process models. Beyond the examples treated here, most of them assume much more familiarity with mathematics and unfortunately, applications of more sophisticated techniques are limited in the social sciences. There are obviously problems with the reality of the Markov process and we are not likely to find a good fit between the model and the data so long as too much unreliability is present in

36. For a Markov model of labor movement through twelve successive quarters, see Isadore Blumen, Marvin Kogan, and Philip J. McCarthy, "Probability Models for Mobility," in *Readings in Mathematical Social Science*, ed. Lazarsfeld and Henry, pp. 318–34.

37. Kemeny and Snell, in *Readings in Mathematical Social Science*, ed. Lazarsfeld and Henry.

panel data. Furthermore, the Markov process treats unidirectional patterns, but beyond that, the models are inapplicable. Generally, the more complex the model, the more complex the technique, and the better they approximate reality. Yet because of the restrictive Markovian assumptions, this model is relatively easy to understand and it serves as a useful introduction to more complex methods.

Research Examples and Introductory Notes

Several examples of time series analysis techniques are presented in the readings to follow. These articles focus on a variety of substantive areas within political science and they are presented in generally the same order as the appearance of analysis techniques in this chapter. They include examples of simple descriptive time series analysis, interrelationships within and between time series, the analysis of age cohorts, and the application of simple Markovian probability models to processes of change.

Selected Bibliography of Applications

Statistical Analysis Within and Between Times Series

Alker, Hayward, and Puchala, Donald. "Trends in Economic Partnership: The North Atlantic Area, 1928–1963." In *Quantitative International Politics*, ed. J. David Singer, pp. 287–316. New York: Free Press, 1968.

Baggaley, Andrew R. "Religious Influence on Wisconsin Voting, 1928–1960." *American Political Science Review* 56 (1962): 66–70.

Banks, Arthur S. "Correlates of Democratic Performance." *Comparative Politics* 4 (1972): 217–30.

Burnham, Walter Dean. *Critical Elections and the Mainsprings of American Politics*. New York: W. W. Norton, 1970.

Butler, David, and Stokes, Donald E. *Political Change in Britain*. New York: St. Martin's Press, 1969.

Campbell, Angus. "Surge and Decline: A Study of Electoral Change." In *Elections and the Political Order*, ed. Angus Campbell et al., pp. 40–62. New York: John Wiley, 1966.

Caporaso, James A., and Pelowski, Alan L. "Economic and Political Integration in Europe: A Quasi-Experimental Analysis." *American Political Science Review* 65 (1971): 418–33.

Carlsson, Gosta. "Time and Continuity in Mass Attitude Change: The Case of Voting." *Public Opinion Quarterly* 29 (1965): 1–15.

Clausen, Aage R. "Measurement Identity in the Longitudinal Analysis of Legislative Voting." *American Political Science Review* 61 (1967): 1020–36.

Clubb, Jerome M., and Allen, Howard W. "Party Loyalty in the Progressive Years: The Senate, 1909–1915." *Journal of Politics* 29 (1967): 567–84.

Feierabend, Ivo K., and Feierabend, R. L. "Aggressive Behaviors Within Polities, 1948–1962: A Cross-National Study." *Journal of Conflict Resolution* 10 (1966): 249–71.

Galtung, Johan. "East-West Interaction Patterns." *Journal of Peace Research* 2 (1966): 146–77.

Haas, Michael. "Social Change and National Aggressiveness, 1900–1960." In *Quantitative International Politics*, ed. J. David Singer, pp. 215–44. New York: Free Press, 1968.

Kanter, Arnold. "Congress and the Defense Budget, 1960–1970." *American Political Science Review* 66 (1972): 129–43.

Key, V. O., Jr. *The Responsible Electorate*. Cambridge: Harvard University Press, 1966.

———. "A Theory of Critical Elections." *Journal of Politics* 17 (1955): 3–18.

Lindeen, James W. "Longitudinal Analysis of Republican Presidential Electoral Trends, 1896–1968." *Midwest Journal of Political Science* 16 (1972): 102–22.

MacRae, Duncan, Jr., and Meldrum, James A. "Critical Elections in Illinois: 1888–1958." *American Political Science Review* 54 (1960): 669–83.

McClelland, Charles A. "The Access to Berlin: The Quantity and Variety of Events, 1948–1963." In *Quantitative International Politics*, ed. J. David Singer, pp. 159–86. New York: Free Press, 1968.

Mueller, John. "Presidential Popularity From Truman to Johnson." *American Political Science Review* 64 (1970): 18–34.

———. "Trends in Popular Support for the Wars in Korea and Vietnam." *American Political Science Review* 65 (1971): 358–75.

Pelz, Donald C., and Andrews, Frank M. "Detecting Causal Priorities in Panel Study Data." *American Sociological Review* 29 (1964): 836–48.

Richardson, Lewis F. *Statistics of Deadly Quarrels*. Chicago: Quadrangle Books, 1960.

Rieselbach, Leroy N. "The Demography of the Congressional Vote on Foreign Aid, 1939–1958." *American Political Science Review* 58 (1964): 577–88.

Rummel, R. J. "Dimensions of Conflict Behavior Within Nations, 1946-1959." *Journal of Conflict Resolution* 10 (1966): 65–73.

———. "Dimensions of Dyadic War, 1820–1952." *Journal of Conflict Resolution* 11 (1967): 176–83.

Rusk, Jerrold G. "The Effect of the Australian Ballot Reform On Split Ticket Voting: 1876–1908." *American Political Science Review* 64 (1970): 1220–38.

Sellers, Charles. "The Equilibrium Cycle in Two-Party Politics." *Public Opinion Quarterly* 29 (1965): 16–38.

Stokes, Donald E. "Some Dynamic Elements of Contests for the Presidency." *American Political Science Review* 61 (1966): 19–28.
Turett, J. Stephen. "The Vulnerability of American Governors, 1900–1969." *Midwest Journal of Political Science* 15 (1971): 108–32.
Wright, Quincy. *A Study of War.* Chicago: University of Chicago Press, 1941.
Zikmund, Joseph. "Suburban Voting in Presidential Elections, 1948–1964." *Midwest Journal of Political Science* 12 (1968): 239–58.

Cohort Analysis

Carlsson, Gosta, and Karlsson, Katarina. "Age, Cohorts and the Generation of Generations." *American Sociological Review* 35 (1970): 710–18.
Converse, Philip E. "Of Time and Partisan Stability." *Comparative Political Studies* 2 (1969): 141–47.
Crittenden, John. "Aging and Political Participation." *Western Political Quarterly* 16 (1963): 323–31.
Glenn, Norval D. "Aging, Disengagement, and Opinionation." *Public Opinion Quarterly* 33 (1969): 17–33.
Glenn, Norval D., and Grimes, Michael. "Aging, Voting and Political Interest." *American Sociological Review* 33 (1968): 563–75.
Glenn, Norval D., and Hefner, Ted. "Further Evidence on Aging and Party Identification." *Public Opinion Quarterly* 36 (1972): 31–47.
Inglehart, Ronald. "The Silent Revolution in Europe: Intergenerational Change in Post-Industrial Societies." *American Political Science Review* 65 (1971): 991–1017.
Klecka, William R. "Applying Political Generations to the Study of Political Behavior: A Cohort Analysis." *Public Opinion Quarterly* 35 (1971): 358–73.
Rintala, Marvin. "A Generation in Politics: A Definition." *Review of Politics* 25 (1963): 509–22.
Zody, Richard E. "Cohort Analysis: Some Applicatory Problems in the Study of Social and Political Behavior." *Social Science Quarterly* 50 (1969): 374–80.

Probability Models

Anderson, T. W. "Probability Models for Analyzing Time Changes in Attitudes." In *Mathematical Thinking in the Social Sciences*, ed. Paul F. Lazarsfeld, pp. 17–66. New York: Free Press of Glencoe, 1954.
Converse, Philip E. "Attitudes and Non-Attitudes: Continuation of a Dialogue." In *The Quantitative Analysis of Social Problems*, ed. Edward R. Tufte, pp. 168–89. Reading, Mass.: Addison-Wesley, 1970.
Davis, Otto A.; Dempster, M. A. H.; and Wildavsky, Aaron. "A Theory of the Budgetary Process." *American Political Science Review* 60 (1966): 529–47.
Estes, W. K. "A Random-Walk Model for Choice Behavior." In *Mathematical Methods in the Social Sciences*, ed. Kenneth Arrow, Samuel Karlin, and Patrick Suppes, chap. 18. Stanford: Stanford University Press, 1960.
Goodman, Leo. "Statistical Methods for the Mover-Stayer Model." *Journal of the American Statistical Association* 56 (1961): 841–68.
Horvath, William J., and Foster, Caxton C. "Stochastic Models of War Alliances." *Journal of Conflict Resolution* 7 (1963): 110–16.
Stokes, Donald E. "Party Loyalty and the Likelihood of Deviating Elections." In *Elections and the Political Order*, ed. Angus Campbell et al., pp. 125–35. New York: John Wiley, 1966.
Stokes, Donald E., and Iversen, Gudmund R. "On the Existence of Forces Restoring Party Competition." *Public Opinion Quarterly* 26 (1962): 159–71.
Ulmer, S. Sidney. "Stochastic Process Models in Political Analysis." In *Mathematical Applications in Political Science*, ed. John Claunch, pp. 1–20. Dallas: Arnold Foundation Monographs, Southern Methodist University, 1965.
Wiggins, Lee M. "Mathematical Models for the Interpretation of Attitude and Behavior Change: The Analysis of Multi-Wave Panels." Ph.D. dissertation, Columbia University, 1955.

*GERALD POMPER**

Classification of Presidential Elections

*This article treats interrelationships within a time series with
multiple observations at each point in time. Pomper's research goal is
to classify presidential elections on the basis of majority party victory
or defeat and on the basis of continuity or change in electoral
cleavage. Victory or defeat is easily operationalized, but one's
ability to distinguish between electoral continuity and change must
rely on several basics of time series analysis. In order to accomplish
his classification goal, the author relies on several time series
analysis techniques.*

    *First, the primary means of analysis is the simple correlation coefficient,
where a set of observations by state (percent Democratic) at one point
in time is correlated with another set of observations at the next point
in time, and this pattern is followed successively throughout the time
series. For example, the correlation between 1828 and 1832 observations
is calculated and graphed, then the correlation between 1832 and 1836 is
calculated and graphed. That is, Pomper utilizes the linear correlation
of state by state results in all successive paired presidential elections
from 1824 to 1964. The variables are measured as the Democratic
percentage of each state's total presidential vote and observations are
across states and through time. When successive correlations are high, it
represents continuity (versus change) between two elections.*

Reprinted from Gerald Pomper, "Classification of Presidential Elections," *Journal of Politics* 29
(1967): 535–66, by permission of the journal and the author.

*I wish to thank the Rutgers University Research Council for financial assistance, Judson James for
many helpful comments, Mrs. Doris Paul for programming, I. H. Pomper for mathematical instruc-
tion, and Barry Seldes for aid in the calculations. Calculations were performed at the Rutgers Center
for Computer Services.

*Second, in order to correct for, or take into account, "temporary
perculiarities" or irregularities in the flow of this electoral time
series, Pomper modifies his original set of correlations by achieving
a minimal "smoothing out" of the data. He does this by considering the
mean Democratic vote in four preceding elections as a normal party vote
where, in effect, he is using a moving average procedure to smooth out
the data — hopefully to eliminate irregular disturbances without hiding
basic and significant changes. A span of four elections was chosen as
most suitable for this averaging process. The author then correlates
the percent Democratic in each election with the previous four election
average for each state.*

*Third, in order to reach an even higher level of generality and
move beyond a focus on individual results, Pomper identifies "electoral
eras" by correlating nonsuccessive elections. The basic idea is that
if a stable coalition is present, there will be high correlations between
nonsuccessive elections. He must therefore move beyond paired correlations
between successive elections to a larger correlation matrix representing
relationships between elections. By isolating subsets of high intercorrelations he is able to identify stable eras, e.g., 1932 to 1948.*

*Finally, to complete his analysis, the author focuses on variations
from "normal" Democratic percentages. A means of measuring these
variations relies on basic descriptive statistical procedures as
described in chapter 2. The author first calculates, for each year
and each state, the percentage difference between percent Democratic in
one year and the statistical normal Democratic percentage (four election
average). All state differences then are averaged to yield an average
national variation from normal Democratic vote. The higher the mean variation
for each year, the greater the change in Democratic regularity. This
procedure makes apparent some voter changes hidden in the previous
analysis. Further information also is provided by measuring the standard
deviations of differences from average state votes. Generally, the
higher the standard deviation from the national mean, the greater the
electoral shift in individual states. Pomper then discusses problems
relevant to his aggregate geographical analysis, such as those evolving
from treating all states equally (without regard for population differences)
and the hiding of electoral shifts within states, and how these problems
and his findings bear on recent survey research procedures and results.*

The accumulation of voting research in the United States[1] has provided a foundation from which we can investigate more than the unique candidates, issues, and
events of a specific election. Rather, we can focus on the similarities between different
elections, attempt to classify them, and abstract some patterns from the historical

---

1. The most notable works are those of the Survey Research Center, particularly Angus Campbell,
et al., The American Voter (New York: Wiley, 1960) and *Elections and the Political Order* (New York:
Wiley, 1966). A recent important work is V. O. Key, Jr., *The Responsible Electorate* (Cambridge:
Harvard University Press, 1965).

realities. This article presents certain methods of classification using aggregate voting statistics, and offers a tentative categorization of presidential elections.

Comparisons between elections can perhaps most usefully be focused on the enduring factors in American politics, the parties, and their sources of support. V.O. Key stimulated such study in "A Theory of Critical Elections." Key pointed to "a category of elections . . . in which the decisive results of the voting reveal a sharp alteration of pre-existing cleavages within the electorate. Moreover, and perhaps this is the truly differentiating characteristic of this sort of election, the realignment made manifest in the voting in such elections seems to persist for several succeeding elections."[2]

Building on this concept, the authors of The American Voter suggested classifying elections into three categories: Maintaining, Deviating, and Realigning.[3] In the first two types of elections, there is no change in the basic patterns of party loyalty. In a Maintaining election, the "normal" majority party wins its expected victory; in Deviating cases, the minority party wins a short-lived tenure because of temporary factors, such as a popular candidate. In the Realigning election, much as in Key's critical election, the basis of voter cleavage is transformed.[4]

There are three important differences between these approaches: (1) Key's scope is narrower, as he is concerned principally with the unusual balloting, while the Michigan researchers attempt a classification of all contests, and tend to emphasize the importance and stability of party loyalty. (2) The methods are quite distinct. Key employs electoral data from geographic areas, such as towns in New England or counties or states in the rest of the nation. Campbell and his collaborators use national sample surveys. (3) Because of the last difference, the historical period considered differs. While the survey method allows greater precision, reliable data of this kind are lacking for the period before 1936. Electoral data, on the other hand, are available in some usable form for most of American history.[5]

Various methods may be employed in analysis of presidential elections which combine elements of these two schemes. Electoral data for geographic areas, states, are employed here in a four-fold categorization based on that of the Survey Research Center. The SRC classification cannot be used without change. As noted by Irish and Prothro,[6] the Michigan typology is based on two different dimensions which

---

2. Journal of Politics, Vol. 17 (February, 1955), p. 4. Key also suggested that critical elections evidenced deep concern and high involvement by voters. However, these characteristics are difficult to establish historically and are not vital to the concept. Further work on the subject includes Key, "Secular Realignment and the Party System," Journal of Politics, Vol. 21 (May, 1959), pp. 198–210; Duncan MacRae, Jr. and James A. Meldrum, "Critical Elections in Illinois: 1888–1958," American Political Science Review, Vol. LIV (September, 1960), pp. 669–683; and Charles Sellers, "The Equilibrium Cycle in Two-Party Politics," Public Opinion Quarterly, Vol. XXIX (Spring, 1965), pp. 16–3⁸.

3. The American Voter, pp. 531–38. The additional category, Reinstating, is best understood as a sub-category of Maintaining. Cf. Philip Converse, et al., "Stability and Change in 1960: A Reinstating Election," American Political Science Review, Vol. LV (June, 1961), pp. 269–80.

4. Further work by the same authors on this subject is included in chapters 4, 7 and 10 of Elections and the Political Order.

5. The Michigan researchers have resorted to this data when attempting to analyze the more distant past. For imaginative use of this material, see Lee Benson, The Concept of Jacksonian Democracy (Princeton: Princeton University Press, 1961). A general discussion of the uses and limits of electoral data is found in Austin Ranney, Essays on the Behavioral Study of Politics (Urbana: University of Illinois Press, 1962), chap. 2.

6. Marian Irish and James Prothro, The Politics of American Democracy, 3rd. ed. (Englewood Cliffs: Prentice-Hall, 1965), pp. 300–1.

are not clearly distinguished. One of these dimensions is power, i.e., continuity or change in the party controlling the White House. The second dimension is electoral support, i.e. continuity or change in voter cleavages. Four combinations of these factors are possible, but the basic Michigan scheme includes but three.

The deficiency is due to ambiguous use of the Realigning category, applied to elections in which "the basic partisan commitments of a portion of the electorate change, and a new party balance is created."[7] This definition confuses two distinct effects: change in partisan commitments, and change in the party balance. Both results are evident when the former majority is displaced, as was the case in the period around the New Deal. It is also possible, however, that the reshuffling of voters can retain the same majority party, although it is now endorsed by a different electoral coalition. Partisan commitments change, while the party balance continues the same party as the majority.

The election of 1896, perhaps the classical critical contest, illustrates the problem. The Republican Party was the majority both before and after this watershed year, winning six of eight Presidential elections in each interval. The basis of its support changed significantly in 1896, even though the party balance was not affected. Given the ambiguities of their classification, the Michigan authors find it difficult to deal with this election. At one point, the contest is included in a series of Maintaining elections but, in the space of a few pages, it is discussed as Realigning.[8]

The classification represented in the diagram below separates the two aspects of elections. The horizontal axis is the power of the "normal" majority party. The vertical dimension is continuity or change in electoral cleavages.[9] The terms Maintaining and Deviating are used in a manner similar to that employed by the SRC. Realigning is reserved for elections in which a new majority party comes to power as the electorate substantially revises its loyalties. If the invention of a new label may be excused, Converting is offered as a term for elections in which the majority party retains its position, but there is considerable change in its voter base.

The problem is one of assigning given elections to the proper category. The horizontal dimension presents no difficulties. There are only two possible outcomes, victory or defeat of the majority party, and these are historical facts. Complexities arise in regard to the vertical dimension, in knowing whether a particular result signifies electoral continuity or change. Since both are partially present in every contest, there can be no simple solution. Some reasonable means is needed to locate critical elections, by distinguishing a Maintaining from a Converting victory of the majority party, and discriminating between Deviating and Realigning triumphs of

---

7. *The American Voter*, p. 534; *Elections and the Political Order*, p. 74.

8. *The American Voter*, p. 531, places Republican victories from the Civil War to the 1920s in the Maintaining category, but on p. 536, the authors write of "the realignment accompanying the election of 1896." In *Elections and the Political Order*, p. 74, the existence of a Republican majority prior to 1896 seems to exclude this election as Realigning, but on p. 76, McKinley is grouped with Lincoln and Franklin Roosevelt as victors in Realigning contests.

9. The "normal" majority party must be assumed at some point in time from historical evidence. For example, we can make the rather safe assumption that the Democrats were the majority party after 1936. After the initial assumption, the election results will indicate when this majority status began and when other changes have occurred. Emphasizing the success or failure of a given party, rather than change as such, avoids the need for a sub-category such as the SRC's Reinstating election. It also avoids the problems, inherent in Irish and Prothro's scheme, of dealing with two consecutive Deviating elections, as in 1912–16.

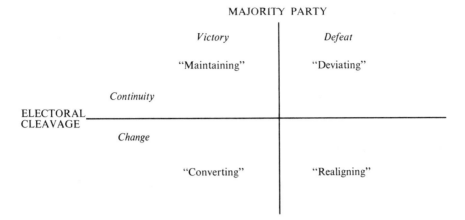

FIGURE A   A Classification of Presidential Elections

the minority. To deal with these questions, various statistical procedures are applied here to presidential state voting results. If these techniques are valid, they should be applicable to more extensive and detailed studies, using elections for other offices and using data more detailed than the state-wide results employed here.

Methods of Classification

A change in the parties' bases of support would be evidenced in various changes in the election returns. The geographical distribution of each party's vote would be different from the past: traditional strongholds would fall, while new areas of strength would become evident. Statistically, the vote in a critical election would not be closely associated with previous results. In individual states, each party's vote would likewise tend to diverge measurably from traditional levels. Taking all states together, each party would experience both gains and losses. The Democratic percentage of the vote, for example, would increase in erstwhile rock-ribbed Republican areas, but would decline in previously Democratic geographical bastions.

Correlation of Successive Elections

The first method employed here is linear correlation of the state-by-state results in paired presidential elections. Linear correlation will indicate the degree to which the results in two elections are similar. The basic data were the Democratic Party's percentage of each state's total vote from 1824 to 1964.[10] Each election constituted a variable, and the Democratic percentage in each state was a case of that variable. Each election, or variable, was then paired and correlated with that in every other election. An additional problem is created by the presence of significant third parties in many presidential elections. The possibility exists that these splinter groups are receiving votes which ordinarily would be cast for the Democrats. To deal with this possibility, separate correlations were made. The third party percentage was added to the Democratic share, and the totals for the given year then constituted a new variable, to be correlated with every other election. In all there are 47 variables, and

---

10. The percentages are from Svend Petersen, *A Statistical History of the American Presidential Elections* (New York: Ungar, 1963); *Congressional Quarterly Weekly Report*, Vol. 21 (March 26, 1965), p. 466.

a total of 46 + 45 ... + 1 pairings, or 595 totally.[11] The resulting coefficients provide a measure of the association of the geographical distribution of votes in paired elections.

Correlation analysis will indicate the relative degree of electoral continuity or change. If there is high geographical continuity between two elections, regardless of partisan victory or defeat, the correlation coefficient should be high. If there is change, even if the same party wins both elections considered, we should find a relatively low coefficient.[12] The basic assumption here is that change in the electorate's party preferences will be revealed by changes in the various states' support of the Democrats.[13]

Figure B pictures the correlation of the Democratic vote in successive elections. The peaks of the diagram indicate that Democratic support in the designated election was highly related to that in the preceding presidential contest. The valleys indicate a change in the sources of support.[14] Significant change in electoral cleavages appear to have occurred five times in American history: (1) Van Buren's victory in 1836; (2) The Civil War and Reconstruction period, with the elections of 1864 and 1872 particularly significant; (3) The Populist and Bryan period of 1892–96; (4) The time of the Great Depression, particularly in the contests of 1928 and 1932; and (5) The current era, most prominently the Kennedy and Johnson victories of 1960 and 1964. Questions can be raised about each of these, but a fuller discussion can be postponed until the other methods of classification have been presented.

Correlation with Average Democratic Vote

Each election is inevitably unique and will always differ somewhat from its predecessor and its successor. A given election may stand out not because it is truly a critical election, marking the end of one era and the beginning of another, but only because of temporary peculiarities. Thus, MacRae and Meldrum, analyzing shifts in the vote between successive elections, show increased dispersion in 1920 and 1940, although there is no reason to believe that these elections revealed any basic change in the electorate.[15]

---

11. The third-party elections are those of 1848, 1860, 1892, 1904 to 1924, and 1948. It should be noted that the number of states (N for a given variable, or election) is not constant. It increased over time as new states were admitted to the Union and as states began to choose electors by popular vote. It decreased temporarily during the Civil War and Reconstruction, when Confederate states were excluded from the balloting. The correlation of any pair of elections, therefore, is only of those states participating by popular vote in both elections.

12. For uses of this method using county data, cf. V. O. Key, Jr. and Frank Munger, "Social Determinism and Electoral Decision: The Case of Indiana," in Eugene Burdick and Arthur Brodbeck, *American Voting Behavior* (Glencoe: The Free Press, 1959), pp. 281–99; and Thomas A. Flinn, "Continuity and Change in Ohio Politics," *Journal of Politics*, Vol. 24 (August, 1964), pp. 521–44.

13. This assumption could prove false if voter realignment occurred within the states, but the net effect of countervailing movements was masked by state-wide returns. The Democratic percentage in a given state might then remain stable, but the party's votes would be quite different from those of the past. Political developments affecting social groups differentially should be reflected, however, by unequal vote changes from one state to another. While the divergences of states have lessened greatly in recent decades, considerable diversity remains.

14. The Democratic percentage of the total vote is used for all years, except 1860, where the Douglas and Breckinridge percentages are combined, and 1948, where the Truman and Thurmond percentages are combined. If the Douglas vote alone is used for 1860, the correlation coefficient drops to -.24. If the Truman vote alone is used, the coefficient decreases to −.41. Since both elections saw a short-lived division of the Democrats, not a real break, it seems appropriate to statistically reunite the factions.

15. *Op. cit.*, Figure 1, p. 671.

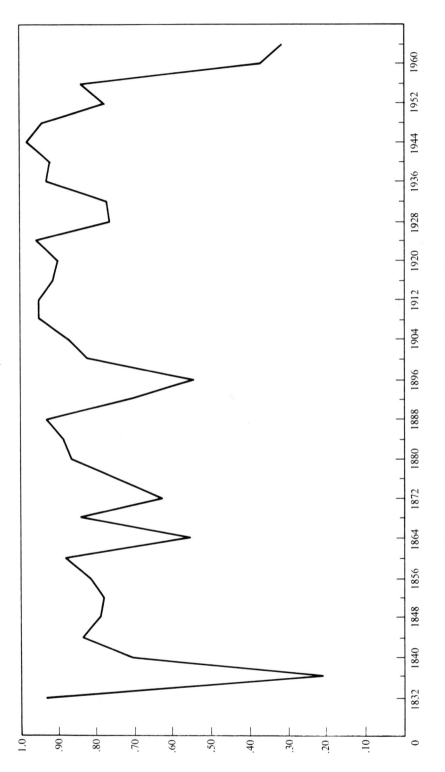

FIGURE B Correlation of Successive Presidential Elections, 1828–1964, Graphed at Latter Year

One means of moderating such eccentricities is to average the party's state votes in past elections. The mean Democratic vote in the four preceding elections is taken here to be the "normal" or traditional party vote. Four elections were chosen as sufficient to eliminate influences due solely to particular candidates or similar factors, while avoiding the inclusion of too many elections, and thereby making it difficult to detect significant changes.[16] In a second operation the Democratic state-by-state vote in each election was then correlated with the averages for each state's vote. Separate calculations were again made for those years in which significant third parties existed. Because of the various combinations of third parties possible, an additional 99 correlations result.

Figure C represents the correlations between the Democratic vote by states in the designated years and the "normal" party vote. The pattern is similar to that in Figure B, with the same dates indicated as critical elections, but there are some refinements. In general, the electoral eras pictured are more distinct from one another. Certain erraticisms are eliminated. The low correlation for 1872 is seen as due largely to the peculiarities of the previously paired contests of 1868 and 1872, rather than any enduring change in the 1872 election itself. In the New Deal period, the election of 1928 stands out as the time of change. In our own time, realignment beginning in 1952 is made more apparent, with the uniqueness of the 1964 election heavily emphasized.

Correlation Matrices

Emphasizing single elections, even critical ones, can be misleading. We cannot assume that all contests between two critical elections are similar, or that no change occurs between them. Instead of focusing on individual results, we can seek to identify periods of voter stability, or electoral eras. These eras are identified by correlations of non-successive elections.[17]

When a stable, persistent voter coalition is established, the vote in non-successive elections will be highly correlated. To identify such eras, the correlation coefficients of the Democratic vote in paired elections over a period of years are placed in a matrix.[18] To be considered in a stable era, the vote in a given year must be related not only to the immediately following or preceding election, but to *every other* consecutive election in that era. Even in a period of change, a large proportion of the voters retain their party loyalty, and spurious correlations may result. Requiring high correlation to a series of elections should avoid inclusion of votes with such meaningless correlations in the designated eras.[19]

---

16. If a state had not participated in all of the four previous elections, its "normal" vote was assumed to be the mean for as many of the four in which it had voted — 1, 2 or 3. The "normal" vote figure is therefore less reliable for the period immediately after a state has joined the Union. New states are not included at all for the first election in which they participated. Confederate states are included immediately upon rejoining the Union, their "normal" vote being the pre-war Democratic percentage.

17. This procedure is suggested by MacRae and Meldrum, p. 670, although they only correlate successive elections. Cf. Benson's discussion, *op. cit.*, pp. 125–31, of "stable phases" and "fluctuation phases."

18. I have adopted this method from David B. Truman, *The Congressional Party* (New York: Wiley, 1959).

19. Of the total of 595 correlations of the 47 variables, relating elections over 140 years, the mean coefficient of correlation is a reasonably high .54, while the mode and median are .65.

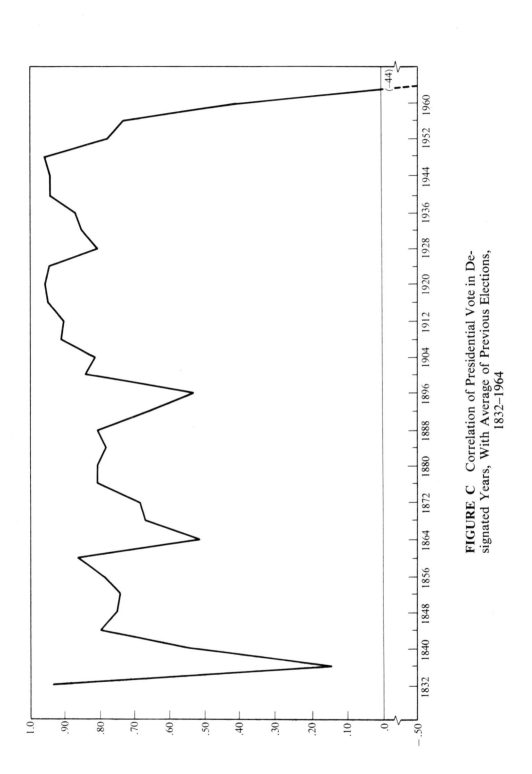

FIGURE C Correlation of Presidential Vote in Designated Years, With Average of Previous Elections, 1832–1964

Table 1, a matrix of the Democratic vote in paired elections from 1924 to 1964, illustrates the method. The core or stable electoral era is the period from 1932 to 1948. Each election in this period is related to every other at a high level, no coefficient being lower than .84. Correlation with the earlier elections of 1924 and 1928 falls below this level, indicating differences in the Democratic Party's geographical sources of support from one period to the next. Correlations with the Eisenhower elections are too low to be included in the core period as well, the 1952–56 votes apparently constituting the postscript to the New Deal Democratic period. A changed basis of support is sharply evident in 1960 and 1964.

TABLE 1   Correlation of Democratic Vote in Presidential Elections, 1924–1964*

	1928	1932	1936	ELECTION YEARS 1940	1944	1948	1952	1956	1960	1964
1924	.77	.79	.78	.88	.86	.88	.72	.54	.18	−.59
	(.79)	(.95)	(.93)	(.87)	(.84)	(.88)	(.57)	(.59)	(.07)	−.73
1928		.78	.76	.80	.82	.85	.58	.43	.22	−.56
1932			.93	.86	.84	.90	.58	.64	.09	−.73
1936				.93	.91	.90	.66	.66	.15	−.74
1940					.98	.94	.78	.64	.27	−.67
1944						.94	.80	.67	.30	−.68
1948							.77	.71	.21	−.68
	(−.43)	(−.29)	(−.32)	(−.36)	(−.41)	(−.33)	(−.16)	(−.08)	(.16)	(.65)
1952								.84	.56	−.39
1956									.38	−.47
1960										.32

*Row figures in parentheses refer to the combined Democratic and Progressive vote in 1924 and the vote of Truman alone in 1948.

Correlation matrices for overlapping earlier periods are presented in reverse chronological order in Tables 2, 3 and 4. The previous stable period seems to be 1900–1920, with the lowest coefficient of any pair of elections .87, a very high degree of association. The coefficients are somewhat lower for 1924, particularly if the Progressive vote is added to the Democratic, and lower still in 1928. Another grouping is found in the period 1876–1888, with all paired elections evidencing a coefficient of .70 or better. A similar relationship is found for the elections from 1844–1860. Coefficients for elections in the nineteenth century tend to be lower than in later periods, perhaps partially because of the changing number of states in each contest.[20] However, the median coefficient in the 1876–88 period is .86 and, in 1844–60, it is .79.

Of the total of 35 presidential elections since the initiation of broad popular participation, we can classify twenty as included within four eras of electoral stability. Critical elections are not usually part of these stable periods, but serve as breaking points, ending one era and leading to the next. Other contests represent

20. Between 1864 and 1896, the number of states participating in the Presidential election increased from 25 to 45. During the stable period of 1876–88, only Colorado entered the Electoral College. In 1844–60, however, coefficients were high even though the number of states increased from 25 to 32. Results for the 1824 election are not included because the data are unreliable and because few states then employed popular votes to choose the President.

TABLE 2 Correlation of Democratic Vote in Presidential Elections, 1896–1928*

				ELECTION YEARS					
	1900	1904	1908	1912	1916	1920	1924		1928
1896	.82	.53	.67	.53	.74	.59	.48	(.70)	.47
1900		.87	.93	.88	.93	.89	.83	(.88)	.77
1904			.94	.95	.89	.95	.96	(.81)	.81
1908				.94	.93	.92	.91	(.88)	.79
1912					.92	.93	.93	(.88)	.79
1916						.91	.85	(.90)	.80
1920							.97	(.83)	.86
1924									.77

*Figures in parentheses in 1924 column refer to the combined Democratic and Progressive vote.

TABLE 3 Correlation of Democratic Vote in Presidential Elections, 1856–1896*

				ELECTION YEARS						
	1860	1864	1868	1872	1876	1880	1884	1888	1892	1896
1856	.89	.60	.53	.71	.80	.82	.84	.73	.61	.79
1860		.55	.63	.68	.78	.83	.86	.79	.54	.84
		(−.06)	(−.26)	(.03)	(−.19)	(−.30)	(−.16)	(−.24)	(−.31)	(−.27)
1864			.85	.55	.65	.62	.60	.67	.17	.09
1868				.62	.64	.68	.57	.56	.38	.33
1872					.75	.58	.47	.33	.29	.22
1876						.88	.80	.70	.49	.47
1880							.90	.87	.68	.63
1884								.93	.61	.61
1888									.71	.64
1892										.54
	(.80)	(.31)	(.41)	(.30)	(.58)	(.75)	(.74)	(.80)	(.70)	(.75)

*Row figures in parentheses refer to the Douglas vote alone in 1860 and the combined Democrat and Populist vote in 1892.

TABLE 4 Correlation of Democratic Vote in Presidential Elections, 1828–1864*

				ELECTION YEARS					
	1832	1836	1840	1844	1848	1852	1856	1860	1864
1828	.93	.05	.38	.68	.60	.67	.82	.79 (−.37)	.39
1832		.22	.50	.77	.65	.74	.77	.77 (−.25)	.08
1836			.71	.62	.46	.48	.24	.17 (.25)	.06
1840				.84	.63	.61	.45	.36 (.14)	−.02
1844					.79	.80	.74	.70 (−.09)	.27
1848						.78	.79	.69 (.15)	.31
1852							.81	.84 (.12)	.46
1856								.89 (−.24)	.60
1860									.55

*Figures in parentheses in 1860 column refer to Douglas vote alone.

transitional elections before and after critical times. The last stable period ended in 1948 with Truman's victory. Since then, we have seen four transitional elections significantly different in the geographical distribution of the vote from the preceding period. This last conclusion is seemingly in conflict with the results of voting surveys, which posit considerable stability in the voters' partisan predispositions. We will return to the consideration of this important question after discussing two other methods of analysis and surveying the overall results.

Variations from State Averages

The remaining methods concern the variations in state votes from "normal" Democratic percentages. Even in periods of stability, the state-by-state vote will vary from one election to the next. In periods of substantial alteration in voting cleavages, however, the changes will be larger and more geographically dispersed. For each year, the absolute difference between each state's vote and its "normal" Democratic percentage was calculated. These state differences were then averaged to yield a single national figure. The expectation was that changes from past voting habits would be reflected in a correspondingly higher national mean.[21]

The results of this procedure are charted in Figure D. The regular pattern of the earlier graphs is not evident here, with relatively high means, or apparent voter change, recorded not only in predictable years such as 1896, but also in such unlikely times as the 1916 election.[22] These anomalies indicate the deficiencies of the mean alone as a measurement of change. High means will exist in critical elections, but may also occur even when there is no basic change in the electorate. In a Deviating election, there is likely to be considerable change from past voting habits, although the change does not persist. Thus, in 1916, the peace issue, the reforms of the first Wilson administration, and the remaining Progressive defections induced a crucial marginal group of voters to defect from the normally dominant G.O.P. This change, however, constituted no essential change in voter loyalties and was short-lived.[23]

The standard deviation provides a means of further distinguishing these two types of elections, by measuring the dispersal of state differences around the national mean. A Deviating election is the result of largely temporary factors, the effect of which is felt generally in the electorate. The shifts of the individual states will therefore tend to be within a relatively narrow range. A low standard deviation will result.[24]

In an election in which cleavages are significantly altered, voters are not equally affected, nor do they tend to be attracted only toward one party. Rather, there are movements of unequal degree and in both partisan directions. The shifts of the

21. It is to highlight such changes that absolute differences are used. If signed arithmetical differences were used, negative and positive variations would tend to cancel one another. This method is different from that of MacRae and Meldrum, who measure changes only from one election to the next, *op. cit.*, p. 670, and also different from that of Sellers, *op. cit.*, p. 33f., who concentrates on the differences in the two parties' votes.

22. It should be noted that this graph and the next are to be interpreted differently from Figures B and C. Change in the earlier graphs was evidenced by a decline in the curve; in the present cases, change is evidenced by an increase in the vertical values.

23. Cf. Arthur S. Link, *Wilson: Campaigns for Progressivism and Peace* (Princeton: Princeton University Press, 1965), esp. chap. 4.

24. The cleavages remain, although the partisan breaking-point may change. For a similar analysis of class voting, cf. Robert Alford, *Party and Society* (Chicago: Rand-McNally, 1963).

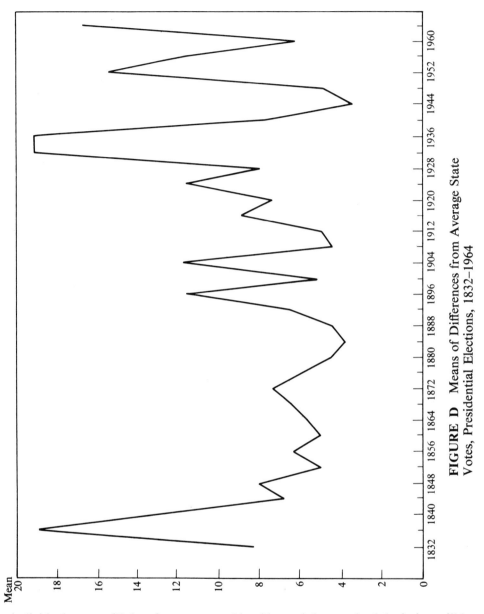

FIGURE D Means of Differences from Average State Votes, Presidential Elections, 1832–1964

individual states will therefore vary considerably, and the standard deviation will be relatively high.

Figure E represents the standard deviation around the national mean of state differences over time. The pattern is pleasantly regular, and there are few anomalies. The standard deviation for 1916, for example, is a low 5.39, substantiating our earlier belief that this was a Deviating rather than a critical election.

Conveniently, the pattern corroborates many of our earlier conclusions. There are peaks in 1836, 1864, 1896, 1924, and 1964, indicating the movement of voters between the parties in these years. However, we find not only isolated critical elections, but periods of assimilation after a decisive vote, indicated by the gradually

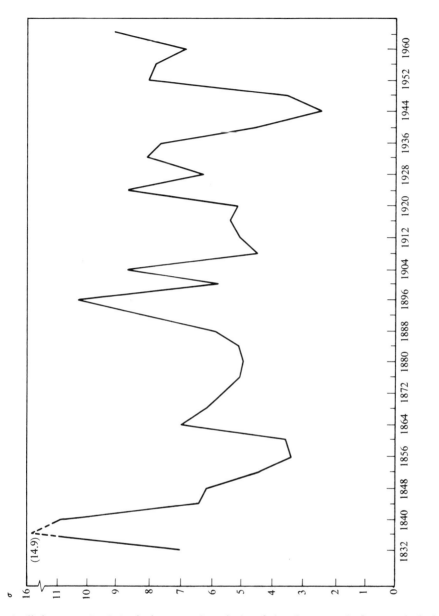

FIGURE E Standard Deviation of Differences from Average State Votes, Presidential Elections, 1832–1964

declining standard deviations, and periods of development before a vital election, with increasing standard deviations. The 1964 increase, for example, was preceded by changes in the four earlier contests.

A Survey of Presidential Elections

We now have five statistical measures available with which to classify elections. To summarize, an ideal Converting or Realigning election would be likely to show a low correlation to the immediately preceding election, to the average of four preceding elections and to the series of individual elections which both precede and follow it. The mean of state differences from the "normal" state votes and the standard deviation would tend to be high. In a Converting election, the majority party would retain its status; in a Realigning contest, the former minority would become dominant. In the model Maintaining or Deviating election, the opposite statistical results would be evident. The majority party would win the White House in the Maintaining case, but would be temporarily displaced in a Deviating contest. (Detailed statistical results are presented in the Appendix.)

By all indications, the victory of Martin Van Buren in 1836 was a Converting election. There is a low correlation to the 1828 and 1832 votes, and sharp increases in the mean of state differences and the standard deviation. Historical evidence indicates a considerable change in the leadership of both parties, the center of gravity of the Democratic party moving away from the South toward the Middle Atlantic states. In the balloting, the basis of party support shifted strongly in the same direction. The Democrats gained 10 or more percentage points in the six New England states, and lost a similar proportion in 10 states, 7 of them slave areas. As McCormick writes of the South in particular, "Although the new alignments did not become firm in some states until after 1837, the basic outlines of what were to be the Democratic and Whig parties had been delineated."[25] By 1844, a period of electoral continuity is evident, relatively undisturbed by the plethora of third parties, the admission of new states, and the substitution of the Republicans as the principal opposition party in 1856.

The second break in electoral continuity resulted from the Civil War. The 1860 vote, in the face of the contemporary upheavals, bears a strong resemblance to the past. If we combine the Douglas and Breckinridge percentages, the total shows a correlation of .89 with the 1856 results. The party did not change its geographical support, in other words, but this support has divided into two opposing factions.

During the War and Reconstruction, changes in party loyalty became evident. The correlation coefficients tend to be low, whatever figure is used to represent the Democratic vote of 1860, and the same conclusion results if we compare later elections or use four-election averages. The net import of these statistics is a definite break in traditional bases of support. The Republican Party became dominant in the nation, making 1864 a Realigning election. The degree of Republican victory in this year is exaggerated by the absence of the Confederate states, but the signs of change are evident in the Northern states alone, as the Republicans assimilated former Whigs, Know-Nothings, Constitutional Unionists and even Democrats. The party bore the new name of Union in 1864, and "it is a much debated question," writes Dennis Brogan, whether it had much "in common with the agglomeration of 'Anti-Nebraska' men of 1854, or even with the Republican Party of 1856 or 1860."[26] Readjustment in the electorate continued for some time after 1864. Stability returned in 1876, when a considerable return to ante-bellum loyalties is evident.[27]

---

25. Cf. Richard P. McCormick, *The Second American Party System* (Chapel Hill: University of North Carolina Press, 1966), for an excellent account of the changes in the party system. The quotation is from p. 339.

26. *Politics in America* (New York: Harper and Row, 1954), p. 55. Cf. David Donald, *The Politics of Reconstruction* (Baton Rouge: Louisiana State University Press, 1965).

27. Correlation of the 1876 vote with that of Douglas in 1860 is -.19, but it is a high .78 with the combined Douglas and Breckinridge tallies.

The post-Reconstruction system was not long-lived. Whatever measurement is used, a transformation of the political order is evident with the Populist movement of 1892 and the Bryan-McKinley presidential contest of 1896. The change is evident in both of these years, not only in 1896, which is often classified as the single crucial election of the period.[28] Transformations in party support were geographically widespread. Nineteen states changed more than 10 percentage points from their "normal" Democratic vote in 1896. Ten states showing Democratic losses were all located in the Northeast. Nine states with large Democratic gains were all in the South and West. Extensive changes also occurred within states and in the leadership of the parties, as evidenced in the splintering of each party and in the campaign appeals to social class.[29]

The Populist Party was a crucial element in the change. In 1892, Populist votes appear to have come largely from former Democrats; in 1896 many Populists then supported Bryan.[30] The decisive break of 1892–96, however, did not immediately result in the establishment of a new electoral coalition. Future years saw additional changes, and Republican dominance was sealed more firmly in 1900 than in the more-noticed first contest of McKinley and Bryan. Thus, 1896 was a great watershed, but it did not by itself fix the future contours of American politics.

Another change in the party system took place, as is well-known, in the period 1924–36. The discontinuity is evident in the measures used here, but it is less dramatic than the revisions of earlier periods. Unlike previous changes, those associated with the time of the Depression and New Deal were not principally sectional in character. Realignment occurred in most states, along lines of social class, residence, and ethnicism.[31] Measurements of state-wide voting can capture some of these changes, but not in the fine detail of sample surveys.

To the extent that aggregate figures are useful, they point to 1924 as a transitional year, and the Progressive Party as a "halfway house" for those leaving their traditional party. Changes in this election are signified by the high mean of differences from "normal" state votes and high standard deviations. The Progressive vote probably came from former adherents of both major parties, but there is some indication that it tended to be more from Republican loyalists.[32]

The transition to a Democratic majority extended over a number of elections, but the most critical appears to be 1928. The correlation coefficients for this election are

---

28. Cf. MacRae and Meldrum, *op. cit.*, pp. 678–81. The change in 1892 did not come only in Western, silver states. Indeed, six of these "radical" states were excluded from the 1892 calculations here, since they were not in the Union in earlier elections.

29. Cf. Stanley L. Jones, *The Presidential Election of 1896* (Madison: University of Wisconsin Press, 1964).

30. A statistical indication of the source of Populist votes is the higher correlation of the 1892 vote with that of 1888 (.81) when Populist and Democratic votes are added together than when Democratic votes alone are considered (.71). The correlation of the combined 1892 vote with that of 1896 is .75, higher than the coefficient achieved if comparison is made to the Democratic vote alone, .54.

31. Cf. *The American Voter*, pp. 153–60; Samuel J. Eldersveld, "The Influence of Metropolitan Party Pluralities in Presidential Elections since 1920," *American Political Science Review*, Vol. XLIII (December, 1949), pp. 1189–1205; Samuel Lubell, *The Future of American Politics* (Garden City: Doubleday Anchor, 1956); Rutch C. Silva, *Rum, Religion and Votes* (University Park: Pennsylvania State University Press, 1962).

32. The coefficient for the Democratic vote alone in 1920 and 1924 is extremely high, .97. If the Progressive vote is added to the Democrats' for 1924, however, the correlation falls to .83.

the lowest for any 20th century contest before 1960. Al Smith lost 10 percentage points or more from the average Democratic vote in seven states, all of them Southern or Border. He gained strongly in seven other states, four of them urban and Catholic, the rest largely rural and Progressive. There was sufficient change in 1928 to constitute it a Realigning election, although the new Democratic majority did not become evident until 1932.[33] The new pattern was then continued for the next four contests.[34]

By the methods employed here, the four most recent presidential contests constitute another critical period, culminating in the 1964 Conversion of the dominant Democratic majority. Strains in the New Deal coalition were already evident in 1948, when the Dixiecrats temporarily split the party. There was no fundamental alteration in that year, but greater change is evident in 1952, when all of our measures indicate discontinuity from the past. Shifts toward the Republicans occurred in all social groups and in all parts of the nation. Geographical variations were evident within the general trend. Differences from the four-election averages were greatest in sixteen states, all in the South or Mountain regions.[35]

The 1964 election represents a radical break from past results, and the statistics strongly suggest that it was a Converting election, retaining the same Democratic party as the majority, but on a new basis of popular support. The correlation coefficients for this election are astoundingly low, given the generally moderate to high figures, even in the case of arbitrarily paired elections. The 1964 Democratic vote is positively related to that of only two years other than 1960, both involving third parties. Johnson's vote is related to Truman's vote alone in 1948 ($r = .65$), and to Douglas' vote alone in 1860 ($r = .40$). In all of these cases, the Democratic vote was highly sectional in character, and severely depressed in the South.

There was large variation from traditional Democratic levels in most states. Of course, the Democratic vote increased substantially, as Johnson gained the largest percentage of the total vote ever achieved by a Democrat. The important point is that the gains were not relatively equal in all states, as would tend to be the case if all areas were reacting only to the temporary oddities of Goldwaterism. The party vote decreased from its four-election average in the five Black Belt states of the South, while it increased over 18 percentage points in eleven states of the Northeast and five of the Midwest.

The final test of a critical election must remain persistence. In the final analysis, 1968 and 1972 will tell if the pattern of 1964 did constitute a true Converting election. It is possible that the great transfer of voters between the parties was only a temporary reaction to the admittedly unusual circumstances of the time. It would be quite remarkable if such were the case. The events of 1964 left their mark in the control of state legislatures by the Democrats, the passage of "great society" legislation, in-

---

33. Key, "A Theory of Critical Elections," and MacRae and Meldrum, also find 1928 to be critical. Smith gained votes in Massachusetts, Rhode Island, New York, Illinois, Wisconsin, Minnesota and North Dakota.

34. When change takes place over a number of years, classification of individual elections becomes awkward. It might be more precise to classify the 1928 election as a Converting or Deviating election to explain Hoover's victory, but it then becomes even more complicated to correctly appraise the 1932 results.

35. For indication of change within the South, cf. Donald S. Strong, "The Presidential Election in the South, 1952," *Journal of Politics*, Vol. 17 (August, 1955), pp. 343–89.

tensification of the civil rights movement, organizational changes and conflicts in both parties, and the memories of the voters. Republican strength in the South continued to grow in the 1966 elections. Democrats lost considerably last November, but these losses were not simply a return to pre-1964 voting patterns. Democrats were elected in areas of former party weakness, such as Maine and Iowa, but were defeated in traditional bastions such as Illinois and Minnesota. The future impact of "black power" and other developments is now uncertain, but clearly significant. Change, not simple continuity, seems evident.

Limits and Problems

The apparent Conversion of the electorate in recent years is generally contrary to the conclusions of sample surveys on the persistence of party identification. After the 1964 election, Stokes found "almost no perceptible shift in the single most important types of response disposition, the electorate's enduring party loyalties."[36] His conclusion both points to the limitations of the methods employed here, and offers an opportunity for discussion of some general problems of electoral analysis.

Geographical units are used here for analysis. We examine the voting patterns of states, not that of individuals, whose behavior must be inferred, rather than directly examined. Evidence of continuity or change in political cleavages is therefore evidence about the persistence of geographical bases of party support, not conclusions about the loyalties of demographic or psychological reference groups.

The use of areal units is partially the simple result of necessity: only these data are historically available. This form of analysis has intellectual validity as well. For much of American history, the important social conflicts have also been geographical, i.e. sectional, conflicts. Party loyalties have been grounded on areal issues, traditions and leadership. Examination of aggregate voting returns can therefore provide insight into individual behavior. Conclusions based on this data will be made even more confidently as smaller geographical units are analyzed, and as social characteristics are correlated with political material.[37] Moreover, in dealing with the Presidency, we are dealing with a geographical system of selection, the Electoral College. Since national parties are centered around the presidential contest, analysis of their support in geographical terms is legitimate.

A real data are nevertheless subject to certain distortions. As the apportionment controversy has reminded us, acres or political units are not people. There can be considerable discrepancy between the voting of states, as units, and of the particular voters within them. The likelihood of such discrepancy would appear to be increased when, as above, all states are counted equally regardless of population. To deal with this possibility, a second analysis was performed, using the same techniques, but weighting the vote of each state by its population. Details are provided in the Appendix. The striking conclusion is that there is very little effect on the results: the same elections are located as critical, and the statistics derived do not differ greatly from those obtained previously.

---

36. Donald E. Stokes, "Some Dynamic Elements of Contests for the Presidency," *American Political Science Review*, Vol. LX (March, 1966), p. 27.

37. The Inter-University Consortium for Political Research is still in the process of obtaining and preparing county electoral data and Census material. When this immense task is completed, fuller national analysis will be possible.

Another possible distortion is the masking of voter changes within a state. Apparent stability in the total state returns might disguise considerable, but counter-vailing, party shifts by individual voters.[38] More relevant to the present discussion is the opposite distortion. When vote shifts are geographically concentrated, the methods employed here will tend to exaggerate the degree of change. In 1948, exclusion or inclusion of the Dixiecrat vote in Truman's total immensely affects all of our statistical indicators, even though the Dixiecrats received less than 3% of the national popular vote. The same factor accounts for the extremity of the shifts evidenced in 1960 and 1964, since vote changes have tended to be geographically concentrated, particularly in the South.

Results obtained using aggregate returns will therefore differ from those of surveys of an approximate random sample of individuals. Other differences are to be expected because this study focuses only on presidential voting, while surveys deal with other offices as well. Furthermore, we have been concerned with actual voting, while surveys emphasize "party identification," the voter's basic loyalty to a particular party. These identifications will show considerably less variation than the vote, and a vote for the opposition party will usually precede a change in identification. As Campbell himself suggests, the critical election provides a party with the opportunity, by its actions in office, permanently to win those voters who have given it power, or to regain its lost adherents.[39] Republicans for Johnson and Democrats for Goldwater may have made 1964 a Converting election, but the evidence in changed party identifications will not be fully apparent until later surveys.

These methodological differences are partially responsible for different conclusions about the meaning of recent elections. This analysis of aggregate election returns indicates a shift in electoral cleavages, with the 1964 election altering the geographical basis of support of the majority Democratic Party. Reported survey results indicate the continuity of past loyalties. Both conclusions can be right, since they deal with different aspects of the political system.

Even the surveys, however, provide some indications that meaningful change is taking place, although it has not been highlighted by scholarly analysis. Even where identifications have not yet altered, "party images" have been modified. In the South, where the vote change has been greatest, Matthews and Prothro find significant revisions in what the voters "like" and "dislike" about the Democrats and Republicans. Such alterations of traditional images may be the prelude to the further step of changing identifications.[40] Outside the South, results both from the Michigan surveys and from other sources also indicate substantial change in voter perceptions of the parties. Some of the variation may be due to purely temporary factors, but "party images" also include tenacious elements, which directly affect the basic identification.[41]

Most importantly, there is evidence that there has been change in party identi-

---

38. See H. Daudt, *Floating Voters and the Floating Vote* (Leiden: Stenfert Kroese, 1961), chap. 2, and the discussion of the New Deal period, above.

39. *The American Voter*, pp. 554–55.

40. Donald Matthews and James Prothro, *Negroes and the New Southern Politics* (New York: Harcourt, Brace and World, 1966), chap. 13.

41. "Some Dynamic Elements of Contests for the Presidency," pp. 19–28; *The Harris Survey*, January 11, 1965; Thomas W. Behnam, *Public Opinion Trends: Their Meaning for the Republican Party* (Princeton: Opinion Research Corporation, 1965).

fications as well. Belief in their immobility has been an unquestioned, but perhaps unjustified, article of faith. The evidence that party identification has been stable is largely based on aggregate figures from the surveys, not on analysis of individual behavior. We find, for example, that the proportion of Republicans from 1952 to 1964 always remained in the range of 24–32% of the total electorate.[42] It is therefore assumed that a given 24% of the voters were always Republicans, that 68% never identified with the G.O.P., and that only 8% ever changed their loyalties. This is a vital error, the same error which is often made in the analysis of aggregate voting data. In both cases, the net change between parties is assumed to be the total change.

The case for stability in party identification is largely based on limited net change. In examining identifications in 1956 and 1960, for example, Converse's data show that 14% of Southerners and 26% of non-Southerners changed their loyalties to some degree. Yet, because there is no strong trend in one direction, he devotes little attention to these conversions.[43]

In theory, virtually all voters could have changed their party identifications from 1952–64, even while the percentage supporting each party remained relatively stable. This is an unlikely situation, but it is also unlikely that the net change and the gross change are the same. Moreover, even marginal shifts can be decisive. An 8 percent change in the vote would usually create a landslide. Similarly, even an 8 percent change in identifications might be indicative of a Converting or Realigning election. In reality, the shifts in party identification are even higher.

The pattern of party loyalties is like a square dance — the important element in the dance is the movement and change of positions. We do not understand the dance by statically noticing that the number of sides to the square is always four or that there are equal numbers of men and women. The action comes when each dancer leaves one partner and takes another. To measure stability in party identifications, it is necessary to examine the behavior of individuals, as the Michigan surveys have indeed done. Ideally, respondents to a previous survey should be reinterviewed, as in the 1960 study. Alternately, persons can be asked to recall past identifications, as was done in the 1956 and 1964 surveys.

The results are interesting. Of the 1956 sample, 18 percent indicated that they had changed their party loyalty at some time in the past. Compare this finding to that upon reinterviewing in 1960. In the intervening four years, using the same categories as in 1956, 11 percent of the total group had changed their identifications. (Changes from Independent *to* either Democratic or Republican, or from strong to weak partisanship are not included, only changes *from* the two parties.) In other words, there were more than half as much change in party loyalty in the four-year period from 1956 to 1960 as in all of the years (perhaps twenty for the average respondent) in which the interviewees had been politically active before 1956.

In 1964, a different sample was interviewed, of which 22 percent indicated some change in party identification in the past. Changes at all elections, not only in the previous four years, are included here. It seems significant that, eight years

---

42. *Elections and the Political Order*, p. 13.
43. *Ibid.*, pp. 224–26.
44. Percentages are calculated from the data in *The American Voter*, Table 7–2, p. 148; *Elections and the Political Order*, Table 12–2, p. 225; and Inter-University Consortium for Political Research, *1964 Election Study Codebook*, Question 51, Deck 6, col. 11–12. SRC is now preparing further materials on this subject.

further away from the realignments induced by the Depression and New Deal, stability in party loyalty had actually decreased in comparison to 1956.[44] Fuller analysis of these responses are necessary before any final conclusions are reached, but there does seem sufficient evidence, in the survey results themselves, to support a suspicion that party identification has not been unchanging, but rather that significant numbers of voters have been altering traditional loyalties.[45]

In recent elections, therefore, statistical analysis of state voting indicates considerable shifts in the geographical bases of party support. The extent of change found in sample surveys is less, but there are numerous clues in that material to justify a tentative belief that the 1964 Presidential contest was indeed a Converting election.

Conclusions

It is now possible to summarize our findings and to attempt a classification of presidential elections. It is obvious that categorization is not a simple matter, for elections are not always of one type or another. Some convenient simplifications are lacking. For example, change in voter loyalties does not fit any neat cyclical pattern, with change occurring after a fixed number of years.[46] There is a tendency, it is true, for critical elections to occur approximately once in every generation, but the length of time between these contests varies considerably. The party system which became stabilized in 1876 lasted only until 1888, while the different party system which began to appear in 1924 still greatly affects politics today. Electoral change is periodic, but the periods are irregular.

Difficulties also exist in isolating the turning points in these periods, the critical elections. It is apparent that electoral change is neither unheralded nor precipitate. In most cases, there is not a single critical election, sandwiched between two periods of great stability. Rather, there are times of unease preceding the most crucial year, and a period of assimilation after it. Typically, the critical election represents a break in electoral continuity, but does not result in the immediate establishment of a new and persistent voter coalition. Thus, the elections identified as critical here do not show high correlations with later ballots, but following contests do demonstrate this stability. Persistence comes after the critical election, and partially as a reaction to its upheavals.

This conclusion is at variance with Key's original definition of a critical election. The disagreement is partially attributable to a difference in method. Key identifies critical elections by focusing on the extreme cases, the areas showing the most change toward or away from the new majority party. The methods used here are based on examination of all areas, and therefore include changes in the middle ranges as well. MacRae and Meldrum, who all also include all areas, show similar results — less

---

45. In a more recent publication, Angus Campbell writes, "The question which the 1964 vote raises is whether we are entering a period of party realignment . . . . There are indications in our survey data of a movement of this kind." However, this conclusion is also based on analysis of the distribution of party identifications, not on changes in these loyalties. Cf. "Interpreting the Presidential Victory," in Milton C. Cummings, Jr., *The National Election of 1964* (Washington: The Brookings Institution, 1966), esp. pp. 275–81.

46. Cyclical explanations are advanced in Louis Bean, *How to Predict Elections* (New York: Knopf, 1948).

precipitous changes coming in the total critical period, rather than in a single election.[47] Key himself recognized the point in his later writings.[48]

Despite the many pitfalls, it may be suggestive to position elections within the categories offered in Figure A. The horizontal dimension clearly represents a nominal classification — the left and right sides are exclusive and exhaustive. The vertical dimension is more in the nature of a continuum — particular elections may not be clearly stable or critical, but may tend to an intermediate position. Therefore, the distinction between a Deviating and Realigning contest, or a Maintaining and Converting election, is somewhat subjective and arbitrary. The change which exists in every election is disguised, as is the existence of critical periods, rather than single crucial ballotings.

On the basis of the data developed here (listed in detail in the Appendix), the elections of 1836, 1896, and 1960–64 are classified as Converting, and those of 1864 and 1928–32 as Realigning. The victories of the first Harrison, Taylor, Lincoln in 1860, Cleveland, Wilson, and Eisenhower are considered Deviating, and the others are classified as Maintaining.[49] In order to isolate a small number of critical elections, fairly strict standards have been applied in making this classification. Modified standards would obviously change the designation of individual elections.

The most accurate characterization of our political history would be one of electoral eras. The life cycle of an electoral era typically begins with, or soon follows, a third-party election. The first such era began with the contest of 1836, in which the Democrats faced three opposition Whig candidates. The period came to an end in 1860 with the division of the Democratic party, and the nation. The next period ended with the emergence of the Populists in 1892, and the Republican dominance that began with the victories of McKinley began to disappear with the 1924 appearance of the LaFollette Progressives. The end of the New Deal era was heralded by the Democratic split of 1948.

Third parties arise when traditional loyalty seems inadequate to many voters. Often, the rise of third parties accompanies or precedes change in these loyalties sufficient to constitute a critical election. This election may continue the same party in power, on the basis of a realigned majority, or result in an overthrow of its power. The changes in the critical year itself, as we have seen, will not necessarily be permanent. Further readjustments are likely in succeeding contests.

After a time, stability is achieved. Stable periods tend to resemble earlier eras. Thus, after the adjustments which result from the critical election, correlations between paired elections of different periods are fairly high. For example, the correlation of the vote in 1876 and 1860 is .78; that in 1900 and 1888, .85; and that in 1932 and 1920, .80. Part of the process of readjustment is an apparent return by the voters in some states to past voting traditions. Even with the transformation of the electoral coalition, a strong degree of continuity is present.

The transition from one electoral era to another, resulting from considerable

---

47. MacRae and Meldrum, *op. cit.*, pp. 681–82.

48. V. O. Key, Jr., *Politics, Parties, and Pressure Groups*, 5th ed. (New York: Crowell, 1964), p. 537

49. Two tests define a critical election: correlation to the last election and to the four-election average of less than .70 (in the 19th century) or .80 (20th century); and a coefficient of variation greater than 75. The latter measure is the standard deviation divided by the mean, with the result then multiplied by 100. Alternately, low correlation to the previous election alone, combined with a high mean (15 or greater) and high standard deviation (8 or greater), would define a critical election.

partisan movement by the voters, is an impressive manifestation of democratic control. Voters intervene decisively to change the political terms of reference. Party support and party programs become more congruent. Old policies and slogans are replaced by new, possibly more appropriate, appeals. The confusions of a waning order give way to the battle cries of an emergent party division. The Eisenhower elections did little to change the content of American politics from the dated themes of the New Deal. The Kennedy-Johnson administration, and the 1960–64 elections, did present new issues and conflicts. If 1964 did indeed constitute a Converting election, it may have provided the electoral foundation for the governmental resolution of long-standing issues.

Appendix

Since this study is basically one of geographical distribution of party support, no special effort was made to compensate for differences among the state in population or votes. Moreover, past work on this subject, from Key onward, has used unweighted data. A number of readers, however, have suggested the desirability of weighting. To investigate the question, the procedures used were adapted for use with weighted data, leading to a new set of statistics, corresponding to those of Figures C, D, and E.

The weight for each state was its number of Representatives in Congress in the designated election year, or in the later of paired years. Although apportionment is not perfectly proportional to population, it is accurate, simple, and a reliable indicator of relative population. The electoral vote, a suggested alternative, was rejected because it is biased toward smaller states. The total vote for each state, another alternative, is more difficult to obtain accurately for distant elections, and harder to use statistically. Weighting by Representatives changes the number of cases for each variable, or election. For 1964, illustratively, the number of cases is no longer the 50 states, but is the 435 Representatives. Nevada and New York are no longer each a case. Delaware is still one case, but New York is 41.

No extended analysis of these results will be offered here; the data are included in the table below. In regard to the location of critical elections, weighted data tend to reinforce the original conclusions. Change in 1836, 1864, 1928 and 1960–64 is even more marked, although the differences are not great. Weighted data reduce the degree of change evident in 1892–96, but do not require any modification of these years' designation as a critical period. The general conclusion one would reach is that the additional computational problems occasioned by weighted data do not seem to bring proportionately increased insights. Indeed, in an unusual case, weighted data can cause new problems. The election of 1848, for example, becomes sharply distinguished by this method. The reason does not appear to be that 1848 was a critical election. Rather, the cause is the concentration of votes for the Free Soil party in New York. Van Buren's personal appeal in a state with nearly a sixth of the nation's Representatives seriously distorts the weighted results, but his local attraction is not decisive if unweighted votes are used.

four elections, the mean of state differences, and the standard deviation. The last three statistics for weighted data are also included in the appropriate columns. The number of "associated elections" denotes the number of consecutive elections before and after the given year which are highly correlated with the results of that year. (A high level is defined as a coefficient of .69 or better for the 19th century, and .82 for 1900 and later elections.) Each election is also provisionally classified as Maintaining, Deviating, Converting or Realigning.

The table below summarizes all of the data obtained. Included for each year are coefficients of correlation with the previous election and the average of the previous

TABLE 5   Data for Classification of Presidential Elections[a]

bYear, Category	r: Last Election	r: Four Elections	Mean State Difference		Standard Deviation		Associated Elections Before	After
1832-M	.93	.93, .93	8.34,	5.90	6.83,	5.11	1	0
1836-C	.22	.14, .05	18.81,	15.73	14.89,	14.92	0	1
1840-D	.71	.54, .38	13.27,	12.37	10.56,	10.19	1	1
1844-M	.84	.79, .81	6.82,	6.69	6.22,	6.08	1	4
1848-D	.79	.75, .57	8.12,	10.04	6.02,	8.13	1	3
1852-M	.78	.74, .74	5.02,	4.22	4.53,	3.60	2	2
1856-M	.81	.78, .79	6.33,	6.39	3.35,	3.53	3	1
1860-D	.89	.86, .77	5.06,	5.25	3.55,	3.35	4	0
	(−.24)	(.02,−.29)	(24.33,	23.80)	(18.58,	18.43)	(0	0)
1864-R	.55	.51, .34	5.70,	5.98	6.78,	6.97	0	1
	(−.06)	(.31, .19)	(6.99,	7.43)	(7.69,	7.40)	(0	2)
1868-M	.84	.67, .63	6.43,	5.61	6.09,	5.93	1	0
1872-M	.62	.69, .61	7.41,	6.57	5.58,	5.19	0	1
1876-M	.75	.80, .78	5.94,	5.76	4.99,	4.69	1	3
1880-M	.88	.80, .78	4.50,	3.69	4.89,	4.34	1	2
1884-D	.90	.78, .77	3.88,	3.45	5.08,	4.79	2	1
1888-M	.93	.80, .79	4.38,	3.63	5.81,	5.38	3	1
1892-D	.71	.66, .73	6.55,	5.67	8.05,	5.67	1	0
	(.80)	(.76, .83)	(9.15,	6.87)	(9.95,	7.86)	(3	6)
1896-C	.54	.53, .70	11.53,	7.62	10.21,	6.85	0	1
	(.75)	(.71, .80)	(9.21,	7.02)	(8.49,	5.97)	(1	1)
1900-M	.82	.84, .94	5.16,	3.80	5.59,	3.30	1	6
1904-M	.87	.81, .91	11.68,	9.50	8.70,	6.17	1	5
1908-M	.95	.91, .96	4.47,	3.27	4.48,	3.19	2	4
1912-D	.94	.90, .95	5.02,	3.50	5.04,	3.77	3	3
1916-D	.92	.94, .95	8.96,	7.17	5.34,	4.49	4	2
1920-M	.91	.95, .95	7.30,	8.51	5.15,	5.19	5	1
1924-M	.97	.94, .96	11.69,	10.96	8.81,	8.04	6	0
	(.83)	(.89, .92)	(6.78,	5.48)	(5.71,	5.41)	(4	0)
1928-R	.77	.80, .77	7.94,	9.02	6.19,	6.18	0	0
	(.79)	(.81, .78)	(7.80,	7.97)	(6.12,	6.48)	(0	0)
1932-R	.77	.85, .89	19.21,	18.98	8.02,	6.86	0	4
1936-M	.93	.87, .89	19.20,	19.92	7.50,	6.97	1	3
1940-M	.92	.94, .94	7.78,	7.89	4.16,	4.27	2	2
1944-M	.98	.94, .96	3.35,	2.61	2.38,	2.06	3	1
1948-M	.94	.95, .95	5.01,	5.18	3.45,	3.26	4	0
	(−.33)	(−.35,−.24)	(12.86,	12.21)	(19.68,	18.15)	(0	0)
1952-D	.77	.77, .73	15.31,	13.62	7.98,	8.21	0	1
	(−.16)	(.76, .68)	(13.36,	11.93)	(5.72,	6.18)	(0	1)
1956-D	.83	.73, .71	11.77,	11.44	7.73,	7.31	1	0
1960-C	.37	.36, .28	6.05,	6.05	6.78,	5.83	0	0
1964-C	.31	−.44,−.55	16.82,	16.37	9.00,	7.91	0	0

[a]The second figure listed in columns 3, 4 and 5 are the statistics derived from state election results weighted by the number of Congressional Representatives.

bThe data in parentheses refer: in 1860 and 1864, to the Douglas vote alone in 1860; and 1896, to the combined Democratic and Populist vote in 1892; in 1924 and 1928, to the Combined Democratic and Progressive vote in 1924; in 1948 and 1952, to the Truman vote alone in 1948. The categories are: M-Maintaining; D-Deviating; C- Converting; and R- Realigning.

PAUL SMOKER[1]

A Time Series Analysis
of Sino-Indian Relations

*More complex methods for testing interrelationships
within time series, and additionally, those between time series, are
presented in a study of communications between decision makers in India
and China from 1959 to 1964. Paul Smoker's primary theoretical interest
in this exercise focuses on factors necessary for system stability. In
his concern for the study of interactions he points to many analyses of
trend ("general rise or fall in mean level") and recognizes the need
to eliminate trend variations in order to better understand serial
relationships ("a tendency for fluctuations about the mean level to
perpetuate themselves"). Specifically, he proposes to use serial
correlations to examine predictability in interaction sequences between
two countries. Data are counts of communiques from India and China
collected weekly from 1959 to 1964. Each year was composed of fifty-two weeks,
thereby depicting seasonal variation in the time series of communications
(reflecting climatic conditions in disputed border regions between the
two countries). Furthermore, trend in the series was related to crises
and probably to economic and political growth. Therefore, seasonal
and yearly trends are eliminated from both sets of data (China and
India) so that serial relationships are more meaningful.*

Reprinted from Paul Smoker, "A Time Series Analysis of Sino-Indian Relations," *Journal of Conflict Resolution* 13 (June 1969): 172–91, by permission of the journal.

1. The author is associated with the Simulated International Processes Project of Northwestern University and the program of Peace and Conflict Research at Lancaster. The research was supported by ARPA–NU Project (Advanced Research Projects Agency, SD 260) on Simulated International Processes conducted at Northwestern within the International Relations program.

These serial relationships or interdependencies within time series are conceptually linked to freedom of decision in crises situations. That is, the more communications at t_1 are related to (determine) communications at t_2, the less the freedom of decision, and subsequently, the more predictable t_3 communications (as they depend on those at t_2). The author is therefore interested in interrelationships within series and the extent to which later observations are dependent on previous observations.

Interaction between countries is defined as the co-occurrence of communications at the same point in time (same week), whereas reaction is defined as one country's response to another at a later date. Therefore, in order to measure reaction, Smoker calculates cross-lagged correlation coefficients between series to see, for example, if China's reaction at a second point is related to India's action at an earlier point in time. Therefore, Smoker is concerned with serial interrelationships within a series (both China and India) to indicate freedom of decision (Index 1 and 2), as well as dependencies between series at the same point in time (Index 3), and dependencies between series with a lag of one week (Index 4 and 5). The latter two indices yield two series of correlations: (1) reflecting the correlation of the China series at $t + 1$ with the India series at t (reaction of China to India), and (2) the correlation of the India series at $t + 1$ with the China series at t (reaction of India to China). He also discusses how partial correlations might help to eliminate the effects (serial) of each variable on itself.

I. Introduction

Many empirical studies of international relations have considered phenomena at a particular time point, or more often over a given time period that is subsequently treated as a single time point in analysis. While such studies have been, and will continue to be, of great value in mapping the field (see, for instance, the outstanding work of Rummel and Tanter), it can be argued that certain aspects of international relations are more amenable to time series analysis than to time point analysis.

It is understandable that time series analysis is not as well developed as time point analysis in the study of international relations. At the technical, data, and theoretical levels greater complexities are involved when time series analyses are attempted, and our present skills as peace researchers, political scientists, and students of international relations are hard pressed as it is.

At the technical level at least three major assumptions are involved in our extensive use of the correlation coefficient and other measures of association:

(1) That the observations are representative of the situation to which they are taken as referring.

(2) That the deviations from the regression line are distributed normally with the same variability.

(3) That the observations are independent of one another.

Sampling theory helps us with the first assumption. Transformation, it is argued, can help us with the second. But how to deal with the third in time series analysis is not obvious, since time series observations are not independent of one another.

At the data level it is difficult enough to collect adequate data for one point in time if a representative sample is sought.[2] When data for many distinct time points are required, the problems can become severe, given present resources.

At the theoretical level time series analysis becomes exceedingly complex, as relationships themselves change over time, and such changes must be incorporated within the theoretical model that serves as the basis for analysis.

Despite these difficulties a number of time series analyses have been carried out by various authors using a variety of methods. The second section of this paper considers some of these studies.

The substance of this paper is communication between decision-making elites of the Republic of India and the People's Republic of China, in population terms the largest nations in the world, during the period 1959–1964. From a study of communications between these decision-makers, inferences are drawn concerning some possibly necessary conditions for system stability. This paper attempts to place crisis-like situations within a general context of "normal" relations between decision making elites. At the same time an attempt is made to relate to findings from laboratory gaming situations (Rapoport, 1965) and to suggest an alternate perspective for such laboratory experiments. Part three of the paper discusses some relevant empirical studies of crisis and normal relations between governmental decision-makers. The fourth part of the paper presents an analysis of the data using a time series technique and the theoretical notions developed in part three. The final section of the paper discusses the results and outlines some possible implications for future research.

II. Examples of Time Series Methods

Pitirim Sorokin (1937) in his studies of social and cultural fluctuations used, for the most part, time series data expressed as frequency counts and analyzed in a graphical way. Such an analysis is able to demonstrate trends, where a trend is defined as a general rise or fall in mean level, but fails to analyze explicitly serial relationships, where a serial relationship is defined as a tendency for fluctuations about the mean level to perpetuate themselves. The distinction between trend and serial relationships is critical in the analysis of time series data, for nonsense correlations often result when overall trends dominate (Hooker, 1901; Yule, 1926).

The intellectual style of Sorokin and of Wright (1941), another pioneer in time series analyses of international processes, retains much of the time-oriented flavor of historians such as Toynbee (1934–61), whereas more recent empirical studies of time series phenomena in international relations tend to be less all-encompassing in content and more rigorous in measurement.

The Stanford studies of crises (Holsti, 1964; Holsti and North, 1964; Zaninovich, 1962) concentrate on relations between a limited number of behavior groups for a relatively short time period. While such content analysis procedures make possible relatively sophisticated indications of tension, the subsequent analysis uses a trend approach where frequencies from time period to time period are compared in the

---

2. When a purposive or directional sample is taken, as in this paper, the data problem is not so severe.

usual way. Similarly, the outstanding work of McClelland and his associates (McClelland, 1968) in time series and crisis analysis, while evolving sophisticated indices of behavior, has been concerned to date with trend-type relationships rather than serial-type relationships. This is not to argue that trend-type analyses are invalid but to suggest that further understanding might be gained if such approaches were exapanded slightly to include the capacity for serial and causal analyses.

Richardson (1960b), in his *Statistics of Deadly Quarrels*, undertook a certain amount of time series analysis by comparing frequencies in successive time periods. Using this approach, he was able to investigate trends in such indicators as the frequency of war. Denton (1966, and Denton and Phillips, 1967) considered the same time period and again used a trend-type analysis, having developed measures using factor analysis. When displayed in graphical form Denton's trend analysis suggested a cyclical pattern of war, where successive peaks increased in size.[3] Galtung (1966), working more from the theoretical level, has also compared indicators from period to period in a trend-analysis fashion. In fact, when time series analysis of any sort is undertaken, trend effects are often the central concern (Singer and Small, 1966a, 1966b; Campbell and Cain, 1965; Rowe, 1964; Naroll, 1966).

Recently at least two additional time series analysis techniques have been used: causal inference and cross-lagged panel correlations. Causal inference has been developed from the work of Simon and Blalock (Simon, 1957; Blalock, 1964) and has been used for political analyses by such authors as Alker (1967) and Tanter (1966b). Boudon (1965b) has suggested a variant of causal inference, dependence analysis. Both causal inference and dependence analysis have become increasingly common in political science, international relations, and peace research.[4] The second method, cross-lagged panel correlations, has been used by Campbell (1963).[5]

Multivariate time series analysis can be undertaken using techniques like canonical analysis (Bartlett, 1948). Such studies have not yet appeared in the peace and conflict literature, but groups such as the Dimensionality of Nations Project are adapting the factor-analytic method to time series problems (Phillips, 1968).

Apart from statistical approaches, many authors have used mathematical models (Moberg, 1966; Rapoport, 1965; Richardson, 1960a; Wolfson, 1966; Smoker, 1963) and simulation (Guetzkow, 1963) to study time series phenomenon in international relations. Even a brief glance at the literature relevant to time series shows that a number of methods have been used. This article suggests still another approach which may be used in addition to and in conjunction with many of the methods mentioned above.

III. Theoretical Considerations

Empirical time series studies of crisis situations are numerous, but the work of Charles McClelland and his associates (McClelland, 1961, 1964, 1968; McClelland *et al.*, 1965) has been of particular value in executing this study.

---

3. Interestingly enough, a possible general systems phenomenon relevant to such a cyclical pattern has been suggested by J. G. Dash (1966).

4. For an outstanding review of causal inference and dependence analysis techniques applied to political science, see Alker (1967).

5. Some recently discovered problems involved with the cross-panel technique have been suggested by Rozelle and Campbell (1966).

Crises, McClelland suggests, were prominent features of international politics in the Cold War era but may be less frequent in the future. They appear to be "intense and periodic manifestations of underlying conflict configurations in international politics and may serve for brief periods as partial sustitutes for war" (McClelland, 1967b).

McClelland argues that there may be a number of definitions of crises, each depending in part upon the particular characteristics singled out for attention. One view sees international crises as passages or sectors in the unceasing flow of political action and response among nation states. The McClelland approach has been to build partial explanations on the basis of observed overt behavior, thus concentrating on the flow of acts and responses between actors.

> An acute international crisis may then be defined in terms of the flow of discrete acts and the response to these acts. Thus, a crisis is a sharp break in the usual flow and pattern of acts in a specific issue-area or arena. . . . This definition of the acute crisis can be specified more completely by stating that a crisis is a transformation that is initiated in a short span of time in the volume and distribution of the stream of event-interaction and that is terminated by a return toward the volume and distribution of event-interaction prevailing before the onset of the crisis [McClelland, 1967b].

McClelland contends that performance characteristics of decision-makers, in both crisis and noncrisis behavior, can be identified, and that phase characteristics of particular crises and of crises in general, as one type of international behavior, can be distinguished.

McClelland summarizes his research to date with a list of nine specific findings:

(1) Crises exhibit increase in volume and variety of acts towards equal proportions of each of the event interaction categories.

(2) Acute crises are brief, never more than three months.

(3) When a second crisis occurs in the same arena, it tends to be shorter than the first.

(4) The total behavior of all parties to a crisis tends to have a repetitive quality. Certain types of acts are employed more frequently and regularly than others.

(5) Experience potential grows faster in crisis than in noncrisis.

(6) The distributions of noncrisis acts across the repertory predict to the crisis in the same arena, but not outstandingly.

(7) The participants in the Berlin crisis employed quite different repertory patterns than those in the Quemoy crisis.

(8) Crisis participants do not show any strong tendency to adopt new combinations of interaction behavior as the crisis progresses.

(9) Specific crisis characteristics can be derived for each participant from the McClelland analyses.

McClelland concludes his summary paper by saying,

> The field should be extended; perhaps an empirically-based typification of crises could be constructed by the study of the interaction patterns of many crises. Increased knowledge about structures and processes of acute crises in international politics might well contribute some increase in the ability to make short-range predictions of crisis mechanisms and crisis outcomes, if conditions in the international system again precipitate a new series of these confrontations [McClelland, 1967b].

This study adopts an approach that has some similarities to the published studies of McClelland. There are, however, at least two significant differences. First, the indicators of interaction used here are not as sophisticated as the battery of interaction indicators employed by McClelland. And second, the method used here is concerned with serial relationships rather than trend. That is, general changes in level are eliminated, and only fluctuations about mean levels and the relationship to other fluctuations are considered. In this way causal relationships can be inferred on a stronger basis.

If it seems appropriate, McClelland-type indicators could be used with the general method suggested here. But because of the effort involved, this limited analysis has been undertaken to explore the method.

Similarly, the content analysis technique used by the Stanford group to exhibit trends in conflict spiral indicators could include the further step of examining relationships between variables from which trend effects have been eliminated.

At a different level of analysis, laboratory experiments furnish some valuable insights into crisis processes as against normal processes in international relations. In particular, the extensive literature on Prisoner's Dilemma[6] has been concerned, among other things, with the so-called "lock-in" effect. Rapoport and Chammah (1965, p. 195), in reporting their experiments, comment that:

> Turning to the final lock-ins ... we see that seventy percent of the male pairs end the sessions locked in, and that of these over four times as many pairs have locked in on CC [cooperative-cooperative responses] than on DD [defection-defection responses].

Using the findings from laboratory experiments as a heuristic, one might hypothesize an analogous phenomena in the relations between governmental decision-makers. Both CC and DD "lock-ins" have a systemic property in common: the notion of predictability as outlined by Galtung (1964) in his discussion of the international system. McClelland relates to the same phenomena when he points out in his summary findings (1967a, p. 7), that:

> The overall, cumulative channeling of event-interaction items becomes patterned in that the same types of acts are employed more frequently and regularly than others and also in the stabilizing of particular distributions of acts after a brief period at the beginning of the crisis.

Thus one might hypothesize that both crisis and stable peace situations will exhibit "lock-in" effects in the sense that DD and CC interaction sequences become more predictable. Intermediary states can be viewed as less predictable on the CC and DD dimensions. The technique of serial correlation is singularly well suited to investigate the degree of predictability in an interaction sequence.

IV. The Analysis

Previous Studies of the Sino-Indian Crisis

A previous paper (Smoker, 1964) used a gross trend analysis to examine the relationship between trade, defense, and communication for decision-makers of India

---

6. The recent section of the *Journal of Conflict Resolution* devoted to gaming is indicative of the epidemic-like interest in such experiments.

and the People's Republic of China during the period 1954–1964. The conclusions of that study are as follows:

(1) From 1950 to 1964 the defense expenditure of India varied inversely with trade except during the period 1959–1961.

(2) India pursued a nonviolent defense policy from 1954 up to September 1962, i.e., increased tension was met with decreasing defense expenditure and increasing communication.

(3) After this period India appears to have adopted the Western position of national security through military strength.

(4) A seasonal variation in communication is apparent.

(5) Up to 1959 there was relatively little communication. The period following 1959, however, shows a steady rise in communication rates, with two peaks. The first peak occurred after the March 22, 1959, conflict in Tibet and the March 31, 1959, entry and asylum of the Dalai Lama in India. The second massive increase took place one year after the publication in February 1961 of the final report of the joint study group.

(6) Since the ending of active fighting in 1962, communications between India and China have declined.

(7) The maximum communication rate was reached just before fighting started; subsequently the letter rate diminished. A similar effect was observed by the Stanford group for the 1914 crisis (Holsti, 1965).

(8) It seems possible that the sheer volume of communication helped precipitate the crisis, as the decision-making apparatus of both governments may have been inundated by a massive increase in communication. Such an overload could have caused a serious lag between information and action.

(9) Many of the disputes were ostensibly over a few soldiers and goats, and violence was usually restricted to activities such as throwing stones.

The series of ten White Papers published between 1959 and 1964 by the Ministry of External Affairs of the Government of India served as data source for the previous study. These White Papers contain all the correspondence between the decision-makers of India and China. The same data source is used for this paper, with the inclusion of the eleventh White Paper covering the period up to January 1965.

A recent, apparently unpublished study by Greaser (1966), entitled "Sino-Indian Border Dispute, 1954–1962," is summarized in a working paper by Martin and Young (1967) and forms part of the interaction studies conducted by McClelland and his associates. Martin and Young summarize the following eleven propositions from the Greaser study:

(1) India committed over three border violations for every one perpetrated by China.

(2) During the dispute, the place of main activity shifted during the three major time periods, rather than being concentrated in NEFA as popularly hypothesized.

(3) Throughout the time period, the first half of each year was comparatively peaceful in the Himalayas, with activity starting in about April, hitting peaks from July through October, and then tapering off again.

(4) Most violations were of small-average magnitude, involving few men and a low number of deaths.

(5) Seventy-six percent of all violations occurred in the air and not on the ground.

(6) In the major 1962 crisis an approximate 700 percent increase in violations plus the presence of the "peak" period should have warned India to be better prepared than she was for trouble.

(7) Both China and India issued about the same number of communiques during the period studied, but the length of messages differed greatly.

(8) Differences in the behavior of India and China in diplomatic matters is readily apparent in their communiques. India's communiques were generally short, moderate in tone, and followed the actual intrusion by a longer period of time than did China's. China's notes were generally a little longer, issued quite rapidly after the intrusion, and vacillated between mild and strong.

(9) In general terms, the three-phase time breakdown followed the predictable activity growth upwards, with little activity indicated for 1954 to mid-1959; a moderate growth from mid-1959 to 1961; and a large jump for 1962.

(10) A good indicator of strain between India and China was the origin of the communiques.

(11) The frequency of communiques correlated highly with the frequency of intrusions and the intensity of the conflict.

Table 1 shows the relatively good agreement between the independent studies of Smoker and Greaser.

TABLE 1   Table of Rough Correspondence of Two
Previous Studies

Greaser's finding (1966)	Smoker's finding (1964)	Agreement
(1)	None	
(2)	None	
(3)	(4)	Good
(4)	(9)	Good
(5)	None	
(6)	(5)	Good
(7)	China: No. = 320	Fair
	India: No. = 370	
(8)	Mean Length China = 9.6″	Fair
	Mean Length India = 9.0″	
(9)	(5)	Good
(10)	None	
(11)	None	
None	(1)	
None	(2)	
None	(3)	
None	(6)	
None	(7)	
None	(8)	

Trend Elimination

Against the background of these previous studies, this paper uses a serial correlation method to reexamine the situation with trend effects eliminated. To begin with, the data collected from the series of White Papers was arranged in the following way. The number of communiques sent by India and by China were coded by the week for the period 1959–1964, which includes the before- and after-crisis periods.

In order to code the data in a form that would show seasonal variations, each year was divided into exactly fifty-two weeks. This was done by coding week one as January 1–7, week two as January 8–14, and so on. Week nine comprised February

TABLE 2 Communication Frequency of China (to India) and India (to China) by Week for Years 1959–1964 Inclusive*

Week No.	1959 China/India		1960 China/India		1961 China/India		1962 China/India		1963 China/India		1964 China/India	
1	0	0	0	0	1	1	1	2	4	5	2	3
2	1	0	0	0	0	0	0	0	4	7	1	6
3	0	1	2	0	0	0	0	4	2	2	0	2
4	1	0	3	0	0	1	3	2	2	5	1	3
5	0	0	0	1	2	0	1	0	0	4	3	0
6	0	0	2	2	1	2	0	0	1	3	1	0
7	0	0	0	1	0	1	0	0	0	1	0	2
8	0	0	0	2	4	0	0	1	4	0	0	0
9	0	0	2	1	0	0	3	2	2	1	1	2
10	0	0	0	0	2	0	2	3	7	4	0	2
11	0	0	0	0	2	1	2	2	2	5	0	1
12	1	3	1	1	1	0	6	1	3	2	1	1
13	0	0	1	1	1	2	0	2	4	6	1	3
14	0	0	3	5	0	0	2	2	3	3	0	0
15	0	0	0	1	0	1	0	2	1	4	0	0
16	0	0	0	0	0	2	1	4	4	0	0	0
17	1	1	1	1	2	1	4	1	6	2	0	1
18	0	1	0	0	2	2	5	2	5	4	0	0
19	0	1	0	0	0	1	3	4	4	1	0	0
20	1	0	0	1	1	0	4	6	2	8	0	0
21	1	2	0	0	1	1	1	7	2	3	1	0
22	0	0	0	0	2	1	10	3	3	9	0	0
23	0	0	1	0	0	3	2	4	3	4	3	0
24	0	0	0	2	0	3	2	3	1	6	0	0
25	1	0	0	1	2	3	3	4	1	1	0	0
26	0	1	1	1	1	0	1	8	5	1	3	0
27	0	1	1	0	0	2	1	3	1	3	2	0
28	0	1	2	1	0	1	2	7	2	2	0	0
29	1	0	0	0	0	1	2	2	3	2	0	2
30	0	5	0	2	0	0	2	9	2	3	1	2
31	0	1	1	1	1	0	8	4	6	2	0	1
32	1	1	1	0	3	1	5	2	1	6	0	2
33	0	3	0	2	1	1	4	6	6	2	0	0
34	1	2	1	2	3	2	3	8	4	3	0	0
35	3	2	3	0	0	3	5	6	2	3	1	0
36	5	1	1	0	0	1	5	5	0	5	1	5
37	2	4	1	0	1	1	4	6	2	1	2	1
38	0	2	1	0	2	1	5	6	3	3	1	0
39	0	5	1	4	2	2	7	6	0	2	2	0
40	0	0	0	0	1	1	3	4	3	2	0	3
41	0	0	0	0	0	0	8	4	2	2	0	1
42	1	0	3	3	0	0	3	4	3	3	1	0
43	4	4	0	2	0	0	2	4	2	2	0	0
44	1	6	0	1	4	1	2	6	1	2	0	0
45	1	2	2	1	0	3	5	2	1	2	1	2
46	3	2	0	0	0	2	4	2	5	2	2	0
47	0	1	0	0	1	1	5	0	1	0	0	0
48	2	0	1	2	4	0	4	3	3	1	0	1
49	0	3	1	0	2	4	5	9	2	3	0	2
50	0	1	4	0	3	1	1	4	1	3	0	0
51	5	2	1	1	0	0	1	1	1	0	0	0
52	3	0	3	1	0	0	13	4	3	2	2	1

*Source: Eleven White Papers entitled "Notes, Memoranda and Letters Exchanged between the Governments of India and China." New Delhi: Ministry of External Affairs Series, 1959-1965, Government of India.

26–March 4 in both normal and leap years (giving one eight-day week in each four years). Other weeks followed in sequence up to week fifty-two, December 24–31, a yearly eight-day "week."

This procedure was adopted for each of the six years, 1959–1964. The data are shown in Table 2. In order to eliminate seasonal and yearly trends, the following procedure was adopted. Seasonal trends had been reported in both the previous Sino-Indian studies mentioned above and appear to be related to climatic conditions prevailing in the border regions. Much of the disputed border is occupied only during the summer. Yearly trends, however, seem to be related in this instance to the occurrence of crisis periods. It also seems reasonable to suppose that a general rise in communication may have occurred in any case due to economic and political growth effects. As the relationship of trend to crisis has been relatively well documented, and as the effects of other trend phenomena may also be involved, the overall yearly trend from these two sources can be eliminated. For both Chinese and Indian communication:

Let $f\,w.y$ be the frequency of communication in week (w) and in year (y).
Then the mean

$$\overline{fw} = 1/N \sum_{y=1}^{y=N} fw.y \text{ for } w = 1 \text{ to } M$$

and the mean

$$\overline{fy} = 1/M \sum_{w=1}^{w=M} f\,w.y \text{ for } y = 1 \text{ to } N.$$

In our particular case, the number of weeks (M) is 52, and the number of years (N) is 6. Thus, we have:

$$\overline{fw} = 1/6 \sum_{y=1}^{y=6} f\,w.y \text{ for } w = 1 \text{ to } 52$$

$$\text{and } \overline{fy} = 1/52 \sum_{w=1}^{w=52} f\,w.y \text{ for } y = 1 \text{ to } 6.$$

This gives us 52 weekly means $\overline{fw}$ and 6 yearly means $\overline{fy}$. The overall mean $\overline{m}$ is also calculated using the formula:

$$\overline{m} = \frac{1}{(6 \times 52)} \sum_{w=1}^{w=52} \sum_{y=1}^{y=6} f\,w.y$$

The trend-free frequencies $F\,w.y$ are then calculated using the expression:

$$F\,w.y = f\,w.y - \overline{fw} - \overline{fy} + \overline{m}.$$

Using this procedure the seasonal and yearly trend effects can, for all practical purposes, be separated from serial effects in the data.[7]

---

7. A computer program has been written for this purpose. The program punches out a serial data deck suitable for use in standard correlational programs. The program is available from the author on request.

Serial Correlation

The analysis of serial relationships can then be undertaken in the following way:

(1) Let F $w.y$ be represented by a one index variable Ft. Here t is the week number during the whole period considered. Thus $F_{30.4}$ (week 30, year 4) becomes F_{186} $[t = (3 \times 52) + 30 = 186]$.

(2) Let the overall time span of N equally spaced time points be divided into $(N + 1 - n)$ overlapping and consecutive time series, each time series being n time points long. In this paper N equals 312 (6 years times 52 weeks), and n has been taken as 50 (weeks). Thus series 1, S_1, comprises time points F_1, F_2, F_3 ... F_{49}, F_{50}, while series 2, S_2, comprises time points F_2, F_3, F_4 ... F_{50}, F_{51}. In general series M, S_M, comprises time points F_M, $F_{(M + 1)}$, $F_{(M + 2)}$ ... $F_{(M + 48)}$, $F_{(M + 49)}$.

(3) Each of the series S_M is treated as a variable having 50 cases in the subsequent analysis. A serial correlation coefficient is simply a correlation between any of the series S.

Because we have 263 series S in our six-year period, and consequently a large number of possible serial correlation coefficients, and more importantly because we are interested in generating theory, it is necessary to introduce some additional theoretical notions to select the serial relationships relevant to this paper.

Freedom of Decision

An important idea in international relations in general, and in crisis and escalation situations in particular, is freedom of decision. It can be argued that the greater the freedom of decision perceived by a particular decision-maker, the better. For as perceived and actual freedom of decision diminish, the decision-maker's control is reduced and the situation becomes systemically deterministic. Put another way, the nature of the situation moves from being game theoretical, in logical terms, to Richardsonian (Rapoport, 1957).

An index of freedom of decision is constructed using the first serial correlation coefficient. The logic is as follows. For a particular set of variables, for example the 263 series S for Indian communications to China, the degree to which the communications of one week determine communications the next week can be taken as an indicator of freedom of decision. The less the freedom of decision, the more predictable the next week's communication, knowing this week's. As the first serial correlation coefficient is calculated by correlating S_M with $S_{M + 1}$, it is possible to calculate 262 first serial correlation coefficients for each of the two sets of variables, Chinese and Indian communication. The second serial correlation coefficients, the correlation between S_M and $S_{M + 2}$, also can be studied to see if second-order processes exist at any time; if such second-order processes are apparent, the third serial correlations can be inspected, and so on.

The concept of freedom of decision, together with ideas of interaction and reaction discussed below, are broadened subsequently, although the simplified indices and model of analysis presented here are maintained for analytical purposes in this paper.

Interaction and Reaction

Interaction, in this paper, is taken to mean a situation in which at least two behavioral entities respond to each other at the same time. Thus, for purposes of analysis, each tends to respond to the other's current actions during the week time point, rather than in a subsequent week, or not at all.

Reaction, in this paper, is taken to mean a situation in which one behavioral entity responds to another at a measurably later date. Thus, the responses of one set of decision-makers in week M will depend on the action of the other set of decision-makers in week M − 1, if a week's reaction lag is present. To index reaction with a week lag, the serial correlations for variables S of one set of variables S_{M-1} of the other are calculated.

Assumptions

Given the above ideas of freedom of decision, interaction, and reaction, it is possible to propose the following tautologies, all other things being equal:

(1) As freedom of decision goes down, systemic causality in the Richardson sense goes up, i.e., behavior becomes more deterministic since the knowledge of past behavior makes possible the prediction of future responses.

(2) As interaction, defined in the above sense, goes up, systemic causality also goes up since the immediate response of one behavioral entity to the actions of the other becomes more predictable.

(3) As reaction, defined in the above sense, goes up, systemic causality also goes up since the delayed response of one behavioral entity to the actions of the other becomes more predictable.

Thus, the terms *freedom of decision*, *interaction*, and *reaction* as defined here imply the above assumptions. There are, however, at least two major problems implicit in the above discussion.

(1) The phrase and frame of mind "all other things being equal," together with the notion of causality implied in the above discussion, leaves much to be desired. It would seem reasonable to suppose that a group of "variables" might be better related causally to a second group of "variables." Canonical analysis may prove to be well suited for such a procedure (Rutherford, 1966), or a variant suggested by Barlett (1948) may be superior for over-time relationships. At a more fundamental level the very idea of a variable may need careful reexamination as time series analysis of human relationships continues, for a group of apparent variables at one level of analysis can become a single variable at another. Further, the degree of differentiation involved in defining "causal" phenomena may be critical in relating one pattern of behavior to a subsequent pattern. Since the very definition of a variable is an expression of the degree of differentiation involved (in the theoretical model), causality may appear lacking at one level of complexity, or rather simplicity, and present at another. This problem may become more important as better indicators such as the more differentiated variables discussed above are used.

(2) This consideration leads to a second related problem concerning the implicit or explicit model of the phenomena under consideration. In the present case it can be argued that before it is possible to test the significance of interaction or reaction between the two sets of decision-makers, it is necessary to eliminate the "effects" each set of decision-makers has upon itself. Thus, if at a particular time the Indian letters to China can be represented by a first-order process, while the China letters to India are second-order, it might seem reasonable to follow standard convention and test the significance of interaction or reaction correlations by first eliminating the

"effects" of each variable on itself, using partial correlations. However, this assumes a model in which the sets of variables are considered separately before they are considered in interactive and reactive terms together, and while it may be standard research practice to work in such a fashion, this is not to say that it is how the world works. We could have started the other way around, taking the interaction and reaction sets first, and considered only the freedom-of-decision variables, having first eliminated the interaction and reaction "components" of freedom of decision. Alternatively, we could adopt the procedure of considering apparent relationships, rather than the segmented levels of partial correlational behavior. A satisfactory approach would probably include a range of perspectives, the above three being typical models.

In the present study apparent relationships will be reported and partial correlations will be mentioned when problems of significance or interpretation arise. However, given the non-*gestalt* nature of most of our statistical and scientific tools, our inadequacies here are the general inadequacies of present statistical methods in the social sciences. Additional work on perception in international relations may provide assistance in choosing more adequate models and appropriate statistical assumptions.

We are now in a position to consider the five indices defined above and illustrated in Figures 1-2-3. A summary statement of each index is given in Table 3. The graph shows the size of the serial correlation coefficients on the Y axis, and time on the X axis.

Time is defined in terms of successive series of 50 weeks, giving some 260 "time points" on the X axis. Shorter series would more adequately approximate conventional time, but problems of index instability might arise. Future studies might use index instability in shorter series to establish the probability terms in standard Markov equations.

During the discussion in the next section the word China refers to the governmental decision-makers of China, and similarly for India. No inferences can be made to total populations or to whole nations as behavioral entities from such a limited study. This obvious point is stressed here because of a concern for accurate-

TABLE 3   Summary of Five Concepts and Indices

Concept	Statistical Index	Key in Figs. 1–3
(1) Freedom of decision of China	Correlation of SC_t with $SC_{(t+1)}$	India → China
(2) Freedom of decision of India	Correlation of SI_t with $SI_{(t+1)}$	China → India
(3) China/India interaction	Correlation of SC_t with SI_t	India ↔ China
(4) Reaction of China to India	Correlation of $SC_{(t+1)}$ with SI_t	China
(5) Reaction of India to China	Correlation fo $SI_{(t+1)}$ with SC_t	India

Note: SC_t is defined as the series for China starting with time point t.
  SI_t is defined as the series for India starting with time point t.
  All series are fifty time points long.

ly identifying the behavioral entities involved in the situation. It could be that the tendency to identify all behaviors as national behaviors, where nations are viewed as single behavioral entities, is not theoretically useful.

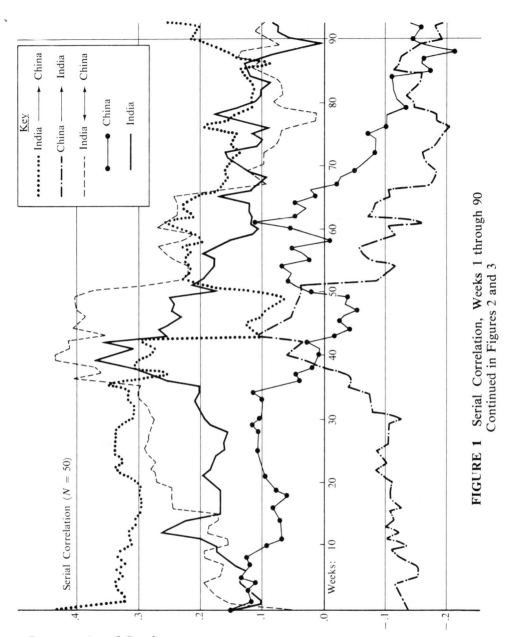

FIGURE 1 Serial Correlation, Weeks 1 through 90
Continued in Figures 2 and 3

Interpretation of Graphs

For normal correlation coefficients the 0.5 level of significance for 50 observations is approximately .28, while the .01 level is .36. These levels may be taken to test significance for normal serial correlation coefficients.[8]

At the beginning of the period under consideration, the graph shows that only the reaction of China to India is significant, although the interaction index also

---

8. In our case it should be acknowledged that group means have been eliminated from the data, and a more exact test of significance developed by J. Durbin and G. S. Watson should be used. However, for present purposes the usual method is sufficiently accurate.

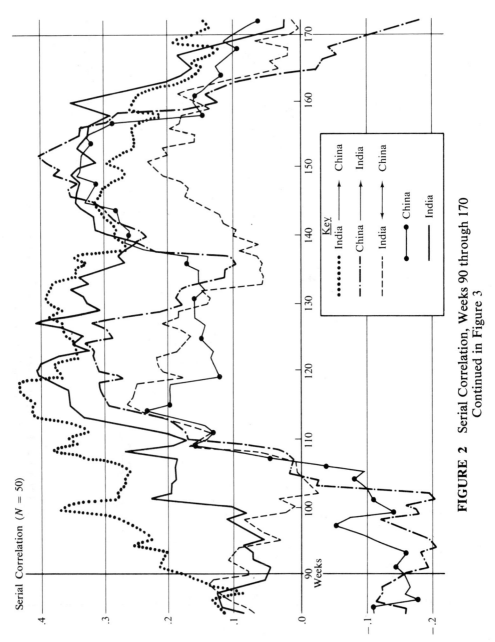

FIGURE 2 Serial Correlation, Weeks 90 through 170
Continued in Figure 3

becomes significant, statistically speaking, around series twenty. At that time both nations appear to have a high freedom of decision, the appropriate serial correlation not being significant and India's reaction to China also not being significant. The situation remains relatively constant up to series thirty, but shortly thereafter comes a noticeable first peak. This peak can be taken as corresponding to the Dalai Lama incident and the delayed crisis-like situation.

Thus by series forty the interaction index is very significant, the reaction of China less significant than previously, and the freedom of decision of India low, the index being significant. China still maintains a high freedom of decision in her relations

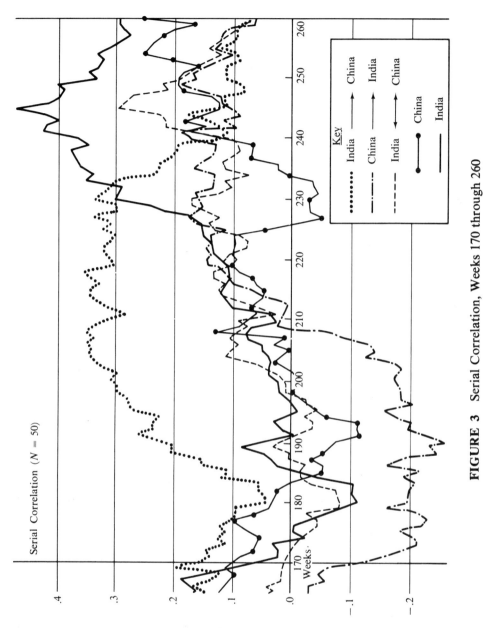

Serial Correlation (N = 50)

Key

India ⋯⋯⋯⋯ China
India --⋅-- China
India ----- China
China ●―――● China
India ―――――

FIGURE 3   Serial Correlation, Weeks 170 through 260

with India, while India, although interacting significantly with China, is not reacting significantly. If we assume that the high reaction score of China is partly a
result of the high interaction, and then calculate the appropriate partial correlation,
we find, indeed, that such an assumption is consistent with the resulting insignificant
partial correlation. Thus at the apparent level the situation is as described above, but
the serial profiles are consistent with a situation in which interaction is high and the
freedom of decision of India is low. "Lock-in" has not occurred, since both freedoms
of decision would be low in such a case, and information overload is not apparent,
since interaction is significant. In an information overload situation one might
expect both parties to be reacting to each other rather than interacting.

After this first peak the freedom of decision of India appears to increase again, while the interaction stays significant. By series fifty interaction alone is significant, although this, too, drops shortly afterwards and gradually loses significance. Series eighty represents a trough, at which time both nations maintain freedom of decision and all significant interaction and reaction have ended.

On theoretical grounds it can be argued that this first small crisis period remained stable (in that violence was avoided) because of the nature of the India-China relationships exhibitied in Figures 1, 2, and 3 and discussed above. Freedom of decision was never lost by both nations at once; the "lock-in" effect and information overload were not apparent. Figure 2 covers the time period in which war occurred and is characterized by patterns of serial relationships that differ from those in Figure 1.

Just before series ninety the China reaction index begins to increase, so that by series ninety-seven statistical significance is achieved almost as if the initial pattern of behavior was reestablishing itself. Just after series 100 an apparent upsurge of all the profiles can be seen, although only the China reaction profile remains statistically significant by series 110. India's freedom of decision continues to fall, however, and is soon significant. At the same time India's reaction to China becomes significant, and by series 120 both nations are reacting rather than interacting, and India's freedom of decision is low. Information overload could have occurred at this time.

Just before series 130 a drop is apparent in the Indian reaction profile, a drop that is mirrored just before series 140 in the China reaction and the Indian freedom-of-decision profiles. It is not clear at this time how this temporary lull relates to the crisis phenomena.

While the China reaction and Indian freedom-of decision profiles are dropping to the border of statistical significance, the Indian reaction profile and the China freedom-of-decision profile are again rising. By series 150, "lock-in" has occurred, as indicated by low freedom of decision, and both nations are reacting rather than interacting. This is consistent with a "lock-in" situation in which information overload is present, particularly since the interaction indicator is not significant. This period corresponds to the crisis that led to one month's hostilities. Subsequently all profiles drop to a second trough of non-interaction and high freedom of decision by series 180.

Figure 3 continues the postcrisis situation up to January, 1965. An interesting phenomenon is apparent here. The China reaction profile once again rises, thus reinforcing our suspicion that this rise might be a characteristic of each new phase. The Indian reaction profile, however, falls almost to a significantly negative value. This implies that deviations about the mean for India's reactions to China might tend to produce a deviation in the opposite direction during the next week. This is almost consistent with a predictable attempt to be unpredictable! However, significance is not reached and soon falls. By series 210, only China's reaction is statistically significant and the situation remains relatively stable up to series 230. At that time India appears to lose her freedom of decision, the profile rising to an unprecedented height. At the same time the Chinese reaction profile drops, while the interaction profile rises to temporary significance. Even statistically this significance cannot be attributed to the effects of the Indian freedom-of-decision profile since the Chinese freedom-of-decision indicator is at that time free of serial correlation, and the correlation between a serially correlated variable and a nonseriallycorrelated variable can be treated in the same fashion as a normal correlation co-efficient. If both had exhibited serial correlation effects then partials could be used to eliminate these effects in testing for significance of the correlation between them.

Figure 3 shows a situation in which both freedoms of decision are falling, possibly suggesting a second "lock-in" effect. Of course, such an effect on its own may be safe, but if reaction were also to become significant our previous experience might warn us to be concerned.

V. Discussion and Summary

A number of possibilities are suggested by this study. In particular:

(1) It may be possible to identify stable and unstable patterns of behavior in terms of such concepts as freedom of decision, interaction, and reaction. It seems likely that a pattern of "variables" rather than a single variable, such as threat, will be of value in discriminating between stable and unstable situations.[9]

(2) Each of the three phases examined here exhibited different patterns of behavior. Using the simple ideas of freedom of decision and information overload, the patterns of verbal behavior are consistent with the violent and nonviolent management of the crisis situations that occurred. During the first period freedom of decision was never lost by both nations at once, "lock-in" was avoided, and information overload was not apparent. The crisis associated with the situation in Tibet did not break down into war. During the second period the profiles were consistent with a "lock-in" situation with information overhead and loss of freedom of decision by both groups. The crisis during this period did break down into war.

(3) The five relationships (two reaction, two freedom of decision, one interaction) undoubtedly changed significantly during the course of the six years studied. This is consistent with the observation that either our models must include the facility for variables, "constants," and relationships to change or we must dig deeper to get to the real constant relationships involved.

(4) The use of better indicators and sets of indicators within the general design used here might make it possible to consider series of much shorter lengths than fifty terms — say ten terms — and thus pinpoint the development of the crisis with much greater accuracy.

(5) Laboratory experiments might well replicate the general time series method used here both to provide linkages between such work and studies of the international system, and to provide an alternate way to consider pre-"lock-in" and "lock-in" behavior. Such replication would, of course, have to be on individual cases and not on aggregated samples, as is the present custom.

---

9. If a regression analysis of the data is undertaken, two methods suggest themselves: (1) Calculate the deviations from a serial regression of the dependent variable upon previous values of itself. Use these deviations in a regression analysis on the independent variables and their previous values. (2) Carry out a regression of the dependent variable upon the independent variables and upon previous values of the independent variables and itself.

Method (1) estimates the extent to which the independent variables might be used to predict the "random" variation in the dependent variable (i.e., nonserial).

Method (2) estimates the best equation for predicting the dependent variable from the independent variables and previous observations.

References

Alker, Hayward R., Jr. "Causal Inference and Political Analysis." In Joseph Bernd (ed.), *Mathematical Applications in Political Science*. Charlottesville: University Press of Virginia, 1967.

Anderson, R. L. "Distribution of the Serial Correlation Coefficient in a Circularly Correlated Universe," *Annals of Mathematical Statistics*, 18 (1942), 80.

Anderson, R. L., and T. W. Anderson. "Distribution of the Circular Serial Coefficient for Residuals from a Fitted Fourier Series," *Annals of Mathematical Statistics*, 21 (1950), 59.

Ando, A., F. M. Fisher, and H. A. Simon. *Essays on the Structure of Social Science Models*. Cambridge: MIT Press, 1963.

Bartlett, M. S. "Some Aspects of the Time-Correlation Problem in Regard to Tests of Significance," *Journal of the Royal Statistical Society*, 98 (1935), 536.

————. "On the Theoretical Specification of Sampling Properties of Autocorrelated Times Series," *Supplement to the Journal of the Royal Statistical Society*, 8 (1946), 27.

————. "A Note on the Statistical Estimation of Supply and Demand Relations from Time Series," *Econometrica*, 16 (1948), 323.

Blalock, H. M., Jr. *Causal Inferences in Nonexperimental Research*. Chapel Hill: University of North Carolina Press, 1964.

Boudon, R. "Méthodes d'analyse causale," *Revue Française de Sociologie*, 6 (1965a), 24–43.

————. "A Method of Linear Causal Analysis: Dependence Analysis," *American Sociological Review*, 30 (June 1965b), 365–74.

Campbell, Donald T. "From Description to Experimentation: Interpreting Trends as Quasi-Experiments." In Chester W. Harris (ed.), *Problems in Measuring Change*. Madison: University of Wisconsin Press, 1963.

Campbell, Donald T., and Julian C. Stanley. "Experimental and Quasi-Experimental Designs for Research on Teaching." In Nathaniel L. Gage (ed.), *Handbook of Research on Teaching*. Chicago: Rand McNally, 1963.

Campbell, Joel T., and Leila S. Cain. "Public Opinion and the Outbreak of War," *Journal of Conflict Resolution*, 9, 3 (Sept. 1965), 318–29.

Cochrane, D., and G. H. Orcutt. "Application of Least Squares Regression to Relationships Containing Autocorrelated Error Terms," *Journal of the American Statistical Association*, 44 (1949), 32.

Coleman, J. *An Introduction to Mathematical Sociology*. New York: Macmillan, 1964.

Dash, J. G. "A Condensation in Warpeace Space," *General Systems Yearbook* (1966), 143–46

Denton, Frank H. "A Handbook of Factor Analysis for International Relations." Los Angeles, California: School of International Relations, University of Southern California, 1965.

————. "Systemic Properties of War 1820–1949." The RAND Corporation, April 1966.

Denton, Frank H., and Warren Phillips. "Some Cyclical Patterns in the History of Violence." The RAND Corporation, 1967.

Durbin, J., and G. S. Watson. "Testing for Serial Correlation in Least Squares Regression. I," *Biometrika*, 37 (1950), 409.

————, ————. "Testing for Serial Correlation in Least Squares Regression. II," *Biometrika*, 38 (1951), 159.

Feigl, H. "Notes on Causality." In H. Feigl and M. Brodbeck (eds.), *Readings in the Philosophy of Science*. New York: Appleton-Century-Crofts, 1953.

Felz, Donald, and Frank M. Andrews. "Detecting Causal Priorities in Panel Study Data," *American Sociological Review*, 29 (Dec. 1964), 836–48.

Galtung, Johan. "Summit Meetings and International Relations," *Journal of Peace Research*, 1 (1964), 36–54.

————. "East-West Interaction Patterns." *Journal of Peace Research*, 2 (1966), 146–77.

Greaser, Connie. "Sino-Indian Border Dispute, 1954–1962." Unpublished master's thesis, University of California, 1966.

Guetzkow, Harold, Chadwick F. Alger, Richard A. Brody, Robert C. Noel, and Richard C. Snyder. *Simulation in International Relations: Developments for Research and Teaching*. Englewood Cliffs, N.J.: Prentice-Hall, 1963.

Holsti, Ole R. "Perceptions of Time and Alternatives as Factors in Crisis Decision-Making," *Peace Research Society (International) Papers*, 3 (1965), 79–120.

——. "External Conflict and Internal Consensus: The Sino-Soviet Case." In Philip J. Stone, Dexter C. Dunphy, Marshall S. Smith, and Daniel M. Ogilvie (eds.), *The General Inquirer.* Cambridge: MIT Press, 1966.

Holsti, Ole R., and Robert C. North. "The History of Human Conflict." In Elton B. McNeil (ed.), *The Nature of Human Conflict.* Englewood Cliffs, N.J.: Prentice-Hall, 1965.

——, ——. "Comparative Data from Content Analysis: Perceptions of Hostility and Economic Variables in the 1914 Crisis." In Richard L. Merritt and Stein Rokkan (eds.), *Comparing Nations: The Use of Quantitative Data in Cross-National Research.* New Haven: Yale University Press, 1966.

Hooker, R. H. "Correlation of the Marriage-Rate with Trade," *Journal of the Royal Statistical Society,* 64 (Sept. 1901), 485–92.

Koopmans, T. C. "Serial Correlation and Quadratic Forms in Normal Variables," *Annals of Mathematical Statistics,* 13 (1942), 14.

—— (ed.). *Statistical Inference in Dynamic Economic Models.* New York: Wiley, 1950.

Lazarsfeld, P. "Evidence and Inference in Social Research," *Daedalus,* 87, 4 (Fall 1968).

Lee, Wooyoung, James H. Christensen, and Dale F. Rudd. "Design Variable Selection to Simplify Process Calculations," *American Institute of Chemical Engineers' Journal* (Nov. 1966), 1104–10.

Leipnik, R. B. "Distribution of the Serial Correlation Coefficient in a Circularly Correlated Universe," *Annals of Mathematical Statistics,* 18 (1947), 80.

Martin, Wayne Richard, and Robert A. Young. "World Event-Interaction Study: Pilot Study Report," University of Michigan, 1966.

MacIver, R. M. *Social Causation.* Boston: Ginn, 1942.

McClelland, Charles A. "The Acute International Crisis," *World Politics,* 14 (Oct. 1961), 182–204.

——. "Decisional Opportunity and Political Controversy: The Quemoy Case," *Journal of Conflict Resolution,* 6, 3 (Sept. 1962), 201–13.

——. "Action Structures and Communication in Two International Crises: Quemoy and Berlin," *Background,* 7 (Feb. 1964), 201–15.

——. "The Acute Crises of Berlin and the Taiwan Straits: A Summary Statement," University of Michigan, 1967a.

——. "World Event-Interaction Survey: A Research Project on the Theory and Measurement of International Interaction and Transaction." University of Michigan, 1967b.

——. "The Access to Berlin: The Quantity and Variety of Events, 1948–1963." In J. David Singer (ed.), *Quantitative International Politics: Insights and Evidence. International Yearbook of Political Behavior Research,* Vol. VI. New York: Free Press, 1968.

—— et al. *The Communist Chinese Performance in Crisis and Non-Crisis: Quantitative Studies of the Taiwan Straits Confrontation, 1950–64.* China Lake, Calif.: Behavioral Sciences Group, Naval Ordnance Test Station, 1965.

Moberg, Erik. "Models of International Conflicts and Arms Races," *Cooperation and Conflict, Nordic Studies in International Politics,* 2 (1966), 80–93.

North, Robert C., Ole R. Holsti, M. George Zaninovich, and Dina A. Zinnes. *Content Analysis. A Handbook with Application to the Study of International Crisis.* Evanston: Northwestern University Press, 1963.

Naroll, Raoul. "Imperial Cycles and World Order." Northwestern University, 1966.

Phillips, Warren R. "Dynamic Patterns of International Conflict: A Dyadic Research Design." University of Hawaii, 1968.

Quenouille, M. H. "A Large-Sample Test for the Goodness of Fit of Autoregressive Schemes," *Journal of the Royal Statistical Society,* 110 (1947), 123.

——. *Associated Measurements.* New York: Academic Press, 1952.

Rapoport, Anatol. "Lewis F. Richardson's Mathematical Theory of War," *Journal of Conflict Resolution,* 1, 3 (Sept. 1957), 249–99.

Rapoport, Anatol, and Albert M. Chammah. *Prisoner's Dilemma.* Ann Arbor: University of Michigan Press, 1965.

Richardson, Lewis F. *Arms and Insecurity.* Pittsburgh: Boxwood Press; Chicago: Quadrangle Books, 1960a.

——, *Statistics of Deadly Quarrels.* Pittsburgh: Boxwood Press; Chicago: Quadrangle Books, 1960b.

Rowe, Edward T. "The Emerging Anti-colonial Consensus in the United Nations," *Journal of Conflict Resolution*, 8, 3 (Sept. 1964), 209–30.

Rozelle, Richard M. "Causal Relations in Attitude Change as Demonstrated through the Cross-Lagged Panel Correlation." Mimeographed research report to the US Office of Education, Project C998, Contract 3-20-001, 1965.

——— and Donald T. Campbell. "More Plausible Rival Hypotheses in the Cross-Lagged Panel Correlation Technique." Mimeographed research report supported in part by Project C-998, Contract 3-20-001, US Office of Education, and the National Science Foundation, grant SS1309X, University of Houston, 1966 (circa).

Rubin, H. "On the Distribution of the Serial Correlation Coefficient," *Annals of Mathematical Statistics*, 16 (1945), 211.

Rummel, R. J. "A Social Field Theory of Foreign Conflict Behavior," *Peace Research Society (International) Papers*, 4 (1966a), 131–50.

———. "Some Dimensions in the Foreign Behavior of Nations," *Journal of Peace Research*, 3 (1966b), 201–24.

Rutherford, Brent M. "Canonical Correlation in Political Analysis." Northwestern University, 1966.

Simon, H. A. *Models of Man*. New York: Wiley, 1957.

Singer, J. David, and Melvin Small. "The Composition and Status Ordering of the International System, 1815–1940," *World Politics*, 18 (Jan. 1966a), 236–82.

———, ———. "Formal Alliances, 1815–1939," *Journal of Peace Research*, 1 (1966b), 1–32.

———, ———. "Alliance Aggregation and the Onset of War, 1815–1945." In J. D. Singer (ed.), *Quantitative International Political Behavior Research*, Vol. VI. New York: Free Press, 1968.

Smoker, Paul. "A Pilot Study of the Present Arms Race," *General Systems Yearbook*, 8 (1963), 67–76.

———. "Sino-Indian Relations: A Study of Trade, Communication and Defense," *Journal of Peace Research*, 2 (1964), 65–76.

Sorokin, Pitirim A. *Social and Cultural Dynamics*, 4 vols. New York: American Book, 1937.

Tanter, Raymond. "Dimensions of Conflict Behavior Within and Between Nations, 1958–1960," *Journal of Conflict Resolution*, 10, 1 (March 1966a), 41–64.

———. "A Systems Analysis Guide for Testing Theories of International Political Development." Northwestern University, 1966b.

Toynbee, Arnold J. *A Study of History*, 12 vols. London and New York: Oxford University Press, 1935–1961.

Watson, G. S., and J. Durbin. "Exact Tests of Serial Correlations Using Noncircular Statistics," *Annals of Mathematical Statistics*, 22 (1951), 446.

Whittle, P. *Hypothesis Testing in Time Series Analysis*. Uppsala, 1951.

Wold, H. "On Least Squares Regression with Autocorrelated Variables and Residuals." Paper read at the meetings of the International Statistical Institute, Berne, 1949.

Wolfson, Murray. "A Mathematical Model of the Cold War." Oregon State University, 1966.

Wright, Quincy. *A Study of War*. Chicago: University of Chicago Press, 1941.

Yule, G. U. "Why Do We Sometimes Get Nonsense-Correlations between Time-Series?" *Journal of the Royal Statistical Society*, 89 (1926), 1.

———. "On a Method of Investigating Periodicities in Disturbed Series, with Special Reference to Wolfer's Sunspot Numbers," *Philos. Trans.*, A. 226 (1927), 267.

Zaninovich, M. George. "Pattern Analysis of Variables within the International System: the Sino-Soviet Example," *Journal of Conflict Resolution*, 6, 3 (Sept. 1962), 253–68.

JOHN CRITTENDEN

Aging and Party Affiliation*

*The next series of two articles and comments by the
authors focuses on an analysis of the effects of aging on party affiliation
and methodological variations in cohort analyses of data relevant to
this research problem. By presenting such a series of research exchanges,
some of the methodological difficulties in cohort analysis will become
apparent.*

*This first article by John Crittenden, which stimulated this exchange
of research ideas and methods of analysis, attempts to isolate aging
and generational effects on partisan identification. While previous
research has pointed to the dominant presence of generational changes
contributing to changes in party identification in the American electorate,
the author attempts to show that aging itself has an effect on this
balance independent of generational change. He utilizes data from four
national surveys with nearly equal intervals and apparently comparable
sampling procedures (yet, it is doubtful that AIPO sampling procedures
were comparable during this period — a factor which probably influences
both sets of analysis presented here). The first evidence for the effect
of aging is presented in Crittenden's table 1. These data offer evidence
for aging effects, yet they do not contain information relevant for*

Reprinted from John Crittenden, "Aging and Party Affiliation," *Public Opinion Quarterly* 26 (1962):
648–57, by permission of the journal and the author.

*This research was made possible by the award of a Law and Behavioral Science Fellowship at the
University of Chicago Law School, 1959–1960. Numerous individuals have provided insights or sug-
gestions, including David Beardslee, John Maher, Allan Sindler, David Easton, Bernice Neugarten,
David Matza, Peter Rossi, Ethel Shanas, and William Buchanan. I am especially grateful to Duncan
MacRae, Soia Mentschikoff, and Hans Zeisel. Of course, none of these persons is responsible for any
errors, whether of technique or interpretation.

a generational comparison. Therefore, the author proceeds to table 2
in order to, in effect, "control the factor of historical experience"
(plus a control for two educational attainment levels). Note that he
also must take into account the overall trend toward the Democratic
party.

It is at this point that Cutler takes Crittenden to task for not
complying with proper cohort analysis procedures. He points to the need
for a diagonal analysis of Crittenden's data in order to compare the
aging effects with the generational changes. He also employs the plus
and minus difference procedures described earlier in this chapter to
offer support for his conclusion pointing to the importance of
generational over aging effects.

As Crittenden's reply to Cutler notes, the differences in findings
rest on tallying procedures where Crittenden's data were "corrected"
for trend. We also are reminded of the need to make both diagonal and
nondiagonal comparisons in a cohort matrix. Furthermore, Crittenden
points to the demanding criteria of a linear increase claimed necessary
by Cutler to justify his findings. In response, Cutler defends his
non-de-trended analysis by pointing to problems in Crittenden's treatment
of trend. While this exchange provides few certain answers (which
would only be forthcoming from an entire reanalysis comparing diagonal
and nondiagonal data, trend and de-trended data with comparisons of
de-trending efforts and more sophisticated methods for assessing effects —
such as those employed by Klecka cited earlier) — the arguments are
more instructive from a methodological point of view than most published
research offers.

Many characteristics related to age can be explained in terms of aging or generations
or both.[1] When variations are observed in the political behavior of age groups, it is
particularly difficult to judge which factor should be stressed. Possibly there has
been a greater tendency, in the case of party affiliation, to emphasize generations.
Thus, in Europe, Heberle and others have regarded World War I and its aftermath
as decisive experiences underlying the appeal to young age groups of the Nazi
political movement.[2] Samuel Lubell, Louis Harris, and the authors of the Elmira
study have suggested that the New Deal marks a dividing point between political

---

1. General statements treating the ambiguity of age-group differences include: Robert P. Hinshaw,
"The Relationship of Information and Opinion to Age," Princeton, Princeton University, 1944, unpublished Ph.D. dissertation; Seymour Lipset *et al.*, "The Psychology of Voting: An Analysis of
Political Behavior," in Gardner Lindzey, editor, *Handbook of Social Psychology*, Boston, Addison-
Wesley, 1954, Vol. II, pp. 1143–1150; Herbert Hyman, *Political Socialization*, Glencoe, Free Press,
1959; Hans Toch, "Attitudes of the 'Fifty Plus' Age Group," *Public Opinion Quarterly*. Vol. 17, 1953,
pp. 391–394; William Evan, "Cohort Analysis of Survey Data," *Public Opinion Quarterly*, Vol. 18,
1959, pp. 63–64.

2. Rudolf Heberle, *Social Movements*, New York, Appleton-Century-Crofts, 1951, pp. 120–121;
Seymour Lipset, *Political Man*, New York, Doubleday, 1960, p. 266.

generations in America.[3] The authors of *The American Voter* have submitted impressive evidence that broadly corroborates this view, but they also suggest that "life cycle changes" account for some of the Republicanism of older groups.[4]

The purpose of this paper is to demonstrate that the aging process has an impact on party affiliation that is independent of any such generational factors. Findings are based on four nationwide surveys by the American Institute of Public Opinion, spanning a period of twelve years at approximately equal intervals, and containing similarly worded items on party identification and vote in previous presidential election.[5] These were selected without prior knowledge of what the pattern of age differences would be, and solely on the basis of the following criteria: (1) similarity of question wording; (2) relevance to direction of party affiliation; (3) comparability of sampling methods; (4) number of surveys available containing given items; (5) length of time spanned by the surveys; (6) punching of age by individual years, rather than grouped intervals.

Criteria were developed in part from a systematic inspection of age breakdowns in published reports of surveys. The inspection had suggested that age differences generally tend to be consecutive, but that in the area of partisan commitment they are somewhat irregular.[6]

In each of the four years, party affiliations of respondents who lived outside the South showed a strong tendency for a simple sequence of increasing Republicanism with increasing age.[7] This is clear from Table 1.[8] The regularity of these age patterns suggests aging. However, historical experience of the groups portrayed varies, and may account for some of the differences.

The best way to demonstrate an aging effect would be to control the factor of historical experience. Panels of respondents interviewed at successive points in time and at different life-span locations would be ideal. An approximation of this is provided in Table 2, where the same data as in Table 1 are arrayed with a control for education, so that the same population cohorts can be identified in each survey.[9]

3. Samuel Lubell, *The Future of American Politics*, New York, Harper, 1951, pp. 28–29; Lipset, *Political Man*, pp. 266–267; Bernard Berelson, Paul Lazarsfeld, and William McPhee, *Voting*, Chicago, University of Chicago Press, 1954, pp. 59–61, 301–302.

4. Angus Campbell *et al.*, *The American Voter*, New York, Wiley, 1960, pp. 154–156, 165–166.

5. AIPO Surveys, No. 384, November 1946; No. 455, May 1950; No. 535, August 1954; No. 603, August 1958. I am grateful both to the American Institute of Public Opinion and to the Roper Public Opinion Research Center for access to these surveys.

6. The method and detailed findings of this inspection are reported in John Crittenden, "The Relationship of Age to Political Party Identification," Chapel Hill, University of North Carolina, 1960, unpublished Ph.D. dissertation.

7. The Southern respondents in these surveys show the same proportion Republican in all age groups, except in 1958, when Republicanism *decreased* with age. See *ibid.*, p. 133.

8. The pattern of age differences in Table 1 is corroborated by special tabulations provided by the Survey Research Center. Probability surveys in 1952, 1954, and 1956 suggest especially good comparability as regards young and middle. However, the SRC data show many fewer Republicans in the old group. There is apparently a pronounced Republican bias among the elderly segments of the AIPO samples. Nevertheless, in 1952 and 1956 there were somewhat more Republicans among non-Southern respondents in the group over sixty-five years old than in the group aged thirty-five to sixty-four. In the Center's survey of October 1954, the group over fifty-five (sic) showed the same proportion of Republicans as the group aged thirty-five to fifty-four.

9. A cohort is a group of persons born in any given time interval. In a series of cross-sectional surveys, one can observe cohort samples at different points in the life span (see Evan, *op. cit.*, pp. 63–64).

TABLE 1   Republicans by Three Age Groups in Non-
Southern States*

Year	Young (21–39)	Middle (40–59)	Old (60–79)
1946:			
Per cent	50	55	61
(N)	(1,164)	(1,045)	(410)
1950:			
Per cent	37	48	62
(N)	(409)	(312)	(129)
1954:			
Per cent	40	48	62
(N)	(512)	(407)	(157)
1958:			
Per cent	43	43	52
(N)	(435)	(425)	(232)

*Interpret the first entry in this table as follows: of the 1,164 respondents between the ages of twenty-one and thirty-nine in 1946, the sum of the percentage Republican and one-half the percentage independent is 50 per cent. The arbitrary assumption that independents are equally split between Republicans and Democrats will be followed throughout this paper and is incorporated in all tables. The resulting percentage index is a conservative one; it portrays slightly smaller differences between age groups than would obtain if the Republican percentage of Democrats and Republicans were used instead. It corresponds analytically to using a plurality percentage, but is easier to comprehend.

Small cohort comparisons pose problems that are shared in part with observations of age groups at a single point in time. Rather wide variation may appear in the way that important subgroups of the population are represented in four-year age-group samples. The distribution of age levels within the groups may also vary. While any given cohort comparison is highly unreliable, the use of a large number of cohort comparisons offsets this unreliability: extraneous factors partially cancel each other as the number of comparisons increases.

A major advantage of age comparisons between cohorts is that, except for sampling variations, the *amount* of aging involved is absolutely uniform. Thus in a cohort comparison of 21–24 in 1950 as opposed to 25–28 in 1954, *everybody* has aged four years. Comparing the same age groups in 1950, the aging component *varies* from one to seven years.[10]

Table 3 summarizes the forty cohort changes of eight years that are available from Table 2. The shifts are portrayed in relation to partisan shifts of subsamples, as explained below. Such a procedure is necessary because the trend was toward the Democratic Party.[11] Since eight-year aging effects are being measured, Table 3 compares 1954 (Time$_2$) observations with those in 1946 (Time$_1$), as well as 1958

10. Cursory inspection of Table 2 reveals that the distributions are not smooth, and that there are numerous exceptions to the hypothesis that older groups are more Republican. In spite of this, the direction of the difference between extreme age groups is quite reliable. For example, every possible comparison of the four youngest groups with the four oldest groups each year yields 128 possible observations. In only 5 of these 128 observations is the older group not more Republican than the younger. Even comparisons between adjacent groups produce many more instances in which the older group is more Republican. One can hypothesize that larger samples would produce consecutive distributions.

11. Four-year cohort shifts relative to trend can also be derived from Table 2. There are a total of 66 such events, of which 37 are in a more Republican direction, 25 more Democratic, and 4 the same.

TABLE 2 Republicans by Four-Year Age Groups
and Educational Level in Non-Southern States

Age Group	1946 Per Cent	(N)	1950 Per Cent	(N)	1954 Per Cent	(N)	1958 Per Cent	(N)
			*High Education**					
21–24	46	(160)	41	(45)	42	(57)	43	(38)
25–28	54	(171)	43	(52)	45	(53)	51	(57)
29–32	51	(145)	44	(53)	39	(87)	49	(71)
33–36	59	(118)	50	(50)	47	(63)	49	(86)
37–40	59	(135)	53	(48)	51	(67)	42	(64)
41–44	70	(87)	58	(30)	56	(52)	44	(50)
45–48	58	(109)	58	(33)	52	(42)	34	(49)
49–52	58	(93)	50	(19)	89	(18)	62	(38)
53–56	60	(74)	60	(15)	66	(32)	47	(36)
57–60	65	(55)	75	(12)	58	(13)	63	(23)
61–64	58	(37)	86	(7)	75	(8)	55	(19)
65–68	70	(20)	60	(5)	90	(5)	66	(19)
21–68	57	(1,204)	51	(369)	50	(497)	48	(550)
			*Low Education**					
21–24	36	(81)	14	(28)	38	(34)	41	(17)
25–28	52	(91)	18	(22)	37	(45)	24	(17)
29–32	43	(101)	26	(35)	29	(40)	38	(33)
33–36	42	(115)	32	(45)	27	(52)	30	(38)
37–40	51	(128)	28	(51)	38	(60)	33	(36)
41–44	40	(105)	40	(46)	36	(52)	39	(54)
45–48	54	(118)	44	(35)	38	(56)	34	(47)
49–52	44	(130)	48	(47)	39	(44)	37	(49)
53–56	59	(128)	37	(32)	45	(32)	46	(41)
57–60	59	(118)	42	(43)	50	(54)	47	(30)
61–64	58	(72)	61	(28)	50	(48)	50	(41)
65–68	52	(63)	58	(26)	59	(28)	45	(49)
21–68	49	(1,250)	38	(438)	40	(545)	39	(452)

*High education: graduated high school or better. Low education: did not graduate from high school. This basis of comparison is used in all subsequent tables employing education breakdowns.

TABLE 3 Eight-Year Cohort Shifts on Party
Identification Relative to Trend*

AGE OF COHORT		TIME₂		
Time₁	Time₂	More Republican	More Democratic	Same
(21–24) — (29–32)		3	0	1
(25–28) — (33–36)		2	1	1
(29–32) — (37–40)		4	0	0
(33–36) — (41–44)		3	1	0
(37–40) — (45–48)		1	2	1
(41–44) — (49–52)		3	1	0
(45–48) — (53–56)		2	1	1
(49–52) — (57–60)		3	1	0
(53–56) — (61–64)		2	1	1
(57–60) — (65–68)		3	1	0
Total		26	9	5

*Derived from Table 2.

(Time$_2$) observations with those in 1950 (Time$_1$). This produces two observations for each change in life-span location. An additional two are provided by virtue of the fact that the four-year cohorts are observed at two educational levels. Observations are tallied in the following manner. Table 2 shows that, in 1946, the low education group aged 21–24 was 36 per cent Republican. Eight years later, in 1954, the corresponding cohort was 29–32 years old, and 29 per cent Republican, a loss of 7 per cent in eight years. The low-education population as a whole had moved from 49 per cent Republican to 40 per cent, a loss of 9 per cent. This figure represents the trend value. Since the cohort remained more loyal to the Republican Party than this segment of the population as a whole, it is tabulated in the "More Republican" column in Table 3.

The total results are fairly satisfactory not only because a significantly[12] higher percentage of observations are as hypothesized, but also because, taking the sets of

TABLE 4   Republican Voters* by Four-Year Age
Groups and Educational Level in Non-Southern States

Age Group	1946 Per Cent	(N)	1950 Per Cent	(N)	1954 Per Cent	(N)	1958 Per Cent	(N)
			High Education					
25–28	44	(175)	43	(54)	61	(49)	64	(55)
29–32	38	(145)	47	(53)	54	(86)	62	(70)
33–36	48	(116)	57	(48)	69	(63)	60	(83)
37–40	51	(134)	55	(47)	62	(66)	57	(63)
41–44	60	(85)	63	(30)	74	(50)	56	(51)
45–48	46	(107)	67	(33)	70	(42)	57	(49)
49–52	53	(92)	58	(20)	94	(18)	70	(38)
53–56	57	(69)	57	(14)	69	(32)	71	(36)
57–60	59	(56)	92	(12)	50	(12)	75	(22)
61–64	53	(37)	93	(7)	94	(8)	65	(17)
65–68	66	(19)	60	(5)	100	(5)	70	(20)
69–72	56	(18)	80	(5)	83	(3)	67	(6)
73–76	85	(13)	50	(4)	100	(3)	71	(7)
25–76	50	(1,066)	57	(332)	66	(437)	63	(517)
			Low Education					
25–28	39	(90)	32	(22)	50	(44)	34	(16)
29–32	41	(102)	25	(36)	45	(40)	56	(33)
33–36	31	(113)	24	(44)	51	(51)	46	(39)
37–40	38	(128)	30	(51)	51	(57)	38	(37)
41–44	31	(101)	35	(47)	47	(50)	58	(53)
45–48	41	(117)	39	(35)	46	(54)	50	(48)
49–52	34	(128)	49	(48)	64	(43)	56	(48)
53–56	44	(125)	35	(31)	64	(33)	61	(39)
57–60	45	(115)	33	(42)	54	(49)	68	(30)
61–64	51	(71)	55	(30)	61	(49)	55	(39)
65–68	38	(66)	46	(24)	63	(27)	61	(48)
69–72	42	(60)	65	(17)	60	(20)	60	(39)
72–76	48	(47)	57	(15)	75	(14)	65	(24)
25–76	40	(1,263)	38	(442)	54	(531)	55	(493)

*Per cent voting for the Republican candidate for president in previous election, plus one-half the percentage not voting.

12. $p < 0.05$.

four-year age-group shifts as a single observation, there was only one reversal of the tendency for cohort aging to result more often (or equally often) in a higher proportion of Republicans than Democrats.

Corroborating evidence may be obtained from the partisan direction of the presidential vote (as revealed in the same surveys). Nonvoters are split equally among Democrats and Republicans, in a manner exactly parallel to the treatment of independents above. Table 4 includes two more four-year groups at the aged end of the continuum even though the numbers are small, since preliminary runs suggested that increasing Republican voting tendencies may be arrested in very old groups. It excludes the 21–24 group because of the high proportions of ineligibles in elections held two years prior to the given survey.

The distributions in Table 4 are somewhat *less* steady than those in Table 3 on party affiliation. Comparisons between extreme age groups tend by a wide margin to favor the hypothesis, but comparisons between groups that are near to each other in the life span are not as satisfactory. Again, however, eight-year aging shifts relative to trend provide fair evidence of a sequential aging effect, as Table 5 demonstrates.[13]

TABLE 5   Eight-Year Cohort Shifts on Republican
Voting Relative to Trend*

AGE OF COHORT		TIME₂		
Time₁	Time₂	More Republican	More Democratic	Same
25–28 — 33–36		2	2	0
29–32 — 37–40		2	2	0
33–36 — 41–44		3	1	0
37–40 — 45–48		2	2	0
41–44 — 49–52		4	0	0
45–48 — 53–56		3	1	0
49–52 — 57–60		3	1	0
53–56 — 61–64		4	0	0
57–60 — 65–68		3	1	0
61–64 — 69–72†		0	3	0
65–68 — 73–76†		3	0	0
Total		29	13	0

*Derived from Table 4.
†Observations omitted where based on one or more cells having less than five cases.

Interpretation

On both available measures of party affiliation, aging seems to produce a shift toward Republicanism in the period from 1946 to 1958. Although identification effects may vary somewhat at different points in the life cycle, the pattern appears to be linear on both measures. With voting, the aging-Republican hypothesis seems to be most pronounced in middle age groups. Large quantities of comparable data

13. With four-year shifts, excluding cells where cases fall below five, of 68 observations, 35 are more Republican, 28 more Democratic, and 5 the same.

are available for replication of the above analysis, so there is no reason why evidence cited here must be final. Findings for any particular part of the life cycle are, of course, only suggestive.

Aging is a complex variable. In the broad sense, an individual's aging may reflect any or all of the following: (1) differences in social roles and statuses (such as go with differing positions within an occupation), which have little to do with physiological aging but instead are a social result of aging in a particular culture; (2) differences in psychology, temperament, or outlook that may result directly from physiological aging; (3) greater experience in given role and status situations; (4) greater total experience; (5) reactions to a variety of particular personal or social events. Data presented here go only part of the way in helping us choose which of these to emphasize.

Apparently, personal events can be removed from serious consideration. The number of respondents is too large for individualized situations to be importantly reflected in the general patterns observed. Moreover, since the samples have been obtained over several four-year intervals, unique social events occurring at single points in time cannot account for the differences.

It is also difficult to believe that experience in the same role or status accounts for a significant amount of the aging effect. With four- or eight-year aging, specific roles and statuses may remain relatively unchanged. But comparisons between extreme groups obviously involve different roles and statuses, unless one conceives them very broadly.

The general role of "elector" indeed covers the entire adult life span. It is possible that experience in this role brings not only an increase in voting but an increase in Republicanism. However, while the role requirement is quite explicit in regard to voting participation, it makes no demands as to the direction voting choices should take. It seems reasonable to suppose that the partisan direction of effects due to experience in other roles would depend on what the roles were — that in settings which predispose in a Democratic direction, such experience would produce a higher, not a lower, proportion of Democrats.

Still a different view of the impact of experience could be maintained. If experience in the broadest sense includes *all* aspects listed, the total effect may be that the individual's values remain much the same as he ages, only with increasing coherence and stability. Differences among age groups may then be attributed to changing appeals of the parties. Since both parties reach a relatively broad range of the value spectrum, many individuals will be able to accommodate such changes by remaining within their political party. However, since there are differences between parties, other people may be under pressure to defect.

The institutional interpretation may be questioned on at least two grounds. For one thing, there may be a tendency for people to change their *values* to bring them into line with their party affiliations.[14] Also, the AIPO data suggest that greater partisan consistency may occur among Republicans *and* Democrats with aging.[15]

---

14. Angus Campbell and Homer Cooper, *Group Differences in Attitudes and Votes*, Ann Arbor, University of Michigan, Survey Research Center, 1956, p. 93.

15. See the forthcoming article by this author, entitled "Aging and Political Participation," *Western Political Quarterly*. Consistency is measured by congruence between party identification and partisan evaluation of the President. Republicans show more consistency with age than Democrats, but the difference is not significant at 0.05.

The institutional explanation requires that Democrats become less consistent, since the Republican Party is available as a major alternative that more nearly represents the political ethos of the past. For most aging Republicans, the Democratic Party is not a comparable alternative.

Unfortunately, with these data there appears to be no way of choosing between a sociological and a psychological interpretation of aging. The sociological interpretation is that aging from twenty-one to sixty brings preferred status in the society at every socio-economic level. For example, people get married and raise children. This increases the distance and independence from the family of origin and provides new prerogatives. Income and job security increase. Families move to new neighborhoods and purchase homes. In the occupational world, aging permits the individual to exploit opportunities for greater prestige and job privileges that may be unrelated to increasing income. Furthermore, during much of this span, a pervasive belief in progress may lead individuals to expect further accretions of status as they stay in given communities and job situations. The direction of the aging effect follows from the fact that preferred status in this society is almost invariably correlated with Republican Party identification.[16]

The psychological interpretation emphasizes change that is dependent on processes of physiological evolution that accompany aging. Reactions to gradual physical deterioration in a culture that strongly emphasizes youth and good health may tend toward pessimism, conservatism, and narrowness. Individuals change party affilation in line with changes in ideology. They more and more identify with the party which is more skeptical about human nature, less bent on finding new things for government to do, and which claims a greater attachment to traditional values.[17]

If sociological or psychological aging explains the age differences reported above, then, given the research strategy of this study, it would appear likely that most of the larger age differences obtained in surveys of the United States population contain an aging component. The design does not provide as powerful a test of the generational interpretation, because of the relative shortness of the time span covered and because it is more difficult to obtain a satisfactory number of observations. Probably there are fairly significant generational effects in the area of partisan affiliation that result from the impact of the Great Depression and New Deal. Aging and generational theories therefore complement each other in explaining why older groups are often more Republican. Although it is not yet possible to make a reliable assessment of the relative importance of each, computers make it increasingly possible to analyze intensively a vast backlog of potentially relevant survey materials.

---

16. Cf. Lipset, *Political Man*, pp. 267–268.
17. Cf. Hinshaw, *op. cit.*, pp. 67–68.

NEAL E. CUTLER

Generation, Maturation
and Party Affiliation:
A Cohort Analysis

While historians and novelists have often used the concept of generation in their writings, there is little research on contemporary patterns of political behavior and attitudes in which the concept of generational differences or experiences plays a central role. A major obstacle to generational attitude and opinion research is, perhaps, the dearth of panel studies of national scope and extensive duration. The isolation of generational trends, it may be argued, can only take place in the context of repeated measurements of the same set of individuals. Yet the study of changes in whole systems can be based upon aggregate trends, and does not necessarily require measurements of individual differences. One such approach to the measurement of systemic change rests upon the analysis of differences among successive generational groups within the polity and society.

In 1959, William Evan suggested a method of secondary data analysis by which generational trends in attitudes and behavior may be empirically traced.[1] This method, called "cohort analysis," is borrowed from demography, wherein the demographer attempts to trace sets of birth cohorts across a number of years, usually on the basis of successive decennial censuses. Evan suggested that students of survey research might easily substitute national sample surveys taken at regular intervals for censuses. At this point cohort analysis in survey research is much like its counterpart in demography. As long as groups of individuals can be identified by their age, they can be traced through a longitudinal series of surveys or censuses. A sample of twenty-five-year-olds in a 1950 survey, for example, is a sample of the same

Reprinted from Neal Cutler, "Generation, Maturation and Party Affiliation: A Cohort Analysis," *Public Opinion Quarterly* 33 (1969–70): 583–88, by permission of the journal and the author.
1. William M. Evan, "Cohort Analysis of Survey Data: A Procedure for Studying Long-Term Opinion Change," *Public Opinion Quarterly*, Vol. 23, 1959, pp. 63–72.

population group represented by the thirty-year-olds in a 1955 survey. In a 1960 survey, this same cohort is represented by the sample of thirty-five-year-olds. The logic is quite straightforward: As five years of history elapse, represented by the successive surveys, the analyst "ages" the cohorts five years by looking at the appropriate cell in an age-by-survey matrix.

The application of cohort analysis to a particular data set may reveal significant information concerning the meaning of observed age differences, since the researcher can simultaneously observe the generational and maturational effects of age. He can then go one step further and compare these effects in an effort to determine the relative explanatory power of each.

The significance of the cohort analysis approach may be clearly seen through a reanalysis of a set of party identification data first presented in the *Public Opinion Quarterly* in 1962. In that study, Crittenden sought to demonstrate that increasing age brought about an increasing identification with the Republican party.[2] The purpose of the study, in the words of its author, was to demonstrate that "the aging process has an impact on party affiliation that is independent of any such generational factors."[3] In other words, as Americans get older they get increasingly more Republican. Fortunately for purposes of reanalysis, Crittenden presented his data in a form amenable to cohort analysis, that is, in an age-by-survey matrix. These data are repeated here in Table 1. The only additions made to Crittenden's table are the diagonal lines, which define the generational cohorts, and the life-stage and cohort labels.

TABLE 1 An Empirical Example of Cohort Analysis[a]

Age Intervals	Cohort[b] Labels	1946	1950	1954	1958	Lifestage[b] Labels
	A					
21–24	B	46	41	42	43	(1)
25–28	C	54	43	45	51	(2)
29–32	D	51	44	39	49	(3)
33–36	E	59	50	47	49	(4)
37–40	F	59	53	51	42	(5)
41–44	G	70	58	56	44	(6)
45–48	H	58	58	52	34	(7)
49–52	I	58	50	89	62	(8)
53–56		60	60	66	47	(9)
57–60		65	75	58	63	(10)
61–64		58	86	75	55	(11)
65–68		70	60	90	66	(12)
Total		57	51	50	48	

[a]Cell entries are the percentage of each cell which identified with the Republican party in the year indicated. Source: John Crittenden, "Aging and Party Affiliation," *Public Opinion Quarterly*, Vol. 26, 1962, p. 651. Data represent the "high" education group in Crittenden's analysis.
[b]Capital letters indicate the cohort diagonals; numbers in parentheses indicate life-stage rows.

2. John Crittenden, "Aging and Party Affiliation," *Public Opinion Quarterly*, Vol. 26, 1962, pp. 648–657.
3. *Ibid.*, p. 648.

Crittenden's own analysis is based on the fact that in each of the four cross-sectional samples the older groups are more Republican than the younger groups. For example, in the 1946 sample the younger groups are about 50 per cent Republican while the older groups are about 60 per cent Republican. For Crittenden these data provide dramatically clear evidence of the influence of aging on increasing Republicanism: "Every possible comparison of the four youngest groups with the four oldest groups each year yields 128 possible observations. In only five of these 128 observations is the oldest group not more Republican than the younger."[4]

While this interpretation of the table is at first convincing, cohort analysis of these same data do not produce the same overwhelming results. The diagonal lines added to Crittenden's table define the cells which represent the "development" of the nine cohorts for which the full complement of four observations is available. Crittenden's hypothesis states that as individuals age there is an increasing tendency to support the Republican party; hence, as any particular age cohort gets older it should be characterized by an increasing percentage of Republicans. Through cohort analysis these nine age groups may be viewed as they get older between 1946 and 1958. As described above, the sample of 21–24 year-olds in 1946 is a sample of the very same cohort of persons represented by the 25–28 age group in the 1950 sample, etc. Crittenden's hypothesis directs the reader to look for a linear increase in Republicanism as each cohort gets older. *In no instance of these nine cohorts is this relationship found.*

Table 2 has been prepared to summarize these data as they pertain to the aging-Republicanism hypothesis. By comparing adjacent observations for each cohort, for example the change from 1946 to 1950, any patterned increases or decreases in Republicanism can be clearly identified. A + in Table 2 indicates an increase and supports the hypothesis; a − indicates a decrease in Republicanism. The first three columns of this table represent the changes in Republicanism between adjacent samples. Not only is there no cohort with the hypothesized pattern of three pluses, but there are more decreases in Republicanism with age than there are increases.

TABLE 2   Alternative Tests of the Aging-Republicanism Hypothesis[a]

Cohort	4-YEAR DIFFERENCES			8-YEAR DIFFERENCES		12-YEAR DIFFERENCES
	1946–1950	1950–1954	1954–1958	1946–1954	1950–1958	1946–1958
A:	−	−	+	−	+	+
B:	−	+	−	−	−	−
C:	−	+	−	*	−	−
D:	−	+	−	−	−	−
E:	−	−	+	−	+	+
F:	−	+	−	+	−	+
G:	−	+	−,	+	+	+
H:	+	−	−	*	−	−
I:	+	*	−	+	−	+

[a]A − indicates that the percentage of Republicans decreased from the first observation point to the second and fails to support the hypothesis; a + indicates that the percentage of Republicans increased, and supports the hypothesis; an * indicates no difference. Cell entries derived from Table 1.

4. *Ibid.*, pp. 650–651.

One may argue that comparison of adjacent samples increases the influence of error or of random fluctuation, and that the effects of aging can best be seen by observing longer-range trends. Therefore, the next three columns in Table 2 have been computed. The fourth and fifth columns represent changes in Republicanism over eight-year intervals for each cohort, 1946–1954 and 1950–1958. Again, as in the first three columns of this table, the *decreases* in Republicanism outnumber the increases. In the sixth column, the twelve-year differences are represented; of the nine cohorts, four demonstrate an increase in Republicanism while five demonstrate a decrease.

It was pointed out previously that the cohort approach allows the analyst to confront directly the aging and generational interpretations of any age-related differences in behavior found in a single set of data. This, too, may be applied to Crittenden's data. The inquiry may be posed in the following way: Is there greater homogeneity in attitudes associated with generational factors or life-stage factors? If it is true that *each successive* life-stage is characterized by greater percentages of Republicanism, then the variation *within* each life-stage should be small, that is, each row in Table 1 should contain a homogeneous set of entries. On the other hand, the generational interpretation of Table 1 predicts that each generational cohort is characterized by a homogeneity of attitudes, since predispositions established early in life have a certain degree of durability.

The application of cohort analysis to Crittenden's data can lead to at least a preliminary answer to this apparent dilemma. The total amount of variability or fluctuation can be calculated for each group vector of Republicanism percentages, rows for the life-stage groups and diagonals for the cohort groups. Operationally, these are the absolute differences between each pair of adjacent percentages, that is, 1946–1950, 1950–1954, and 1954–1958. By then calculating the average fluctuation associated with cohorts, a decision can be made as to which of these two aspects of the age variable produces greater homogeneity in attitudes, that is, which effect provides the more powerful explanation.

Table 3 presents these calculations as derived from Table 1. The entries for Cohort A, for example, are derived as follows: $46 - 43 = 3$, $43 - 39 = 4$, and $39 - 49 = 10$. In the ideal hypothetical situation, if the generational effect imposed a perfect homogeneity of attitudes, these "fluctuations" would all be zero. But given both behavioral changes and sampling error, there is in fact fluctuation both for cohorts and for life-stages. The question then becomes one of determining which effect more nearly conforms to the hypothetical case. As Table 3 demonstrates, there is on the average less fluctuation, or more homogeneity, associated with generational cohorts than with aging process or life-stage groups.

This application of cohort analysis to a published data set demonstrates the need to consider both the maturational and generational interpretations of observed age differences in patterns of human behavior. What may at first appear to be clear and dramatic evidence of one phenomenon, when analyzed in a cross-sectional manner, may turn out to be convincing evidence of an alternative effect when the appropriate longitudinal methodology is employed.[5] As survey research has matured over the

---

5. Based upon his own analysis of these party identification data Crittenden concluded as follows: "Aging seems to produce a shift toward Republicanism in the period from 1946 to 1958 . . . the pattern appears to be linear." *Ibid.*, p. 654.

TABLE 3 Cohort and Life-Stage Fluctuation in Republicanism[a]

Age Groups	1946–1950		1950–1954		1954–1958		Total
Cohorts							
A:	3	+	4	+	10	=	17
B:	10	+	3	+	5	=	18
C:	1	+	1	+	7	=	09
D:	6	+	3	+	22	=	31
E:	1	+	6	+	10	=	17
F:	12	+	31	+	42	=	85
G:	8	+	16	+	3	=	25
H:	2	+	2	+	3	=	07
I:	15	+	0	+	9	=	24
Life-Stages							
1:	5	+	1	+	1	=	07
2:	11	+	2	+	6	=	19
3:	7	+	5	+	10	=	22
4:	9	+	3	+	2	=	14
5:	6	+	2	+	9	=	17
6:	12	+	2	+	12	=	26
7:	0	+	6	+	18	=	24
8:	8	+	39	+	27	=	74
9:	0	+	6	+	19	=	25
10:	10	+	17	+	5	=	32
11:	28	+	11	+	20	=	59
12:	10	+	30	+	24	=	64

Mean Cohort Fluctuation = 25.9
Mean Life-Stage Fluctuation = 31.9

[a]The change values represent the absolute value of the difference between each pair of adjacent percentages as found in Table 1 — in the diagonals for the Cohorts, in the rows for the Life-stages.

past three decades, there has grown a wealth of data that can now serve as an empirical basis for the determination of longitudinal trends. The collection of much of these data in archives, such as those at Ann Arbor, Williamstown, Chapel Hill, and Berkeley, facilitates the systematic secondary analysis of old survey data.[6] In the years during which the art and science of survey research were developing there was a necessary focus upon development of valid and reliable approaches to the collection of new data. Given the environment in which survey researchers now find themselves, however, there is a need for the development of approaches and methodologies of secondary analysis of existing data sets. Cohort analysis is one such approach.

6. See Ralph Bisco, "Social Science Data Archives: A Review of Developments," *American Political Science Review*, Vol. 60, 1966, pp. 93–109; David Nasatir, "Social Science Data Libraries," *The American Sociologist*, Vol. 2, 1967, pp. 207–212; and Ralph Bisco, "Social Science Data Archives: Progress and Prospects," *Social Science Information*, Vol. 6, 1967, pp. 39–74.

JOHN CRITTENDEN

Reply

In challenging the thesis of my 1962 article, Dr. Cutler asserts that "when the appropriate longitudinal methodology is employed" (cohort analysis), the aging-Republican hypothesis cannot be sustained with these data on nonsouthern respondents. Why do we differ? Not because of my alleged use of cross-sectional analysis in contrast to his use of cohort analysis. While I regarded cross-sectional comparisons as suggestive, Dr. Cutler knows that the bulk of my study was taken up with cohort analysis. The real issue therefore concerns which application of the technique is correct.

His method is basically the same as mine except that I corrected for trend. For example, the age group 41–44 is 1 per cent *less* Republican in 1950 than the 37–40 group in 1946. However, the 1946 sample (age 21–68) was 57 per cent Republican, while the 1950 sample, with the same age limits, was 51 per cent Republican. These values appear in the "Total" row of Dr. Cutler's Table 1. The difference between them (the trend value) is −6 per cent. Since the Democratic trend between samples of identical age limits is greater than the cohort Democratic change, I tallied this particular aging event as confirming the hypothesis. The fact that the cohort was *relatively* more Republican in 1950 than in 1946 seemed more pertinent than the absolute loss of 1 per cent.

Dr. Cutler comes to a different conclusion because he prefers not to make the correction, and because he omits all cohort comparisons not contained within the diagonal lines of Table 1. Thus the cohort change cited above ends up as a minus in his Table 2, and each of the eight comparisons outside the diagonal lines — all of them positive — is left out of Table 2 entirely.

Reprinted from John Crittenden, "Reply to Cutler," *Public Opinion Quarterly* 33 (1969–70): 589–91, by permission of the journal and the author.

I feel certain that my method can be improved upon, but not by ignoring the trend problem. Surely it is obvious that with surveys showing a consistent trend, the uncorrected cohort comparisons will tend to move in the same direction, showing Republican "aging" effects over periods of increasing Republicanism, but Democratic "aging" effects when the trend is Democratic. This can be illustrated by referring to data on Republican *voting* in my 1962 article. Here the question had to do with voting in the previous presidential election, and the trend was from 50 per cent Republican in 1946 to 57 per cent Republican in 1950 in the high education group. Now if we score the various cohort changes by Dr. Cutler's method, we find that eleven are positive and only one is negative. This sharply contradicts his findings on party affiliation contained in the first column of his second table. My method yields six pluses, three minuses, and three the same in voting, and seven pluses, three minuses, and one the same on identification — *a consistent finding* that does not overstate the aging effects.

Regardless of whether aging has an impact that surmounts all short-run trend effects (including sampling error), it is essential to think of aging in a way that permits us to distinguish it from such effects. For example, the data suggest that there was a general shift toward the Democratic party among persons of higher education in nonsouthern states between 1946 and 1950. In searching for an explanation, one might wish to hypothesize that higher status organized groups were moving away from virulent hostility to the New Deal. Since such a change has nothing to do with aging, we still want to know if there was a contrary tendency for people to become more Republican as they got four years older. We expect both "pressures" to affect the difference in level of Republican voting for the relevant segment of any given cohort. Dr. Cutler's implicit conceptualization does not recognize the need to identify such pressures separately.

In correcting for trend, two kinds of misunderstanding may arise. The reader may (1) suspect that such correction jiggles the data to make the analysis come out right. He may also (2) feel that aging is a variable of minor importance since so much control is needed to demonstrate its impact. With the first problem, we are probably dealing with a psychological reaction against correcting for trend in a period of decreasing Republicanism. If levels of Republicanism were increasing, it would be quite natural to insist that aging effects be conceded only where cohorts had become relatively more Republican than the sample as a whole. In the present context, the procedure seems generous in attributing the hypothesized aging effects; in the other context it seems rather stringent. These appearances about stringency ought not to be relevant, since the logic of my method is precisely the same regardless of the direction of trend. Dr. Cutler's more direct approach appeals to the psychological disadvantages of my method under the trend conditions in the data segment chosen, but it does not meet the issue.

In regard to the second problem, the aging-Republican hypothesis does not require that party shifts take place with increased age "no matter what." Rather, it suggests that aging effects constitute one of many discernible tendencies in a complex process. We should be prepared to find that the effects of aging, though discernible, were in some cases overpowered by other pressures on voting. If aging effects appear to be small, it should be remembered that aging increments are also small. When we use cohort analysis on these data, none of the aging exceeds twelve years. This goes a long way toward explaining the more consistent cohort pattern noted by Dr. Cutler.

Confirmation of a *linear* increase in cohort Republicanism across each of the four surveys should probably not be expected with these data. The test appears to be valid if corrections are made for trend, but it is also extremely demanding, since we have both small N's and small aging increments. If a sampling error throws off only one value in a series, the linear pattern is destroyed.

The analysis centering upon Table 3 represents a possibly significant departure from what I reported in 1962. Unfortunately, measures of fluctuation are quite sensitive to number of cases in the comparisons. Excluding life stage groups 10, 11, 12, and cohort I because of small N's, the mean cohort fluctuation is very close to mean life-stage fluctuation — in fact slightly exceeds it. This technique seems more appropriate for pooled samples, perhaps with statistical corrections for differences in N. It is too bad that Dr. Cutler did not use all of the data easily at hand from my article to corroborate or qualify his analysis.

Actually, Dr. Cutler employs only a quarter of the data which I submitted to the *Quarterly* in 1962. The segment he has chosen is the only one in which trend values move in a consistently Democratic direction. He is, of course, entitled to use any data and methods he wishes, but he should have provided some criteria. Also, since he did not choose to go beyond the data I presented in dealing with the problem I analyzed, he might at least have provided an approximately correct characterization of my study.

NEAL E. CUTLER

Comment

While Crittenden's 1962 hypothesis argues that aging will precipitate a conversion to the Republican party, his "adjustments for trend are in fact measures of Democratic party identifications. His own operational definitions (1962, p. 652) demonstrate this: If age-cohort X becomes *more Democratic* between Time 1 and Time 2 by 7 per cent while the whole population has become more Democratic by 9 per cent, Crittenden scores this as a Republican increase on the part of age-cohort X. If, theoretically, aging predicts a conversion to Republicanism it should do so despite (and maybe even because of) a national Democratic trend. Instead, Crittenden's data demonstrate that the aged are becoming more Democratic in a Democratic era; certainly no evidence is found that aging is making people more Republican. Interestingly, Crittenden's presentation juxtaposes *increasing Democratic identification* of an age group with the increasing Democratic identification of the whole sample (p. 654), yet concludes that "aging seems to produce a shift toward Republicanism in the period 1946 to 1958 . . . the pattern appears to be linear" (p. 654). I believe that my cohort analysis of these same data calls for rejection of the aging-Republicanism hypothesis.

Reprinted from Neal E. Cutler, "Comment," *Public Opinion Quarterly* 33 (1969–70): 592, by permission of the journal and the author.

LEO A. GOODMAN

Statistical Methods for
Analyzing Processes of Change[1]

The final readings example is an application of simple
probability models to test the process of attitude change toward presidential
candidates (vote intention) among panel respondents in six waves of
interviews. It represents an attempt to determine whether certain models
(Markovian) fit the actual changing distributions of vote intention
throughout a campaign and to make predictions of future responses. Goodman's
analysis is not unlike the simple Markovian example presented earlier in
this chapter (as well as that developed by Wilkenfeld in chapter 4);
however, six time periods (months) are involved and respondents may respond
in three categories each time: Republican, Democratic, or don't know.

The first model to which the data were fit is a first order Markov
chain. At any two consecutive months the process is represented by a
total of nine transition probabilities (see chart 1). For example, the
probability of a Republican intention changing to a Democratic intention
in the next month, and so on, is shown throughout all combinations of Republican,
Democratic, and uncertain categories. Chart 2 presents the actual
distributions of responses for each pair of successive months and these
values are translated into transition probabilities in chart 3. If the
transition probabilities remain the same (or nearly so), i.e., where
one month's responses are dependent on the preceding month's responses,
the process resembles a first order chain.

Reprinted from Leo A. Goodman, "Statistical Methods for Analyzing Processes of Change," *American Journal of Sociology* 68 (1962): 57–58, by permission of the author and The University of Chicago Press. Copyright 1962 by The University of Chicago Press.

1. Research carried out at the Statistical Research Center, University of Chicago, under sponsorship of the Statistics Branch, Office of Naval Research. Reproduction in whole or in part is permitted for any purpose of the United States Government.

*Second, data relevant to a second order chain are presented,
where the model tests for one month's responses dependency on the* two
*preceding months. The combination of two preceding months' relationship
to a third requires twenty-seven transition probabilities. If the matrices
of second order transition probabilities are constant, there is evidence
of a second order chain. In addition, Goodman suggests the possibility
that the probability laws governing change may vary from one segment
of the population to another (e.g., among those of high, moderate,
and low political interest).*

*The next phase of Goodman's paper is a series of predictions
of distributions based on the first and second order chain assumptions,
as well as a consideration of predictions for different strata in the
population. In the first order case, for example, the transition
matrix for one period is examined for its accuracy in predicting the
next month's responses. Similarly, assuming constancy in the second order
transition probabilities, a second order chain can be tested by
predicting one month's responses from the two preceding months. In
a final section of the paper, the "closeness" of the predictions
to the actual data, i.e., the degree of fit between the model and actual
distributions, is tested using the chi square statistic. This
procedure enables judgements about the interdependence of successive
responses, the constancy of the transition probability matrices, the
fit of first or second order chains, and the presence of different
forms of change in several population strata.*

1. Introduction

In this paper we present probability models relating to the study of certain kinds
of processes of change, and suggest statistical methods for analyzing them. Our
point of view concerning probability models is similar to that presented by T. W.
Anderson in his interesting study of attitude changes.[2] However, the statistical
methods given here are different. Many research workers will find the methods
presented here easier to understand and to apply than the corresponding methods in
Anderson's paper. Some of these methods will also permit a more detailed analysis
of the data than did the methods given in the earlier paper.

Some of the methods to be discussed here were first mentioned in a brief abstract
by the present author,[3] and the mathematical theory necessary for their justification was given in a joint paper by Anderson and the author.[4] Several techniques
which are included here were not discussed in the earlier publications.

In order to describe our methods and facilitate their comparison with those in
Anderson's paper, we shall use, as illustrative material, data on attitude changes

2. "Probability Models for Analyzing Time Changes in Attitudes," in Paul F. Lazarsfeld (ed.), *Mathematical Thinking in the Social Sciences* (Glencoe, Ill.: Free Press, 1954).

3. Leo A. Goodman, "On the Statistical Analysis of Markov Chains" (abstract), *Annals of Mathematical Statistics*, XXVI (1955), 771.

4. T. W. Anderson and Leo A. Goodman, "Statistical Inference about Markov Chains," *Annals of
Mathematical Statistics*, XXVIII (1957), 89–110.

given in his article. It should be emphasized, however, that the application of these methods need not be limited to the study of attitude changes. We expect the general approach presented here, or some modified version of it, to prove useful in the analysis of a number of different processes of change.[5]

Usually there will not be exact agreement between observed phenomena (the data) and the corresponding expectations derived from a probability model (a theory) relating to them, even if the model does in fact provide a true "explanation" of the phenomena. However, probabilistic aspects of the model will often make it possible to determine how much lack of agreement is probable. This will then provide a natural basis for the development of statistical tests to determine whether the model actually does fit the data sufficiently well. If the model is not congruent with the data, then the manner in which the data differ from the expectations could be studied further and modified models developed that might provide better representations of the phenomena, better descriptions and predictions. In this paper, we present specific illustrations of this process of model building, testing, modifying, etc.

The methods presented here can be applied to data obtained from case studies where each individual studied is asked a given set of questions in successive interviews, or where each individual is classified with respect to a given set of categories at successive time points. Do these case histories exhibit certain kinds of statistical regularities? We provide methods for answering this question for such case studies or for panel studies where a random sample of individuals respond to a set of questions in a series of interviews. Most of these methods can also be applied, with only slight modification, to a rotating panel study, in which after several interviews some individuals in the original sample are replaced by others. The particular kinds of inferences that can be made will, of course, depend upon the method of selection of the individuals studied and the population from which they were selected.[6]

The data we shall use here were obtained in a panel survey of potential voters in Erie County, Ohio.[7] A group of people were interviewed in May, June, July, August, September, and October. One of the questions dealt with which party (candidate) the respondent intended to vote for. Data for 445 people who responded to all six interviews were used in Anderson's analysis and will be used here.[8]

For each month, each of the 445 responses can be classified as either "Republican" (R), "Democratic" (D), or "Don't Know" (U). The monthly response fre-

5. See, e.g., Isadore Blumen, Marvin Kogan, and Philip J. McCarthy, *The Industrial Mobility of Labor as a Probability Process* (Ithaca, N.Y.: Cornell University, 1955), and Leo A. Goodman, "Statistical Methods for the Mover-Stayer Model," *Journal of the American Statistical Association*, LVI (1961), 841–68, where data on mobility are analyzed using methods somewhat similar to, though different in technical detail (mathematical and substantive) from, the methods given here.

6. If a random sample of individuals is drawn from a specified population, and if the interviewing procedure itself does not affect those in the panel study in a significant manner, then the methods presented here can be used to make inferences concerning the population sampled. The assessment of the possible effects of the interviewing procedure (repeated questioning) can be determined by a carefully designed experiment.

7. For a description of this survey, see Anderson's article and also Paul F. Lazarsfeld, Bernard Berelson, and Hazel Gaudet, *The People's Choice* (New York: Columbia University Press, 1948).

8. The problem of non-response was not considered in Anderson's article and will not be considered here, since it would complicate the exposition of the general point of view. Of course, this problem may be important, and it must be kept in mind by the research worker interested in making inferences from a panel study of a set of individuals to a larger population.

quencies (i.e., the number of R, D, and U responses) form a partially condensed report of the dynamic process of individual changes recorded in successive interviews. For each individual, his responses in the six interviews could be listed, and since there are three possible responses (R, D, U), there will be $3^6 = 729$ possible response patterns, some of them occurring more frequently than others. We now propose and test a variety of models (hypotheses) that, if found to be correct, would help us to explain these pattern frequencies and to make predictions of future responses.

2. Probability Models

2.1. First-Order Chain

Let $p\,(R,\,R)$ be the probability of an R response in a given month among those who were R in the preceding month; let $p\,(R,\,D)$ be the probability of a D response in a given month among those who were R in the preceding month; let $p\,(R,\,U)$ be the probability of a U response in a given month among those who were R in the preceding month; let $p\,(D,\,R)$ be the probability of an R response in a given month among those who were D in the preceding month; let $p\,(D,\,D)$ be the probability of a D response in a given month among those who were D in the preceding month; etc.[9] In this way, nine transition probabilities are obtained, which we list in Chart 1. If these transition probabilities determine the basic mechanism of the process for a single individual, then this process is called a "first-order Markov chain."[10]

CHART 1   Matrix of Transition Probabilities for
First-Order Chain

		A GIVEN MONTH			
		R	D	U	Total
The Preceding Month	R D U	$p(R,\,R)$ $p(D,\,R)$ $p(U,\,R)$	$p(R,\,D)$ $p(D,\,D)$ $p(U,\,D)$	$p(R,\,U)$ $p(D,\,U)$ $p(U,\,U)$	1.00 1.00 1.00

The relevant data for estimating the matrix of transition probabilities for, say, the June interview, given the May interview, are summarized in a 3×3 cross-classification of responses in May and June. These data for the successive pairs of months — May–June, June–July, July–August, August–September, and September–October — are given in Chart 2.

---

9. This notation differs somewhat from that appearing in the mathematical statistical literature, but it seems best for our present exposition.

10. For further details about Markov chains, the reader is referred to William Feller, *An Introduction to Probability Theory and Its Application*, Vol. I (New York: John Wiley & Sons, 1950), and to Anderson's article.

CHART 2

		JUNE						JULY			
		R	D	U	Total			R	D	U	Total
May	R	125	5	16	146	June	R	124	3	16	143
	D	7	106	15	128		D	6	109	14	129
	U	11	18	142	171		U	22	9	142	173
Total		143	129	173*	445	Total		152	121	172	445

		AUGUST						SEPTEMBER			
		R	D	U	Total			R	D	U	Total
July	R	146	2	4	152	August	R	184	1	7	192
	D	6	111	4	121		D	4	140	5	149
	U	40	36	96	172		U	10	12	82	104
Total		192	149	104	445	Total		198	153	94	445

		OCTOBER			
		R	D	U	Total
September	R	192	1	5	198
	D	2	146	5	153
	U	11	12	71	94
Total		205	159	81	445

*The numerical value 179, rather than 173, is given in Anderson's article, but this is obviously a typographical error.

The transition probabilites are estimated by dividing each cell entry in the tables by the corresponding row total; for example, the probability of an R response in June among those who were D in May, $p(D, R)$, can be estimated by 7/128 (5.5 per cent), the proportion of R responses in June among those who were D in May. Chart 3 gives the estimated transition probabilities for the five successive pairs of months.

A cursory inspection of the five matrices in Chart 3 would seem to indicate that the first two are similar, and that they are different from the last two. The same process of change seems to have taken place in the May–June period as in the June–July period. The process of change appears to be different in the July–August period from the earlier periods (the probability of holding to a specific party intention is higher and the probability of reserving judgment is lower). It is interesting to note that the Democratic convention was held in the period between the July and the August interviews; the Republican convention had been held in an earlier period. The process of change seems not to have varied much until both conventions were held. With respect to the difference between the third matrix and the fourth and fifth matrices, Anderson states that this difference is essentially a matter of the time scale (i.e., the July–August matrix seems to represent changes at twice the speed of the August–September and September–October matrices), and he suggests that an interpretation is that the second convention sets into operation a different process of change that slows down as the campaign progresses.[11]

If the process of change were alike for the May–June and June–July periods, then the estimated matrix of transition probabilities obtained for the May–June period could be used with the data on June responses to predict the responses in the July interview. The quality of the predictions for successive months depends on whether the successive transition probability matrices are alike, that is, on whether they are constant. These predictions would be rather good for the July interview, since the data indicate that the matrices for May–June and June–July were quite similar. However, if the May–June or the June–July matrix were used along with the data on July responses to predict the August responses, the predictions might be poor since the matrix for July–August differed from the earlier ones. The question of constancy of the transition probability matrix is therefore an important one. Methods for studying this question (i.e., for testing the hypothesis) will be presented in section 4.2 and compared with the corresponding tests suggested in Anderson's paper.

If the process were alike for August–September and September–October, then the two estimated matrices could be combined into a single matrix estimating the constant matrix of transition probabilities. If this single matrix describes how responses in a given month are dependent on responses in the preceding month, then applying the data on October responses to this matrix we can attempt to predict what would be the responses if the group of persons could have been interviewed again in November concerning their vote intention. This prediction method, which assumes that the matrix will apply to the October-November period, will be discussed further in section 3.1.

We have noted that the basic mechanism of the first-order chain (model) is the matrix of transition probabilities, where responses in a given month are dependent on responses in the immediately preceding month. This model does *not* assume that responses in a given month are independent of responses in the month before the immediately preceding month, but one of the consequences of the model is that if knowledge about responses in the two preceding months is available, then it is the information about the immediately preceding month that is relevant. (This is a consequence of the fact that transition probabilities as given in Chart 1 form the basic mechanism of the process.) This model may not be realistic enough, and so we now consider the case where knowledge about responses in the two preceding months, rather than just the responses in the immediately preceding month, may be necessary in order to understand the changes in response that take place in a given month.

11. In sec. 4.2 we shall test the statistical significance of the differences and similarities mentioned above and shall analyze these matrices in more detail. We note there, e.g., that the only significant difference between the third matrix and the fourth and fifth is with respect to the people who "Don't Know" (the undecided in July are more likely to decide by the time of the next interview than are those who are undecided in August), thus providing a quite different interpretation from that given in Anderson's paper for the difference between the July–August period and the August–September and September–October periods.

CHART 3

		JUNE					JULY		
		R	D	U			R	D	U
May	R	.856	.034	.110	June	R	.867	.021	.112
	D	.055	.828	.117		D	.047	.845	.108
	U	.064	.105	.831		U	.127	.052	.821

		AUGUST					SEPTEMBER		
		R	D	U			R	D	U
July	R	.961	.013	.026	August	R	.958	.005	.037
	D	.050	.917	.033		D	.027	.940	.033
	U	.233	.209	.558		U	.096	.115	.789

		OCTOBER		
		R	D	U
September	R	.970	.005	.025
	D	.013	.954	.033
	U	.117	.128	.755

2.2. Second-Order Chain

We shall now be concerned with the transition probabilities of a particular response, say D, in a given month among those who had a particular pattern of responses, say R and then U, in the two preceding months. In this case, a transition probability matrix is obtained containing $3 \times 3 \times 3 = 27$ probabilities, which can be arranged in a cross-classification table with $3 \times 3 = 9$ rows to describe the possible patterns in the two preceding months and 3 columns to describe the response in the given month. If this matrix of transition probabilities determines the basic mechanism of the process for a single individual, then the process is called a "second-order Markov chain."

The relevant data for estimating the matrix of second-order transition probabilities for, say, the July interview, given the responses in May and June, are summarized in a 9×3 cross-classification of responses in May, June, and July. Estimated matrices could be obtained for the successive triplets of months May–June–July, June–July–August, July–August–September, August–September–October. The estimated matrices for these four periods could then be compared to see how similar they are. Differences between these matrices might tend to suggest that the process of change varied with the time period considered. However, since some of the cells in each of the four 9×3 cross-classification tables, from which the estimated matrices are computed, would contain in the case considered here only a small number of observations, we might expect quite a large amount of variation in the four matrices as a result of sampling fluctuation alone. In order to decide whether the differences in the four estimated matrices can be attributed to sampling fluctuation or to real variation in the process of change, statistical tests are required. The hypothesis that the matrices of second-order transition probabilities are constant was not discussed in Anderson's paper; we shall present methods for testing this hypothesis in section 4.2.

If the four matrices of second-order transition probabilities are constant (which seems doubtful), then there is some justification for combining the four estimated matrices into a single matrix estimating the constant matrix of transition probabilities. This single matrix was given in Anderson's paper and is reproduced in Chart 4. This table indicates, for example, that among those people who were R in one month and then D in the next month, 27.3 per cent were R in the following month.

It is of interest to know whether use of the two preceding months in describing transition probabilities is any more helpful than merely use of just the immediately preceding month. A cursory glance at Chart 4 would seem to indicate that we gain by taking account of responses two time points back. For example, among those persons who were R and then R again in two successive months, 96.2 per cent were also R in the following month; among these persons who were D and then R in two successive months, only 78.3 per cent were R in the following month; among those persons who were U and then R in two successive months, 85.5 per cent were R in the following month. Hence, the response in a given month may not depend on the response in the preceding month alone. If Chart 4 does describe how responses in a given month are statistically dependent on the responses in the two preceding months, then applying the data on responses in September and October to this matrix we can attempt to predict what would be the responses if the people were reinterviewed in November. This will be discussed further in section 3.3.

CHART 4

TIME	TIME	TIME t		
$t-2$	$t-1$	R	D	U
R	R	.962	.010	.028
	D	.273	.727	.000
	U	.395	.116	.489
D	R	.783	.000	.217
	D	.019	.934	.047
	U	.105	.263	.632
U	R	.855	.012	.133
	D	.080	.840	.080
	U	.134	.117	.749

2.3. Models for Different Strata

It may well be that the models we have considered above are still not realistic enough. For example, the population may be sufficiently heterogeneous, with different strata within the population subject to different processes of change, so that an analysis that did not explicitly take this into account would go awry. If this is the case, a separate analysis of the kind described here could be carried out for each known stratum separately. As an example of this use of separate analyses, Anderson stratified the population studied with respect to their interest in the campaign, classifying individuals into one of three groups: high, moderate, and low interest. For each group, estimated matrices of transition probabilities were obtained, and are given here in Chart 5.

CHART 5

	HIGH INTEREST				MODERATE INTEREST				LOW INTEREST		
	R	D	U		R	D	U		R	D	U
R	.976	.000	.024	R	.968	.016	.016	R	.932	.000	.068
D	.011	.978	.011	D	.019	.953	.028	D	.030	.910	.060
U	.125	.333	.542	U	.182	.151	.667	U	.081	.074	.845

The differences between the estimated matrices for the different groups may be examined. For example, in comparing any two groups in Chart 5, the more interested group had a higher proportion of persons who were R in a given month among those who were R in the preceding month; a higher proportion of persons who were D in a given month among those who were D in the preceding month; and a lower proportion of persons who were U in a given month among those who were U in the preceding month. Statistical methods are given in Anderson's paper for testing whether the estimated matrices for two different groups estimate a common matrix of transition probabilities; that is, we are able to test whether two different groups have a similar process of change. These statistical methods will be discussed further in section 4.4, where alternative procedures are mentioned and where methods are presented for comparing any number of groups.

If there are essential differences among the three groups, it should be possible to obtain more accurate predictions of future responses by taking into account these differences. Information concerning the response frequencies of the three groups in October could be applied to the matrices in Chart 5 to predict what the responses would be if the groups were interviewed again in November. This matter will be discussed further in section 3.4.

The general approach of stratifying the population and then studying the pattern of change for each of the strata can be used to study different social classes or different races, individuals with different religious affiliations or different educational backgrounds, individuals subject to different mass media, individuals that have different psychological characteristics, activities, interests, amounts of influence or leadership, etc. A similar kind of statistical analysis of the patterns of change for different groups of individuals can also be used to determine, from the results of an experiment, the effect of different experiences on the process of change. In other words, if the population, or a sample from it, is divided into different groups at random and each group is then subject to a different kind of experience, the subsequent patterns of change for the different groups can be analyzed by the methods given in section 4.4 to study the effect of the different experiences on the process. Of course, the more detailed stratifications and/or experiments will require samples of larger size for their analysis.

2.4. General Remarks

We have been discussing the analysis of the changes in responses to a single question concerning vote intention. The models discussed so far attempt to explain changes in a given response (attitude) only in terms of the past history of changes in this one response (though we did relate changes in the transition matrices to other events — the conventions). These models can be generalized to carry out a simultaneous analysis of several responses (attitudes). Anderson's paper includes an illustrative example dealing with the process of change of two attitudes. He presents a statistical method for testing whether changes in two attitudes are independent. We shall present in section 4.5 other methods for studying the mutual relations among several attitudes. The statistical techniques used in the analysis of relations among several attitudes may also be used in the analysis of the relations between attitudes and actions (e.g., preference for a party and actual vote) or among several actions in a study of the mutual interactions of a number of variables.

The use of certain probability models will, of course, imply certain assumptions about the phenomena studied. For example, use of the first- or second-order chain model will imply, in the case where a random sample of individuals is studied, that only a certain amount of past history affects the present attitudes of the population from which the sample was drawn (while this past history is in turn affected by earlier history). Also, these particular models do not deal directly with social interdependencies, which may affect the relationship between the individuals studied and their response patterns. For some purposes these may be serious limitations; for other purposes, it will not matter.

The models are rather general and describe a number of different processes. In studying any particular empirical phenomenon, it is sometimes desirable to construct models based on more specific theories related to it. By an examination of the general models and data, we hope to be able to see what are the apparent complications in the data and how to develop more specific models that will help us to understand the phenomena more fully.

The first-order chain model, the second-order model, and models that are based, in part, on a stratification of the population can all lead to quite different interpretations of the same set of data. Other models, which are different from those we have presented, will lead to still other interpretations of the data. We mention one such model now.

As we have seen, one interpretation of the data in Chart 2 for the May–June transitions is in terms of a first-order chain model. However, the following model may be closer to reality. There are three latent classes — R, D, U — in the population, and there are certain probabilities that an individual in the R latent class will be classified as D or U in the May interview, certain probabilities that an individual in the D latent class will be classified as R or U in the May interview, and certain probabilities that an individual in the U latent class will be classified as R or D. There are similar probabilities associated with the June interview, and the responses for an individual in a given latent class are assumed to be independent in the two time periods. Some further assumptions can be made concerning the relations between the probabilities. This latent class model may be interpreted either as an "error of measurement model," where the probability that an individual in the R latent class will be classified as a D is interpreted as an error rate, or more directly in terms of the existence of real latent classes, where the individuals in the R latent class can, with a given probability, give a D response, which is his true response in that given interview. For this model, methods quite different from those discussed here will be appropriate, and predictions based on this model will also be quite different.[12]

Since the questions asked and the answers obtained from a set of data depend on the model used, it therefore is important to obtain a reasonable model. For a given set of data, it may be difficult to choose between different models. For example, for the data in Chart 2 for the May–June transitions, the first-order chain model and the latent class model may seem equally reasonable. However, it is possible, by examining the individual response patterns from May to July, to study the question of which of the two models fits the data better. For any two really different models, it should be possible to determine the kinds of data that would be necessary to distinguish which model fits the data better.

3. Methods of Prediction

3.1. First-Order Prediction

Summing the cell entries in the 3×3 cross-classification of responses in August and September with the corresponding cell entries in the cross-classification of responses in September and October, we obtain a single 3×3 cross-classification table that can be used to estimate the matrix of first-order transition probabilities, assuming that this matrix is constant during the periods August–September, September–October.[13] The matrix of estimated transition probabilities is given in Chart 6. Applying the results of the October interview (i.e., the number of R, D, U responses) to this estimated matrix, Anderson obtained the following predictions of vote intention in November: 209.4, 161.3, 74.3, for R, D, U, respectively, while the actual vote in November was 204 Republican and 146 Democratic, with 95 among the 445

CHART 6

Time	Time t		
$t-1$	R	D	U
R	.964	.005	.031
D	.020	.947	.033
U	.106	.121	.773

12. For a discussion of simple models of this kind, the reader is referred to Patricia Kendall, *Conflict and Mood* (Glencoe, Ill.: Free Press, 1954); Eleanor E. Maccoby, "Pitfalls in the Analysis of Panel Data: A Research Note on Some Technical Aspects of Voting," *American Journal of Sociology*, LXI (1956), 359–62; Leo A. Goodman and William H. Kruskal, "Measures of Association for Cross Classifications. II: Further Discussion and References," *Journal of the American Statistical Association*, LIV (1959), 123–63.

13. Mathematical justification for this estimation procedure is presented in Anderson and Goodman, "Statistical Inference about Markov Chains," *op. cit.*

in the study not voting. In the following sections, an attempt will be made to improve predictions of voting behavior by developing methods for modifying the predictions given in Anderson's paper.

3.2. Action Predictions

Anderson has pointed out that a possible explanation of the discrepancy between his predictions and the actual vote may be the difference between verbalizing a vote intention and the action of voting. (Since Anderson's data related to vote intention, his predictions were also of vote intention.) We now consider how his predictions might be modified to take account of the difference between vote intention and voting. Let $p(R)$ represent the probability that a person will vote among those who would have said that they intended to vote Republican if they had been interviewed in November. Let $p(D)$ represent the probability that a person will vote among those who would have said that they intended to vote Democratic if they had been interviewed in November. For simplicity, we shall assume that if a person who would have been Republican in a November interview actually voted, he would vote Republican (in the November election), and we shall also assume that if a person who would have been Democratic in a November interview actually voted, he would vote Democratic. Let $p(U)$ represent the probability that a person will vote among those who would have said that they didn't know in a November interview. Then the prediction for the number of R votes among those (209.4 people estimated) who would have said they intended to vote R is $209.4 \times p(R)$; the prediction for the number of D votes among those (161.3 people estimated) who would have said they intended to vote D is $161.3 \times p(D)$; and the prediction for the number of people voting among those (74.3 people estimated) who would have said that they didn't know is $74.3 \times p(U)$.

We must now consider for which party the $74.3 \times p(U)$ people would vote. From the estimated matrix of transition probabilities (Chart 6), we note that among those people who state that they don't know in a given month, 10.6 per cent will be R in the following month, 12.1 per cent will be D in the following month, and 77.3 per cent will be U in the following month. Hence, 22.7 per cent will be either R or D in the following month. Among those who will be either R or D, we find that 46.7 per cent ($10.6/22.7 = 0.467$) will be R, and 53.3 per cent ($12.1/22.7 = 0.533$) will be D. Therefore, we might attempt to predict that, among those who say they don't know and do vote, 46.7 per cent will vote R and 53.3 per cent will vote D. Hence among this group of $74.3 \times p(U)$ people, $74.3 \times p(U) \times .467$ people would vote R and $74.3 \times p(U) \times .533$ people would vote D.

In order to predict actual voting behavior, numerical estimates of the probabilities $p(R)$, $p(D)$, and $p(U)$, must be obtained. One difficulty is that these probabilities depend on the particular people studied in a given election. These probabilities might be estimated for a particular election from supplementary information, obtained possibly in the panel study, concerning registration, intentions, strength of interest, activities and attitudes of the given population, or from any other relevant information concerning the relations among voting behavior, voting intention, population composition, and other factors. If the probabilities $p(R)$, $p(D)$, p(U) remain constant for a series of elections, then these probabilities can be estimated from data concerning past elections and used to estimate the next election. If they do not remain constant, the relation between the changes in these probabilities and various other factors (e.g., strength of interest) may be examined and used for estimating the probabilities in a given election. Since appropriate data from such studies of voting behavior were unavailable to this writer, the following estimates will be used for illustrative purposes only: $p(R) = .951$, $p(D) = .855$, and $p(U) = .235$. These estimates were obtained by examining the actual voting behavior of the people in the panel study, and so the predictions based on these estimates cannot be taken very seriously because of this element of circularity; for the people in the study, 95.1 per cent ($195/205 = 0.951$) actually voted among those who said they intended to vote Republican in the last interview, 85.5 per cent ($135/159 = 0.855$) actually voted among those who said they intended to vote Democratic, 23.5 per cent ($19/81 = 0.235$) actually voted among those who said they didn't know. If these estimates had been based on supplementary information, available before the time of the actual voting period, then they could have been used to modify the predictions of intentions in order to obtain predictions of voting behavior. Of course, supplementary information available only after the voting time cannot be used in practice except for purposes of research and prediction relating to later elections.

We might predict that

$209.4 \times .951 + 74.3 \times .235 \times .467 = 199.1 + 8.2 = 207.3$ people would vote R, $161.3 \times .855 + 74.3 \times .235 \times .533 = 137.9 + 9.3 = 147.2$ people would vote D, and $445 - (207.3 + 147.2) = 90.5$ people would not vote.

When compared with the actual voting behavior, these predictions are more accurate than those given in the preceding section. (The element of circularity in this particular case should, of course, not be overlooked.)

We now discuss another method of dealing with the differences between verbalizing a vote intention and action. Let $p'(R)$ represent the probability that a person will vote among those who said in the October interview that they intended to vote Republican; let $p'(D)$ represent the probability that a person will vote among those who said in the October interview that they intended to vote Democratic; let $p'(U)$ represent the probability that a person will vote among those who said in the October interview that they didn't know. Then the prediction for the number of people voting from among the 205 people (see Chart 2) who were R in October is $205 \times p'(R)$; the prediction for the number voting from among the 159 who were D in October is $159 \times p'(D)$; and the prediction for the number voting from among the 81 who were U in October is $81 \times p'(U)$.

We must now consider for which party the $205 \times p'(R)$ people (the people who were R in October and actually do vote) would vote.[14] From the estimated matrix of transition probabilities (Chart 6), we note that, among those people who were R in a given month, 96.4 per cent will be R in the following month, 0.5 per cent will be D in the following month, and 3.1 per cent will be U in the following month. Hence, 96.9 per cent will be either R or D in the following month. Among those who will be either R or D, we find that 99.5 per cent ($.964/.969 = .995$) will be R and 0.5 per cent ($.005/.969 = .005$) will be D. Therefore, we might attempt to predict that, among those who were R in October and do vote, 99.5 per cent will vote R and 0.5 per cent

14. We shall not assume here that a person voted Republican if he was R in October and did in fact vote. In the preceding analysis it was assumed that a person voted Republican if he would have been R in a November interview and did in fact vote, which is quite reasonable since the election took place in November.

will vote D. Hence among this group of $205 \times p'(R)$ people, $205 \times p'(R) \times .995$ people would vote R and $205 \times p'(R) \times .005$ would vote D. We also find from Chart 6 that, among those who were D in a given month and who will be either R or D in the following month, 2.1 per cent $(.020/.967 = .021)$ will be R and 97.9 per cent $(.947/.967 = .979)$ will be D. Hence, among those people who were D in October and do vote (i.e., $159 \times p'(D)$ people), we might attempt to predict that $159 \times p'(D) \times .021$ would vote R and $159 \times p'(D) \times .979$ would vote D. We also find that, among those who were U in a given month and who will be either R or D in the following month, 46.7 per cent will be R and 53.3 per cent will be D. Hence, among those who were U in October and do vote (i.e., $81 \times p'(U)$ people), we might attempt to predict that $81 \times p'(U) \times .467$ would vote R and $81 \times p'(U) \times .533$ would vote D.

In order to predict actual voting behavior, we must now obtain numerical estimates of the probabilities $p'(R)$, $p'(D)$, and $p'(U)$. Since appropriate data from studies of the relation between voting behavior and other factors were unavilable, the estimates $p'(R) = .951$, $p'(D) = .855$, and $p'(U) = .235$ will be used here, as earlier in this section, for illustrative purposes only. (The element of circularity is present here as in the earlier discussion.) We might predict that

$$205 \times .951 \times .995 + 159 \times .855 \times .021 + 81 \times .235 \times .467 = 194.0 + 2.9 +$$
$$8.9 = 205.8 \text{ people would vote } R, \text{ and that } 205 \times .951 \times .005 + 159 \times .855 \times$$
$$.979 + 81 \times .235 \times .533 = 1.0 + 133.1 + 10.1 = 144.2 \text{ people would vote } D.$$

As with the method presented earlier in this section, there is close agreement between our predictions and the actual vote. The predictions based on the two methods of this section are more accurate than the predictions in the preceding section; the element of circularity will, however, affect to some extent our assessment of these results.

We have indicated two methods for modifying predictions in order to take account of the difference between verbalizing a vote intention and action. Other methods could be developed that might actually lead to still better results.

3.3. Second-Order Predictions

The predictions given in Anderson's paper were based upon a first-order chain model. We now present predictions based upon the second-order chain model.

Summing the cell entries in the 9×3 cross-classification of responses in May–June–July with the corresponding cell entries in the three other 9×3 cross-classifications (June–July–August, July–August–September, August–September–October) we obtain a single 9×3 cross-classification table that can be used to estimate the matrix of second-order transition probabilities, assuming that this matrix is constant during the four time periods. The estimated matrix of second-order transition probabilities was given in Chart 4. If we assume the constancy of these matrices (a test for this hypothesis is given in sec. 4.2), the results for the September and October interviews (i.e., the frequency of the nine possible responses in the two interviews) as given in Chart 2 can be applied to this estimated matrix (Chart 4) to obtain predictions of vote intention in November. Carrying out these quite straightforward calculations, the following predictions are obtained: 212 people would be R, 159 would be D, and 74 would be U.

These predictions are not very different from those based upon the first-order chain model given in section 3.1. Specifically, both methods predict about the same number of people would be U; that is, 74.0 or 74.3. Therefore, in comparing these methods, we shall study how the methods differed in their predictions of the R and D responses. Among those who would be either R or D, the first-order method predicts, that 56.5 per cent $(209.4/370.7 = 0.565)$ would be R, while the second-order method predicts that 57.1 per cent $(212/371 = 0.571)$ would be R. Among those who actually did vote in this group of people, the panel study data indicate that 58.3 per cent $(204/350 = 0.583)$ voted R. Hence, the second-order method has resulted in a quite good prediction of the percentage of the vote that was Republican. The second-order prediction was somewhat more accurate in this particular case than the first-order prediction. It should be remembered, however, that the second-order method, like the first order method, could not predict accurately the number who actually did not vote.

In this discussion of second-order prediction, we have not taken into account the difference between verbalizing a vote intention and action. Methods similar to those described in section 3.2 could be used to make the appropriate modifications.

3.4. Predictions for Different Strata

The prediction methods presented in the preceding sections could be applied separately to different strata in the population. For example, assuming that the three matrices given in Chart 5 estimate the first order transition probabilities for the three strata — high, medium, and low interest groups, respectively — then information concerning the response frequencies of each of these groups in the October interview could be applied to the corresponding matrices to predict the November vote intention for each group. Since the information concerning the October responses for the different groups was not given in Anderson's paper, we are unable now to actually compute these predictions. If such information had been available, the computations would be quite straightforward. If, in addition, information is available concerning the proportions of people in the population under consideration who belong to the various strata, the predictions for the separate strata could then be combined to obtain predictions for the entire population.

3.5. Remarks on "Stationary State" Predictions

If the matrix of transition probabilities describing the process of change is constant, and if the process of change were to continue for a large number of time periods, we would usually find that a "stationary state" was finally reached. In other words, after a long time, the proportions in the various categories would be approximately constant and would not depend upon the proportions that were in these categories at an initial time point. For example, if the estimated matrix of transition probabilities given in Chart 6 described the process of change, and if the process were to continue for a large number of time periods, we would find that finally the proportions of R, C, and U responses in an interview would be approximately constant, and these constant proportions would be 54.3 per cent R, 33.4 per cent D, and 12.3 per cent U.[15]

---

15. These numbers can be determined either by successive application of the matrix (Chart 6) to an initial set of proportions, or by use of formula (2.12) in Anderson's paper. They appear as n. 13 in his paper and were used to make predictions there.

Since 445 people were interviewed, we might expect that $445 \times .543 = 241.7$ people would be R, $445 \times .334 = 148.6$ would be D, and $445 \times .123 = 54.7$ would be U in an interview after a very long period of time, if the process of monthly change could be described by the matrix given in Chart 6. This does not mean that we might expect that 24.7 would "settle down" to being R after a long period of time; but rather that, in an interview after a long time, 24.7 people can be expected to be R, and in another interview after some time, the same number (24.7) of people, who are most probably not all the same ones as in the earlier interview, can also be expected to be R.

The proportions computed for the "stationary state" might be useful as an aid to understanding the process of change and the implications of a given matrix of transition probabilities. These proportions tell us what the results would be if the same process of change continued for a much longer time. Under the assumption that the matrix remains constant, the proportions computed for the "stationary state" are predictions about the far future; that is, long-range predictions. If the assumption of a constant process of change is unrealistic in a particular situation, which is often the case, then these long-range predictions may be subject to large errors. Furthermore, we would not expect these predictions to be accurate if they were used to predict the responses that would occur after only a single period — for example, from October to November. In fact, we find that these long-range predictions (i.e., 241.7 R's, 148.6 D's, 54.7 U's) are very inaccurate for predicting actual voting behavior in November.

If the matrix of transition probabilities is applied once in the first period, twice during the second period, three times during the third, etc., then the process of change is not constant but accelerates as time passes, and the "stationary state" for the process can be reached without a very long passage of time. Hence, the proportions given for the "stationary state" may also be interpreted as a description of the proportions that would be obtained if the particular process of change accelerated by the successive application of the given matrix of transition probabilities. For the actual data studied here, the process did not accelerate. In fact it may have decelerated from the July–August to the August–September period. Hence, this is an added reason why the predictions based on the "stationary state" proportions were very inaccurate.

The information concerning "stationary states" might be useful in comparing various processes of change and various given matrices. For example, if the process of change described by Chart 4 were to continue for a long period of time or if the process accelerated, then the proportions of R, D, and U responses that would be obtained can be computed, and would be .621, .271, and .108, respectively. For the 445 people in the group, we might expect that $445 \times .621 = 276.3$ would be R, $445 \times .271 = 120.6$ would be D, and $445 \times .108 = 48.1$ would be U in an interview after a very long period of time if the process of monthly change might be described by Chart 4. Thus, the long-range implications (assuming either a constant matrix or an accelerating process) of this process of change are somewhat different from the results using the matrix in Chart 6.

4. Tests of Hypotheses

The methods we shall now present are closely related to the commonly used χ^2 test of independence in a contingency table (i.e., a cross-classification table). The standard χ^2 test of independence is a "large sample" test, and the tests we shall now present are also large sample tests. The sample sizes necessary for the use of the methods given here are probably about the same as those required for the related standard χ^2 test.[16]

The commonly used measures of the amount of dependence in a cross-classification table, some of them related to the χ^2 statistic for testing independence in the table, can be applied to the various tables given in the charts in the following sections (where the χ^2 test is made) to measure the amount that the data actually differ from the corresponding expectations derived from the null hypotheses considered there.[17] For each null hypothesis considered, we shall present the appropriate χ^2 test. The standard estimated expected value computed for each cell in the cross-classification table used to obtain the appropriate χ^2 statistic will be the corresponding expectation derived from the null hypothesis, and standard measures of dependence for this cross-classification table will measure, in a certain sense, the difference between the data and the corresponding expectations.

4.1. The Hypothesis That Responses in Successive Interviews Are Independent

Assuming the first-order chain model, the first simple, though not very promising, hypothesis that comes to mind is that the transition probabilities relating to the responses in a given month may in fact be independent of the responses in the preceding month. We mention this hypothesis since there are many situations where it will be of interest, although for the pre-election panel data, it is quite unrealistic. Even a cursory glance at the relevant data in Chart 2 or the corresponding data in Chart 3 will indicate that the hypothesis will be rejected. It is not necessary to present the numerical calculations here, though we shall describe the general procedure for testing this hypothesis.

Suppose we wish to test that the responses in June are independent of the responses in May. The data given in Chart 2 for the May–June period describe a two-way classification table, and we are concerned with testing the hypothesis of independence in this table. Hence, the usual χ^2 test may be performed. The χ^2 statistic will have $2 \times 2 = 4$ degrees of freedom.[18]

Suppose we wish to test the hypothesis that the responses in each month are independent of the responses in the preceding month. A separate χ^2 test can be performed on each of the five tables (see Chart 2), and the five values of χ^2 obtained might be added together. The sum of these five values will also have a χ^2 distribution with $4 \times 5 = 20$ degrees of freedom, if the hypothesis is true. A statistical test of

16. For a discussion of χ^2 tests of independence in contingency tables, see, e.g., Wilfred J. Dixon and Frank J. Massey, Jr., *Introduction to Statistical Analysis* (New York: McGraw-Hill Book Co., 1951). This topic is covered in many textbooks in elementary statistics.

17. For a discussion of the measurement of association in cross-classification tables, see Goodman and Kruskal, "Measures of Association for Cross-Classifications," *Journal of the American Statistical Association*, XLIX (1954), 732–64, and "Measures of Association for Cross-Classifications. II: Further Discussion and References," *ibid.*, LIV, 123–63.

18. In addition to the standard χ^2 test of independence in a contingency table, there are different statistical tests appropriate for other hypotheses relating to the contingency table. For example, the hypothesis that the marginal distributions (i.e., the response frequencies for different months) are the same would be of particular interest with respect to the tables considered here. See Alan Stuart, "A Test for Homogeneity of the Marginal Distributions in a Two-Way Classification," *Biometrika*, XLII (1955), 412–16. A related though different hypothesis is studied by Albert H. Bowker, "A Test of Symmetry in Contingency Tables," *Journal of the American Statistical Association*, XLIII (1948), 572–74.

the hypothesis of independence can be obtained by determining the sum of these five values and seeing if it is significantly large.

If it is assumed that the matrices of transition probabilities for the five periods are the same (see sec. 4.2), then a different test of the hypothesis of independence should be performed. The data given in Chart 2 for the five periods should be combined into a single 3×3 table by summing the corresponding cell entries in each of the five tables. To test the hypothesis that the responses in each month are independent of the responses in the preceding month, we need only test the hypothesis of independence in the combined 3×3 table. Hence, the usual χ^2 test can be performed. The χ^2 statistic will have $2 \times 2 = 4$ degrees of freedom.

4.2. The Hypothesis That the Transition Probability Matrices Are Constant

A method for testing this hypothesis is given in Anderson's paper. A simpler method will be presented here.

Suppose we wish to test the hypothesis that the matrix of transition probabilities for the May–June period is the same as for the June–July period, assuming that the process can be described by a first-order chain. Using the data for May–June and June–July periods given in Chart 2, we form a new set of tables as shown in Chart 7.

CHART 7

		R	D	U	Total
May	R	125	5	16	146
June	R	124	3	16	143

		R	D	U	Total
May	D	7	106	15	128
June	D	6	109	14	129

		R	D	U	Total
May	U	11	18	142	171
June	U	22	9	142	173

We now have a 3×2 table for the R category, a 3×2 table for the D category and a 3×2 table for the U category. The hypothesis of independence can be tested in each of these three tables by computing the value of χ^2 for each of the tables.[19] Each of these χ^2 values (.47, .15, 6.65 for R, D, U, respectively) has $2 \times 1 = 2$ degrees of freedom, and the sum of the three χ^2 values (7.27) has $3 \times 2 = 6$ degrees of

---

19. A simplified method for computing χ^2 in a table with 2 rows and c columns is given, e.g., on p. 189 of Dixon and Massey, op.cit.

freedom. Using these χ^2 values we can test whether the transition probabilities in the May–June period are the same as in the June–July period. We can also determine, by studying the three separate χ^2 values (each with 2 degrees of freedom), for which of the three categories (R, D, or U) the transition probabilities are different.

The method that has just been described may be used to compare the transition probabilities for any two periods, for example, May–June with September–October. We now indicate how to test the hypothesis that the matrices of the transition probabilities are the same for all five periods, assuming that the process is a first-order chain. An analogous procedure can be described to compare any three periods, or any four periods.

Using the data in Chart 2, we form a new set of tables (Chart 8).

CHART 8

		R	D	U	Total
May	R	125	5	16	146
June	R	124	3	16	143
July	R	146	2	4	152
August	R	184	1	7	192
September	R	192	1	5	198

		R	D	U	Total
May	D	7	106	15	128
June	D	6	109	14	129
July	D	6	111	4	121
August	D	4	140	5	149
September	D	2	146	5	153

		R	D	U	Total
May	U	11	18	142	171
June	U	22	9	142	173
July	U	40	36	96	172
August	U	10	12	82	104
September	U	11	12	71	94

We now have a 3 × 5 table for the R category, a 3 × 5 table for the D category, and a 3 × 5 table for the U category. Assuming that the sample sizes are sufficiently large (which may be somewhat doubtful for the R category table), the hypothesis of independence can be tested in each table by computing the value of χ^2 for each of them (30.64, 22.85, 49.85 for R, D, U, respectively). Each of these χ^2 values has 2 × 4 = 8 degrees of freedom, and the sum of the three χ^2 values (103.34) has 3 × 8 = 24 degrees of freedom. Using these χ^2 values, we can test whether the transition probabilities are alike for all five periods. We can also determine, by studying the three separate χ^2 values (each with 8 degrees of freedom), for which of the three categories ($R, D,$ or U) the transition probabilities are different. Each of these three values of χ^2, in this particular case, is significant at the 1 per cent level. Thus, for each of the three categories ($R, D,$ and U), the null hypothesis that the transition probabilities are alike in all five periods is rejected at the 1 per cent level of significance. If small values of χ^2 had been obtained, rather than significantly large values, and if the sum of the three values was also small and not significant, then the null hypothesis would have been accepted. (Rather than state that the null hypothesis would have been "accepted," some research workers might prefer to state that the null hypothesis would not have been rejected or that it would have still been "entertained after the data had been analyzed.") When the sample size is sufficiently large so that errors of the second type, as well as errors of the first type, can be small, this would have served as confirmation of the fact that the data could be fitted by a first-order chain model with a constant transition probability matrix.

Let us now make some numerical comparisons between the method just described and the formula given in Anderson's paper. For hypotheses of the kind described in this section, all the numerical results for significance tests that appear in his paper are given in column A of Table 1.

TABLE 1*

Time Changes	A	Degrees of Freedom	χ^2	Decision
May–June, June–July	7.64	6	7.27	Accept
May–June, June–July, July–August	27.96	12	64.77	Reject at 1 per cent or 5 per cent level of significance
July–August, August–September, September–October	21.86	12	24.63	Reject at 5 per cent level of significance
August–September, September–October	1.50	6	1.48	Accept

*The results given in the rows of this table are not statistically independent. Also, the particular hypotheses discussed in Anderson's paper were chosen on the basis of the data, which will affect the risks associated with the procedure.

When the sample is large, some of the tests given in Anderson's paper are statistically equivalent (under the null hypothesis) to, although from the point of view of the formulas and computations they are quite different from, the corresponding methods given here. We would therefore expect that the results given in column A would not differ much from those given in the χ^2 column, though for those who are familiar with the usual χ^2 test for contingency tables the computation leading to the values in the χ^2 column (based on the methods given here) will be preferable to the corresponding computation given in Anderson's paper. The only large difference that actually appears in the table is for the May–June, June–July, July–August comparison, 64.77 versus 27.96. This difference seemed puzzling to us, and so we recomputed these values, using both the method given here and the formula in Anderson's paper, discovering that the value of 27.96 given in his paper was in error; it should have been 70.28. Hence, here too, the difference between the A and the χ^2 columns is not large; that is, 64.77 versus 70.28. It was simpler for us to compute the χ^2 values than the corresponding A values, and so this computation might replace the formula given in his paper. (Research workers who may be more familiar with the use of the "likelihood ratio test" for independence in contingency tables rather than with the χ^2 test, and with the computation of likelihood ratio statistics using available tables of logarithms rather than with the computation of χ^2 statistics, might find Anderson's formula preferable.)

In Table 2 we give the χ^2 values for all the relevant comparisons, for the separate hypotheses relating to R, D, and U, and also for the total data.[20] The hypotheses considered in Anderson's paper were related only to some of the results given in the total column of this table.

TABLE 2

Time Changes	Degrees of Freedom	R	D	U	Total
May–June, June–July	2	.47	.15	6.65*	7.27
June–July, July–August	2	8.93**	5.32	30.31**	44.56**
July–August, August–September	2	.89	.97	15.28**	17.14**
August–September, September–October	2	.41	.74	.33	1.48
May–June, June–July, July–August	4	11.27*	6.79	46.71**	64.77**
June–July, July–August, August–September	4	14.38**	10.35*	35.84**	60.57**
July–August, August–September, September–October	4	1.45	3.29	19.89**	24.63*
May–June, June–July, July–August, August–September	6	20.42**	14.40**	49.45**	84.27**
June–July, July–August, August–September, September–October	6	20.61**	15.91**	37.35**	73.87**
May–June, June–July, July–August, August–September, September–October	8	30.64**	22.85**	49.85**	103.34**

*Significant at the 5 per cent level.
**Significant at the 1 per cent level.

We notice that the significant result for the total data in the July–August, August–September, September–October comparison is almost completely due to the U data and does not appear at all in the R and D data. Also, in the July–August, August–September comparison, a similar result is obtained. Hence, the process of change in the July–August period appears to be similar to the August–September period

---

20. I am indebted to Judah Matras for carrying out these computations.

except for the behavior of the undecided people. The undecided in July are more likely to decide by the time of the next interview (the Democratic convention took place in this period) than are those who are undecided in August (both conventions had already taken place by then).[21] We might also point out that, although the total data do not indicate significance for the May–June and June–July comparison, the U data do indicate differences between these two periods. The undecided in May are more likely to be D in June, while the undecided in June are more likely to be R in July (the Republican convention was held between the latter two interviews). Those who are R in July (after the Republican convention) are more likely to remain R than are those who were R before July. It should be pointed out that, in comparing any two successive periods, the D data indicate no significance, the R data indicate significance only for the June–July and July–August comparison, while the U data indicate significance for all comparisons except the August–September, September–October periods (when both conventions had taken place).

An approach similar to the one presented in this section can be used to test the hypothesis that the four estimated matrices for the second-order transition probabilities (May–June–July, June–July–August, July–August–September, August–September–October) are the same. It should be mentioned that the sample of 445 people is actually rather small for testing this particular hypothesis; there may not be enough data to indicate significance.[22]

4.3. The Hypothesis That a Model Is First-Order Rather Than Second-Order

A method for testing this hypothesis was given by formula (4.10) in Anderson's paper.[23] A different, and simpler, method for testing this hypothesis is presented here.

Assuming that the process can be described either by a first-order or a second-order chain and that Chart 4 describes the estimated matrix of second-order transition probabilities, we form a new set of tables (Chart 9).

We now have a 3×3 table for the R category at time $t - 1$, a 3×3 table for the D category at time $t - 1$, and a 3×3 table for the U category at time $t - 1$.[24] The proportions in each row must now be multiplied by the denominator of the proportion (i.e., the number of cases used to compute the proportion) to change the proportions to frequencies. When the proportions have been changed to frequencies, we then have 3×3 cross-classification tables. The hypothesis of independence can be tested in each of these three tables by computing the value of χ^2 for each of the tables. Each of these χ^2 values will have $2 \times 2 = 4$ degrees of freedom, and the sum of three χ^2 values has $3 \times 4 = 12$ degrees of freedom. Using these values, we can test whether the transition probabilities depend on the response pattern at both the two preceding time periods or only on the response in the immediately preceding

---

21. Causation, of course, cannot be inferred from this kind of statistical analysis alone.

22. For further details concerning this test see Anderson and Goodman, "Statistical Inference about Markov Chains," op. cit.

23. This formula was given incorrectly in Anderson's paper, but has been corrected in Anderson and Goodman, op. cit.

24. It would have been more convenient, for hypothesis testing, if the table of frequencies rather than proportions were available, as was the case for the tables considered in the preceding section, but these data were not given in Anderson's paper.

CHART 9

Time $t-2$	Time $t-1$	R	D	U
R	R	.962	.010	.028
D	R	.783	.000	.217
U	R	.855	.012	.133

Time $t-2$	Time $t-1$	R	D	U
R	D	.273	.727	.000
D	D	.019	.934	.047
U	D	.080	.840	.080

Time $t-2$	Time $t-1$	R	D	U
R	U	.395	.116	.489
D	U	.105	.263	.632
U	U	.134	.117	.749

time period; that is, whether the model is second-order or first-order. We can also determine, by studying the three separate χ^2 values (each with 4 degrees of freedom), for which of the three responses (R, D, or U) at the immediately preceding time period the transition probabilities actually depend on responses for the two preceding periods.

If the data that appear in the three 3 × 3 tables were obtained from a given set of three successive months, then the conclusions based on the application of the statistical method described here would apply to the process in this given time period. However, if the data in these tables were obtained as the sum of several such sets of tables for several sets of three-month periods, then it will be necessary to assume that the transition probability matrix for the second-order chain is constant in time, in order to justify the procedure of using the sum of these tables as the data to which the statistical method described here is applied.

4.4. The Hypothesis That Several Strata Have the Same Process of Change

To test the hypothesis that two strata have the same process of change, a formula is given in Anderson's paper. We shall now present a version of this formula that is somewhat easier to compute and shall also indicate how to test the hypothesis when more than two strata are to be compared. For simplicity, it is assumed here that the process in each stratum is a first-order chain, although the same general approach can be applied to more general situations.

Let us first compare the patterns of change given in Chart 5 for two of the strata, high interest (*H*) and low interest (*L*). We form a new set of tables from the data given for these two strata (Chart 10).

CHART 10

	R	D	U
H R	.976	.000	.024
L R	.932	.000	.068

	R	D	U
H D	.011	.978	.011
L D	.030	.910	.060

	R	D	U
H U	.125	.333	.542
L U	.081	.074	.845

We now have a 3 × 2 table for the *R* category, a 3 × 2 table for the *D* category, and a 3 × 2 table for the *U* category. The proportions in each row must now be multiplied by the denominator of the proportion (i.e., the number of cases used to compute the proportion) to change the proportions to frequencies. When the proportions have been changed to frequencies, we then have three 3 × 2 cross-classification tables. The hypothesis of independence can be tested in each of these three tables by computing the value of χ^2 for each of the tables.[25] Each of these χ^2 values will have 2 × 1 = 2 degrees of freedom, and the sum of the three χ^2 values has 3 × 2 = 6 degrees of freedom. Using these χ^2 values, we can test whether the transition probabilities are the same for the two groups. We can also determine, by studying the three separate χ^2 values (each with 2 degrees of freedom), for which of the three responses (*R*, *D*, or *U*) are the two groups different.

To test the hypothesis that three (or more) groups have the same process of change, an analogous procedure may be followed. We shall indicate how this is done using the data for the three strata (high, medium, and low interest) given in Chart 5. We form a new set of tables from the data given for these three strata (Chart 11).

25. See n. 19.

A value of χ^2 (with $2 \times 2 = 4$ degrees of freedom) may be computed for each of the three tables (after the tables have been modified by changing the proportions to frequencies), and an analogous analysis of these values of χ^2 may be made.

4.5. The Hypotheses That Two Attitude Patterns and the Changes in Two Attitudes Are Independent

A method for testing the hypothesis that the changes in attitudes are independent is given in Anderson's paper, and it is pointed out that even if changes in attitudes are independent, this does not imply that the attitudes themselves are independent. We now present a method for testing that the patterns of attitudes are independent: this method and hypothesis are different from those given in Anderson's paper.

Let us consider data relating to the responses to two questions: (A) whether or not the respondent had seen an advertisement of a particular product and (B) whether or not he had bought the product. The data are arranged in Chart 12.[26]

CHART 11

	R	D	U
H R	.976	.000	.024
M R	.968	.016	.016
L R	.932	.000	.068

	R	D	U
H D	.011	.978	.011
M D	.019	.953	.028
L D	.030	.910	.060

	R	D	U
H U	.125	.333	.542
M U	.182	.151	.667
L U	.081	.074	.845

26. These data, from the files of the Bureau of Applied Social Research, were presented in Anderson's paper. The arrangement (i.e., tabulation) of these data in his paper is quite different from Chart 12 here. We note that the consideration of different (though related) hypotheses leads to different arrangements of the data and to different statistical tests.

Each column represents a different pattern of response to Question A, and each row represents a different response pattern to Question B. The column heading, say, $1 \rightarrow 2$, indicates that the column represents those people who had a "1" response on Question A (they said they saw the advertisement) on the first interview and a "2" response on Question A (they said they did not see the advertisement) in the second interview. Similarly, the row heading, say, $2 \rightarrow 1$, indicates that the row represents those people who had a "2" response on Question B (they said they did not buy the product) in the first interview, and a "1" response on Question B (they said they did buy the product) in the second interview. To see if the pattern of response in the two interviews is independent, we test the hypothesis of independence in the above 4×4 cross-classification by computing χ^2 for the table. The χ^2 statistic will have $3 \times 3 = 9$ degrees of freedom. Since the χ^2 value is 205 and is highly significant, the response patterns for the two questions are not independent. However, if we examine the chart further, we see that the distribution of response patterns to Question B for the first column does not differ very much from the distribution in the second column. The χ^2 value, with three degrees of freedom, for the 2×4 cross-classification table consisting of the data in the first two columns of Chart 12 is 2.06, and is not statistically significant.[27] Hence, the response pattern on Question B for those who were $1 \rightarrow 1$ on Question A was approximately the same as the response pattern for those who were $1 \rightarrow 2$ on A. In other words, for those who said in the first interview that they had seen the advertisement, their patterns of response to Question B did not depend on whether or not they said in the second interview that they had seen the advertisement. Also, the response patterns on Question B for those who were $1 \rightarrow 2$ on Question A did not differ significantly from the response pattern for those who were $2 \rightarrow 1$ on A. The χ^2 value, with 3 degrees of freedom, was 2.71. That is, among those persons who changed their responses to Question A on successive interviews, the response pattern on Question B among those who were $1 \rightarrow 2$ on A did not differ significantly from those who were $2 \rightarrow 1$ on A. A still more detailed statistical analysis of this table can be carried out, but we shall not do that here.

CHART 12   Reponse Patterns to Two Questions on Two Interviews

		RESPONSE PATTERN TO QUESTION A			
		$1 \rightarrow 1$	$1 \rightarrow 2$	$2 \rightarrow 1$	$2 \rightarrow 2$
Response Pattern To Question B	$1 \rightarrow 1$	83	35	25	95
	$1 \rightarrow 2$	8	7	10	15
	$2 \rightarrow 1$	22	11	8	6
	$2 \rightarrow 2$	68	28	32	493

5. The Analysis of Total Responses

In this paper we have dealt with the analysis of data concerning response patterns. If the monthly totals (i.e., the number of R, D, U responses) are available,

27. The χ^2 values given in this section are not independent of each other; they are all based on the data in Chart 12.

but the response pattern data are not, the methods presented here cannot be applied. For this situation, George A. Miller has suggested a method of analysis, although he presented it in a somewhat different context.[28] His method is applicable to the case where it is known a priori that the process of change can be described by a first-order chain with a *constant* matrix of transition probabilities. For the data analyzed here, we noted that the matrix of first-order transition probabilities was constant for, at most, two time periods. To apply Miller's method of analysis to the monthly totals for these data, the matrix of transition probabilities must be constant for at least three specified consecutive time periods in this particular case, and to obtain quite satisfactory results the matrix should be constant for many consecutive time periods. Miller's method cannot be applied satisfactorily to our data. Nevertheless we have mentioned it here since it may be of interest to the research worker who is unable to obtain data concerning response patterns but has response frequencies for specified time periods.

It should be mentioned that data concerning response frequencies will in general provide little information concerning the frequency of various response patterns.[29] For example, if the response frequencies were the same in two different time periods, this could mean that no individuals changed their responses or that some or many changed their responses but the changes "canceled out." In the light of present knowledge, the study of processes of change should be based on data concerning changes in individual response patterns whenever possible, rather than on the partial condensation of these data given by the response frequencies for a number of time periods.

---

28. "Finite Markov Processes in Psychology," *Psychometrika*, XVII (1952), 39–47. See also Leo A. Goodman, "A Further Note on 'Finite Markov Processes in Psychology,' " *Psychometrika*, XVIII (1953), 245–48, where Miller's method and proof are discussed further, and Albert Madansky, "Least Squares Estimation in Finite Markov Processes," *Psychometrika*, XXIV (1959), 137–44.

29. This comment is somewhat related to the point of view presented (in a different context) by W. S. Robinson, "Ecological Correlations and the Behavior of Individuals," *American Sociological Review*, XV (1950), 351–57. The discussion by Goodman, "Some Alternatives to Ecological Correlation," *American Journal of Sociology*, LXIV (1959), 610–25, is also related in a general sense to this problem, though it too is presented in the context of ecological correlation.